THE CURSE OF HAM

The painting on the book jacket is reproduced from folio 33r of the Alba Bible, a fifteenth-century illuminated translation of the Hebrew Bible into Castilian, accompanied by Jewish and Christian commentaries. The work was commissioned by the churchman Don Luis De Guzmán, the text was prepared by Rabbi Moses Arragel de Guadalajara, and the paintings were executed by Spanish Christian artists. The miniature reproduced on the book jacket depicts the biblical story recounted in Genesis 9. While Noah's son Ham "looks at his father's nakedness," Noah's other sons, Shem and Japheth, respectfully avert their gazes and cover their father. Ham, the father of Kush/Ethiopia, is shown as a black African. Reproduced by courtesy of Mauricio Hatchwel Toledano. Full details of the facsimile edition of the Alba Bible may be found at www.facsimile-editions.com or Facsimile Editions Limited, 40 Hamilton Terrace, London NW8 9UJ, England.

THE CURSE OF HAM

RACE AND SLAVERY IN EARLY JUDAISM, CHRISTIANITY, AND ISLAM

David M. Goldenberg

PRINCETON UNIVERSITY PRESS

PRINCETON AND OXFORD

Published by Princeton University Press, 41 William Street, Princeton, New Jersey 08540

In the United Kingdom: Princeton University Press, 3 Market Place, Woodstock,

Oxfordshire OX20 1SY

British Library Cataloging-in-Publication Data is available

This book has been composed in Galliard type

Printed on acid-free paper. ∞

www.pupress.princeton.edu

Printed in the United States of America

1 3 5 7 9 10 8 6 4 2

10 9 8 7 6 5 4 3 2 1

Library of Congress Cataloging-in-Publication Data

Goldenberg, David.

The curse of Ham : race and slavery in early Judaism, Christianity, and Islam / David M. Goldenberg.

p. cm.

Includes index.

ISBN 0-691-11465-X (alk. paper)

1. Ham (Biblical figure). 2. Bible. O.T. Genesis 9, 18–25—Criticism, interpretation, etc.,—History—To 1500. 3. Blacks in the Bible. 4. Blacks—Public opinion—History—To 1500. 5. Jews—Attitudes—History—To 1500. 6. Christians—Attitudes—History—To 1500. 7. Muslims—Attitudes—History—To 1500. 8. Slavery—Justification—History 9. Black race—Color. I. Title.

BS580.H27 G65 2003

291.1′7834896—dc21

2002042713

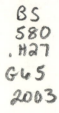

For

Bernard Lewis

Friend

And

In Memory of My Mother

שרה בת יצחק אייזיק הכהן ז״ל

CONTENTS

PART FOUR AT THE CROSSROADS OF HISTORY AND EXEGESIS

ACKNOWLEDGMENTS

A WORK OF THIS SORT, which attempts a historical synthesis covering different time periods, cultures, and languages, is naturally dependent upon the help of others. Several are mentioned and thanked in the notes to this work. In addition, I am indebted to Annalisa Azzoni, William Brinner, Ephraim Dardashti, Joseph F. Eska, Gilad Gevaryahu, Moshe Lazaar, Nehemiah Levtzion, Bernard Lewis, Renee Levine Melammed, Uri Melammed, Vera Moreen, Yudah Nahum, Ann Macy Roth, Everett Rowson, Yehudah Ratzaby, and Liliane Weissberg for help in their respective disciplines. I am sure that Lewis and Brinner regret ever having occupied an office next to mine.

The various librarians who have suffered my excessive requests often went beyond the call of duty on my behalf. My thanks to the indefatigable Judith Leifer at the Center for Judaic Studies and Hilda Pring at the Van Pelt Library (University of Pennsylvania). At the center I was also helped by Etty Lassman, who prioritized her work to my benefit and tutored me in the arcane and very frustrating world of computer formatting. It is a pleasure for me to acknowledge my thanks to Tel Aviv University, which twice awarded me a summer fellowship, and to Hebrew University, where I spent a year's sabbatical and was provided an ideal academic environment. At Tel Aviv Gideon Spiegel and Mina Rosen were exceptionally helpful in making my stay comfortable and productive.

Some people were of particular help to me and I especially wish to thank them. Three colleagues and friends read and commented on drafts of this work. Arthur Kiron read the entire manuscript and, chapter by chapter, discussed its contents with me. His comments were particularly helpful in developing the structure of the book. Mark Smith read the chapters dealing with the Bible; his knowledge of biblical and other ancient Near Eastern literature was an invaluable resource. Richard Steiner read the chapter on philology, dealing with the etymology of Ham, patiently correcting my errors. Others were equally helpful in various ways. Peter Frost put at my disposal some of his published and unpublished material on topics directly relevant to my work. This material—especially his valuable collection of early Christian sources—was very useful. The reader will notice that the name Sol Cohen appears in this study several times. Not infrequently he is cited in the footnotes for alerting me to one source or another. I was fortunate to have him as my colleague and daily traveling companion for many years; his wide-ranging knowledge served this study to good effect. If the analyses of Jewish sources in this study are clear, and if the conclusions turn out to be correct in the light of subsequent discussion, it is due in no small measure to Tsvi Groner. During my sabbatical in Jerusalem Groner and I met two evenings a week to study Talmud together. Our discussions invariably ranged far beyond the talmudic text and helped sharpen the questions that underlie this study. In many ways I am indebted to this *talmid ḥakham.* My wife Jennie read the entire manuscript of the book and commented from the perspective of someone from a different discipline; she is also responsible for considerable improvements in style. The thanks that I give to my wife and to my children, Joshua, Tirzah, and Shifra, is tinged with regret. They put up with a missing spouse and father for long stretches of time. They may forgive me, but I cannot. Lastly, I am grateful to Brigitta van Rheinberg of Princeton University Press for her close reading of the manuscript and insightful comments toward its improvement. I am sorry that my mother, *zikhronah li-vrakhah,* could not live to see the completion of this work. To her and to my father, *yibadel le-ḥayim ṭovim,* with gratitude I give thanks.

One person has been more helpful to me in more ways than I can even begin to recount. Bernard Lewis entered my life in 1986. I had been president of Dropsie College, a graduate school devoted to Judaic Studies in Philadelphia. The college had ceased to exist as a graduate school and was being reborn as a postdoctoral research institute on the model of the Institute for Advanced Study at Princeton. Lewis, an expert in Islamic history with a strong knowledge in Judaic studies, was then at Princeton (both the IAS and the university), and was a perfect choice as the first director of the new institution. As associate director, I worked closely with him in developing the programs and policies of what became the Annenberg Research Institute for Near Eastern and Judaic Studies. Having a world-renowned scholar at its helm assured the new institution immediate success. Indeed, those were heady days, with some of the world's leading academics in Jewish and Islamic studies converging in Philadelphia.

In our new jobs, Lewis saw to it that I was afforded every opportunity to return to the scholarship of my preadministrative years. In many different ways, some known only to the two of us and some undoubtedly only to him, he assured my return. This book took seed when Lewis, writing his *Race and Slavery in the Middle East,* asked my advice about Jewish texts. From that moment on, as the book germinated and took shape, Lewis was at my side, a source of information for matters Islamic and Arabic, an inspiration for what could be achieved, and a constant encouragement (he would say *nudge*) when things looked bleak.

I have been privileged to know him. I have been more privileged to call him a friend. May the dedication of this book to him be a token of that friendship.

ABBREVIATIONS

Biblical Literature

Gen	Genesis
Ex	Exodus
Lev	Leviticus
Num	Numbers
Deut	Deuteronomy
Josh	Joshua
Judg	Judges
1 Sam	1 Samuel
2 Sam	2 Samuel
1 Kgs	1 Kings
2 Kgs	2 Kings
Isa	Isaiah
Jer	Jeremiah
Ezek	Ezekiel
Hos	Hosea
Obad	Obadiah
Nah	Nahum

Hab	Habakkuk
Zeph	Zephaniah
Hag	Haggai
Zech	Zechariah
Mal	Malachi
Ps	Psalms
Prov	Proverbs
Job	Job
Song	Song of Songs (Canticles)
Lam	Lamentations (Eikhah)
Qoh	Qohelet (Ecclesiastes)
Est	Esther
Dan	Daniel
Ezra	Ezra
Neh	Nehemiah
1 Chr	1 Chronicles
2 Chr	2 Chronicles

Rabbinic Literature

Ar	*ʿArakhin*
ARNa, b	*Avot de-Rabbi Natan,* recensions a and b
AZ	*ʿAvodah Zarah*
b	Babylonian Talmud; e.g., *bBer* = Babylonian Talmud, *Berakhot*
BB	*Bava Batra*
Bekh	*Bekhorot*
Ber	*Berakhot*
Bik	*Bikurim*
BM	*Bava Meṣiaʿ*
BQ	*Bava Qama*
Dem	*Demai*
ʿEr	*ʿEruvin*
GenR	*Genesis Rabba*

Giṭ	*Giṭin*
Ḥag	*Ḥagigah*
Hor	*Horayot*
Ḥul	*Ḥulin*
Ker	*Keritot*
Ket	*Ketubot*
Kil	*Kilayim*
m	Mishna; e.g., *mBer* = Mishna, *Berakhot*
Maʿas	*Maʿasrot*
Mak	*Makot*
Meg	*Megilah*
Men	*Menaḥot*
MidPs	*Midrash Psalms*
MQ	*Moʿed Qaṭan*
Naz	*Nazir*

Ned	*Nedarim*
Neg	*Negaʿim*
Nid	*Nidah*
Oh	*Ohalot*
Pes	*Pesaḥim*
PesR	*Pesiqta Rabbati*
PesRK	*Pesiqta de-Rav Kahana*
PRE	*Pirqei de-Rabbi Eliezer*
Qid	*Qidushin*
QohR	*Qohelet (Ecclesiates) Rabba*
R	Rabba, e.g., *GenR* = *Genesis Rabba;* Rabbi, e.g., R. Yannai
RH	*Rosh Hashanah*
San	*Sanhedrin*
Shab	*Shabbat*
Sheq	*Sheqalim*
Shevi	*Sheviʿit*
Shevu	*Shevuʿot*
Soṭ	*Soṭah*
Suk	*Sukah*
t	Tosefta; e.g., *tBer* = Tosefta, tractate *Berakhot*
Taʿan	*Taʿanit*
Tam	*Tamid*
Tanḥ	*Tanḥuma*
TanḥB	*Tanḥuma,* ed. S. Buber
Ter	*Terumot*
Tg	Targum; e.g., *TgQoh* = Targum to Qohelet
y	Palestinian (*Yerushalmi*) Talmud; e.g., *yBer* = Palestinian Talmud, *Berakhot*
YalqSh	*Yalqut Shimʿoni*
Yev	*Yevamot*
Zev	*Zevaḥim*

Secondary Literature

AB	*Anchor Bible* series (Garden City, N.Y., 1964–)
ABD	*Anchor Bible Dictionary,* ed. David Noel Freedman et al. (New York, 1992)
ACW	*Ancient Christian Writers* (Westminster, Md., 1946–)
ANF	*The Ante-Nicene Fathers,* ed. A. Roberts and J. Donaldson; rev. A. Cleveland Coxe (1885–87, 1896 ["American edition"], repr., Peabody, Mass., 1994)
ANRW	*Aufstieg und Niedergang der römischen Welt* (Berlin, 1972–)
ANT	*The Apocryphal New Testament,* ed. M. R. James (Oxford, 1924); ed. J. K. Elliott (Oxford, 1993)
APOT	*Apocrypha and Pseudepigrapha of the Old Testament,* ed. R. H. Charles (Oxford, 1913)
BASOR	*Bulletin of the American Schools of Oriental Research*
BJRL	*Bulletin of the John Rylands Library*
CAD	*Assyrian Dictionary of the Oriental Institute of the University of Chicago,* ed. Ignace J. Gelb et al. (Chicago, 1964–)
CANE	*Civilizations of the Ancient Near East,* ed. J. Sasson et al. (New York, 1995)
CC	*Continental Commentaries* series (Minneapolis, 1990–)

CCL	*Corpus Christianorum,* Series Latina (Turnhout and Paris, 1953–)
CPL	*Clavis patrum Latinorum,* ed. Eligius Dekkers and Aemilius Gaar (Steenbrugis, 1995)
CSCO	*Corpus scriptorum Christianorum orientalium* (Louvain, 1903–)
CSEL	*Corpus scriptorum ecclesiasticorum Latinorum* (Vienna, 1866–)
DJD	*Discoveries in the Judaean Desert: The Texts from the Judaean Desert,* vols. 1–39 (Oxford, 1955–2002)
EB	*Encyclopaedia Biblica* [Hebrew: *Enṣiqlopedyah Miqraʾit*] (Jerusalem, 1950–88)
EI[1]	*The Encyclopedia of Islam,* 1st ed. (Leiden, 1913–36)
EI[2]	*The Encyclopedia of Islam,* 2nd ed. (Leiden, 1960 –)
EJ	*Encyclopedia Judaica* (Jerusalem, 1972)
FC	*Fathers of the Church* (New York, etc., 1947 –)
FHN	*Fontes Historiae Nubiorum,* ed. T. Eide, T. Hägg, R. H. Pierce, and L. Török (Bergen, Norway, 1994–)
FS	Festschrift
GCS	*Die griechischen christlichen Schriftsteller der ersten drei Jahrhunderte* (Leipzig, 1901–)
HBOT	*Hebrew Bible, Old Testament: The History of Its Interpretation,* ed. Magne Sæbø (Göttingen, 1996)
HTR	*Harvard Theological Review*
HUCA	*Hebrew Union College Annual*
IB	*The Interpreter's Bible,* ed. N. B. Harmon (New York, 1956)
IBWA	*The Image of the Black in Western Art,* ed. Ladislas Bugner, trans. William G. Ryan (Cambridge, Mass., 1976)
ICC	*International Critical Commentary* series (New York, 1895–)
IDB	*The Interpreter's Dictionary of the Bible* (Nashville, 1962); Supplementary volume (1976)
IEJ	*Israel Exploration Journal*
JANES	*Journal of the Ancient Near Eastern Society*
JAOS	*Journal of the American Oriental Society*
JBL	*Journal of Biblical Literature*
JCS	*Journal of Cuneiform Studies*
JE	*The Jewish Encyclopedia* (New York, 1901–6)
JJS	*Journal for Jewish Studies*
JNES	*Journal of Near Eastern Studies*
JPSC	*The Jewish Publication Society Torah Commentary* (Philadelphia, 1989–96)
JQR	*Jewish Quarterly Review*
JRT	*Journal of Religious Thought*
JSJ	*Journal for the Study of Judaism*

JSOT *Journal for the Study of the Old Testament*
JSP *Journal for the Study of the Pseudepigrapha*
JSQ *Jewish Studies Quarterly*
JSS *Journal of Semitic Studies*
JTS *Journal of Theological Studies*
KBL L. Koehler and W. Baumgartner, *Hebräisches und aramäisches Lexikon zum alten Testamant,* Mitarbeit von B. Hartmann und E. Kutscher, 3rd ed. (Leiden, 1967–96); English translation: Koehler, Baumgartner, and Johann J. Stamm, *The Hebrew and Aramaic Lexicon of the Old Testament,* trans. M.E.J. Richardson (Leiden, 1994–2001)
KJV King James Version of the Bible (London, 1611)
LCL Loeb Classical Library (London, 1912–)
LSJ Henry G. Liddell and Robert Scott, rev. Henry S. Jones, *A Greek-English Lexicon* (9th ed., 1940; rev. suppl. 1996)
LXX The Septuagint (see Glossary)
MGWJ *Monatsschrift für Geschichte und Wissenschaft des Judenthums*
MT Masoretic Text (see Glossary)
NAB New American Bible (Washington, D.C., 1970, 1987)
NASB New American Standard Bible (1977, 1995)
NEB New English Bible (Oxford–Cambridge, 1970)
NIV New International Version of the Bible (Grand Rapids, Mich., 1978, 1983)
NJB New Jerusalem Bible (Garden City, N.Y., 1985)
NJPS *Tanakh,* New Jewish Publication Society translation of the Bible (Philadelphia, 1985)
NKJV New King James Version of the Bible (New York–Oxford, 1982, 1990)
NPNF1 *Nicene and Post-Nicene Fathers,* 1st ser., ed. Philip Schaff (1886–89 ["American edition"], repr., Peabody, Mass., 1994)
NPNF2 *Nicene and Post-Nicene Fathers,* 2nd ser., ed. Philip Schaff and Henry Wace (1890–99 ["American edition"], repr., Peabody, Mass., 1994)
NRSV New Revised Standard Version of the Bible (New York–Oxford, 1989)
NTA *New Testament Apocrypha,* ed. Wilhelm Schneemelcher, rev. ed., English translation, ed. R. McL. Wilson (Cambridge, 1991–92; based on the Hennecke-Schneemelcher German edition, 1959)
NTS *New Testament Studies*
OEAE *The Oxford Encyclopedia of Ancient Egypt,* ed. Donald B. Redford (Oxford, 2001)
OhT *ʿOlam ha-Tanakh* Bible commentary series (Tel Aviv, 1993)

OLD *Oxford Latin Dictionary*, ed. P.G.W. Glare (Oxford, 1982)
OTL *Old Testament Library* series (Philadelphia, 1961–)
OTP *Old Testament Pseudepigrapha*, ed. James Charlesworth (Garden City, N.Y., 1983)
PAAJR *Proceedings of the American Academy for Jewish Research*
PG *Patrologiae cursus completus . . . series Graeca*, ed. J. P. Migne (Paris, 1857–66)
PL *Patrologiae cursus completus . . . series Latina*, ed. J. P. Migne (Paris, 1844–55)
PO *Patrologia Orientalis* (Paris, 1907–)
Q Qumram (see Glossary)
RB *Revue Biblique*
RE *Paulys Real-Encyclopädie der classischen Altertumswissenschaft neue Bearbeitung begonnen von Georg Wissowa* (Munich, 1980)
REB Revised English Bible (Oxford–Cambridge, 1989)
REJ *Revue des Études Juives*
RLA *Reallexikon der Assyriologie* (Berlin and Leipzig, 1932–)
RSV Revised Standard Version of the Bible (New York, 1952)
SC *Sources Chrétiennes* series (Paris, 1946–)
TDNT *Theological Dictionary of the New Testament*, ed. G. Kittel; trans. and ed. Geoffrey Bromiley (Grand Rapids, Mich., 1964–76)
TDOT *Theological Dictionary of the Old Testament*, ed. G. Johannes Botterweck and Helmer Ringgren; trans. David Green (Grand Rapids, Mich., 1990–)
VT *Vetus Testamentum*
WBC *Word Biblical Commentary* series (Waco, Tex., 1982–)
ZAW *Zeitschrift für die Alttestamentliche Wissenschaft*
ZDMG *Zeitschrift der deutschen morgenländischen Gesellschaft*

THE CURSE OF HAM

INTRODUCTION

Blackness and Slavery

> The sons of Noah who went forth from the ark were Shem, Ham, and Japheth. Ham was the father of Canaan. These three were the sons of Noah; and from these the whole earth was peopled. Noah was the first tiller of the soil. He planted a vineyard; and he drank of the wine, and became drunk, and lay uncovered in his tent. And Ham, the father of Canaan, saw the nakedness of his father, and told his two brothers outside. Then Shem and Japheth took a garment, laid it upon both their shoulders, and walked backward and covered the nakedness of their father; their faces were turned away, and they did not see their father's nakedness. When Noah awoke from his wine and knew what his youngest son had done to him, he said, "Cursed be Canaan; a slave of slaves shall he be to his brothers."
>
> (Gen 9:18–25, RSV)

THIS BIBLICAL STORY has been the single greatest justification for Black slavery for more than a thousand years. It is a strange justification indeed, for there is no reference in it to Blacks at all. And yet just about everyone, especially in the antebellum American South, understood that in this story God meant to curse black Africans with eternal slavery, the so-called Curse of Ham. As one proslavery author wrote in 1838, "The blacks were originally designed to vassalage by the Patriarch Noah."[1]

This book attempts to explain how and why this strange interpretation of the biblical text took hold. It does so by looking at the larger picture, that is, by uncovering just how Blacks were perceived by those people for whom the Bible was a central text. What did the early Jews, Christians, and Muslims see when they looked at the black African? Clearly, the biblical interpretation is forced. How, then, did the biblical authors view Blacks and what were the postbiblical forces that wrung such a view from the Bible?

This is a book about the ancient link between black skin color and slavery. It is, thus, a study of perceptions, symbolic associations, and historical ramifications. It explores how dark-skinned people were perceived in antiquity, how negative associations attached to the color black were played out on the stage of history, and how the connection between blackness and slavery became enshrined in the Curse of Ham.

In 1837 the painter and theorist Jacques Nicolas Paillot de Montabert wrote:

> White is the symbol of Divinity or God;
> Black is the symbol of the evil spirit or the demon.
> White is the symbol of light . . .
> Black is the symbol of darkness and darkness expresses all evils.
> White is the emblem of harmony;
> Black is the emblem of chaos.
> White signifies supreme beauty;
> Black ugliness.
> White signifies perfection;
> Black signifies vice.
> White is the symbol of innocence;
> Black, that of guilt, sin, and moral degradation.
> White, a positive color, indicates happiness;
> Black, a negative color, indicates misfortune.
> The battle between good and evil is symbolically expressed
> By the opposition of white and black.[2]

De Montabert wrote these words in a manual for artists. For us, they starkly demonstrate how deeply and in how many varied ways black-white symbolism is part of Western culture.

Some scholars argue that these associations were the cause of Black enslavement for centuries. They claim that the negative value of blackness—whether due to a psychological association of darkness with fear of the unknown or due to some other cause—underlies the negative sentiment toward dark-skinned people that resulted in Black slavery.[3] The historian Winthrop Jordan especially assigns a great deal of weight to the Africans' skin color. The associations of black and white as symbolic of evil and good, sin and purity, and the like, Jordan argues, were transferred to human beings when the light-skinned English came into contact with the dark-skinned Africans.[4] Speaking of the slaves in antebellum America, Toni Morrison put it this way:

> The distinguishing features of the not-Americans were their slave status, their social status—and their color. It is conceivable that the first would have self-destructed in a variety of ways had it not been for the last. These slaves, unlike many others in the world's history, were visible to a fault. *And they had*

> *inherited, among other things, a long history on the meaning of color; it was that this color "meant" something.*[5]

"Color meant something." Indeed, it meant a great deal. And it conveyed the same negative associations in many different cultures. The same black-white color symbolism seen in Western traditions is found in China and South Asia.[6] It has been found among the Chiang (a Sino-Tibetan people), the Mongour (a Mongolian people), the Chuckchees of Siberia, and the Creek Indians of North America.[7] It is in Sanskrit, Caledonian, and Japanese, as well as Western, literature.[8] Indeed, according to many anthropology reports, the phenomenon is common even in black Africa.[9] It appears that the symbolism of black-negative and white-positive is widespread among peoples of all colors.[10]

The same associations of black and white are also found in our earliest written records in the ancient Near East and the classical world.[11] In Christianity these associations played a large role in the meanings given to light and darkness. "There is continual conflict between the world of darkness, that is sin, error and death, and the figure of Christ who is light, truth and life."[12] Jesus is "the light of the world" (John 8:12, 9:5). "God is light and in him there is no darkness at all" (1 John 1:5). It played an even larger role when the church fathers in the third century began to allegorize the scriptural Black (the "Ethiopian") as sin, as we shall see later. The common patristic depiction of devils as Ethiopians was of one cloth with this symbolism in the service of exegesis.

The negative symbolism of the color black may indeed have influenced how the light-skinned European came to perceive the dark-skinned African. Some sociologists, however, have questioned whether black-white symbolism "must necessarily transfer to social relations"; to see blackness as a metaphor for negative values, they claim, is not the same as seeing black people negatively.[13] We cannot so easily jump from abstract metaphor to human reality.

Whether or not the negative value of blackness was the cause of anti-Black sentiment, and whether or not anti-Black sentiment led to Black slavery, it is clear that already by the beginning of the Atlantic slave trade in the fifteenth century Black and slave were inextricably joined in the Christian mind. Over and over again one finds Black enslavement justified with a reference to the biblical story of the curse of eternal servitude pronounced against Ham, considered to be the father of black Africa.

This book looks at the relationship between color symbolism and color prejudice and asks whether the former must lead to the latter, and whether color prejudice, strictly defined, must lead to ethnic prejudice. It seeks to uncover that point in time when blackness and slavery were first joined and it tracks the Western justification for the join in an evolving biblical interpretation. The focus of the study is on those civilizations that accepted the Bible as a basis of life.

It begins the investigation by examining the ancient Jewish world. This is not accidental. If a biblically rooted Western civilization came to exhibit anti-Black sentiment over many centuries, could the origin of such sentiment lie in the Bible? If Christian exegesis from the earliest centuries interpreted the scriptural Black as sinner and understood the devil to be an Ethiopian, could these interpretations derive from Christianity's cradle, ancient Judaism? The question takes on even greater importance in light of recent writings by scholars and nonscholars alike who have concluded that there is indeed an underlying anti-Black sentiment in early Jewish society.[14]

Was Jewish antiquity where anti-Black attitudes originated and became fixed in Western civilization? To answer this question I examine how Jews of the ancient world perceived black Africans over a fifteen-hundred-year period, from about 800 B.C.E. until the eighth century C.E. after the appearance of Islam. What images of Blacks are found in Jewish literature of this period and what attitudes about Blacks are implicit in those images? How did Jewish society of the biblical and postbiblical periods relate to darker-skinned people, whether African or not? The examination of the ancient Jewish world will provide the necessary framework in which to examine and understand the biblical Curse of Ham text and its later interpretations in Jewish, Christian, and Islamic exegesis. If the biblical Curse reflects an anti-Black sentiment, that sentiment should be found elsewhere in early Jewish literature. If it is not, then we must account for the development of such sentiment and for its expression in the various biblical interpretive traditions.

From Exegesis to History

The importance of the Hebrew Bible (Old Testament) for Judaism, Christianity, and even Islam is obvious and can be gauged by the enormous quantity of biblical interpretation and expansion generated by these three faith-cultures and their offshoots. More than the quantity, it is most striking how the same interpretive traditions with and without variation are so widely disseminated among these monotheistic faiths. How can one account for this melting pot of biblical interpretation? Of course, when Christianity and Islam accepted the Jewish Bible as part of their heritage, they inherited as well some of Judaism's interpretations of its sacred text. It is often noted that the Qur'an and later Islamic stories about biblical personalities and events (*isrāʾīliyyāt*) reflect much of ancient Jewish biblical interpretation. As the ninth-century traditionist, al-Bukhārī, wrote: "The Jews used to read the Torah in Hebrew and to interpret it to the people of

Islam in Arabic."[15] The same is true for Christianity in Asia Minor and the lands of the Near East. The Christian Syriac Bible translation, the Peshiṭta, has been shown to contain many Jewish interpretations embedded in its translation. The church fathers of the East, especially, but not only, Ephrem (d. 373), transmit Jewish midrashic explanations again and again. Origen (d. ca. 253), who wrote in Greek, not Syriac, lived in the Near East, first in Alexandria, then in Caesarea, and his works too contain many Jewish interpretations. So do the writings of Jerome, who lived in Bethlehem.[16] Sometimes these church fathers quote a contemporary, usually anonymous, Jewish source (e.g., "the Hebrew"). Many times they transmit a Jewish interpretation without attribution.

Of course, there are uniquely Christian and Islamic biblical interpretations. Jewish midrash, for example, sees no foreshadowing ("types") of Jesus or Muḥammad in the Hebrew Bible. But even many of the unique Christian or Islamic interpretations can often be seen to reflect earlier, Jewish, thinking. The concept of the *logos,* for example, which John 1:1–18 applies to Jesus ("In the beginning was the word [*logos*], and the word was with God, and the word was God. . . . Through him all things were made. . . . The Word became flesh and made his dwelling among us"), is used by the Jewish philosopher Philo (b. ca. 25 B.C.E.) as a device by means of which the infinite, transcendent God was able to create a finite, real world—the way an immaterial God can make contact with a material world. Similarly, the metaphor of light and darkness used by the early Christians ("You are all children of light," 1 Thessalonians 5:4–5; the Two Ways of Light and Darkness, *Barnabas* 18–20) is an echo of the dualistic theology of the Dead Sea sect (the "children of light" and the "children of darkness").[17] In other words, Hebrew Scripture together with its early Jewish interpretation became part of the common heritage of all biblically based cultures in the Near East during the first several centuries of the Common Era. If the church fathers transmit originally Jewish expansions and explanations without attribution, it is not because they want to hide their Jewish source, but because these interpretations had become part of the biblical package lived and studied by all, the way one read and understood the Bible. It was the vehicle of intellectual intercourse and commonality as much as the basis of, and impetus for, differentiation.

Whether Jewish, Christian, or Islamic, biblical exegetical traditions moved freely among the geographically and culturally contiguous civilizations of the Near East. It is precisely the fluidity of the various interpretations and legends that provides a unique opportunity for cross-cultural investigation. When we can determine the direction of a tradition, the very confessional permeability of biblical exegesis becomes a historical witness to changes in attitudes and perceptions. For as exegesis crossed denominational lines it took on new coloring reflecting its new environment. By recognizing "the interactive character of such inter-hermeneutic encounters," we can "elucidate the dynamics by which religions incorporate, idealize, repress, deny, and otherwise remake their inheritance, as that inheritance is recreated."[18] "Tracing the threads" while tracking the changes provides evidence of the new attitudes and views conditioned by the new environment, just as within one culture exegetical changes over time reflect changes in attitudes due to different historical circumstances. In other words, following biblical interpretation synchronically as well as diachronically provides us a picture of changing views, opinions, and attitudes within and among the monotheistic cultures. By tracking exegetical traditions concerning black Africans across confessional lines, we can see how and why the original Jewish biblical interpretations change as they move into the different cultural orbits, and we can trace the trajectory as they move back into Judaism.

The main traditions on which I focus in this regard revolve around the biblical figure of Ham and the infamous Curse of Ham. I follow the exegetical changes in Jewish, Christian, and Islamic literature, showing the origin of this postbiblical idea, how and when it took root, and how it was exegetically integrated into the biblical text. In other words, I show how non-Blacks began to look at Blacks as slaves and how this new perspective was reflected in biblical exegesis. In a related section, I track a second group of traditions that reflect another change, one of far-reaching consequences still with us today, that is, a new way of categorizing humanity—not by language, or religion, or citizenship, but by physiognomy, especially skin color. In sum, in this book I attempt to uncover the origins and development of anti-Black sentiment in Western civilization as reflected in the Bible and in postbiblical exegetical tradition, and how biblical exegesis was used to justify Black slavery.

The Plan of the Book

The book is structured in four parts. In Part I, where the investigation focuses on early Jewish views of the black African, the material is investigated chronologically rather than thematically, that is, biblical evidence is looked at first and then the postbiblical texts. This approach allows us to see continuities and discontinuities more clearly. It also allows for an informed approach to later ambiguous material. A prime example of what can happen when this approach is not taken can be seen in the claim of a recent work that in a rabbinic text "black people are described as drunken people."[19] I show later in this work that this reading of the rabbinic text is based on a scribal error; that the manuscripts and first printed edition speak of blackness rather than drunkenness; and that the correct reading was already incorporated into a number of modern translations.[20] The text, in other words, describes Blacks as being black, not drunk. What is of importance here is that had the author considered the chronologically prior material, he would have found nothing to indicate that such a perception should appear in the rabbinic corpus. That conclusion would have led him to question the text as he understood it and, perhaps, to discover the correct reading. As a West African saying puts it, "If you do not know where you are or where you have been, you cannot know where you are going."[21]

This study documents several such examples of misreading of the sources, many of which cases are ultimately due to an assumption that the way things are now is the way things were in the past. The tendency is strong to read the past from the perspective of one's own time and place. It is especially important, however, to avoid this mistake when dealing with the topic of this book, for our perceptions of the Black have been conditioned by the intervening history of centuries of Black slavery and its manifold ramifications. Unfortunately, in too many cases we shall see that that mistake has not been avoided by those who attempt to read the past with the limited tools at their disposal.

In Part II, I move the inquiry from Black as an ethnic group to black as a color, and examine Jewish views of, and attitudes toward, dark skin color. The question is necessarily broader than asking about attitudes toward black Africans. Dark- and darker-skinned people are found in a variety of ethnic groups, and within the same ethnic group. Do we find in the Jewish sources disapproving attitudes toward dark skin color irrespective of the ethnic group? Does ancient Jewish literature exhibit a particular sentiment toward the color of one's skin?

Part III steps back from the examination of Jewish perceptions and attitudes and asks a more general and more concrete historical question: how early can we date Black slavery? Here I seek to determine if and when the black African became identified as slave in the Near East. The question is important for this study because an identity of Black with slave would be expected to influence views and opinions of the Black found in the literature. If we find no such influence in the Bible, it would indicate that such an identification did not take place in the biblical period. If it can then be demonstrated, as I believe it can, that an identification of Black and slave occurred in the postbiblical period, we should expect to find reinterpretations of biblical literature to coincide with the new historical situation and view of the black African as slave. Such reinterpretation, of course, happens in every age to every people who seek to live by the Book.

Part IV focuses on the reinterpretation of the Bible that occurred as a result of this new historical situation, that is the identification of Black with slave. The primary interpretive enterprise reflecting the new historical situation concerns the Curse of Ham. I track the exegetical changes in Jewish, Christian, and Islamic literature, showing how these interpretations became historically possible, how they were textually implemented, and what views and attitudes underlie the exegesis. Methodologically, this section is the heart of the study. It shows how postbiblical literature, even if informed by the biblical world and even if formally structured around the Bible, nevertheless greatly reflects its own world. The Bible is not so much a framework, conceptual and structural, into which all subsequent thinking must fit (conform), as it is a grid upon which postbiblical thinking asserts itself, and in the process changes the biblical blueprint. The metaphor is equally applicable to all Bible-based religions. Judaism, Christianity (west and east), Islam, and even Samaritanism all refashioned the biblical grid, which, when read carefully, becomes a network of historical data. By looking at how the Bible is reinterpreted at different times and places we can detect shifting *mentalités,* and under them we can delineate historical changes. Conversely, if we know when and where crucial historical changes occur, we can explain how and why the interpretation-shaping attitudes began. Playing the two sides of the equation against each other, I show how history and exegesis are intimately related and how the exegetical mirror can act as a lens focusing on historical changes.

The set of views, opinions, beliefs, and attitudes regarding black Africans and how they have been perceived has a long and complex development. The history of Western perceptions of the black African has many tributaries, and we today are the most recent inheritors of this long accumulating history. In this sense, the results of this study are diametrically opposed to the view expressed by John Ralph Willis in his study "The Image of the African in Arabic Literature." Willis wrote that "there is no need to dwell on the unpleasant statements in Arabic literature regarding peoples of African descent. . . . The matter which concerns us here is the origin of the unfavorable attitude. . . . Those Arab writers showing antagonism to people of dark color echoed the external traditions of the Jews, Greeks and perhaps others."[22] As if discovering origins will reveal Truth. As if the support mechanisms that keep an idea in place over millennia are irrelevant.[23] Given the body of common Near Eastern traditions and the permeability of each culture in admitting and transmitting these traditions, to speak of origins, even were it possible, is not enough.

The Question of Racism

Throughout my research for this book I have had two models in mind, Frank Snowden's *Blacks in Antiquity* (1970) and Lloyd Thompson's *Romans and Blacks* (1989). The question both authors sought to answer was whether the world of classical antiquity was racist. Snowden was not the first to address the question, but he was the first to do so comprehensively. His attempt to examine every reference to black Africans, both literary and iconographic, in that world remains unsurpassed. With this magisterial work in mind, I have aimed for the same type of comprehensiveness in the Jewish world of antiquity. Thompson's contribution was to bring greater methodological nuance to the question of racism in antiquity. The main critique that has been leveled against Snowden was that he closed his eyes to obvious expressions of anti-Black sentiment in a world in which he believed there was none. Where Snowden refused to see anti-Black sentiment, Thompson saw it but explained it not as racism but as "ethnocentric reactions to a strange and unfamiliar appearance," and "expressions of conformism to the dominant aesthetic values."[24] Snowden saw this distinction too, but Thompson made it an important methodological basis of his work: "[Racism is evidenced by] reactions to an ideologically ascribed, and so almost infallibly predictable, social significance of a given set of somatic characteristics," whereas ethnocentrism, "a natural and universally evidenced human response," would allow for negative reactions to a strange and unfamiliar somatic appearance.[25] Ancient Roman society was indeed ethnocentric, but it was not racist.

The conclusion, shared by both classicists, that the ancient world was not racist hinges on their acceptance of the definition of racism as a socially defined creation. Racism exists when social structures assign "inferior and unalterable roles and rights" to a specific group; when this group cannot, practically speaking, assume the superior roles and rights of the dominant group; when a belief system or ideology supports these social structures; and when the group is defined by biological descent and perceptions of somatic and cultural identity. Looked at from the other direction, racial prejudice defines a set of attitudes that underlie discriminatory social structures. It is an attitude "that rests on an ideological perception of the individual as necessarily possessing particular desirable or undesirable qualities by virtue of his or her membership in a given socially defined group, in a social context in which the individual can do nothing to alter the basic situation."[26] This definition assumes two crucial differences between racism and ethnocentrism: biology and socially embedded discrimination.

Not everyone, however, agrees with this definition of racism. Others would consider any kind of social discrimination to be racist. Not biological hierarchy, but any hierarchy defines racism, for example, the cultural hierarchy of citizen-barbarian practiced in the Greco-Roman world, what others call ethnocentrism—in other words, institutionalized discrimination of any sort.[27] Still others would keep the biology and remove the social structures. To them, racism is "an ideology based on the conception that racial groups form a biogenetic hierarchy" period. Attributing inferiority or superiority to people on the basis of biological traits, "congenital inferiority" in the language of philosopher Harry Bracken, is the essence of racism.[28]

It seemed to me that if I would try to determine whether ancient Jewish society was racist, I would soon be up to my neck in theoretical quicksand. As an African American student once said in my class, racism is like obscenity, with which it is closely related: you know it when you see it, although it may be hard to define. When dealing with the Jewish material, therefore, I decided not to ask whether ancient Judaism was racist but instead to ask a simpler question: how did ancient Jewish society look at the black African? Only in the concluding chapter do I come back to the issue of racism to see how the answer to this question does or does not accord with various definitions of racism. I reasoned that to approach the topic this way would in any event lead to richer results, for it would attempt to describe in all its colors how Jews of antiquity, and then Christians and Muslims, perceived Blacks.

Some Remarks on Sources and Terminology

The Nature of the Evidence

The first half of this study explores the images of the black African found in Jewish society of the biblical and postbiblical periods. What is the nature of these images? As opposed to the Greco-Roman, and then Christian, world, they are not iconographic. There are some examples of representational art in early-century mosaics and in the wall paintings of the third-century Dura-Europas synagogue, but these depictions (mostly biblical scenes) contain no Blacks and thus provide no evidence for our purposes. Our images are all literary, starting with the Hebrew Bible of ancient Israel, continuing with Jewish writings in Greek, apocryphal and pseudepigraphical works, and the Dead Sea (Qumran) literature in the Hellenistic-Roman periods, and concluding with the rabbinic corpus (Talmud and Midrash) composed during the first seven or eight centuries C.E. The Bible consists of several different genres of literature, from the creation epics in Genesis to the love poem of Song of Songs, from the national founding narrative of Exodus to the universal wisdom of Proverbs. These many different genres and topics were gradually brought together and canonized as the core document of Judaism. But even before canonization occurred, and even while there were variant versions of some of its parts, this body of literature assumed a deep centrality in Jewish society. As a consequence, the vast majority of postbiblical Jewish literature consists of interpretation, expansion, commentary, discussion, and paraphrase of the Bible. Whether pseudepigraphic expansion or rabbinic interpretation, whether Philo's allegory or Pseudo-Philo's paraphrase, postbiblical Jewish literature generally takes the Bible as its starting point and its focus.

Determining a society's attitudes and perspectives from its literary remains is fraught with methodological difficulties. As Lloyd Thompson put it, "We depend almost entirely on the surviving remarks of a few long-dead people, none of which remarks was made in response to any carefully-worded question put to them by us."[29] Not only may the remains not properly represent the society, or even one group in the society, but the attitudes and views may never have been put into literary or iconographic form. In addition to these general methodological problems, much of postbiblical Jewish literature has its own set of difficulties for the historian, especially when we seek to uncover ideas and attitudes. This is particularly the case with regard to rabbinic literature, for the nature of this literature is such that it does not present systematic expositions of ideologies or attitudes. Such expositions may or may not have occurred in the rabbinic academies or study circles, but what we have in the extant literature does not record them. Furthermore, rabbinic literature is transmitted in a uniquely rhetorical discourse that presents barriers to historical inquiry.[30] The rabbinic medium does not allow for individual expression of the type that we find in the contemporaneous Greco-Roman world.[31] We do not find a parallel to Juvenal who would express his prejudices and preferences without mediation or mitigation.

Nevertheless, any interpretation of the biblical text will be influenced, however unconsciously, by the time and place of the interpreter, even as it attempts to explain or expand (also an interpretation) the text it is interpreting. Depending on the literary genre, the reflections of the interpreter's world may be explicit, like the *pesher* commentaries of the Dead Sea Scrolls or the homilies of the modern-day rabbi or preacher, or they may be implicit and hard to detect. Sometimes the influences of the interpreter's world may not be found in the content of the interpretation at all but only in the choice of one interpretation over another, or sometimes in the choice of one biblical verse to be interpreted over another. But the interpreter's world will surely be reflected in his work, one way or another.

And that world is not as narrowly defined as we tend to think from our perspective two thousand years later. The Jews of antiquity and late antiquity did not live in a vacuum but were part of a larger society and culture, a point abundantly reflected in the literature. The Hebrew Bible and the Hebrew-Aramaic Talmud and Midrash are suffused with foreign words and ideas. Rabbinic literature contains thousands of Greek loanwords that became part of the Jewish lexicon, reflecting social, literary, economic, and even theological influence. The opening chapters of the Bible are a uniquely Jewish theological statement fashioned from, and on the framework of, common ancient Near Eastern (Mesopotamian) material. The idiom, linguistic structure, and underlying concepts of Psalms, to take another example, are part and parcel of a larger ancient Near Eastern (Ugaritic) literary world. And, of course, Jewish literature written in Greek is thoroughly

Hellenistic. Two thousand years ago, as today, the Jewish world was constantly creating its world within a world, drawing on and reshaping foreign ideas. If Jewish literature, therefore, is a mirror of Jewish thought, as it is, then Jewish thought is a lens through which we may also perceive the non-Jewish surrounding environment.

Rabbinic Literature and Terminology

Much of the rabbinic source material used in this study will be unfamiliar to many readers. For this reason I have included a Glossary in which I briefly present the dates, place of composition, editions, and translations of the material, as well as definitions of unfamiliar terminology. Where available I have used critical editions of ancient texts, in which case the text is cited by the traditional section division, followed by the page number of the edition in parentheses. Thus *GenR* 36.7 (p. 341) refers to section 36.7, which is on p. 341 in Theodor and Albeck's edition of *Genesis Rabba*. For many of these texts, dating cannot be precise and is often given within the parameters of one or two centuries. Rabbinic texts and traditions chronologically belong either to the period of the *tannaim* (70–220 C.E.) or the *amoraim* (220–500). Beyond that gross classification, dating of rabbinic traditions is notoriously difficult, because anonymous early traditions may appear in works that were redacted much later than the traditions themselves. Even traditions that are attributed to named authorities may be much earlier than these authorities.[32] On the other hand, some scholars, emphasizing the role played by tradents and redactors of rabbinic traditions, accept the only certain date as the one of the final document in which the tradition is embedded.[33] My practice in this study is to date a tradition to the time of the authority in whose name the tradition is recorded. For our purposes, however, it matters little whether a tradition can be dated to, say, the year 135 or to the tannaitic period in general. Chronologically broad strokes in this regard will suffice. If the tradition is recorded anonymously, then I assign it the date of the redaction of the composition in which the tradition appears. An exception is made in the case of anonymous statements preceded by introductory markers of the tannaitic period, for example, *tanya*ʾ ("it is learned"), *teno rabanan* ("our Rabbis have taught"), and so on. Such traditions appearing in works of the amoraic period are regarded as being authentically tannaitic. All dates that appear in this study are C.E. unless otherwise noted.

The Rabbis

At times in this study I will speak of "the rabbinic view" of such-and-such a matter. This does not mean that all Rabbis over more than four hundred years agreed on a particular point. That would be unlikely were it even possible to ascertain a full documentation of rabbinic opinions. It means rather, in the words of Jay Harris, "that there is a certain conception of the past that finds expression in a number of rabbinic documents, that is not explicitly challenged and that serves as the basis for other discussions in the literature. . . . [It] shows the compatibility of certain claims and the broader culture."[34] The results of my research claim that there are indeed certain rabbinic conceptions (and lack of conceptions) concerning the black African; that these conceptions and perceptions are in agreement with the antecedent Jewish cultures of the biblical and Hellenistic-Roman periods, as they are with Near Eastern cultures generally. Not until after the rabbinic period in the seventh century do these views begin to change.

Cushite/Kushite/Nubian/Ethiopian/Black/Black African

The area south of Egypt descending into central Africa and extending east to the Red Sea was known to the ancient Near Eastern cultures as Kush. This is the name found in the Hebrew Bible. In Greek writing the name for this land was Ethiopia. We also find the name Nubia in the earlier sources. A more general term for the sub-Saharan inhabitants of Africa is Black or black African, terms commonly used in Greco-Roman studies. In this study I use all terms interchangeably as called for by the context. My preference is to avoid the use of Ethiopia as much as possible because of the association of the name with the modern nation-state, which is not the same as the ancient land of Kush. The capitalization of Black is intended to distinguish individuals whose ancestry is from sub-Saharan Africa from other dark-skinned people. In most translations of the Bible the name Kush is written with a *c:* Cush. This is due to the influence of Latin, which acted as an intermediary between the ancient and modern languages. Today, however, more and more scholars are writing Kush, which reflects the original spelling of the name in pre-Latin texts. I prefer this for consistency, since the phoneme *k* in ancient Near Eastern languages is transliterated with *k* and not *c*. Sometimes (infrequently), to avoid confusion, I will change Cush to Kush in a quotation.

Israel/Palestine/The Land of Israel

Due to today's political climate many scholars are reluctant to use the terminology of previous generations for the name of the Land of Israel in late antiquity and the rabbinic period. In the past "Palestine" was the term commonly used but the political connotations of the name today have led some to avoid it. "Israel" is linguistically the simplest alternative, and some have adopted the term, but the name is historically problematic since it connotes the State of Israel, which came into existence only some fifty years ago. "The Land of Israel" (or its Hebrew counterpart "Eretz Israel") is historically accurate but stylistically cumbersome. The same problem of terminology obtains for the rabbinic composition known as the "Palestinian Talmud." Some use the alternative "Jerusalem Talmud," an accurate translation of the Hebrew title of the work. But "Jerusalem Talmud" never did become universally accepted, even in the past, for good reason: this Talmud was created primarily in Tiberius. I have not shied away from using the chronologically inaccurate but reader-friendly "Israel"; nor have I totally avoided the mouthful "Land of Israel." Nor, when dealing with the postbiblical period, have I rejected the older usage of "Palestine."

Translation and Transliteration

Bible translations usually follow one or more of the English versions, as noted. Translations of other sources are my own unless otherwise stated. Hebrew transliteration generally follows a popular format, for example, Hebrew *shin* is rendered *sh* and not *š*, vowel length is not indicated (*ḥam* and not *ḥām; kush* and not *kûsh*), nor are reduced vowels (*shaḥarut,* not *shaḥ*ᵃ*rut*), nor doubled consonants and initial *alef* (*afriqiyim* and not *ʾafriqiyyim*). But when the discussion moves to philological issues these indications are preserved and a modified system of scientific transliteration of the consonants is adopted (*ʾ, b* or *v, g, d, h, w, z, ḥ, ṭ, y, k* or *kh, l, m, n, s, ʿ, p* or *f, ṣ, q, r, š, ś, t* or *th*). Arabic transliteration follows standard practice, and vowel lengthening and doubled consonants are shown. Syriac transliteration generally is shown without vowels. Other languages follow standard rules for those languages. Egyptian and Epigraphic Hebrew do not indicate vocalization, and when transliterating such texts, depending on the context, vowels may or may not be supplied: for example, *Kš* (*Kɜš*) or *Kuš* for Kush. Spellings of biblical names differ from English Bible translations only in having *k* and not *c* represent Hebrew *kaf;* thus Kush, Sabteka. Names not generally found in the Bible are transliterated (Yoḥanan, not Johanan), unless the names are commonly found in English, in which case the familiar spelling is used (Akiba, not ʿAkiva or Akiva).

PART I

IMAGES OF BLACKS

ONE

BIBLICAL ISRAEL: THE LAND OF KUSH

HOW DID THE ancient Israelites view the black African? Our main body of evidence for ancient Israel is the Hebrew Bible. Although other evidence is also found, the Hebrew Bible is the main repository of information for ancient Israel, including its views of the black African. Indeed, the Bible refers to these people a number of times, which should not be surprising as they were part of the ancient Near East and played a role in its history. Of course, before we can say anything about biblical views of the black African, we must first know when the biblical text refers to black Africa and its people. This is not as easy as it seems. If we look at modern translations of the Bible, we often find the terms "Ethiopia" and "Ethiopian," which go back to the early Greek and Latin translations of the original Hebrew. In the Greek- and Latin-speaking world of antiquity "Ethiopia" meant black Africa. These terms are always translations of the original Hebrew "Kush" and "Kushi," but are they correct translations? Do Kush and Kushi in the Hebrew Bible always refer to "Ethiopia," that is, black Africa? Our first task, then, will be to determine when the Bible means black Africa. Once we have done that, we will look at what the text says and try to determine what attitudes the Israelites had of this land and its people.

Kush was the Egyptian name (*kȝš*) for the area to the south of Egypt extending deep into East Central Africa. Its border with Egypt ranged from between the first and second cataracts (waterfalls) of the Nile during the early Egyptian dynasties down to the fourth cataract in the biblical period. The name Kush, first found in Egyptian texts from the twentieth century B.C.E., was taken over into several languages of the ancient Near East, including Babylonian (*kūšu*), Assyrian (*kūsu*), Old Persian (*kūšā*), Old Nubian (*kas*), and Hebrew (*kûš*).[1] Some Christian fathers and onomastic lists give the meaning "darkness" or "blackness" for the name Kush.[2] This interpretation seems to go back to Origen, who is apparently dependent on Philo's etymology of the name from the Greek word χοῦς 'dust, dirt'.[3] The name Kush, however, is not Greek, and its etymology therefore cannot be derived from Greek vocabulary.[4] Contrary to what some moderns suggest,[5] we do not know the meaning of the name. The Greeks usually called the area Ethiopia, sometimes Nubia. Between approximately 760 B.C.E.

and 320 C.E., Kush was the center of an empire and civilization, whose capital was first at Napata (near the fourth cataract) and then further south at Meroe (between the fifth and sixth cataracts). For about the first hundred years of this period the Kushite kings ruled Egypt and were known as the twenty-fifth or Ethiopian (or Nubian or Kushite) Dynasty.[6]

In the Hebrew Bible the term Kush usually designates this area in Africa south of Egypt including the lands bordering the Red Sea. So, for example, Ezek 29:10 indicates that Kush was geographically situated in an area south of Egypt, beginning at Syene (i.e., Aswan).[7] The same information is provided by the Greek geographer Strabo (b. 64/63 B.C.E.).[8] References to this African Kush in the Bible are common, especially where Kush is paired with Egypt (Isa 20:3–4, 43:3, 45:14; Ezek 29:10, 30:4, 9; cf. Dan 11:43; Nah 3:9; Ps 68:32).[9] Similarly, the line from Jeremiah (13:23), "Can the Kushite change his skin?" refers to the dark-skinned Nubian. The Kushite dynasty of Egypt is referred to a few times in the Bible, most notably in 2 Kgs 19:9 (= Isa 37:9) where Tirhaqa, who reigned as one of the Kushite pharaohs of Egypt between 690 and 633 B.C.E., is called "King of Kush."[10]

In several instances in the Bible, however, "Kush" seems to refer to a location not in Africa. The Table of Nations in Gen 10:7 (and 1 Chron 1:9) lists "the descendants of Kush: Seba, Havilah, Sabtah, Raamah, and Sabteka; the descendants of Raamah: Sheba and Dedan." Are these descendants or locations in Africa, which would seem to be required, if Kush, the ancestor, is located in Africa? In regard to Seba there are indeed a number of indications arguing for a location in Africa. Isa 43:3 groups together Egypt, Kush, and Seba, thus pointing to an African location.[11] Isa 45:14 has the same grouping (Egypt, Kush, Sebaites) and characterizes the Sebaites as "tall," which further points to an African location in view of Isa 18:1–2, "Beyond the rivers of Ethiopia . . . to a people tall and smooth."[12] In addition, Josephus (first century C.E.) and Strabo locate Seba in Africa.[13] Consider also the early Christian traditions that identify the queen of Sheba (= Seba) with the queen of Ethiopia, and the onomastic lists that define Saba, Sabaeans as "Ethiopians."[14] Some scholars have therefore concluded that Seba is indeed to be located in Africa.[15] Despite this, there is general agreement that the other names of Kush's descendants (according to some even Seba) correspond to names of peoples who inhabited areas not in Africa but in the southern and southwestern parts of the Arabian peninsula.[16]

This, however, does not necessarily mean that the descendants of Kush in Arabia and the African Kushites are of different ethnic stock, for historically there was always movement across the Red Sea and the Sinai peninsula between Africa and Arabia.[17] The biblical conception informing the Table of Nations, therefore, that the people on both sides of the Red Sea were ethnically related and descended from the same Kushite ancestor probably reflects the historical situation. This relationship between the peoples on either side of the Red Sea is, incidentally, paralleled in the field of linguistics, where scholars now see a relationship between the respective families of languages and refer to a parent family as Afro-Asiatic (formerly called Hamito-Semitic). "In recent years the feeling has grown in linguistic circles . . . that the linguistic criteria for dividing the Semitic and Hamitic languages into two distinct blocks do not exist. All these languages have certain common elements in vocabulary, morphemes and patterns of grammatical behavior (especially in verb conjugation), which are characteristic of the whole family."[18] Whether original Arabian Kushite tribes migrated into eastern Africa and gave their name to the land, or African Kushites migrated into Arabia, in the biblical view the peoples on either side of the Red Sea were regarded as of the same Kushite stock.[19]

Today we see the Red Sea as separating two distinct lands, Africa and Arabia. But in antiquity it was not seen that way. Indeed, in the world of classical antiquity, from Herodotus to Strabo, the term Arabia included the area across the Red Sea up until the Nile. It wasn't the Red Sea but the Nile that constituted the boundary between Africa and Asia.[20] The same perspective may well lie behind the Palestinian Targums that associate Arabia with Kush in Gen 10:6 and translate "Arabia" for "Kush" in 1 Chr 1:8.[21] It may also account for the Septuagint's refusal to translate Kush in Gen 10:6–8 as "Ethiopia," which is its translation everywhere else in the Hebrew Bible. Only here does the Septuagint simply transliterate the name of the land as Kush (Χούς). Lastly, note that in Herodotus's description of the various ethnic units that composed Xerxes' army, the Ethiopians and Arabs are grouped together in one unit under a single commander.[22] These Greek and Roman (and, perhaps, Aramaic) sources point to the same phenomenon as do the ancient Near Eastern sources—that the Red Sea did not serve as an ethnic boundary and land on both its sides shared the same name, whether that name was Arabia in the Greek sources or Kush in the Bible (and perhaps, the Targum). Indeed, according to some Latin sources, "Ethiopia" extended eastward as far as the Indus.[23]

In addition to Kush in Africa and South or Southwest Arabia, there is another people of that name known from the ancient Near East. A group of nomadic or seminomadic tribes located in the Negev or on the southern border of Israel identified as Kushu (*kwšw*) is mentioned in Middle Egyptian execration texts (nineteenth or eighteenth century B.C.E.), and possibly in other Egyptian sources as well.[24] Scholars have variously identified these bedouin people behind some of the biblical references to Kush or Kushite, such as Zerah the Kushite (2 Chron 14:8–14, 16:8), the Kushites who were "neighbors of Arabs" (2 Chron 21:16), Kushan in

Habakkuk 3:7,[25] and the Kushites in the service of the kings of Judah (2 Sam 18.21ff., Jer 38.7ff.).[26] It has also been pointed out that the biblical reference (1 Chron 4:40) to the area of Simeon's territory near Gedor (or Gerar) as having been formerly inhabited by descendants of Ham (*min ḥam*), would support the notion of a Kushite people in the northern Negev at the southern borders of Israel. Simeon's territory was located in the southern part of ancient Israel bordering on the Negev.[27] The existence of a Kushite people in this general area and references to it in the Bible have become well accepted in biblical scholarship.[28]

Whether these Kushites were related to the African and Southwest Arabian Kushites is not clear. There may have been a Kushite migration to the southern border area of Judah.[29] Or there may have been no ethnic connection at all, and the same name was applied to northern Arabia because one had to pass through it to get to Kush in Africa or the southern part of Arabia, just as, for the same reason, the northern region of Arabia was called Miṣir or Muṣri (i.e., Egypt) by the people of western Asia.[30]

Finally, there is yet one other Kushite people whose echo is found in the Bible: "Kush also begot Nimrod. . . . The mainstays of his kingdom were Babylon, Erech, Accad" (Gen 10:8–12). It is unlikely that this Kush, who is associated with the lands of Mesopotamia, is related to either an African or an Arabian Kush. Most scholars feel, rather, that the Nimrod Kush is associated with the Kassites (*Kaššu/Kuššu* in the cuneiform texts, Greek *Kossaioi*) of Mesopotamia who overthrew the first Babylonian dynasty in 1595 B.C.E. and ruled Babylon for the next 450 years.[31] During this long period, Babylonia was known as the land of the Kassites. The biblical Kush who "begot Nimrod" of Mesopotamia is seen as a literary echo of these Kassites.[32]

In sum, Kush in the Hebrew Bible usually refers to East Africa or Southwest Arabia, sometimes to North Arabia or South Israel, and, at least once, to Mesopotamia. The early Greek and Latin translations of the Bible do not distinguish between the different areas, translating them all as "Ethiopia," that is, Nubia. Through these translations the name Kush became exclusively identified with Africa.

Descriptions and images of the African Kush, preserved in the Hebrew Bible, will give us a picture of how the land was perceived by the Jews of antiquity. In only a few places does the Bible describe aspects of the topography, resources, and geographical location of Nubia. Gen 2:13 refers to a river called Giḥon, "that winds through the whole land of Kush."[33] Some claim that Giḥon is the Egyptian *giyon,* which is the Amharic name given to the springs and waterfalls of the Blue Nile.[34] Isa 18:2 describes Kush as "*bazʾu* by rivers." Some early versions (Old Greek recensions, Peshiṭta, Vulgate) translate "plundered," assuming a relationship to the Hebrew root *bzz.* A recent attempt connects the word to the Arabic *bazza* 'pull along forcibly', and renders the Hebrew "wash away."[35] Most modern translations, however, assume that the word is related to the Syriac *bzʿ* 'to pierce, cleave' and translate the verse accordingly, giving the sense of the rivers dividing the land.[36] To his translation "cut through by streams" Wildberger adds that "everyone who visits the country is impressed by the way the southern part of Kush is crisscrossed with mighty rivers."[37] Indeed, Isa 18:1 mentions "the region of the rivers of Kush." The phrase "cut through by streams," however, may not be a reference to the crisscrossing of many rivers but to the division of the land into two by the Nile. This is precisely how Homer described Ethiopia according to Strabo. Homer referred to the Ethiopians "who dwell sundered in twain," which Strabo understood as meaning the division of the land by the Nile.[38]

Job 28:19 indicates that gold and topaz (chrysolite) were among the natural resources of Kush/Nubia. Pliny parallels this report in regard to chrysolite, which, he says, Ethiopia exports.[39] Regarding gold, there is a plethora of evidence. Indeed, Upper Egypt and Kush had the richest gold mines in antiquity and Kush "was principally renowned for its gold production."[40] Gold was a major Kushite import to Egypt during the eighteenth to twentieth Dynasties (1570–1090 B.C.E.) and ancient Egyptian paintings show captured Kushites bringing gold to the pharaoh.[41] Herodotus speaks about the gold wealth of Ethiopia (3.114), and he adds that prisoners in Ethiopia are bound with fetters made of gold (3.23, cf. 22; Mela 3.86). Agatharchides of Cnidus (second century B.C.E.) mentions the "many large gold mines, where gold is extracted in great quantity."[42] If Sheba is to be located in Africa, the biblical story of the queen of Sheba bringing gold and precious stones to King Solomon (1 Kgs 10:2, 2 Chr 9:1) may be another indication of the wealth of gold in this area (see also Ezek 27.22 and Dan 11:43). As late as the first century C.E. we find Pliny referring to a district in Ethiopia that "produces a large amount of gold" and Strabo mentioning the gold mines of Meroe in Ethiopia.[43] It should also be noted that the name "Nubia," first attested in Eratosthenes in the third century B.C.E., may derive from the Egyptian word for gold, *nbw*—that is, Nubia is the Land of Gold.[44]

One enigmatic passage in the Bible may also point to a Nubian natural resource, although it is not clear what that resource is. Apparently describing those who will recognize God and come to worship him, Ps 68:32/31 states that "*ḥashmanim* will come out of Egypt; Kush shall stretch out its hands to God."[45] The difficult Hebrew word, which occurs but once in the Hebrew Bible, has been translated as meaning either princes, nobles, envoys, or some sort of rich tribute (or those who bring tribute), such as bronze vessels, red cloth, or blue-green wool.[46] Although the *ḥashmanim* are said to derive from Egypt, not Kush, the parallelism of the two names would indicate an association between them, most probably placing the psalm at the time of the Nubian dynasty of Egypt.

The one perception of the land of Kush that has been very influential in subsequent depictions of Kush and its inhabitants is found in Amos 9:7. This verse has also been subject to, not coincidentally, serious misinterpretation. Certainly for this study, which attempts to examine ancient Israelite and Jewish attitudes toward the Kushites, a verse that states "Are you not like the Kushites to me, O Israelites?" takes on added significance.

What does Amos mean by this comparison? A common interpretation by Bible scholars until recent times claimed that the prophet meant to denigrate Israel. Just as the dark-skinned Kushites were held in contempt, so too were the Israelites. Take William R. Harper for example: "Israel, says the prophet, is no more to me than the far distant, uncivilized, and despised black race of the Ethiopians."[47] How did Harper know that the Ethiopians were despised? "Their color and the fact that slaves were so often drawn from them added to the grounds for despising them."[48] S. R. Driver can serve as another example: "The Kushites, or Ethiopians, are mentioned as a distant people, far removed from the grace and knowledge of God, despised on account of their dark colour (cf. Jer 13:23), and perhaps also on account of slaves being often drawn from them. Degenerate Israel is no more in Jehovah's eyes than these despised Kushites."[49] There is, however, no evidence from the ancient Near East in general or ancient Israel in particular that Ethiopians were "despised on account of their dark color. . . . There is, of course, no slightest suggestion that the colour of their skin is the point at issue; there is no warrant anywhere in the Bible for that kind of idea."[50] Nor is there any warrant anywhere in the Bible that black Africa provided a disproportionate number of slaves in the ancient Near East or that black Africans were known to the Israelites "mostly as slaves."[51] It appears rather that Harper and Driver and others like them were interpolating the assumptions and prejudices of their time into the biblical text. "[The] statement reflects Driver's own attitude rather than that of Amos . . . or the ancient Israelites."[52]

Harper and Driver were not the first to express these views. The negative interpretation of Amos 9:7 has a old pedigree. Two hundred years before them the Puritan Bible scholar Matthew Poole (d. 1679) explained the word "Ethiopian" in the text this way: "i.e. most vile and ignoble," an explanation that ultimately goes back to early Christian exegesis.[53] For example, Augustine's (d. 430) explanation of "Ethiopians" in Ps 72/71:9 as "the remotest and foulest of mankind" couples geographic and moral distance.[54] This kind of interpretation became so well established that even the scholar of Ethiopia in antiquity, Edward Ullendorff, accepted it.[55] Probably the most egregious examples of such an interpretation are those involving Bible instruction for the religious. Driver's work was part of a series called *The Cambridge Bible for Schools and Colleges.* Unfortunately, even in recent times we can find similar cases. In 1979 the American Bible

Society published *A Translator's Handbook on the Book of Amos*, which explains our verse by virtue of the fact that the Ethiopians are a "despised people."[56]

However, another interpretation is gaining ground among scholars of the Hebrew Bible today and appears dominant: the purpose of the verse is to reject the belief that Israel has a special status before God; the Israelites are just like any other people. The Kushim/Ethiopians are specifically mentioned as representative of the other nations because of their remote distance. "Are you not like the Kushites to me, O Israelites" proclaims, in other words, that the Israelites are no more special to God than the most remote people on the face of the earth. "Even the most inaccessible nation is still under God's surveillance and sovereignty, as is Israel."[57] This interpretation has much in its favor.

The idea that the Ethiopians, that is, the black Africans, are the most remote peoples in the world is commonly found in classical sources, as in Homer's description of them as "the farthermost of men" (ἔσχατοι ἀνδρῶν).[58] The very term "Ethiopian" in ancient Greek sources, came to designate the remote southern peoples, just as "Scythian" came to designate the remote northern peoples.[59] These designations underlie a common topos in the classical world, that is, the use of a Scythian-Ethiopian pairing as a way to refer to the geographical extremes of the inhabited world. The topos is most frequently found in the widespread environmental theory of anthropological differentiation. The extremes of weather and environment in the remote north and south provided the explanation for different racial traits, including skin color. Since the peoples in the far north and far south were the lightest- and darkest-skinned people known to the Greeks and Romans, the Scythian-Ethiopian pairing came to be used to designate anthropological and racial, as well as geographical, extremes.[60] Sometimes other northern peoples (Thracians, Gauls, Saxons, Germans) were substituted, or "Egyptian" replaced "Ethiopian," but in general the Scythians and Ethiopians became the formulaic expression of racial extremes in the Greco-Roman world.[61] "The Ethiopian-Scythian formula had appeared as early as Hesiod and had become a frequent, if not the favorite, Hellenic illustration of the boundaries of the north and south as well as of the environment theory."[62] Thus from the earliest days of Greek literature, that is, as early as the eighth century B.C.E., the Kushim/Ethiopians were considered to be the most remote (southern) people on the face of the earth. It should not be too surprising that the same idea circulated in the eastern Mediterranean, in Israel, at the same time. The prophet Amos and the poet Homer are both said to have lived in the eighth century.

It would seem that this connotation of remoteness, which so defined the Ethiopians in the ancient world, underlies Amos 9:7. Not only do the classical sources support this interpretation, but so do some ancient Near Eastern and biblical sources, in which Kush indicates the ends of the earth. The Assyrian usage of the name Meluḫḫa to mean Ethiopia, according to the regnant view, is due to the fact that Ethiopia was thought to be the most remote land.[63] An Aramaic text in demotic script dating from the fourth century B.C.E. pairs Ethiopia and Elam to indicate "the ends of the known world."[64] Apparently the combination of Syria-Palestine (*Khзrw*) and Kush have the same meaning in a fourteenth-century B.C.E. Egyptian text, the Hymn to Aton.[65] The Persian king Darius describes the extent of his empire by reference to its geographic extremes in the north, south, east, and west: "Saith Darius the King: This is the kingdom which I hold, from the Scythians who are beyond Sogdiana, thence unto Ethiopia (*Kāšū*); from India (*Hidauv*), thence unto Sardis."[66] This inscription, of course, is reminiscent of a similar formula found in the biblical book of Esther (1:1), "from India (*Hodu*) to Ethiopia (*Kush*)," indicating the great extent of Ahasueres' kingdom of Persia.[67] It would appear that the connotation of remoteness also underlies the choice of Kush in Zephaniah's prophecy against the nations (2:12), thus indicating God's universal reach to the most remote parts of the world.[68] Similarly the names of "Egypt, Kush, and Seba" in Isa 43:3 and 45:14 were "probably chosen because they represent the most remote regions known to Israelites."[69] Apparently the same may be said for Ps 68:32/31, "Kush shall stretch out her hands to God." By the choice of Kush in this verse, the psalmist indicates that those from the farthest reaches of the world will come to know God. Compare also the NJPS translation of Isa 18:1–2, "Ah, land . . . beyond the rivers of Nubia! Go, swift messengers, to a nation far and remote, to a people thrust forth and away."

This ancient view of the geography of the inhabited world probably also explains the two references to Ethiopians found in the Greek and Latin versions of Psalms but not in the Hebrew original. Psalm 72/71, "a prayer of David son of Jesse" concerning Solomon, entreats God that "the king" be endowed with righteousness, that he may champion the lowly, the poor and the needy who cry out. Verses 8–11 ask that the king be powerful and rule over a great empire:

> Let him rule from sea to sea, from the river to the ends of the earth.
> Let desert dwellers kneel before him, and his enemies lick the dust.
> Let kings of Tarshish and the island pay tribute, kings of Sheba and Seba offer gifts.
> Let all kings bow to him, and all nations serve him.

Where the Hebrew has "desert dwellers" (*ṣiyyim*) the Greek texts of the Septuagint, Aquila, and Symmachus, as well as the Vulgate have "Ethiopians" (*Aithiopes*).[70] Substitution of "Ethiopian" for "desert dweller" is a natural interpretation of the difficult Hebrew word because these verses describe the "ends of the earth" from where all kings will come and pay tribute to the king of Israel. Furthermore, the combination of Kush, Seba, and Sheba occurs elsewhere in the Bible (Isa 43:3 and 45:14), as noted earlier.[71] The substitution of "Ethiopians" for "desert dwellers" having been made, it was then automatically made again two chapters later for the same difficult Hebrew word (*ṣiyyim*) in Ps 74/73:14, where we find *Aithiopes* once again in the Septuagint, the Vulgate, and other versions.[72]

The belief that Kush is found at end of the earth lies behind the choice of an Ethiopian as the first gentile convert to Christianity (Acts 8:26–40). Nothing could more visibly indicate the universalist posture of the early church than the conversion of those from the most remote parts of the world. Indeed, Philip's conversion of the Ethiopian became a symbol of Christianity's conversion of the world, and in Christian metaphor (beginning with Origen in the third century) the "Ethiopian" became the symbol for the church of the gentiles. As Augustine said explaining "Ethiopians" in Ps 72/71:9, "By the Ethiopians, as by a part the whole, He signifies all nations, selecting that nation to mention especially by name, which is at the ends of the earth." And Augustine explained that the same interpretation is to be given also to our verse in Ps 68:32/31, "Ethiopia, which seems to be the utmost limit of the gentiles."[73] Given the evidence from classical, ancient Near Eastern, and biblical sources, it appears quite certain that the connotation of Ethiopians/Kushites as being the most remote southern peoples on the face of the earth is the key to Amos 9:7.[74]

In summary, biblical references to the place Kush or the people Kushites, usually mean Nubia/Ethiopia and its inhabitants, including the territory and people on the (south or southwestern) Arabian side of the Red Sea, but may on occasion refer to the Semitic Kushu on the southern borders of Israel in the Negev and the North Arabian desert. In addition, the Kush who is the father of Nimrod is to be associated with the Mesopotamian Kassites. Whether or not the biblical author in compiling the genealogy of Kush in Genesis 10 "sought dexterously to explain" the existence of different peoples or geographical entities sharing the same name, it appears that the biblical references to Kush do not all indicate the same people or land.[75] The Bible knows that African Kush is "sundered in twain" by the Nile (and/or it is crisscrossed by a multitude of rivers); that it is a rich source of gold and topaz; and, most important, that it is the land at the furthest southern reach of the earth. The image of Kush as being at the end of the earth, we shall see, has important ramifications for the image of the black African that develops in the postbiblical period.

TWO

BIBLICAL ISRAEL:
THE PEOPLE OF KUSH

NOW THAT WE have determined when the Bible refers to Nubia/Kush, what the ancient Israelites knew about the land, and how they perceived it, we can begin our investigation into the biblical views of, and attitudes toward, the people of that land. Kushites are mentioned in a number of places in the Hebrew Bible, but we cannot, of course, restrict our investigation to the Bible. Ancient Israel's attitudes and perceptions must be located within the larger ancient Near Eastern context, of which it was part. In addition, as we saw in the last chapter, Greco-Roman perceptions of the Black can also help illuminate contemporaneous Jewish perceptions.

Numbers 12:1

One of the most interesting Kushite passages in the Bible is the reference to Moses' wife. Much has been written against and in favor of Blacks based on this passage. Some have seen this biblical event as the first recorded instance of racism; others, as a divine declaration for a color-blind brotherhood; yet others, as both; and still others, as neither.

> Miriam and Aaron spoke against Moses because of the Kushite woman whom he had married (for [*ki*] he had indeed married a Kushite woman); and they said, "Has the Lord spoken only through Moses? Has he not spoken through us also?" (Num 12:1–2; NRSV)

The translation given, that of NRSV (similarly RSV and NEB), presumes that the clause "for he had indeed married a Kushite woman" is the narrator's parenthetical remark providing the reader with necessary background information.[1] As the medieval Jewish exegete Bekhor Shor (twelfth century) said: "Since nowhere were we told that Moses had married a Kushite, Scripture tells us 'for indeed he had married a Kushite.'"[2] This translation is commonly found in modern as well as medieval biblical commentators.[3] Other translations are, however, possible. NJPS, based on Ibn Ezra's (d. 1164) statement that *ki* introduces direct discourse, translates: "Miriam and Aaron spoke against Moses because of the Kushite woman he had married: 'He married a Kushite woman.'"[4] It is also possible to interpret *ki* as indicating indirect discourse: "Miriam and Aaron spoke against Moses because of the Kushite woman he had married, that he had married a Kushite woman."[5]

Whether we understand the *ki* clause as explanatory, as direct discourse, or as indirect discourse, the complaint against Moses was that he had married a Kushite woman. Who was this woman and what was the reason for the complaint? Until recently biblical scholars had commonly understood "Kushite" in this verse to refer to the African Kushites. This understanding is not surprising. After all, that is the common biblical meaning of the name, and it has been enshrined in Bible translations since the Septuagint's "Ethiopian" rendering of Num 12:1 over two thousand years ago. What is somewhat surprising, however, is the degree to which scholars—biblical and otherwise—have read their modern day assumptions and prejudices into the biblical text. Thus many have understood this incident in the Bible as an ancient example of racism, for it shows Aaron and Miriam's disapproval of Moses' marriage to a Black.[6] Or, if Moses' wife is not actually Black, Aaron and Miriam mean to insult her by characterizing her as one.[7]

Even more surprising is how some scholars have assumed that because Moses' wife was a black African (as they think), she was therefore a slave. In Hastings's well-respected *Dictionary of the Bible* (1911), D. S. Margoliouth remarked that the reason for Miriam and Aaron's objection to Moses' marriage is that the woman he married was a "black slave-girl."[8] Ullendorff, who wrote a book on Ethiopia and the Bible, also speaks of "the obvious interpretation that Moses had married an Ethiopian slave-girl."[9] The Bible, however, says nothing of the Kushite being a slave.

Many scholars became convinced of the Black or racist interpretation of Numbers because of the punishment of leprosy God inflicted on Miriam for speaking against her brother Moses (Num 12:10). The "snow-white" leprosy is seen as an apt response to a racist slur about a black African. This is a common interpretation of Miriam's affliction, which is found in writings by both Blacks and non-Blacks, whether theologically or scholarly based, over many years.[10] Biblicists, however, now generally agree that the Hebrew term (*ṣaraʿat*) used to describe the punishment of Moses' sister is not leprosy, nor is it a category of diseases that includes leprosy. It is doubtful that leprosy even existed in the ancient Near East at the time of the Hebrew Bible. The evidence presented by the Bible indicates rather that *ṣaraʿat* is a disease or group of diseases that exhibit a flaking or exfoliation of the skin, symptoms that are common to several skin diseases (psoriasis, eczema, seborrhea, etc.). The biblical description of the disease in our passage and in others (Ex 4:6, Num 12:10, 2 Kgs 5:27) as "like snow" does not refer to the color of the disease but to its characteristic flakiness. The adjective "white" that accompanies the "like snow" description in various translations is *not* in the original Hebrew text.[11] The passage in Numbers actually provides evidence of a nonwhite color of the disease, as well as its flaky characteristic, for it describes the condition as similar to a "dead [fetus] when it comes out of its mother's womb." The color of a fetus that has died in the womb is reddish, which turns brown-gray after a few days out of the womb. As for its flaky condition, a dead fetus in utero sheds its skin in large sheets.[12]

Finally, even if *ṣaraʿat* did mean "snow-white" leprosy, why should that punishment be an apt response to a racist slur against black Africans? The disease is found in the Hebrew Bible as God's punishment for different sorts of sins, none of which have anything to do with Blacks. Joab and his descendants are cursed with it for the crime of murder (2 Sam 3:29); Gehazi is afflicted with it for acting deceitfully (2 Kgs 5); King Azariah, for not removing the high places (2 Kgs 15:5); and King Uzziah for improperly offering incense in the temple (2 Chr 26:16–21).

In short, the interpretation of Num 12:1 that sees Miriam and Aaron deprecating black Africans is a product of modern assumptions read back into the Bible. Looking at the biblical sources without the skewing prism of postbiblical history provides no such reading of the text. There is no evidence here that biblical Israel saw black Africans in a negative light.

What then was the complaint against Moses, and who was the Kushite whom he had married? As we saw in the previous chapter, there was a people, or group of people, inhabiting the Negev and northern Arabia, known as Kushites. Now the prophet Habakkuk parallels Kushan with Midian: "The tents of Kushan . . . the dwellings of Midian" (Hab 3:7). Because Midian is located in the same general area as these Negev or North-Arabian Kushites, that is, northwest Arabia, and because the name Kushan is a lengthened form of Kush, scholars have therefore concluded that there is some historical connection between Kush(an) and Midian.[13] It is generally thought that the Arabian Kushites assimilated among the Midianites, just as the Midianites later assimilated among the Ishmaelites, and the Ishmaelites among the Arabs. Thus, Kush(an) is the ancient name of Midian or the name of a tribe that had close ties to Midian.[14]

This identity of the Arabian Kush with Midian is the key to understanding the passage in Numbers that speaks of Moses' Kushite wife. According to the earlier biblical narrative, Moses indeed had a wife, Zipporah, who was a Midianite (Ex 2:21). When the Bible says, therefore, that Moses had a Kushite wife, it is referring to the same Midianite wife Zipporah, but is using the ancient name of her people. "The Kushite" of Num 12:1 is just another name for the "the Midianite." The identity of the names is found in Christian sources as early as the fifth century and in Jewish sources of the Hellenistic period and the later Middle Ages.[15] It has become very well accepted among modern-day biblicists.[16]

If the translations of RSV, NRSV, and NEB ("for he had indeed married a Kushite woman") are correct, it would imply that at the time of the composition of these verses in Numbers, this ancient name for Midian was no longer so well known, and the biblical author therefore interjects the parenthetical remark, "for he had indeed married a Kushite woman." If the direct discourse (Ibn Ezra and NJPS) or the indirect discourse translation is correct, I argue that the identification of Kush(an) with Midian may still have been known, and therefore occasioned no biblical explanation. In any case, the identification of Kush(an) with Midian allows the biblical narrative to make sense on its own terms and does not force us to posit events not provided by the narrative, that is, a second marriage by Moses.

Whether we understand "Kushite" in Num 12:1 as another name for Midianite or whether we understand the word to mean Ethiopian, the point of Miriam and Aaron's complaint was that Moses had taken a non-Israelite wife. In having God punish Miriam for arguing against the marriage, the Bible implicitly acknowledges the acceptability of foreign marriage.[17] The story of Moses' marriage to the Kushite, then, is neither the first recorded instance of racism nor a divine declaration for a color-blind brotherhood. Still less is it both of these. Whether the Kushite is a black African or not, color is not the issue of concern in the text.

Isaiah 18:1–2 (18:7)

A passage in Isaiah (18:1–2; repeated in verse 7) describes one aspect of the land of Kush and several characteristics of the Kushites. In fact, these two verses contain the Bible's most detailed description of the black African. While the passage, however, is reasonably clear regarding its description of the land of Kush, as we saw in the previous chapter, its description of the people of Kush is full of linguistic problems and has been the subject of a multitude of different interpretations. By way of illustration, to its translation of these two verses ICC (G. B. Gray) inserts six question marks, and even the more recent NJPS version provides an alternate translation to one line and admits "meaning of Hebrew uncertain" to two others. A sense of the difficulties may be gained by looking at two different recent translations, those of the Continental Commentaries series (H. Wildberger) and the New Jewish Publication Society.

Ha! The land of the winged boats
[which is situated] in the region
  of the rivers of Kush,
which sends envoys on the river,
and [in] papyrus canoes on the water.
Go, you nimble messengers,
to a tall, smooth nation,

Ah, land in the deep shadow of wings,
Beyond the rivers of Nubia!
Go, swift messengers,
To a nation far and remote,
To a people thrust forth and away—
A nation of gibber and chatter—
Whose land is cut off by streams;

to a people feared far and wide, to a nation, which tramples down with muscle power, whose land is cut through by streams. (CC)[18]	Which sends out envoys by sea, In papyrus vessels upon the water! (NJPS)

The historical context of these verses is an attempt by Kush-Egypt and Judah to join forces in an alliance against Assyria.[19] At this time Egypt was ruled by the Kushite or twenty-fifth Dynasty, which had sent emissaries to Judah to discuss the possible alliance. Isa 20:5–6 also refers to attempts (either Judahite or Philistine) to make alliance with "Kush, their hope" against Assyria. In Isaiah 18 the prophet sends the delegation back to its own country with the message that it is not the right time for political alliances and military action against Assyria. In the first two verses Isaiah describes the land and the people who would make alliance with Judah.[20]

Land of the winged boats / land in the deep shadow of wings; Hebrew *ṣilṣel kenafayim.*

The second Hebrew word, *kenafayim* 'wings', presents little problem. The difficulty is with the word *ṣilṣel,* which has generally received one of four interpretations by moderns: the word is related to Arabic *ṣalla, ṣalṣala* 'to whir, to rattle'; it is equated with *ṣrṣr* 'a locustlike creature'; it derives from *ṣl* 'shadow'; or *ṣilṣel* 'ship, boat'. Together with *kenafayim* 'wings', these interpretations inform most translations, ancient and modern. So we have "whirring wings" (RSV, NRSV), "buzzing insects" and "whirring locusts" (NAB and NJB); "deep shadow of wings" or "a most sheltered land" (NJPS, similarly KJV), following LXX and Targums; and "winged boats," meaning either sailboats or speedy boats found in REB and some modern commentaries.[21] Although the Hebrew *kenafayim* has generally not been the subject of dispute, this word too has not entirely escaped debate. A recent interpretation understands the word in the sense of "side," one meaning it has in Hebrew, and translates the phrase "land of shadows on both sides"—that is, "near the equator, shadows fall on one side of an object during the summer and on the other during the winter."[22]

It seems to me that a translation "whirring of wings," or something similar, is most likely correct. Not only is there an Arabic cognate to *ṣilṣel,* as indicated earlier, but the word itself, although not found in Biblical Hebrew, is found in Tannaitic Hebrew as a reduplicated form of *ṣll* 'to resonate, ring, tremble'.[23] Although this translation has an ancient tradition, being found in the Greek translation of Symmachus, and has been incorporated in RSV and NRSV, it has not become universally accepted.[24] A new find, however, may support the translation and help to explain its meaning. A hieroglyphic stela dating from the end of the twenty-fifth (Kushite) Dynasty in Egypt was found in 1977 along a desert road in Egypt. The stela, dated to the years before the conflict with Assyria (i.e., just at the time when Isaiah gave his message recorded in Isaiah 18), describes the army of the Kushite king, Tirhaqa (690–664 B.C.E.): "[(The army) is coming] like the coming of the wind, like falcons flapping the wings with [their] wings."[25] The description "like falcons flapping the wings" may well be the intended meaning of Isaiah's *ṣilṣel kenafayim,* that is, "whirring of wings."[26] It is not clear from the inscription precisely what action of the army is being compared with the flapping of falcons' wings, but it may be a reference to the Kushites' legendary running speed, to which Isaiah next refers. As Heliodorus (fourth century C.E.) said of the Ethiopian Trog(l)odytes, "Their swift feet carry them like wings."[27]

GO, YOU NIMBLE MESSENGERS / GO, SWIFT MESSENGERS;
HEBREW *MALʾAKHIM QALIM.*

The Kushite messengers are characterized by their speed, an attribute of the ancient Ethiopians noted also in Egyptian and Greek texts. The stela of Tirhaqa, mentioned earlier, indicates that Kushites were known for their running ability. The inscription describes how Tirhaqa had commanded that his army run every day and how the king had gone out "to observe the running of his army": "When the person of the king is on the way to the camp (*bj3*) to see the beauty of his army, [(The army) is coming] like the coming of the wind, like falcons flapping the wings with [their] wings." It further describes how the army ran the fifty kilometer distance, from Memphis to the Fayum, in five hours, and how it was rewarded by the king.[28] Herodotus (fifth century B.C.E.) says that the "Ethiopian Troglodytes [cave-dwellers] are swifter of foot than any men of whom tales are brought to us," and Pliny quotes Crates of Pergamum (second century B.C.E.) as saying that "the Trogodytes beyond Ethiopia are swifter than horses."[29] Heliodorus, a few centuries later, speaks about these same people saying that "they have from nature the gift of running swiftly, which they train from childhood."[30] Given these attestations of Kushite speed, it may not be coincidental that Joab, David's commander in chief (tenth century B.C.E.), employed a Kushite runner (2 Sam 18:21–23).

TO A TALL, SMOOTH NATION / TO A PEOPLE THRUST FORTH AND AWAY;
HEBREW *MEMUŠAKH U-MORAṬ.*

The first Hebrew word is apparently a passive participle of the root *mšk* 'to draw', but it is not clear what sense the word has. Some would see it as a reference to the famed Kushite ability with the bow, that is, "drawing [the bow]," a sense the word has elsewhere in the Hebrew Bible.[31] Others, such as RSV, NRSV, and REB, prefer "tall" (i.e., drawn out), a translation that is supported by the remarks of several classical authors about the Ethiopians' height. Herodotus's remark that the Ethiopians are said to be the tallest people in the world is often mentioned.[32] This depiction is echoed by Pseudo-Scylax in his *Periplus* (fourth cent B.C.E.).[33] And the remark in the *Periplus Maris Erythraei* (first–second century C.E.) that the inhabitants of the East African coast near Zanzibar are "big of body" (μέγιστοι δὲ ἐν σώμασιν), an expression that refers to stature, reminds one of Isaiah's (45:14) comment about "Egypt's wealth and Nubia's gains and Sabaeans, men of stature" (*yegiaʿ miṣrayim u-seḥar kush u-sevaʾim anshe midah*).[34] Although Pliny's description of the Ethiopian Syrobotae as being about twelve feet tall is fantastic, as is Diodorus of Sicily's (first century B.C.E.) reference to the height (about ten feet) of those people south of Ethiopia near the equator, both writers clearly reflect reports of very tall Ethiopians.[35] Notice of the height of some East Africans is not restricted to the ancients. Medieval Muslim writers often noted this feature, as did some moderns.[36] Given this evidence, it would seem that the LXX translation of *memušakh* in Isa 18:2 by the word μετέωρον (lit. "raised up") captures the same sense of height.[37]

With the second word, *moraṭ* 'smooth' or 'burnished, polished', some think that Isaiah was referring to the appearance of the Kushites' skin after it has been rubbed with oil, "which would have been especially eye-catching when seen on the dark skin of the Kushites."[38] This interpretation may perhaps be supported by observations made by ancients as well as moderns. Herodotus (3.23; cf. Mela 3.88) noted that the Ethiopians have shining skin, and the anthropologist Dominique Zahan described the body care practiced by men in some black African societies this way: "Great emphasis is placed on the smoothness and brilliance of the skin. Its luster and sheen are a sign of vigor and good health. Plant and animal fats are used to contribute to this exaltation of the skin and black colour. Often people use the remains of gravy fat on their fingers to grease their thighs and legs."[39] Other scholars understand the Hebrew word to have the same meaning that the Semitic root *mrṭ* has in cognate languages: "to pull out hair, to depilate," a meaning that is commonly found in the Hebrew Bible and which is given to our passage by a number of biblicists.[40] If this is the meaning, we may point to the notice of Diodorus of Sicily that those near the equator "have absolutely no hair on any part of their bodies except on the head, eyebrows and eyelids, and on the chin," a report echoed much later by the Arabic geographer Dimashqī (d. 1327), who wrote that the black African "Zanj, the Sūdān, the Ḥabasha and Nūba and the like" are "hairless and smooth."[41] These writers describe a characteristic of black Africans that has been noted by scientists—that Negroids tend to have less body hair than Caucasoids.[42]

These two possible descriptions of the Kushites as being "hairless" or "oiled" are not mutually exclusive and Isaiah may have had both ideas in mind when he said that the Kushites are *moraṭ*, that is, "smooth" *and* "burnished." Such an appearance may have made a favorable impression on the ancient Israelites. "There is no reason why the Hebrews should not have admired the burnished copper colour of the Ethiopians."[43] "Isaiah would seem to have been struck by the fine physique of the ambassadors."[44] Several biblical scholars have suggested that this may have been what Herodotus (3.20) had in mind when he described the Ethiopians as the best-looking people in the world.[45] If this is Herodotus's meaning, then his statement "The Ethiopians are said to be the tallest and best-looking (μέγιστοι καὶ κάλλιστοι) of all people" would parallel two of the Kushite features (*memušakh u-moraṭ*) noted by Isaiah.[46]

Wildberger's translation "to a tall, smooth nation," then, not only makes philological sense but is supported by extrabiblical evidence. On the other hand, the NJPS translation "to a people thrust forth and away" understands both Hebrew words *memušakh* and *moraṭ* to be saying the same thing and to be referring to the distant land of the African envoys. This translation is apparently based on the work of H. L. Ginsberg, who translates "distant (in space) and thrust away," noting the meaning of "distant in time" for *nimšakh* in Isa 13:22 and Ezek 12:25 and 28, and "thrust away" for *moraṭ*, as derived from *yrṭ*, drawing attention to Job 16:11 and the Arabic *wrṭ*.[47] This translation has not found acceptance among biblical scholars today.

To a people feared far and wide / To a nation far and remote; Hebrew *el ʿam nora᾽ min hu᾽ wahal᾽ah.*

"The invasions into Egypt, which led to the Twenty-fifth (Ethiopian) Dynasty seizing control over the land, would undoubtedly have brought with it a respect for Cush from the surrounding countries that was commensurate with its power."[48] Not only this, but once Kush controlled Egypt it exhibited an aggressive geopolitical thrust northward. Among other events, in 701 B.C.E. Kush battled the Assyrian king Sennacherib to a standstill and a few years later engaged in military campaigns in Asia Minor. "The awareness of the strength and fighting potential of the Kushites which appears suddenly in the Bible (Isa 18:1, Jer 46:9, Ezek 38:5, [Isa 37:9 = 2 Kgs 19:9, Isa 45:14]) dates from these halcyon days of the 25th Dynasty dominion."[49]

No doubt the Kushites' dominion over Egypt and their subsequent military activities brought in its wake a reputation of the Kushites as a power to be reckoned with, but Kushite fighting ability was respected even before the period of the twenty-fifth Dynasty. Egyptian literature and art from the

Middle Kingdom (ca. 2133–1786 B.C.E.) onward reflect a view of the Kushites as a powerful force in resisting Egyptian intervention into their land. "Nubia as a military power on the periphery of the Mediterranean world was by far the most prominent feature of the ancient profile of blacks."[50] And Egyptians had a long history of recruiting Kushites as mercenaries from the First Intermediate Period (ca. 2258–2040 B.C.E.) down to the Hellenistic period.[51] We find Kushites as mercenaries in the service of the Egyptian army in Canaan in the fourteenth and the tenth centuries B.C.E. The same is true after the period of the twenty-fifth Dynasty in the sixth and fifth centuries B.C.E.[52] There were Kushite contingents also in the Persian army of Xerxes.[53]

One aspect of the Ethiopians' military prowess was particularly well known in the ancient world—their skill with the bow. Herodotus (3.21) tells the story of how the Ethiopian king defied the Persian king Cambyses, who had conquered Egypt and was preparing to invade Ethiopia. He sent Cambyses an Ethiopian bow with the message that when the Persians could draw the bow as easily as he does, then they might stand a chance against the Ethiopians (and even then only with overwhelming odds); until then they should thank the gods that the Ethiopians do not have it in mind to attack the Persians. These bows must have been very large, for Herodotus (7.69) describes them as being four cubits long—about six feet—and Strabo (first century C.E.), who also gives this measurement (17.2.3), says that they were used for hunting elephants with two men holding the bow and the third drawing the arrow (16.4.10).[54] It wasn't only the size—and thus the power—of the bow that gained a reputation in the Greco-Roman world; it was also the accuracy of the Ethiopian aim. Pliny describes the "Ethiopian coast-tribes, the Nisicathae and Nisitae, names that mean 'men with three' or 'with four eyes'—not because they really are like that but because they have a particularly keen sight in using arrows," and he says that the Ethiopians are famous among all peoples for their archers.[55] Heliodorus later reports that the Ethiopians were able to hit their target right in the eye, an echo of which is found in the later Arabic term for their Nubian opponents as "pupil smiters."[56] Strabo (16.4.9) refers to another Ethiopian people who "have the custom of setting up a contest in archery for boys who have not yet reached manhood." These literary references have now been confirmed by iconographic evidence. A group of forty wooden figurines representing a troop of Nubian archers was recovered from an Egyptian tomb dated about 2000 B.C.E.[57] And these figures are only the most dramatic representation of Nubian archers, for the depiction of Nubians with bows (and arrows at times) is very common in Egyptian iconography.[58] One of the Egyptian names for the land to the south, Ta-Sety (*t3-stj*) Land of the Bow, may even derive from this famed ability.[59] It is interesting that this characteristic of the Kushites has continued into relatively modern times. In 1790 James Bruce wrote about the Shankella at the lower end of the Blue Nile that "they are all archers from their infancy. Their bows are all made of wild fennel thicker than the common proportion, and about seven feet long."[60]

It is possible that the Kushites' fame as archers is reflected in two biblical verses. In a description of the foreign contingents in the Egyptian army at the battle of Carchemish in 605 B.C.E., Jer 46:9 says: "Let the warriors go forth, Kush and Put who grasp the shield. And the Ludim who grasp and draw the bow." Isa 66:19 may also have a reference to Put and Lud. Although the Hebrew reads "From them I will send survivors to the nations, to Tarshish, Pul, and Lud—which draw the bow," several scholars, on the basis of the reading "Put" (Φουδ) in the LXX, as well as the association of Lud and Put elsewhere (Ezek 27:10, 30:5), would see an original "Put" rather than "Pul."[61] In any case, the Ludim are said to be practiced with the bow. Who are the Ludim? An ancient people by that name inhabited Asia Minor, and some earlier scholarship believed that Jeremiah and Isaiah have these people in mind.[62] However, because Lud is grouped with Kush in Jer 46:9 and Ezek 30:5 and because Put, whether it is to be identified with modern Somalia or Libya, is in Africa, most scholars today agree that Lud too is in Africa.[63] And just as the bows, so too the shields of the Kushites must have made an impression. Apparently their striking feature was also their size.[64] Similarly, Strabo (17.1.54) mentions the Ethiopians' long oblong shields.[65]

The NJPS translation "to a nation far and remote" is that of H. L. Ginsberg, who refers to Ibn Janaḥ and the Arabic *waraʾa* 'to repel'.[66] However, Ibn Janaḥ provides no support for his explanation except for the context in both Isa 18:2 and 21:1. This translation has not found acceptance among biblical scholars today.

TO A NATION, WHICH TRAMPLES DOWN WITH MUSCLE POWER / A NATION OF GIBBER AND CHATTER; HEBREW *GOY QAW-QAW U-MEBUSAH.*

The main problem in this line is the Hebrew word *qaw-qaw,* which occurs in the Bible only here (and repeated in Isa 18:7). The translation "a nation which tramples down with muscle power" understands the word as meaning "sinewy muscle power" on the basis of the Arabic *quwwa* 'strength, power' and *qawiya* 'stretched tight, be strong'.[67] So also J. Blenkinsopp's new translation in the Anchor Bible series: "a nation strong and conquering."[68] Note Mela's (first century C.E.) remark, ultimately deriving from Herodotus, that the Ethiopians are admirers of bodily strength and that their custom is to choose their leader partly on the basis of his strength.[69] The NJPS translation, "a nation of gibber and chatter," on the other hand, sees *qaw-qaw* as semantically similar to the Greek *barbar,* which is traditionally understood as deriving from the sound of foreign and unintelligible speech on the ears of the Greeks who coined the word. The nonsensical repetition of the syllable was meant to mimic the sound of incomprehensible foreign speech. The same linguistic phenomenon is seen to be behind Isaiah's *qaw-qaw*.[70]

Another translation is possible, which is based on the meaning of Biblical Hebrew *qaw* or *qāw* 'measuring line' or (possibly) 'measure'.[71] Some commentaries and translations have thus rendered the text as "a nation of line by line," or "a nation meted out."[72] Although these explanations don't make much sense, perhaps we may see an extended meaning of *qaw* in the difficult word *qaw-qaw* in the sense of "tall." Such a semantic development is found in the Syriac *mšwḥtʾ*, which the Peshiṭta uses to translate both *qāw* in Isa 28:17, where the meaning is "measuring-line," and *anshe midah* in Isa 45:14 where the meaning is "tall men" (*gbrʾ dmšwḥtʾ*). Our passage then would provide a parallelism between *goy memušakh* and *goy qawqaw*, assuming *memušakh* to mean "tall."

There is yet one other possibility for the word *qaw-qaw*. It is suggestive that the Arabic geographers, from the ninth century C.E. onward, commonly refer to a black African people and place by the name of Kawkaw or Qawqaw, "the greatest of the realms of the Sūdān" (Yaʿqūbī). Two objections might be raised to an identity of these people with Isaiah's *qaw-qaw*. The first is geographic: the name Kawkaw (Qawqaw) in the Arabic sources is identified with the toponym Gao, which, situated on the Niger, is considerably west of Kush. The second is chronological: the earliest references to a people and place called Kawkaw are geographers who lived more than fifteen hundred years after Isaiah. As far as the geographic objection is concerned, however, we must remember that biblical Kush (i.e., Isaiah's perspective) meant black Africa in general. On the other hand, from the Arabic perspective, al-Zuhrī (twelfth century) puts Kawkaw on the Nile and makes it the capital of Ḥabasha, that is, Kush.[73] I have shown elsewhere, as have others, that in the early centuries of the Common Era there was a lack of accurate geographic knowledge about Africa.[74] The chronological objection, on the other hand, does not mean that the Kawkaw did not exist before the Arab geographers wrote about them, or even before there was a place by that name. It is true that the name Kawkaw is similar to other reduplicated names by which the Arabs refer to distant peoples deep in Africa, such as Damdam, Namnam, and Lamlam, as Nehemiah Levtzion and John Hunwick observe.[75] But, once again, this does not mean that the Arab geographers of the ninth century invented those names. The names could have been long known among the Semites, whether heard from the Africans themselves or not, and Isaiah therefore could have referred to one of them as the Qawqaw people (*goy qaw-qaw*). Nonetheless, I would not push this theory too hard because it requires spanning more than fifteen hundred years with conjecture. Since we have no evidence of a Kawkaw/Qawqaw people contemporaneous with Isaiah or for a long time after Isaiah, the theory must remain only suggestive.

The Hebrew word *mebusah* was translated with a negative nuance in the LXX and the Peshiṭta as "trodden down" (καταπεπατημένον and *dyš* respectively) and is reflected in the KJV, which has the same translation. The negative cast has affected also the translation of the associated word *qawqaw* in these versions: "without hope" (ἀνέλπιστον) and "dishonored, disgraced" (*mškr*).[76] The translation of *mebusah* as "trodden down" assumes the word to be a passive form of the verb *bws,* but as scholars have realized, *mebusah* is rather a nominal form with the active meaning of "trodding down" or "trampling."[77] Thus we have "conquering" in RSV and similarly in REB, NAB, NJB, *La Sainte Bible,* von Orelli, and so on.

A review of what Isaiah had to say about the Kushites indicates that they were considered to be a people feared for their military might with a reputation for conquest and prowess with the bow. They were known for their speed of foot, their height, and their smooth skin, which may have taken on a burnished appearance. They may have also struck Isaiah as a people with sinewy muscle power (or, alternatively, as a people whose language sounded strange). Finally, their nautical accomplishments were noted. Given this description it should not be surprising to find biblical scholars concluding, "In Isa 18:1–2 the Ethiopians are regarded with something akin to admiration," or "One detects in [Isaiah's] words a certain measure of admiration for this exuberant, youthful people, which had so recently entered on the stage of world history."[78] The one characteristic that comes across most strongly in Isaiah's words is military prowess, a feature for which the Nubians were apparently well known in the ancient world. Speaking of the First Intermediate Period in Egypt (2258–2040 B.C.E.), Henry Fischer said: "It . . . seems likely that the Nubians enjoyed considerable prestige among the Upper Egyptians at Gebelein on account of their prowess as hunters and warriors."[79] As Strabo said (17.1.53), the ancients believed the Ethiopians to be warlike. Even the characteristic of swiftness is associated with this ability, as we saw in the Taharqa inscription and as we can see in Ps 19:6/5, "rejoicing like a warrior to his course." Such an association goes back a long way, for several Egyptian inscriptions from about the First Intermediate Period, including one speaking of Nubians, link running speed with military prowess.[80]

Jeremiah 13:23

No doubt the best-known line in the Bible about the Kushites/Ethiopians is Jer 13:23 "Can the Kushite change his skin or the leopard his spots? Just as much can you do good, who are practiced in doing evil." A straightforward reading of this verse cannot uncover any negative sentiment toward the Kushite, or toward black skin. Jeremiah is simply using the Kushite's black skin as a metaphor for that which is unchangeable.[81] Although Jeremiah's perspective is that of a non-Kushite, who assumes that black is not the normal skin color, there is no value judgment implied in the use of the metaphor. However, less literal interpretations, more homiletical in nature, saw the prophet as playing on the color symbolism of blackness when he compared Ethiopians and leopards to sinners who "whether totally black or only spotted" are still sinners.[82] With these kinds of interpretations, it is not surprising that an African American Christian author, Alfred Dunston, could say, "The passage . . . is almost always used to say that one must be content with the misfortune of being what he is. . . . [This understanding presents] the picture of the poor unfortunate Ethiopian who would most certainly change his skin if he could; but alas he cannot."[83] Dunston refutes this meaning: "Jeremiah was not commiserating either with the Ethiopian or the leopard."[84] Jeremiah's rhetorical question implying nothing more than immutability has its parallel in an ancient Egyptian wisdom saying, "There is no Nubian who leaves his skin,"[85] as well as in the Greek proverb, "It's like trying to wash an Ethiopian white."[86]

Jeremiah 38:7–13

In addition to Moses' wife, another biblical personality identified as a Kushite is Ebed-melech. "Ebed-melech the Kushite" was in the service of the Judahite king Zedekiah (*ʿebed-melekh* literally means "servant, or vassal, of the king") and saved the prophet Jeremiah's life (Jer 38:7–13).[87] He is rewarded for this deed by God's promise that he would survive the coming destruction of the kingdom: "You shall escape with your life, because you trusted Me—declares the Lord" (Jer 39:15–18). The Hebrew text calls Ebed-melech a *saris,* which may mean either "eunuch" or "palace official."[88] In any case, the Bible presents him as a righteous man and casts him in a heroic role.

Jeremiah 36:14 (LXX 43:14), Zephaniah 1:1, Psalms 7:1

Aside from *kushi* as an ethnic designation (gentilic) for Moses' wife (Num 12:1) and Ebed-melech (Jer 38:7–13), Kush or Kushi is found elsewhere in the Bible as a personal name. A Yehudi son of Nethanyahu son of Shelemyahu son of Kushi is employed by the royal court of Yehoiakim, king of Judah (Jer 36:14). The father of the prophet Zephaniah is named Kushi: "The word of the Lord that came to Zephaniah son of Kushi son of

Gedaliah son of Amariah son of Hezekiah, during the reign of King Josiah son of Amon of Judah" (Zeph 1:1). A psalm of David begins with the ascription "which he [David] sang to the Lord, concerning Kush, a Benjaminite" (Ps 7:1).[89]

There are three opinions as to the origin of the personal name Kush or Kushi in the Bible. First, some say that it was originally a gentilic indicating land of origin, which in time became a personal name. One might compare the name of Kashta, the second Kushite king known to us (reigned ca. 760–747 B.C.E.), which probably means "the Kushite," or the names Kusaia, Kusaiu, Kusi, and Kusitu (feminine), all meaning "Kushite," which occur in various Akkadian documents.[90] On the basis of this explanation, Roger Anderson has argued that the Kushi names in the Bible indicate that dark-skinned Africans (Saharan and sub-Saharan) had settled in some areas of Palestine, were incorporated into the mixed population of Syria-Palestine, and became accepted as members of Israelite society.[91] The Bible scholar Gene Rice has gone further and attempted to pinpoint a specific historic incident for the arrival of some biblical Kushites. He thinks that as a result of the alliance between the twenty-fifth (Kushite) Dynasty of Egypt and the kingdom of Judah against Assyria, a number of Kushites came to Judah.[92] Whenever their arrival, it is not difficult to conceive of Kushites or black Africans in ancient Israelite society. Evidence for such may be indicated from the "negro head" seals found in ancient Israel from as early as the thirteenth century B.C.E.[93]

Second, some scholars are of the opinion that the personal name Kushi found in the Bible is a common West Semitic name found in several languages (Epigraphic Hebrew, Aramaic, Akkadian, and Phoenician) and has nothing to do with a land of origin.[94] Finally, a third opinion holds that the name could indeed mean "Nubian" but was given to a non-Nubian for other reasons, for example, for political purposes (to identify with the Egyptian-Nubian dynasty), or as a nickname referring to one's work (a merchant, say, trading with Nubia) or one's dark complexion.[95] A similar situation exists with the Egyptian name *Pꜣ-nḥsy,* familiar to us from its biblical form Pinḥas (Phinehas), which literally means "the Nubian." The name may be used in Egyptian for someone whose skin is dark but who is not a Nubian.[96]

To summarize the ancient Israelite perception of the black African, references to Kushites in the Bible fall into three categories: one comment about skin color, several statements about specific Kushites living among the Israelites, and Isaiah's description of the people of Kush living in their own land. The comment about skin color is a proverb about immutability drawn from the permanent genetic dark skin of the African as opposed to the temporary dark skin acquired from the sun or from dirt. It implies no value judgment about the African's skin color. Of statements about individuals, a few Kushites served in the Judahite royal court; one was a runner for David's army, another was a trusted attendant of the prophet Jeremiah, who is portrayed by the biblical author as a hero and is rewarded by God. If the name Kushi, father of Zephaniah, indicates an African origin, then one of the biblical prophets had black African ancestry. If the LXX translation of the Kushite in Num 12:1 as "Ethiopian" is correct, Moses had a black African wife. While we cannot be sure of the ethnicity of Zephaniah's father and Moses' wife, the fact that there is no biblical statement indicating a negative sentiment speaks loudly. No biblical writer thought it necessary to say of Zephaniah's father or Moses' wife, "but they were only Midianites; they were not Africans." No writer thought it necessary to comment about their skin color. That precisely is what is so noticeable by its absence in the Isaiah passage. The prophet reflects the Israelite perception of the black African as a militarily powerful people—a feared people with muscle power, fast of foot and accurate with the bow. Isaiah says that they are tall and good-looking. He mentions their accomplishments with boat construction. But in his descriptive catalog of these people, he "did not think it worth while to mention that their skins were dark."[97] Nor is skin color ever mentioned in descriptions of other biblical Kushites. That is the most significant perception, or lack of perception, in the biblical image of the black African.

THREE

POSTBIBLICAL ISRAEL:

BLACK AFRICA

HAVING EXAMINED how biblical Israel viewed black Africa and its people, we are ready to investigate the postbiblical period. As we did with the earlier material, we first look at the land and then the people. We saw that in the Hebrew Bible the name Kush referred to several different places. In trying to assess attitudes toward black Africans, our first task was to determine when "Kush" meant the African location. In postbiblical literature we have a similar problem. Here Kush almost always refers to black Africa but two other names—Afriqa (or Afriqi) and Barbaria—can refer to black Africa and can also refer to other places. Our first task, then, will be to ascertain when Afriqa and Barbaria mean black Africa. Before we can determine what images of and attitudes toward black Africans are reflected in the sources, we must be clear about the nomenclature and know when the material is talking about Blacks and when it is not. So we start with the names of the land.

Aside from the targumic traditions associating Arabia with Kush in Gen 10:6 and 1 Chron 1:8, and the possibility of an indirect reference to Midian being called Kush in Hellenistic-Jewish writings, postbiblical Jewish sources primarily know Kush as Nubia.[1] This identification is assumed in the LXX, which consistently translates Kush as Ethiopia—that is, black Africa—and in Hellenistic, rabbinic, and targumic literature.[2] We have direct evidence for this identification at the beginning of the rabbinic period in the words of Josephus, who says that biblical Kush is represented by the Ethiopians of his day, and toward the end of the rabbinic period in the words of Jerome (d. 420): "Up to the present day, Ethiopia is called Chus by the Hebrews."[3] In short, the Hebrew and Aramaic sources use "Kush" in a way very similar to the way "Ethiopia" is used in Greek and Latin sources, that is, to mean black Africa.[4]

Afriqa/Afriqi

In addition to the name Kush, however, rabbinic and targumic literature also refer to the land of Nubia/Ethiopia as Africa and as Barbaria. References to *afriqa* (or *afriqi*) in these sources do not always mean black Africa, and sometimes not Africa at all.[5] In some cases manuscript evidence indicates that the reading *afriqa/i* may be incorrect.[6] In other cases, the reading is correct, but the word refers to a place in Babylonia (Persian: Abriq; Arabic: Difriqi; Greek: Afriki, Tephrike), which is today in Turkey and is called Divrigi. This is the place mentioned by Mar Zuṭra (fourth century) as the area to which the Ten Tribes were exiled.[7] Elsewhere the reading *afriqa/i* apparently refers to Phrygia in Asia Minor.[8] In still other cases, *afriqa/i* indeed refers to Africa, but to North Africa, more precisely Carthage and the surrounding area, the same meaning that Arabic "Ifrīqiya" has.[9] In fact, in some of these cases, a number of manuscripts or editions read *ifriqiya* (or *afriqiya*) for *afriqa/i*.[10]

Afriqa/i, however, can also mean sub-Saharan black Africa in rabbinic and targumic literature. One of the place-names mentioned in the Bible that has thus far eluded definite identification is Tarshish. Scholars generally offer two or three candidates for the identification of this ancient site: Tartessos in the Iberian peninsula, Tarsus in Cilicia (Asia Minor), and sometimes Taros in Sardinia.[11] Three times the Targum translates "Tarshish" as *afriqa* (1 Kgs 10:22 = 2 Chr 9:21, 1 Kgs 22:49, and Jer 10:9). It is possible that the Targum's author was thinking of Tarsus (an identification made in *GenR* 37.1), and that *afriqa* here means Phrygia, a meaning the word sometimes has, as we have seen. Nevertheless, although both the city of Tarsus and the province of Phrygia are in Asia Minor, they are not in the same area, for Tarsus is in the province of Cilicia southeast of Phrygia. While we cannot assume that the Targum's geographic knowledge was accurate, we should not be too hasty in assuming that it was not.

A second possibility is that the Targum's *afriqa* means North Africa. The Arabic geographer Idrīsī (d. 1165) wrote that the ancient name of Tunis in North Africa was Tarshish, which was near Carthage.[12] Johann Vater noted this passage in Idrīsī almost two hundred years ago, and he also pointed out that several ancient Bible translations agree with this identification, probably having in mind the LXX and Vulgate, both of which translate "Carthage" for "Tarshish" in Ezek 27:12; perhaps Vater also had in mind our Targum. If Tarshish was indeed the ancient name of Tunis, this may be the key to the Targum's identification of biblical Tarshish as *afriqi*. In other words, here we must understand *afriqa* as meaning North Africa, the meaning often given to this place-name in rabbinic literature.

But there is yet a third possibility, that by *afriqa* the Targum meant black Africa. There are several reasons why the Targum would have made this identification. Those biblical verses in which Tarshish is translated as *afriqa* mention several products of Tarshish or closely connected with Tarshish, such as gold, ivory, and apes, which are commonly seen as products of black Africa. We have seen, especially, how Kush was a great source of gold in antiquity and was well known for this product.[13] Furthermore, in these verses the ships of Tarshish are said to bring gold from Ophir (1 Kgs 22:49), which was reached by going south from Israel along the Red Sea and was presumably situated either in Kush or across the Red Sea in Arabia.[14] Lastly, the Bible elsewhere (Ezek 38:13, Ps 72/71:10) parallels Tarshish with Sheba, Seba, and Dedan, locations at the southern end of the Red Sea, either in Arabia or Africa.[15] Given these associations, it is likely that when the Targum translated *afriqa* for Tarshish, it meant black Africa.

There are other places in the Targum and in rabbinic literature where *afriqa/i* means black Africa. According to some scholars, we must assign this meaning to the Targum's translation of *afriqaʾei* for *kushim* in 2 Chr 21:16.[16] In the next chapter, which is concerned with the people of Africa, I deal with three other rabbinic references to *afriqi,* which appear to mean black Africa: a story about Alexander the Great and the inhabitants of *afriqi,* an exchange between Hillel (beginning of the Common Era) and an interlocutor about the *afriqiyim,* and two references to the language of *afriqi.*[17] I show that in these cases the various elements in the accounts point to black Africa. Thus, while the place-name *afriqa/i* in targumic and rabbinic texts may refer to North Africa (if the meaning is not Phrygia), the term may also refer to black Africa. Such a double meaning for the name is found also in Greek and Roman texts of late antiquity where "Africa" may mean either North Africa or the continent as a whole.[18]

Barbaria

An abundance of evidence from antiquity through modern times attests to the toponym Barbaria in what is today Sudan and Somalia in East Africa. Barbaria or its inhabitants the Barbarians are mentioned in Egyptian, Greco-Roman, Christian, Arabic, and even Chinese sources. The names are also found in Jewish sources of late antiquity and the Middle Ages. Although usually confused with Barbary or the Berbers in North Africa, or with the common noun and adjective "barbarian," Barbaria(n) in these texts often refers to the country and people of that name in East Africa, as I have shown elsewhere.[19]

To the ancient Greeks the Scythians, Sarmatians, Germans, and Goths were the remote northern races of antiquity. Geographically near to one another, they were often grouped together under the term "Scythians," which by the third century B.C.E. no longer had an ethnic or national connotation and had come to designate the peoples of the remote north. In the same way, the southern peoples were often grouped together under the term "Ethiopians" to designate those peoples living at the southern end of the world. Scythian and Ethiopian thus became general terms to denote, respectively, the remote northern and remote southern peoples. These two gentilics then came to be paired together as a kind of literary shorthand to refer to the geographic extremes of the inhabited world.

Rabbinic literature uses the same literary topos to refer to the people from the ends of the known world, but it sometimes substitutes Barbarians for Ethiopians and Sarmatians, Goths, or Germans for Scythians. So, for example, to the question how the messiah can appear if the Jews have not yet been subjugated to the rule of "the seventy nations," that is, all the nations of the world, a necessary condition in some rabbinic thinking, God is made to answer: "If one of you is exiled to Barbaria and one to Sarmatia, it is as if you had all been exiled. Furthermore, this kingdom [= Rome] levies troops from throughout the world, from every nation. If one *(s)kuthi* and one *kushi* subject you, it is as if all the seventy nations had done so."[20] The pairings of Barbaria/Sarmatia and (S)cythian/Kushite are merisms representing the extent of the nations and peoples of the world. Thus, if one Jew is exiled to Barbaria and another Jew to Sarmatia, it is as if the Jews had been exiled to all the nations of the world; if one Scythian and one Kushite subjugate the Jews, it is as if all the seventy nations had done so.

A similar usage of Kushite, this time paired with German, another distant northern people, is found in a midrashic fragment discovered in the Cairo Genizah. Isa 66:18 describes the messianic age as one in which "all nations [or, people: *goyim*] and tongues" will be brought together to the temple in Jerusalem to worship God. The rabbinic paraphrase of the verse puts it this way: "Isaiah said: In the messianic period the *germani* will take hold of the hand of the *kushi* and the *kushi* will take hold of the hand of the *germani* and arm in arm they will walk together."[21] Here too we seem to have the same merism, with German being used instead of Sarmatian, Scythian, or Goth, to indicate all the people of the world. The two peoples from the opposite ends of the world (the far north and far south) thus signify the entire world, Isaiah's "all nations."

Another example—this time with Barbari instead of Kushi—is found in a midrashic expansion to Ps 25:19, "See how numerous my enemies are, and how unjustly they hate me": "If Esau hated Jacob, he had good reason—for Jacob had taken the birthright from him. But as for the Barbarians, the Goths and the other nations, what have I ever done to them that they should 'hate me so unjustly'?"[22] Here again, the gentilic pairing indicates a merism representing the extent of the world ("and the other nations"). A similar statement about undeserved hatred by the nations is found in a comment on Ps 109:3, "They fought against me without cause." The rabbinic explanation claims that this refers to Barbaria and "S(h)tutia" = Scythia.[23]

We can use the knowledge gained from these rabbinic texts to explain a long-standing enigma in the New Testament. In a series of antitheses the author of Colossians (3:11) states: "Here is no more Greek and Jew, circumcised and uncircumcised, *barbaros*, Scythian, slave, free; but all are in Christ." Assuming *barbaros* to be a common noun "barbarian," scholars have long been bothered by the apparent lack of antithesis in the barbarian-Scythian pairing, and therefore concluded that the two terms are synonymous, with Scythian being a sort of "super-barbarian." But the author of this text was actually using the place-name Barbaria in opposition to the place-name Scythia, and his antithesis, then, was geographic (north-south), according with the national (Greek-Jewish), religious (circumcised-uncircumcised), and social (slave-free) antitheses in the passage. Precisely the same figure of speech that we saw in the rabbinic texts appears in Colossians with the same sense of geographic extremes. The Ethiopian-Scythian topos was part of the literary world of the eastern Mediterranean of late antiquity with the "Barbarian" variation appearing in Jewish texts.[24]

In short, we see that the place-name Barbaria has the same meaning in rabbinic literature as it has in other sources. It refers to an area in East Africa corresponding to today's Sudan and Somalia. Its substitution for Ethiopia in the Scythian-Ethiopian formula indicates that Judaism of late antiquity considered black Africa to lie at the southern end of the earth, a view held in common with the larger Hellenistic culture and which goes back, on the one side, to classical Greece, and on the other, to biblical Israel (Amos 9:7 etc.) and the ancient Near East, as we have seen.[25]

To summarize the results of this chapter, postbiblical sources have little knowledge of Kush outside of Africa. The Targums do twice associate Arabia with Kush, and the biblical name of Kush for Midian may have been known into the Hellenistic period and perhaps even later. Otherwise, postbiblical literature assumes that the land of Kush refers to black Africa. Two other names for black Africa found in the rabbinic corpus are Africa (*afriqa, afriqi*) and Barbaria, as they are also found in Greek and Roman texts of late antiquity. The biblical image of Kush as a land at the farthest southern reach of the earth continued into postbiblical literature, where the end-of-the-earth location became the basis for various expressions denoting geographic extremes, just as in classical writings. Probably related to the idea that Kush extends to the southern end of the world is the rabbinic notion that the Land of Kush covers a very large territory: "Egypt is one-sixtieth the size of Kush and Kush is one-sixtieth the size of the world."[26]

FOUR

POSTBIBLICAL ISRAEL: BLACK AFRICANS

NOW THAT WE have defined the various names for black Africa used in postbiblical Jewish literature, we are ready to look at the references to the people who lived in, or came from, this part of the world to see how they were perceived by the Jews of late antiquity. We saw that in the biblical period Kush played a role in the history of Israel and the ancient Near East, and that the Kushites were known to biblical Israel primarily as a militarily powerful people. There were also some Kushites who had assimilated into Israelite society such as Ebed-melech (Jer 38:7–13). It is possible that Moses' Kushite wife and Zephaniah's father were also black Africans. Whether in regard to the Kushites in Africa or in Israel, we find in the Bible no value judgments expressed regarding their ethnicity or color. Ethnicity and color apparently were not relevant in determining the image of these people as reflected in the literature. Do these images and attitudes continue into the postbiblical period or do they undergo change? To answer the question, I examine references to Ethiopians/Kushites in Jewish literature of late antiquity, beginning with the Hellenistic period in the third century B.C.E. and continuing through to the end of the talmudic period, about 500 C.E. At the end of the chapter I draw together the results of this inquiry and see what they imply about attitudes toward Blacks.

Ethiopians as Cowards

In his allegorical interpretation of the Bible, the first-century Jewish philosopher, Philo of Alexandria, says that the etymology of "Ethiopia" is ταπείνωσις 'lowness', and that this symbolizes cowardice.[1] This etymology has not yet been adequately explained. Lester Grabbe, who admits that it "is very puzzling," is forced to explain it as either a scribal error or "visual etymology," reading *r* for *k* in Hebrew *kush*.[2] Various other explanations whether based on the Hebrew *kwš/kbš,* or the Arabic *qāsa,* or assuming a derivation of Hebrew *šaḥ* from *šaḥor* are equally unconvincing.[3]

We saw that in both classical and biblical antiquity Ethiopia/Kush was considered to lie at the ends of the earth, that is, at the remote southern end of the inhabited world. This conception carried over into the postbiblical period, where Barbaria, the land in East Africa in the general area of today's Sudan and Somalia, sometimes substituted for Ethiopia as the most distant land in rabbinic writings.[4] In the classical world, the environmental theory provided the explanation for different physical features of humanity. The remote southern location of Ethiopia, where the sun was at its hottest, was believed to be the cause of the Ethiopians' dark skin and tightly curled hair.[5]

But not only physical features were conditioned by the extremes of the environment, for the Greeks believed that the climate was responsible also for nonphysical differences among the various ethnic groups.[6] In the cold north, the inhabitants were dim-witted but courageous, while the intense heat of the south endowed the Ethiopians with sharp intelligence and cowardice. In regard to the last characteristic, Pseudo-Aristotle wrote that "those who are too dark are cowardly; this refers to Egyptians and Ethiopians," "an excessively black color signifies cowardice," and "those with wooly hair are cowardly; this applies to the Ethiopians."[7] A work of late antiquity also ascribed to Aristotle, *Of the Constitution of the Universe and of Man,* claims that "those governed by black bile are indolent, timid, ailing, and, with regard to body, swarthy and black-haired."[8] Philo's contemporary, the first-century Roman Vitruvius, wrote that black Africans fear to resist the sword, that they have no courage because their strength is drained away by the sun.[9] The idea that the extreme heat of Africa caused cowardice in its inhabitants is also found several centuries after Philo, in the works of Vegetius (fourth to fifth century), and it continues into the Middle Ages and later.[10]

This common perception of the Ethiopian as coward explains the difficult passage in Philo, whose intellectual world was shaped by Greek thought. Underlying Philo's etymology is the contemporaneous, climatically based view that the Ethiopians were cowards. Philo cleverly drew on the phonetic similarity in the *t(h)-p* base found in ***aithiops*** and ***tapeinos*** and concluded that the name Ethiopia is derived from the word ταπείνωσις, which symbolized cowardice.[11]

Color Symbolism: Ethiopian Blackness as Evil

Elsewhere Philo allegorizes the blackness of the Ethiopians as evil. In a passage interpreting Gen 10:8–9 ("Kush was the father of Nimrod, who grew to be a mighty hunter on the earth"), Philo explains why it was Kush who fathered Nimrod. He says that it was right that Nimrod, who was evil and rebelled against God, should be the son of Kush. Nimrod's evil nature, reflected in his occupation as hunter, which "is as far removed as possible from the rational nature," is hinted in his father's blackness, "because pure evil has no participation in light, but follows night and darkness."[12]

Raoul Lonis, a historian of classical antiquity, has claimed that the only exception to a lack of racism and prejudice in the ancient Greek world is Philo.[13] Lonis refers the reader to a thesis by Babacar Diop, who argued that Philo's thinking derives from a negative Egyptian-Ethiopian theme found in first-century Hellenistic Judaism in Alexandria, although he admits that other Hellenistic-Jewish sources portray the Ethiopian in a positive light.[14] The same opinion of a negative attitude on the part of Philo was expressed more recently by Emmanuel Tonguino in another French thesis.[15]

Philo is of course drawing on the common metaphor of darkness as evil. The application of the metaphor to dark-skinned people was also made in rabbinic and patristic exegesis. An anonymous amoraic interpretation of Amos 9:7 ("Are you not like Kushites to me, O Israelites?") states: "When Israel sins against God, He calls them Kushites," probably taking the Kushite dark color as a metaphor for sin (moral evil).[16] I assume this understanding of the Kushite color because of a second anonymous midrash, also amoraic, that associates Amos 9:7 with Song 1:5 ("I am black but beautiful"), which the Rabbis took as referring to Israel.[17] The most extensive use of the metaphor of darkness as sin as applied to dark-skinned people was made by the church fathers in their allegorical interpretations of the Bible. Undoubtedly, the most ramified of such interpretations, as well as the one with the greatest influence, was that of Origen (d. ca. 253). Using the metaphor of blackness as sin, he identified various biblical references to Ethiopia or Ethiopian(s), as well as the black maiden in Song 1:5–6, as symbols ("types") for the church of the gentiles, who, not having known God, were born and lived in sin. Building on this foundation, Origen then erected an exegetical superstructure, beginning with the verses in Song, that saw the "daughters of Jerusalem" (the born Jews) mock the black maiden for her blackness (her gentile birth), who, although indeed black, is beautiful ("black but beautiful") through faith in Jesus and conversion to Christianity. Eventually, the maiden's blackness diminishes and she "becomes white and fair" (based on a reading of Song 8:5 found in the Old Greek translation: "Who is she that comes up having been made white?").[18] Similarly, Moses' marriage to the Kushite (Num 12:1) represents God's embrace of the gentiles; "Ethiopia shall stretch out her hands to God" (Ps 68:32/31) means that the gentiles outstrip the Jews in their approach to God; God's words to the prophet Zephaniah, "From beyond the rivers of Ethiopia will I receive the dispersed ones" (Zeph 3:10), means that although the Ethiopian, typologically the gentile church, "has been stained with the inky dye of wickedness [and] has been rendered black and dark," he will nevertheless be accepted by God; Ebed-melech, the Ethiopian (Jer 38:7–13), who is "a man of a dark and ignoble race," represents therefore the gentiles; and when Matthew (12:42) speaks of "the Queen of the South . . . who condemns the men of this generation," he means the queen of Sheba who, being identified by Origen as an Ethiopian, represents the gentiles who will condemn the Jews.[19]

Origen's biblical exegesis, in general, and his works on Song, in particular, were enormously influential on the church fathers who followed.[20] Not surprisingly, his interpretation of Song's maiden as an Ethiopian, and his use of this and other biblical Ethiopians as a metaphor for those in sin (i.e., the gentiles), became widespread in later patristic literature. It "set the tone of all later exegesis."[21] With the single exception of Theodore of Mopsuestia, who did not read Song allegorically, the entire Christian tradition followed Origen on this interpretation.[22] An indication of the appreciation of Origen's work on Song can be seen in Jerome's comment in the prologue to his translation of Origen's *Homilies on Song:* "Origen, who surpassed everyone in his other books, has surpassed even himself in the Song of Songs."[23]

The popularity of this exegetical theme of Ethiopian blackness can be gauged by a sampling of Fathers from Origen's time through the sixth century, in whose writings we find his interpretation of biblical Ethiopians as sinners, usually meaning the unbaptized gentiles, in one form or another, on one verse or another. Peter of Alexandria,[24] Didymus the Blind,[25] Apollinaris,[26] Ambrose,[27] Paulinus of Nola,[28] Ephrem,[29] Apponius,[30] Gregory of Nyssa,[31] Jerome,[32] Augustine,[33] Cyril of Alexandria,[34] Cassiodorus,[35] Cyril of Alexandria,[36] Faustus, bishop of Riez,[37] Gregory the Great,[38] and Ennodius[39] all draw on this allegory. Even Theodoret of Cyrrhus, of the supposedly nonallegorizing Antiochene school, explains Moses' Ethiopian wife as meaning the gentiles.[40] In sum, the patristic hermeneutic tradition saw the biblical Ethiopian as a metaphor to signify any person who, not having received a Christian baptism, is black in spirit and without divine light. In a similar way "Ethiopia" came to symbolize the "as yet unevangelized, and spiritually unregenerated world of sin."[41] As Jean Marie Courtès has shown, Christian patristic literature refers to Blacks mostly as metaphors for evil and sin, either as exegetical interpretations of the unconverted or as demons.[42]

Was the rabbinic interpretation the source for Origen? The evidence is not determinative in establishing lines of influence. Some scholars think that Origen's commentary on Song reacts to, and builds on, rabbinic exegesis; others that the rabbinic exegesis is a reaction to Origen.[43] Could Philo's allegorization of the Ethiopians' blackness as evil have been the source for both the Rabbis and Origen? In regard to the Rabbis, the answer is unequivocal: there is no evidence here or elsewhere that they drew on Philo. In regard to Origen, however, the answer is not so clear-cut, for we know that the Fathers did draw on Philo.[44] Clement of Alexandria (second century) was the first to do so extensively, being "greatly influenced by Philo" in his allegorical method of exegesis.[45] Ambrose (fourth century) made heavy use of Philo, as has been noted often.[46] As Courtès pointed out, it is clear that Ambrose drew on the Philonic passage when he wrote that, "the color of the Ethiopian signifies darkness of the soul and the squalor which is opposed to light, dispossessed of brightness, covered in darkness, and more similar to night than day."[47] More to the point, Origen drew on Philo and "most scholars have seen Philo's influence on Origen operating predominantly in the area of allegorical exegesis."[48] So was Philo the source for Origen and the Fathers on this point?

We cannot say with certainty, for darkness as a symbol of evil is "an almost universal phenomenon, common among black as well as white peoples."[49] The symbol was certainly as well established in the Hebrew Bible as in Egyptian, Greco-Roman, and Arabic literature.[50] Furthermore, allegorical interpretations that saw the black maiden of Song as sin (unconnected to Kushites) existed by Origen's time among both Christian and Jewish writers.[51] We cannot therefore draw a direct line between Origen and Philo on this point of interpretation. As Dölger remarked, both Philo and the early Christian writers drew on the same universal symbol.[52] Origen did use Philo and was most probably influenced by his color symbolism in a general way. But we cannot claim a direct dependence for Origen on Philo's metaphorical use of Ethiopian black skin as evil in *Quaestiones in Genesim* 2.82.[53]

Irrespective of who drew on whom, can we say with Lonis that Philo was racist? (Of course, Lonis's anachronistic terminology as applied to the first century C.E. is problematic.) Can we claim the same for the rabbinic interpretation or for Origen and his successors? There is no question that the Christian metaphor of the Ethiopian as sinner, and as devil, a related phenomenon, had a negative effect over time and did contribute toward a developing racism. "The linking together of the four ideas—black, other, sinner, danger—runs throughout all the manifestations of medieval Western Christian thought."[54] And even if, as many point out, such thought was restricted to the realm of metaphor, whether as exegetical interpretations of evil or the unconverted or as demons—"a mark of identity . . . in the diptychs of darkness and light," as Courtès put it—nevertheless these themes "were destined for a long life" and Blacks "suffered nonetheless by their metaphorical relationship with the demons."[55] "Although the theological intent is to gloss sacred text, the result . . . is to encourage attention to . . . the blackness of Ethiopians . . . overlaid with the metaphoric associations of contemporary divines linking the African to sin and slavery."[56] These "texts were repeated again and again, and it is undeniable that they inspired the later interpretations that invariably identified blackness with sin, Ethiopia with the land of sin, and the Ethiopian with the collective sin of a people."[57] When exegesis became iconographic and depicted the Black as executioner and torturer, the effect of these interpretations had even greater force. "How many generations of Christians have been conditioned by looking at a grimacing black man torturing Christ or his saints?"[58] As Devisse says, "A whole mental structure, unconscious for the most part, was erected to the detriment of the blacks."[59] It is, Landislas Bugner concludes, "beyond question that this pejorative extension of the symbolism of black color reflected unfavorably on the person of the African."[60]

Nevertheless, can we claim that the church fathers were racist? Frank Snowden argued that patristic exegesis from Origen to the sixth century leaves no doubt about the equality of the Black in the eyes of the church fathers.[61] Even if Origen's exegetical framework, which indeed included the Ethiopian within the Christian dispensation, was founded on the basis of interpreting Ethiopian as sinner, a point that Snowden does not consider, nonetheless Snowden is right: Christian theology does not harbor anti-Black sentiment. The accumulating negative effects of Black-as-sinner-or-devil exegesis, which cannot be denied, does not, however, necessarily implicate those who initiated the exegesis as racists. In allegorizing the biblical text the early Fathers drew on the common metaphor of darkness or blackness as evil, and, unless there is evidence to the contrary, we cannot assume that such exegesis reflects an antipathy toward black Africans. The same can be said for the Rabbis and Philo.

Elsewhere, Philo allegorizes the raven that Noah sent from the ark, as "a symbol of evil, for it brings night and darkness upon the soul. . . . And so it was right to expel beyond the borders whatever residue of darkness there was in the mind. . . . Why, after going out, did the raven not return again? . . . The passage is to be interpreted allegorically, for unrighteousness is the adversary of the light of righteousness."[62] Does this imply that Philo was anti-raven? Or, to ask the question from the opposite direction, when Philo gives a positive allegorical interpretation of the color of the Ethiopian whom Moses married ("resolve unalterable, intense, and fixed," who, black like the pupil of the eye represents the soul's power of vision),[63] does this imply that Philo was pro-Ethiopian. Neither "pro" nor "anti," Philo was using the universal symbols of color in his allegorical arsenal. Lonis, Diop, and Tonguino have read modern-day assumptions and terminology back into history.

Moses' Kushite Wife: Miscegenation or Denigration

One of the most prominent biblical passages mentioning a Kushite is the story of Moses and his Kushite wife. Here are the crucial lines of this enigmatic story.

> (1) Miriam and Aaron spoke against Moses because of the Kushite woman whom he had married (for he had indeed married a Kushite woman); (2) and they said, "Has the Lord spoken only through Moses? Has he not spoken through us also?" And the Lord heard it. (3) Now the man Moses was very humble, more so than anyone else on the face of the earth. (Num 12:1–3; NRSV)

In our earlier examination of this text, we saw that it is most likely that Moses' Kushite wife was Zipporah the Midianite, whom Moses had married as reported previously in the biblical narrative. Kush was the ancient name of the area in Northwest Arabia, which later became known as Midian. We saw evidence of the use of this name in the Egyptian execration texts and in the prophet Habakkuk's parallel "The tents of Kushan . . . the dwellings of Midian" (Hab 3:7). However, even if we accept the minority view among Bible scholars today and understand "Kushite" in Num 12:1 to mean Ethiopian, the point of Miriam and Aaron's complaint was that Moses had taken a non-Israelite wife. The purpose of the story is to advocate the acceptance of foreign marriage; thus God punished Miriam for arguing against such acceptance. There is no evidence that color or black African ethnicity was in any way relevant.

This is how Bible scholars today understand the events in Num 12:1–3. How did postbiblical Judaism understand them? Was the Kushite woman identified with Zipporah, the Midianite wife of Moses, or was the Kushite Moses' second wife? Was Kushite understood to mean black African? If yes, what is the meaning of Miriam and Aaron's complaint and God's punishment of Miriam? Finally, what can we learn about Jewish views of Blacks from how these events were understood in postbiblical Judaism?

Hellenistic-Jewish and rabbinic literature preserves four exegetical traditions that address the issue of the Kushite: (1) Moses married only one woman, Zipporah the Midianite, who is called a Kushite because Kush is another name for Midian; (2) Moses married two women, Zipporah the Midianite and the unnamed Kushite/Ethiopian; (3) Moses married only Zipporah, and the Hebrew term *kushit* does not refer to a place, either Midian or Ethiopia, but is to be understood metaphorically as something distinctive or different; (4) Moses married only Zipporah and *kushit* means "beautiful." Let us look at each of these traditions.

Moses married only one woman, Zipporah from Midian, and Kushite means Midianite. This view is expressed by two Hellenistic-Jewish writers living in Alexandria: Demetrius, the chronographer and exegete of the late third century B.C.E., and Ezekiel, the poet of the second century B.C.E. Here is Demetrius:

> Moses fled to Midian and there was married to Zipporah . . . of the stock of Abraham. . . . They lived in the city of Midian which is named after one of the children of Abraham. For [Scripture] says that Abraham sent his sons to the East to make their home. For this reason, too, Aaron and Miriam said at Hazeroth that Moses had married an Ethiopian woman.[64]

In this passage Demetrius attempts to reconcile the report of Moses' marriage to a Kushite (Num 12:1) with the report of his marriage to a Midianite (Ex 2:21) and he does so by simply equating the two, without further explanation.

Similarly, Ezekiel identifies Zipporah with the Kushite. In his *Exagoge* 60–65 he has Zipporah say to Moses, concerning her homeland:

> Stranger, this land is called Libya.
> It is inhabited by tribes of various peoples,
> Ethiopians, black men [Αἰθίοπες ἄνδρες μέλανες].
> One man is the ruler of the land:
> he is both king and general.
> He rules the state, judges the people,
> and is priest. This man is my father and theirs.[65]

The description of Zipporah's father as priest—and probably also the description as judge—is based on the story in Exodus 18, where Zipporah's father, the priest of Midian, advises Moses on a judicial system. Ezekiel says that the inhabitants of Zipporah's homeland are Ethiopians of Africa ("Libya" is the Greek term for the continent of Africa), thus making Zipporah a Kushite/Ethiopian. Unlike Demetrius, Ezekiel does not explicitly name Midian as Zipporah's homeland. But Ezekiel was certainly familiar with the biblical identification of Zipporah as a Midianite (witness his knowledge of the biblical story in these lines), and yet he makes Zipporah an Ethiopian. As with Demetrius, it appears that Ezekiel's intent in this passage is to reconcile the biblical verses reporting Moses' marriage to Zipporah and his marriage to the Kushite, and he does so by equating Zipporah's unnamed homeland (Midian) with Ethiopia.

Demetrius and Ezekiel thus equate Midian with Ethiopia. They cannot be accused of trying to "pull the wool over the eyes" of their readers, certainly not Demetrius, who blatantly mentions Zipporah's Midianite origins. Apparently they saw no problem in making the equation, probably because they still knew the ancient name of Kush to designate Midian, the designation we encountered in biblical and Egyptian sources.[66] They therefore saw no problem in claiming that a Midianite could be called a

Kushite/Ethiopian. Some scholars assumed that Ezekiel was geographically confused and thought that Midian was in Africa where the Ethiopians live.[67] But, given the fact that the people in Northwest Arabia (Midian) were called Kushites, we need not suspect Ezekiel's geographic knowledge. Because Ezekiel knew that the people who lived in Midian were called Kushites, he may have considered Midian to be part of "the land called Libya [Africa]." Hundreds of years later we find Augustine (d. 430) saying that Moses' Ethiopian wife was a Midianite, but that "almost no one now calls them Ethiopians, as names of places and peoples often undergo a change of name in time."[68] Augustine's language does not necessarily indicate that *at his time* some people knew Midian by its ancient name Kush or Ethiopia (although that possibility cannot be ruled out), but it would seem to imply that Kush/Ethiopia was known as a name for Midian after the biblical period.[69] It is, therefore, not unlikely that the name was still known at the time of Demetrius and Ezekiel. In any case, and for whatever reason, Demetrius and Ezekiel both equate Moses' Kushite wife with Zipporah.

The following lines from the *Exagoge* may also indicate Ezekiel's identification of the Kushite as Zipporah. At Moses' meeting with Sepphora (= Zipporah), Ezekiel presents a dialogue between her and a person named Chum (Χουμ):

Chum: Sepphora, you must reveal this.
Sepphora: My father has given me as spouse to this stranger.[70]

Who is Chum? Based on the context and parallel literary motifs in Greek and Latin literature, scholars have concluded that he is either Zipporah's brother or her (soon to be jilted) fiancé. Where did Ezekiel get the name Chum? Holladay thinks that the name is a variant spelling for Chus (i.e., Kush). Because Ezekiel identifies Zipporah as a Kushite, he introduces Zipporah's brother/fiancé as "Kush" (Chum).[71] Jacobson believes that "Chum" is a deliberate "hybrid" of Kush and his father Ham (Χους + Χαμ = Χουμ), the two Ethiopian ancestors, motivated by a wordplay on the Hebrew *ḥum* 'black, dark', thus inventing "an appropriate name [Χουμ] for an Ethiopian or an ancestor of the dark-skinned Ethiopians."[72] Robertson also assumes that Chum is Kush.[73] If these scholars are right that Chum derives from the name Kush, it would provide further evidence of Zipporah's identity as a Kushite. In any case, Demetrius and Ezekiel clearly identify the biblical Kushite as Zipporah. Thus the first exegetical tradition explaining Num 12:1 assumes that Moses married one woman, Zipporah.

The second exegetical tradition on Num 12:1 does not identify the Kushite with Zipporah, but understands Kush in its common biblical meaning as Ethiopia: Moses had a second wife, an Ethiopian. This view is represented by the Moses-Ethiopia romance that is found recorded, in various versions, in sources from antiquity to the late Middle Ages. Josephus (*Ant.* 2.242ff.) transmits the story, in which Moses, on behalf of the Egyptians, leads an army against the invading Ethiopians. Moses is successful and marries the Ethiopian king's daughter, who had fallen passionately in love with him.[74] Even earlier than Josephus, the story is told by the Hellenistic-Jewish writer Artapanus, who does not however record the marriage of Moses with the Ethiopian princess.[75]

An echo of the story is heard in the paraphrase of *Targum Pseudo-Jonathan* to Num 12:1,

> And Miriam and Aaron spoke improper words against Moses concerning the matter of the Kushite woman whom the Kushites had married to Moses during his flight from Pharaoh, but he had separated from her; because they had given [him] the Queen of Kush in marriage, but he had separated from her. Then they said: "Does God speak only with Moses, that he abstained from a sexual life? Behold, He speaks with us too."

Similarly a rabbinic tradition, found only in a later, medieval quotation, claims that Moses married a Kushite but never slept with her.[76] The same medieval source preserves another rabbinic tradition that Zipporah was a Kushite from her mother's side.[77] The marriage to the queen of Ethiopia is clearly based on the Hellenistic romance, but the source of the addition that Moses stopped having sexual relations with his Ethiopian wife is derived from an element found in tannaitic midrash, which fills in the gaps of the biblical story: Miriam and Aaron learned that Moses had stopped sleeping with his wife, so they confronted him with their complaint, "Are you so high and mighty that because God speaks with you, you consider yourself too holy to have sex? 'Has the Lord spoken only through Moses? Hasn't he also spoken through us?' (Num 12:2) and we haven't stopped sleeping with our spouses!"[78] At first, this behind-the-scenes reconstruction of events seems preposterously imaginary. But it is actually a clever reading of the biblical text. Miriam and Aaron's complaint against Moses had something to do with his wife (Num 12:1); yet it is expressed as "God speaks to us too, not only to Moses" (12:2); furthermore, the nature of the complaint must be related to what it says in the immediately following verse, which is apparently explanatory: "The man Moses was very humble, more than anyone else on the earth" (12:3).[79] In other words, the complaint must have had something to do with Moses' marriage, his relationship with God, and his humility. The rabbinic reconstruction accounts for all three points: the complaint against Moses was his "holier than thou" attitude, which was detected by his relationship with his wife, which was misread by Miriam and Aaron because Moses was in reality a very humble man. The reconstruction is then neatly tied up with the midrashic comment (echoed in *Targ Ps-Jon*) to 12:8, "*Mouth to mouth do I speak with him,* and I told him to separate from his wife."

Scholars are divided as to whether the story of Moses' Ethiopian campaign originated in an attempt to answer the enigma of Moses' otherwise unknown wife in Num 12:1, or whether the verse preserves a distant echo of an extrabiblical story about Moses.[80] Whatever the case, whether it be an extrabiblical echo or a postbiblical expansion, the story and its preservation in the Hellenistic, Roman, and rabbinic periods are important for assessing Jewish attitudes toward black Africans. Neither Josephus nor the Targum nor the rabbinic source saw anything denigrating in African origins or in miscegenation. Neither source indicates any irregularity in, or even slightly apologizes for, the marriage of Moses to the Ethiopian princess or queen. This would suggest a similar attitude on the part of their Jewish audience and/or readers.[81] If marriage to a black African woman was, in and of itself, considered demeaning, it is unlikely that Josephus, the Targum, and the Rabbis would have mentioned that the Jews' greatest leader and prophet married the Ethiopian woman.[82]

The third exegetical tradition on Num 12:1 interprets the word "Kushite" in the verse metaphorically. Moses married only one woman, Zipporah the Midianite, and the passage in Num 12:1 refers to her, with the word "Kushite" being understood as a metaphor for that which is different or distinctive, usually in beauty or good character: "Just as the Kushite is distinctive [*meshuneh*] in skin color, so Zipporah was distinctive [*meshunah*] in beauty and character."[83] This midrashic interpretation of the biblical word *kushi(t)* is said not only concerning Zipporah but also of others whom the Bible refers to as Kushites. In this manner, the Rabbis said of King Saul ("Kush the Benjaminite" in Ps 7:1 is understood to mean Saul) that he was handsome: "Just as the Kushite is distinguished by his skin color so Saul was distinguished by his appearance (or appearance and character)." Similarly, the people of Israel (Amos 9:7, "Are you not like Kushites to me, O Israel?") is distinctive in fulfilling God's commandments. Ebed-melech the Kushite (Jer 38:7) is distinctive by his good deeds in saving the prophet Jeremiah.[84] In these cases biblical "Kushite" is not taken literally but metaphorically, as that which is different in a positive way.[85]

Why did the midrash interpret "Kushite" metaphorically? Does it indicate, as some have argued, a rabbinic unwillingness to accept the plain sense of the passage, that Moses' wife and some other biblical personalities were black Africans?[86] To ask this question is to ask about the nature of midrash. Metaphoric explanations of names and descriptions of biblical figures are widespread in midrashic literature and are driven by several factors, some internal to the text and some external.[87] Of the internal reasons, the factor that comes into play in the case of Moses' wife is the midrashic aversion to anonymity in the Bible—that is, the attempt to identify anonymous biblical figures and to do so, often, by identifying them with known figures. Such a technique is not peculiar to midrashic literature but is part of a universal literary phenomenon. In our case, the unknown Kushite is thus identified with the known Zipporah.[88] What pushes the midrash in this direction is the fact that the Bible had not recorded a second marriage for Moses up to this point.

Rabbinic sources preserve another explanation of the Hebrew word *kushi(t):* that it means "beautiful." This opinion is recorded in the tannaitic midrashim *Sifre Numbers* and *Sifre Zuṭa,* where it appears independent of the distinctiveness midrash.[89] According to R. Eliezer b. Yose ha-Galilee (second century), the interpretation is based on wordplay (*noṭariqon*): *Ṣipporah: ṣefu u-reʾu,* "Zipporah: look and gaze" at her beauty.[90] From these early texts it appears that the definition of *kushi(t)* as "beautiful" was well accepted, although it is hard to imagine that the basis for the definition was a wordplay that does not even contain the word "beauty" in the play.

Indeed, there is evidence that R. Eliezer b. Yose ha-Galilee's explanation may not have been the source of the definition. Zeʾev Ben-Ḥayyim has shown that in Samaritan tradition, *kushit/kaśita* means "beautiful." The Samaritan Targum translates *kushit* of Num 12:1 this way (*yʾyrth,* var. *nhyrth, kšyrth*), as it does *kaśita* of Deut 32:15 (*ṣprt,* var. *ʾšpryt, ʾtrbrbt*).[91] Marqe, the Samaritan poet and exegete (third or fourth century), glosses the latter passage in a similar way: "Whoever sees *anything good* will be blessed." In a Samaritan trilingual (Hebrew/Arabic/Samaritan-Aramaic) dictionary the two words of Num 12:1 and Deut 32:15 are translated "beautiful": *ḥsnt, ʿgbt* (= *ʿājibu / ʿājabu*) in Arabic; *kšyrh, ʾtrbrbt* in Aramaic. Finally, the word appears (undeclined) in three Samaritan *piyyuṭim* with the same apparent meaning: *wkl ʿwbdyw kšyth* 'and all his actions are beautiful', *wmmlkwtk kšyt* 'and your kingdom is beautiful', *hlwky šbyl kšyt* 'those going in the beautiful way'.[92] Clearly, the Samaritans had a tradition that the word *kushit* (and *kaśita*) meant "beautiful."

And not only the Samaritans. Cognate languages also support such a definition, for in Arabic *kuwayyis* means "beautiful." The word is attested in a ninth-century Arabic papyrus (referring to cloths), in *A Thousand and One Nights,* and in modern colloquial Arabic.[93] In his study of early Arabic preserved in papyri, Simon Hopkins noted that the close correspondence between the language of the papyri and Middle Arabic "speaks of a very impressive continuity in colloquial Arabic usage, and the roots of the modern vernaculars are thus seen to lie very deep. This conclusion may also be supported by pointing to items of vocabulary, such as *kwys,* 'good' . . . very common in modern dialects, but almost unknown in literary Arabic."[94] In other words, *kuwayyis* is part of the early Arabic vocabulary.

Years ago some scholars suggested that the rabbinic explanation of Kushite as "beautiful" may have been based on Arabic *kuwayyis*.[95] It would certainly not be the first time that the rabbinic authors referred to Arabic to explain Hebrew words.[96] Nevertheless, the scholars' suggestions, based at the time on late colloquial Arabic, were not very convincing.[97] However, now that we have recovered Arabic *kwys* in a ninth-century papyrus, and Hopkins has concluded that this word has an early pedigree, and since we are aware of a similar Samaritan definition of the word as early as the third or fourth century, it is clear that the midrashic interpretation is based on a Semitic cognate. Eliezer b. Yose ha-Galilee's wordplay (*Ṣipporah: ṣefu u-reʾu*) now makes more sense as explaining a definition that was already known rather than being the basis for a new, midrashically originated definition.

A late midrash, *Tanḥuma*, provides two explanations as to why Zipporah was called Kushite meaning "beautiful," one based on the fear of the "evil eye," and one based on *gematṛiya* (numerical value of letters).[98] As to the first, *Tanḥuma* says, "Because of her beauty she was called Kushite, as a man calls his son 'Kushi' to ward off the evil eye."[99] The custom of language circumlocution as a defense against the evil eye is a universal phenomenon, whose purpose is "to undo compliments or to render the complimented person or object unworthy of praise."[100] Implicit in *Tanḥuma*'s explanation is the assumption that a Kushite is the opposite of beauty.[101] This circumlocution may be similar to the use of the color black in Arabic literature as "a kind of homeopathic magic . . . used as a charm against 'the evil eye.'"[102] *Tanḥuma*'s other explanation, that of *gematṛiya*, is based on the equal numerical values of the words *kushit* and *yefat marʾeh* ("beautiful").

Some have argued that the interpretation of Kushite as "beautiful," as found in the midrashim and Targum, is based on these explanations.[103] This, however, is rather unlikely, since the explanations cannot be traced earlier than the eleventh century. Their appearance in *Tanḥuma* is deceiving; this section of *Tanḥuma* is not original to the work and derives from a later source. S. Buber showed that there are considerable additions in the *Tanḥuma* sections *Wa-Yiqraʾ*, *Ṣaw*, and *Shemini* that come from later sources including Maimonides, Saadia, *Pirqei deR. Eliezer*, and Rashi; our section is one of those that derive from Rashi (d. 1105).[104] More than three hundred years before Buber, Meir b. Samuel Benveniste argued that the source for this section in *Tanḥuma* was Rashi's *Commentary to the Torah*.[105] The *gematṛiya* and evil-eye explanations are thus late, medieval additions to the text and do not reflect the classical rabbinic world view, with which we are concerned.[106]

In summary, the biblical reference to Moses' Kushite wife required explanation, for there had been no earlier mention of such a marriage. In Judaism of late antiquity, we find four answers. Two early Hellenistic-Jewish authors simply equated the Kushite with Zipporah, seemingly recognizing that Zipporah's country of origin, Midian, could be called Kush. The second explanation, beginning in the Hellenistic period, recorded by Josephus, and echoed in the Targum and, possibly, rabbinic tradition sees the Kushite as an Ethiopian. The third explanation, seen in rabbinic midrash, interprets Kushite metaphorically as meaning "distinctive." The last explanation claims that the Hebrew word *kushit* means beautiful. The meaning "beautiful" given directly in explanation four and indirectly in explanation three may preserve an echo of the ancient view of the Ethiopians as a particularly handsome people.[107]

Postbiblical Interpretation of Isaiah 18:1–2

We saw that the difficult lines in Isa 18:1–2 reflect a positive appreciation of the Kushites, both from the military point of view (a strong people with great speed and prowess with the bow) and their physical appearance (a handsome people, tall, smooth-skinned). *Targum Jonathan* renders the Isaiah verses as follows:

> (1) Ah, the land to which they come in ships from a far land, their sails spread out as the eagle which soars on its wings, which is beyond the rivers of India, (2) which sends messengers by the sea and in fishing boats upon the waters! Go, swift messengers, to the people robbed and plundered, to the people which was strong before and continually, the people robbed and plundered, whose land the Gentiles plundered."[108]

The interpretations embedded in the Targum have been encountered above as various alternative translations to Isaiah's puzzling words, which are offered by today's biblical scholars.[109] Such is the interpretation of *ṣilṣel kenafayim* as "sailboats." The rendering of *memušakh u-moraṭ* as "robbed and plundered" echoes the same idea as that put forward by Ibn Janaḥ and the Peshiṭta, which found recent expression in the NJPS rendering. So too, apparently, *MidPs* 120.5, which translates *memušakh* as "carried away." It appears that the Targum did not know what to do with *qaw-qaw u-mebusah* and so preferred to repeat "robbed and plundered" (unless the repetition is a dittographic error). Despite understanding the verse to mean that the Ethiopians' land was robbed and plundered, the Targum nevertheless saw these people as strong and powerful, translating *ʿam noraʾ min huʾ wahal-ʾah* as "a people which was strong before and continually," an interpretation that carried over into later medieval commentators, such as Rashi and Joseph ibn Kaspi.[110]

Chilton believes that in translating the Hebrew *Kush* as "India," the Targum shifted the geographical focus from Ethiopia to India.[111] However, the targumic translation "India" does not indicate a different location at all; the Targum may not have even realized that Kush and India are two different locations, for the confusion or interchange between the names Kush/Ethiopia and India is as old as antiquity and continues into and beyond the Middle Ages, cutting across Greco-Roman, Jewish, Christian, and Islamic boundaries.[112] There is no question that with the translation "India" the Targum to Isa 18:1 meant East Africa; he did not shift his geographical focus as Chilton thinks.

Righteous Ethiopians

We recall that the Bible describes Ebed-melech the Kushite, servant of the Judahite king, as one who saved Jeremiah's life and was rewarded by God. In the postbiblical period Ebed-melech's reputation as a righteous hero seems to have grown greater. *4 Baruch,* a pseudepigraphical work of the second century C.E., casts Abimelech, as he is called in this work, in a central role and portrays him in a very favorable light. Jeremiah asks God to spare Abimelech the sight of Jerusalem's destruction and desolation and God complies by putting Abimelech to sleep for sixty-six years until the exiles return from Babylonia. According to some manuscripts of the work, Abimelech and Baruch, Jeremiah's scribe, are both prevented from seeing the exile of the Jews on the analogy of a father whose son is punished and who covers his face so as not to see his son's grief. Jeremiah, in writing to Baruch (or, Baruch and Abimelech), asks the two to pray for the Jews in Babylonia.[113] Certainly the character of Ebed-melech as a righteous man is built upon the biblical narrative, but his reputation and stature have grown from being a relatively minor biblical personality who saved Jeremiah's life, to playing a central role with Jeremiah and Baruch as one of three righteous heroes. In rabbinic literature, Ebed-melech's reputation has taken on even greater luster. He is considered to be one of the select few who did not die but entered paradise alive. He is also described as one of ten rulers (*melekh* "king") who became proselytes to Judaism.[114] In some midrashic texts he is identified with Baruch and/or with Zedekiah.[115] Similarly Zephaniah's father, about whom the Bible says nothing other than that his name was Kushi, is considered by the Rabbis to have been a righteous man.[116]

Idealized Ethiopians

The idea that Ethiopia/Kush was located at the ends of the earth had various consequences, some positive and some negative, in terms of how the black African was perceived. The Greco-Roman world and the Jewish world shared both perceptions. Both cultures believed that those furthest away from society with its corrupting influences lived in a state of pristine innocence, "beloved of the gods" as Homer put it, exhibiting innate wisdom, justice, and righteousness. And both cultures shared the contradictory belief that those who lived furthest away from society were the most barbaric and least civilized of people.[117]

We can see the idealized, positive view of the black African in a rabbinic legend about Alexander the Great:

> Alexander of Macedon visited King Qaṣya [*qṣyʾ*] beyond the Mountains of Darkness. He came to a certain province [*medinta*] called *qrṭygnʾ*, which was inhabited entirely by women. They came out to meet him and said: "If you make war against us and defeat us, you will have a reputation as one who conquered a province of women; and if we make war upon you and defeat you, you will be known as one who lost a war to women. In any case you will always be ashamed to face any king." At that moment his face fell. When he left, he wrote upon the city gate: I, Alexander of Macedon, was a foolish king until I came to the principality of *qrṭygnʾ* and learned wisdom from women.
>
> He then went to another province [*medinta*] which was called *afriqi*. The people came out to greet him with golden apples, pomegranates, and bread. He said to them, "Is this what you eat in your land?" They replied, "Do you not have it in your own land that you come to us for it?" He said to them, "I have not come to see your wealth but to observe your laws [*din*]." While they were standing there, two men appeared before the king [of the land] for a judgment. They were both concerned about avoiding theft. One said: "I bought a ruin from this man and while digging in it found a treasure, and so I said to him 'Take your treasure. I bought a ruin, not a treasure.'" The other said to the king: "My lord, when I sold that man the ruin, I sold him everything that was in it."
>
> The king turned to one of them and asked him: "Do you have you a son?" He replied: "Yes." The king asked the other: "Have you a daughter?" He replied: "Yes." "Go, then," said the king, "marry them one to the other, and let them both share the treasure." Alexander was amazed at what he heard. The king asked: "Why are you amazed? Have I not judged well?" Alexander replied: "Yes." The king asked: "If such a case had come up in your country, how would you have handled it?" Alexander replied: "We would have removed both of their heads, and the treasure would have gone to the palace." The king asked: "Does the sun shine where you live?" Alexander replied,

> "Yes." "Does the rain fall where you live?" "Yes." "Are there small cattle in your land?" "Yes," Alexander replied. "May your breath be extinguished!" exclaimed the king. "Don't you realize that it is on account of the small cattle that the sun shines and the rain falls? It is only on account of the small cattle that you remain alive!"
>
> This is the meaning of the verse "Man and animal You save, O Lord" (Ps 36:7/6)—that is, because of the merit of the animals God saves man. On account of the animals God saves man."[118]

What is of interest to us is the term *afriqi*—what does it mean? Before attempting to answer this question, it is necessary to say a few words about the Alexander stories in late antiquity. The historical accounts of Alexander's (d. 323 B.C.E.) conquests were early elaborated with various fabulous elements, taking the form of a romance, that is, a prose narrative set in distant lands recounting the sensational exploits of its central character(s). The Alexander romance, called by scholars "Pseudo-Callisthenes," may have first appeared as early as a century after Alexander's death, although the earliest existing manuscript dates from around 300 C.E. First in the Greco-Roman world, then in the East (sixth century), and finally in the West (tenth century) various versions of the romance developed and became very popular, eventually being translated into dozens of languages.[119] One of the most common and prominent themes in all the versions is Alexander's desire to go to, and beyond, the ends of the earth (διῆλθεν ἕως ἄκρων τῆς γῆς).[120] Stoneman remarks that "the fundamental idea, that Alexander is proceeding beyond the boundaries of the known world, is expressed even in Alexander's lifetime," and he quotes the Athenian orator Aeschines that "Alexander had withdrawn to the uttermost regions of the North, almost beyond the borders of the inhabited world."[121] Although Aeschines puts the "uttermost regions" in the north, and Pseudo-Callisthenes locates it where the Amazons live at the river Thermodon near the Black Sea, later versions of the Alexander romance elaborated this theme and put Alexander in various ends-of-the-earth locations.[122]

The ends-of-the-earth locations are often indicated by references in the romance to Alexander's arrival at the Land of Darkness.[123] In several versions the Land of Darkness is associated with mountains remarkable for their height or their darkness. The rabbinic version quoted here, as well as the medieval, Hebrew *Yosippon,* mentions Mountains of Darkness.[124] Other versions speak of a "great mountain" in the Land of Darkness.[125] The Persian *Iskandarnamah* has Alexander reach the Qāf mountains, which encircle the world, in the Land of Darkness.[126] The earlier Latin version of *Alexander's Letter to Aristotle* has Alexander come to high mountain ranges and the world-encircling Ocean.[127] The Land of Darkness and

Mountains of Darkness are not unknown in ancient Near Eastern literature. In Mesopotamian geography the ends of earth are found at the horizons where the sun rises and sets over mountains. The mountains are thus known as mountains of sunrise and sunset and as light and dark mountains. The "dark mountain" and the "light mountain" mentioned in the Sumerian Tablet XII of Utukku Lemnutu is translated in Akkadian as "mountain of sunset" and "mountain of sunrise." The dark mountain of sunset is presumably the same as Mount Mashu in the Gilgamesh epic. This mountain is found at the ends of the earth connecting the heavens and the netherworld, and contains regions of deep darkness.[128] The Ugaritic Baal Cycle also mentions two mountains at the ends of the earth, which cover the entranceway to the underworld. Baal sends messengers to Mot, god of the underworld: "Then you shall head out / To Mount TRGZZ / To Mount THRMG / The two hills at Earth's edge. / Lift the mountain on your hands, / The hill on top of your palms. / And descend to Hell."[129] Probably, later references to the Mountain(s) of Darkness on the way to hell found in other cultures are echoes of these dark mountains connecting the netherworld. In Mandaic literature "Mountain(s) of Darkness is where sinners go after death, and in rabbinic literature it is the place beyond which Gehenna is found.[130] Note also that in later midrashic literature the fallen angels Uzza and Azael are suspended between heaven and earth, chained to the Mountains of Darkness.[131] In any case, we see a fairly widespread notion in the ancient Near East that situates mountains of darkness at the ends of the earth, standing between heaven and earth and leading to the netherworld.

These ancient Near Eastern dark mountains at the ends of the earth are the literary ancestors of the Land of Darkness and the Mountains of Darkness located at the ends of the earth in the Alexander romance. The relationship to the ancient antecedents is seen even more clearly in the Syriac and Ethiopic versions of the romance that describe Alexander's approach to the Mashu (Musas, Masis, Masas) mountain, which, in the Ethiopic version, is "where the sun sets in the west."[132] In the Gilgamesh epic Mashu is the dark mountain of sunset at the ends of the earth. J. T. Milik noticed the evocation of Mesopotamian mythic geography in Enoch's journey to the boundaries of the universe, as described in the pre-Maccabean Book of Watchers, "to a mountain whose summit reached to heaven," to the great encircling Ocean in the west "as far as the Great River and as far as the Great Darkness."[133] These geographic notions are found also in the Alexander romance, which has its origins as early as, if not earlier than, the Book of Watchers.[134] The parallels with Mesopotamian mythic geography is even closer if Reinink's explanation of the Syriac version of the romance is correct. The phrase translated "Land of Darkness" in the Syriac text is *hmt* (or *hmwt*, *hmty*, *ʾhmt*) *dḥšk*ʾ. Reinink thinks that *hmt* is related to the

Syriac *hmn* 'death' or 'place of death' and that "*hmt* of darkness" is, therefore, a reference to the underworld.[135] This explanation would accord perfectly with the ancient Near Eastern concept of Mount Mashu, the dark mountain, located where the sun sets, at the entrance to the underworld.[136]

As we have seen, Alexander was perceived as having reached the ends of the earth, where he found the Land of Darkness and the Mountain(s) of Darkness. As more and more fabulous elements were added to versions of the romance, Alexander was put in increasingly more ends-of-the-earth locations; Alexander's "desire to go beyond the limits of the known world . . . receive growing attention."[137] Because black Africa was considered to lie at the ends of the world, we would not be surprised to find that later versions of the romance put Alexander there, whether or not he actually went there.[138] Thus, although in the historical accounts the furthest south Alexander reached was the oasis of Siwa in Egypt, later legendary versions have him going much further southward into Nubia. Lucan (d. 65 C.E.) reports that Alexander sent Callisthenes on a mission "to the furthest reaches of Ethiopia" (*per ultima terrae Aethiopum*), but in many versions of the romance, Alexander himself is reported as having gone to Ethiopia.[139] Pseudo-Callisthenes has Alexander meet with Queen Candace of Meroe, in her territory, and a later recension of the Greek text speaks of Alexander's battle with black men.[140] The Latin version of *Alexander's Letter to Aristotle* puts Alexander at "the Ocean in Ethiopia."[141] The medieval Hebrew versions of the romance speak of Alexander's conquest of Kush.[142] Thomas of Kent's thirteenth-century *Roman de toute chevalerie*, drawing on the Alexander stories, had Alexander go to Ethiopia.[143] In other words, the tradition that Alexander went to the ends of the earth naturally gave rise to the view that he went to black Africa. The association of black Africa with distant lands may also lie behind the geographic impossibility found in the third *Sibylline Oracle* (mid-second century B.C.E.), where "the land of Gog and Magog was situated in the midst of the Ethiopian rivers."[144] Gog and Magog, the peoples whom Alexander imprisoned behind gates of iron, were situated in the northern end of the world, yet are here put in the midst of Ethiopian rivers. David White notes this conflation of the far north with the far south at a later time: "From the 9th century [C.E.] onwards, 'Ethiopia' was used to designate the lands north of the Caucasus, between the Black and Caspian seas—the very location, in legend, of Alexander's Gate!"[145] Apparently this conflation of the edges of the earth began much earlier.

Let us now return to the rabbinic text of "Alexander of Macedon [who] visited King Qaṣya beyond the Mountains of Darkness," first going to *qrtygn'*, the province of women (i.e., the Amazons), and then to *afriqi*, where he witnessed the trial. These two stories appear individually in other rabbinic sources, as noted by Theodor and Margulies.[146] In the separate accounts, it is the Amazon story that takes place in *afriqi,* while the trial before King Qaṣya takes place beyond the Mountains of Darkness. In the combined, presumably later, version the trial is in *afriqi,* the women are in *qrṭygnʾ,* and Qaṣya/Mountains of Darkness frame the entire unit. The following table shows this information in tabular form.

	bTam	*GenR*	*yBM*	*LevR/PesRK*
Amazons	*afriqi*			Qaṣya, Mountains of Darkness *qrṭygnʾ*
Trial		Qaṣya, Mountains of Darkness	Qaṣya	*afriqi*

Previous generations of scholars debated whether *afriqi* means Iberia, Phrygia, or Africa, and if the latter, whether it is North Africa or black Africa.[147] Those who argued for North Africa did so primarily on the basis of the name *qrṭygnʾ,* which they understood to mean Carthage.[148] However, the Amazons of Greek myth are found in ends-of-the-earth locations. Their placement at the edge of the known world "is a spatial expression of their reversal of patriarchal culture: Amazons blur the categories that classify the domains of male and female";[149] It indicates a "reversal of patriarchal culture: Amazons blur the categories that classify the domains of male and female"; they represent a "structural reversal of the Greek paradigm of civilization and organization of power."[150] At the edges of the world the categories, whether human-divine, human-animal, or male-female, break down. "The rule of women . . . can exist only on the margins of the Greek and Roman *politikon.*"[151] By putting the Amazons beyond the Mountains of Darkness, the editor of the rabbinic text (*LevR/PesRK*) indicates that he understood this.

Carthage is not at the ends of the earth. What then can *qrṭygnʾ* mean? There are several other places in rabbinic literature where a place *qrṭygnʾ* is mentioned (as in our text with a multitude of variant readings) and is understood by many scholars to refer not to Carthage but to some place east of Babylonia, or in Spain, or Armenia, or Persia.[152] In other words, whatever *qrṭygnʾ* may mean, we need not take it to refer to Carthage, and we are not, therefore, forced to understand *afriqi* as North Africa. There is also another possibility. Many years ago the suggestion was made that the word *qrṭygnʾ* in our text is an artificial term composed of Aramaic *qarta* 'city' + Greek γύνη 'woman' (the sources vary between *t* and *ṭ* in the spelling of *qrṭygnʾ*).[153] As the suggestion was proposed, without any supporting evidence, it sounded a little too ingenious. But, it should not be too quickly rejected, for there was a city in the Egyptian delta by the name of Gynaeconpolis 'Woman City'.[154] The editor or author of the combined account, therefore, did not necessarily fabricate a name of a city. Rather, he may have incorporated the name of a known city into his story because the name perfectly fit the story. He either assumed that Gynaeconpolis was the place of the Amazons, or he played on its name for his literary presentation, translating it to *qarta*-γύνη, *qrṭygn'*, not knowing or caring about geographic niceties.

If it is not necessary to understand *afriqi* in these stories as referring to North Africa, what else could the term mean? Some have argued for sub-Saharan Africa on the basis of the personal name Qaṣya, which, they say, is a fictitious creation derived from the Hebrew *qeṣ* 'end'—that is, the king of the end of the world, where, as we have seen, black Africa was considered to be.[155] Although the Amazons are variously located, Diodorus Sicilus (first century B.C.E.) writes that the original Amazons were in Africa. These Amazons lived in the western parts of Africa, on the bounds of the inhabited world, "near Ethiopia and that mountain by the shore of the ocean which is the highest of those in the vicinity and impinges upon the ocean and is called by the Greeks Atlas."[156] In other words, the Amazons lived near Ethiopia, one of the ends-of-the-earth locations in Greek thought. Other indications in the rabbinic account also point to an Ethiopian location. Saul Lieberman noted that the trial story depicts the characters in idealized ways as just, pious, and wise, precisely as the Greco-Roman sources portray the Ethiopians living at the ends of the earth.[157] The traits of justice, piety, and wisdom are indeed found among the classical writers as characteristic themes regarding the Ethiopians. "An image of pious, just Ethiopians became so imbedded in Graeco-Roman tradition that echoes are heard throughout classical literature."[158] And this image continued into late antiquity and the Byzantine period. As the sixth-century Lactantius Placidus said of the Ethiopians, "Certainly they are revered by the gods because of justice. Even Homer indicates this when he says that Jupiter frequently leaves heaven and feasts with them because of their justice and equity."[159] Therefore, whether or not the name Qaṣya points to a land at the end of the world,[160] the stories of the Amazons and the trial in *afriqi* would perfectly fit a location in the land of the Ethiopians, considered to lie at the ends of the earth, whether that refers to the western Ethiopians or the southern Ethiopians.

In this regard, it should be noted that another rabbinic text explicitly connects *afriqi* with distant lands:

> Diocletian oppressed the inhabitants of Paneas. They said to him, "We are going to leave!" His sophist said to him, "They will not leave. And [even] if

> they leave, they will return! Now, if you want to test [my claim], take some gazelles and send them to a far-away land [*arʿaʾ de-raḥiqaʾ; arʿaʾ raḥiqah*]. In the end they will return to their [original] home." [Diocletian] did [as instructed]. He took some gazelles, gilded their horns with silver, and sent them to *afriqi*. And, at the end of thirteen years, they returned to their [original] home.[161]

Here *afriqi* is identified as *the* faraway land.

The rabbinic story of the trial is not found in any other source from late antiquity. The earliest parallel is found in an eleventh-century Arabic collection of wise sayings.[162] Although we find elements of the story in other Alexander and non-Alexander accounts, there is no contemporaneous or early parallel to the story as a whole.[163] Whether it is a Jewish-Hellenistic creation or it derives from a no-longer-extant Greek source, it is clear that the rabbinic story of the trial incorporates the Greek notion of Homer's "blameless Ethiopians."[164] The rabbinic Alexander legend thus reflects the classical idea that those furthest away from society, those at the edges of the earth, specifically the Ethiopians, are wise, just, and righteous people who live in a utopian world.

Uncivilized Ethiopians

On the other hand, the idea that Ethiopia/Kush was located at the ends of the earth had negative consequences in how the black African was perceived. This perception, also paralleled in the Greco-Roman world, regarded those who lived furthest away from society as the least civilized. Greco-Roman tradition saw distant peoples—whether from the north, south, east, or west—as barbaric and primitive. This classical ethnocentrism was determined by geographic parameters, which can be conceived of as concentric circles emanating from the writer's region and encompassing ever more primitive and barbaric peoples. As we move outward, the people are barely or only partly human, until, at the furthest extremes, we get to Pliny's monstrous races, which are most commonly found in Africa, in the outermost districts (*extremitates*) of Ethiopia. In this scheme, Ethiopians—Homer's "farthermost of men"—were often considered to be savage and as having "the nature of a wild beast." They went about naked, kept their women in common, and practiced cannibalism.

To the best of my knowledge, Jewish literature of late antiquity does not have such an ends-of-the-earth catalog of barbaric characteristics. It does, however, echo the general classical idea that those living at the southern ends of the world—the Kushites or the Barbari—are less civilized. We find this expressed in a midrash that discusses Eliezer, the servant of Abraham

(Gen 15:2), who is considered to be a descendant of Canaan according to rabbinic tradition. In an exegesis of Prov 17:2 ("A servant who deals wisely . . . "), Eliezer is said to have preferred serving Abraham, because as a descendant of Canaan he was doomed to a life of slavery (Gen 9:25) and, should he leave Abraham, his chances for a better master would not improve. In fact, they might considerably worsen. In the words put in Eliezer's mouth, "A Kushi or a Barbari might enslave me! It is better for me to be a slave in this household and not in some other household."[165] The connotation of "*kushi* or *barbari*" in this context would seem to be clear. The people of Barbaria and Kush, considered to live at the remote southern end of the earth, are set in antithesis to Abraham, the model of piety and proper behavior,[166] and would seem to represent the uncivilized barbarian.

Another rabbinic text apparently conveys the same idea, although it is impossible to say for certain, because all that is extant of this text is the fragmentary line "even Sarmatians and even Barbarians," that is, the people at the northern and southern ends of the earth. The line is quoted from a *Yelamedenu* midrash by Nathan b. Yeḥiel of Rome in the eleventh century, who explains that these gentilics are meant to represent uncivilized peoples, a view presumably based on the *Yelamedenu* context, which he had before him.[167]

Ethiopians as Archers

A late rabbinic anthology of earlier material, *Leqaḥ Ṭov,* authored by Ṭoviah b. Eliezer of Bulgaria at the end of the eleventh century, contains a unique text that associates the twelve signs of the zodiac with twelve specific peoples or lands. In what may be an echo of the ancient Kushite reputation with the bow, Saggitarius, the archer, is associated with the Kushites.[168]

Hillel and the Broad-Footed Africans

A tannaitic series of traditions about Hillel includes the story of one who attempted to try the sage's legendary patience with various questions, one of which was, "Why do Africans [*afriqiyim*] have broad feet?" Hillel answered: "Because they live in marshes and walk about in water."[169] Rashi (d. 1105) offered two possible explanations of Hillel's answer. Either, in an adumbration of natural selection theory, the feet of the *afriqiyim* broadened to allow them to walk in the marshes and not sink; or since they walk in marshes and do not therefore wear shoes, their feet are broader than those of others who have the lifelong constriction of shoes. In any case, Hillel's answer was that the *afriqiyim* walk about in marshes.

Although *afriqa* often means North Africa in rabbinic literature, it can also refer to black Africa south of the Sahara, as already shown.[170] It will be seen that in this text about Hillel, the *afriqiyim* are indeed black Africans. Sub-Saharan Africa was well known in antiquity for its marshes. A stele recording the Nubian campaign of the Egyptian king Psammetich II in 593 B.C.E. tells how the king was "roaming the marshes."[171] Note also Herodotus's (2.32) story of the Nasamonians of Libya who ventured into inner Africa, going first through the inhabited areas along the coast of North Africa, then to the region of wild beasts, then over the desert until they came to an area of trees. There they were captured by men of small stature who led them across great marshes (ἑλέων μεγίστων) to a city "where all the people were of like stature . . . and black." Elsewhere Herodotus (2.137) again refers to the marshes of Africa, as does Agatharchides (in Diodorus Sicilus 3.8.6, 3.9.1, 3.10.1) in mentioning the marshy places where the Ethiopians live. Strabo (16.4.9), describing the various Ethiopian tribes, mentions "the Root-eaters (Ῥιζοφάγοι) and Marsh-dwellers (Ἕλειοι)." In the first century C.E., Seneca (*Naturales Quaestiones* 6.8.3–4) mentions a Roman expedition to Africa to discover the source of the Nile, which took place during Nero's reign and which, penetrating deep into Africa, encountered immense marshes, "which were impassable on foot or by boat." This is the Sudd, an area on the White Nile more than a thousand kilometers upstream from Meroe, which is "a vast and virtually impenetrable swamp."[172]

Not only does the description of the land point to sub-Saharan Africa; so too does the description of the people. The question put to Hillel echoes a perception of black Africans found in contemporaneous classical sources as well as later Arabic ones. The *Virgilian Appendix* describes Africans (*Afer genus*) as having "broad and ample feet" (*spatiosa prodiga planta*).[173] Similarly, some descriptions of black Africans in Arabic literature mention broad feet. Luqmān, the qur'anic legendary pre-Islamic hero, is described by Thaʿlabī (d. 1036) as being a Black with *mushaqqaq al-qadamayn*, which Sale translates as "splay feet."[174] Note also Masʿūdī's quotation of Galen (the original is not extant) describing one of the characteristics of black Africans as "long [*tashqīq*] feet and hands."[175] Frank Snowden finds that this perception has a physiological basis in anthropological descriptions of flat feet said to be characteristic of black Africans.[176] In any case, broad feet has been recorded as a characteristic of black Africans from the time of Hillel until our own days.[177] Note Maya Angelou's description of "a cruel fairy stepmother, who was understandably jealous of my beauty, [and] had turned me into a too-big Negro girl, with nappy hair, broad feet."[178]

Blemmyes and Nobae

An indirect reference to two black African peoples, the Blemmyes and the Nobae, can be found in a tannaitic text of the third century. Deut 32:21 describes the punishment God has decided to inflict on Israel for its disloyalty to him: "I will incense them with a no-folk [*be-loʾ ʿam*]; I will vex them with a nation of fools [*be-goy nabal*]." In a previous study I attempted to show that the tannaitic exposition of this passage interprets the biblical term *be-loʾ ʿam* as Blemmye, and possibly also the word *nabal* as Nobae (Nubae, Nobatae, Nobadae), the black African peoples of antiquity who were well known, especially during the third and fourth centuries, as a major threat to Roman rule in Upper Egypt.[179] Here is the tannaitic text: "'And I will incense them with a *be-loʾ ʿam.*' Do not read *blʾ ʿm,* but *blwy ʿm,* this refers to those who come from among the nations and kingdoms and expel them [the Jews? the Romans?] from their homes. Another interpretation: This refers to those who come from *barbaria* and *mrṭnyʾ,* who go about naked in the marketplace."[180]

The Blemmyes' period of political importance extended over three hundred years, approximately during the years 250–550 C.E. During this time they are mentioned again and again in Roman sources as a fierce nomadic people who inhabited the desert south of Egypt between the Nile Valley and the Red Sea and often invaded Egypt. Their raids finally forced Diocletian in 297 to cede control of Roman territory south of the first cataract, even though the raids later continued. The Nobae were also known for their raids into Roman territory and they are regularly mentioned by Roman writers together with the Blemmyes as threats to Roman security.[181] For almost three hundred years the Blemmyes and the Nobae are the two best-known peoples of East Africa on the borders of Upper Egypt. In the tannaitic text the Rabbis use the names of these contemporary peoples, well-known as warriors, to depict the punishments that will come to Israel, in essence saying, "I will incense them with the Blemmyes; I will vex them with the Nobae."

The indication that the text is referring to these black African peoples is found in the "other interpretation," which continues the initial identification of *be-loʾ ʿam* as *blwy ʿm* (Blemmye) and which refers "to those who come from *barbaria* and *mrṭnyʾ,*" that is, from Barbaria in East Africa to Mauritania in West Africa.[182] As is the case among many Greek and Roman writers, the Rabbis may not have realized that the Blemmyes were a specific ethnic or political group, but may have understood the term as referring to several nomadic tribes inhabiting the Nubian desert east and west of the Nile. "Blemmye" may thus have merely connoted dark-skinned Africans in general. Such lack of specific geographic knowledge may account for the rabbinic description of the "Blemmyes" as inhabiting all of sub-Saharan Africa from the east to the west. Or the Rabbis may have had accurate ethnic and political information, but hermeneutically increased the size of the Blemmyes' land to heighten the sense of fear their words would impart to their listeners. Similarly, their depiction of the Blemmyes and Nobae as not wearing clothes—a historically accurate characterization commonly found in classical sources, medieval Christian writers, and Arab geographers—would further add to the image of a fearsome people.

Michal bat Kushi

A tannaitic tradition states that "Michal the daughter of Kushi used to don phylacteries and the Sages [*ḥakhamim*] did not object; and the wife of Jonah used to make pilgrimage and the Sages did not object."[183] Who was this Michal the daughter of Kushi (or, "the Kushite") who was so devout that she put on phylacteries? The commentators (e.g., Rashi to *bʿEr*) claim that she is to be identified with Michal the daughter of King Saul (1 Sam 14:49), and one source (*yʿEr*) actually reads "the daughter of Saul," instead of "daughter of Kushi." It is clear, however, that this view is based on the midrashic tradition that equates "Kush the Benjaminite" of Ps 7:1 with Saul, because of the similarity of name and the place of origin of Saul's father, Qish the Benjaminite (1 Sam 9:1).[184] If Michal the daughter of Saul were truly the one referred to in the tradition, her name would have been transmitted as "Michal the daughter of Saul." There is no reason why her name would have been transmitted as "Michal the daughter of Kushi."

Rather, it seems that the tannaitic tradition preserved the memory of a certain pious woman who was the daughter of a Kushite or of one whose name was Kushi. Some time later, when there was no longer a memory of this Michal and she was consequently identified as Saul's daughter, the story of her piety was joined with that of Jonah's wife as examples of two biblical women whose religiosity compelled them to practice the law beyond what was required of them as women.[185] If this reconstruction is correct, we have evidence of a pious Jewish woman of late antiquity who was the descendant of a Kushite, or of one whose name was Kushi, which may, in any case, indicate Nubian origins.[186]

The Language of Kush

As far as the Greeks were concerned the language of the Ethiopians was only one of many barbaric languages. Statements, therefore, that speak of this language (or languages) as barbaric—such as the *Sibylline Oracles:* "Maurians and Ethiopians and peoples of barbarous speech [βαρβαροφώνων]," or the inscription found in Egypt that speaks of βαβαρικην λεξιν απ'Αι-θιοπων, "the barbarous speech of the Ethiopians"—merely represent the Greek idea of foreign speech in general being barbarous-sounding (e.g., *Iliad* 2.867).[187] One Jewish passage, however, may go beyond this idea and may imply that the language of the Ethiopians is particularly incomprehensible and difficult.

The Hebrew *Testament of Naphtali* elaborates the biblical story of the Tower of Babel and the confusion of languages. Seventy angels, we are told, taught the different languages to the seventy nations of the world. When God asked the nations whom they would worship, Nimrod chose the angel who taught him the language of Kush, his father, for he said, "There is none greater than he who taught me and my nation *kefi shaʿah* the language of Kush. Similarly Put, and Miṣraim, and Tubal, and Yavan, and Meshech, and Tiras. And every nation chose its own angel." The meaning of *kefi shaʿah,* lit. "as (or, according to) the hour," in this context is difficult. M. Gaster, who first published and translated the text, merely omitted the words in translation, as did L. Ginzberg in his *Legends.* Charles translated "in one hour," as did Hollander and De Jonge.[188] A similar and similarly enigmatic statement occurs in a midrashic comment to the words "Kush the Benjaminite" of Ps 7:1, where David is made to say that Saul "changes toward me in every hour [*be-khol shaʿah*] and pursues me."[189] It would appear that in both cases we are looking at wordplay (*noṭariqon*) on the word ***kush: kol shaʿah*** and ***kefi shaʿah.***

When the *Hebrew Naphtali* recounts the nations' choices of whom to worship, only Nimord is given voice: "There is none greater than he who taught me and my nation in one hour [*kefi shaʿah*] the language of Kush." Is this only because the author wished to pun on the name Kush, or was the Ethiopian language considered to be especially difficult, such that teaching it in one hour was extraordinary? Apparently some ancients thought that the language was unusual. Herodotus says of certain Ethiopian people that "their speech is like no other in the world; it is like the squeaking [τετρίγασι] of bats," a comment echoed by Pliny (first century), who reports that "they have no voice, but only make squeaking [*stridor*] noises."[190] Diodorus Sicilus (first century B.C.E.) says that those who live in the interior of Africa speak "with a shrill [ὀξεῖαν] voice."[191] In an article dealing with those languages thought to be difficult in various societies (such as "It's Greek to me" in America or "C'est de l'Hébreu pour moi" in France), Ullendorff said that he found "no recorded early instances of the language of Abyssinia serving as the embodiment of unintelligible speech."[192] He cited the passage from the *Hebrew Naphtali,* but he did so from Ginzberg's translation and thus missed the proof he was looking for that would regard the Ethiopian language as particularly difficult. The line in *Hebrew Naphtali* may be paraphrased as "Nimrod said that there is no one greater than the angel who taught him the language of Kush because he did so *in one hour*."

If this conjecture is correct, we may say that the society that produced *Hebrew Naphtali* saw Ethiopian as a difficult language. Which society is that, and can it be placed in late antiquity? There is indeed a (Greek) pseudepigraphical work called *Testament of Naphtali,* dated to the second century B.C.E., but it does not parallel the *Hebrew Naphtali* text from which our quotation is taken. It was therefore thought that the *Hebrew Naphtali* is a medieval creation.[193] Now, however, a fragment of a Hebrew *Naphtali* has been discovered among the Dead Sea material, and Michael Stone, who studied the fragment, has concluded that it is from the original Hebrew (or Aramaic) *Testament of Naphtali,* which, in one form or another, survived from the Second Temple period and was the source for the medieval Hebrew quotations.[194] It is not unreasonable, then, to suggest that the statement, "There is none greater than he who taught me and my nation in one hour [*kefi shaʿah*] the language of Kush" may derive from the original *Testament of Naphtali* of late antiquity.[195]

Rabbinic literature mentions three words as being of the language of "Africa." R. Akiba (second century) is attributed with saying that in *afriqi* (or *afriqiya*) they call a *meʿah* (a monetary unit) a *qeśiṭah,*[196] and R. Levi (third century) reports that in *afriqi* (*afriqiya*) they call a menstruous woman a *galmudah.*[197] Both of these words, however, are also reported to be, or are found in, other languages. *Qeśiṭah* is said to be of the language of Arabia, and the word is preserved in texts written in Biblical Hebrew, Samaritan Aramaic, and Neo-Syriac, in all cases with the meaning of something used as a value of exchange.[198] As far as *galmudah* is concerned, in addition to *afriqi,* it is said to be part of the vocabulary of Galia (*glyʾ*), Arabia, and the "sea-towns," where the meaning in all cases is definitely or apparently "menstruous woman."[199] The word is extant in Biblical Hebrew, where it means "barren"; in Palestinian Amoraic Hebrew, where the meaning, although not specified, is apparently "menstruous woman"; and in three Ethiopic languages (Geʿez, Amharic, Tigrinya), where it means "prostitute."[200] The various meanings of this word belong to the same semantic range related to a woman's reproductive physiology. Clearly, then, the two words *qeśiṭah* and *galmudah* are part of the shared Semitic lexicon, with appearances in a number of languages. One of the words, *galmudah,* is found in several Ethiopic languages, that is, in some of the Semitic languages of black Africa. It is, therefore, not impossible that although *afriqi* in rabbinic texts may refer to various locations, here the word could very well mean black Africa.[201] The third "African" word is more problematic and has so far eluded any convincing interpretation. In explaining why the biblical *ṭoṭafot* (Ex 13:16, Deut 6:8, 11:18), understood as referring to the phylactery, consists of four sections, R. Akiba said: "*ṭṭ* in *ktpy* means 'two' and *pt* in *afriqi* means 'two.'"[202] To my knowledge, *pt* does not mean "two" in any African language. Neither this word nor *ṭṭ* nor *ktpy* (*gdpy*) has yet been satisfactorily explained.[203]

Conclusion: Postbiblical Images of and Attitudes toward the Black African

What do these various postbiblical references to Kushites, Ethiopians, and Africans tell us about ancient Jewish images of, and attitudes toward, the black African? The image of the Ethiopians as warriors, which we saw in biblical and Greco-Roman literature, is possibly found in two places in rabbinic literature. The first, in a medieval anthology of earlier material, may draw on the ancient Kushite reputation as archers. The second apparently reflects the reality of the Blemmye and Nobae military threat to Rome more than it echoes the biblical and classical image of the Ethiopians as fearsome warriors.

Other Greco-Roman and biblical themes make their appearance much more prominently in Judaism of late antiquity. The notion that Ethiopia was at the ends of the earth gave rise to two contradictory images of the people who lived there: they are pious, unsullied by civilization; and they are barbaric, unenlightened by civilization. Both of these classical images are echoed in rabbinic literature. The opinion of Hillel's interlocutor that Africans have "broad" feet, and Hillel's answer that their country has marshes, also reflects classical views, although it is not impossible that these statements were based on firsthand knowledge, as was the rabbinic knowledge of some African vocabulary, and perhaps also the view of the Kushite language as particularly difficult. Not surprisingly, we find that the allegorical treatment of the Bible authored by Philo, the Hellenistic-Jewish philosopher, echoes ideas found in Greco-Roman literature. Thus we find Philo etymologically playing on the environmental-climatic theme of Ethiopians as cowards, and utilizing the metaphor of blackness as evil in regard to the Ethiopian skin color.

The negative color symbolism of black is found also in rabbinic as in biblical and ancient Near Eastern literature. Its particular application to the Ethiopian received its widest play in patristic exegesis (Origen especially), although it was made also in classical and rabbinic sources. Apparently the Greco-Roman writers, Philo, the Rabbis, and the church fathers drew on the universal symbol and independently applied it to the Ethiopian. We cannot say that application of the blackness-as-evil metaphor to scriptural Ethiopians necessarily implies a derogatory view of real Ethiopians. Unless we have evidence to the contrary, we cannot assume that such allegorical exegesis reflects an antipathy toward black Africans.

In regard to Moses' Kushite wife, the overwhelming driving force behind the interpretations was exegetical, that is, the need to resolve the biblical enigma. Some Hellenistic-Jewish writers apparently assumed an identification between Kush and Midian, probably based on knowledge of earlier place-names. This view cannot tell us anything about attitudes toward the Black because it assumes that the Kushite was not a black African. On the other hand, those interpretations (Josephus, Targum Pseudo-Jonathan, rabbinic midrash) that understood Moses' Kushite wife to have been a black African do not see anything worthy of note in marriage to a Black. The complaint against Moses was not because he married a Black but because he married a non-Israelite.[204] Miscegenation was clearly not an issue for Josephus, the Targum, and the midrash. In the targumic expansion, Miriam and Aaron not only find nothing wrong with Moses' marriage to a black African, but they complain that he should not have abstained from sex with his Ethiopian wife. Clearly, color and miscegenation were irrelevant.[205]

Rabbinic midrash interpreted "Kushite" metaphorically not because the Rabbis found the idea of miscegenation objectionable, but because the dictates of the hermeneutic and literary process demanded it. In any case, the application of allegory does not imply the rejection of the simple meaning of the text. For the Rabbis, it is rather an additional exegetical tool; both methods reveal the word of God—Moses married a Kushite *and* "Kushite" is a metaphor. The metaphorical meaning given to the term Kushite ("distinctive" in good character or good looks) may have evolved from the rabbinic explanation of Kushite as "beautiful," another rabbinic interpretation, which was probably based on etymological considerations (*kuwayyis*). The explanation "beautiful" may preserve an echo of the biblical and classical image of the Ethiopians as a particularly handsome people.

Postbiblical treatments of other Kushites also show no negative evaluations of Blacks. Ebed-melech the Kushite's stature as a righteous man grows ever greater as we move from biblical to pseudepigraphic to rabbinic literature. So too is Kushi, the father of the prophet Zephaniah, considered to have been righteous by the Rabbis, who may well have understood his name to point to black African origins. In any case, nowhere do we find a statement denying the possibility that the father of this biblical prophet may have been a black African. Nor is any anti-Black sentiment expressed in regard to Michal bat Kushi, a pious Jewish woman most probably the descendant of Kushites, of whom rabbinic tradition preserved vague knowledge. Apparently Kushite ancestry did not matter one way or the other.[206]

PART II

THE COLOR OF SKIN

FIVE

THE COLOR OF WOMEN

Mislike me not for my complexion,
The shadow'd livery of the burnish'd sun
—Shakespeare, *Merchant of Venice*

One passage in the Bible does not speak of black Africans and yet is very important in any discussion of attitudes toward skin color: "I am black but beautiful" (Song of Songs 1:5). As the historian Harold Isaacs wrote forty years ago, "'I am black *but* comely,' sang the Shulamite maiden to the daughters of Jerusalem and on that *but* hangs a whole great skein of our culture."[1] As we shall see, although the passage is not about the black African, it is very definitely about aesthetic evaluations of skin color. More specifically, it concerns women's skin color and perceptions of feminine beauty. The biblical text will lead us to other ancient Jewish expressions of feminine beauty and ugliness in regard to skin color, and thus help us to construct a complete picture of how Jews of antiquity looked at skin color and, consequently, at black Africans.

Biblical Images of Feminine Beauty: Song of Songs 1:5–6

I am black [*sheḥorah*], but [*we-*] comely,	I am dark [*sheḥorah*], but [*we-*] comely,
O ye daughters of Jerusalem,	O daughters of Jerusalem—
As the tents of Kedar,	Like the tents of Kedar,
As the curtains of Solomon.	Like the pavilions of Solomon.
Look not upon me [*al tir'uni*],	Don't stare at me [*al tir'uni*]
because I am black [*sheḥarḥoret*],	because I am swarthy [*sheḥarḥoret*],
Because the sun hath looked upon me;	Because the sun has gazed upon me,
My mother's children were angry with me,	My mother's sons quarreled with me,
They made me the keeper of the vineyards;	They made me guard the vineyards;
But mine own vineyard have I not kept.	My own vineyard I did not guard.
(KJV)	(NJPS)

As can be seen from the two translations, one centuries old and Christian, the other modern and Jewish, the sense of the passage has generally been understood in an apologetic way ("I am black, but beautiful") with the Hebrew *we-* understood adversatively.[2] Although *we-* may also be translated as a conjunctive "and," verse 6 seems to force the translation "but."[3] "Don't look at me that I am dark, because the sun has burned me" is a reply to an apparently critical and disapproving attitude. Thus, "I am black, *but* beautiful."[4]

Nevertheless, several biblical scholars are lately favoring a nonadversative "and," for otherwise (if we assume a literary unity to the composition) this verse is the only negative comment, even if implicit, about the woman's appearance in a work which throughout praises her beauty. Such translations have the advantage of according with the overall tone in Song, which describes the bride's appearance in "language of boldness, praise, and delight, not of reticence, apology, and disparagement."[5] So, for example, Marvin Pope translates our verses:

> Black am I and beautiful,
> O Jerusalem girls,
> Like the tents of Qedar,
> Like the pavilions of Salmah
> Stare not at me that I am swart,
> That the sun has blackened me.
> My mother's sons were incensed at me,
> They made me a vineyard guard;
> My own vineyard I did not guard.

Pope explains: "The bride is both black *and* beautiful, like a Bedouin tent." The translation "stare not" is meant to convey the ambiguity of the Hebrew, which can convey interest and fascination as easily as disdain or revulsion. Pope's understanding is that fascination is intended: "The blackness is striking and beautiful."[6] Similar to this interpretation are those of the biblicists Othmar Keel and Roland Murphy, who translate "black I am and beautiful." Keel considers the blackness to be "frightening and fascinating; she is mysteriously different," and Murphy says that the Daughters of Jerusalem find "fascination with her black complexion and striking beauty."[7]

Other recent "positive" translations are those of Mitchell Dahood, Cheryl Exum, and Dianne Bergant. While Pope, Keel, and Murphy understand *al tir'uni* as "not to look with fascination," Mitchell Dahood understands the phrase as "not to look with envy," a meaning he gives the verb elsewhere in the Hebrew Bible.[8] More traditionally, Bergant sees *al tir'uni* as reflecting a negative evaluation on the part of the daughters of Jerusalem, but in response the maiden asserts her own standard: black and beautiful.[9] Exum takes *al* not as a negative particle ("do not"), but as an asseverative, "indeed": "Black am I and beautiful. . . . Indeed, look at me that I am black."[10] Reflecting the recent scholarship, the NRSV replaced its earlier rendering "I am very dark, but comely" (RSV) with "I am black and beautiful," and the REB translated "I am dark and lovely."

Whether we accept these positive interpretations or the traditional adversative explanation, it is important to realize, as both Murphy and Fox note, that the blackness in the verse has nothing to do with ethnicity. The maiden is dark due to her long hours in the sun-baked fields.[11] In her study of color in the Bible, Athalya Brenner has shown that Biblical Hebrew *shaḥor* has a wider range of meanings than "black." The term originally implied the color of burned things, from which it came to mean "dark," including the colors of brown and gray as well.[12] To determine the meaning of any particular usage of *shaḥor,* therefore, "syntagmatic relations" and general context are crucial. In Song 1:5, "I am *sheḥorah* but beautiful" is defined by an explanatory equivalent in the next verse, *sheḥarḥoret,* which indicates a lighter color than *shaḥor,* and by the larger context, which indicates the color of sunburned skin. She concludes that the word in our text means "the color of sunburnt skin, that is, 'brown.'"[13]

When we place the sun-darkened maiden within the sociological context required by the biblical text, the meaning of Song 1:5–6 becomes clearer, for sun-darkened skin was associated with a rural life (guarding the vineyards) while urban dwellers (daughters of Jerusalem) retained lighter complexions. Iconographic parallels to this verse are found in Egyptian art. Henry Fischer claims that some ancient Egyptian paintings that deviate from convention and depict Egyptian men in yellow or lighter colors than the normal reddish-brown, do so to indicate a type of individual who has led a sedentary life indoors such as bureaucrats or the elderly or the very young. He refers to one painting in which a "chocolate-red" land owner is depicted beside his darker, "chocolate" field workers.[14] A similar color contrast is found in two tomb paintings where the officials have a light yellow complexion and those plowing the field or herding the cattle are dark brown.[15] Several scholars have noted a theme in early Arabic poetry, where white feminine skin is indicative of the noble, beautiful woman, who spends her time within the home and thus does not get blackened by the sun.[16] Even closer to the imagery of Song 1:5–6 is the parallel found in the urban-rural contrast of feminine beauty in modern Arabic erotic poetry of Palestine, in which the theme of a controversy between brown bedouin women and white urban women plays a prominent role.[17]

By itself, this sociological explanation cannot determine whether the verses should be read with a positive or negative nuance. That determination would depend on whether we see the maiden's response as accepting the urban ideal of beauty ("I am black but beautiful") or as asserting her own rural ideal of dark, sunburned beauty ("I am black and beautiful").[18] In the latter case, as Marcia Falk puts it, although the daughters of Jerusalem, being urban dwellers, see dark sunburned skin as not beautiful, the maiden, being a country dweller, doesn't see it that way. She "defies them to diminish her own self-esteem. No, she argues, I will not be judged by your standards, I am black *and* I am beautiful." Not, in other words, "I am black but beautiful anyway," but "I am black and for that reason I am beautiful."[19] In short, interpretations generally agree that the dark-fair contrast is sociologically determined and reflects, respectively, the rural-urban ideals of beauty. But the adversative translators ("but") understand that a negative value judgment of dark skin is implicitly accepted in the text as the single standard of beauty, while those translating "and" would maintain that in the Bible there is no single ideal of human beauty.

No matter how we read Song 1:5–6, it is clear that lighter-skinned women were preferred among the urban elite as implied by the daughters of Jerusalem. Such a color preference (by men) for women is found in other ancient societies as well. Egyptian painting followed a convention of skin color contrast with men colored dark red-brown and women light yellow.[20] In discussing the ideal skin color of women and men, Aristotle referred to "fair-skinned women who are typically feminine, and not . . . dark women of a masculine appearance."[21] This preference is seen also in an Alexander romance known as the *Letter to Aristotle,* written about 300 B.C.E., which tells how on the way back from India Alexander's men were entrapped and killed by some women. "Since the women were extraordinary in appearance, the men, who were completely overcome with their fond feeling (for them), the women treated violently or killed during sexual pleasure." What was so beautiful about these women? "Their complexion was snow-white [*colore niveo*], (and) like nymphs their hair spread over their backs."[22]

Others have noted that ancient Greek art reflects the same color distinction noted by Aristotle: "The Greeks admired a deep tan in men, white skin in women. . . . Vase-painters in the genre which uses white, use it for women and goddesses."[23] Whether in literature or art, Aphrodite, the goddess of love, is regularly depicted as having very white skin.[24] On black-figure vases, all male figures are dark; female figures light.[25] Eleanor Irwin points out that this color distinction is maintained also in Mycenaean wall-paintings.[26] We find the same situation in a sixth-century mosaic found on the island of Lesbos: the male (Demeas) is dark and the female (Chrysis) light.[27] Whether in literature or art, "[this] differentiation between the sexes was very clearly marked."[28]

As in Greece, so too in Rome. In his study of color in Roman poetry, Hugo Blümner showed that white (*candor*) skin was commonly used to depict beauty in women and girls (and young boys).[29] Lloyd Thompson concluded that in ancient Rome the somatic norm, and thus the preferred image, excluded "dark or bronzed complexions in women of the 'Caucasian' type." An example of this preference is provided by Martial's (first century C.E.) Lycoris, a dark-complected woman who bleached her skin in line with "the dictates of contemporary fashion to seek to acquire a lighter complexion." In Rome prior to the first century B.C.E., the Mediterranean pale-brown (*albus*) skin represented the somatic norm, "but a somewhat paler complexion symbolized feminine aristocratic privilege, and this *femineus pallor* was accordingly regarded in polite society as an essential mark of the feminine ideal of beauty." Beginning in the first century B.C.E., due to the importation of northern lighter-skinned female slaves and the influence of Hellenistic fashions, the feminine ideal took on an even lighter "milk-white" complexion.[30]

The paler complexion that "symbolized feminine aristocratic privilege" in Rome parallels Song 1:5–6. In fact at one point, Thompson, in speaking of Roman literature, sounds as if he were precisely describing the situation in Song: "[The Roman writers lauded] the 'ivory-white' or 'snow-white' or 'milk-white' faces, arms, necks, breasts and legs of this *candida* ['white'] ideal, and mocked the deep ruddy tan of the peasant woman, whose colour betrayed regular exposure to the sun."[31]

Because this was the preferred feminine somatic norm in Greco-Roman antiquity, we find in classical literature, just as we found in Song of Songs, apologetic "black but beautiful" justifications for dark beauty. Asclepiades (third century B.C.E.), for example, says of one Didyme: "If she is black [μέλαινα], so what? / So are coals, but when we light them, they shine as bright as roses."[32] While Asclepiades is close in sentiment to Song 1:5–6, another justificatory classical text comes even closer when it says that dark, sunburned women are called "Syrian": "Charming Bombyca, all call thee the Syrian, lean and sun-scorched, and I alone honey-hued. Dark is the violet and the lettered hyacinth [ἁ γραπτὰ ὑάκινθος], yet in garlands these are accounted first."[33] The geographical—if not ethnic—proximity of Syria to Israel and the use of similar terms to describe the skin color of their inhabitants [ἁλιόκαυστον 'sun-scorched' and *shezafatni* 'sun-gazed') immediately bring to mind the biblical text of Song.

Closest of all to the Song passage is Virgil. He not only conveys the same apologetic "black but beautiful" sense as does the Bible but also situates the dark-complected woman in a vineyard just as we find in Song: "Indeed I wish I had been one of you, a shepherd of your flocks, or a vineyard hand. Phyllis might then have been my sweetheart, or Amyntas, or some other love. . . . And is Amyntas dark [*fuscus*]? Well, what of that? Violets are dark [*nigrae*], and so are hyacinths [*et vaccinia nigra*]."[34] In sum, Song 1:5–6 exhibits the same upper-class preference for fair skin as a marker of feminine beauty that we find in the Greco-Roman world of antiquity, and the literary expression in Song finds close parallels in Greco-Roman writings. Furthermore, just as in the classical world so too in ancient Israel we can find rejection of this aesthetic and assertion of different criteria for determining feminine beauty.[35]

Song of Songs 8:5 (LXX)

Another reference to the maiden's skin color occurs in the Old Greek and Old Latin versions of Song 8:5, "Who is she that comes up having been made white?" A similar reading is found in Ethiopic manuscripts of Song ("Who is she that glances forth like the dawn white and shining?"), as well as the *Biblija Ostrozska,* the Church Russian Bible (1580–81), both of which are dependent upon the Greek. Several church fathers, including Origen, Jerome, Augustine, Ambrose, and Cyril of Jerusalem, had the same reading.[36] The Hebrew text, however, is entirely different: "Who is she coming up from the desert" (*mi zoʾt ʿolah min ha-midbar*)?

As is indicated by the citations in the church fathers, the reading "having been made white" is closely connected with the Christian exegetical tradition.[37] We cannot, however, ascribe the origin of this reading to Christian circles, for the Greek translation of Song is presumably a Jewish enterprise.[38] The question then is, how did the Greek reading arise? Pope reviews various unconvincing suggestions that assume an original Hebrew text different from MT that would account for the Greek translation.[39] Perhaps, however, the Greek reading is not based on a variant Hebrew text but on an interpretation of the existing Hebrew text.

Ariel Bloch points out that the formula "Who is that / Who are these?" occurs three times in Song and refers to the maiden "in terms of a supernatural phenomenon, a fantastic apparition that 'rises' from the east" like the dawn: "Who is she that shines through like the dawn [*šaḥar*], beautiful as the moon, radiant [*barah*] as the sun?" (Song 6:10, NJPS). He notes that *ʿalah* 'to rise' is the verb commonly used in the Hebrew Bible for the rising dawn.[40] "Who is she coming up" would thus have been understood as referring to the dawn as a metaphor for the maiden, who is thus "made white." The inclusion of "desert" in the metaphor would have only strengthened this understanding, for in the Bible, according to Shemaryahu Talmon, the desert is a place of darkness (Jer 2:6, *ṣalmawet;* 2:31, *maʾpelyah*). Furthermore, the desert can function as an image of the underworld, as it does in Mesopotamian and Ugaritic myths.[41] Now, since in Mesopotamian myth it was believed that each evening when the sun set, it entered the western entrance to the underworld, passed through the underworld during the night, and reemerged at the eastern end in the morning,[42] "who is she coming up from the desert?" might well have been understood as referring to the rising sun at dawn, and thus interpreted or translated as "who is she that comes up having been made white?"

In any case, once the reading "having been made white" entered the (Greek) text of Song 8:5, and thus became part of the Christian Bible, it further strengthened the Christian exegetical tradition that allegorized the maiden as representing the (black) gentile church who, by accepting

Christ, had become whitened. It strengthened the tradition because feminine beauty was equated with white skin.

On the other hand, the Hebrew (MT) version of Song 8:5 in association with 1:5 may lie behind an unexplained etymology reported by several church fathers. Apponius (fourth–fifth or seventh century) and some early Christian onomastic lists claim that the Hebrew word for "black" means "ascent," an etymology that, on the face of it, appears inexplicable.[43] Indeed, neither the recent German translation of Apponius by H. König, nor the recent edition by B. de Vregille and L. Neyrand in the Sources Chrétiennes series, nor Wutz in his edition of the onomastica offers an explanation.[44] The strange etymology would seem to be based on the MT version of 8:5, which Apponius (and the onomastica, or their source) transferred to the description of the maiden in Song 1:5, which is where we find Apponius's etymology: "*Nigra sum sed formosa, filiae Hierusalem. . . . Nigra scilicet 'ascendens' interpretatur hebraica lingua.*" The result is that the black maiden is the one who rises, which consequently produced the notion that the Hebrew word for "black" meant "ascent."[45]

Postbiblical Images of Feminine Beauty

The classical preference for lighter skin in women continued into late antiquity. We saw examples of this preference from the pagan Roman world. Other examples from later periods can be added, such as the biographer of the early third-century emperor Elagabalus, who refers to "Ethiopian hags" (*Aethiopibus aniculis*), thus "suggest[ing] a widespread upper-class conception of the least attractive woman as one who is both old and black," and the sixth-century Carthaginian poet Luxorius, who takes white as typifying feminine beauty and black as feminine ugliness (*informes et foedas puellas* 'hideous and ugly black girls').[46]

Just as in Rome so too in Judaea of late antiquity. In an expansion of Gen 12:11, where Abraham tells Sarah, "Now I know that you are a beautiful woman," the *Genesis Apocryphon* (20.4), one of the Dead Sea scrolls, lauds Sarah's beauty with: "How beautiful is all her whiteness."[47] These words are then followed by a detailed description of Sarah's body beginning with "Her arms, how beautiful," which is reminiscent of "white arms" used as an epithet of beauty by Homer, Hesiod, and Pindar when speaking of Hera, Persephone, and others.[48] In Latin literature Virgil describes Venus as having "snow-white arms" (*niueis lacertis*).[49] "Snowy" skin is a common classical description of feminine beauty.[50]

The same aesthetic is found later than the *Genesis Apocryphon* in a number of rabbinic texts. One tannaitic source, in discussing vows, posits a situation where one has vowed "not to marry a particular woman who is ugly, but it turns out that the woman is beautiful; or black (dark; *sheḥorah*), but it turns out that she is white (fair; *levanah*); or short, but she is tall. Even if she was ugly, but became beautiful; or black, and became white." The antitheses in this text clearly show the preferred complexion for a woman.[51]

Reminiscent of the *Genesis Apocryphon,* are the words of R. 'Azariah in the name of R. Yuda ben R. Simon (fourth century). In recounting the biblical story of how, when Abraham came to Egypt, he feared that the Egyptians would covet his wife Sarah, he explained Abraham's strange words to Sarah, "Now I know that you are a beautiful woman" (Gen 12:11). The Rabbi wondered how it was possible that, after so many years of marriage, Abraham seems to have noticed Sarah's beauty for the first time. His answer: relative to the dark-skinned Egyptians, Sarah's light skin stood out for its beauty. "Now I know" is thus paraphrased as "Now we are about to enter a place of ugly and dark [people]."[52] Once again, we see that a light complexion was considered a mark of beauty in women.

In an extrabiblical expansion of the war against Midian recounted in Numbers 31, R. Isaac (third century) states that the Israelites blackened (*mefaḥem*) the faces of the Midianite women and removed their jewelry in an attempt to counteract their seductive charms.[53] The opposite treatment is told of the dark-skinned daughter of R. Bebai (third to fourth century). *Omphacinon,* an oil made from unripe olives, was applied to her body to lighten her skin and make her more desirable.[54] Unlike the case of Martial's Lycoris it worked. R. Bebai could have used another technique, for according to R. Ḥiyya (third century), "He who wishes to whiten his daughter's complexion, let him give her milk and young fowl."[55] A similar view of feminine beauty is expressed in the midrashic story that tells of Nehemiah's return from the Babylonian exile. He found that the men did not want to marry the Jewish women who returned with them, for on the long journey back to Israel, their faces had been darkened by the sun and they were found to be unattractive. The men therefore married gentile women. This midrash, ascribed to R. Ḥanan (third–fourth century), assumes a dark complexion to be undesirable in a woman but not in a man.[56] The statement put in the mouth of another fourth-century Rabbi opposes beauty and blackness. "R. Isaac b. Elyashuv said, 'May Hanah become beautiful' and she became beautiful. . . . 'May Hanah revert to her blackness' and she reverted to her blackness."[57]

The figure of a *kushit* maidservant (*shifḥah kushit*) appears in three parables in the rabbinic corpus. Two of the parables are relevant for our discussion of feminine skin color and will be discussed here.[58] In the first, the maidservant is set in literary opposition to her mistress who is a townswoman. The story is transmitted by R. Isaac who lived during the second half of the third century.

> A townswoman [*qartanit*][59] had a *kushit* maidservant who went with her friend to draw water from the spring. The maid said to her friend: "Tomorrow the master will divorce his wife and marry me." Her friend asked why and she replied, "Because he saw that his wife's hands were dirty." Her friend replied: "Listen to what you are saying! If your master will divorce his wife, whom he loves, because of dirty hands, how will he stay with you who are black from birth?!"[60]

The parable is meant to illustrate Song 1:5–6, which speaks of the temporary skin darkening due to suntan. The lesson of the parable is drawn of Israel who sins temporarily (dirty hands of the naturally light-skinned mistress) and thus cannot be compared to the gentiles who are permanently immersed in sin (blackness of the naturally dark-skinned maidservant). The point of the story revolves around the opposition between the dark skin of the maidservant and the light skin of her mistress, with light skin being the preferred complexion.

The same skin-color contrast and the same preference is found in a second parable, where, once again, a *kushit* maid is set in opposition to her mistress, who in this instance is a *maṭronah.*

> Come and see the difference "between the righteous and the wicked, between him who serves God and him who doesn't serve him" (Mal 3:18). A parable of a *maṭronita* who had a *kushit* maidservant, and whose husband went overseas. All night long the maid said to the *maṭronah,* "I am more beautiful than you and the king loves me more than you." The *maṭronah* answered her: "Come the morning and we'll know who is more beautiful and whom the king loves more." So too the nations of the world say to Israel: "Our deeds are beautiful and God delights in us." Therefore Isaiah said: "Come the morning and we'll know in whom He delights," as it says, "The watchman said: The morning is coming and also night" (Isa 21:12), i.e. at the arrival of the World to Come, which is called "morning," we'll know in whom He delights.[61]

A *maṭronah* is a free woman, generally one of high social standing,[62] or a "matron, lady (mostly used of Roman women of quality)."[63] In this parable the *kushit* maidservant represents the nations of the world in contrast to the *maṭronah*/Israel. Just as night prevents one from seeing the distinction of skin color between a dark-skinned and a light-skinned woman, so does this world blur the distinction between the deeds of the gentiles and of Israel. Only in the light of the World to Come will the difference be apparent. The operating, but unstated, assumption in the midrash is that light skin is the more beautiful and that in the dark, where the difference of skin color is not apparent, one might choose a dark-skinned companion. The assumption is made explicit in a parallel source quoted in the later (twelfth- or thirteenth-century) anthology *Yalquṭ Shimʿoni,* which states: "All night long she argued with the *maṭronah* and said, 'I am whiter [*levanah*] than you,'" and ends the story with: "She said to her, 'Come the morning and we'll see who is black [*shaḥor*] and who is white [*lavan*].'"[64]

Some scholars argue that these two parables show a preference by some Jewish men for dark-skinned women over their lighter-skinned wives.[65] Perhaps so, but it is clear that the general opinion, as represented by the author of the story, did not agree with this assessment. In Judea of late antiquity, as in biblical Israel and the Greco-Roman world, a fair complexion in women was generally considered desirable.

The preference for lighter skin in women is commonly found also in early Christian writings. The fourth-century prostitute-turned-convert, Pelagia of Antioch, is described as a woman of extraordinary beauty, which "stunned those who beheld her." The main physical characteristic in her description is "her skin [which] was as dazzling as snow."[66] Another example from the Christian world comes from the church father Theodore of Mopsuestia (in Cilicia; d. 428). Although Song of Songs was regularly interpreted as an allegory in both Jewish and Christian tradition, Theodore wrote one of the very few literal interpretations of this biblical book. He understood Song to be a love poem written by King Solomon for his wife, Pharaoh's daughter (and not an allegory of the relationship between Christ and the church).[67] The line in 1:5, "I am black but beautiful," according to Theodore reflects popular disapproval of Solomon's marriage to a dark-skinned woman. "She was dark [*šḥmtʾ*] as all the Egyptians and Ethiopians, and the Hebrews and their beautiful women, as well as the other princesses, mocked her on account of her ugliness and smallness and black color [*snywth wkrywt qwmth* wʾ*wkmwt gwnh*]. To avoid her being irritated, and a consequential enmity between him and Pharaoh," Solomon built her a special palace (as recorded in 1 Kgs 9:24) and composed Song of Songs for her, in which he said that she is black and beautiful.[68] This interpretation reflects a fourth or fifth-century view of fair skin as the desired feminine ideal (even if the story is not original to Theodore and even if the story itself also reflects a contrary view).

Even the Christian allegorical exegesis of Song of Songs, introduced by Origen and commonly accepted afterward, which spoke of symbolic blackness (i.e., sin) and whiteness (God's grace), "reflect[s] the values of the temporal and secular world in which whiteness of skin was generally regarded as an essential element of beauty . . . while generally finding '*Aethiops* beauty' a difficult concept to comprehend and accorded little favour to it, even as an acknowledged reality."[69] That is why Gregory of Elvira (late fourth century) was confused with Origen's interpretation of the black maiden in Song of Songs as allegorically meaning the gentiles who are black and beautiful: "I confess to being troubled. How can the church be at once black and beautiful? . . . How can it be black if it is beautiful, or beautiful if it is black?"[70] Gregory reflected the "socio-cultural ambience dominated by a value system which holds whiteness of skin as a more or less essential constituent of beauty (especially female beauty)."[71] Similarly, when Jerome (d. 420) compares Jesus' love for lowly humanity with the love one would have for an Ethiopian woman ("Your bridegroom is not arrogant. He is not proud. He has married an Ethiopian woman"), for our purposes it does not matter whether Jerome's statement is based on Origen's allegorical interpretation (Ethiopian maiden = gentile church), for it reflects the same value system.[72] Augustine (d. 430) shares the same aesthetic as Jerome when he writes of the relationship between the church and God: "First he loved us and granted us to love him. We did not yet love, but by loving we were made beautiful. What will a deformed and facially distorted person do if he loves a beautiful woman? And what will a deformed and distorted and black woman do if she loves a beautiful man? By loving can she become beautiful?"[73] The association of light skin with feminine beauty and, conversely, black skin with ugliness is clear in these texts.

Peter Frost adds several further examples from early Christian literature that regard the dark-skinned Ethiopian "as being the very antithesis of female beauty," such as this description in the *Apophthegmata Patrum* of a couple's reunion after many years' separation: "She recognized her husband, but he could not recognize her; so much her beauty had disappeared, to the point where she looked like an Ethiopian woman."[74]

Frost also feels that those Christian texts depicting the devil as an Ethiopian woman reflect the same view. These texts were created "for the purpose of inculcating disgust for the pleasures of the flesh," as an antidote to the monks' visions of sexual temptation. He cites the following story of a desert monk:

> And he looked, and behold, the work of fornication came and drew nigh unto him, and it stood up before him in the form of an Ethiopian woman whose smell was exceedingly foul, but he was unable to endure her smell, and he drove her away from his presence. Then she said unto him, "In the hearts of men I am a sweet smell, and a pleasant one, but because of thine obedience and labor God hath not permitted me to lead thee astray, but I have, nevertheless, made thee acquainted with my smell." And the young man rose up, and came to his father, and said unto him, "I no longer wish to go into the world, for I have seen the matter of fornication, and I have smelled its foul odor."[75]

Other examples mentioned by Frost include Pachomius's temptation by an Ethiopian woman, and Ennodius's maxim, "Do not let the body of a black girl soil yours, nor lie with her for her hellish face."[76]

Throughout the Middle Ages and into modern times, across a wide chronological and geographic spectrum, Western literature reflects the view that light skin in a woman is beautiful and dark skin is ugly.[77] We also find the same preference if we move eastward. Two medieval Armenian apocryphal works indicate that feminine beauty was associated with white skin. *The History of the Creation and Transgression of Adam* 27 says of Eve: "Even though she had been stripped of the [heavenly] light, she was nonetheless beautiful, for her flesh was dazzling white like a pearl because she was newly created." *Concerning the Good Tidings of Seth* 21 reports that the women of Cain's generation would whiten their faces to make them more beautiful.[78]

Examples from the Islamic world can easily be added to this list. The complaint of Nuṣayb ibn Rabāḥ (d. 726), who was black, to the Caliph ʿUmar ibn ʿAbd al-ʿAziz reflects the same societal view of black skin: "O Commander of the Faithful! My years have increased and my bones have become thin and I am afflicted with daughters. My color has rubbed off on to them and they are left on my hands."[79] The *Qiṣaṣ al-anbiyā* of Kisāʾī describes the birth of Eve, who had skin that was "tender and white": "She was of the same form as Adam, except that her skin was softer and purer in color.[80] Al-Bakrī (d. 1094) speaks about "pretty slave girls with white complexions, good figures, firm breasts, slim waists, fat buttocks, wide shoulders and sexual organs so narrow that one of them may be enjoyed as though she were a virgin indefinitely."[81]

Abduh Badawī wrote that in Arabic literature "one of the signs of beauty in a woman was also whiteness. It was also a proof of her nobility. In the same way a man could be eulogized as 'the son of a white woman.' Similarly, they would boast that they had taken white women as captives."[82] There is much evidence in Arabic literature and art indicating a preference for light-skinned women. The etymology of "houri," the beautiful virgins who, according to the Qurʾan, will be given to the faithful in Paradise, is based on the root *ḥwr* 'white', and may refer to their white skin; in other words, houri means "white ones."[53] As K. Vollers said, the early Arabs preferred women with light skin.[84]

Indeed the phenomenon would seem to be universal. Peter Frost has conveniently summarized the similar findings of modern scholarship on Roman literature, Etruscan paintings, medieval Europe, and Aztec, Egyptian, Chinese, and Japanese art. The historical and cultural association between light skin and femininity is verified by Frost's investigation of anthropological data, which "reveal a consistent worldwide association of fairness with femininity."[85] Carl Degler has similarly noted that in Chinese and Japanese writings of the nineteenth and twentieth centuries, a woman's beauty is marked by her white skin color, and H. Wagatsuma has shown the same to be true in Japanese literature of much earlier periods, for example in the eleventh century.[86] In a later article, Frost added information from medieval peasant folklore of the British Isles, Italy, Serbia and Croatia, Rumania, and Macedonia. All these considered "fair skin to be a prerequisite of feminine beauty."[87] One can add also the various folktales that contrast a beautiful and good white princess/bride/maiden with an ugly and evil black princess/bride/maiden.[88]

A recent study of art from a large cross section of cultures across time has shown the same results. Paintings, mosaics, and sculptures from ancient Egypt, Greece, and Italy, and from medieval and modern Europe and Asia, often depict females as lighter skinned than males.[89] The same association between fairness and femininity exists among societies in our time. Studies of fifty-one different societies found in sub-Sahara Africa, Europe, Asia, the Middle East, Muslim Africa, North America, South America, the Caribbean, and the Insular Pacific show an overwhelming cross-cultural preference for lighter skin as an indicator of beauty, especially in women.[90] Most surprising, we find the same association of feminine beauty with lighter skin even among dark-skinned people, including also black Africans. Dominique Zahan has reported that in black Africa "the whiter a child is at birth, the more splendid it is," and that "this predilection for white and light skin also becomes manifest in connection with young girls of marriageable age. The light-skinned girl is in fact considered to possess more charm than one whose skin is jet-black."[91] Among the Ibo of eastern Nigeria, whose skin pigmentation includes a range of tones, lighter-skinned brides are preferred and get a higher price. The perfect wife is of a café au lait color.[92]

Over and over again we see a preference for lighter-skinned women, no matter the time, the culture, or the ethnic group. Why should this be the case? A number of scientific studies show that in any given ethnic group the women are in fact slightly lighter skinned than the men. This may be due either to women's greater need during pregnancy and lactation for the sun's vitamin D, therefore giving them less sun-blocking dark skin (melanin), or to the fact that historically women stayed at home while men generally were outside more often, in either case resulting in an evolutionary development of lighter-skinned women. In any case, the evidence indicates that women are lighter skinned than men and this, Frost and Tegner both hypothesize, would have produced a mental association of light skin with femininity and thus the universal preference for lighter skin in women.[93]

For the purposes of this study, the transcultural preference for lighter-skinned women would indicate that expressions of light skin as a marker of feminine beauty ought to be put outside the parameters of our investigation. For such expressions do not necessarily reflect a view of the ethnic Other; they reflect rather a view of the gendered Other, a transcultural preference. Because there is no indication that a preference for fair skin in women would have influenced a preference for lighter-skinned people in general, we cannot cite examples of the former as proof for the latter. If we are rigorously to assess the ancient Jewish view of darker-skinned ethnic groups, including black Africans, we must therefore exclude evidence of a preference for lighter-skinned women.

SIX

THE COLOR OF HEALTH

OTHER REFERENCES to skin color in both biblical and postbiblical literature may also fall outside the parameters of our investigation, for they are not markers of a person's natural complexion. These instances, rather, refer to transitory changes in the brightness or color of a person's skin brought on by various physiological or psychological causes (such as our "pale with fright," "red with shame," "ashen with gloom," etc.). Sometimes, however, positive or negative aesthetic judgments are made of these color changes, temporary though they may be, and it is therefore necessary to examine these cases to see whether they can provide us a window into ancient Jewish views of skin color.

The most common physical causes of a change in color, whether it be black or white, are hunger, illness, or weakness. The biblical book of Lamentations describes the devastation of Jerusalem by the Babylonians in 586 B.C.E. and says that the people were "blacker than soot" on account of the famine raging in the country. In this passage, the gaunt, dark look of hunger is contrasted with a white complexion according to many translations: "[Jerusalem's] elect [*nezireha*] were purer [*zaku*] than snow, whiter [*ṣaḥu*] than milk. . . . Now their faces are blacker than soot [*ḥašakh mi-šeḥor toʾaram*]. Better off were the slain of the sword than those slain by famine" (Lam 4:7–9).[1] Here black skin is associated with hunger and contrasted with white skin, which is given a positive evaluation. Again, in Song of Songs we find a preference for white skin when the maiden praises her lover's appearance as, "My beloved is white [*ṣaḥ*] and ruddy" (Song 5:10).[2]

It is important to realize that, contrary to the translations cited here (and others also), the Hebrew word *ṣaḥ(u)* does not mean "white." The word is rather related to the Arabic cognate *ṣḥḥ,* which indicates a clear, glowing complexion of radiant health.[3] In other words, we are dealing with luminosity, not chromaticity. Some translations of Song, both ancient and modern, have recognized this by rendering the Hebrew as "radiant," "dazzling," "gleaming," "shiny," or even "clear-skinned."[4] It is not surprising that many translations of Lamentations have replaced luminosity with the color white, for the verses compare *ṣaḥu* with milk and snow and contrast it with blackness. Radiance appears as white, the most reflective of colors. We see the same semantic development in Akkadian references to slaves who are described as *namru,* literally "white," meaning "healthy."[5]

The association of black or dark skin with hunger and weakness is found in postbiblical literature as well. Josephus describes Sabinus the Syrian who scaled the walls of Jerusalem for Titus: "His skin was black, his flesh shrunk and emaciated."[6] Rabbinic literature several times refers to the darkened skin of one who fasts or is deprived of food.[7] Even angels, according to the mystical Hekhalot Rabbati texts, when weakened by God's glorious splendor, "their strength weakens, their face blackens [*ki taš(aš) koḥam we-hišḥiru peneihem*], their hearts wander, and their eyes darken."[8] The association of dark skin with ill health, weakness, or hunger is similarly found in Arabic and Christian literature.[9]

The rabbinic corpus also associates pale or pallid skin coloring (*panim moriqot*) with weakness deriving from illness, hunger, or other causes. The suspected adulteress's (*soṭah*) face is said to turn pale after she takes the ordeal drink, women are said to be pale for the first three months of pregnancy, a lack of food is the reason for Naomi's pale color, and bloodletting followed by seeing a corpse, it is said, will cause one to become pale.[10] Just as both light and dark skin color can reflect the same physiological condition, such as hunger or illness, so also light and dark skin color are found describing the same psychological or emotional condition, such as shame, embarrassment, sadness, despair, distress, or fright.[11]

In two of these cases of color change an aesthetic judgment is expressed. The woman's skin color in the early stages of pregnancy is considered "pale and ugly" (*panim mekhuʿarot u-moriqot*), and the pale color of the *soṭah* is considered her punishment for beautifying her face in seeking to attract men (*tSoṭ* 3.3), which implies a deprecation of the pallid color. Such judgments, however, may not be of the color per se as much as they may be of the underlying ill health reflected in the color change. Aesthetic evaluations of temporary color change due to a physical or psychological condition may say nothing, therefore, about a somatic aversion toward lighter- or darker-skinned people. On the other hand, when we come to ethnic color variation, the evidence from rabbinic literature is unequivocal.

SEVEN

THE COLORS OF MANKIND

Wer den Dichter will verstehen
Muss in Dichter's Lande gehen.
—Heine

What should they know of Judaism who only know Judaism?
—with apologies to Kipling[1]

A RABBINIC TEXT commenting on the skin diseases mentioned in the Bible (Leviticus, chs. 13–14; Deut 24:8), states: "An intensely bright white spot [*baheret*] appears faint on the very light-skinned [*germani*], while a faint spot appears bright on the very dark-skinned [*kushi*]. Rabbi Ishmael said: 'The Jews—may I be like an expiatory sacrifice for them [an expression of love]—are like the boxwood tree [*eshkeroaʿ*], neither black nor white, but in between.'"[2] This statement records a second-century (R. Ishmael) perception that the skin color of Jews is midway between black and white.[3] More precisely it is light brown, the color of the boxwood tree.[4] This early perception of the intermediate, light-brown shade of the Jewish complexion is corroborated by a number of papyri from the Ptolemaic period in Egypt that describe the complexion of various Jews as "honey-colored."[5] A similar self-perception is found among other Mediterranean peoples, the Greeks and Romans of antiquity, who saw their skin color as midway between the dark African and the fair German, *inter nigrum et pallidum*.[6] "The Mediterranean type of 'Caucasian' physiognomy with pale-brown (*albus*) skin . . . represented the Roman somatic norm image."[7]

R. Ishmael's expression of love was for the Jews, not their skin color.[8] Nevertheless, we may assume that he, and the Jews in general, were partial to the color of their own skin, for such partiality is a universal phenomenon and is found in all cultures and at all times. As Sextus Empiricus (ca. 200 C.E.), the Greek philosopher put it when speaking of feminine beauty, all men agree that beautiful women exist but disagree about what constitutes beauty, "the Ethiopian preferring the blackest and most snub-nosed, and the Persian approving the whitest and most hook-nosed, and someone else declaring that she who is intermediate both in feature and in coloring is the most beautiful of all."[9]

Neither the Greeks and Romans nor the Jews saw very dark skin or very light skin as aesthetically pleasing. Expressions of distaste for the darker or lighter complexion, a reflection of the somatic norm image, are commonly found in Greco-Roman sources and have been thoroughly documented by Snowden and by Thompson.[10] Judaism of late antiquity evinces the same aesthetic tastes, as can be seen from the following quotations.

A tannaitic extension of the biblical (Lev 21:18–20) disqualifications for Temple service among the priests has the following: "[Priests who are] very dark, very red, very white, very tall and thin, the dwarf . . . cannot serve in the Temple."[11] Deviations of any sort from the physiological mean disqualify a priest for Temple service. E. C. Wertlieb understands this priestly requirement in a psychological and symbolic way. The unblemished priest is a national symbol of perfection and thus represents "each person's striving for wholeness and fulfillment," an accomplishment the priest himself would find difficult if he were "blemished."[12] Whether or not the priest represented the individual's striving for wholeness, clearly Wertlieb is right in seeing the priest as a symbol of perfection, or at least as reflecting human (Jewish) perfection. This is just another way of saying that the priest had to reflect the physiological mean.

The same catalog of mean-deviations is found in another tannaitic text speaking of humanity in general. "He who sees the very dark, the very white-spotted, the very red, the very white, the very tall and thin, and the dwarf, says the blessing 'Blessed [is He who] creates such varied creatures [*meshaneh ha-beriyot*].'"[13] As I explain in the next chapter, the blessing means to praise God for the variety of human complexions and forms that He introduced into the world. In regard to complexion, the text expresses this idea by referring to the shades of color that differed most markedly (very dark, very white, very red) from the Jewish somatic norm.

Thus these two tannaitic texts referring to physiological mean-deviations, one concerning the priests and the other humanity in general, implicitly privilege the Jewish somatic norm. Other examples in rabbinic literature reflect one side of the equation only, showing disparagement for dark skin. A rabbinic tradition stemming from the second century states that the *soṭah* who has gone through the judicial ordeal and was found to be innocent will undergo the following physiological changes: "If she formerly gave birth in pain, she will now do so in ease; if she formerly gave birth to girls, she will now bear boys; if she formerly bore ugly babies, she will now bear beautiful babies; if she formerly bore dark [*sheḥorin*] children, she will now bear fair [*levanim*] children; if formerly short, she will now bear tall; if formerly she bore children one at a time, she will henceforth bear twins."[14] This text may not provide clear proof for a disdain of dark skin, because the subject is a newborn baby. The somatic image for newborns may be different from that of the general population and may be similar to that for women, for whom we find a transcultural lighter-skin preference.[15] Recall Dominique Zahan's remark that in black Africa a lighter skin is preferred in newborns and young girls of marriageable age.[16]

However, a number of rabbinic texts disapprovingly describe a man's complexion that is too dark. In a text to be discussed shortly (*GenR* 36.7), Noah is said to have cursed Ham with the words, "May your progeny be dark and ugly [*shaḥor we-khaʿor*]." The same language is found describing the Egyptians (*GenR* 40.4).[17] Another expression encountered a few times in the Babylonian Talmud and apparently used in mild derision to describe someone short and dark is "black bucket" (*patya ukhma*). This expression is used by one Rabbi (amora) to deride another Rabbi.[18] Elsewhere the amora Samuel is described in insulting terms: "fat, black, and toothy."[19] It is clear that in rabbinic circles, whether in the Land of Israel or in Babylonia, a dark complexion was not preferred.[20] Just as in Greece and Rome, so too in Jewish Palestine the flip side of the somatic norm image was a dislike for a noticeably darker or lighter complexion.

The Greek and Roman preference for their own "intermediate" color underlies the widespread environmental theory of anthropological differentiation found in classical sources, that is, the theory that the environment determines the physical and nonphysical characteristics of humanity and thus accounts for differences among peoples.[21] The ancient Greeks noticed that those who lived in the remote northern regions of the world were the lightest-skinned people and those in the remote south had the darkest skin, and they developed the theory that the extremes of weather and environment in the far distant areas caused the different ethnic traits, including skin color. The extreme cold and lack of sun in the north produced light skin while the extreme heat and rays of the sun in the south produced dark skin.[22] The closer one came to the center of the world—that is, Greece and Rome—the more balanced was the environment and thus the effects of the environment on people. In the center humans were the most beautiful physically, in complexion and features, and nonphysically, in temperament (e.g., courage), character (e.g., intelligence, morality), and culture.[23] In this way the Greco-Roman world developed an explanation to account for the origin of people who looked different from them, especially in skin color.

The environmental theory is the most common explanation found in classical sources accounting for human color variation, but the Greeks and Romans also recount the myth of Phaeton, who brought the sun chariot too close to the earth. "It was then, as men think, that the peoples of Aethiopia became black-skinned."[24] Such myths are known as etiologies, that is, stories of ancient times that account for the existing state of the world. Generally, the thing requiring explanation is seen as an unusual or nonideal aspect of the world or of life.[25] Thus Phaeton accounts for the "unusual" skin color of the black Africans. Another example of an etiology—this from the Bible—is the Garden of Eden story. It explains the snake's unusual (legless) anatomy, as well as the labor pains that women suffer and the reason why one must toil to make the land produce its bounty.[26] An important feature in ancient Near Eastern etiologies is the curse. "Curses . . . served as explanation for enigmatic physiological or environmental peculiarities. The ancestor or proto-type of those exhibiting such abnormalities was considered to have been cursed by God . . . or by some ancient hero."[27] Thus, to take the Garden of Eden story, the peculiarities of the snake, labor pains, and toil have their origin in God's curses. Another biblical example is the curse of slavery pronounced against the Canaanites (Gen 9:25), which is seen by Bible scholars as an etiology accounting for Canaan's low and servile status at the time of the story's composition.[28] Which historical-political situation of which ancient Near Eastern period best fits the background of the Genesis story is disputed, but there is general agreement that the curse of Canaan is meant to explain the situation of Canaanite servitude.[29]

An etiology explaining the variety of human skin colors is found in the first- or second-century Jewish paraphrase of the Bible, *Biblical Antiquities* by Pseudo-Philo. In this work the author adds to the Tower of Babel story an element absent in the biblical account (Genesis 11): "God divided up their languages and changed their appearances [*mutavit eorum effigies*], and a man did not recognize his own brother and no one heard the language of his neighbor."[30] "Changed their appearances" refers to ethnic skin color variation, as Louis Ginzberg and Howard Jacobson recognized.[31] Some argue that the term points to individual variation in facial features rather than to variation between different ethnic groups.[32] Others claim that it means a change from human likeness into that of animals or monsters.[33] But both of these latter interpretations miss the etiological point of the biblical story, which is intended to explain the diversity of human groupings throughout the world. Jacobson points out that not only do "the natural demands of both the Latin and the context" support this interpretation, but so too does the preceding text, where "so that one man will not recognize the other" is immediately preceded by "I will . . . scatter them into all regions." This juxtaposition implies that "the dispersal of the people over various parts of the world is connected to their 'non-recognizability,' i.e. that people living in different places have different appearances."[34] Clearly, the point of the biblical story is to explain the diversification of human groups around the world ("The Lord scattered them from there over all the earth"), and not individual human differentiation. It is even clearer in one of the Dead Sea scrolls that describes the Tower of Babel event as "the confusion of tongue and separation of nations, the settling of clans and allotment of lands."[35] The point of the biblical story is to explain human variation writ large. As the biblical text says, "Behold they are *one people* [*ʿam eḥad*] and they all have one language." By means of God's punishment they have now become many peoples with many languages. When Pseudo-Philo said, therefore, that God "changed the appearance" of humanity, he did not mean variation in facial characteristics or a change to animal or monsters, but a change that would visibly mark human differentiation by its various groupings—ethnic differentiation by skin color.[36] While the Bible used only speech to illustrate the point, Pseudo-Philo added color.

A rabbinic midrash implicitly subscribes to the same idea, that is, the introduction of skin color variation at the Tower of Babel. Isa 66:18 describes the messianic age as a time when all "peoples [*goyim*] and languages" will be brought together, thus depicting a reversal to humanity's pretransgression state "of one people and one language." As in Genesis, Isaiah's indicator of differentiation among human groupings is language. But here is how the rabbinic midrash interpreted the Isaiah passage: "Isaiah said: In the messianic period he who is light-skinned will take hold of the hand of him who is dark-skinned and the dark-skinned will take hold of the hand of the light-skinned and arm in arm they will walk together."[37] The same description of anthropological variety by reference to language and skin color is found in very early ancient Near Eastern texts. The fourteenth-century B.C.E. Egyptian Hymn to Aton, for example, says: "O sole god, without another of your kind, you created the world according to your desire. . . . You set every man in his place. . . . Their tongues are separate in speech, and their nature [or, form] is likewise; the color of their skin is different: you distinguish the peoples."[38] By using the topos of language-color differences to indicate human diversity and by attaching it to the biblical Tower of Babel story, Pseudo-Philo (explicitly) and the midrash (implicitly) provide an etiology for the different human (ethnic) skin colors.

Other etiologies that focus only on dark skin are far more common, turning up all over the Near East—from the third century up until our own time.[39] As is to be expected in Bible-dominated societies, these origin stories are often built around biblical personalities and events. A statement attributed to the Syriac Christian church father Ephrem (d. 373) is quoted in a catena of patristic explanations and exegeses to the Pentateuch.[40] The comment describes the story of Noah's drunkenness in Genesis 9, including the curse of slavery on Canaan, but has the following addition to the biblical account:

> Mar Ephrem the Syrian said: "When Noah awoke and was told what Canaan did . . . Noah said, 'Cursed be Canaan and may God make his face black [*sawwada allāhu wajhahu*],' and immediately the face of Canaan changed; so

> did the face of his father Ham, and their white faces became black and dark [*wa-ʿāda bayāḍ wajhuhumā sawādan wa-qatamatan*] and their color changed."[41]

Whether Ephrem actually authored this statement is questionable because it is not found in his *Commentary on Genesis and Exodus*.[42] The same can be said for a similar statement about the raven, which the catena also ascribes to Ephrem. The raven was originally "white in color, . . . beautiful in appearance." However, when Noah sent the raven from the ark and it did not return for three months, Noah cursed it: "Cursed shall you be of all the birds . . . you and your offspring after you. May God change your color to black. . . . From the moment that Noah spoke these words, the raven's form altered, his color ceased and his face and head became black, and he remained disgraced among all the birds."[43] This too is not found in Ephrem's *Commentary*. Nor are two other quotations also attributed to Ephrem.[44] Indeed, a leading scholar of Syriac Christianity, Sebastian Brock, doubts that Ephrem wrote the lines about Canaan turning black.[45] It should not surprise us to find statements falsely attributed to Ephrem, the most important Father of the Syriac Christian Church. Common but anonymous traditions would thus receive an imprimatur of authority, and the curse of dark skin was one such tradition known in eastern Christian circles. The same tradition makes an appearance later in the same Syriac Christian world. Ishodad of Merv (ninth century, bishop of Hedhatha) records it, although not accepting it: When Noah cursed Canaan, he says, "instantly, by the force of the curse . . . his face and entire body became black [*ukmotha*]. This is the black color which has persisted in his descendants."[46]

Similar stories are told by many others. One of the earliest is transmitted by the third or fourth century Samaritan Marqe:[47] "When Kush saw the nakedness of his father, he was cursed and he wore darkness [*wlbš qblh*]—he and all his descendants forever."[48] As in the Ephrem account, the framework for this story is the biblical narrative of Noah's drunkenness and curse, but the one cursed is not Canaan, as in the Bible, but Kush. Some scholars, apparently seeking to harmonize Marqe's statement with the Bible, say that by "Kush" Marqe meant Ham, the father of Kush.[49] But it little harmonizes Marqe with the Bible to make Kush Ham when in the Bible it was Canaan who was cursed, and furthermore, the biblical curse is one of slavery, not blackness. Additionally, elsewhere in the same work Marqe refers to the sinful behavior of Kush, or to the Kushites as cursed, or he puts Kush in the company of other major biblical villains and sinners: Cain, the Sodomites, the Egyptians, Amalek, and Balaam.[50] Clearly, when Marqe wrote Kush he meant Kush. It would seem, rather, that the cause for the change from biblical Canaan to Kush is the same as that for the addition of Ham in the passage attributed to Ephrem (and in the writers to be quoted later): Canaan and his descendants were not black. If the curse was to be one of dark skin, a dark-skinned population would have to be found to carry the curse. Ham, as the biblical ancestor of the dark-skinned Egyptians and Kushites would fit the bill, and so, of course, would Kush.

Marqe's explanation for the origin of black skin illustrates another common feature of etiologies: the close connection of the punishment to the crime, in a measure-for-measure association. This aspect is cleverly put into play by Marqe with his use of the metaphor "to wear darkness": Kush sinfully looked at his father uncovered and was therefore punished with a permanent covering of darkness. The punishment was made to accord with the crime. As Marqe said: "He received recompense according to his action. . . . Kush saw his father's nakedness, and he was cursed and he wore darkness."

Etiologies of dark skin involving the biblical personalities of Noah and his son Ham are very common in Islamic literature. An elaboration of the theme is reported by Wahb ibn Munabbih (d. ca. 730):

> Wahb ibn Munabbih said: Ḥām the son of Noah was a white man, with a handsome face and a fine figure, and Almighty God changed his color and the color of his descendants in response to his father's curse. He went away, followed by his sons, and they settled by the shore, where God increased and multiplied them. They are the blacks [*sūdān*]. Their food was fish, and they sharpened their teeth like needles, as the fish stuck to them. Some of his children went to the West [Maghrib]. Ḥām begat Kūsh ibn Ḥām, Kanʿān ibn Ḥām and Fūṭ ibn Ḥām. Fūṭ settled in India and Sind [*al-hind wal-sind*] and their inhabitants are his descendants. Kūsh and Kanʿān's descendants are the various races of blacks [*sūdān*]: Nubians [*nūba*], Zanj [*zanj*], Qarān [*qarān*], Zaghāwa [*zaghāwa*], Ethiopians [*ḥabasha*], Copts [*qibṭ*] and Barbars [*brbr*].[51]

An even more involved elaboration is reported by Kaʿb al-Aḥbār (d. ca. 652):

> When Noah died, Ham lay with his wife; and God opened his gaul-vesicle and that of his wife also so that they mingled and she conceived a black boy and girl. Ham despised them and said to his wife, "They are not mine!"
>
> They are yours!" said his wife, "for the curse of your father is upon us." After that he did not approach her until the children had grown, when he again lay with her, and she bore two more black children, male and female. Ham knew that they were his, therefore he left his wife and fled.
>
> When the first two children grew up, they went out in search of their father; but when they reached a village by the edge of the sea, they stayed there. God sent desire to the boy so that he lay with his sister, and she conceived.

> They remained in that village with no food except the fish they caught and ate. Then she gave birth to her brother's children, a black boy and girl.
>
> Ham, meanwhile, returned seeking the two children and, not finding them, died soon afterwards of anxiety over them. His wife also died, and the other two children set out in search of their brother and sister until they came to a village by the shore, where they stayed. Then they joined the other two along with their own two children. They remained there and each brother lay with his sister, begetting black [*aswadayn*] male and female children until they multiplied and spread along the shore. Among them are the Nubians [*nūba*), the Negroes [*zanj*], the Barbars [*brbr*], the Sindhis [*sind*], the Indians [*hind*] and all the blacks [*sūdān*]: they are the children of Ham.[52]

Several other Muslim writers report a curse of dark skin but do not have such elaborations. Abu ʿAli Muḥammad Balʿamī (tenth century) extends the results of the curse beyond Ham: "Noah said to Ham: 'May God change the semen of your loins.' After that all the people and fruit of the country of Ham became black.'"[53] Most, however, just include Ham and his descendants. Such are Ibn Ḥakim (d. 1014) in the name of Ibn Masʿūd (d. 956),[54] Ibn Khalaf al-Nīshāpūrī(before 1100),[55] Ibn al-Jawzī (twelfth century)[56] and Zakariya b. Muhammad al-Qazwīnī (d. 1283),[57] both of whom report the story but reject it as the cause of dark skin,[58] and al-Dimashqī (thirteenth century).[59] It is also found in *The Thousand and One Nights:* Noah blessed Shem and cursed Ham. The result: Shem's face turned white and from him came the prophets, caliphs, and kings; Ham's face turned black, he fled to Abyssinia, and from him came the Blacks.[60] Lastly, among Muslim authors, mention should be made of al-Jāḥiẓ (d. 868/9), himself most probably a Black, who, in a work he wrote in defense of Blacks, refers to the curse of blackness commonly believed in his time but, like Ibn al-Jawzī and al-Qazwini, he rejects it: "They say: We have knowledge of philosophy and theory; we are the cleverest of people and have reasons for blackness [?]. We say: God, may he be exalted, did not make us black to disfigure us, but the land did this to us. . . . [This has] nothing to do with deformity or punishment, disfigurement or shortcoming."[61]

Rabbinic literature preserves two etiologies accounting for the origin of dark-skinned people. The first, a tannaitic tradition transmitted by the third-century Rabbi Ḥiyya, is based on the legend that God prohibited Noah and all the creatures in the ark from engaging in sex during the flood ("I have decided to destroy my world and you would create life?!"), a legend found in many Jewish sources, both rabbinic and Hellenistic, as well as in Christian literature. The underlying idea was already explained by Philo in the first century as "it was fitting to sympathize with wretched humanity." In the midrashic sources as well as in Philo the legend is built exegetically upon a comparison of Gen 6:18, 7:7 and 8:16, where the command to enter the ark is addressed to "you [Noah], your sons, your wife and your sons' wives," with males and females grouped separately, while the command to exit is addressed to "you, your wife, your sons and your sons' wives."[62] Thus, after the flood males and females were permitted to come together again.

With this legend as a self-understood background, the tannaitic text says that three creatures transgressed the prohibition of sex. The account is preserved in two versions, Palestinian and Babylonian—a common feature of rabbinic literature. The Palestinian version tells it this way: "Ham, the dog, and the raven had sexual relations [in the ark]. Ham went forth darkened/blackened [*mefuḥam*], the dog went forth with the characteristic of publicly copulating [or, of copulating in a well-known manner]; and the raven went forth different from other creatures."[63] The Babylonian version: "Three had sexual relations in the ark and they were all punished; the dog, the raven, and Ham. The dog is connected, the raven spits, and Ham was punished in his skin [*laqah be-ʿoro*]."[64] It would appear that the Palestinian and Babylonian versions do not disagree in the various elements of the story except, possibly, regarding the dog's punishment. And although the Palestinian account is clear enough, if not always specific ("different from other creatures"), the Babylonian is specific but unclear. What do "connected," "spit," and "punished in skin" mean?

By the ninth to eleventh century a set of explanations for these three expressions seems to have become well accepted and is commonly found in Jewish literature from that period onward. Accordingly, "connected" refers to the dog's physiological inability to disengage from the bitch immediately after ejaculation; "spit" refers to what was believed to be the raven's unique manner of inseminating the female by spitting the semen into her mouth; and "punished in skin" means that Ham's skin turned dark, as stated in the Palestinian version.[65]

The close connection of the punishment to the crime, the measure-for-measure association, is seen clearly in the case of the dog and raven. They are punished in sexual ways for their sexual sins—that is, the story is framed as sexual transgressions to explain the unusual sexual behavior of the dog and raven. Both versions of the dog's punishment, that is, publicly copulating or being unable to disengage immediately, are recognizable today as natural characteristics of the dog. The postcopulation attachment of the dog was already noted by Aristotle (d. 322 B.C.E.) and Pliny (d. 79 C.E.): "Dogs, seals, and wolves . . . still remain coupled against their will."[66] Although oral insemination may not be seen today as a sexual characteristic of the raven, it was a common belief in the ancient and medieval worlds. Aristotle records it—"ravens [κόρακες] and ibises"—as a belief alleged by "Anaxagorus and some of the other physiologers"; Aristophanes of Byzantium (third–second century B.C.E.) thought that pigeons (περιστερά) copulated orally, and Pseudo-Clement (third century C.E.) claimed it of the raven.[67] "Many birds were thought by the ancients to have intercourse orally."[68]

Thus for the dog and raven, but how is Ham's dark skin a sexual punishment? It was commonly believed in antiquity that once the sun had "scorched" the Ethiopians black, the transmission of this characteristic to subsequent generations occurred due to a change in the composition of the Ethiopians' semen, since "the seed comes from all parts of the body,"[69] and the altered seed was then imparted to the next generation. Strabo (15.1.24), for example, says that after the sun had darkened the Ethiopians, "already in the womb children, by seminal impartation, become like their parents in color." Perhaps the clearest statement to this effect is that by the church father Origen (d. ca. 253): "Among the whole of the Ethiopian race . . . there is a certain natural blackness because of seminal inheritance [*ex seminis carnalis successione nigredo*], that in those parts the sun burns with fiercer rays, and that having once been scorched, the bodies remain darkened in the transmission of the inborn defect [*infuscata corpora genuini vitii successione permaneant*]."[70] There was even the belief, which goes back as far as Herodotus, that the semen of Ethiopians (and dark-skinned Indians) "is not white like other men's, but black like their skin," although Aristotle pointed out Herodotus's error.[71]

Rabbinic literature does not have anything about "black semen," but the etiology of sex-in-the-ark does implicitly subscribe to the idea that dark skin derives from a changed seminal composition. This is seen clearly in Arabic literature, which incorporated the rabbinic story of Ham turning black in the ark and added explanatory glosses such as "then his semen was altered and he brought forth blacks" or "God changed [Ham's] semen such that his wife gave blacks to the world."[72] Although the idea is not explicitly stated in the rabbinic accounts, it underlies R. Levi's (third century) explanation of the ark etiology: "This may be compared to one who [dared to] mint coins with his own image in the palace of the king. The king said: 'I decree that the image be blackened [*yitpaḥamu*] and [therefore] the coin be invalidated.' Thus Ham and the dog [each] had sexual relations in the ark and [each] was punished."[73] As Theodor notes in his comments to the passage, the process of minting coins is elsewhere used as both metaphor and parable in rabbinic literature to illustrate the act of procreation. The engraved cast stamps out coins all similar to the engraving on the dyecast, just as human semen produces children all similar to its "encoded" characteristics.[74] Levi's parable thus explains the relationship between Ham's punishment (blackness) with his sin (prohibited sex) according to the measure-for-measure principle: a procreative (i.e., seminal) punishment for a procreative (i.e., sexual) sin. It would seem, therefore, that the ancient notion of dark skin originating in a changed seminal composition was cast in third-century rabbinic literature in the form of an etiology involving Ham.[75]

The notion of changed semen may account for the location of the rabbinic etiology in Noah's ark. It was believed in antiquity that climate at the time of conception affects the semen, which consequently impacts on the physical form (and character) of the resulting birth. Thus Hippocrates explained why the physique of Europeans varied more than that of Asians: the change of seasons in Europe was more violent and frequent than that in Asia, and "it is not the same for the same seed in summer as in winter nor in rain as in drought . . . for there arise more corruptions in the coagulation of the seed when the changes of the seasons are frequent."[76] The dramatic change in weather during the flood may have suggested to the rabbinic authors the right environmental conditions for the sex-in-the-ark etiology, the scriptural basis of the midrash (Gen 6:18, 7:7, and 8:16) notwithstanding.

In any case, the rabbinic etiology saw dark-skinned people originating with Ham. Why Ham? Because according to biblical genealogy Ham was the ancestor of the dark-skinned Egyptians and Kushites. Furthermore, by this time it was believed that the name Ham derived from a Hebrew root meaning "dark," "brown," or "black."[77] Thus the Rabbis were able to account for the existence of dark-skinned people while at the same time explaining, implicitly, the etymology of the name Ham.[78]

A second rabbinic etiology of dark skin also involves Ham, and for the same reasons. It builds on an earlier midrashic tradition that Ham had castrated his father Noah, an elaboration of the narrative in Genesis 9 ("And Ham saw [Noah's] nakedness"), making the measure-for-measure aspect more obvious.[79] In retaliation Noah said to Ham: "You prevented me from doing that which is done in the dark [the sexual act], therefore may you be dark and ugly."[80]

Let's look more closely at Ham's punishment of dark skin. I mentioned earlier that by the ninth to eleventh century, explanations of the three punishments had become well accepted in Jewish sources. The explanation given for "Ham was punished in his skin" in these later sources is that "Kush descended from him"—that is, Ham's punishment was that his descendant Kush became dark-skinned. Since Kush is the ancestor of the black Africans, the black-skinned punishment refers specifically to the black African. The earliest sources that offer this explanation connecting Kush to Ham's punishment, and which can be definitely dated, are Rashi and Nathan b. Yeḥiel, both of the eleventh century.[81] I push the range for the explanation back to the ninth century because of its appearance in a work called *Pirqei de-Rabbenu ha-Qadosh,* whose composition is judged to be from about the ninth or tenth century.[82] However, the probably earlier

Ḥupat Eliyahu Rabba, which may have served as the basis for *Pirqei,* does not offer this explanation, nor does the medieval cycle of Ben Sira stories, which also date from this period and which also may have served as the basis for *Pirqei.*[83] In addition to the Jewish sources, the interpretation is found in an Islamic text. Ibn Hishām (d. 828 or 833) in the name of Wahb ibn Munabbih records the sex-in-the-ark tradition this way: "Noah placed the women in isolation. . . . Ham went to his wife one night and had intercourse with her. . . . When Noah awoke . . . he said to God, 'Allah, blacken his face and the face of the descendants of the one who disobeyed and had intercourse with his wife.' So Ham's wife had a black son and he named him Kūshā."[84] The earlier sources, however—the Palestinian and Babylonian Talmuds and *Genesis Rabba,* and even *Tanḥuma*—assign the punishment of blackness to Ham himself and make no mention of Kush.[85] This is clearly the meaning of the midrash as noted by later Jewish commentators, contra Rashi.[86]

This is significant because Ham is the ancestor not only of the black African people of Kush/Ethiopia, but also, according to the Bible, of other dark-skinned people, such as the Egyptians. In other words, that the punishment of dark skin refers to black Africans and black Africans alone is a view found in Jewish sources not earlier than the ninth century. Due, however, to the overwhelming influence of Rashi's commentary on the Talmud, his explanation of "Ham was punished in his skin" by "Kush descended from him" became accepted as standard. It is found in works of all sorts ranging from the midrashic anthology *Yalquṭ Shimʿoni* (twelfth or thirteenth century) and the Yemenite *Midrash ha-Gadol* (thirteenth or fourteenth century), to various sixteenth and seventeenth-century Christian writers, to Eisenmenger's notorious antisemitic tract *Entdecktes Judenthum* (1700), to Jewish encyclopedias, to works of modern scholarship, and it has even made its way into the talmudic text in one manuscript.[87] The original rabbinic etiology of sex-in-the-ark, however, meant to explain why there are darker-skinned people in the world, and these people consisted of all the dark-skinned descendants of Ham, not just the black Africans.[88]

We can see that this is the intended meaning of the etiology by, once again, examining the Arabic writers who adopted the midrash. They speak of Ham's seed being altered on account of his sin in the ark, as noted, as a result of which the "Sūdān" came into the world.[89] Ismaʾil al-Beily has shown that the term Sūdān in early Arabic writings was not restricted in meaning to the sub-Saharan black African but rather referred to various dark-skinned people including the Copts, Fezzan, Zaghawa, *Brbr,* Indians, Arabs, the people of Marw, the inhabitants of the islands in the Indian Ocean, even the Chinese, as well as the Ethiopians (Ḥabash), Zanj, Buja, and Nubians. In other words, "the coloured people of the world."[90] Other scholars have more recently echoed his conclusion.[91] Note too that the early Arab (not African) leader ʿUbāda ibn al-Sāmit is described as a black (*aswad*) man, and consider the expression used by the Arabic writers to mean "non-Arabs and Arabs" (i.e., the whole world), *al-aḥmar wa'l-aswad,* "the red and the black" respectively.[92] Similarly the explanation of al-Jāḥiẓ, which he puts in the mouths of the Zanj (black Africans): "The Arabs belong with us and not with the whites, because their color is nearer to ours. . . . For the Prophet, God bless and save him, said, 'I was sent to the red and the black,' and everyone knows that the Arabs are not red." Jāḥiẓ concludes: "Our blackness, O people of the Zanj, is not different from the blackness of the Banū Sulaym and other Arab tribes."[93]

Al-Beily mentions Jāḥiẓ, Yaʿqūbī Ṭabarī, Masʿūdī, Ibn Rosteh, and others, who use the word Sūdān with the meaning "colored people." We can add several other authors including those who use the term in the context of Ham's curse of dark skin. Kaʿb al-Aḥbār (d. ca. 652), a Jewish Yemeni convert to Islam, spoke of the cursed descendants of Ham "begetting black [*aswadayn*] male and female children until they multiplied and spread along the shore. Among them are the Nubians [*nūba*], the Negroes [*zanj*], the Barbars [*brbr*], the Sindhis [*sind*], the Indians [*hind*] and all the blacks [*sūdān*]: they are the children of Ham."[94] We saw earlier that Wahb ibn Munabbih (d. ca. 730), "a celebrated authority on the traditions of the *ahl al-kitāb,*" reported that God "changed [Ham's] color and the color of his descendants in response to his father's curse," and that Ham's descendants are Kush, Canaan, and Fut; Fut's descendants are the Indians; and Kush and Canaan's descendants are the various races of blacks [*sūdān*]: Nubians, Zanj, Qaran, Zaghawa, Ethiopians, Copts and Barbar.[95] In another source Wahb is reported to have said that Canaan's descendants were the blacks [*al-asāwid*], Nubians [*nūba*], Fezzan [*fazzān*], Zanj [*zanj*], Zaghawah [*zaghāwa*], and all the peoples of the Sudan [*sūdān*]."[96] The *Akhbār al-zamān* counts "among the descendants of Sūdān, son of Kanʿān . . . the Ishbān, the Zanj, and many peoples that multiplied in the Maghrib, about 70 of them."[97]

Clearly, the rabbinic story of sex-in-the-ark is an etiology that is meant to account for the existence of all dark-skinned people, not just the black African. This is true as well for the sex-in-the-dark story, which is also an etiology directed toward Ham, that is, toward darker-skinned people in general, and not restricted to Kush and his descendants, the black Africans.[98]

Although, to the best of my knowledge, rabbinic literature does not mention the skin color of the Putites and Canaanites, who descended from Ham, it does refer to the dark skin of Ham's other descendant, the Egyptians.[99] In the next chapter, we will see two examples of Egyptians referred to as Kushites because of their dark skin color.[100] Here are some examples of Egyptians being described as dark-skinned. In a midrashic expansion of the biblical story of Abraham's sojourn in Egypt (Gen 12:10ff), R. ʿAzariah in the name of R. Yuda ben R. Simon (fourth century) has Abraham say to his wife Sarah on their entrance to Egypt, "Now we are about to enter a place of ugly and dark [people]."[101] Another rabbinic text that sees the Egyptians as dark-skinned occurs in a midrash on Ps 68:32/31, "*Ḥashmanim* will come out of Egypt; Kush shall stretch out its hands to God." We have seen that in this description of those who will recognize God and come to worship Him, the word *ḥashmanim,* occurring but once in the Hebrew Bible, has proved to be problematic. Ancient and modern attempts to understand the word have come up with envoys, nobles, ambassadors, or some sort of precious cloth or metal as tribute.[102] The Rabbis in this midrash tried a different approach: "*Ḥashmanim* is interpreted as *ʾashmanim,* dark men [*ʾanashim sheḥorim*] as it is written '[The children of Ham were] Kush and Egypt' (Gen 10:6); (*ḥet* interchanging with *ʾalef*)."[103]

This text understands *ḥashman* to be related to *ʾashman,* through an interchange of *ḥ* and *ʾ*, and translates *ʾashman* as "dark man." How does the midrash derive this meaning of *ʾashman*? The word occurs elsewhere (only once, Isa 59:10) in the Hebrew Bible, in a passage where, based on the context, the traditional interpretation of the word—from the LXX, Targum Jonathan, and Saadia on through the medieval period—was "darkness, place of darkness (the grave), gloom."[104] In addition, the connection to "dark men" may have suggested itself to the Rabbis through an association of *ʾashman* and *ʾaswan,* that is, Aswan, with a phonetic interchange of *m* with *w* (a not uncommon occurrence).[105] *ʾAshmanim* is then a deliberate although unstated reference to the place-name Aswan (**ʾaswanim*), the traditional border between Egypt and Kush.[106] Note that the verse speaks of both Egypt and Kush. All this, lastly, should not make us lose sight of the fact that the Rabbis are probably engaging in wordplay, reading *ʾashmanim* as *ʾanashim sheḥorim.* In any case, in this rabbinic interpretation, which is reflected in some versions of the Targum,[107] we see that dark skin is considered to be a common characteristic of both Kushites and Egyptians.

In seeing the Egyptians as dark, the Rabbis were echoing a view commonly found in Asia Minor, Syria, Greece, and Rome.[108] Herodotus, Aeschylus, Martial, and Ammianus Marcellinus, among others, describe the Egyptians as a dark-skinned people.[109] Literary notice of the dark Egyptian skin color may go back as far as Hesiod if he had in mind the Egyptians when he wrote of the "land and city of dark-skinned men," as some think.[110] Pseudo-Aristotle referred to the "too dark" Egyptians and Ethiopians, and while Manilius and Arrian describe the Egyptians as less dark than the Ethiopians, the comparison implies a dark color categorization for both peoples.[111] Coming closer to the time of R. ʿAzariah, in fact contemporaneous with him, is the Christian father Theodore of Mopsuestia (d. 428). In his commentary to the biblical book Song of Songs, Theodore understood the maiden of the Song to be Pharaoh's daughter, and to verse 1:5, "I am black and beautiful," he explained, "She was dark [*šḥmtʾ*] as all the Egyptians and Ethiopians."[112] Even before Theodore, the church father Origen also saw the Egyptians as dark-skinned. In one of his homilies he referred to the Egyptians as "the discolored posterity" of Ham.[113] Note should also be taken of the ancient Egyptian tomb paintings that depict Egyptian men conventionally reddish brown and the Nubians black or black-brown in contrast to the lighter-skinned Asians and Libyans.[114]

These Greco-Roman, Jewish, and Christian sources depicting the Egyptians as a dark-skinned people, parallel the Islamic accounts that consider the Copts, that is, the Egyptians, as one of the Sūdān. It should not be surprising, therefore, if we find a rabbinic etiology that sees the origin of dark-skinned people beginning with the ancestor of the Egyptians and Ethiopians. Similarly, Greek myth has an etiology accounting for the dark-skinned Egyptians and Ethiopians. Zeus disguised himself by becoming black (κάρβανος αἰθός) and seduced Io.[115] From this union was born black (κελαινός) Epaphus, whose daughter was Libya (Africa), whose grandsons were Egyptus and Danaus and, according to Euripides, also Cepheus and Phineus (Nubia).[116] In a different genealogy Zeus had four grandchildren: the Blacks (Μέλανές), the Ethiopians (Αἰθίοπες), the Undergrounders (Κατουδαῖοι), and the Pygmies (Πυγμαῖοι).[117] As Stephanie West says, the story is "an explanation for the swarthiness of [Zeus and Io's] descendants, the Egyptians and Libyans."[118] And again, "Sophocles offers us an aitiology for Egyptian appearance and national character based on the circumstances in which the founding father of the race was conceived."[119] Both the Jewish and the Greek etiologies show that in regard to skin color, the Kushites/Ethiopians were not considered in a separate category but were seen as part of a larger class of dark-skinned peoples. As Snowden said, in the classical color scheme Ethiopians are described as the blackest of mankind, the Indians less so, the Egyptians next in order as mildly dark, and finally the Moors.[120] Thus in both cultures, the Jewish and the Greek, we find etiologies accounting for the anomaly of all dark-skinned people in a lighter-skinned world.

What do the dark-skin etiologies imply about the Jewish, and in general the Near Eastern, view of darker-skinned peoples? Do such stories imply a deprecation of dark skin color? Undoubtedly. They obviously indicate that the authors of the stories considered their own lighter skin color to be the norm and, therefore, the preferred. Such human conceit is universal. People everywhere find most desirable that which most closely resembles themselves. The two major studies of ancient Greco-Roman attitudes toward black Africans concluded that preference for the Mediterranean somatic norm of light brown skin was largely responsible for any expressions of anti-Black sentiment in the classical world, which was explained as an ethnocentric manifestation of conformism to dominant aesthetic tastes.[121] Near Eastern attitudes were no different in this regard.

Nor did black African etiologies of light-skinned people express a different attitude. Veronika Görög-Karady studied the various skin-color etiologies of the Vili in the Congo and concluded: "The texts thus manifest a fundamental ethnocentrism. . . . The Black constitutes the prototype of humanity from which all the 'races' have issued. What is more, [the Black] appears as the normal condition by which humanity is measured where all the other species of mankind—mixed breeds (*métis*) or whites—figure only as deviations or incomplete or unsatisfactory forms. . . . The thematic nucleus of the majority of these Vili texts consists of a fault or misdeed imputed to the ancestor or one of the ancestors and to which the deviation of humanity issues directly. [. . .] The racial differentiation flows directly from the nature of the crime. . . . The transformation of skin color appears as the punishment for an evil action. . . . All these texts affirm the culpability and justified mythic damnation of the white ancestor."[122] In both light-skinned and dark-skinned societies ethnocentric-driven folktales saw the origin of "nonnormal" skin color in divine punishment for disobedience. Only the colors are reversed.

Environment and Etiology

The Near Eastern etiological folktales thus provide us a window into the authors' view of dark skin. While accounting for the variety of human color in the world, these stories see dark skin color as a deviation from the somatic norm and thus aesthetically displeasing. There is no doubt that the authors preferred their own skin color.

It is instructive to compare the two explanations for the origin of dark skin, that is, the Near Eastern etiologies and the Greco-Roman environmental theory. Despite its more scientific sounding explanation, the environmental theory also favored the authors' somatic norm. Implicit in the theory is its ethnocentric character, which viewed others' skin color as an aberrant result of extreme conditions on the normal complexion. Always behind this theory stood the assumption that the changed color was a kind of degeneration, and characteristic of inferiority. The Latin term *decolor* 'discoloration', often used to describe the phenomenon, conveys "a distinctly pejorative connotation, describing something that ought to be fair and gleaming but is unnaturally darkened. . . . Since white is the proper and natural color for human beings, to be *decolor* is to be stained and flawed."[123]

This point was emphasized by William Cohen when discussing France's later adoption of the classical explanation in the seventeenth and eighteenth centuries. "On a theoretical level, environmental theories . . . were egalitarian; in practice they were not. Being black was definitely less desirable than being white. The climatic theory posited people who were originally white and who turned black only as a result of exposure to extreme forms of temperature; in varying degrees it was thought that this transformation was a form of degeneration, implying a departure from the norm."[124] Cohen's point was made also by Jean Devisse, but for the Islamic world. Commenting on Ibn Khaldūn's (fourteenth century) rejection of the curse theory of blackness in favor of the climatic theory, Devisse says: "This position is not . . . so favorable as it may at first seem. True Ibn Khaldūn . . . did attribute the blackness of the Sūdān to the action of the sun. . . . But this theory itself was turned against the Sūdān! A few lines further on, Ibn Khaldūn very seriously explains that, due to the very nature of climate, only the men of the 'temperate' zone can be characterized by *balance*. Thus we are brought back to the Mediterraneocentrism we have already talked about. Beyond the 'temperate' zone, whether to the north or to the south . . . climatic excesses engender dangerous excesses of character."[125] We can clearly see the nonegalitarian character of the environmental theory in the words of Aristotle: "The nations inhabiting the cold places and those of Europe are full of spirit but somewhat deficient in intelligence and skill. . . . The peoples of Asia on the other hand are intelligent and skillful in temperament, but lack spirit. . . . But the Greek race participates in both characters, just as it occupies the middle position geographically, for it is both spirited and intelligent."[126] Like Goldilocks, one extreme is too hot, the other too cold; the one in the middle is just right.

In short, somatic norm preference dictated that neither the Greeks and Romans nor those people living in the Near East, whether Jews, Samaritans, Christians, or Muslims, saw darker skin as aesthetically pleasing. The Greeks and Romans expressed this view by means of the environmental theory, the biblically based monotheists by means of etiology with divine curse. The negative aesthetic sentiment is the same; the culturally conditioned literary expression differs.[127]

Let us summarize the results of our investigation thus far into early Jewish views of human skin color. We have seen that expressions of preference or disfavor for darker or lighter skin fall into three categories: feminine skin color, color as a reflection of health or sickness, and color as ethnic variation. We have seen a transcultural preference for lighter-skinned women in many different places and times. We have also seen an expressed aversion to dark and light skin color as reflective of ill health, adverse psychological or emotional conditions, and hunger. Evaluations of color in these categories are different from somatic evaluations of skin color that derive from the *ethnos*. In this last category—that is, variations of skin color among different peoples—we saw expressions of preference for the somatic norm, which was considered to be a shade between the dark Kushite and the light German. The favoring of the somatic norm underlies various etiologies that account for the existence of darker-skinned people in the world. We found such stories throughout the Near East, in Samaritan, Christian, Islamic, and Jewish sources. They also appear in Greek myth.

EIGHT

THE COLORED MEANING OF KUSHITE IN POSTBIBLICAL LITERATURE

THROUGHOUT THE COURSE of this study, we have seen that the dark color of the Kushite was noted and commented on, to one degree or another, by both Greco-Roman and Near Eastern writers from antiquity onward. It is, after all, the most noticeable feature of the Kushite in a lighter-skinned society. We recall one view that the biblical personal name Kush or Kushi may have even been given to non-Kushites because of their dark complexion.[1] Whether or not this opinion is correct for the biblical sources, it is certainly true for rabbinic literature. There, as we shall presently see, the term *kushi* is commonly applied to dark-skinned individuals who are not Kushites, and it is applied even to dark things.[2] The following twelve cases will substantiate my claim and will also lead to a discussion of dark skin as a social construct.

1. The biblical disqualifications for Temple service among the priests are listed in Lev 21:18–20. The rabbinic extension of that list includes the following physiological extremes: "[Priests who are] *kushi,* or who are very red [*giḥor*], very white [*lbkn/lwkn* = λευκός], very tall and thin [*kipeaḥ*], the dwarf [*nanas*] . . . cannot serve in the Temple."[3] *Kushi* here must refer to complexion (very dark), and not to a particular race or ethnic group—in other words, it cannot mean black African. This can be shown from several directions. First, the grouping of *kushi* with other extreme color terms indicates that the concern of this part of the text is with color, not ethnicity. Second, if *kushi* meant a black African who was a Jew, he (women cannot be priests) would have to be a convert or a descendant of converts and could therefore never be a priest, since priestly status in rabbinic law is acquired via patrilineal descent from the priestly families of Aaron. Third, an equivalence between the term *kushi* in this text and the color term *shaḥor* 'dark', 'black' was made shortly after the composition of the text, by the Palestinian amora Resh Laqish (third century), who advised against the very short, the very tall, the very light (*lavan*), and the very dark (*shaḥor*) marrying those having similar characteristics.[4] The fact that Resh Laqish made this statement apropos of our mishnah, or that the talmudic redactor(s) of this tractate connected his statement to our mishnah, shows that he—or they—also understood the mishnaic *kushi* to refer to skin com-

plexion and not to race. Fourth, this understanding of *kushi* as "very dark" is confirmed by the talmudic discussion concerning the relationship between the mishnah under discussion and the one before it. In the prior mishnah R. Ḥananiah b. Antigonos (first half of the second century) explains the difficult words of Lev 21:20 *maruaḥ ashekh* ("crushed testes") by metathesis, that is, by transposing the last letter of the first word and the first letter of the last word to get *mar᾿aw ḥoshekh* 'dark-complexioned'. To the amoraic objection (*bBekh* 44b) that *kushi* is taught in the next mishnah and need not, therefore, be repeated, we are told that R. Ḥananiah b. Antigonas excludes the reading *kushi* in the following mishnah. We thus see that the equivalency of the terms "dark-complexioned" and *kushi* is assumed. In sum, *kushi* in the mishnaic text means "very dark skinned (Jews)."[5]

2. The same catalog of physiological extremes is found again in another tannaitic text, which deals not with priests but humanity in general: "He who sees the *kushi*, the very white-spotted [*bohaq*], the very red [*giḥor*], the very white [*lbkn/lwkn*], the very tall and thin [*kipeaḥ*], and the dwarf [*nanas*], says the blessing 'Blessed [is He who] creates such varied creatures [*meshaneh ha-beriyot*].'"[6] Some think that *kushi* here means black African.[7] We shall see, however, that this cannot be the meaning of the term.

In this text, that which is unusual is seen as an expression of God's greatness and is accordingly worthy of a blessing, that is, of praising God.[8] The underlying idea is the same as that expressed in the Qur᾿an (30:22), which sees the greatness of God expressed in "the creation of the heavens and earth, and the variety of [human] languages and colors," or in a number of Egyptian texts that refer to the creator god distinguishing humanity by assigning different languages and skin colors to different peoples. For example, from the Temple of Hibis in the Oasis of Khargeh comes the following Hymn to Amun-Re: ". . . their physical aspect being different from that of their neighbors; he has modified their [physical form]; he has given colors to their skin, he has changed their language for self-expression; he has opened their noses; he has brought breath to their throat."[9]

The most complete and famous of these kinds of texts, and one in which praise of the god is manifest, is the Hymn to Aton from the fourteenth century B.C.E.: "How various are the things you have created, and they are all mysterious to the sight! O sole god, without another of your kind, you created the world according to your desire. . . . You set every man in his place. . . . Their tongues are separate in speech, and their nature [or, form] is likewise; the color of their skin is different: you distinguish the peoples."[10]

Another example of praising God for the variety of peoples and languages in the world has recently turned up in a fragment of the Damascus

Document (4Q266 11 9–10), discovered in the Dead Sea caves at Qumran: "Blessed are you, almighty God, in your hand is everything, and who makes everything. You established [pe]oples in accordance with their families and tongues for their nations."[11] Similarly in another Qumran text, the War Scroll (10.8–15), a prayer-petition to God begins with praise:

> Who is like thee, O God of Israel, in heaven and earth, that he can do according to Thy great works and Thy powerful might . . . that created the earth and the boundaries of her divisions into wilderness and plain-land, and all that springs from her, with the bu[rstings-forth of her waters], the compass of the seas, the reservoirs of the rivers and rift of the depths, the shaping of living beings and winged creatures, the forming of man and the is[sue of his ri]b, the confusion of tongue and the separation of peoples [בלת לשון ומפרד עמים] the settling of clans and the allotment of lands [מושב משפחות ונחלת ארצות].[12]

Clearly the idea that God's greatness is seen in the variety of peoples and languages in the world was not uncommon in the Near East of antiquity and late antiquity. While in some texts (Qumran) human differentiation is stated generally ("[pe]oples in accordance with their families," "separation of peoples, the settling of families"), in others (Qurʾan, Egyptian hymns) skin color is specified as a marker of human variety ("the variety of . . . colors"; "the color of their skin is different: you distinguish the peoples"). These texts indicate that the different skin colors among the world's population was a most visible manifestation of the varieties of humanity, for which God ought to be praised. The rabbinic blessing praising God for "creating varied creatures" when one sees the *kushi,* the very white spotted, the very red, and the very white is of one piece with the expressions of God's greatness in the Qurʾan, the Egyptian hymns, and the Qumran documents.[13] Accordingly, *kushi* is a color term and must be translated "the very dark," a meaning that is confirmed by the grouping of the term with other color terms: the very white spotted, the very red, and the very white. Just as the same grouping in the list of priests' disqualifications refers to complexion, so too in the blessing text the terms refer to complexion, and *kushi* means "very dark skinned," a category that includes, but is not limited to, the black African. This meaning of *kushi* in the text was already given by medieval and modern commentators alike.[14]

3. In the tannaitic exposition of the skin diseases recorded in Scripture (Leviticus, chs. 13–14; Deut 24:8), the Mishnah and *Sifra* state: "An intensely bright white spot [*baheret*] appears faint on the *germani,* while a faint spot appears bright on the *kushi.* . . . R. Judah says: The colors of the disease are judged leniently; not stringently. Thus, a *germani* is judged according to the shade of his skin to give a lenient ruling; a *kushi* is judged according to an intermediate shade to give a lenient ruling."[15]

The *baheret* mentioned in Lev 13:2 is described previously in the Mishnah (*m Neg* 1.1) as a skin discoloration that is "bright white as snow." This description gave rise to the obvious objection that the color of the diseased skin would appear relative to the color of the surrounding healthy skin: "A bright *baheret* appears faint on a *germani,* while a faint one, bright on a *kushi.*" We can see, then, that the text quoted here is concerned with the difficulty of determining an absolute color value among the various shade differences of the Jewish population (the law applies only to Jews). Thus, *kushi* and *germani* are meant to indicate the dark-skinned and light-skinned Jews. It could be argued that the terms retain their original meaning of Nubian and German and that these peoples are meant to exemplify extreme skin color, rather than that by transference the terms have come to mean "very dark skinned" and "very light skinned."[16] Most medieval commentators, however, including Hai Gaon, assume that *germani* and *kushi* have a transferred meaning of light-skinned and dark-skinned.[17]

4. In an earlier chapter I discussed another *germani-kushi* text, the Genizah fragment paraphrasing Isaiah's description of the messianic age as one in which "all peoples [*goyim*] and tongues" will be brought together to the temple in Jerusalem to worship God. The rabbinic paraphrase of Isaiah 66:18 put it this way: "Isaiah said: In the messianic period the *germani* will take hold of the hand of the *kushi* and the *kushi* will take hold of the hand of the *germani* and arm in arm they will walk together."[18]

In this picture of the world's recognition of God, it is probable, as noted earlier in chapter 3, that the author used *germani* and *kushi* in their original sense of German and Kushite as a merism to mean all the people in the world. In addition to this meaning, however, in light of the common Near Eastern topos of indicating human variety by skin color and language (note Isaiah's "all nations and tongues"), and in light of rabbinic usage of *germani* and *kushi* to mean dark-skinned and light-skinned, it is probable that the author had in mind the complexions, and not just the geographic distance, of those ethnic groups living at the opposite ends of the earth. In the same way, the picture in Colossians 3:11 of all those who recognize Christ included the dark-skinned Barbari (*barbaros*) and the light-skinned Scythian in order to express the ethnic-color extremes of the world's populations.[19]

5 and 6. The term *kushi* used in a transferred sense of "dark" was even used for inanimate objects. Rabbinic texts from the second and third centuries speak of *kushi* citrons (*etrog*) and *kushi* wine to indicate a dark color:[20] "A *kushi* citron [*etrog ha-kushi*] is not acceptable [for performance of the *mitzvah*]."[21] "Dark," and not "Kushite," is how the text was understood by Abaye (d. 338), a leading amoraic scholar in Babylonia.[22] This understanding is confirmed by a distinction made in the Palestinian Talmud be-

tween "a *kushi* citron" and "a citron that comes from Kush" (*pSuk* 3.6, 53d).[23] A tannaitic statement that distinguishes between "a *kushi* citron" and "a citron that is like a *kushi*" (*bSuk* 36a) may be a corrupt version of the Palestinian Talmud distinction, or "a citron that is like a *kushi*" may refer to a Kushite, with the meaning "as dark as a Kushite," as some medieval authorities believe.[24] In any case, both the tannaitic and the talmudic statements use the adjective *kushi* in the sense of "dark" as opposed to *kush(i)* meaning "Nubia(n)."

The adjectival use of *kushi* as "dark" is also found in the following texts:

> One may not offer as libation on the altar wine that was left in the sun too long [*elisṭon* < ἡλιάζω], *kushi* wine, white wine, raisin wine, cellar wine; but if it was offered, it is acceptable.[25]

> R. Zuṭra b. Ṭuviah in the name of Rav (mid-third century): "One may sanctify the Sabbath and festivals only with wine which would be fit for use as libation on the altar." What does this exclude? . . . Wine that is *kushi*, white [*boreq*] wine, wine left in the sun too long [*helisṭon*], cellar wine, or raisin wine.[26]

As an example of the common and obvious explanation of *kushi* as "dark" in these passage, I mention only Isaac ibn Ghiyyat (d. 1089).[27]

7. In aggadic literature of the amoraic period we find other examples of *kushi* referring to complexion ("dark") and not ethnicity ("Nubian"). Ḥanina bar Papa (third to fourth century) interprets the heading in Psalm 7, "Concerning the matter of Kush the Benjamite," by having King David say, "Just as the Kushite, the wife of Joseph's patron [*paṭronato*], lied about him, so Saul the Benjamite lied about me."[28] The text is alluding to the biblical story (Genesis 39) of how the wife of the Egyptian official, Potiphar, sought to sleep with Joseph and then lied to entrap him. According to the midrashic interpretation, David is made to say to God, "Just as the Kushite lied about Joseph, so Saul lied about me."

There is no indication in the biblical story, or anywhere else, that Potiphar's wife was a black African. Presumably she was an Egyptian, although the midrashist terms her a Kushite. Another example of Egyptians being called Kushites is found in a liturgical poem discovered in the Cairo Genizah. In this *piyyuṭ* of the Palestinian rite, God is praised for His triumph over the Egyptians at the Red Sea:

> A complete salvation the holy people saw,
> The saved rejoiced over their enemies;
> The Awesome hastened to shake off,
> The *kushim* He sank as one.[29]

Clearly the Egyptians are meant but the author has called them Kushites.

In an earlier chapter we saw a few examples in the Bible where Kush appears as a synonym for, or in place of, Egypt.[30] I do not think, however, that the midrashic text and the *piyyuṭ* represent a continuation of this biblical practice. The usage of "Kush" for Egypt in the Bible seems to have been restricted to the period of the Kushite dynasty in Egypt, and, with the exception of our two texts, the usage does not appear to have continued in later biblical or postbiblical periods. On the other hand, Greco-Roman, Jewish, Christian, and Islamic sources commonly depict the Egyptians as a dark-skinned people.[31] It would seem, therefore, that the midrash and the *piyyuṭ* drew on the common perception of the Egyptian as dark and on the rabbinic usage of *kushi* to mean dark-skinned, and thus referred to Potiphar's dark-skinned Egyptian wife and the Egyptians generally as *kushim*.

8. An important case of *kushi* meaning "dark" without an ethnic connotation occurs in an anonymous expansion of the biblical story of Joseph. According to this account, when Potiphar bought Joseph from the Ishmaelites (Gen 39:1), at first he refused to believe that Joseph was a slave, for he knew that "usually the *germani* sells the *kushi*, but here the *kushi* sells the *germani*."[32] Obviously we cannot translate *kushi* as "Ethiopian" and *germani* as "German," for the Ishmaelites were not the former, nor Joseph the latter. As in the preceding examples, we must translate "light-skinned" and "dark-skinned" for *germani* and *kushi*. As Theodor notes, this was the understanding of several medieval scholars, including Hai Gaon (d. 1038), Nathan b. Yeḥiel of Rome (d. ca. 1110), and the unknown author of the commentary printed in the first edition of *Genesis Rabba*.[33]

A thematic parallel to this midrash occurs, surprisingly, in medieval Scandinavian literature. Saxo Grammaticus (early thirteenth century) recounts the story of two Swedish princes who are forced by their stepmother to become slaves to the Danish king. When the daughter of the king is told by one of them that he is a slave, she responds: "The shimmering glow of your eyes pronounces you the progeny of kings, not slaves. Your form reveals your race. . . . the handsomeness which graces you is a manifest token of your nobility. . . . your visage testifies your true family, for in your gleaming countenance may be observed the magnificence of your ancestors. . . . your face reflects your innate rank."[34]

Ruth Karras discussed this passage as part of a larger investigation of the image of the slave in medieval Scandinavian literature. She showed that the slave was stereotypically depicted as ugly and dark-skinned and that the stereotype did not correspond to a reality of ethnically different, darker-skinned people, but was rather a social construct of the underclass by the elite. Physical beauty reflected nobility of birth, while ugliness reflected slave ancestry. The dark skin color was perceived as unattractive and in contrast to the ruddy skin of the freeborn or the bright white skin of the noble born.[35] Slave names also reflect this stereotype, such as Svart (black) or Kol (coal). Dark skin became part of the slave stereotype because it was associated with manual labor done under the sun, or with dirtiness, ugliness, and sickliness in contrast to the healthy good looks of the ruddy free man.[36] Whatever the reason(s), Karras thoroughly documents the depiction of the slave in this literature as dark-skinned, and she convincingly shows that the depiction does not correspond to ethnic distinctions but is, rather, part of a social construct, "the attribution by the elite of all ugliness to the underclass."

Even those who disagree and think that ethnic distinctions may have played a role in Scandinavian depictions of slaves as black nevertheless maintain that the color designation was "more important as a symbolic device for distinguishing in this way what was already socially set apart. . . . Natural markers of difference, such as colour of skin, are often noted as a means of stating social distinctions."[37] The same view is held in regard to depictions of foreign nonslaves as black, such as the American Indians or Inuit peoples, whom the Greenland explorers at the end of the tenth century described as "dark-complected and ugly" (*svartir menn ok illiligir*) when they first met them. The color term is seen as less an ethnic physiological marker than a marker of otherness, an "emblem of contrast."[38]

Ugliness and dark skin that are thought to describe the slave (or the foreigner) are not unique to medieval Scandinavia. The same belief existed in the Roman world of antiquity. Lucian (second century C.E.) speaks of one "pleasing in his complexion, neither dark [μέλος] nor fair [λευκός] of skin; for the one befits a woman, and the other a slave."[39] Lucian cannot be equating slave with black African because there was no such equation in the Roman world; slaves were not identified with any one ethnic group.[40] Furthermore, μέλος by itself, without further identification, does not indicate a black African in Greek texts.[41] Lucian's equation was one of color, not ethnicity. Similarly in regard to ugliness: Quintilian (end of the first century C.E.) quotes Sulpicius Longus's statement concerning a slave that "even his face was the face of a slave." The facial feature that gave the slave away was ugliness. Keith Bradley has remarked about this passage, "While utterly illogical, the assumption of a physical difference between slave and free was part of the process by which slaves were visualised in the Roman mind . . . one that simply distinguished between ugliness and beauty, between what was seemly and what was not."[42]

The same association of ugliness and dark skin with the lower classes or the Other is found also in other cultures. A folk saying recorded in *Leviticus Rabba* states, "The *qibl'ai raʿaya* hangs up his jar in the same place that the master of the house hangs up his armor." Although the term *qibl'ai raʿaya* is not clear—neither in the reading, of which there are variants, nor in the meaning—M. Margulies thinks that it means "black shepherd" with the connotation of "common shepherd."[43] In early Arabic poetry, blackness (*asfaʿ*, *aswad*) and "black face" are used metaphorically to describe the vulgar rabble and people of low character or ignoble origin.[44] Ibn Ezra notes that nobility are compared to white color and the lower classes to black.[45] In Middle English literature we find the expression, "the white and the black" meaning the "high-born and the low-born."[46] Finally, it has recently been shown that whiteness and blackness as social constructs operated as well in sixteenth-century England to represent and categorize the Other. The racial discourse that was then emerging involved "a degree of classification and exclusion used to exercise or to justify control over (or exploitation of) people of other cultures. . . . The trope of blackness had a broad arsenal of effects in the early modern period, meaning that it is applied not only to dark-skinned Africans but to Native Americans, Indians, Spanish, and even Irish and Welsh as groups that needed to be marked as 'other.'"[47] Even in modern times we find this distinction. Nederveen Pieterse notes that the English upper classes claimed that the lower classes had darker skin and hair.[48]

The midrash on Joseph stands between the ancient Roman world and medieval Scandinavia and is explained by both. The terms *kushi* and *germani* mean dark-skinned and light-skinned respectively, and have the sense of ugly and beautiful. This explanation not only accords with perceptions of slave and free in other cultures (ancient Rome and medieval Scandinavia), but it agrees with the rabbinic usage of the terms *kushi* and *germani* as dark-skinned and light-skinned and makes sense of the midrash, which cannot bear an ethnic meaning, for, as said earlier, the Ishmaelites were not Ethiopians and Joseph was not a German.[49]

The earliest versions of this midrash are found in Philo and the pseudepigraphic *Testaments of the Twelve Patriarchs*, in both of which Joseph's slave status is characterized by his physical appearance, confirming the visualization of slaves found in the other cultures. The *Testament of Joseph* has the following conversation taking place when Joseph was sold to the Ishmaelites: "As I was going with the Ishmaelites, they kept asking me, 'Are you a slave?' And I replied, 'I am a slave out of a household,' so as not to disgrace my brothers. The greatest of them said to me, 'You are not a slave; even your appearance discloses that.' But I told them that I was a slave."[50] It is clear that "your appearance" means physical appearance and not behavior or manner of bearing. The Greek text of the *Testament* reads ὄψις which has this meaning, which is also conveyed by the Armenian translation ("face").[51] The particular characteristic that indicated Joseph's nonslave status was his beauty and light skin. This is seen by the line, "And I replied, 'I am a slave out of a household,' so as not to disgrace my brothers," which means, in essence, "I am indeed a slave although I am light-skinned and beautiful, as you noticed, but that is only because I am slave out of the household," a reference to the class of slave known in the Greek world as οἰκέται, slaves who were taken into the master's home, as opposed to the lower classes who worked in the fields or otherwise outside the home.[52] Those who worked outside were darkened by the sun, whereas the house slaves retained a lighter complexion. Joseph said "I am a slave out of a household" so as not to disgrace his brothers with the imputation of kidnapping: he was indeed a slave, but a light-skinned house slave.

Ὄψις is the term used as well in Philo's account of the Joseph story, where the Pharaoh, although having purchased Joseph as a slave, nevertheless "judg[ed] him by his appearance [ἐκ τῆς ὄψεως] to be a man of free and noble birth."[53] Just as in the *Testament of Joseph,* so also in Philo Joseph's appearance is not described, but the key characteristic must have been beauty, which is indicative of the "free and noble" born, and is opposed to the ugliness of the slave as we saw. The imagery is explicit in the Ethiopic *History of Joseph:* "Then when those merchants looked upon Joseph as they were taking him out [from the pit], and gazed upon his appearance and beauty, they loved him with great love. They [then] asked him saying, 'Are you a servant [slave], a messenger, or a free person?'"[54]

Similarly, in some medieval versions of the story from Spain, Jewish and non-Jewish, beauty is specified as that characteristic which indicated Joseph's nonslave status. *Sefer ha-Yashar* (fifteenth or sixteenth century) has the Midianites say to Joseph's brothers: "Is he your slave? Maybe instead all of you are his slaves, for he is a very handsome and very good-looking and very beautiful lad—much better-looking than all of you! Why do you tell us such lies?" It also has Potiphar say: "Perhaps he was stolen, for this lad is no slave, nor is he the son of a slave; for I can see that he comes from a good bloodline and is very handsome."[55] The Spanish-Arabic (*aljamiado*), fourteenth- or fifteenth-century *Story of Yusuf* reports in the name of Kaʿb al-Aḥbar that the merchants saw Joseph's beauty and refused to believe the brothers' claim that Joseph was a slave. One of the merchants said: "By Allah, be He exalted, I swear that this youth is not these people's slave; I think not but that he is the son of kings."[56] Alfonso X (thirteenth-century king of Castile) wrote a *General History* drawing on earlier sources, in which some women are struck by Joseph's beauty and say to his mistress, Potiphar's wife, "This is no servant. He looks more like a noble king."[57] Joan Roiç de Corella (Spain, fifteenth century) wrote a *Story of Joseph* in which the merchants who had bought Joseph "gaz[ed] upon his face, his noble, elegant figure, which was not that of a slave but of a free man."[58] We find the same perception in fifteenth-century Yemen, where Zechariah b. Solomon ha-Rofé commented succinctly on the biblical description of Joseph as a slave (Gen 41:12), "i.e. ugly."[59]

In sum, the imagery of a slave as dark and ugly and of nobility as light and beautiful is found in different cultures in various periods. Joseph's beauty, mentioned in the Bible (Gen 39:6), therefore indicated a nonslave status to those reading the story and consequently provided the spur for the midrashic developments seen in *Genesis Rabba,* Philo, and the *Testament of the Twelve Patriarchs.*[60] The terms *kushi* and *germani* used in *GenR* 86 thus have the same meaning as they do in the other rabbinic texts we have examined, that is "dark-skinned" and "light-skinned," with the connotative sense, respectively, of ugly and beautiful.[61]

9. Another example of dark-skinned Semites being called *kushi* occurs in a story told about the second-century R. Akiba, but recorded only in later literature: "The king of the Arabs asked R. Akiba: 'I am a *kushi* and my wife is a *kushit* and yet she gave birth to a white [*lavan*] son. Shall I have her killed because she committed adultery?' "[62] Some scholars, assuming that *kushi* meant "black African" were forced to construe this text to say that the Arabs had an Ethiopian king ruling over them.[63] On the face of it, that is not an impossibility. Ethiopians did rule over parts of South Arabia in the fourth and fifth centuries for extended periods and established temporary authority at times during the second and third centuries.[64] Since the story is recorded in works that were redacted after that time, it is possible that the story reflects a historical event. However, we have seen enough examples in rabbinic literature of *kushi* meaning "dark-skinned" to realize that such an interpretation is not necessarily required. More important, there are indications that the account is fictitious.

This story of R. Akiba is one of many similar stories commonly found across cultures and times, from classical Greece to eighteenth-century England.[65] The motif of a dark child born to light-skinned parents, or, less frequently, a light child born to dark-skinned parents, provides the framework for suspicions of adultery, which are then proved to be unwarranted. The proof is shown in one of two ways: either the child's skin color is an atavistic peculiarity inherited from an earlier ancestor or, as in most accounts, it is due to the mother looking at an image of a dark-skinned (or light-skinned) person at the moment of conception, the so-called maternal impression. Given the wide temporal and geographical distribution of these stories, it would appear that we are dealing with a literary topos, and the account of R. Akiba should therefore not be taken as a historical datum as some wish to do.[66]

In most of these stories the dark-skinned child is identified as a black African, and, of course, a black African child born to a Caucasian couple would more greatly emphasize the suspicion of adultery.[67] But the child need not be African to raise the suspicion; wide color difference would do the trick. In fact, this is the case in an Arabic story similar to that found in the rabbinic source but with the colors reversed and with Muḥammad taking the place of R. Akiba. Bukhārī (d. 870) reports a *ḥadīth* in the name of Abū Hurayra, a companion of the Prophet: Muḥammad was asked by a bedouin (*aʿarābī*) whether the birth of a black (*aswad*) child by his wife was evidence of adultery on her part.[68] The term *aswad* was used in Arabic literature to describe any dark-skinned person, not necessarily a black African.[69] The Arabs are depicted as white-skinned in the *ḥadīth* and as dark-skinned in the midrash, but the perception of color is relative and in the eye of the perceiver. To the Jew the Arab was dark, as we saw in several other examples, and for our purposes the important point is that in the rabbinic story the dark-skinned Arab is called *kushi.* Such usage is echoed in Byzantine sources, in which we find, after the fourth century, that the terms "India" and "Indians" refer to three different places and its peoples: the Indian subcontinent, South Arabia, and Ethiopia.[70] Some would date this usage as early as the third century.[71] Note also that the Trogodytes, on the east coast of Africa, were variously classified as Ethiopians, Arabs, or Indians by classical writers.[72] The confusion in antiquity and late antiquity of the terms India and Ethiopia, and the use of "Indian" to refer to South Arabians, thus parallels the rabbinic usage of Kushi for Arab.[73]

The rabbinic view of the Arab as dark-skinned is, perhaps, echoed in the name of Abgar V Ukkama, the king of Edessa in the first century C.E. Many of the Abgar dynasty were ethnically Arab, and "Abgar" itself is an Arabic name.[74] Tacitus specifically refers to Abgar V as an Arab who led Arab troops.[75] The name Ukkama is Syriac (the language of Edessa) and means "black." Although there is some dispute as to why Abgar was called "the black," there is a good possibility that his skin color was the reason.[76] We know of a number of individuals in antiquity and late antiquity who were nicknamed "the black." Josephus, for example, mentions a Niger of Peraea who was a general of the Jewish army in the war against Rome, as well as a onetime governor of Idumaea.[77] "Niger" and various derivatives were Latin cognomina chosen for the color of one's hair, eyes, or skin.[78] The prophet or teacher at Antioch, "Simeon called Niger" (Acts 13:1), apparently got his cognomen because of his dark complexion.[79] In Syriac we know of a Mar Ukkama who was one of the founders of a monastery in the seventh (?) century.[80] Indeed, such nicknames seem to be a universal phenomenon.[81] It is therefore not unlikely that Abgar Ukkama was so named because of his Arab dark complexion in the eyes of the surrounding population, just as the Jews of Palestine considered the Arabs to be dark-skinned.[82]

10. Use of the term *kushi* to refer to a dark-skinned Arab continued into the Jewish Middle Ages. A Hebrew poem found in the Cairo Genizah records the Fatimid campaign against the Banū Jarrāḥ in the early eleventh century. Written by Menaḥem be-Rabbi Yom Ṭav [*sic*] he-Ḥazzan shortly after the event, it refers to the Banū Jarrāḥ, who were from southern Ara-

bia and had very dark skin, as *kushim*.[83] According to Ezra Fleischer, who published the poem, a contemporaneous source, the poem *Bekhu aḥay vegam sifdu* by Joseph ibn Abitur, also refers to the Banū Jarrāḥ in this way, calling them *kushim*, while a letter from Ṣadoq Halevi ben Levi in Israel calls them *sheḥorim* 'blacks.'[84] Another example from the Middle Ages is afforded by several medieval exegetes who commented on the biblical identification of Moses' wife as a "Kushite" (Num 12:1). Following the line that Moses' wife was Zipporah (Ex 2:21), they said that since Zipporah was a Midianite/Arab ("Ishmaelite"), she was called a Kushite because she was "very dark like the Kushites."[85] This view of the Arab as dark-skinned is also found among other peoples, as is indicated by the term *arap* (i.e., Arab) meaning "black African" in modern Turkish, Greek, and Russian, as well as in Yiddish.[86]

11. The meaning of *kushi* as dark-skinned occurs also in a tenth-century apocalyptic Genizah fragment dealing with the Byzantine emperors from Michael III to Romanus I (842–944 C.E.). According to this text, Emperor Leo VI, "the Wise," made a close favorite of his, a *kushi*, coemperor for twenty-two years of his reign.[87] Who was this "coemperor" and what does *kushi* mean? Samuel Krauss thought that the reference must be to Stylian Zaoutzes, who indeed shared power with Leo as *basileopater*.[88] An anonymous Byzantine text (fourteenth-century manuscript) strikingly confirms Krauss's suggestion and provides the key for understanding the Genizah document, for in this text Stylian Zaoutzes is called Αἰθίοψ 'Ethiopian'.[89] But Krauss's explanation as to why Zaoutzes, who was an Armenian, is called *kushi* (the author was either misinformed or, for stylistic reasons, he chose to call him *kushi* in order to prevent a possible graphic confusion between "Armenian" and "Roman") is very weak. Steven Runciman thought that the name Zaoutzes, which he says is derived from Armenian *zaoutch* 'Negro', indicated Zaoutzes' ethnic origins.[90] Romilly Jenkins thought that Zautzes was part Armenian and part black African.[91] As far as I can tell, however, aside from this one reference in the Byzantine text, there is no evidence to support the assumption that Zaoutzes was a black African.

E. Kurtz, who edited the Greek text, suggested that the term was used as a nickname for someone with a dark complexion, and for this reason Zaoutzes was called an Ethiopian. This view has since been accepted by the Byzantine scholars Patricia Karlin-Hayter and Shaun Tougher.[92] We see, therefore, another indication that the Hebrew *kushi*, just as the Greek Αἰθίοψ, could designate someone of a dark complexion and was not necessarily restricted to the meaning "black African."

12. Probably another indication of the general meaning "dark-skinned" for *kushi* can be seen in the usage of the term "black *kushim*" (*kushim sheḥorim*)

in the ninth-century story of Eldad ha-Dani. This is the way Eldad described his captors, who lived "beyond the rivers of Ethiopia."[93] Such usage precisely parallels the term "Blackamoor" in English literature, and possibly also *Leukaethiopes* in classical sources. In the first case, "Moor" (from Greek *mauros* 'black') had originally been used to designate the darker-skinned people from the Barbary coast, and when the much darker black African appeared in English literature, the same word was made to do double duty. Soon, however, it became necessary to distinguish between the two different complexions, and so the "Black Moore," "Blackmoore," "Blackamoore" came into being.[94] According to Jehan Desange and Lloyd Thompson a similar linguistic phenomenon happened in classical sources with the term *Leukaethiopes* 'white Ethiopians'. Since, according to them, the term *Aethiopes* referred to a wide range of dark-skinned peoples, not necessarily black Africans from south of the Sahara, the term *Leukaethiopes* was coined to describe the lighter dark skinned people of Africa.[95] In both cases, the secondary development occurred because Moor and *Aethiops* referred to any dark-skinned people. When it became necessary to distinguish between darker and lighter shades, Blackamoor and *Leukaethiops* were coined. If Eldad's "black *kushim*" represents a similar semantic development, it would provide another indication of *kushi* being a term of color, not ethnicity.[96]

In conclusion, these examples of the use of *kushi* in classical rabbinic literature—in all periods and genres—and continuing into the Middle Ages, show that the term may designate any dark-skinned person and not necessarily a black African (it may even be used to describe dark things, such as wine or fruit).[97] It is instructive to compare these conclusions with the research done on the term "Ethiopian" in Greco-Roman sources. Lloyd Thompson wrote that "the terminology is comparable with the ancient Egyptian *Ta-Nehesiu* and the Arabic *Bilad es-Sudan:* 'land of the Blacks.' An *Aethiops* was essentially a person whose skin-colour was considerably darker than the Graeco-Roman norm, and ignorance of geography led to a rather wide application of the term to all the little known peoples beyond North Africa. The nearest English equivalent is 'coloured people.' "[98] Frank Snowden came to a similar conclusion: "The term A[ithiopes] embraced a wide variety of brown, dark, and black peoples, including . . . Negroes and various gradations of mixed black-white types."[99] Also Jehan Desanges argued that *Aethiops* referred to any dark-skinned individual, not necessarily having Negroid features, and that the term was not restricted to describing those people from sub-Saharan Africa. He would thus translate *Aethiops* as "people of color" rather than as "Black."[100] Accepting Desanges' conclusions, François de Medeiros wrote that in antiquity as well as the Middle Ages the term "Ethiopian" was often used to mean dark-skinned people in general.[101] Similarly, J. W. Gardner.[102] The parallels between the rabbinic and the Greek terms extend to things as well as to people. We noted the rabbinic references to "Kushite wine" and "Kushite citrons," and we find in Greek literature—in addition to Homer's αἴθοπα οἶνον, mentioned above—that the cicada's skin color is called αἰθίοπι, the "crow-fish" is named for its αἶθοπι color, a species of ivy is called αἶθοπι ivy, and even dark-skinned Indians are described as αἴθοπες.[103]

Having shown that in rabbinic literature *kushi* has lost its exclusively ethnic definition and has come to have also a color definition, meaning dark-skinned people, we now return to the figure of a *kushit* maidservant (*shifḥah kushit*), which appears in the rabbinic corpus in three parables, illustrating various biblical verses. We examined two of the parables earlier when discussing concepts of feminine beauty in ancient Israel.[104] Now we look at all three together in an attempt to understand the precise meaning of the term *shifḥah kushit* in light of our discussion of the wider meaning of *kushi* and in light of the history of Black slavery.

> A townswoman [*qartanit*] had a *kushit* maidservant who went with her friend to draw water from the spring. The maid said to her friend: "Tomorrow the master will divorce his wife and marry me." Her friend asked why and she replied, "Because he saw that his wife's hands were dirty." Her friend replied: "Listen to what you are saying! If your master will divorce his wife, whom he loves, because of dirty hands, how will he stay with you who are black from birth?!"

The parable is meant to illustrate Song 1:5–6, which speaks of the temporary skin darkening due to suntan. Israel who sins temporarily (dirty hands of the naturally light-skinned mistress) cannot be compared with the gentiles who are permanently immersed in sin (blackness of the naturally dark-skinned maidservant). The same contrast is found in the second parable, where, once again, a dark-skinned *kushit* maid is set in opposition to her light-skinned mistress:

> Come and see the difference "between the righteous and the wicked, between him who serves God and him who doesn't serve him" (Mal 3:18). A parable of a *maṭronita* who had a *kushit* maidservant, and whose husband went overseas. All night long the maid said to the *maṭronah*, "I am more beautiful than you and the king loves me more than you." The *maṭronah* answered her: "Come the morning and we'll know who is more beautiful and whom the king loves more." So too the nations of the world say to Israel: "Our deeds are beautiful and God delights in us." Therefore Isaiah said: "Come the morning and we'll know in whom He delights" as it says, "The watchman said: The morning is coming and also night" (Isa 21:12), i.e. at the arrival of the World to Come, which is called "morning," we'll know in whom He delights.

This parable illustrates the falseness and obfuscation of this world as opposed to the truth and clarity of the World to Come. Just as night obscures the difference of skin color between a dark-skinned and a light-skinned woman, so does this world blur the difference between the deeds of the gentiles and of Israel. Only in the light of the World to Come will the difference be visible. The third parable also opposes a *maṭronah* to a *kushit*, but in this case they are both servants:

> "And Moses said to God: Who am I [that I should go to Pharaoh and take out the Israelites from Egypt]" (Ex 3:11)? R. Joshua b. Levi said: It is like a king who married off his daughter and promised her a province and a *maṭronah* maidservant, but gave her instead a *kushit* maidservant. His son-in-law said to him: "But you agreed to give a *maṭronah* maid!" So did Moses say to God: "Lord of the Universe, when Jacob went down to Egypt didn't you say 'I'll go down with you into Egypt and I will bring you out' (Gen 46:4)? And now you say: 'Go, I'll send you to Pharaoh [and take my people Israel out of Egypt]'" (Ex 3:10).[105]

Because a *maṭronah* is generally understood to be a free woman, some have suggested emending the text to read either *morṭanit* 'Mauritanian', or *briṭanit* 'Britain'.[106] Emendation, however, is not necessary, for the parable may be drawing on knowledge of the *pseudomeretrix*, a woman of free status who had been enslaved by some unusual circumstance, such as war or kidnapping by pirates.[107] Or *maṭronah* may merely mean a "woman of quality and refinement," free or not. Whatever the case, the *maṭronah* is meant to represent God, and the *kushit* is meant to represent Moses, God's emissary.[108]

In the first two parables skin color explicitly defines the difference between the maid and her mistress: permanent dark skin versus temporary dirty skin, and the distinction between light and dark skin, which cannot be seen at night. It is, of course, possible that in these two parables *kushit* refers to a black African; but it is not essential. Any naturally dark-skinned person can illustrate the points being made. In the third parable, however, skin color is not explicitly mentioned, nor does it seem to be the point at all. The point of this parable is rather one of status and social standing (matron vs. maid, God vs. Moses), with the *kushit* maidservant representing a low status as opposed to the high status of the *maṭronah* maidservant. Why would a *kushit* be of a lower status? It may be that this parable reflects a social situation in which the dark-skinned slaves (black Africans or not) were the lowest class among the slave population. It is also possible that *kushit* refers to a peasant woman who has become dark by her work in the field, and she is contrasted with the light-skinned woman who stays at home. This, of course, is exactly the point of Song 1:5–6. We saw earlier that the social construct of a dark-skinned underclass by the elite was widespread, appearing in Roman, Scandinavian, Hellenistic-Jewish, rabbinic, and Arabic literature, and that the origins of this construct derive from the reality of working outdoors under the sun, or with the dirtiness and sickliness associated with the underclass. The same biblical-midrashic contrast between the dark-skinned peasant woman and the lighter-skinned woman of the urban classes is also found in other cultures. Wolfdietrich Fischer noted that in early Arabic poetry white feminine skin is indicative of the refined, noble, beautiful woman, who spends her time within the home and thus does not get blackened by the sun.[109] In Arabic literature a women's light complexion was "proof of her nobility."[110] We recall also the contrast in modern Arabic poetry between the dark bedouin and the light urban women.[111]

In these cases the upper class (or urban) woman is characterized by light skin and the lower class (or peasant, rural) woman by dark skin. It is therefore possible that in the third rabbinic parable *kushit* refers to a peasant woman darkened by the sun, and that *kushit* and *maṭronah* are terms that, in explicating the biblical text, are meant to signify class status, which would serve well the moral drawn of the contrast between God and Moses. In regard to the meaning of *kushit,* then, these three parables are ambiguous. But because parables reflect the society in which they occur, an examination of Jewish society at the time may help us determine whether *kushi/t* has a general meaning of dark-skinned person or whether it refers to a specific dark-skinned person, that is, a black African.

PART III

HISTORY

NINE

EVIDENCE FOR BLACK SLAVES IN ISRAEL

Certain great crimes stain the centuries.
—Andrew Sinclair, *The Savage*

WERE THERE BLACK slaves in Israel in antiquity and late antiquity? If there were, did they constitute a minority or a majority of the slave population? Was there an implicit identity of the Black as slave? Do Jewish sources, specifically the three *shifḥah kushit* parables, reflect this identity? In order to get a better handle on the historical picture in Israel at this time, let us first see what the situation was like in other countries of the Mediterranean basin and the Near East.

There were black African slaves in ancient Greece and Rome, but amid the large numbers of Asian and European slaves, Blacks were relatively rare.[1] The principal source of slaves in antiquity came from prisoners taken in war, and most probably a significant percentage of the Black slaves came to Greece and Rome this way, whether as part of the captured Ethiopian contingent in Xerxes' army during the Persian War in the fifth century B.C.E., or as captives in campaigns against Nubia in the Hellenistic and Roman periods.[2] In addition to war captives, there is some evidence of a Black slave trade out of Africa. Stanley Burstein notes the following:[3] The late first-century or early second-century C.E. *Periplus of the Erythrean Sea* reports that the town of Opone at the end of the Horn of Africa (today Ras Hafun in Somalia) exports "better-quality slaves, the greater number of which go to Egypt."[4] Pliny (first century C.E.) says that at Adule on the east coast of Africa there was a "very large trading center" of ivory, rhinoceros horns, hippopotamus hides, tortoise shell, apes, and slaves.[5] The slave name Meroe (eleven documented cases) indicates, as with other geographic slave names, that "Meroe [in Nubia] was thought of as a typical slave-supplying region by the inhabitants of the Roman empire."[6] A sixth-century contract for the sale of a Nubian slave girl refers to her purchase from "the other slave traders of the Ethiopians."[7] This evidence points to the existence of a slave trade carried on along the East African coast. Burstein further notes several examples in late antiquity of prisoners taken by the Meroitic and Napatan kingdoms in Nubia in conquests of peoples to their south and west. He concludes that "a significant number of the African slaves encountered in Greek and

Latin texts began their long journey to the Mediterranean as prisoners captured in Meroitic raids against their neighbors in the central and southern Sudan."[8]

Archaeological and epigraphic (South Arabian) evidence in East Africa indicates that already in the early first millennium B.C.E. there were strong trade contacts between East Africa and Arabia.[9] Similarly, "topographical names with Sabaean foundations testify . . . to the relations between ancient Yemen and Abyssinia."[10] The anonymous author of the *Periplus* says that in his time a significant part of the East African coast ("Azania") was subject to the kingdom of Arabia "by ancient right" and that Arab (Ἀραψιν) traders "through continual intercourse and intermarriage, are familiar with the area and its language."[11] Thompson thinks that "this was clearly a long-standing situation, going back to the third century B.C., and probably even earlier."[12] Lewicki notes that the name Azania itself indicates the existence of South Arabian traders in East Africa, "many centuries BC," for the name is a Greek transcription of the Arabic name Ajam.[13] In light of the evidence from Greek and Latin texts of a slave trade in black Africans during the first six centuries of the Common Era, it is likely that these earlier trade contacts between Africa and Arabia included slaves. We hear of black African slaves imported into China by professional Arab traders, who had established a base at Canton as early as 300 C.E., and Chinese literature during the T'ang period (618–907) has many references to Black slaves.[14] On the basis of these facts, and with indications of a slave trade in the early Islamic period, some scholars conclude that the Arab slave trade in black Africans existed also during the pre-Islamic era.[15]

We have explicit references of Black slaves being exported to Arab lands from the beginnings of Islam. A pact (*baqṭ*) made between Muslim Egypt and Christian Nubia, which began according to tradition in 652, required Nubia to furnish 360 slaves annually to Egypt.[16] Whether this tribute was "unquestionably a continuation of an ancient tradition, which was furnished to Egypt, well-nigh regularly for many hundreds of years," as some think, we know of the tribute with certainty from the beginnings of the Islamic era.[17] Another indication of the exportation of slaves is the Zanj rebellion in Iraq. The Zanj were black Africans (apparently from Zanzibar) who were brought to Iraq and labored under miserable conditions in slave gangs. In the eighth century, Hārūn al-Rashīd observed that the number of Black slaves in Baghdad was countless.[18] We first hear about the Zanj in 689 when they arose in the first of three rebellions, although we don't know when they were first shipped to Iraq. The Muslim conquest of Zanzibar and capture of the Zanj around 750 undoubtedly replenished the Zanj population in Iraq,[19] but if there was a revolt already in 689, it implies the export of Black slaves somewhat earlier, probably from the beginning of the Islamic period, if not before.[20] The association of Zanj with slave goes back to the first known use of the name in Arabic writings. The author of a seventh-century poem says: "I am being led in Damascus without honor as though I am a slave from Zenj."[21] Another text records that sometime before 715 the Muslim ruler of Ceylon sent eight boatloads of presents, pilgrims, orphans, and "Abyssinian slaves" to the caliph Walīd I and his ruler of Iraq, al-Ḥajjaj.[22] A mid-eighth-century source, John the Deacon (d. ca. 770) reported that "the Muslims were in the habit of kidnapping the Nubians, and selling them as slaves in Egypt," a practice reported by a number of subsequent writers.[23] From the ninth century onward we have more information about the export of Black slaves to Arab lands.[24] There is no question that the Islamic conquest of parts of Africa brought in its wake a constant and large supply of slaves. Muslim merchants, whether Arab, Berber, or Persian, came to the gateways of Sudan, where they traded in slaves, as well as other commodities.[25] In these early centuries of Islam, "*Al-Nūba* became almost synonymous with 'black slaves,' because of the vast number of slaves bought from *Bilād al-Sūdān,* which includes *Bilād al-Nūba.*"[26] It was the purchase of these large numbers of slaves that instituted the commercialization of slavery on a regular basis.[27] Military conquest followed by commercial development of a Black slave trade occurred also in North and West Africa.[28] Lovejoy explains: "Slavery was conceived of as a form of religious apprenticeship for pagans," providing the means for conversion of non-Muslims. As more and more African lands became Muslim, holy wars were pushed further to the frontiers and slaves were taken from those areas. Because Islam required that slaves be taken only from pagan societies, because there was a continual need to replenish the slave population, and because sub-Saharan Africa was not yet Muslim, "black Africa [became] an important source of slaves for the Islamic world."[29]

What can this information tell us about the black African slave population in Arab lands? It is thought that at the time of the Prophet of Islam there were many Black slaves in Arabia.[30] Some think that they may have even constituted the majority of the slave population.[31] Robert Brunschvig speaks of large numbers of Blacks, far more numerous than white slaves. Such claims, however, have been called into question.[32] Bernard Lewis is of the opinion that in pre-Islamic Arabia Black slaves indeed existed, but they were in the minority among other slaves. The gradually increasing percentage of Blacks among the slave population can be traced to the Arab conquest of Africa. "In antiquity, most slaves had been of local provenance—enslaved for crime, debt, or money. . . . Islam created a new situation by prohibiting the enslavement not only of freeborn Muslims but even of freeborn non-Muslims living under the protection of the Muslim state. . . . The growing need for slaves had to be met, therefore, by importation from beyond the Islamic frontier. This gave rise to a vast expansion of slave raiding and slave trading in the Eurasian steppe to the north and in tropical Africa to the south of the Islamic lands. It is for this reason, no doubt, that the massive development of the slave trade in black Africa and the large scale importation of black Africans for use in the Mediterranean and Middle Eastern countries date from the Arab period."[33] We may conclude that there certainly were Black slaves in pre-Islamic Arabia as there were in ancient Greece and Rome. Due to its proximity to Africa, it is likely that there were more Blacks in Arabia than there were in Greece or Rome. Once the Muslim conquests of Africa began in the mid-seventh century, the numbers of Blacks exported to Arabic-speaking lands increased dramatically.[34] Nevertheless, there is no clear evidence for a preponderance of Blacks among the slave population in either Arabia, Greece, or Rome.

Even if most slaves were not Black in these countries, the evidence indicates that most Blacks, as most foreigners in general, were slaves.[35] This is reflected in the literature that assumes black Africans to be slaves. In Rome we can see this in a passage from Petronius's (first century C.E.) novel *Satyricon*. Two characters think of disguising themselves by appearing in blackface in order to elude an enemy. Standing together with their companion, the three will be able to pass "as Ethiopian slaves" with a master.[36] Their companion rejects the plan; the only way it could work, he says, is if they could also grow other black African features such as thicker lips and tightly curled hair. What is debated in this short conversation is the set of characteristics that defines an Ethiopian. What is not at issue is that Ethiopians were commonly considered to be slaves in Rome of the first century. From the late second century, the Christian *Acts of Peter* indicates that the figure of a Black in chains (i.e., enslaved) is a well-recognized motif in the Roman world at this time. This source depicts a demon as "a most evil-looking woman, who looked like an Ethiopian, not an Egyptian, but was all black clothed in filthy rags, dancing, with an iron collar about her neck and chains on her hands and feet."[37] A Syriac Christian work that originates in the fourth century, the *Cave of Treasures,* connects slavery with dark-skinned people, such as the Kushites, the Egyptians, the Indians, and (in some versions) "all those whose skin color is black."[38]

Another proof of an association of Black with slave may come from the descriptions we have of the life of Abba Moses, a fourth-century Christian ascetic, if various elements of his biography are meant as allegories, as Jean Devisse thinks.[39] Abba Moses was a black African who lived in the Egyptian desert as one of the "desert fathers," but Devisse thinks that those aspects of his life presenting him as having come from the lowest level of society and advancing to the highest ("the power of penance . . . transformed a serving-man, a black slave, impious, murderous, lecherous, a thief, and made him a father superior, a doctor, a consoler, a priest") and of being shunned and treated with contempt by the other monks because of his black skin—that these details are allegorical additions to the original narrative.[40] They mean "to epitomize the *Aethiops*-sinner's symbolic road from the darkness of sin to the light of grace." If Devisse is right, perhaps the element of Moses' former status as a slave was also an allegorical addition, which naturally suggested itself not only because of the slave's low status, which is required by the allegory, but also because of the common association of Black with slave. Finally, we have a sixth-century source, which does not assume the Black to be a slave but states so explicitly. The Alexandrian Christian, John Philoponus, wrote: "The Scythians and Ethiopians are distinguished from each other by black and white color, or by long and snubbed nose, or by slave and master, by ruler and ruled," and again, "The Ethiopian and Scythian . . . one is black, the other white; similarly slave and master."[41] Taken together, these citations indicate that between the first and sixth centuries C.E., Blacks were commonly thought to be slaves in Rome, Mesopotamia, Egypt, and perhaps Asia Minor.

In regard to Arabia, the words of the Arabic poet Suḥaym (d. 660), a Black slave, who referred to himself as "a naked negro such as men own," indicate clearly that Blacks were generally slaves in Arabia of the seventh century.[42] Rotter notes several indications of a Black slave population in pre- and early Islamic Arabia, and concludes that the black African was already known as a slave at that time.[43] The Arabic *Life of Shenoute* (a fourth- to fifth-century desert father) may also provide proof that Blacks were generally slaves. This work depicts the devil as "a black slave of great height and very terrifying" (*ʿbd aswad ṭawīl al-qāma hāʾil jiddan*). The original Sahidic Coptic, however, has "an Ethiopian of great height having the appearance of a lion." It would seem that "Ethiopian" became "black slave" when the Black was commonly understood to be a slave. We cannot, unfortunately, date the Arabic *Shenoute* with any degree of certainty. The original Coptic was written by Besa, Shenoute's disciple and successor, in the fifth century, but the Arabic version, containing elaborations and additions to the Coptic, could have been done any time from after the Islamic conquest of Egypt in 640/1 to the thirteenth century.[44] Even without the Arabic *Shenoute,* however, there is sufficient evidence to claim that during the first six and a half centuries of the Common Era most black Africans in Greece, Rome, and the Near East were slaves.

To say that most Blacks in these countries were slaves is not to say that most slaves were Black. They were not. "In antiquity . . . bondage had nothing to do with physiognomy or skin color."[45] That is an important distinction. If the black African is more commonly identified as a slave than is any other ethnic group, it may not be due to the Black's predominance in the slave population, but due to his or her easy identification as a foreigner, and thus a slave. The physiognomy of the black African is more readily distinguishable from the Greek, Roman, and Arab than, say, the physiognomy of the Syrian or the Persian. For this reason, and since most foreigners were slaves, the Black would more commonly be identified as a slave. Lewis used this argument to explain why the Arabic word for slave, *ʿabd,* eventually came to mean 'black African,' whether slave or not: "One reason for the change is surely that those who were of black or partly black origin were more visible."[46] The same point is made by Lloyd Thompson about the Roman declamation theme *matrona Aethiopem peperit* ("A Roman married woman has given birth to an Ethiopian"). Ethiopian infants appear in this declamation of adultery not because having a black African child is a particular disgrace, but because the adultery is most obviously seen when the child of Roman parents is Black.[47]

If there were Blacks (even if a minority) among the slave populations of Greece, Rome, Syria, Arabia, and, possibly, Asia Minor, during the first several centuries C.E., it is not unreasonable to think that the same situation obtained in the Land of Israel. The Bible mentions Kushites in the service of King David (2 Sam 18:21–32) and the Judahite kings Zedekiah (Jer 38:7–13, 39:15–18) and Yehoiakim (Jer 36:14).[48] At the other end of the period we are investigating, there may be indications of a Black-slave association in the Targum to Qohelet, which probably dates from the seventh century.[49] To Qoh 2:7, "I acquired male and female slaves," the Targum adds, "from the children of Ham [*mi-bneihon de-ḥam*] and other foreign peoples." This addition to the biblical text would indicate an association between slaves and Blacks if we can show that the term *bnei ḥam* meant "black Africans." The earliest Jewish source I can find to support this definition is *Exodus Rabba:*

> *I will strike all your border with frogs* (Ex 7:27 [8:2]). Our Rabbis said: The plagues which God brought on the Egyptians had the effect of bringing peace among them. How so? At that time there was a dispute between the Egyptians and the Hamites [*bnei ḥam*]. The Egyptians said: Our border is at such-and-such a place. And the Kushites said: Our border is at such-and-such a place. When the plague of frogs came they made peace between them: the area into which the frogs entered—they knew that it was Egyptian land, as it says "your border" and not the border of Ham.[50]

Although the redaction of *Exodus Rabba* (from earlier materials) is dated to the tenth century at the earliest, similar Arabic usage of the term goes back earlier. Rotter says that during the first three Islamic centuries *banū ḥām* appears quite often as a synonym for black African.[51] The terminology is also common among medieval Jewish authors living in, or influenced by, the Islamic world, such as Benjamin of Tudela and Maimonides (both twelfth century).[52] Reflecting the Indian-Ethiopian confusion, Ibn Ezra (also twelfth century) uses the term to refer to the Hindus.[53] Based on the Arabic usage of *banū ḥām* meaning "black African" in the early centuries of Islam, perhaps we can argue for the same meaning for the term *bnei ḥam* in Targum Qohelet, even if the Hebrew parallel term is first recorded later.

Between the Bible and Targum Qohelet, however, the only evidence I know of from Jewish sources that mentions Kushite slaves consists of the three parables of the *shifḥah kushit*. Clearly, in these parables the *kushit*, set in literary opposition to an upper-class woman, whether a townswoman (*qartanit*) or a matron (*maṭronah*), reflects a position of low status in society, but was this *kushit* a black African? Since, as we have seen, in the rabbinic corpus the term *kushi(t)* means a dark-skinned person, not necessarily a black African, and since, furthermore, slaves in several cultures were seen as dark-skinned, whatever their ethnic origin, it is difficult to tell whether the *kushit* of the parables means Black or black, that is, a black African or any dark-skinned person.[54]

Evidence for an African identity may possibly be found by comparing the exegesis of the church father Origen with the midrashic parables. Origen is close to the Rabbis geographically, chronologically, and exegetically. He lived in Alexandria and then Caesarea, where many of his biblical commentaries were composed; he died in 253/4 and two of the three rabbinic parables were transmitted by third-century sages (the third is anonymous); and both Origen and two of the three parables used a dark-skinned woman as a metaphor for sinning gentiles. Their worlds of exegetical discourse have much in common, as has been noted by several scholars.[55] Now, because the rabbinic parables assume a low status for the *kushit* and Origen's allegorization assumes a low status for the Ethiopian, we may be justified in equating the two and concluding that *kushit* in the parables means Ethiopian.[56]

The equation, however, is not free of problems. Origen's exegesis revolves, for the most part, around the scriptural word "Ethiopian," which means black African, while the rabbinic parables, presumably modeled on the real world, speak of a *kushit*, which means "dark-skinned," a category that was not limited to the black African. Origen's assumption, therefore, of a low status for the "Ethiopian" may have been drawn from the low status of dark-skinned, but not black African, slaves in Palestine at the time. (Remember: his primary exegetical basis is the non-African dark-skinned maiden of Song 1:5.) Or he may have simply drawn on the negative symbolism of the color black without reference to social structures in third-century Palestine. Nevertheless, given the historical situation in the Near East, in which there were Black slaves and most Blacks outside of Africa were slaves, it seems likely that Origen's exegesis of scriptural Ethiopians reflected the situation of real Ethiopians in the world around him. Because there are significant correspondences between Origen and the Rabbis, we may perhaps therefore conclude that the rabbinic *shifḥah kushit* parables, or at least the first two of them, similarly referred to black Africans.[57]

If this conclusion is correct, one rabbinic text requires explanation. In *GenR* 60.2 the Canaanite servant of Abraham, Eliezer, is made to say that a Kushite might enslave him.[58] If this statement is not just exegetical rhetoric, it reflects a belief that black Africans could be masters of lighter-skinned Canaanites. This would seem to contradict our conclusion that Blacks in the Near East were commonly slaves. Perhaps Blacks were generally slaves but some were not and may have had White slaves. Or, perhaps the midrashist is referring to black Africa, and he either knew or assumed that the master-White and slave-Black relationship was reversed there as has been documented for later periods.[59] I have shown elsewhere that the Rabbis had some knowledge of black Africa.[60] Perhaps the midrashist's statement grew out of that knowledge.

In any case, and to summarize, we have seen that black Africans were a minority among the slave populations in ancient Greece and Rome. Despite this, and because most nonindigenous peoples were slaves and because of the Blacks' noticeable somatic distinction, black Africans were readily identified as slaves. The same situation was true in pre-Islamic Arabia with even greater force, since there was undoubtedly a significantly higher percentage of Blacks among its slaves. This was due to the proximity of Arabia to Africa and to the long-established trade contacts between the two countries, which intensified after the advent of Islam. The Islamic conquest of Egypt and parts of the East African coast in the seventh century greatly increased the numbers of black African slaves in Arabic-speaking lands. This background allows us to fill in the blanks between the meager evidence extant from Israel in late antiquity. The situation in Israel was probably similar, that is, black Africans constituted a minority among the slave population but were readily identified as slaves, as in other countries outside of black Africa.[61] Because most slaves came from captives taken in war, the slave population in Israel, Blacks included, must have been significantly less than that in Rome or Arabia. Further reducing the percentage of Black slaves in Israel as compared with Rome and, especially, Arabia is the fact that Israel, as far as we know, did not have long-standing, established trade contacts with Africa as Arabia had. And yet there were Blacks in Israel and, for the same reasons as in the Greco-Roman and Arab worlds, they were commonly identified as slaves.

PART IV

AT THE CROSSROADS OF HISTORY AND EXEGESIS

TEN

WAS HAM BLACK?

FOR THE HUMANITIES, philology is a fairly exact science. To be sure, people have forever been devising their own derivations of words and hanging all sorts of ideologies on their creations. But the development of language follows specific linguistic laws, the proper examination of which can lead to firm conclusions about the origin of words and, consequently, about the world represented by those words. In a wonderful parody of the loose etymology used by Jacob Bryant in 1807 to prove that Egyptians, Indians, Greeks, and Romans were descended from Kush, William Jones, the English jurist and philologist of the time, wrote:

> I beg leave, as a philologer, to enter my protest against conjectural etymology in historical researches, and principally against the licentiousness of etymologists in transposing and inserting letters, in substituting at pleasure any consonant for another of the same order, and in totally disregarding the vowels: for such permutations few radical words would be more convenient than CUS or CUSH, since, dentals being changed for dentals, and palatials for palatials, it instantly becomes *coot, goose,* and by transposition, *duck,* all water-birds, and *evidently* symbolical; it next is the *goat* worshipped in *Egypt,* and, by a meta-thesis, the *dog* adored as an emblem of SIRIUS, or, more obviously, a *cat,* not the domestick animal, but a sort of ship, and, the *Catos,* or great sea-fish, of the *Dorians.* . . . [A]lmost any word or nation might be derived from any other, if such licences, as I am opposing, were permitted in etymological histories.[1]

Despite the attempts documented by Jones, the etymology of the name Kush to this day has not yet been established. But we are in a position to say something about the biblical name of Ham. The meaning of the name Ham is important to this study because the infamous Curse of Ham (Gen 9:25) depends upon it. Those who assumed that the Curse condemns black Africans to eternal slavery based their understanding on the supposed meaning of Ham as "dark, black" or "hot." If their etymological assumptions are correct, it may indeed imply that the ancient Israelites saw a connection between black Africans and slavery. Here is the biblical verse in context:

> The sons of Noah who went forth from the ark were Shem, Ham, and Japheth. Ham was the father of Canaan. These three were the sons of Noah; and from these the whole earth was peopled. Noah was the first tiller of the

> soil. He planted a vineyard; and he drank of the wine, and became drunk, and lay uncovered in his tent. And Ham, the father of Canaan, saw the nakedness of his father, and told his two brothers outside. Then Shem and Japheth took a garment, laid it upon both their shoulders, and walked backward and covered the nakedness of their father; their faces were turned away, and they did not see their father's nakedness. When Noah awoke from his wine and knew what his youngest son had done to him, he said, "Cursed be Canaan; a slave of slaves shall he be to his brothers. He also said, "Blessed by the Lord my God be Shem; and let Canaan be his slave. God enlarge Japheth, and let him dwell in the tents of Shem; and let Canaan be his slave." (Gen 9:18–27, RSV)[2]

There are a number of difficulties with this story as the Bible has it, the most obvious being that Ham sinned but Canaan was punished. Despite the inherent problems, this text has for centuries provided divine justification for the enslavement of black Africans, the so-called Curse of Ham. As an American proslavery writer, J. J. Flournoy, declared in 1838: "The blacks were originally designed to vassalage by the Patriarch Noah."[3]

Of course, the biblical text does not describe anyone as Black. Nonetheless everyone assumed that Ham was Black and that he was somehow affected by the curse of slavery. It didn't matter whether one supported the institution of Black slavery or not, or whether one was Black or not; everyone in nineteenth-century America seemed to believe in the truth of Ham's blackness. As Edward Blyden, a Black scholar, clergyman, and statesman, wrote in 1869: "It is not to be doubted that from the earliest ages the black complexion of some of the descendants of Noah was known. Ham, it would seem, was of a complexion darker than that of his brothers."[4] This was a "fact" accepted by almost all, including both abolitionists and a large number of Black clergy. "That the black race . . . are the descendants of Ham, there can be no reasonable doubt."[5] No one did doubt it; Ham was the progenitor of the black African. In a study of the mythic world of the antebellum South vis-à-vis Blacks, Thomas Peterson showed that the notion of Blacks as "the children of Ham" was a well-entrenched belief: "White southern Christians overwhelmingly thought that Ham was the aboriginal black man."[6] It was a notion well-entrenched in the North as well as the South.[7] And it was a notion that went back, at least, to the year 1700, when the Puritan Samuel Sewall published one of the earliest antislavery tracts and argued against the idea that "these Blackamores are the Posterity of Cham, and therefore are under the Curse of Slavery."[8]

Nor did the Curse of Ham die with the emancipation of slaves and the Civil War. The belief that Ham was the ancestor of black Africans, that Ham was cursed by God, and that therefore Blacks have been eternally and divinely doomed to enslavement had entered the canon of Western religion and folklore, and it stayed put well into the twentieth century. A 1969 study of the educational materials (Sunday School lessons, primers, teachers' manuals, catechisms, etc.) of the American Lutheran Church found that the church had interpreted Gen 9:25–27 in a way that justified Black slavery and/or segregation, and it had done so both intentionally and inadvertently. "There is no doubt left that the 'curse of Ham' has been taught to our [i.e., American Lutheran] children as well as our adults, and application has been made of this curse to our black population. And this teaching is one which has been handed down from generation to generation."[9] The Lutherans were not alone. The Curse of Ham was commonly taught and believed in America up to recent times. As James Baldwin, the African American writer, said: "I knew that, according to many Christians, I was a descendant of Ham, who had been cursed, and that I was therefore predestined to be a slave."[10]

But why should that be the case? Even putting aside for the moment the difficulty that according to the Bible, it was Canaan, not Ham, who was cursed, why was Ham identified with black Africa? Why the persistent, centuries-long identification of Ham with the Black? The answer has to do with the name Ham itself, which was understood to be related to the Hebrew word for "black" or "brown," and thus indicated associations with the black African.

When Josiah Priest, whose works were very popular, wrote in 1843 that Ham was born a Negro, his proof rested on the meaning of Ham as "black."[11] One writer later summarized Priest's position this way: "If Ham's name meant *black* and his descendants were *black,* these two circumstances will go far to prove the proposition in hand: viz., that *Ham was a Negro.*"[12] That is why Ham was given the name Ham—because he was black and the name means black. James A. Sloan, a Presbyterian minister, put it this way in 1857: "Ham's name means 'Black'. . . . There must, then, have been some peculiarity of color in the skin of Ham, which caused his father to give him the name which he received."[13]

But still another piece to the etymological puzzle deepened the identity of the Black with the son of Noah. For the Hebrew name Ham also meant "hot," or so these writers thought. And that, of course, corroborated the "black" evidence from etymology, for weren't the Blacks situated in the hot countries of the world, that is, in Africa? In his 1837 sermon in South Carolina, Samuel Dunwody preached: "It is by no means improbable that the very name Ham, which signifies burnt or black, was given to [Ham] prophetically, on account of the countries that his posterity were destined to inhabit." Samuel A. Cartwright, an American southern physician writing in the middle of the nineteenth century, said the same thing.[14] These arguments from etymology are commonly cited in the literature of that time. Indeed, "almost every Southern writer on the Ham myth" used the philological argument that Ham meant "black," "dark," and "hot."[15]

The Bible then was crystal clear to these writers. Because Ham's name meant both "black" and "hot," Ham's descendants had to come from black Africa. This line of reasoning provided the underpinning for the Curse of Ham. In a study of American proslavery and antislavery writings (mainly by clergy) written between 1837 and 1864, Ron Bartour found that the key pentateuchal passage used to justify slavery was the Curse of Ham story and that the racial character of the story was born of the meaning of the Hebrew word *ḥam* as "hot" and "dark."[16] The authoritative *Cyclopaedia of Biblical, Theological, and Ecclesiastical Literature* summed it up in 1872: "*Ḥam* (from the root *ḥamam*) combines the ideas *hot* and *swarthy*."[17]

Eighteenth-century Americans did not invent these theories. The argument from etymology was imported from Europe. Christopher Hill quotes its use (Ham "signifies black") in England in 1660.[18] Augustin Calmet, a French Benedictine, mentioned it in his *Dictionnaire historique, critique, chronologique, geographique et litteral de la Bible* (Paris, 1722–28), where he gives the same two proofs for Ham's blackness: the Hebrew *ḥam* means "burnt," "swarthy," "black," and God had given Ham Africa as his portion of the world. Both of these points indicate Ham's race and color. Calmet's *Dictionnaire* was a highly popular work, with a second French edition appearing in 1730, an English edition appearing (London) two years later, and finally an American edition in 1812–17.[19]

Was the etymological argument correct? Did the Hebrew word for Ham mean "dark," "black," and "hot"? If it did, then there would seem to have been some relationship between Ham and the black African. That relationship may have been tenuous, for Ham's other sons are not all identified with black Africa, but it must have existed at some level. And if it did, it means that the ancient Hebrews may indeed have identified Ham with the Black. We shall see that this identification became a crucial element in later deprecatory attitudes toward the Black, for when the ancestor of all Blacks is said to have been divinely cursed with slavery, the Curse of Ham is born. In tracing ancient Jewish attitudes toward the Black, it is therefore of great importance to see if and when Ham was considered to be black. In other words, did the name Ham mean "dark," "black," or "hot" to the ancient Israelites?

The Etymology of Ham: Ham in the Bible

The meaning of the name Ham (Hebrew, *ḥām*) has long been a problem in biblical scholarship. After looking at the evidence for various explanations, William F. Albright, the great scholar of the Bible and the ancient Near East, said with some understatement more than fifty years ago: "Plausible etymologies are wanting."[20] But it wasn't for lack of trying. Over the past century various theories have been suggested.

One study concluded that the name was related to *Ḥammu,* allegedly the name of the West Semitic sun god.[21] A more recent investigation saw a possible derivation for Ham from the Semitic *ʿamm* 'kinsman' (Hebrew, Aramaic, Ugaritic) or 'paternal uncle' (Arabic, Old South Arabian).[22] A third theory derived the name from another common Semitic word *ḥam* 'father-in-law'.[23] Yet another possibility, mentioned for personal names with the element *ḥam,* is a derivation from the Arabic *ḥmy* 'to protect'.[24] Earlier generations of Bible scholars had proposed still more possibilities: Ham is derived from the Hebrew root *ḥmm* 'to be hot' (*ḥom* 'heat', *ḥam* 'hot'); or from the Hebrew *ḥwm* (*ḥūm*) 'black, dark'; or from the Egyptian name for "Egypt," *kmt.*[25] Finally, some recent studies suggested a connection with the Egyptian *ḥm,* either *ḥm* 'servant', thus reviving an old theory,[26] or with *ḥm* 'majesty'.[27]

Several of these theories were attractive for more than phonetic reasons. For example, according to the biblical genealogy, Ham's descendants, with the exception of Canaan, inhabited the southern, hot regions of the world, parts of Africa and Arabia. A derivation of the name Ham from *ḥmm* 'to be hot' thus seemed a natural choice and is, in fact, the traditional Jewish and Christian interpretation of the name, found as early as Philo two thousand years ago.[28] Even more inspiring to some was the fact that *ḥmm* and the related Semitic root *yḥm* or *wḥm* carried a sexual connotation, "to be sexually excited, to be in heat,"[29] a characteristic, many were sure, that defined Blacks.[30]

A derivation from the root *ḥwm* 'black, dark' also seemed like a natural choice, for were not Ham's descendants in Africa and Arabia dark-skinned? This Hebrew word appears in only one form (as an adjective) and in only one context in the Hebrew Bible—in the story of Jacob and the sheep (Gen 30:25–43)—so it is difficult to pin down its exact meaning. The most important and up-to-date dictionary of Biblical Hebrew, therefore, not very helpfully defines the adjective *ḥum* as an "undefined color between black and white."[31] Others were more daring. Ever since the Middle Ages it has been assumed that *ḥwm* is related to the root *ḥmm* 'to be hot', and designates the color of that which becomes hot and burned—that is, "dark" or "black," "blackened."[32] The connection between heat and blackening would appear to be obvious and is found in the Semitic languages, where the meaning of "blackness, soot, charcoal," and the like is commonly ascribed to words based on the root *ḥmm* 'to be hot'.[33] Furthermore, the biblical context seems to argue for dark-colored sheep, which are not common in the Near East and thus explain the point of the story.[34] Based on this evidence, most scholars agree that the *ḥwm* (*ḥum*) defining Jacob's sheep represents a dark color.[35] The name Ham, then, according to this explanation, would mean dark-skinned people.

One ramification of the "dark" or "black" theory was the view of some scholars that Noah's sons represented three pigmentations of humanity: Ham, the dark races; Shem, the ruddy races (Akkadian *sāmu* 'red'), and Japhet (Heb. *yaphet*) the white races, since Hebrew *yapheh* means "beautiful" and, according to these scholars, the most beautiful pigmentation is white.[36]

A derivation of Ham (*ḥam*) from *kmt* 'Egypt', also seemed like a good choice despite the differences between the first and last letters of the two words, and scholars until about a generation ago entertained the notion that Ham was a Hebraized form of this Egyptian word for "Egypt."[37] The phonetic differences were only apparent, for the final consonant of *kmt* was no longer pronounced in Egyptian as early as the New Kingdom (ca. 1560–1070 B.C.E.) and the initial *k* was aspirated in the later Bohairic dialect of Coptic. Egyptian *kmt* was thus pronounced as *khemi* (with a short exhalation of breath following the *k*) in Bohairic.[38] Not only Coptic documents provide us this information, but Plutarch (d. after 120 C.E.) does too. He noted that the Egyptians call Egypt "Chemia" (Χημία).[39] With the loss of the final *t* and the realization of *k* as *kh* or as the Greek χ, the word looked very much like the biblical *ḥam*. This theory too had more than phonology on its side. First, from a political-geographic perspective, the extent of Egypt's rule during the New Kingdom is neatly circumscribed by the four areas that the Bible allocates to Ham's sons: Miṣrayim (Egypt, i.e., the Nile Valley), Put (either Somalia or Libya), Kush (Nubia, the land south of the first cataract), and Canaan.[40] The inclusion of Canaan as a Hamite in the Table of Nations (Genesis 10) is otherwise problematic, as has long been noted. Second, the Bohairic dialect was spoken in the delta, the area of Egypt closest to (and according to the biblical account, for a time the home of) biblical Israel and where the Israelites would have heard the pronunciation of the name for Egypt. Third, Egypt is actually called "Ham" or "the Land of Ham" four times in Psalms (78:51, 105:23, 27, 106:22).[41]

Finally, the old-new theory of Ham deriving from Egyptian *ḥm* 'servant' was attractive because of its perceived ability to explain the biblical punishment of slavery incurred for Ham's sin. Even more, Richard Hess notes that *ḥm* in Egyptian was a personal name and an element in personal names. If we accept this derivation of biblical Ham, we then have the names of Noah's three sons properly associated with the geographic areas of the world known in the biblical text: *shem* is a common Semitic name element, *yephet* is found as a Greek name (Iapetos), and *ḥam* occurs as a name element (and as a name by itself) in Egyptian.[42] Thus the entire world begins with Shem, Ham, and Japhet. Gordon makes the same point to buttress his theory of a derivation from Egyptian *ḥm* 'majesty'.[43]

Despite the attractions of the various theories, however, not one of these etymological suggestions is acceptable.[44] Recent research has shown conclusively that ancient Hebrew retained two distinct sounds from Proto-Semitic, *ḫ* (a velar fricative) and *ḥ* (a pharyngeal fricative), as indeed modern Arabic still does. The alphabet that the early Hebrews inherited from the Phoenicians, however, had only a sign for the *ḥ* sound. The *ḥ* sign (Hebrew ח) therefore had to do double duty representing both sounds, the *ḥ* as well as the *ḫ*, and it was up to the ancient reader to know when to pronounce the sign one way and when the other way.[45] The same situation, incidentally, occurred with the Proto-Semitic ʿ and *ǵ*, respectively a pharyngeal and a velar sound. While Arabic preserved both of these sounds and represented them by two different signs by means of diacritics (*ʿayn* and *ghayn*), Hebrew had only one sign (ע), which did double duty.[46]

Although two originally distinct sounds are represented today by one sign, whether a ח or an ע, we can sometimes know which sound was meant and heard by the ancient reader by looking at the early Greek transcriptions of Hebrew names. J. W. Wevers and Joshua Blau have independently shown that the Greek translation of the Pentateuch, especially of Genesis, reflects the Proto-Semitic *ḫ* sound by transliterating it as χ while the proto-Semitic *ḥ* sound is not transliterated at all or is transliterated by a vowel (*a* or *e*; e.g., Nῶε for *Noaḥ*)—that is, it was not heard as a distinct consonantal sound. In other words, the Greek transliteration captured the two different sounds represented by ח by rendering it as either χ or zero. By examining the Greek transliteration of Hebrew names one could therefore determine whether a particular name spelled with ח originally had a *ḫ* or a *ḥ*. Now, the biblical name Ham (Hebrew: חם, *ḫam*) is always transliterated as Χαμ in Greek, thus indicating that the initial letter of the name was *ḫ*.[47] Similarly we can know when ע represents *ghayin* by looking at the LXX transcription of names—for example, Biblical Hebrew *ʿAza* (עזה) is written in the LXX as *Gaza* (Γαζα). These conclusions are well accepted among Semitic linguists today.[48]

This new information forces us to reject all of the suggested etymologies for the name Ham. As we shall now see, the name could not derive from Semitic *Ḥammu*, or *ḥmm*, or *ḥam*, or *ḥum*, or *ʿamm*, nor from Egyptian *kmt* or Egyptian *ḥm* because none of these words begins with the letter *ḫ*, as does the name Ham (*ḫam*). The root *ḥmm* 'to be hot' and its derived forms are common Semitic words[49] and are always written with a *ḥ*, even in those languages (Old South Arabian, Arabic, Ugaritic) that preserved the *ḫ*. Similarly *Ḥammu*, derived from *ḥmm*, is spelled with *ḥ*. An origin based on the Semitic *ḥam* 'father-in-law' must be ruled out because this word is consistently spelled with *ḥ* in the various Semitic languages (Arabic, Hebrew, Syriac, Ethiopic).[50] We must also reject a derivation from the Hebrew root *ḥwm* 'to be black' or 'dark'. This theory has been particularly attractive to those who see the descendants of Ham as being dark-skinned peoples. However, the discovery that the initial phoneme of the name Ham was *ḫ* forces us to reject this suggestion, for, in those Semitic languages that preserve both phonemes *ḥ* and *ḫ*, the word for black is consistently written with *ḥ*. The North Yemenite dialect of Arabic has the word *ḥōm* 'charcoal', which derives from the root *ḥwm*.[51] And in Arabic in general a number of words based on the geminated root *ḥmm* 'to heat' have the meaning "to become black, become charcoal" (e.g. *ḥammama*), "to blacken" (*aḥamm*), "charcoal" (*ḥumamu*), etc., that is, "to become black by means of being heated."[52] So whether we look at words meaning "black" based on the root *ḥwm* in the North Yemenite dialect of Arabic or based on the root *ḥmm* in Arabic in general, we can see that the words always have the pharyngeal fricative (*ḥ*) and are thus unrelated to the name Ham (*ḫam*), which begins with a velar fricative (*ḫ*). For the same reason, the proposed derivation of Ham from Egyptian *ḥm* 'servant' or 'majesty' must be rejected: in Egyptian, which preserves both phonemes *ḥ* and *ḫ*, these words are spelled with the letter *ḥ* and are thus unrelated to Ham, whose initial letter was originally *ḫ*.[53] Nor can we entertain a proposed derivation of Ham from Semitic *ʿamm*, which begins with an *ʿayin*, for Hebrew, as opposed to Akkadian, retained the *ʿayin* sound and would not have represented it with *ḫ*.[54]

In regard to the *kmt* theory, scholars had earlier abandoned the suggestion that this Egyptian word is the origin of the name of Ham. The change of opinion can be seen in Hastings's *Dictionary of the Bible*. In its 1911 edition the entry "Ham" stated that Ham derives from Egyptian *kmt*, while the revised edition of the *Dictionary* (1963), explicitly rejects the possibility: "The name 'Ham' cannot be derived from any known Egyptian word for 'Egypt' or 'Nubia.'"[55] The four references in Psalms to the Land of Ham meaning Egypt are explained in one of two ways: either Egypt was poetically called after the name of its ancestor, Ham, or the references refer to the period from the fifteenth to the twelfth century B.C.E. when the Egyptian empire controlled other areas and peoples descended from Ham (i.e., the Canaanites), and thus the Psalmist used the name Ham to convey this broader geographic-ethnic sense.[56] In any case, Ham was etymologically unrelated to *kmt*, and this for the following reason. We now know that the first letter of Ham derives from an original *ḫ*, as said earlier, and that the Egyptian *k* was aspirated, as in the Bohairic *kh* of *khemi*. Plutarch's transcription of the *kh* of *khemi* with a Greek χ does not prove otherwise because the pronunciation of Greek χ as a fricative (the *ch* sound in "Loch Ness monster") did not occur until the Byzantine period. Until then it was pronounced as aspirated *k*, exactly like the Egyptian *k*. Now Hebrew has the same aspirated sound in its phonetic inventory, which is represented by the letter *kaf*. The Egyptian *k* (Bohairic *kh*) and the Hebrew *k* thus represented the same sound (an aspirated *k*). Therefore, if the word *kmt* (Bohairic *khemi*) had been taken over into Hebrew, it would have been pronounced and written with a *k* (an aspirated stop), not with a *ḫ* (a velar fricative). A recent study confirms this conclusion, for it shows that Egyptian *k* always becomes either *k* or *q* (a stop) in Hebrew; never *ḫ* or *ḥ* (a fricative).[57]

In sum, not one of the suggested etymologies for Ham can be accepted. If we want to be on firm linguistic ground, we must search for an etymology of Ham that begins with a velar fricative (*ḫ*), as does the original Hebrew name of Ham (*Ḫām*). Among those languages that preserved this phoneme graphically, in Epigraphic Arabic we do indeed find personal names bearing a *ḫam* element. Old South Arabian preserves *Ḫamāmat, Ḫammu, Ḫimmān, Ḫammat, Yaḫumm, Yaḫumm'il,* and Old North Arabian has *Ḫummy,* possibly *Ḫamim,* and, in an exact parallel to our biblical name, *Ḫm bn Blm* (*Ḫāmm* son of *Balam*).[58] Regarding the etymologies of these names, we find the root *ḫmm* in Modern and Epigraphic Arabic with the meaning "to feel bad, ill," "to stink," "to go bad (of food)."[59]

Whether the name of biblical Ham is derived from such a root, whether it is related at all to the other *ḫmm*-based personal names we find in Epigraphic Arabic, whether it is a Semitic name at all, we do not know. To arrive at a sure conclusion further investigation would be necessary, not only on the philological and onomastic levels, but also at the interpretive level of the relevant biblical passages against the background of ancient Near Eastern literature. At this stage of our knowledge, however, with the texts that have thus far come to light we can go no further.

We must conclude, therefore, that the origin of the name Ham is still unresolved. Albright's conclusion that "plausible etymologies are wanting" still stands and has been recently confirmed by Blau's remark that the name is of "uncertain etymology."[60] And when it comes to the original sense of the biblical names of Noah's three sons in context, we must still accept Skinner's seventy-year-old conclusion: "Only vague conjectures can be reported."[61]

One thing is, however, absolutely clear. The name Ham is not related to the Hebrew or to any Semitic word meaning "dark," "black," or "heat," or to the Egyptian word meaning "Egypt." To the early Hebrews, then, Ham did not represent the father of hot, black Africa and there is no indication from the biblical story that God intended to condemn black-skinned people to eternal slavery.

It was inevitable, however, that once two different sounds (*ḥ* and *ḫ*) were represented by one sign (ח), it would only be a matter of time before etymological confusion would reign. This is what happened with the name Ham. Although based on a *ḫ*-root, it was confused with *ḥ*-based roots, which all looked the same in Hebrew (חם, חום, חמם). It was then that Ham was thought to derive from the roots *ḥmm* 'to be hot', or *ḥum* 'to be dark, black'. When did this occur? At what point, in other words, was Ham understood to have been black?

Ham in Postbiblical Literature

Once the graphic distinction between *ḫ* and *ḥ* was lost, the name Ham (חם) looked exactly like the Hebrew adjective *ḥam* (חם) 'hot', and before long the two words were equated.[62] The fact that Ham fathered the ancestor of the Kushites who lived in hot, sub-Saharan Africa only helped to cement the etymology. When did this equation occur? Several early church fathers, such as Origen, Jerome, and Ambrose have it, as do some Christian onomastic lists.[63] But the earliest source in which I find the identification is Philo, the first-century Alexandrian Jewish philosopher, from whom the Fathers drew their information.

In interpreting various biblical names allegorically, Philo says that Ham represents quiescent, passive vice, and Canaan represents vice in the active state. This interpretation allows him to answer the question why Canaan was cursed if it was his father, Ham, who sinned:

> Ham the son of Noah is a name for evil (κακίας) in the quiescent state and the grandson Canaan for the same when it passes into active movement. For Ham is by interpretation "heat," and Canaan "tossing." Now heat is a sign of fever in the body and of evil in the soul. . . . No legislator fixes a penalty against the unjust when in the quiescent state, but only when they are moved to action and commit the deeds to which injustice prompts them. . . . It is natural enough, then, that the just man [Noah] should appear to lay his curses on the grandson Canaan. I say "appear," because virtually he does curse his son Ham in cursing Canaan, since when Ham has been moved to sin, he himself becomes Canaan, for it is a single subject, evil, which is presented in two different aspects, rest and motion.[64]

A good description of what Philo is doing in this passage comes from David Dawson:

> Philo . . . evades the constraints of literalism by suspending the personal identity of important biblical characters. Read allegorically, these characters become . . . personifications of various types (*tropoi*) of souls or of faculties (*dynameis*) within the soul. . . . Ham and Canaan denote two sorts of vice (passive and active). So when Noah curses Canaan for Ham's sin . . . he is in effect ignoring his sons' literal individualities in order to make an allegorical point. . . . Philo's allegorical readings turn specific characters who speak and act according to ordinary narrative realism into the impulses and faculties of the inner world of the human soul. [Thus] the suspension of narrative time and space, [and] the reading of scriptural characters as personifications of psychological dispositions and faculties.[65]

By means of this allegorical interpretation, Philo explains the apparent anomaly of Canaan being cursed for Ham's sin. Punishment is rightly administered against action, not against thought of action. Ham means "heat," which represents evil thoughts, and Canaan means "tossing," which represents the action that brings the thoughts of evil into reality. Ham and Canaan, therefore, at this allegorical level represent the relationship between thought and action. So when the Bible says that Canaan was punished (cursed), it is saying that only action, not thought, is punishable. Furthermore, Ham is essentially punished when Canaan is punished, "since when Ham has been moved to sin, he himself becomes Canaan, for it is a single subject, wickedness, which is presented in two different aspects, rest and motion."[66]

So much for Philo's allegory. Note, however, that while Philo provides an etymology for Ham from "heat," he makes no connection between heat and black Africa. Nor do the early church fathers. In other words, we do not yet have a Black Ham, or even a black Ham. For that we have to wait for the development of another mistaken etymology for the name Ham, that is from *ḥwm* (*ḥum*) 'black' or 'dark'.

Some writings from the Hellenistic period at first glance seem to provide evidence of a Ham-black equation in the second century B.C.E., but the evidence is only apparent. Pseudo-Eupolemus and the poet Ezekiel mention an individual by the name of Chum, which may be a reference to Kush in the opinion of some scholars.[67] Ben Zion Wacholder argued that Pseudo-Eupolemus deliberately changed the name of Kush (Chus) to Chum for etymological reasons, to relate Kush to the Hebrew *ḥum* or *ḥmm* "denoting blackened by the sun or heat, which would explain the pigmentation of the Ethiopians."[68] While Wacholder implies a connection with the name Ham, Howard Jacobson makes the connection explicit by arguing that Ezekiel, in addition to a play on *ḥum,* had in mind also the name of Kush's father, Ham, and so created the new name by combining Chus and Cham to get Chum (Χους + Χαμ = Χουμ).[69] Whether implicit or explicit, these explanations assume that behind the associations of Kush, Ham, and *ḥum* lies an etymology of the name Ham based on the root *ḥwm* (*ḥum*) 'black, dark'.

These reconstructions of the name Chum, however, are too conjectural at several levels. Neither the identification of Pseudo-Eupolemus's and Ezekiel's Chum with Kush nor the creation of the name Chum based on Hebrew *ḥum* is certain. Furthermore, even if both of these suppositions are correct, the association of Ham with *ḥwm* (*ḥum*) need not be required for the invention of "Chum." Kush as the father of the black Africans is always assumed to be dark-skinned and, therefore, a play on his name and the Hebrew word for dark (*ḥum*) would of itself produce the desired Chum. If Ham is thrown into the equation, as Jacobson thinks, it may have been because of his relationship to Kush, not because of the etymology of his name. The evidence, then, from Pseudo-Eupolemus and Ezekiel is too uncertain a foundation upon which to base the claim that Ham was understood to have been black during the Hellenistic period.

The second-century B.C.E. text, known as the "Animal Apocalypse," has been interpreted by some to refer to a black-skinned Ham. This text was originally an independent composition but is now part of the Jewish pseudepigraphical work known as 1 Enoch (chs. 85–90) and is dated to the mid-second century B.C.E.[70] The Animal Apocalypse was so named because it recounts biblical history from Adam onward, only substituting various animals for biblical characters or groups, a sort of ancient *Animal Farm,* to use Bryan's apt analogy to George Orwell's novel.[71] The relevant text reads as follows: "The white bull which had become a man came out of the vessel and the three bulls with him, and one of those three bulls was white like that bull, and one of them was red as blood, and one black."[72]

The white bull that came out of the vessel (i.e., the ark) is Noah and the three bulls with him are Shem, Ham, and Japheth.[73] Matthew Black and Siegbert Uhlig believe that the author means to describe the different skin colors of the three races that populated the world after the flood. They think that, although elsewhere in the Animal Apocalypse colors of animals are meant symbolically, in this instance they realistically indicate skin color: the Semites are white, the Japhetites red, and the Hamites black.[74] This view has received some support from Devorah Dimant, who incorporates both a symbolic and a racial interpretation. She understands the black and white colors in this passage to be symbolic of bad and good, but "the description of Ham as black is certainly related to the fact that he is the father of Kush."[75]

The idea that Noah's sons, whose descendants populated the world, were of different skin colors is an old theory in biblical scholarship, which was long ago discarded. When it was first propounded, about one hundred years ago, it was thought that the names of the sons were etymologically related to the names, or values, of colors. This theory has been discarded for good reason, as discussed earlier. Reviving the theory now in the Animal Apocalypse, we are confronted with an additional, and insuperable, problem: throughout the work these colors have only symbolic nonphysical meaning.[76] Thus the white and black animals symbolically represent good-righteousness and evil-wickedness, or, as Tiller puts it, inclusion in or exclusion from the chosen line. Adam, Seth, Noah, Shem, Abraham, Isaac, and Jacob are all white and all considered to be good, whereas Cain, Ham, and Esau are black and evil.[77] The symbolic use of colors in the Animal Apocalypse, which is in accord with the allegorical nature of this apocalypse, is also found in several other ancient Near Eastern sources, perhaps the most famous being the four horsemen of another apocalypse, Revelation 6:1–8.[78]

The symbolic significance of black and white in these texts follows the universal pattern of negative and positive values for these colors.[79] The color red is more problematic, for it is usually understood to represent violence and bloodshed.[80] Red, the color of fire and blood, as symbolically pointing to violence, murder, and the enemy has an ancient history,[81] which continues into the Middle Ages.[82] Some would argue that a similar meaning of the color must be applied to the depiction of Japhet, and also Abel, as red bulls in the Animal Apocalypse—that is, the color symbolizes Abel's murder and Japhet's violent character.[83]

This explanation, however, is problematic. First, we would expect Cain, the murderer, not Abel, to be colored red, as he is in Mani's account recorded by al-Nadīm.[84] Second, why is Japhet chosen to represent violence?[85] None of the commentaries offer a satisfactory solution to the problem of why Abel and Japhet are colored red.

The answer may lie in a statement by Philo that Noah's sons are "symbols of three things in nature—of the good, the evil and the indifferent. Shem is distinguished for good, Ham for evil, and Japhet for the indifferent."[86] Shem, ancestor of the Jews, is allegorized by Philo as good; Ham, who committed the crime against his father Noah, as evil; and Japhet as "indifferent," or morally neutral. Certainly, the colors of white and black in the Animal Apocalypse correspond to Philo's good and evil. So too does the apocalypse's red color correspond to Philo's indifference, for red as a symbol of neutrality is found in several cultures of the Near East and elsewhere, understood as either a combination, or a lack, of both good and bad.[87] In ancient Egypt "the color that regularly embodied both positive and negative meanings was red."[88] A study of bedouin color terms claims that the classification of white-positive, black-negative, and red-ambiguous is "very suggestive vis-à-vis symbolic values assigned to these colors by several Bedouin communities in the Middle East including the Negev Bedouin."[89] Although this study was carried out in recent times, the Arabic dialects spoken by the bedouin are known to be conservative, especially in the lexicon, including color classification.[90] In the Arabic *Qiṣaṣ al-anbiyyā* of Kisāʾī, the color of saffron (orange to yellow-orange) seems to represent a symbolic position between good (white) and evil (black).[91] Among some Central African peoples "the indeterminate value is symbolised by the colour red, while the determinate values of 'good' and 'evil' are symbolised by the colours white and black, respectively."[92] In the ritual system of the Ndembu people in Zambia, symbolically red "shares the qualities of both white and black," and thus "whiteness is positive, redness ambivalent, and blackness negative."[93] Also in Hausa literature red symbolizes ambiguity.[94] The same tricolor symbolism underlies the hierarchical depiction of the social classes we saw earlier in several medieval European texts, that is white for nobility, black for slave, and red for the middle position of the free born commoner.[95] In Jewish sources, Athalya

Brenner notes that the symbolism of the color red in the Hebrew Bible, "is ambivalent; it sustains its own antithesis."[96] In postbiblical literature, R. Yannai (third century) told his children not to bury him in white shrouds (*kelim*), which would indicate righteousness, nor in black shrouds, which would indicate wickedness, "but bury me in *ʾwlyyryn* shrouds," which the talmudic editors glossed as "red (*swmqy*)."[97] It would seem, then, that in the Animal Apocalypse red represents ambiguity or neutrality, and the color symbolism of Shem, Ham, and Japhet as white, black, and red is meant to represent the good, bad, and neutral, the same representation as given by Philo in his allegorical interpretation of Noah's sons.[98]

In any case, Ham's blackness in the Animal Apocalypse is meant as a metaphor for evil, as is the blackness of Cain and Esau, and does not indicate that Ham was seen as having a dark complexion. We can conclude with Tiller that there is nothing to support the pigmentation theory in the Animal Apocalypse.[99] In sum, therefore, the Animal Apocalypse gives no evidence for the belief that Ham was black. Nor is there any evidence that I could find at all in the Hellenistic period.

A natural place to look for the meaning of the name Ham is in the lists of Hebrew names and their meanings compiled by early Christian writers. In these patristic onomastic lists Ham is usually understood to mean "hot" or something similar. One list offers the meaning *nubilum* 'dark', but this list appears in two manuscripts that were written in the sixth to seventh century.[100] None of the earlier onomastica gives this meaning.

Another source of potential evidence in Christian literature might come from representations of the three magi who appear at Jesus' birth, for Christian writers often draw a parallel between the three magi and Noah's three sons. "The three magi, with gifts from the people to honor the Trinity, signify the three sons of Noah."[101] The basis for the analogy is the idea that the three figures in both cases represent all humanity in a new world. It would stand to reason, then, that if one of the magi was believed to have been Black, it would indicate that one of Noah's sons was considered to have been Black. According to Paul Kaplan, Hilary of Poitiers (d. 367/8) implied that one of the magi was Black when he commented on Ps 68/67:32, "Ambassadors shall come out of Egypt; Ethiopia shall soon stretch her hands to God," with the remark that "this was indeed fulfilled both by the coming of the Magi from the East and then by the coming of the holy spirit into the Apostles in the form of fire," and then followed it by a reference to the Ethiopian eunuch who was the first to convert to Christianity (Acts 8:26–40).[102] After Hilary, Kaplan next finds a trio of writers from the sixth century who suggest that "one of the Magi may have been an Ethiopian."[103] Hilary and the others, however, do not say that one of the magi was Black. They say, rather (having in mind the story in Acts), that "the Ethiopians, who represent the gentiles, were the first to come to Christ" (*ad Christum primum Aethiopes, id est gentiles, ingrediuntur*). The Ethiopians are mentioned in a magian context because the magi represent the entire gentile world and the Ethiopians represent the gentiles, following Origen's influential exegesis that took the blackness of the Ethiopians as a metaphor for sin, and thus the Ethiopians as gentiles, who, not having known God, live in sin.[104] This is clear from the immediately following words in Pseudo-Sedatus, one of these writers: "The first fruits of the gentiles are consecrated to acknowledgment of truth, the church of the gentiles preceded the synagogue of the Jews taking off the blackness of sin and putting on the whiteness of faith" (*gentium primitiae consecrantur in agnitionem veritatis, synagogam iudaeorum praecedit ecclesia gentium peccati exuta nigritudine et fidei induenda candore*).[105] Thus there is no indication of a Black magus, and consequently no implication of a Black Ham, from the work of Hilary and those sixth-century writers.[106]

The two rabbinic etiologies that speak of Ham's skin being darkened, which I discussed earlier, clearly indicate that Ham was considered to be dark-skinned. One of these etiologies ("sex-in-the dark") is reported in the name of R. Joseph of the fourth-century, and the second ("sex-in-the-ark"), which apparently assumes an etymological link between the name Ham and the meaning 'dark,' is tannaitic.[107] While the version of the tannaitic tradition preserved in the Babylonian Talmud says vaguely that "Ham was punished in his skin," the Palestinian Talmud specifically states "Ham [*ḥam*] went forth darkened [*mefuḥam*]," apparently punning on the name and thus implying an etymology of the name Ham from the Hebrew root *ḥwm* 'dark', 'brown', or 'black'. Does the Palestinian version with the "black" etymology represent a variant tannaitic tradition, thus originating not later than 220 C.E., or does it represent a later amoraic gloss of the original tannaitic statement (as recorded in the Babylonian Talmud) and therefore should be dated no later than ca. 370 C.E. when the Palestinian Talmud was redacted? With the evidence before us today, we cannot say. It is possible that the idea that "Ham [*ḥam*] went forth darkened [*mefuḥam*]" goes back to the tannaitic period, but given the textual situation before us today we cannot establish a sure dating before the redaction of the Palestinian Talmud.[108]

A passage in the work of the Samaritan Marqe may show that during the third and fourth centuries, when Marqe lived, Ham was considered to have been black. In commenting on the biblical Ten Plagues, Marqe says about the fourth plague (Ex 8:17): "The *ʿrb* came and thus a great darkness was revealed there. A very heavy *ʿrb* ruled over the Egyptians. A great darkness was revealed there. The partner of Ham [*šwtpyw dḥm*], destroyer of his children. 'And the land was destroyed because of the *ʿarob*' (Ex 8:20)—it ate their [i.e., the Egyptians'] children and they [the parents] remained alive."[109] In his commentary to *Tibat Marqe,* Ben-Ḥayyim notes on this passage that the Samaritan Aramaic *ʿrb* is ambiguous in meaning. However, because the *Samareitikon* (presumably a Greek translation of the Samaritan Pentateuch; quoted in Origen's *Hexapla*) translates biblical *ʿarob* as κορακα (κόραξ) 'raven', and because Marqe here emphasizes the darkness attendant to this plague, Ben Ḥayyim feels that Marqe's *ʿrb* means "raven."[110] Thus, he says, "partner of Ham" means that Ham and the raven are partners in their black color.[111]

The explanation "raven" is not without difficulties, for as Ben Ḥayyim points out, Marqe elsewhere describes the biblical plague of *ʿrb* as "large birds," which Ben Ḥayyim takes to mean "a mixture of birds," a meaning confirmed by a *piyyuṭ* of the Samaritan liturgist Aaron ben Meir (thirteenth–fourteenth century), which defines the *ʿarob* as "of different large kinds."[112] Despite this difficulty, I think it likely that Ben Ḥayyim's explanation of *ʿrb* as referring to the raven is correct, for it is precisely the raven that, according to a contemporaneous belief, is a "destroyer of his children." A common rabbinic folktale (also found in Islamic sources) speaks of the raven that abandons its newborn chicks, who would die were it not for God's intervention in providing them food.[113] Marqe is silently, subtly, and cleverly drawing on this folkloristic association to say that the biblical *ʿarob* 'raven' destroyed the children of the Egyptians. If this explanation is correct, it implies that Ham was considered to have been black in third or fourth-century Palestine, for, as Ben Ḥayyim thought, it is the color of the raven that makes it the "partner of Ham."[114] Thus, the earliest evidence we have for the notion that Ham was considered to be black dates certainly to the fourth century (R. Joseph; redaction of the Palestinian Talmud), probably to the third–fourth century (Marqe), and possibly to the second or third century (tannaitic etiology).

To summarize the results of this chapter, the biblical name Ham does not mean "dark, black" or "heat." The name is not related to the Egyptian *km(t)* 'black' nor to the Semitic words for "dark, black" or "heat." Ham, which begins with *ḫ,* derives from a different root than these words, which begin with *k* or *ḥ* respectively. When Hebrew was put into written form, however, the two different phonemes *ḫ* and *ḥ* were represented with one graphic sign (the letter ח) and, as a consequence, the distinction between the name *ḫam* (Ham) and words based on the roots *ḥwm* 'dark, black' and *ḥmm* 'heat' was lost, and it was eventually assumed that these words were related since they were all written with ח. We don't know when this assumption first occurred, but we begin to see the confusion with the word for "heat" in the first century and with the word for "dark, black" somewhere between the second and the fourth centuries.

ELEVEN

"HAM SINNED AND CANAAN WAS CURSED?!"

And Ham, the father of Canaan, saw the nakedness
of his father. . . . When Noah awoke from his wine
and knew what his youngest son had done to him,
he said, "Cursed be Canaan; a slave of slaves
shall he be to his brothers."
(Gen 9:22, 24–25, RSV)

THE BIBLICAL ACCOUNT of Noah's drunkenness and his curse of slavery is very clear about who was cursed. Although it was Ham who behaved improperly toward his father, Noah, it was not Ham whom Noah cursed. Rather, Noah cursed Ham's son Canaan. Why Canaan was cursed if it was Ham who sinned is a question that has been debated for well over the past two thousand years. Nevertheless, it was Canaan who was cursed. And yet, despite the Bible's explicit statement, we find writers who claim that although the curse was pronounced against Canaan, it affected Ham and/or all of Ham's children—not just Canaan. In what follows I cite and discuss the various authors—Jewish, Christian, and Muslim—who interpret the verse in this strange way, attempting to understand what motivated them to do so.

One reason for the interpretation of the biblical text so contrary to its plain sense would seem to lie in an attempt to explain the problematic passage: If Ham sinned, Ham should be punished. This obvious problem was even cause for an altered reading of "Ham" for "Canaan" ("Cursed be Ham") in some Greek and Latin manuscripts of the Bible, as well as some patristic quotations of the verse.[1] For the most part, however, the enigmatic biblical text spawned a number of extrabiblical explanations. Philo's solution—"virtually he does curse his son Ham in cursing Canaan"—is embedded in his allegorical interpretation of the Bible, which we have seen in the previous chapter: Ham represents potential (for evil), whereas Canaan represents action. Although the mind (soul) reasons, only the effects of such reasoning—that is, potential brought into action—are properly punished. In other words, Ham was indeed punished and biblical "Cannan" is really Ham in a different form.[2]

Josephus (first century C.E.) had a different solution to the question of why Canaan was cursed: "Noah, on learning what had passed, invoked a blessing on his other sons, but cursed—not Ham himself, because of his nearness of kin, but his posterity. The other descendants of Ham escaped the curse, but divine vengeance pursued the children of Chanan."[3] As T. W. Franxman says, by means of this interpretation Josephus obviates two unstated problems: not only why Ham was not cursed, but why the curse affected only Canaan and not also Ham's other sons. This second problem with the biblical story was not any less severe than the first, as noted by later writers.[4] Josephus's answer was that Canaan, in fact, was not the only one cursed; all of Ham's progeny were.[5] For reasons unknown, however, the curse stuck only to the Canaanites and the other sons of Noah managed to escape the curse.

The church father Justin Martyr (d. ca. 165) was also concerned with both problems. His solution: "The spirit of prophecy would not curse the son that had been by God blessed along with [his brothers]. But since the punishment of the sin would cleave to the whole descent (ὅλου τοῦ γένους) of the son that mocked at his father's nakedness, he made the curse originate with his son."[6] Justin claims that Ham could not be cursed since he had already been blessed by God (Gen 9:1). The curse was therefore transmitted to (all) his descendants instead, with Canaan alone being mentioned in the Bible, apparently, as a sort of representative of Ham's descendants.[7]

The argument that Ham could not be cursed because he had already been blessed by God is very commonly found, appearing as early as Qumran and then later in rabbinic and patristic literature.[8] Here is the way it reads in the Qumran fragment: "And he said, 'Cursed be Canaan. . . .' And he did not curse Ham, but only his son, because God had blessed the sons of Noah." The rabbinic text is only slightly more expansive: "Ham sinned and Canaan was cursed?! . . . R. Judah [second century] said, 'Since it is written, "And God blessed Noah and his sons" (Gen 9:1), and there cannot be a curse where a blessing has been given, therefore He said "Cursed be Canaan, etc."'"[9] Does this mean that the curse was transferred to Canaan and that Ham was unaffected by it or does it mean that, in some way, Ham was also affected by the curse although it was pronounced only against Canaan? Some ancient writers understood that indeed Ham was affected. The Syriac church father Ephrem (d. 373), for example, citing "others," says that the curse of slavery was pronounced against Canaan, since Ham had been blessed, but fell also upon his father Ham.[10] On the other hand, in the Qumran and rabbinic sources, the explanation is laconic and gives no indication that Ham was involved in the curse. These texts merely say that since Ham could not be cursed, the curse fell on Canaan.

In addition to Ephrem, references to Ham being cursed with slavery or being affected by the curse of slavery are found in patristic literature from the second century, and commonly from the fourth century, onward. Irenaeus (b. ca. 150) quotes a "presbyter" who says that Ham laughed at his father's shame and came under the curse.[11] Hippolytus of Rome (d. 235) says that "because Ham saw his father naked and mocked him, he was cursed."[12] Pachomius, one of the desert fathers (d. 346/7), says that Ham was cursed along with his descendants;[13] Ambrose (d. 397), that Ham "was condemned by his father's curse."[14] Note also Ambrose's remark that "he who mocked [Noah] for being naked, himself remained bound by the reproach of everlasting shame," which probably refers to the shame of slavery.[15] Similarly Epiphanius (d. 404): "[Noah's] mocker received the curse."[16] "Ambrosiaster" also speaks of "Ham the son of Noah, who first deservedly received the name of slave";[17] Chrysostom (d. 407), of "the son of Noah, when for a freeman he became a slave";[18] Sulpicius Severus (d. ca. 420), of Ham who was cursed by Noah; Vincent of Lerins (d. before 450), of the curse that fell on Ham and his descendants; and Augustine (d. 430), of Ham who "was cursed through his son."[19]

If we look at later versions of the biblical story in Christian works not authored by the fathers of the church, we find the same thing: Ham, not Canaan, was cursed. Both Caedmon, the early English poet (seventh century), and the Anglo-Saxon poem *Genesis,* which may be from the hand of Caedmon, have Noah curse Ham, not Canaan.[20] So also a Latin version of the *Acts of Andrew and Matthew,* the *Recensio Vaticana* (dating to the seventh or eighth century) refers to "Ham cursed by his father,"[21] as does *The Book of Adam and Eve, Also Called The Conflict of Adam and Eve with Satan* (not before the seventh century).[22] The ninth-century version of the *Historia Britonum* by Nennius speaks of "Cam the son who was cursed for ridiculing his father."[23] In a ninth-century riddle book, the question is posed as to the origin of slaves and the answer given is "from Ham."[24] Also the *Kebra Nagast,* the Ethiopian national epic, in recounting the biblical story has Ham, not Canaan, cursed with slavery: "[Shem] was blessed by Noah, saying, 'Be God to thy brother.' And to Ham he said, 'Be servant to thy brother.'" And, "By the will of God, the whole of the kingdom of the world was given to the seed of Shem, and slavery to the seed of Ham, and the handicrafts to the seed of Japhet."[25]

Exegetes who understood that Ham was cursed assumed that all of Ham's descendants inherited the curse—that is, Egypt, Kush, Puṭ, and Canaan, and not just the line of Canaan as the Bible would have it. Indeed, this notion is common in patristic and rabbinic literature, especially in regard to Egypt. Beginning in the second and third centuries we find Christian literature referring to the Egyptians as a cursed people. Tertullian (b. ca. 155) does not mention the nature of the curse, only saying that biblical "Egypt" sometimes symbolizes the whole world marked by superstition and "malediction" (*superstitioneis et maledictionis elogio*).[26] The nature of the curse, however, and indeed the connection to Ham's punishment is made explicit by Origen (d. ca. 253):

> But Pharao easily reduced the Egyptian people to bondage to himself, nor is it written that he did this by force. For the Egyptians are prone to a degenerate life and quickly sink to every slavery of the vices. Look at the origin of the race and you will discover that their father Cham, who had laughed at his father's nakedness, deserved a judgment of this kind, that his son Chanaan should be a servant to his brothers.[27]

Origen claims that the Egyptians are slavish by nature; thus Pharaoh easily reduced them to bondage. The proof for this claim comes from the story of Ham, whose son was cursed with slavery. That the son who was cursed was Canaan and not Egypt does not seem to bother Origen. Perhaps Origen's thinking was similar to Justin's: Canaan was mentioned in Scripture only as a representative of all the descendants of Ham, including Egypt. In any case, Origen says that the Egyptians are slaves, and he relates that to Ham's sin against Noah.[28]

Just as the Fathers, so too the Rabbis often assume that all the descendants of Ham, and especially the Egyptians, are slaves:

> "[I am the Lord, your God, who took you out of the land of Egypt] from the house of slavery" (Ex 20:2)—R. Tanḥum b. Ḥanilai in the name of R. Berakhiah: Only Canaan was cursed with slavery, "[And he said: Cursed be Canaan], a slave of slaves shall he be to his brothers" (Gen 9:25). Nonetheless, how do we know that *all the families of Ham are called slaves?* For it says, " . . . out of the land of Egypt, from the house of slaves."[29]

Based on the description of Egypt in Ex 20:2 as "a house of slavery," literally "a house of slaves" (*ʿavadim*), and reading the phrase as a subjective genitive rather than an objective genitive, R. Berakhiah understands "slaves" to refer to the Egyptians rather than the Israelites.[30] He thus concludes that, although only the line of Canaan was cursed with slavery, the term "slave" can refer to all the descendants of Ham, of which Egypt was one line.

Several other midrashic passages, although not relying—at least, not explicitly—on the Ex 20:2 prooftext, yet assume that the Egyptians had been cursed with slavery. *Lamentations Rabba:* "'Slaves ruled over us' (Lam 5:8)—This refers to the Egyptians."[31] A *yelamedenu* text has Moses declare that Pharaoh is a slave, "for it says: 'And the children of Ham are Kush and Egypt [and Phut and Canaan]" (Ex 10:6).[32] The one adduced biblical text (Ex 10:6) in this midrash merely proves that Egypt was the son of Ham. In other words, the midrash takes it as a given that all of Ham's descendants were affected by the curse and seeks to prove that Egypt was one of those descendants. Similarly, *Tanḥuma,* without any prooftext, assumes that Pharaoh was a slave.[33] Lastly, *Pirqei de-Rabbi Eliezer* has Jacob say, in debating whether to go to Egypt: "Shall I go to an unclean land, among slaves, the children of Ham?"[34]

The notion that the Egyptians were slaves became so strongly embedded in rabbinic exegesis that a later medieval writer used it—instead of the explicit biblical text!—to prove that the Canaanites were also slaves. Speaking of Canaan, David b. Amram of Aden (thirteenth or fourteenth century) says: "And the curse was implanted in him for all future generations, for you find that when the Israelites left Egypt God was revealed to them and he said to them, 'I am the Lord your God who brought you out of the land of Egypt, from the house of slavery.'"[35] David says that Canaan was eternally enslaved and his proof is from a text showing that the Egyptians were enslaved. This statement makes sense only if we assume that all of Ham's descendants were cursed with slavery so that the enslavement of one descendant (Egypt) could offer proof for the enslavement of another descendant (Canaan).

These texts, whether explicitly relying on Ex 20:2 or not, assume that the Egyptians were slaves because all of Ham's descendants were affected by the curse. The following rabbinic text assumes that the Kushites were slaves for the same reason: "R. Akiba said: [The descendants of Noah] threw off the kingdom of Heaven and set as king for themselves Nimrod, a slave son of a slave, for *all the descendants of Ham* [*bnei ḥam*] are slaves."[36] Nimrod, son of Kush, is called a "slave, son of a slave." Kush was a slave because as a son of Ham he was affected by Noah's curse.[37] Other texts, when speaking of slaves, refer to them as "the descendants of Ham" rather than "the descendants of Canaan." Such is the case in the following text from *Tanḥuma:*

> "And he said: Cursed be Canaan, [a slave of slaves. . . .]"—R. Shimʿon b. Laqish said: But also the descendants of Shem were slaves, for it says, "If your brother Hebrew, male or female, be sold to you" (Deut 15:12)? The descendants of Shem go free after six years, as it says, "On the seventh year he shall go free" (Ex 21:2), whereas *the descendants of Ham* [*mi-shel ḥam*] do not go free, for it says, "If he shall say to you: I will not leave you. . . . You shall take the awl . . . and he will be your slave forever. (Deut 15:16–17)[38]

Another example may be seen in a midrashic commentary to Lev 16:22, which states that the expiatory goat sent into the wilderness would go to "the land of the Hamites" (*ereṣ bnei ḥam*). The biblical spur for this exegesis is the "land of the *gezerah*" mentioned in the verse as the place to which the goat was sent: "Why did [God] level this decree (*gezerah*) against the Hamites (*bnei ḥam*) rather than against all the other nations of the world? The Sages said: In order for God to fulfill Noah's curse against *the descendants of Ham* [*bnei ḥam*], for he said, 'Cursed be Canaan.'"[39] Here too Noah is said to have cursed the "descendants of Ham" despite the fact that the prooftext quoted states "Cursed be Canaan"! Apparently the underlying thinking is that "all the descendants of Ham were cursed . . . and it was only because God had previously blessed Ham that the [Torah] did not say explicitly that he was cursed."[40] Another midrashic text, which does not mention either Ham or Canaan, implies that all the descendants of Ham (or Ham himself, or both) were affected by the curse: "Just as He cursed the earth on account of the snake, as it says 'May the earth be cursed because of you" (Gen 3:17), so *a third of the world was cursed* on account of wine, as it says, 'And Noah awoke from his wine. . . . (Gen 9:24).'"[41] "A third of the world" must refer to Ham, who together with his two brothers, Shem and Japheth, divided the world among them. Whether the intention is to Ham himself or to his descendants or to both is not clear. What is certain is that in this passage the curse is not restricted to the descendants of Canaan as in the Bible.

Other texts specifically state that Noah's curse affected both Ham and all his descendants. In the following *Tanḥuma* midrash neither of the "slave" verses (Gen 9:25 and Ex 20:2) is interpreted. Indeed the context is altogether different, but in the course of discussion we learn that Ham and all his descendants were cursed. "Our Rabbis taught: Since Ham saw the nakedness of his father, although he did not curse him, *he and his descendants were nevertheless distanced* [*nitraḥeq*] forever, how much more so will this occur to one who curses his father."[42] "Distanced" means distanced by slavery as we can see in the parallel midrash in *Exodus Rabba*, which explicitly mentions slavery: "God said: Ham the father of Canaan did not hit, but only looked at [his father]. Now *he and his descendants are slaves forever.* How much more so one who curses or hits his father."[43] The references to cursing and hitting derive from Ex 21:15 and Lev 20:9, which require the death penalty for these acts committed against a parent. Ham did neither, yet he and his descendants were cursed with eternal slavery. How much greater, then, the punishment for cursing or hitting a parent.[44]

Perhaps the same midrash is echoed in a text found among the Genizah fragments, which includes Ham and his descendants in the curse of slavery. In any case, it too sees Ham and his descendants affected by the curse: "He sinned with his eyes and was made as an abject slave [*ke-ʿeved meshuʿebad*], *he and his descendants* until the end of time. . . . And who is this? Ham."[45]

We see a curse of slavery on all the descendants of Ham also in a Jewish nonrabbinic text, the pre-eleventh-century *Chronicles of Moses* (*Divrei ha-Yamim shel Mosheh*), which describes the story of Moses' Ethiopian campaign with great elaboration.[46] From this source, the story was incorporated into the later medieval anthologies *Sefer ha-Yashar, Sefer ha-Zikhronot,* and *Yalquṭ Shimʿoni.*[47] In these accounts, the king of Kush, Ki(r)kanos, asks

Moses' help in suppressing a rebellion.[48] Moses was successful and subsequently ruled over Kush for forty years. Upon the death of Kirkanos, the army declares Moses his successor and gives him Kirkanos's widow to wed.

> But Moses feared the Lord, the God of his fathers, and he did not come into her, nor did he even turn his eyes to her, for he remembered that Abraham had sworn his servant, Eliezer, to an oath saying "Do not take a wife for my son Isaac from among the daughters of the Canaanites" (Gen 24:3). And so too did Isaac command Jacob "Do not take a wife from among the daughters of the Canaanites" (Gen 28:1), and do not marry with any of the descendants of Ham, for the Lord, our God, has made Ham the son of Noah, his children, and all their issue, as slaves to the descendants of Shem and the descendants of Japheth and to their issue after them forever. Therefore Moses did not turn his heart or his eyes to Kirkanos's [former] wife all the days he ruled over Kush.[49]

There is no biblical proscription against marrying descendants of Ham. That is why the author of this text felt the need to add the explanation of slavery. The earlier rabbinic explanation for Moses' abstinence from sex as due to his increased state of holiness has been replaced by a new explanation: Moses would not marry a slave, and his Kushite wife was a slave since she descended from Ham who was cursed with slavery.[50]

The same substitution of Ham for Canaan occurs in another medieval nonrabbinic work, the Ben Sira cycle of stories. It will be recalled that in the midrashic exposition of Prov 17:2 ("A servant who deals wisely . . . "), Eliezer, the servant of Abraham, is said to have preferred serving Abraham, since he was doomed to a life of slavery anyway and he would rather serve Abraham than an idol worshiper.[51] The unstated reason why Eliezer was doomed to slavery is that he was a Canaanite, and Canaan was cursed with eternal slavery (Gen 9:25). Remarkably, however, in the incorporation of this midrash in the medieval Ben Sira stories, Canaan becomes Ham, as the one cursed with slavery:

> Eliezer the servant of Abraham said, "I am a descendant of Ham whom Noah his father cursed to be a slave forever. It is better that I serve [Abraham] forever rather than an idol worshiper." (Version A)

> Eliezer the servant of Abraham was a [descendant] of Ham. When Noah cursed him and said "May you be a slave of slaves to your brothers (Gen 9:25)," Eliezer said, "I am doomed to be a slave in any case." He went and enslaved himself to Abraham our father. (Version B)[52]

Eliezer is said to be a descendant of Ham who was cursed, even thought it was Canaan who was cursed, and version B even quotes the verse from Genesis in which Canaan is cursed with slavery!

Just as in Christian and Jewish sources, so too in Islamic sources do we find that it was not Canaan whom Noah cursed with slavery, but Ham instead of or in addition to Canaan. So, for example, Ṭabarī (d. 923) quoting Ibn Isḥāq (d. 768), Masʿūdī (tenth century), and Dimashqī (thirteenth century).[53] Ham appears as the recipient of the curse so regularly, that the only Arabic author Gerhard Rotter could find who specifically limits the curse to Canaan is Yaʿqūbī (d. ca. 900). In all others all the descendants of Ham were enslaved.[54]

In all these texts, whether Jewish, Christian, or Islamic, whether from the East or the West, Ham and/or Ham's descendants replace Canaan as the recipient of Noah's curse. This in spite of the biblical text to the contrary, and sometimes quite blatantly, as in the quotation above from *Pitron Torah:* " . . . in order for God to fulfill Noah's curse against the descendants of Ham, for he said, 'Cursed be Canaan.' " How could this be? How could a tradition that stands opposed to the plain sense of the biblical text become so well established among biblically based societies? It is true that some authors held up the words of Scripture and emphasized that it was only Canaan who was cursed. As one of the tosafists says, "Ham, who didn't do anything, was neither cursed nor blessed. . . . He cursed [Canaan] alone."[55] But their very emphasis only shows how well accepted was the notion that Ham and his progeny were the ones cursed, contrary to the Bible.

I think that there are four factors operating simultaneously that account for this counterbiblical interpretation: explanation, error, etymology, and environment. In regard to the first, it is clear that the enigmatic biblical verses demanded explanation, for it made no sense that Canaan was cursed for his father's sin. The interpretations of Philo and Josephus are clearly attempts to reconcile the problematic texts. Probably the same can be said for another line of Jewish exegesis, introduced much later by Saadia Gaon (d. 942) and apparently based on an Arabic custom of calling a father by the name of his best-known son. "Canaan," therefore, in the biblical curse means "father of Canaan."[56] In the words of *Numbers Rabba,* accepting Saadia's explanation, " 'Cursed be Canaan'—This was Ham . . . and he was called 'the father of Canaan' (Gen 9:22). This is the way they used to curse."[57]

As we saw, the most common exegesis, found in Qumran, rabbinic, and patristic writings was that Canaan was cursed because Ham had been blessed previously, and he therefore could not be cursed. Victor Aptowitzer argued that this interpretation assumed that although the curse was thus shifted to Canaan, Ham was nonetheless affected by the curse. Aptowitzer quoted Ephrem and other church fathers who made this claim explicitly, although when it came to the Rabbis all Aptowitzer could say was that their exegesis "too must be interpreted to mean that the curse undoubtedly applied to Ham likewise."[58] Indeed, it would be very strange for the Rabbis to let the guilty (Ham) go free and assign punishment to the innocent (Canaan) because of some technicality. Samuel Yaffe Ashkenazi (sixteenth century) put the matter bluntly when he protested against the midrashic explanation that Ham could not be cursed because God had already blessed him: "Nevertheless, why punish Canaan? He didn't sin!"[59] Ham must have been punished. But Aptowitzer could find no statement to that effect. It is, in fact, remarkable that in all the rabbinic exegeses explaining why Canaan was cursed, nowhere does it say *explicitly* that Ham was also affected. Yet, we have seen that it is often assumed. Nonetheless, Aptowitzer's assumption was right, although he provides no proof. The unstated rabbinic exegesis is this: *Cursed be Canaan; a slave of slaves shall he be to his brothers*—The curse couldn't be pronounced on Ham because he had been blessed. So Noah cursed Canaan by saying not "May you be a slave" but "May you be a slave of slaves," understanding the genitive (*of*) as indicating a biological relationship (son of the father) and thus implying that Canaan's father, Ham, was to be a slave. The exegetical fulcrum is the expression *a slave of slaves.*[60] If Canaan was to be a slave, then his father Ham, by virtue of the language "slave of slaves," would have to be one too. The sentence "Ham couldn't be cursed because he had been blessed" does not mean that Ham couldn't be cursed, but that a curse could not be pronounced against him. Canaan was thus cursed explicitly and Ham implicitly. Explanation then, spurred by the textual difficulty, was one factor in the claim that Ham was cursed despite what the Bible said.

There is also the strong possibility that many writers simply erred in claiming Ham as the one cursed, the result of confusion arising from the enigmatic biblical text. There is considerable evidence that such mistakes occurred. Among eastern Christian writers, Aphrahat (fourth century, Persia) in his *Demonstrations* 14.7 and 14.25 states that Ham became a slave to his brothers, although elsewhere (*Demonstrations* 3.8) he says that it was Canaan who was the recipient of Noah's curse.[61] The same confusion is found in Narsai, the fifth-century Syriac church father (the most important after Ephrem). He quotes the Bible and has Canaan as the recipient of Noah's curse, but he also says elsewhere that the curse fell on Ham: "[Noah] made Ham a servant to his brothers, bound to serve them."[62] We find the same fluctuation much later in Eutychius (= Saʿīd ibn Biṭrīq), the Alexandrian Melkite patriarch (d. 940). In his *Book of the Demonstration,* he quotes the biblical verse as: "Cursed be Canaan; a servant who serves his brethren shall he be. And he said, Blessed be the Lord God of Shem; and Canaan shall be his servant."[63] However, in his *Annales,* he quotes the verse as: "Cursed be Ham and may he be a servant to his brothers."[64] And even in the *Book of the Demonstration* one manuscript (MS Sinai) reads "Ham" for the first "Canaan."[65] The medieval Jewish exegete, Baḥya b.

Asher (thirteenth century), when explaining the verses in Genesis, says that Canaan alone was cursed, but when he discusses Ex 20:2 he implies that Ham was cursed.[66]

It is not surprising that the biblical text caused such confusion. Because Ham sinned, it is natural to think that Ham was punished. Anyone quoting the story of Noah's drunkenness from memory is likely to substitute Ham for Canaan as the one cursed. Perhaps the best example of such an error may be cited from a work much closer to our own time. In 1861 the abolitionist rabbi Gustav Gottheil delivered a discourse, subsequently published, in which he, undoubtedly in error, changed the biblical text: "Was it not when Cham, the son of Noah, for his anti-filial and utterly unnatural conduct, brought down upon himself the curse of his outraged parent? 'Cursed be Cham; a servant of servants shall he be unto his brethren.'"[67] Gottheil was answering Morris Raphall, a rabbi from New York, who had delivered a proslavery sermon declaring that Blacks, as Ham's descendants, had been condemned to eternal slavery. The last thing Gottheil would want to say would be that Ham, the Blacks' ancestor, was cursed with slavery. On the contrary, abolitionist writers often argued that the Bible specifies Canaan, not Ham, as the one cursed. Gottheil simply got confused. Even scholars today make the mistake. Mahmoud Zouber, a scholar of Arabic literature, said that "après la Bible, Nūḥ (Noé) avait maudit son fils Ḥām (Cham)."[68] Michael Banton, a sociologist who studies race and ethnicity, speaks of "the curse upon Ham and his descendants," Robert Graves, a novelist, and Raphael Patai, an anthropologist, refer to the biblical account that "sentences Ham to perpetual servitude under his elder brothers," and Anthony Pagden, in his work on comparative ethnology, mentions the curse on Ham, although in a footnote he quotes the biblical text referring to Canaan.[69]

In addition to factors of explanation and error, however, we must also look at the influence of the social environment in which the early-century writers lived. We have seen that at this time in the Near East and in the Roman world the black African was becoming increasingly identified as a slave.[70] Once this equation was made, it forced a reinterpretation of the biblical story from Canaan to Ham as the ancestor of the slaves. Ham, not Canaan, was the father of the dark-skinned peoples of the world. Even according to Islamic traditions, which indeed saw Canaan as the ancestor of various groups of black Africans, Ham was the ancestor of other dark-skinned (*sūdān*) peoples, such as the Sind, Hind, Barbars/Berbers, Copts, and the Kushites (*Ḥabasha*).[71]

A final, and strong, impetus for the reinterpretation of Scripture was the etymological factor, for by the time the Black was becoming identified as a slave, it was understood (incorrectly) that the very name Ham meant "black, dark."[72] Not long afterward, in the seventh century, we begin to see the expressions *banū ḥām* (Arabic) and *bnei ḥam* (Hebrew) being used as synonyms for "black African."

In sum, in regard to Noah's curse, four factors were at play during the first six or seven centuries of the Common Era: explanation—an attempt to make sense of the Bible; error—a mistaken recollection of the biblical text; environment—a social structure in which the Black had become identified as slave; and etymology—a mistaken assumption that Ham meant "black, dark." The combination of these factors was lethal: Ham, the father of the black African, was cursed with eternal slavery. The Curse of Ham was born.

TWELVE

THE CURSE OF HAM

First, let her Face with some deep Poys'nous Paint,
Discolour'd to a horrid black be stain'd.
Then say 'twas as a mark of Vengeance given,
That she was blasted by the Hand of Heaven.
—Elkanah Settle, *The Empress of Morocco,* 1687

THE CURSE OF HAM is the assumed biblical justification for a curse of eternal slavery imposed on Black people, and Black people alone. Earlier we examined various Near Eastern curse-of-blackness etiologies accounting for the existence of dark-skinned people in a lighter-skinned world. We saw, too, that the Greeks had their own etiologies as well as an environmental explanation to account for the phenomenon of dark-skinned people. Other etiological explanations are found elsewhere.[1] What distinguishes the Curse of Ham from a curse of blackness is the link between dark skin and slavery. In this chapter I attempt to trace the development of a Curse of Ham, that is, the idea of a biblically mandated curse of slavery imposed on black Africans.

The Bible makes no mention of a curse of blackness; it knows only a curse of slavery. Pseudo-Philo (first or second century), on the other hand, records an etiology explaining the origin of different skin colors but does not mention the biblical slave etiology.[2] Rabbinic sources that record a curse-of-blackness etiology distinguish between it and the biblical curse of slavery. This can be seen in the transmission of two traditions by R. Huna in the name of R. Joseph (fourth century) in *Genesis Rabba,* one speaking of a curse of slavery on Canaan and the other of a curse of dark skin on Ham.[3] We do not find a link between skin color and slavery in the Jewish sources of antiquity and late antiquity.

Nor is a link found in early Christian sources. The church father Origen does mention skin color and slavery together, but the connection would seem to be incidental. In one of his homilies on Genesis he explains the servile condition of the Egyptians under Pharaoh:

> But Pharao easily reduced the Egyptian people to bondage to himself, nor is it written that he did this by force. For the Egyptians are prone to a degenerate life and quickly sink to every slavery of the vices. Look at the origin of the race and you will discover that their father Cham, who had laughed at his fa-

> ther's nakedness, deserved a judgment of this kind, that his son Chanaan should be a servant to his brothers, in which case the condition of bondage would prove the wickedness of his conduct. Not without merit, therefore, does the discolored posterity imitate the ignobility of the race [*Non ergo immerito ignobilitatem generis decolor posteritas imitatur*].[4]

Based on the biblical account in Genesis 9, Origen says that due to Ham's sin, his descendants were punished with everlasting servitude of various kinds. He seems to include all of Ham's descendants, including Egypt, in the curse pronounced against Canaan, as I have shown in the previous chapter.[5] Origen describes the Egyptians as dark-skinned (*decolor*), but he does not say that their skin color was a result of Ham's sin. It is not the Egyptians' *decolor* that "imitate[s] the ignobility of the race," but their bondage and "slavery of the vices." *Decolor* is merely meant as a description of the Egyptians, not as an external manifestation of their ancestor's sin. There is thus no explicit statement that dark-skinned people are meant to be enslaved by Noah's curse on Canaan. Nevertheless, one must ask why Origen chose to mention the Egyptians' skin color while describing their bondage. Even if he shared the common view of the Egyptians as dark-skinned, why was it relevant to mention it here?[6]

The answer, I think, can be deduced from Origen's extensive exegetical treatment of dark skin elsewhere in the Bible. He explains the dark color of the maiden of Song 1:5 by saying that the darkening is due to a prior sinful condition, and, using the same language as he does in the Egyptian homily just quoted, Origen compares the maiden of Song of Songs to Moses' Ethiopian wife who is "black because of the ignobility [*ignobilitate*] of birth."[7] These statements are part of Origin's overarching exegetical construction that interpreted dark-skinned biblical personalities as allegories for people living in sin or for the sinful soul.[8] For Origen, dark skin was metaphorically equated with sin, and it thus served his purpose in this passage to describe the Egyptians as *decolor*. Thus, although Origen's exegesis may be a disquieting adumbration of things to come, it is not a Curse of Ham.

Indeed, it is difficult to see how such a notion could develop out of the biblical text. In the Bible Ham is the father of four sons: three (Miṣrayim/Egypt, Puṭ, Kush) who became the ancestors of various dark-skinned African people, and Canaan. Only Canaan, the nonblack ancestor of the Canaanites, was cursed with slavery. Given this scenario, there are two ways that one could, by deft manipulation of the text, link blackness and slavery: either push the curse of slavery back onto a genealogically and etymologically black Ham, or make the biblically enslaved Canaan the ancestor of black Africans. In the previous chapter we saw the earliest stages in the development of the first alternative. When Bible readers began to see

Ham in place of Canaan in Noah's curse, we have an implicit link between blackness and slavery. As the Black became increasingly identified as slave the link became increasingly explicit, thus serving to maintain—by divine mandate—the social order.

We first see this kind of explicit link between skin color and slavery in Near Eastern sources beginning in the seventh century. Some writers claim that Noah pronounced a dual curse of slavery and blackness, although the Bible mentions only slavery. Others keep the biblical story of a single curse of slavery but, they say, as a consequence the one cursed turned black. Still others would have a curse of slavery pronounced on someone who is already black. The common denominator of all these variations is the linkage of blackness and slavery.[9]

The tradition that Noah uttered a dual curse against his son Ham, cursing him with blackness and with slavery at the same time, is very widespread in Islamic sources. An example is afforded by Kisāʾī: "'May God change your complexion and may your face turn black!' And that very instant his face did turn black. . . . 'May He make bondswomen and slaves of Ham's progeny until the Day of Resurrection!'"[10] Similarly, a dual curse is mentioned by ʿAṭāʾ (d. 732/3) as quoted by Ṭabarī (d. 923)[11] and Thaʿlabī (d. 1036),[12] an anonymous opinion recorded by Ṭabarī,[13] a work called *Akhbār al-zamān* of the tenth or eleventh century,[14] "genealogists" recorded by Ibn Khaldūn (d. 1406),[15] and *The Book of the Zanj*, which claims that the story of the dual curse is widely found in history books, as is recorded in the "Book of the Gold Ingot" (*Sabāʾik adh-dhahab*).[16] The belief in a dual curse continues into modern times.[17]

The variation on the theme, in which the curse of slavery causes an incidental change of skin color may be illustrated by Rashīd al-Dīn (d. 1318): "Noah cursed Ham with slavery and his anger caused Ham to turn black. Noah's anger was then abated, but he asked God that Ham and his descendants be black."[18] Another variation of the Curse of Ham has only a curse of slavery, but the one being cursed is already black. The following, recorded by C. Snouck Hurgronje from Abyssinian slavewomen of Mecca in the late nineteenth century, serves also to show the continuity of these traditions into modern times: "Very widespread is the naive tale that Adam and Eve were going about naked in Paradise when of all the girls present only the Abyssinian girls and some negresses laughed at them, and therefore they were turned into a slave race."[19]

The common denominator in all these stories is a linkage of black skin color and slavery. Precisely when and where the earliest of these traditions began to appear—that is, in seventh-century Arabia—is when the Black became strongly identified with the slave class in the Near East, after the Islamic conquest of Africa. The two independent Near Eastern etiologies of slavery and dark skin were joined to create a new etiology of the Black slave, thus underpinning the new social order.[20] Etiologies explain existing phenomena. A new phenomenon will spawn a new etiology.

The second way one could link blackness and slavery is to blacken the biblically enslaved Canaan. This alternative is commonly found among Near Eastern writers, both Christian and Muslim. Ibn al-Ṭaiyib (Baghdad, d. 1043), a Nestorian Christian, put it this way: "The curse of Noah affected the posterity of Canaan who were killed by Joshua son of Nun. At the moment of the curse, Canaan's body became black and the blackness spread out among them."[21] In the continuation of the passage, Ibn al-Ṭaiyib makes it clear that the nature of the curse was one of eternal slavery for the posterity of Ham, although Ham himself was unaffected by the curse. The ninth-century bishop of Hedhatha, Ishodad of Merv, records a similar tradition (although he rejects it), as does the thirteenth-century Christian Ibn al-ʿIbrī (Bar Hebraeus).[22] This approach is also commonly found in Islamic sources, which make Canaan the ancestor of the various black African peoples,[23] or relate him, as son or father, to Kush.[24] This alternative method of linking blackness and slavery was not constructed ex nihilo.

An unknown Samaritan, called by scholars "Pseudo-Eupolemus," living in the mid-second century B.C.E., records the following:[25]

> The Babylonians say that first there was Belus (who was Kronos), and that from him was born Belus and Canaan. This one fathered Canaan, the father of the Phoenicians. To him was born a son, Chum, whom the Greeks called Asbolus, the father of the Ethiopians and the brother of Mestraeim, the father of the Egyptians.[26]

There are several obvious difficulties with this text, which I have translated literally, but we shall be concerned only with those issues relevant to a Ham-Canaan-Kush relationship. (1) Who is *Chum* (variant: *Chun*)? Most scholars believe that the name is a corruption of Chus (possibly by means of an accusative *Chun*), that is, Kush.[27] Two facts lead to this conclusion. First, the statement that "Chum [is] the father of the Ethiopians and the brother of Mestraeim [= Miṣrayim], the father of the Egyptians" accords with the biblical genealogy that makes Kush the father of the Ethiopians and the brother of Miṣrayim (Egypt). Second, in Greek *asbolos* means "soot," the color of which well describes the father of the dark-skinned Ethiopians.[28] (2) But if *Chum* is Kush, then Pseudo-Eupolemus does not agree with the Bible, which makes Ham the father of Kush. In our text Canaan is made the father of Kush. For this reason, some would emend the first reference of Canaan (*Chanaan*) to Ham (*Cham*).[29]

This emendation is based on a perceived need to bring Pseudo-Eupolemus in line with the Bible. Robert Doran, however, notes that the text need not accord with the biblical account, since it purports to be a Babylonian genealogy, not a biblical genealogy.[30] In a similar way René Dussaud long ago argued for a Phoenician origin for this text.[31] Support for the non-biblical character of Pseudo-Eupolemus's account may come from Greek genealogies. In Greek mythology Kronos's son Zeus had a son Epaphus, who had a daughter Libya, (i.e., Africa), whose son Belus sired Egypt and Nubia among others. (In a different genealogy Zeus's grandchildren included the Blacks and the Ethiopians.) Epaphus was called κελαινός 'black' or 'dark', and in one papyrus fragment Zeus is described as κάρβανος αἰθός 'coal' and 'burnt black, sooty'.[32] Not only is Kronos the ancestor of the Egyptians and Ethiopians in both the Pseudo-Eupolemus and the Greek genealogies, but some of the intermediary links in both (Zeus, Epaphus, Chum/Asbolus) are characterized as sooty or black. Furthermore, although Canaan is not mentioned in the Greek genealogy, Libya's other son, Agenor, was the ancestor of the Phoenicians, just as Canaan is said to be the ancestor of the Phoenicians in the Pseudo-Eupolemus genealogy. Clearly Pseudo-Eupolemus's account is influenced by Greek sources, as we can see from the names Kronos and Asbolus. I do not mean to equate Canaan with any Greek character, as some have done; I merely want to use the parallels from Greek myth to argue that Pseudo-Eupolemus's genealogy need not accord with the Bible. It reflects, rather, an extrabiblical Near Eastern tradition (whether it be Eupolemus or Pseudo-Eupolemus), according to which Canaan was seen as the father of the Ethiopians and/or the Blacks, exactly as the Arabic sources claim.[33] In other words, the Islamic sources preserved this counterbiblical tradition.[34]

And not only the Arabic sources. The Eastern Christian work, *The Cave of Treasures,* whose composition goes back probably to the fourth, and perhaps the third, century, makes Canaan the ancestor of the dark-skinned peoples, that is, the Egyptians, the Kushites, the Indians, and the Musdaye, and, according to the Arabic version, "other blacks [*sūdān*]," or according to the Ethiopic version, "all those whose skin color is black."[35] Thus we have a counterbiblical Near Eastern tradition preserved in the Samaritan (?) Pseudo-Eupolemus, the Christian *Cave of Treasures,* and a number of Islamic writers, according to which Canaan was genealogically linked to many dark-skinned people, especially of Africa. Because this genealogy goes back to, at least, the second century B.C.E., well before there is any evidence of an identification of the Black as slave, which seems to begin in the first century C.E.,[36] we cannot argue that the genealogy must have its origins in a time and place in which the Black was assumed to be a slave. In other words, it was not created to justify Black enslavement. But it was the ancient raw material out of which was fashioned a link (via Canaan) between Black and slave. Like the dual curse of blackness and slavery on Ham, it drew on preexisting traditions. In a biblically anchored society in which the Black had become identified as slave, a genealogy that linked

Canaan (the biblical slave) with the Black would well serve that society's interests.

The various recensions of the *Cave of Treasures* provide us a fascinating look at the interplay between the two justifications (via Ham or Canaan) for Black slavery. The work explains that Canaan invented musical instruments, by means of which sin had multiplied in the world through song and "lewd play and . . . lasciviousness." In the earliest, Syriac, version of the work, it then continues:

> And Canaan was cursed because he had dared to do this, and his descendants were reduced to slavery, and they are the Egyptians [*egupṭaye*], the Kushites [*kušaye*], the Indians [*hinduye*], and the Musdaye [*musdaye*; variants: Muṣraye, Musraye, etc.].[37]

The author draws on the ancient nonbiblical tradition of a Canaan-black genealogy and relates it to the biblical curse of slavery pronounced on Canaan. This is even clearer in the Arabic and Ethiopic versions of the work, which include all blacks:

> [Noah] was angry with Ham and said, "Let him and Canaan be cursed, and let him be a slave to his brethren. . . . [Noah] increased in his curse of Canaan, wherefore his sons became slaves. They are the Copts [*qibāṭ*], the Kushites [*kūšīn*], the Indians [*hind*], the Mysians [*mūsīn*], and other blacks [*sūdān*].[38]

> . . . they are the Egyptians, the Kuerbawiens, the Indians, the Mosirawiens, the Ethiopians, and all those whose skin color is black.[39]

This version was probably the source for Eutychius (Saʿīd ibn Biṭrīq), the Alexandrian Melkite patriarch (d. 940), who specifies the "other blacks":

> Cursed be Ham and may he be a servant to his brothers. . . . He himself and his descendants, who are the Egyptians, the Sūdān, the Abyssinians [Ḥabash], the Nūbians, and (it is said) the Barbari.[40]

By the time we come to the Georgian version of the *Cave of Treasures*, done between the ninth and the eleventh centuries, any implicit connection of black and slave is made absolutely explicit with the introduction of blackness as a result of the curse of slavery, one of the variations of a dual curse:

> When Noah awoke . . . he cursed him and said: "Cursed be Ham and may he be slave to his brothers" . . . and he became a slave, he and his lineage, namely the Egyptians, the Abyssinians, and the Indians. Indeed, Ham lost all sense of shame and he became black and was called shameless all the days of his life, forever.[41]

As the *Cave of Treasures* passed through its various recensions, moving from the fourth–sixth to the ninth–eleventh centuries, two changes occurred, one regarding the person cursed and the other regarding the curse itself. At first, Canaan was cursed, which then became Canaan and Ham, and finally just Ham. In regard to the curse, an original curse of slavery gradually became a dual curse of slavery and blackness together. In the first stage (Syriac) the biblical curse of slavery on Canaan was attached to the nonbiblical genealogy of Canaan, thus affecting the Egyptians, the Kushites, the Indians, and the Musraye.[42] In the second stage (Arabic/Ethiopic) more black Africans are subsumed under the curse, which must then include Ham, the ancestor of "all whose skin color is black." Here we see the move from the justification for Black slavery based on a nonbiblical genealogy to one based on a biblical genealogy, the Curse of Ham, in which both Canaan and Ham are cursed with slavery. Finally, in the third stage (Georgian), in a version of the Curse of Ham, the nonbiblical genealogy is discarded entirely, only Ham is cursed, and the curse is of dual character encompassing both slavery and blackness.

The dual curse brings us back to the Muslim writers who commonly reported such a tradition. Could they have drawn on the *Cave of Treasures*? It is certainly not out of the range of possibility. The work was very popular in the Near East.[43] Gary Anderson calls it a "witness to the Christian roots of Islamic traditions about the biblical prophets," and L. Chiekho thinks that works such as the *Cave of Treasures* did leave an impact on pre-Islamic Arabic literature.[44] More specifically, Camilla Adang has shown that the *Cave of Treasures* influenced several Islamic writers, among them Ibn Saʿd, Yaʿqūbī ("shows a marked preference for [it]"), Ibn Qutayba, and Ṭabarī.[45]

To sum up the results of this chapter thus far, we have seen a Near Eastern tradition going back at least to the second century B.C.E. (Pseudo-Eupolemus) that sees Canaan as the ancestor of Kush and other dark-skinned people. As the black African became increasingly identified with the slave in the Near East, this tradition was joined to the biblical story of the curse of slavery on Canaan. Thus, blackness is gradually introduced into the fourth-century retelling of the biblical story in the *Cave of Treasures.* At first (Syriac version) the connection made between blackness and slavery in this retelling is implicit. As subsequent versions of the *Cave of Treasures* are made, shifting the black genealogy to Ham in accord with the Bible, the implicit becomes ever more explicit until we see a dual curse make its appearance. By this time, the Christian paraphrases of biblical stories, such as those reflected in the *Cave of Treasures,* have influenced the Islamic world and we begin to see in its literature the dual curse in several variations. From the seventh century onward, the Curse of Ham is commonly found in works composed in the Near East, whether in Arabic by Muslims or in Syriac by Christians. The increasing reliance on the Curse coincides with the increasing numbers of Blacks taken as slaves into the Islamic world.

The Curse of Ham, in its various forms, became a very powerful tool for maintaining the existing order in society. Its importance for explaining, and thus justifying, the enslavement of Blacks cannot be underestimated. We can clearly see the close relationship between social order and biblical justification by tracking the appearance of the Curse. We note its first appearance in the Christian West as soon as Europe discovered black Africa and began to engage in the slave trade of its inhabitants. In fifteenth-century Portugal, Gomes Eannes de Zurara wrote about black African slaves he had seen: "These blacks were Moors like the others, though their slaves, in accordance with ancient custom, which I believe to have been because of the curse which, after the Deluge, Noah laid upon his son Cain [read: Cham], cursing him in this way: that his race should be subject to all the other races of the world."[46] In the Arabic-speaking world, where the enslavement of black Africans was extensive and early, reliance on the Curse never ceased. Among Jewish writers in the Christian West, we begin to see a Curse of Ham mentioned at the same time that Christian writers mention it, for example, in Moses Arragel's fifteenth-century Castilian commentary to the Bible (on Gen 9:25): "And Canaan was a slave from slaves [i.e., his father, Ham, was a slave]: Some say that these are the black Moors who, wherever they go, are captives."[47] It is not clear who the "some say" are. In any case, beginning in the fifteenth century Jews too rely on the Curse in their explanations for the state of things in the world.[48] In regard to Jewish literature written within the Islamic orbit, Ibn Ezra (d. 1164) seems to be quoting the view of the surrounding culture when he says, "Some say that the Blacks are slaves because of Noah's curse on Ham."[49] In the Islamic East at a later time I find the Jewish-Yemini scholars Nathaniel ibn Yeshaya and Zechariah b. Solomon ha-Rofe (fourteenth and fifteenth centuries) incorporating the Curse of Ham into their writings.[50]

As the Black slave trade moved to England and then America, the Curse of Ham moved with it. An English author wrote in 1627: "This curse to be a servant was laid, first upon a disobedient sonne *Cham,* and wee see to this day, that the *Moores, Chams* posteritie, are sold like slaves yet."[51] There can be no denying the fact, however, that the Curse made its most harmful appearance in America, and there can be no denying the central role it played in sustaining the slave system. It was *the* ideological cornerstone for the justification of Black slavery, "the major argument in the proslavery arsenal of biblical texts," "certainly among the most popular defenses of slavery, if not the most popular."[52] Its place in American thought of the time was succinctly described in 1862 by Alexander Crummell, a man born in the United States to freed slaves. In a learned article he refers to "the opinion that the sufferings and the slavery of the Negro race are the consequence of the curse of Noah" as a "general, almost universal, opinion in the Christian world." This opinion, says Crummell,

> is found in books written by learned men; and it is repeated in lectures, speeches, sermons, and common conversation. So strong and tenacious is the hold which it has taken upon the mind of Christendom, that it seems almost impossible to uproot it. Indeed, it is an almost foregone conclusion, that the Negro race is an accursed race, weighed down, even to the present, beneath the burden of an ancestral malediction.[53]

In America this "ancestral malediction" took on a most sinister expression. It is in this country that one finds descriptions of the Curse as that made in 1857 by James A. Sloan, a Presbyterian minister:

> Ham deserved death for his unfilial and impious conduct. But the Great Lawgiver saw fit, in his good pleasure, not to destroy Ham with immediate death, but to set a *mark of degradation* on him. . . . All Ham's posterity are either *black* or dark colored, and thus bear upon their countenance the mark of *inferiority* which God put upon the progenitor. . . . *Black, restrained, despised, bowed down* are the words used to express the condition and place of Ham's children. Bearing the mark of degradation on their skin.[54]

Or that made by Buckner Payne ("Ariel") ten years later, who in great detail described the effect of the Curse on Ham:

> The curse denounced against him, that a servant of servants should he be unto his brethren; and that *this* curse, was denounced against Ham, for the accidental seeing of his father Noah naked—that this curse was to do so, and did change him, so that instead of being long, straight-haired, high forehead, high nose, thin lips and white, as he then was, and like his brothers Shem and Japheth, he was from that day forth, to be kinky headed, low forehead, thick lipped, and black skinned; and that his *name,* and this *curse* effected all this.[55]

The form of the Curse that simultaneously generated both slavery and blackness (the "dual" curse), as Sloan and Payne describe it, was commonly found in antebellum America and continued well into the twentieth century.[56] If Thomas Peterson is right, the Curse entered America via a work by Bishop Thomas Newton, chaplain to King George II, published in London in 1759, who drew on Augustin Calmet's *Dictionary of the Holy Bible,* published in Paris about thirty years earlier.[57] Calmet's source was Ṭabarī's (d. 923) *Taʾrīkh,* mentioned earlier: "The author of Tharik-Thabari says that Noah having cursed Ham and Canaan, the effect was that not only their posterity became subject to their brethren and was born, as we may say, in slavery, but likewise that the color of their skin suddenly became black; for they [i.e., the Arabic writers] maintain that all the blacks descend from Ham and Canaan."[58]

Of course, anyone could look in the Bible and see that the Curse of Ham was a chimera. But it didn't matter how patently absurd was the argument from Scripture. When the Bible states that Canaan was cursed, it really means that Ham was cursed. And what was the proof? The fact that Blacks are enslaved, as Abbé Louis Fillion (d. 1927), onetime professor of exegesis at the Institut Catholique of Paris, explained.[59] These arguments are, of course, irrational (Canaan means Ham) and circular (it must have been black Ham who was cursed with slavery because the Blacks are all enslaved), but that did not matter.[60] The Curse of Ham myth legitimized and validated the social order by divine justification. No matter then how irrational or circular, the arguments were accepted because they supported society's beliefs and practices, and with God's approval.[61]

The element of divine authorship was what gave the Curse its force and prevented any rebuttal. Perhaps the clearest and most succinct expression of this belief are the words of the Dominican Fray Francisco de la Cruz, who may have played an influential role in developing New World attitudes toward Blacks. He reported to the Inquisition in 1575 that, "the blacks are justly captives by just sentence of God for the sins of their fathers, and that in sign thereof God gave them that color."[62] The Curse of Ham became so well entrenched as God's word, that it was even used to legitimate the enslavement of some black Africans by other black Africans. Ethiopian Christians see themselves as descendants of Shem, not of Ham; they consider themselves to be red and the surrounding peoples whom they enslaved to be black.[63]

THIRTEEN

THE CURSE OF CAIN

HAM IS NOT the only biblical figure who was supposedly marked by a change of skin color. So was Cain, the son of Adam, according to some writers. Several authors in antebellum America refer to a then-current idea that Cain was smitten with dark skin as punishment for killing his brother, Abel. To some, this was the unspecified "mark" that God put on Cain "so that no one who found him would kill him" (Gen 4:15). David Walker, an African American writing in 1829, reflects this view common at the time when he says, "Some ignorant creatures hesitate not to tell us that we (the blacks) are the seed of Cain . . . and that God put a dark stain upon us, that we might be known as their slaves!!!"[1] The black mark of Cain, although far less common than the Curse of Ham, is nevertheless found among a number of antebellum writers from 1733 onward.[2] Phyllis Wheatley, the African American poet, in 1773 recorded this belief in verse: "Remember Christians, Negroes black as Cain / May be refined, and join the angelic train."[3]

The Cain theory had an advantage over the Curse of Ham, since the Bible mentions a "mark" put on Cain, even if it doesn't specify what is was. Furthermore, Cain, history's first murderer, was a far more sinister character than Ham, who merely looked at his father's nakedness. On the other hand, as a link between skin color and slavery, the theory had a problem, for, as opposed to the Curse of Ham, there is no mention of slavery in the Cain narrative. How could slavery be brought into play? One answer was to make Ham a descendant of Cain, but a quick look at the biblical genealogy made that thesis untenable.[4] The answer that took hold was to claim that Ham must have married a descendant of black Cain.[5] This way Ham's descendants, through Canaan, would be both black and enslaved, conveniently coinciding with the situation current at the time. Joseph Smith, founder of the Mormon Church, incorporated this genealogy into his thinking, and from his time onward Cain's blackness became part of Mormon theology: "The seed of Cain were black and had not place among [the seed of Adam]"; "a blackness came upon the children of Canaan, that they were despised among all people."[6] Thus, Brigham Young taught that Blacks would "continue to be the servant of servants until the curse is removed."[7] The Curse of Cain, both in and out of the Mormon Church, continued well into the twentieth century.[8]

As with the Curse of Ham, the Curse of Cain did not originate on American soil. A curse of blackness on Cain, from whom the Blacks are descended, is often noted in European literature of the seventeenth to nineteenth century. In England Thomas Peyton referred to the black African as "the cursed descendant of Cain and the devil" in his *The Glasse of Time* published in 1620, and in 1785 Paul Erdman Isert more expansively recorded the view that the Black's skin color "originated with Cain, the murderer of his brother, whose family were destined to have the black colour as a punishment."[9] In France the Curse is mentioned in a 1733 *Dissertation sur l'origine des nègres et des américains,* and is recorded by Jean-Baptiste Labat, the Dominican missionary and explorer (d. 1738), as also by Nicolas Bergier in his *Dictionnaire Théologique* in 1789.[10] It is also found in the seventeenth- and eighteenth-century Portuguese empire.[11] And just as in America, Cain's black color continued, at least in some parts of Europe, into our times. A modern Greek folk legend sees Cain in the cycle of the moon, which, like Cain becomes dark (as it wanes monthly).[12]

In seventeenth-century Europe and eighteenth-century America we begin to see the Cain myth quite frequently. But the notion of Cain's darkness can be found much earlier, if less frequently, in European literature and art. The Irish *Saltair na Rann* (tenth century) has God send the angel Gabriel to Adam to announce: "Dark rough senseless Cain is going to kill Abel" (*Caín cíar garbdai cen chéil a-tā ic tríal marbtha Abéil*).[13] The *Vienna Genesis,* an eleventh-century (or early twelfth-century) German poetic paraphrase of Genesis, says that some of the evil descendants of Cain "lost their beautiful coloring; they became black and disgusting, and unlike any people. . . . [They] displayed on their bodies what the forebears had earned by their misdeeds. As the fathers had been inwardly, so the children were outwardly."[14] A thirteenth-century English psalter depicts Cain with Negroid features, as it does another figure—one of the men who arrested Christ at the Betrayal.[15] If one scholar's reading is correct, the black women in Hieronymus Bosch's (d. 1516) *Garden of Earthly Delights* are the biblical "daughters of man" who are descended from Cain.[16] And a Greek poem dated to about 1500 C.E. and containing earlier traditions describes God's curse of Cain as consisting of a change of color to black and a loss of power (μαύρος πολλὰ και ἀδύναμος σαν τὸν λυσάριν σκύλον).[17]

So, the idea that Cain was smitten by God with a dark skin has an early pedigree, but where did the idea come from? It is true that the Animal Apocalypse (second century B.C.E.) depicts Cain as black, but we saw that colors in this text are meant symbolically, with blackness standing for Cain's sin and wickedness in killing his brother.[18] It is also true that some manuscripts of the Greek *Apocalypse of Moses* 1.3 claim that Cain was born "without light" (ἀδιάφωτος), but other manuscripts as well as the Latin have "full of light" (διάφωτος, *lucidus*), and anyway being born without light is not the same as losing a light skin color and becoming black.[19] From where, then, comes the idea that Cain became black? In one of the Armenian "Adam-books," dated "probably to the fifth or sixth century, but in any case prior to 1000," we find this interesting addition to the biblical story: "And the Lord was wroth with Cain. . . . He beat Cain's face with hail, which blackened like coal, and thus he remained with a black face."[20] The idea of Cain's blackness, then, goes back to earlier eastern Christian traditions. Where did they get it from?

Let's look at the biblical text. Gen 4:5 reads: "And Cain was greatly saddened (or, distressed) and his face fell [*wa-yiḥar le-qayin me'od wa-yipelu panaw*]." "Saddened (or distressed)" is the correct translation for the Hebrew *wa-yiḥar le-*, as several scholars have shown.[21] This is also the way the LXX translated the phrase (ἐλυπήθη 'he was saddened, grieved, distressed').[22] "His face fell" is a literal translation of the Hebrew *wa-yipelu panaw*, which idiomatically means in Biblical Hebrew, as in Akkadian, "to be sad." A good translation might be "and he was downcast" as in NJB and NIV. Some Palestinian Targums (Neofiti and Fragment Targum) translate *wa-yipelu panaw* as *ištane ziwhon de-apoy* 'the countenance of his face changed', which, despite its general sounding sense in English, has a very specific meaning in several ancient Near Eastern languages (Akkadian, Biblical Aramaic, Biblical Hebrew, and Ugaritic): "to be gloomy or sad."[23] So Cain was sad, distressed, gloomy. Still, however, no color.

Some think that the missing chromatic link is supplied by a midrashic comment to the verse. Taking the *me* of the word *me'od* in the verse as a preposition and playing on the similarity, both phonological and morphological, of the remainder (*'od*) with the word for ember, or firebrand (*'ud*), the midrash says: "For it [his face] became like an ember [*ke-'ud*]."[24] Now we have color, for an ember is burned black. A different midrash will confirm this point. On 2 Sam 6:8, "And David was saddened [*wa-yiḥar le-dawid*]," a midrash comments: "His face changed as a grill cake [*ništanu panaw ke-ḥararah*]."[25] Once again color, for something grilled (*ḥararah* < *ḥrr* 'to burn, heat') is dark. The Rabbis are trying to determine the meaning of *wa-yiḥar le-*and they do so by means of exegesis, in the one case interpreting the word *me-'od/mi-'ud*, in the other by interpreting the word *wa-yiḥar/ḥararah*. Apparently, they mean to say that Cain's face, and David's as well, turned dark or black. Both Theodor and Ginzberg think that the statement in the Armenian Adam-book that Cain's face became black was based on the midrashic tradition that Cain's face "became like an ember."[26] In general the Armenian Adam-books "inherited a wealth of elements of tradition which were widespread in Jewish and Christian literature from pre-Christian times into the Middle Ages," and ours, according to them, is one example of the Jewish bequest.[27]

What does the midrash mean when it says that Cain's (or David's) face became black? Does it mean that Cain turned black and became the ancestor of dark-skinned people, as was later understood in Europe and America? A clue to the meaning of the midrash is found in its language: "his face became like . . . " and not "his body" or "he" (as in the sex-in-the-ark midrash), for postbiblical Jewish literature commonly uses the expression "his or her face became black" as a figure of speech to indicate distress, including embarrassment, or sadness.[28] *Ben Sira:* "The wickedness of a woman darkens the face of her husband";[29] *Thanksgiving Hymns:* "The light of my face has become gloomy with deep darkness, my countenance has changed into gloom . . . I am eating the bread of weeping, my drink is tears without end . . . Agony and pain surround me, shame covers my face";[30] the Similitudes of *1 Enoch:* "Their faces will be filled with shame, and the darkness will grow deeper on their faces";[31] and several times in rabbinic literature, for example, *bShab:* "The faces of all of David's enemies turned black as the bottom of a pot" when they saw that God favored him.[32] The same meanings of black face are found also in Akkadian and early Arabic literature.[33]

From the foregoing, it is clear that the midrash does not mean that Cain turned black literally as in the Armenian Adam-book, but that Cain was deeply saddened, an interpretation that agrees with the LXX and Targum translations as well as with the current scholarly understanding of the biblical text. It is, of course, possible that the Adam-book misunderstood the midrash, but that requires us to assume that the Adam-book knew this midrash. A simpler and more direct solution may be offered. Lipscomb thinks that the sources for much of the extrabiblical elements in the Armenian Adam-books came originally from Judaism via eastern Christianity, "perhaps via Syria." "Indeed," he says, "the bulk of Jewish and Christian literature translated into Armenian came from Greek and Syriac sources."[34] If this is so, we ought first to look at the Peshiṭta, the Syriac translation of the Bible, and when we do we find the answer to our problem. The Peshiṭta renders the text in Gen 4:5 *wʾtbʾš lqʾyn ṭb wʾtkmr ʾpwhy* "and Cain was very displeased and his face *ʾtkmr*." The Syriac word *ʾtkmr* is a form of the root *kmr*, which commonly means "to be black" and then, in a transferred sense, "to be sad."[35] These two meanings of *kmr* are behind Cain's change of color in the Adam-book, which would have understood *ʾtkmr* to mean "became black" rather than "became sad."[36]

There is also another reason for thinking that the Adam-book's black Cain derived from the Syriac *ʾtkmr*. The Syriac church father Ephrem developed an interpretation of the Cain-Abel story as symbolic of a dualistic theology in which the two biblical figures are intertwined with images of darkness and light. They are prefigured by the creation of natural light and darkness; they are born from the spiritual world of light-darkness (Christ-Satan); and in turn, they serve as prototypes of the children of light and children of darkness. "Abel was *ʾtpṣḥ* as the light, / but the murderer was

ʾtkmr as the darkness." Cain is the firstborn of Darkness and thus performs works of darkness; he is the image of Darkness, and Christ is the Father of Light, the contrary image.[37] Certainly, Ephrem drew on the Peshiṭta's *ʾtkmr* when he wrote that Cain "was *ʾtkmr* as the darkness." Whether Ephrem had in mind the meanings "to be sad, gloomy" for *ʾtkmr* and "to be cheerful" for *ʾtpṣḥ,* or he meant that "Abel was bright [*ʾtpṣḥ*] as the light [*nhyrʾ*], / but the murderer was dark [*ʾtkmr*] as the darkness [*ḥšwkʾ*]," as Kronholm translates, or he had both meanings in mind, Ephrem's influence on Syriac Christian interpretation was in any case strong and his theological interpretation of Cain representing and prefiguring darkness probably impacted on the interpretation found in the Adam-book.[38]

In addition to the Armenian Adam-book, Cain's blackness may possibly be found in Arabic sources. In the Qurʾan the name for Cain is Qābīl. Goldziher thinks the origin of this name lies in an Arabic practice to create assonant pairs of names. So Qābīl is joined with Hābīl (Abel), and we get Hābīl wa-Qābīl, just as Hārūt wa-Mārūt, Yājūj wa-Mājūj, and so on.[39] Perhaps so, although with these other qurʾanic pairs the repetition of the second syllable is more closely linked to the original name of the figure: Hārūt wa-Mārūt is Haurvatāt-Ameretāt (Zoroastrain archangels), Yājūj wa-Mājūj is Gog-Magog. Even Ṭālūt's (Jālūt wa-Ṭālūt, Goliath-Saul) second syllable is based, at least partially, on the original name. Qābīl for Qayin, however, shares nothing in the second syllable. Perhaps in addition to assonance another factor was behind the creation of the name: the root *qbl* in Aramaic means "black." Note, in this regard, that the name or title of the king of Nubia in some Arabic sources was *qabil.*[40] If Islamic tradition, as Armenian/Syriac tradition, believed that Cain was black, it would account for the name Qābīl.

Whether or not the Arabic name Qābīl indicates a knowledge of Cain's blackness, the Armenian Adam-book seems to be the first record of the notion that Cain was punished with a change of skin color. If my theory is correct, the explanation for this novel idea lies in a textual misunderstanding. The Syriac *ʾtkmr* 'he became sad', said of Cain, was incorrectly understood as "he became black," a related meaning of the word, possibly influenced by Ephrem's interpretation of Cain as representing spiritual darkness (which itself, it seems clear, is based on a play of the biblical *ʾtkmr*). This linguistic confusion would have been the source of the tradition in the Adam-book that Cain became black, which then traveled through Western thought.[41]

FOURTEEN

THE NEW WORLD ORDER: HUMANITY BY PHYSIOGNOMY

WE HAVE SEEN how the new historical circumstances, that is, the increasing identification of the Black as slave, brought in its wake reinterpretations of Scripture. Although only Canaan is cursed with slavery in the Bible, Ham, the father of colored people, shares that fate in the later interpretations. Peculiarities in the graphic representation of the Hebrew language also played a very significant role in these reinterpretations, for at least as early as the third century C.E. the name Ham was understood incorrectly to mean "black, dark." The combination of these two factors—the historical and linguistic changes—built a massive wall of misunderstanding of the biblical text that remained impenetrable for close to fifteen hundred years, up until recent times. The Curse of Ham, however, was not the only exegetical child of changed historical circumstances.

Categorization by Color

Recognition of humanity's various skin colors can be traced as far back as ancient Egypt. Several tomb paintings, dating from the thirteenth and twelfth centuries B.C.E., depict different ethnic groups as four human figures. The figures are identified by their ethnic names and painted in different colors: the Egyptian (*rmṯw*) is red-brown, the Kushite (*nḥsyw*) black, and the Libyan (*tmḥw*) and Syrian/Asian (*ʿ3mw*) are painted in two different light colors (pink, yellow, or white).[1] Other tomb paintings also depict one or more of these ethnic groups by skin color.[2] Although the Egyptians did make use of color symbolism, such as black in funerary contexts, and artistic conventions, the ethnic differentiation by skin color is based in reality.[3] As the Egyptian empire expanded its borders, it came into contact with peoples of different skin colors, who were at various times represented iconographically.

The same happened in the Islamic world, except that in Islam, of course, the representations are literary, not iconographic. As the boundaries of the Muslim world expanded, we begin to see an emphasis on skin color as a marker of differentiation among peoples. Bernard Lewis has shown that in early Arabic literature, color terms used to describe people generally have a personal rather than an ethnic sense (like our "sallow" or "ruddy"), and even when they are used ethnically, the terms are relative—for example, the Arabs might describe themselves as black compared with the red Persians but as red or white as compared to the black Africans. However, following the Muslim conquests of large areas of Asia and Africa in the seventh century a change took place in Arabic color descriptions of people. There is a "narrowing, specializing, and fixing of color terms applied to human beings. In time almost all disappear apart from 'black,' 'red,' and 'white'; and these become ethnic and absolute instead of personal and relative."[4]

Kim Hall has drawn attention to a similar phenomenon in sixteenth-century England. She noted that descriptions of blackness and whiteness, dark and light, in English Renaissance texts do not merely reflect Elizabethan standards of beauty of complexion or a European aesthetic tradition or moral categories, but "become in the early modern period the conduit through which the English began to formulate the notions of 'self' and 'other.'" Hall explains this development against the backdrop of England's movement from insularity to encounters with other peoples. These encounters brought about the "process by which preexisting literary tropes of blackness profoundly interacted with the fast-changing economic relations of white Europeans and their darker 'others' during the Renaissance." Thus these preexisting tropes were conveniently used to represent and categorize the other.[5]

The situations described by Lewis and Hall, although existing among different peoples and at different times, point to the same phenomenon. Both the Arabs and the English, who originally used color terms to depict individual complexion contrast, begin to use these terms in fixed ways as ethnic markers in order to describe themselves over against foreign peoples of darker or lighter skin when they discovered such people.

In the Islamic world we can see this recognition of human color variation in a tradition that God created Adam from black, white, and red (or, dark) colored earth, which accounts for the different colors of humanity.[6] It is possible that two Jewish texts composed in the Islamic world refer to the same tradition. Some readings in *Pirqei R. Eliezer* state that Adam was created from red, black, white, and green-yellow (*yaroq*) earth, which accounts for the different colors of parts of the human body, and *Targum Pseudo-Jonathan* has it that God created Adam in red, brown (*sheḥim*), and white colors.[7] There is enough in common with the Islamic tradition to lead some to the conclusion that the Jewish material was originally the same as the Islamic.[8] Supporting this suggestion is the current scholarly view that both *Pirqei R. Eliezer* and *Targum Pseudo-Jonathan* were probably composed or redacted in Israel after the Islamic conquest.[9]

Be that as it may, the notion that all humanity is color-coded is expressed in Jewish, Christian, and Muslim biblical interpretations that see Noah's sons as representing the three human skin colors of the world's population. *Pirqei R. Eliezer* depicts God as dividing the world among Noah's sons and decreeing different skin colors for them.

> [God] blessed Noah and his sons—as it says: "And God blessed them" (cf. Gen 9:1)—with their gifts, and he apportioned the entire earth to them as an inheritance. He blessed Shem and his sons [making them] *sheḥorim* and beautiful and he gave them the habitable earth. He blessed Ham and his sons [making them] *sheḥorim* as the raven and he gave them the sea coasts. He blessed Japheth and his sons [making] them all *levanim* and he gave them the desert and fields. These are the portions he gave them as an inheritance.[10]

I have not provided the conventional translations of "white" for *lavan* (pl. *levanim*) and "black" for *shaḥor* (pl. *sheḥorim*), for Athalya Brenner has shown that these words have a wider range of meanings. Biblical Hebrew *lavan* "denotes a property of brightness more than of hue." As such it covers a range that is equivalent to "light-colored" or "pale." It "designates any colour property from 'clear, light in colour' to 'white' proper." "The consistent interpretation of *lavan,* wherever it occurs, as its modern parallel 'white' is misled and misleading. . . . ['White' is] much narrower in scope than biblical *lavan*." The same range of meaning continued into Tannaitic Hebrew (e.g., *sdeh lavan* 'field of grain').[11] Similarly, *shaḥor* means not only "black" but "dark" as well, including the colors brown and gray, meanings that continued into the tannaitic period.[12] "The lack of biblical terms which are peripheral to 'white' or 'black' makes the utilization of *lavan* for 'light coloured' and *shaḥor* for 'dark' almost inevitable."[13] "Syntagmatic relations" as well as general context are necessary for determining the precise meaning of these words.

As we saw earlier, in Song 1:5 the meaning of *shaḥor,* which in context describes sunburned skin, is "brown."[14] In Song 5:11, the meaning of *shaḥor,* which describes the lover's hair as the color of the raven, is "black." The author of *Pirqei R. Eliezer* drew on these two verses to designate the complexion of the Hamites and the Semites.[15] Adding also the light-skinned (*levanim*) Japhetites, he depicted the world's populations as divided by complexion: the light-colored Japhetites, the medium dark colored (brown) Semites, and very dark colored (black) Hamites.

In all of the Jewish material we have examined up to this point, we have not come across this kind of categorization of humanity by color. To be sure, we have seen evidence that ethnic color differences were recognized, but we have not come across this type of cataloging of the world's populations by skin color. Classification of humanity certainly occurred, but it was of a religious nature, polytheists (idolaters) as opposed to monotheists, or gentiles as opposed to Jews. Categorization by skin color appears uniquely in this text.

This passage from *Pirqei R. Eliezer*, a work which, as said, was composed in Israel after the Islamic conquest, is strikingly paralleled in an Arabic text of approximately the same period. The historian Ṭabarī (d. 923) quotes Ibn ʿAbbas (d. 686/8) as saying: "Born to Noah were Shem, whose descendants were tawny white [*bayāḍ wa-ʾadma*]; Ham, whose descendants were black with hardly any whiteness [*sawād wa-bayāḍ qalīl*]; and Japheth, whose descendants were reddish-white [*al-šuqra wal-ḥumra*]."[16] The tradition is repeated in the thirteenth century by the Christian Ibn al-ʿIbrī (Bar Hebraeus), known for the "fidelity with which he reproduces earlier writers."[17] He writes in his commentary to Gen 5:32, "'And Noah begat Shem and Ham and Japheth.' That is Shem is the father of the swarthy [*šḥmʾ*] and Ham of the blacks [*ʾkmʾ*], and Japheth of the whites [*ḥwrʾ*]." And to Gen 10:32, " . . . the red [*smqryʾ*] sons of Japheth . . . the black [*ʾkmʾ*] sons of Ham . . . and the swarthy [*šḥmʾ*] sons of Shem."[18] Again in another work, Bar Hebraeus speaks of Noah dividing the world among his three sons, with Ham getting the Land of the Blacks (*sūdān*), Shem the Land of the Browns (*sumra*), and Japheth the Land of the Reds (*šuqra*).[19]

This categorization of the world's population by skin color seems to begin with the Islamic conquests in Africa and Asia. With the encounter of large numbers of darker- and lighter-skinned peoples in different parts of the world, color terms are no longer used as indications of relative complexion but as ethnic markers to describe the new populations, as Lewis said. This way of looking at humanity is captured by the story of Noah's sons who represent the three skin colors of all people in the world.

This new way of classifying people will explain the medieval interpretations of the rabbinic sex-in-the-ark story, which I discussed earlier.[20] We saw that, although in that third-century story it was Ham who was darkened and became the ancestor of all dark-skinned people, by the eighth to ninth century in Islamic sources and the ninth to eleventh century in Jewish sources it was understood that it was really Kush, one of Ham's four sons, who was darkened and became the ancestor of dark-skinned people. In the Islamic version we can actually see how the Kush interpretation is grafted onto the earlier story mentioning only Ham: "When Noah awoke . . . he said to God, 'Allah, blacken his face and the face of the descendants of the one who disobeyed [i.e., Ham] and had intercourse with his wife.' So Ham's wife had a black son and he named him Kūshā" (Ibn Hishām). Noah curses Ham and his descendants but the result is a blackening of Kush alone. In regard to the Jewish (Rashi et al.) interpretation, we saw that later commentators objected to it, arguing that it stood contrary to a plain reading of the midrashic story. The explanation for the interpretation in both Islamic and Jewish sources lies in the changed perception of skin color from a marker of complexion to a marker of ethnicity. Since skin color had now become an ethnic marker with black marking the

Kushites, the person who became darkened in the story had to be Kush, the black African ancestor. If the story explicitly mentioned Ham, it could be interpreted away in the face of the way the world and its peoples were now perceived. Blackness was no longer seen as a complexion with varying shades, which might encompass several peoples, the Jew and Arab included. Skin color, as Lewis says, became fixed, narrowed, and specialized.

Categorization by Physiognomy

In addition to darker skin color, other perceptions of the black African are recorded. After the Greeks encountered the peoples south of Egypt, they, and later the Romans, recorded their impressions in both literature and iconography.[21] The same happened later in Arabic literature after the Muslims penetrated Africa. Arabic writings, beginning in the ninth and increasingly in the tenth century, contain many descriptions of the Black physiognomy. In both Greco-Roman and Muslim, as also in later medieval Christian writings, the most common perceptions of black African features include dark skin, tightly curled hair, thick lips, red eyes, nakedness, and a large phallus, as we shall presently see. The same perceptions are apparently also recorded in the following Jewish text:

> Ham's eyes turned red, since he looked at his father's nakedness; his lips became crooked, since he spoke with his mouth; the hair of his head and beard became singed, since he turned his face around; and since he did not cover [his father's] nakedness, he went naked and *nimshekhah ʿorlato*. For all of God's punishments fit the sin measure for measure [*midah keneged midah*].[22]

Clearly based on the biblical narrative of Ham's sin against his father Noah (Gen 9:22–23), this midrash has often been understood by both medieval and modern scholars as an etiology of the black African physiognomy.[23] Is this view correct? Does this text mean to describe the black African, whose ancestor is assumed to be Ham? When I first dealt with the text I was not sure.[24] Now, however, I am convinced that it does. An examination of the description of the physical features in the passage in comparison with Greco-Roman, Muslim, and Christian descriptions of the Black will indeed show that the black African is intended.

The depiction of the hair would clearly seem to refer to the black African. The adjective used to describe it, *nitḥarekh* 'singed' or 'scorched', is comparable with other descriptions of the tightly curled hair of the black African.[25] Classical Greek and Roman explanations of the African hair quality (and skin color) refer to the effects of the scorching heat of the sun, and the consequent burning of the skin and singeing of the hair. This explanation is given in the myth of Phaeton, who brought the sun chariot too close to the earth and "discolored the bodies of men with a murky dark bloom and curled their hair," as well as in the environmental theory of anthropological differentiation.[26] Similar descriptions of heat-singed, tightly curled hair of those who lived closest to the sun are also found in Arabic writings and in later Christian literature.[27]

Nakedness would also seem to refer to black Africans, for it is a description commonly given by writers from the period of the ancient Greeks through the European discovery of black Africa. Many pagan, Christian, and Muslim accounts across this wide chronological range were struck by the lack of clothes of black African natives.[28]

The description of the lips in the Midrash appears strange. At first reading, I did not think that the word "crooked" could describe the shape of human lips.[29] However, "crooked" is that which is not straight, and that which is not straight can be curved. Indeed, in Tannaitic Hebrew *ʿaqum* is used in this sense referring to a "palm branch curved like a sickle" (*lulav ʿaqum domeh le-magal*).[30] Even closer to our text, in referring to human physiognomy, is the derived Aramaic word *ʿaqmumita* 'hump'.[31] In regard to Negroid physiognomy, *ʿaqumot* could then be describing lips, which would appear to curve outward from the face and look thicker. Abraham Epstein captured this sense of the Hebrew word in our passage with his "retroussées," that is, turned up lips.[32] We find thick lips mentioned as a black African characteristic by Galen in the second century C.E., as well as in Arabic writings from the ninth century onward and Christian works from the thirteenth century onward.[33]

We would not think of red eyes as a feature of black Africans, but earlier writers disagree. From the medieval through the modern periods Muslim, Christian, and Jewish writers often describe black Africans as having red eyes. Some examples: Masʿūdī (tenth century) from the Arab world, "Their color is black, they have red eyes . . . because the hot atmosphere burns the infant in the womb; their hair is curly." A frequently cited anecdote in medieval Iranian literature states: "A Zangi [i.e., black African] found a mirror and viewed his reflection in it. He saw a flat nose, an ugly face, a charcoal complexion, and inflamed eyes." Albertus Magnus (thirteenth century), the Christian scientist and theologian, provides an explanation: because of the extreme heat of Africa, the Blacks' "flesh is suffused with blood as if they are [*sic*] glowing coals, as is apparent in their tongues and throats. . . . And they have . . . reddened eyes, veins and eye lids on account of the heat."[34] Albert's contemporary, Marco Polo, says of the inhabitants of Zanzibar: "They are all black, and go stark naked . . . their mouths are so large, their noses so turned up, their lips so thick, their eyes so big and bloodshot, that they look like very devils."[35] From the Jewish world the

Andalusian-Hebrew poet Jacob ben Eleazar (twelfth–thirteenth century) describes a Black woman as having "eyes like flames" (*reshafim*) and a Black man as having "eyes like (glowing) coals."[36]

The most difficult phrase in the *Tanḥuma* text is *nimshekhah ʿorlato,* which I have deliberately left untranslated. This Hebrew expression literally means "his foreskin was extended," usually in the sense of having the foreskin extended over a circumcised penis, whether by means of a restorative technique or by natural regrowth.[37] But this translation could not be correct in our text if the passage is indeed an etiology, for such stories intend to explain features of the human anatomy that appear unusual from the standpoint of the storyteller, such as thick lips, tightly curled hair, or red eyes. The reextension of a foreskin over a circumcised penis is not a feature of any human anatomy.[38]

The Hebrew expression, however, can bear another meaning: "to be or remain uncircumcised," that is, to have the foreskin retained ("extended") naturally. This meaning is found in the following two midrashic texts, the first of which describes Pharaoh's behavior toward the Israelites in Egypt: "He decreed against them enactments one more severe than the other: he prohibited the Israelites from having sexual intercourse, *u-mashakh lahem ba-ʿorlah,* and he made them plait their hair [in the non-Jewish style]."[39] The Hebrew words in this text must mean that Pharaoh prevented circumcision, that is, *nimshekhah ʿorlato* means to remain uncircumcised rather than to extend surgically or otherwise the foreskin of an already circumcised penis.[40] Were the intended meaning one of foreskin restoration, the passage could only have been referring to the first generation of Jews in Egypt, who would have arrived there circumcised. But the context of the passage depicts the Israelites' condition in Egypt during their entire sojourn in the land (Moses and the Exodus are part of the exegetical package), thus including subsequent generations of newborn uncircumcised children. The point of the passage is that Pharaoh prohibited the circumcision of newborn boys. This interpretation would accord with another midrashic tradition, exegetically based on Josh 5:5, that after the first generation in Egypt the Jews no longer practiced circumcision or were prohibited from practicing circumcision.[41]

The second text in which the Hebrew term has the sense of "remaining uncircumcised" compares the practices of Jews and gentiles: "It is the way of the gentiles that when you [God] give a son to one of them, *moshekh lo ʿorlah*. But when you give a son to one of the Jews he circumcises him on the eighth day."[42] This passage describes the characteristic behavior of Jews as opposed to gentiles. *Moshekh lo ʿorlah* in this passage apparently refers to the gentile practice of remaining uncircumcised, a meaning that may be implied in one version of the text that has *megaddel lo ʿorlah* for *moshekh lo ʿor-*

lah, where the meaning of *megaddel* would be similar to *megaddel śeʿar* 'to let the hair grow', that is, to allow natural growth to occur.[43]

Thus the Hebrew term *mashakh* (or *nimshekhah*) *ʿorlah* can mean "to be uncircumcised," as in these two texts.[44] If *Tanḥuma* is an etiology of Negroid physiognomy, can it have this meaning? In other words, is the passage saying that the black African is born with an uncircumcised penis?[45] This suggestion is patently absurd, for an etiology explains how and why the natural order (in our text, the usual anatomy) was changed by God. In *Tanḥuma,* however, this explanation would be stood on its head, for the usual human anatomy includes a foreskin. God does not have to change anything. Therefore, even if a foreskin appeared "unusual" to the Jewish storyteller, its existence would not be the result of extranatural intervention and could not, therefore, figure in an etiological story.

What then can the Hebrew term *nimshekhah ʿorlato* mean in the text of *Tanḥuma*? An aggadic passage dealing with Nebuchadnezzar, the king of Babylonia, may provide the answer. In this text it is claimed that Nebuchadnezzar would commit sodomy on those kings he captured. When he tried to sodomize Zedekiah, the last king of Judah (ca. 597–586 B.C.E.), however, he ran into trouble, for "*nimshekhah ʿorlato* 300 cubits!"[46] Shall we translate literally "his foreskin became extended 300 cubits"? While such a translation is possible, it is more likely that "foreskin" in this passage should be understood as a metonymy, standing for penis.[47] Thus Nebuchadnezzar's punishment fit his sexual crimes. His instrument of sexual gratification become so grossly enlarged that he could no longer commit sodomy. Nebuchadnezzar was ironically and aptly punished (*midah keneged midah*), and Zedekiah was saved.

If this interpretation is correct, we have derived a meaning of the Hebrew expression *nimshekhah ʿorlah* that makes sense in an etiology of the Black physiognomy, for it conforms to the image of the Black as found in other cultures. Snowden, Thompson, and others have noted this for the classical world.[48] "The black with an oversize phallus was a traditional theme" in Greco-Roman art.[49] And not just art: Galen in the second century C.E. considered a "long penis" as one of ten characteristics of the black African.[50] Such depictions, whether in art or literature, were continued in the Islamic and Christian worlds.[51]

In sum, given the fact that the physical features detailed by *Tanḥuma*—red eyes, thick lips, tightly curled hair, nakedness, and a large phallus—are commonly given by pagan, Christian, and Muslim writers over many centuries to describe the black African, we may conclude that the *Tanḥuma* text is similarly meant to depict the black African.

There is, however, an argument that can be raised against this conclusion. If the midrash is meant to be an etiology of the black African physiognomy, why are two other distinguishing features not mentioned, the broad nose and the black skin color, the latter being the most distinguishing feature of all? Just as the English, when they first encountered Blacks, were struck by their skin color and "disfigured" lips and nose, or just as Galen's list of the Black's attributes included black skin and a "flat nose," as did those of the Arab writers, so too we would expect an etiology of the Black physiognomy to mention the unusual (to the author of the etiology) shape of the nose and color of the skin.[52] It was undoubtedly this omission in the *Tanḥuma* passage that led the scholar of rabbinic literature, Louis Ginzberg, to paraphrase the text as referring only to Canaan, thus excluding the black African: "The descendants of Ham, through Canaan therefore, have red eyes."[53]

Another problem with the *Tanḥuma* text concerns the framework of the biblical story. According to the midrash "the hair of [Ham's] head and beard became singed, since he turned his face around." In the biblical account it is not Ham, but Ham's brothers, Shem and Japheth, who turn their faces around as they went to cover their father with looks averted: "But Shem and Japheth took a cloth, placed it against both their backs and, walking backwards, they covered their father's nakedness; their faces were turned the other way, so that they did not see their father's nakedness" (Gen 9:23; NJPS). It was Ham who did *not* turn his face around and thus saw what he should not have seen. This basic difficulty clearly was the cause for the readings of *Tanḥuma* "he did *not* turn his head around," found in some text witnesses.[54] But this obvious "correction" only exchanges one difficulty for another, for if Ham did not turn his head, why was his hair made curly or twisted ("singed")?

Nevertheless, these two textual difficulties do not undermine our conclusion that the midrash means to be an etiology of the black African physiognomy. For, as to the second objection, clearly the subject of the etiology is Ham, and even if the Bible implies that he did not turn his head around, the midrash says explicitly that he did. The author of the midrash may have been confused in his recollection of the biblical story, but he is, in any case, describing a people with "singed" hair. As to the first objection—that skin color and nose shape are not mentioned—there are several possible explanations for the omissions. It may be that the author could not find in the biblical story a suitable act by Ham corresponding to these physical features; or the author may have relied on the ark etiology of dark skin and/or assumed an already dark-skinned Ham, an assumption hinted at by Ham's name; or the broad shape of the nose may not have been a common feature of those black Africans known to the author (many Blacks from East Africa do not have this feature).[55] Whether or not any of these possibilities has merit, the descriptions that *are* found in *Tanḥuma* correspond to descriptions of black African features reported by many others in different cultures over a long period of time. There is no reason to assume that this Jewish author should have seen things differently.

I conclude then that the characteristics of Ham as described in *Tanḥuma* are in agreement with descriptions of the black African physiognomy familiar to the world of the midrashic author. It is significant, however, that these descriptions, either as a group or individually, are not found elsewhere in the corpus of rabbinic literature. Nor have I found them in early Christian writings. As said earlier, they are found in Greco-Roman literature and art and again in Arabic writings beginning in the ninth and tenth centuries. We recall Lewis's comment about how Masʿūdī's quotation of Galen is repeated by later Muslim writers.[56] Now, the most recent scholarly analysis of *Tanḥuma* literature puts the redaction of our text in Iraq (Babylonia) during the Islamic period.[57] Another recent study differs and puts its redaction in Israel between the end of the eighth to the end of the tenth century.[58] Nevertheless, since both works agree on the Islamic time frame, and since the *Tanḥuma* description of the Negroid physical features is unique in rabbinic literature and common in Arabic literature, it would appear that the passage transmitting an etiology of black African physiognomy derives from and is influenced by the Islamic cultural environment in which it was composed. Recently Steven Wasserstrom has written about the "seemingly fluid interconfessionalism" in seventh- and eighth-century Iraq. Wasserstrom was dealing specifically with gnostic ideas, but his comments about the "syncretism between Muslim and non-Muslim minorities" and "interreligious amalgamation" would well explain our *Tanḥuma* text.[59]

To summarize this chapter, the Greek and Muslim hegemonies over large areas of the world, and their subsequent encounters with people of different color and physiognomy, naturally generated descriptions of the new population groups. Greco-Roman authors and sculptors exhibited a keen interest in these features, as documented fully by Snowden. No less did the Arab geographers note and record their observations. Both Greek and Arab relied on the climatic-environmental theory to explain the different colors and other physical features of the peoples to the north and south of them. The Arab three-color scheme of brown, black, and red-white, a result of encounters with Africans and Asians, was grafted onto the biblical story of Noah's three sons, ancestors of all humanity. The colorization of Shem, Ham, and Japhet is, thus, another exegetical result of new historical circumstances. In addition to skin color, other perceptions of human physiognomy became increasingly common as markers of differentiation as the borders of the Arab world expanded and subsumed ever more people of different appearance. Gerhard Rotter noted that while the biblical Table of Nations (Genesis 10) divides humanity by political-historical criteria, "the typical Arabic-Islamic Table of Nations, as opposed to this, uses a purely racial division on the basis of external features."[60] This new Arabic-Islamic way of looking at the world's population was then incorporated into the thinking and literature of others in the Near East, whether they be Jewish, such as the authors of *Tanḥuma* and *Pirqei R. Eliezer,* or Christian, such as Bar Hebraeus.

CONCLUSION

JEWISH VIEWS OF BLACK AFRICANS AND THE DEVELOPMENT OF ANTI-BLACK SENTIMENT IN WESTERN THOUGHT

WHAT WERE THE images of black Africans in the ancient Jewish perception? How did Jews in the biblical and postbiblical periods think about Blacks? What were the attitudes underlying these views? Was there an overriding color prejudice? Did early Jewish attitudes toward Blacks influence later Christian and Islamic views? How did postbiblical Jewish interpretation of Scripture influence Christian and Islamic exegesis in regard to the black African? This study has attempted to answer these questions. What follows is a summary of the findings.

To biblical Israel, Kush was the land at the furthest southern reach of the earth, whose inhabitants were militarily powerful, tall, and good-looking. These are the dominant images of the black African in the Bible, and they correspond to similar images in Greco-Roman culture. I found no indications of a negative sentiment toward Blacks in the Bible. Aside from its use in a proverb (found also among the Egyptians and Greeks), skin color is never mentioned in descriptions of biblical Kushites. That is the most significant perception, or lack of perception, in the biblical image of the black African. Color did not matter.

Some of these images and themes continued into the postbiblical period. Black Africa was still considered to lie at the furthest southern extreme of the world. Just as in the classical world, this location generated contradictory images of the Kushites. They are pious and just but also barbaric and uncivilized, both images being literary constructs of ends-of-the-earth peoples found also in Greco-Roman literature. Apparent rabbinic knowledge of the Blemmye and Nobae as persistent enemies of Rome recalls the biblical allusions to the Kushites as a warrior people of significance. The midrashic depiction of Saggitarius as a Kushite may draw on the related biblical image of Nubian archers. Another reflection of biblical imagery may be indicated in the midrashic play on the Arabic word *kuwayyis* to describe the Kushites as a particularly handsome people. In Jewish-Hellenistic and rabbinic/targumic literature miscegenation was clearly not an issue, as is indicated by the exegetical treatment of Moses' marriage to a Kushite woman. Another biblical Kushite, Ebed-melech, is highly praised in biblical, and even more so, in postbiblical literature. Two figures whose fathers were called Kushi (the biblical Zephaniah and the talmudic Michal) also come in for praise in postbiblical expansions, which may have well understood the name Kushi to indicate African ancestry. In any case we find no expressions of concern that these praiseworthy individuals may have been black Africans. In short, no negative evaluations of real Blacks (as opposed to imaginary literary constructs) were found either in biblical or postbiblical sources. Race did not matter.

In our investigation of skin color as a signifier of a person, aside from what seems to be a cross-cultural preference for lighter-skinned women, we found an ethnocentric partiality for the skin color of one's own ethnic group. This universal bias for the somatic norm found expression in rabbinic literature in two etiologies accounting for the existence of dark-skinned people, including, but not limited to, black Africans. We saw a similar somatic preference expressed in the Greco-Roman world, especially underlying the common environmental theory. Use of the color black as a metaphor for evil is found in all periods of Jewish literature. Application of the metaphor to the skin color of the black African is made in Jewish-Hellenistic and rabbinic literature to a limited extent, and in patristic allegory more extensively. In all cases the image does not transfer to the black African, that is, there is no indication that the negative symbolism of the color black translates to antipathy toward black Africans. The patristic metaphorical representation of the black African as demon is not found in Jewish literature.

We saw that there were trade contacts, including a Black slave trade, between Arabia and East Africa from the earliest centuries of the Common Era. As a consequence of this trade and of wars and conquests, Blacks were among the slave populations in the Near East, as they were also in Greece and Rome. Although there was probably a greater proportion of black Africans among the slaves in Arabia than elsewhere due to geographical proximity and the established trade routes, there is no clear proof that most slaves in Arabia were black Africans. Still, most black Africans there, as in Greece and Rome, and we can assume also in Israel, were slaves. This was the lot of most nonindigenous peoples anywhere in antiquity and late antiquity. Nevertheless, the noticeably different skin color of the Africans in a lighter-skinned environment created a ready association of Black with slave.

An important aspect of this study concerns the nexus of history and exegesis. Social, cultural, and linguistic developments are reflected in biblical interpretation (as true fifteen hundred years ago as today) and, therefore, these developments can be tracked by decoding the exegetical interpretations. I applied this methodology diachronically (in Jewish literature) and synchronically (in Jewish, Christian, Samaritan, and Islamic literature) to the interpretations of the biblical story concerning Noah's curse of eternal servitude. The results showed that the increasing association of Black with slave in the Near East was one of two primary factors that influenced exegetical changes. The second factor was a perceived etymology of the name Ham as derived from a root meaning "dark, brown, black," which, while incorrect, was nevertheless assumed to be true due to linguistic peculiarities of Hebrew (the single graphic representation for two originally distinct sounds). These social and linguistic developments influenced interpretations of the biblical story of Noah's curse of slavery on Canaan, which now also included Ham, or was even replaced by Ham. We saw these exegetical changes from the first century onward.

A second exegetical change was the gradual introduction of blackness into the retelling of the biblical story, which was originally colorless. Beginning with the fourth-century Syriac Christian *Cave of Treasures,* a biblical tradition that saw Canaan as cursed with slavery now included a statement informing the reader or listener that Canaan was the ancestor of dark-skinned people. The link of blackness and slavery in the various versions of this work is clear, though implicit, while an explicit link, in the form of a dual curse of both blackness and slavery, begins to appear in seventh-century Islamic texts. This exegetical innovation coincides with the seventh-century Muslim conquests in Africa, which brought an increasing influx of black African slaves to the Near East. From this time onward, the Curse of Ham, that is, the exegetical tie between blackness and servitude, is commonly found in works composed in the Near East, whether in Arabic by Muslims or in Syriac by Christians. The increasing reliance on the Curse coincides with the increasing numbers of Blacks taken as slaves.

The Arab conquests also had another consequence. Where skin color in Arabic literature previously described personal complexion, it is now used to designate ethnic groups, with "black" referring to the dark-skinned peoples. The same phenomenon occurred in sixteenth-century England. After England's encounter with black Africans, white and black became the terminology for "self" and "other." Both Arabs and English begin to use color terms as ethnic markers to distinguish others of darker or lighter skin when they discovered such people. This new way of categorizing humanity by skin color was also mapped onto the biblical grid. Beginning in the seventh century, it is found in Jewish, Christian, and Muslim biblical interpretations that see Noah's sons as representing the three human skin colors of the world's population.

The Bible scholar Jon Levenson remarked that the modern-day tendency to "define ethnicity according to physical characteristics (such as skin color) . . . seems to have played no role whatsoever" in ancient Israel during the biblical period.[1] As we have seen, this is true as well for postbiblical Israel. The apostle Paul reflects this clearly when he describes the followers of the new faith as "not Jewish, nor Greek; not slave, nor free; not male, nor female; but all are one in Christ Jesus."[2] Of course Paul's theology was his own, but the parameters that he uses to frame the idea of universalism come from the religious-cultural world of Judaism. "Black/White" is not one of those parameters. Nothing in the sources examined in this study has led to the conclusion that black Africans were seen as a species apart.

The lack of correspondence between color and ethnicity is clear also in the rabbinic use of the term *kushi(t)*. We saw that in rabbinic literature the word referred to any dark-skinned person or thing. The difficulty sometimes encountered in deciding on a meaning of Black or black for this word (e.g., in the *shifḥah kushit* parables) arose not because it was impossible to decide between two mutually exclusive categories, but because there were *not* two different categories. In other words, the Black was not seen as a separate classification of humanity; he or she was, rather, part of a large class of dark-skinned people. To make a judgment of Black or black on the basis of the term *kushi(t)* alone would be to impose our categorization artificially upon a culture that had no such categories. The only times that *kushi(t)* definitely means Black in rabbinic literature are when the references are to, or derive from, biblical passages mentioning the people of Kush, or when they are based on the biblical image of the Kushites as those who live at the ends of the earth. In the latter case, Kushite is paired with a people from the northern ends of the earth (Sarmatian, Goth, German) in a usage that parallels the Greek Scythian-Ethiopian topos of ends-of-the-earth people. Aside from these fixed usages, the term *kushi* as employed in the rabbinic corpus apparently always means dark-skinned. It may include a black African, but the term itself is not an ethnic designation. In other words, *kushi* is always used as a color term without any ethnic implication. This is significant, for it indicates that, as far as the evidence allows us to go, Judaism in late antiquity up until the Islamic period did not view the black African as a separate order of being. He was simply the darkest of a variety of dark-skinned people in the world.

Lloyd Thompson points out that a major flaw of many studies on racism in classical antiquity is the confusion between aesthetic preference and racial prejudice. Disparagement of black somatic features is not in and of itself racist. Only when a society's internal structures are discriminatory and its ideology justifies such discrimination can that society be considered racist. Otherwise we are merely looking at "ethnocentric reactions to black otherness and mere expressions of conformism to the dominant aesthetic values."[3] Ethnocentrism is not tantamount to racism. The former recognizes physical reality, the latter orders that reality into a hierarchy of domination. Gayraud Wilmore, an African American theologian, put it this way:

> If one prefers one skin color over another, whether white over black, or black over white, with the implication of aesthetic, genetic or cultural superiority,

> the seeds of racial prejudice are already present. And when that preference is not simply a natural, almost subconscious ethnocentrism, but a self-justifying concomitant of economic, political and cultural domination and exploitation, color prejudice is raised to the level of an ideology that stretches from a rather benign "racial thinking" to full-blown racial hatred, brutality and potential genocide.[4]

In other words, the difference between ethnocentrism and racism is "a self-justifying concomitant of economic, political and cultural domination and exploitation." Without it the seeds of racial prejudice will not germinate and take root.

I referred earlier to Kim Hall's study that showed how the colors black and white "become in the early modern period the conduit through which the English began to formulate the notions of 'self' and 'other.'" It wasn't a recognition of color difference, or even an ethnocentric preference, that was new in sixteenth-century England. It was the appropriation of these differences to support a racial ideology. "Traditional terms of aesthetic discrimination and Christian dogma become infused with ideas of Africa and African servitude," serving as racial signifiers.[5] A similar argument was made by Audrey Smedley about the very word "race," which

> from the beginning of its use in the English language . . . reflected a particular way of looking at and interpreting human differences, both physical and cultural. It was intricately linked with certain presuppositions of thought held by European colonists from the sixteenth to the eighteenth centuries. During that period the word was transformed in the English language from a mere classificatory term [of biophysical variation] into a folk idea. This idea expressed certain attitudes toward human differences as well as prejudgments about the nature and social value of these differences.[6]

The attitudes that evolved from the sixteenth to the eighteenth century were a product of the political dominance of various European states during this time. The conquered peoples were physically different from the Europeans, thus allowing for the linking of social status with physical difference. "Race was a social mechanism for concretizing and rigidifying a universal ranking system that gave Europeans what they thought was to be perpetual dominance over the indigenous peoples of the New World, Africa, and Asia."[7]

We thus come back to Wilmore's definition of racism as requiring domination and exploitation. The Jews of antiquity and late antiquity did not politically dominate physically distinct people. They did not conquer Africa and its people, who were markedly darker in skin color. During this period of time, Jewish society did not consequently mark ethnicity by color, nor did its categories of human differentiation serve as a social mechanism for perpetual dominance over another people. Therefore its literature, as shown in this study, did not reflect attitudes of denigration or disdain toward the black African. When, in later periods, Jews were part of larger cultures that did politically dominate physically distinct peoples, its literature began to equate ethnicity with skin color and began to exhibit the anti-Black sentiment of the surrounding culture.

It is by now a commonplace that all historical writing is a representation of the past as seen through the world of the writer. Yet, what struck me as I read through hundreds of modern biblical commentaries and historical and cultural studies of ancient Judaism was how strongly the perspective of one's own time and place shapes one's view of another time and place. We today are heirs to centuries of anti-Black sentiment, which has greatly conditioned our perspective. As a consequence, people—in and out of the academic world—readily assume that Blacks were always viewed pejoratively. But as I immersed myself in the literary remains of ancient Judaism, it became increasingly apparent that a different way of thinking about humanity was operating in the Mediterranean and Near Eastern civilizations of earlier times. Lewis did not find anti-Black sentiment in Arabia until the seventh-century conquest of Africa and the enslavement of its inhabitants.[8] Snowden and Thompson similarly did not find a prejudiced view of Blacks in ancient Greece and Rome.[9] Approaching the ancient texts without preconceived notions of anti-Black sentiment leads to the same conclusion for the Jewish world of antiquity and late antiquity. In those earlier times color did not define a person and was not a criterion for categorizing humanity. It was irrelevant in taking the measure of man.

APPENDIX I

WHEN IS A KUSHITE NOT A KUSHITE? CASES OF MISTAKEN IDENTITY

SOMETIMES a black African will appear in a text as a result of a misreading of the source or as a scribal error. A first-century Jewish work in Greek, the *Testament of Abraham,* refers to a meeting of the archangel Michael with Abraham at the biblical site of Oaks of Mamre (δρυὶ τῇ Μαμβρῇ). An eighteenth-century Romanian version of this work puts the meeting at a place called Driea the Black. How did Oaks of Mamre become Driea the Black? Moses Gaster suggested that the Greek δρυί 'oaks' was misunderstood as a proper name Driea, and Μαμβρῇ was misread as Μαυρῇ 'black'. So we get Driea the Black.[1] Whether this particular explanation is acceptable or not,[2] scribal errors of all sorts are very common in the transmission of texts before the age of printing. In the area of interest to this study, such misreadings and scribal errors have created a number of otherwise unknown Kushites.

Solomon's Scribes

In a story found in the Babylonian Talmud, King Solomon's two scribes, Eliḥoref and Aḥiyah, who are mentioned in 1 Kgs 4:3, are called Kushites.[3] On the other hand, in the version of the story recorded in Palestinian sources—the Palestinian Talmud and *Qohelet Rabba*—they are not called Kushites, but *secretarii* (or *exceptores, scriptores*) 'copyists'.[4] While *secretarii* is a straightforward translation of the biblical "scribes" (*soferim*), "Kushites" seems inexplicable.[5] Louis Ginzberg noted the difference between the two versions but did not attempt an explanation for the designation "Kushites."[6]

We do know that some Black slaves and freed slaves in the Roman Empire became secretaries, as did their white counterparts, but they also took on many other professions.[7] There is nothing to suggest a particular association between Blacks and secretaries. This being so, it would appear that "Kushites" may only be a textual corruption of some sort. It is possible that the confusion came about by a mistaken association of Aḥiyah the scribe with Aḥiyah the son of Shemḥazaʾe, who was said to have had intercourse with Ham's wife.[8] But an identity between the one who had intercourse with Ham's wife and Ham's son Kush is somewhat loose. It is more likely that "Kushites" represents a graphic or phonetic error: one of the Greek or Latin words in the Palestinian tradition (*secretarii, exceptores, scriptores,* etc.) was misread or misheard as the Greek σκοτερόι (or some other derivative of σκότος), that is, "dark ones" and that, in turn, became "Kushites."[9]

Caesar's Blacks

Another rabbinic reference to Kushites is recorded by Joshua Boaz (sixteenth century) as a variant reading in *bQid* 39b–40a (*Masoret ha-Shas,* ad loc.). The text states that R. Ḥanina b. Papa (Papi) spent the night in a bath house that was dangerous "even during the day" but he was protected by "two bearers of the Caesar" (*shnei nośeʾei qeisar shemaruni*). The variant has "Kushites" (*kwšʾy*) for "bearers" (*nwśʾy*).

Although Jewish sources elsewhere refer to the physical dangers of the baths (floor collapse, fire, etc.), "even during the day" indicates that the danger in this story derives from demons, who seem to be particularly active at night, as was understood by Rashi and other commentators.[10] A number of Christian and Greco-Roman sources indicate a belief in late antiquity that bath houses were haunted by demons and that various measures had to be taken by the bather for protection. The Christian texts mention the efficacy of prayer, and various symbols on the mosaics and paintings of Greco-Roman bath houses have been interpreted as apotropaic devices against the bath demons.[11] At first glance, the reading "Kushites" would seem to confirm a theory that Ethiopian images found in the baths also served an apotropaic function.[12] Upon consideration, however, it becomes clear that this reading cannot be accepted. First, "Kushites" is found only in the late anthology *Haggadot ha-Talmud;* all extant manuscripts of *bQid*—Munich 95, Vatican 111, Oxford 367—as well as ed. pr. have *nwśʾy* or obvious corruptions of it.[13] Second, the sentence in which the Hebrew word *nośeʾei* appears is Hebrew, where one would not expect the Aramaic *kushaʾei* (cf. *bSuk* 53a: *beʿo minʾai hanei tartei kushaʾei . . .*). On the other hand, the reading "bearers," which apparently refers to litter-bearers, the φορεαφόροι, has manuscript and linguistic support and makes good sense. At the time in which this story is put—Ḥanina b. Papa lived from the end of the third to the beginning of the fourth century—litters (*lectica*) were commonly used by the upper classes in Rome as well as in the provinces, so that "bearers of the Caesar," referring to the local Roman authority, were a known feature of the Palestinian social landscape. As would be imagined, litter-bearers were particularly chosen for their strength, so that their role in the story as protectors makes good sense.[14] The difference between *kwšʾy* (Kushites) and *nwśʾy* (bearers) is in the two very similarly written letters, *k* (כ) and *n* (נ). Clearly, "Kushites" is just a scribal error.

Drunken Kushites

A talmudic passage reads: "Ten measures of drunkenness were given to the world: nine were taken by Kushites and one by the rest of the world."[15] So according to the standard printed versions. However, a marginal annotation in the editions notes a variant reading "blackness" in place of "drunkenness," and this is the reading also in MSS Munich 95, Oxford 367, Vatican 111, and the first printed edition. Undoubtedly "blackness" is the correct reading, for it makes perfect sense, while "drunkenness" makes no sense at all. In Hebrew the difference between the two words (*škrwt–šḥrwt*) is slight—in one letter only—and scribal corruption readily occurred. The reading "blackness" was noted as a variant in the English translation published by the Soncino press (ed. I. Epstein; London, 1938), while the German translation (ed. L. Goldschmidt; Leipzig, 1912) already incorporated "blackness" as the correct reading. A similar mistake occurred in another passage that deals with drunkenness.[16]

Kushites Who Are Kuthites

At times in rabbinic texts the word *kushi* appears to be a scribal error for *kuthi* (originally 'Samaritan,' which then came to mean 'non-Jew' in general). This is a fairly common phenomenon in rabbinic literature and can be determined by context and textual witnesses. Such is the case in the following instances: *bNaz* 39a, where MS Vat 110, MS Moscow Günzberg 1134 (MS Munich 95 is lacking the clause), and a quotation in R. Asher and later writers read *goyim* 'gentiles';[17] *bMak* 24a bottom, where MS Munich 95, *YalqSh*, and *Haggadat ha-Talmud* read *goyim*, and *ʿEin Yaʿaqov* reads *ʿakum* and *kuthim;*[18] *bBer* 52b;[19] *bBQ* 113a-b;[20] *NumR* 19.3 toward the end; the midrashic citation in *Menorat ha-Maʾor,* ed. Enelow, 1:51 (also in one manuscript of *GenR* 70.7); the talmudic quotations of: Maharam of Rothenberg (d. 1293), *Responsa* (ed. Prague), vol. 4, sec. 982; Moses Sofer (d. 1839), *Responsa Ḥatam Sofer,* vol. 4 (*Even ha-ʿEzer*) sec. 8; and Israel Joshua Trunk (d. 1893), *Responsa Yeshuʿot Malko,* sec. *Yoreh Deʿah* 68. As can be seen clearly in the case of *bNaz* 39a or *bBer* 52b, censorship was responsible for the change from *goy* to *kuthi*. From there to *kushi* is probably no more than a scribal error, if it is not a deliberate substitution for *kuthi,* after the latter was commonly understood to mean "Christian."[21]

The *kushi* for *kuthi* error is also responsible for a reading found in some versions of a midrash telling how a few biblical personalities made a request of God in an improper manner, yet all but one were answered favorably. The midrash says that when Abraham sent his servant Eliezer to find a wife for Isaac, Eliezer said to God: "Here I stand by the spring as the daughters of the townsmen come out to draw water. Let the maiden to whom I say, 'Please lower your jar that I may drink,' and who replies, 'Drink, and I will also water your camels'—let her be the one whom You have decreed for Your servant Isaac" (Gen 24:13–14). This was considered an improper request, for a "slave, gentile, or prostitute" (*shifḥah, goyah, zonah*) might have appeared. Nevertheless, the request was answered favorably when Rebekah appeared. Similarly King Saul declared that whoever kills Goliath would receive great wealth and the king's daughter in marriage. Even though Goliath's slayer might have been a "slave, gentile, or bastard" (*ʿeved, goy, mamzer*) and thus an inappropriate husband for the king's daughter, Saul was answered favorably and God sent David (1 Sam 17:25ff.). Caleb too was fortunate. He declared that he would give his daughter in marriage to the man who conquers Kiriath-sepher (Judges 1:12). Although this request was also improper, for a "slave, bastard, or gentile" (*ʿeved, mamzer, goy*) might have appeared, yet God sent Othniel, Caleb's kinsman. When Jephthah, however, vowed to God, "If you deliver the Ammonites into my hands, then whatever comes out of the door of my house to meet me on my safe return from the Ammonites, shall be the Lord's and shall be offered by me as a burnt offering" (Judg 11:30–31)—also an improper request, since an animal unfit for sacrifice could have appeared—the request was answered unfavorably. Jephthah's daughter greeted him.

This account is recorded in *Leviticus Rabba* and in some manuscripts of *Genesis Rabba*.[22] Other manuscripts of *GenR*, however, include *kushi* among those who would be inappropriate husbands for Saul's daughter. Some read "*kushi, barbari*" (or "*kushi, barbari, mamzer*"); others "*ʿeved, goy, kushi*." The various readings in the manuscripts and later citations are shown in the table on the next page.[23]

The fact that *kushi* does not appear in any manuscript or edition of *LevR* nor in two important witnesses to *GenR*—MSS London and Vatican 60—strongly indicates that *kushi* in *GenR* is not original to the text. In regard to the reading "*kushi* and *barbari*" I have already shown that this phrase was transferred from the immediately preceding section, *GenR* 60.2.[24] The reading "*ʿeved, goy, kushi*" is not found in the better manuscripts of *GenR* (Vatican 30, Vatican 60, and London), and while "*goy, kushi*" is found in a Genizah fragment, it is one of the latest of the *GenR* Genizah fragments, one that contains many errors.[25] I believe that the key to the origin of this reading is to be found in a medieval compilation that I have not seen cited as a

		אליעזר	כלב	שאול
1	ויקרא רבה	שפחה גויה זונה	עבד גוי ממזר	עבד גוי ממזר
2		שפחה גויה	עבד גוי ממזר	גוי ממזר
3		שפחה זונה	עבד גוי ממזר	עבד גוי
4		שפחה זונה ממזרת	עבד גוי ממזר	עבד גוי ממזר
5		שפחה זונה	עבד גוי ממזר	עבד גוי ממזר
6	בראשית רבה	שפחה גויה זונה	גוי ממזר	עבד גוי ממזר
7		אמה	עבד	עבד
8		שפחה	עבד ממזר	עבד ממזר
9		אמה	עבד	עבד עכו"ם כושי
10		אמה	עבד	עבד גוי כושי
11		שפחה	עבד ממזר	עבד גוי כושי
12		אמה	עבד גוי ממזר	עבד גוי כושי
13		אמה	עבד	כושי ברברי
14		אמה ממזרה	עבד (?)	כושי ברברי
15		אמה ממזרת	עבד ממזר	כושי ממזר ברברי
16			כושי ברברי	גוי כושי
17	ספר והזהיר	שפחה	עבד כותי ממזר	
18	פדר"ה (גרינהוט)	שפחה		גוי ממזר
19	מדרש אגדה	שפחה ממזרת נתינה		עבד גוי נתין
20	מדרש הגדול	שפחה	כושי מואבי	עבד גוי
21	תענית	סומא חגרא		עבד ממזר
22	יל"ש : בראשית	אמה	עבד	עבד גוי כושי
23	יהושע	סומא חגרת	עבד	עבד ממזר
24	לקח טוב	אמה גידמת	עבד	עכו"ם כושי
25		סומא חיגרת גידמת	עבד	עכו"ם כושי
26	פדר"ה (שענבלום)	שפחת ממזרת סומא חיגרת		עבד ממזר שאול בן כושי

1–5 Variant readings following Margulies, ed. *LevR*.
6 MS Vat. 60 (p. 221)
7 MSS London, Adler
8 MS Paris
9 Edd.
10 MS Stuttgart
11 *Midrash Ḥakhamim* (MS)
12 MS Munich
13 MS Vat. 30 (p. 93b)
14 MS Oxf. 2335
15 MS Oxf. 147
16 MS Genizah 7 in Sokoloff, p. 147
17–26 Editions noted in text
20 כושיומואבי: *MT*, *Issurei Biʾah* 12.
25 Ms Florence as cited by Buber.

parallel source of our midrash—*Sefer We-Hizhir*.[26] This work transmits the Caleb tradition this way: "Had a *mamzer, kuthi,* or *ʿeved* conquered Kiriath-sepher . . . " In other words, *ʿeved, goy, mamzer* of *LevR* (and *GenR* MS Vatican 60)[27] became *ʿeved, kuthi, mamzer* in *We-Hizhir* in accordance with the common substitution of *kuthi* for *goy* in rabbinic literature. This last reading then probably became, by scribal corruption, *ʿeved, kushi, mamzer* (a reading not found in its entirety, but cf. *GenR* MS Oxford 147 which has *kushi* and *mamzer*). At the last step, *ʿeved, kushi, mamzer* may then have become *ʿeved, kushi, goy* (the inferior *GenR* manuscripts) in order to include the category of non-Jew, which had been lost by the change from *kuthi* to *kushi*.[28] The reconstruction of the scribal changes would look something like this: *ʿeved, goy, mamzer* > *ʿeved, kuthi, mamzer* > [*ʿeved, kushi, mamzer*] > *ʿeved, kushi, goy* or *ʿakum* [idolater], *kushi, goy*. Whether the last step of this reconstruction is correct or not, it seems clear that the original reading of *GenR* did not have *ʿeved, goy, kushi,* and that *kuthi* was substituted for *goy* (as in *Sefer we-Hizhir*), which via scribal error became *kushi*.[29] The introduction of *kuthi/kushi* was probably also the prompt for the "*kushi, barbari*" reading copied from the preceding section of *GenR*. Note that MS Oxford 147 has both *kushi, barbari,* and *mamzer,* and the Genizah fragment has both *goy, kushi* (for Saul) and *barbari, kushi* (for Caleb).[30]

In the texts quoted in this section, the word *kushi* is a scribal error for *kuthi*. On the other hand, the place-name ʿEin Kushi(n), mentioned in rabbinic sources (*bAZ* 31a; *yAZ* 5.4, 44c; *tShevi* 4.4; *yShevi* 5.5, 36a top), is not an error and yet has nothing to do with black Africa. Arabic writers mention a Samaritan sect called the Kushanis (*kūshānīyya*). Although these authors are writing in the posttalmudic Islamic period, according to Moshe Gil their information derived from pre-Islamic sources.[31] If Gil is right, then the rabbinic ʿEin Kushi(n) may be related to the Kushanis.[32] In any case, there is no indication that the name of the place has anything to do with Kush in Africa.

The Black Heads

Both Tannaitic Hebrew and Amoraic Hebrew have a term *sheḥorei roʾsh,* which literally means "black heads."[33] The term, however, does not refer to skin color. The context of the tannaitic source indicates a meaning of "men" as opposed to women and children, while the context of the amoraic source indicates a meaning of "youth" as opposed to old age.[34] The same term occurs in Akkadian (*ṣalmāt qaqqadi* 'black heads'), where the meaning is "mankind."[35] The semantic development of the term is obvious in Soqoṭri, where we can see that the term *ḥoriš* 'man' is derived from *ḥor riš* 'black-headed'.[36]

The Black Monk

The following case derives from a time after the close of the rabbinic period, and thus outside the purview of this study, but I include it here as another example of how a misreading of texts can create a black African where none was intended. A medieval Jewish folktale tells the story of a Jewish community endangered by an antisemitic sorcerer, who is defeated by a saintly Jew commanding divine powers by virtue of his piety. The tale is found in a variety of versions, in both Hebrew and Yiddish, extending over an eight-hundred-year period and having its origin apparently in twelfth-century France-Germany (Ashkenaz). Although the versions contain a variety of different elements, the common core of the story consists of a public competition of magic between the Jew and the gentile. In two of the seventeenth-century Yiddish texts the antagonist of the Jews is termed a "black monk" (*shvartzer munk*), and in two of the Hebrew texts (one a translation from Yiddish), from the same time period, he is called a kushite monk (*komer kushi*).[37]

It would be strange were *komer kushi* (or *shvartzer munk*) to refer to a black African. We would not expect a Black monk, or a black African in general, to be part of the Jewish world in which this legend was born and developed, that is, from twelfth-century Ashkenaz through medieval, premodern, and modern Eastern Europe. And while there is reason enough during this period to cast the Jews' adversary as a monk, there is no reason to see him as a black African.

It seems to me that there are, rather, three possibilities (not mutually exclusive) to explain the monk's blackness. (1) It may derive from the monk's practice of "black magic" as opposed to the divinely aided miraculous magic of the Jewish hero. This antithesis of good and bad magic constitutes the heart of the folktale and is seen, as well, in the association of the antagonist with demons and with his depiction as a practitioner of the "black arts" (*der shvartz kuntzter*).[38] (2) A second possibility is that the black color of the enemy may be a literary antithesis to the description of the hero in some of the versions as "a little red Jew." According to a recent study, the legend of "the red Jews," apocalyptic destroyers of Christendom, originates in circa twelfth-century Germany, precisely the time and place in which our story originated.[39] (3) The most likely possibility is that the blackness derives from the monk's habit, just as the Benedictines were known as the Black Monks, or the Dominicans as the Black Friars, or the Alexian (or Cellitine) nuns as the Black Sisters.[40] The last suggestion would stand or fall on a correlation of "black" with "monk" in the various versions of the story; in at least one (Yasif, no. 2), the black man is not described as a cleric. In any case, there are sufficient explanations to account for the appearance of a "black monk" without having to assume an

African heritage, which would be an unlikely scenario in a twelfth-century Ashkenazic-Jewish folktale. It would appear, then, that the translation *komer kushi* is a misunderstanding of the Yiddish *shvartzer munk* or that *kushi* is being used as a color term, "black."

Ein Grosser Schwarzer Mann

This case also derives from a time beyond the chronological framework of this study, but I include it here not only as another example of misreading but also because its origin is in a talmudic story, and because it continues the aesthetic distaste for dark skin color we saw operating in the earlier period. Illustrating the evil of proud behavior, the sixteenth-century anonymous Yiddish collection of stories and folktales known as the *Maʿaseh Buch* tells of "a big black man" (*ein grosser schwarzer mann*) who greeted Rabbi Eleazar b. Shimʿon and said to him:

> "Peace unto you O master." Rabbi Eleazar did not return the greeting and said to him, "Tell me, you wretch, are all the people of your town as black as you are?" The man replied, "I do not know, but go and say to the Master who made me, 'Why have you made such a contemptible vessel?'" When the man replied to him so strangely, Eleazar realized that he had spoken improperly and that he had sinned against God. So he dismounted from his ass and fell down at the feet of the man and said, "My dear friend, forgive me for having spoken disrespectfully to you, I did not consider what I was saying." But the man replied, "I cannot forgive you until you go to the Artisan who made me and ask Him why He made such a black article?"

The story continues with Eleazar's attempts to seek forgiveness.[41]

The origin of this story is a tannaitic *baraita* recorded in several rabbinic sources.[42] However, in all these sources, as well as in later quotations in R. Ḥananel's (d. 1050) commentary to *bTaʿan,* Abraham Zacuto's (d. ca. 1515), *Sefer ha-Yuḥasin,* and the *Haggadot ha-Talmud* and *ʿEin Yaʿaqov* anthologies there is no mention of "black"; the man is just "ugly."[43] Indeed, if Yonah Frenkel's literary analysis of this story is correct, there is a crucial play on words implied in the use of *mekhuʿarin* and *bene ʿirkha,* the point of which would be lost if "black" replaced or supplemented "ugly."[44] Apparently, the description of the man as black or dark is a later development.

In a further development of the story, the color term becomes an ethnic term, just as in the case of the Black Monk. In his commentary on the passage from the Talmud, Samuel Edels (Maharsha) says that the man may have been a *kushi,* since "he was ugly and very black."[45] Edels (d. 1631, Poland) lived at about the same time and place as the author the *Maʿaseh*

Book, and there may therefore be a connection between the two works—either they both drew on the same (no longer extant) source, or Edels was dependent upon the *Maʿaseh Buch.* In any case in the early sources the man is not identified as an African and not even as dark; he is just ugly (in *Derekh Ereṣ Rabba* he is an ugly Jew).

Kush(i) = Cochin?

Finally, I include another case of a (possibly) non-African *kush(i)* found in some medieval Jewish sources. Although these sources also derive from a later period, I mention them here because one of them, Benjamin of Tudela, is commonly cited in studies dealing with rabbinic texts.[46] Yehudah Ratzaby has noted that a reference to *kush* and *kushi* in the writings of the Yemeni, Zechariah al-Ḍāhrī (sixteenthth century) "almost certainly" means Cochin.[47] If this is so, I would suggest that the "Kushites" (*bnei kush*) mentioned by Benjamin of Tudela as living in Khulam (Quilon) on the Malabar coast of India to the south of Cochin similarly may not refer to black Africa but to Cochin.[48]

APPENDIX II

KUSH/ETHIOPIA AND INDIA

THE CONFUSION OR interchange between the names Kush/Ethiopia and India is found from antiquity to the modern period in Greco-Roman, Jewish, Christian, and Islamic sources.[1] Already Herodotus called the Indians "Ethiopians," distinguishing between the wooly-haired Ethiopians (Africans) and the straight-haired Ethiopians (Indians).[2] Similar confusion between Ethiopia and India is found in *The Sibylline Oracles* (first century B.C.E.).[3] The pseudepigraphon *Joseph and Aseneth* 22.7 (first century B.C.E. to second century C.E.) describes Jacob as having hair thick as an Ethiopian, but the variant "Indian" occurs in an Armenian version.[4] The *Expositio totius mundi et gentium* (fourth century) refers to the Sudanese as "Indians."[5] Compare also the statement in *The Chronicle of John, Bishop of Nikiu* 5.1 (seventh to eighth century): "There was a man from India, named Qanturgus, an Ethiopian of the race of Ham . . . ,"[6] and the version of Moses' "Ethiopian" war found in the *Palaea historica* (ninth to tenth century), in which India is substituted for Ethiopia.[7] In targumic and medieval Jewish literature, A. Epstein lists the following translations of "Kush" as "India": Targum to Isa 11:11, 18:1, Jer 13:23, Zeph 3:10; *QohR* and *TgQoh* to Qoh 2:5 (= *Tanḥ, Qedoshim* 10); Rashi on *bBer* 36b, *bYoma* 34b, 81b, and *bQid* 22b.[8] The interchange between India and Ethiopia is also found, Epstein notes, in travel literature such as the writings of Marco Polo and Benjamin of Tudela.[9] In the Judeo-Persian version of Targum Song 1:5 ("When the Israelites made the Golden Calf their faces became as black as the Kushites"), "India" replaces "Kush" of the Targum.[10] In the Prester John legends India is presented as "Ethiopia."[11]

Writing about the confusion between the names India and Ethiopia (and Himyar) in Syriac authors, Alphonse Mingana concluded that the Indians' dark skin led to their being confused with the Ethiopians. "Indian," he says, seems to be a "generic name for all the dark peoples of the East." He notes that this conflation, which he finds first in Aphrahat (fourth century), is far more frequent among West Syrians than East Syrians (Nestorians), among whom India is almost always what we today consider India.[12] We should note that the same confusion—if that's what it is—exists in the Peshiṭta, which renders "India/Indians" for Biblical Hebrew "Kush/Kushites" in 2 Chr 14:8/9, 14:11/12, 14:12/13, 16:8, 21:16 and Jer 13:23.[13] The Syriac seventh-century Pseudo-Methodius uses *hendwaie, hendū* with the meanings "Ethiopians," "Ethiopia."[14] The Ethiopian-Indian confusion is very common and continued well into the modern period.[15]

NOTES

INTRODUCTION

1. J. J. Flournoy, *A Reply to a Pamphlet . . .* (Athens, Ga., 1838), p. 16.

2. Quoted in William B. Cohen, *The French Encounter with Africans: White Response to Blacks, 1530–1880* (Bloomington, Ind., 1980), p. 222.

3. See Anthony J. Barker, *The African Link: British Attitudes to the Negro in the Era of the Atlantic Slave Trade, 1550–1807* (London, 1978), pp. 44, 208 and sources cited there. Also Alden T. Vaughan, *Roots of American Racism* (New York, 1995), p. 6; Cohen, *French Encounter*, pp. 14–15, and Eulalio R. Baltazar, *The Dark Center: A Process Theology of Blackness* (New York, 1973), p. 7.

4. Winthrop Jordan, *White over Black: American Attitudes toward the Negro, 1550–1812* (Chapel Hill, 1968), pp. 6–11. A summary of Jordan's view is provided by George M. Fredrickson, who disagrees with it, in the *New York Review of Books*, 7 February 1974, pp. 23–24.

5. Toni Morrison, *Playing in the Dark: Whiteness and the Literary Imagination* (New York, 1992), pp. 48–49 (emphasis added).

6. Harold R. Isaacs, "Blackness and Whiteness," *Encounter* (London) 21 (August 1963), p. 14, n. 4.

7. Kenneth J. Gergen, "The Significance of Skin Color in Human Relations," *Daedalus* 96 (1967) 397–98, reprinted in J. H. Franklin, *Color and Race* (Boston, 1968), p. 119. See also Jeffrey Russell, *The Devil: Perceptions of Evil from Antiquity to Primitive Christianity* (Ithaca, N.Y., 1977), p. 65. Arrah B. Evarts, "Color Symbolism," *Psychoanalytic Review* 6 (1919) 124–57, provides many examples of color symbolism from different cultures and times.

8. Studies cited in Cohen, *French Encounter*, pp. 13–14 and 299, n. 63.

9. Dominique Zahan, "White, Red and Black: Colour Symbolism in Black Africa," in *The Realms of Colour*, ed. A. Portmann and R. Ritsema, Eranos 1972 (Leiden, 1974), pp. 375–76; L. Cracco Ruggini, "Il negro buono e il negro malvagio nel mondo classico," in *Conoscenze etniche e rapporti di convivenza nell'antichità*, ed. M. Sordi (Milan, 1979), p. 114, n. 26; Isaacs, "Blackness and Whiteness," p. 14, n. 4 (according to Isaacs, these conventions predate contact with Western man); Victor Turner, *The Forest of Symbols: Aspects of Ndembu Ritual* (Ithaca, N.Y., 1967), pp. 57, 60, 65–74, 77, and see also 60, 81–84; Carl N. Degler, *Neither Black nor White: Slavery and Race Relations in Brazil and the United States* (New York, 1971), pp. 211–12. Gergen, "Significance of Skin Color," pp. 397–98; Pauline M. Ryan, "Color Symbolism in Literature," *Journal of Anthropological Research* 32 (1976) 141–60, esp. 144–47; John S. Mbiti, *Concepts of God in Africa* (London, 1970), pp. 41, 106, 112, 118, 155–56, 184, 189, 222.

10. See also Frank Snowden, *Before Color Prejudice: The Ancient View of Blacks* (Cambridge, Mass., 1983), pp. 82ff., the literature cited on p. 139, n. 94, and his "Asclepiades' Didyme," *Greek, Roman, and Byzantine Studies* 32 (1991) 251, n. 30. For explanations as to why this symbolism is so common, in addition to the literature cited thus far, see J. Kovel, *White Racism: A Psychohistory* (New York, 1970).

11. See the entries under *ʾôr* and *ḥāšak* in *TDOT* 1:149–65 (S. Aalen) and 5:246–58 (L. A. Mitchel, H. Lutzmann), and under λευκός, σκότος κτλ., and φῶς κτλ. in *TDNT* 4:241ff. (W. Michaelis), 7:424ff. (H. Conzelmann), and 9:312ff. (H. Conzelmann). See also Lloyd Thompson, *Romans and Blacks* (Norman, Okla., 1989), p. 110, with literature cited at n. 96; Christopher Rowe, "Conceptions of Colour and Colour Symbolism in the Ancient World," Portmann and Ritsema, *The Realms of Colour,* pp. 354–56; J.P.V.D. Balsdon, *Romans and Aliens* (Chapel Hill, N.C., 1979), p. 217; and Jeffrey Russell, *Satan: The Early Christian Tradition* (Ithaca, N.Y., 1981), p. 40, n. 26.

12. Francis X. Gokey, *The Terminology for the Devil and Evil Spirits in the Apostolic Fathers* (Washington, D.C., 1961), p. 50. The symbolism is very common in John, but also in the Synoptics and Paul, e.g., Matthew 18:7, 1 Corinthians 2:12, 11:32, 2 Corinthians 7:10, Galatians 1:4.

13. See St. Clair Drake, *Black Folk Here and There* (Los Angeles, 1990), esp. 2:206–23. Gergen also argues that the evidence is not conclusive to support the proposition; see his "Significance of Skin Color," p. 121.

14. See David Goldenberg, "The Curse of Ham: A Case of Rabbinic Racism?" in *Struggles in the Promised Land,* ed. Jack Salzman and Cornel West (New York, 1997), pp. 22–24, and David Aaron, "Early Rabbinic Exegesis on Noah's Son Ham and the So-Called 'Hamitic Myth,'" *Journal of the American Academy of Religion* 63 (1995) 721–29. A new book, Abraham Melamed's *The Image of the Black in Jewish Culture* (London, 2003), makes similar claims. This book is, unfortunately, full of mistakes of all sorts. Almost every page exhibits the author's misreadings and misunderstandings of the primary sources. I review the work in *JQR* 93 (2003) 557–79.

15. In M. J. Kister, "Ḥaddithū ʿan banī isrāʾīla," *Israel Oriental Studies* 2 (1972) 238. Kister's article itself provides evidence of transmission of such extrabiblical traditions.

16. Jay Braverman, *Jerome's Commentary on Daniel: A Study of Comparative Jewish and Christian Interpretations of the Hebrew Bible* (Washington, D.C., 1978), pp. 1–10, gives a short introduction to the issue of rabbinic influence on patristic exegesis with the focus on Jerome.

17. Most notably in the *War Scroll.* On the logos, see T. Tobin in *ABD* 4:350–52; on light and darkness, see *TDOT* 5:258–59 (Ringgren, Mitchel), and John J. Collins, *The Apocalyptic Imagination,* 2nd ed. (Grand Rapids, Mich., 1998), pp. 153–57. Regarding the Christian application of light and darkness, cf. also the Qumran terminology "Prince of Lights" and "Angel of Darkness" (1QS 3:20–22).

18. Steven Wasserstrom, "Jewish Pseudepigrapha in Muslim Literature: A Bibliographical and Methodological Sketch," in *Tracing the Threads: Studies in the Vitality of Jewish Pseudepigrapha,* ed. John C. Reeves (Atlanta, 1994), p. 100. See also Wasserstrom's remarks about the "seemingly fluid interconfessionalism" in seventh–eighth century Iraq, quoted later, p. 192.

19. Yaacov Shavit, *History in Black: African-Americans in Search of an Ancient Past* (London, 2001), p. 178. Similarly, Melamed, *The Image of the Black in Jewish Culture,* p. 97.

20. See Appendix I.

21. Quoted by C. Tsehloane Keto, *The Africa Centered Perspective of History and Social Sciences in the Twenty First Century* (Blackwood, N.J., 1989), p. 38.

22. In John Ralph Willis, ed., *Slaves and Slavery in Muslim Africa* (London, 1985), 1:66.

23. See Sara Mills, *Discourse* (London, 1997), p. 49.

24. Thompson, *Romans and Blacks,* pp. 8, 19.

25. Ibid., pp. 5–8.

26. Ibid., pp. 17–18.

27. See, e.g., Jan Nederveen Pieterse, *White on Black: Images of Africa and Blacks in Western Popular Culture* (New Haven, 1992; originally in Dutch, 1990), p. 51. So also Stephen J. Gould would separate biological determinism from a definition of racism; see his *Mismeasure of Man* (New York, 1981), p. 31.

28. Harry Bracken, "Philosophy and Racism," in his *Mind and Language: Essays on Descartes and Chomsky* (Dordrecht, 1984), p. 51. The essay originally appeared in *Philosophia* 8 (1978) 241–60.

29. Lloyd Thompson, *Rome and Race,* University Lectures, 1981, University of Ibadan (Ibadan, Nigeria, 1987), pp. 17–18.

30. See the comments of Steven Fraade, "Rabbinic Views on the Practice of Targum, and Multilingualism in the Jewish Galilee of the Third–Sixth Centuries," in *The Galilee in Late Antiquity,* ed. Lee Levine (New York, 1992), p. 253.

31. See William Scott Green, "What's in a Name?—The Problematic of Rabbinic 'Biography,'" in *Approaches to Ancient Judaism: Theory and Practice,* ed. W. S. Green (Missoula, Mont., 1978), pp. 89–90.

32. See Ephraim E. Urbach, "The Homiletical Interpretations of the Sages and the Expositions of Origen on Canticles and the Jewish-Christian Disputation," *Scripta Hierosolymitana* 22 (1971) 251, and Y. Sussman in *Meḥqerei Talmud* 1 (1990) 109, n. 204. Note Menahem Kister's comment that "sometimes underlying the traditions of rabbinic midrash are products of a different, earlier era reflecting an ancient Hellenistic heritage" ("Observations on Aspects of Exegesis, Tradition, and Theology in Midrash, Pseudepigrapha, and Other Jewish Writings," Reeves, *Tracing the Threads,* p. 19).

33. See, e.g., Green, "What's in a Name?" esp. pp. 80–84.

34. Jay Harris, "From Inner-Biblical Interpretation to Early Rabbinic Exegesis," in *Hebrew Bible, Old Testament: The History of Its Interpretation,* ed. Magne Sæbø (Göttingen, 1996), 1:266.

CHAPTER ONE

1. See Yoshiyuki Muchiki, *Egyptian Proper Names and Loanwords in North-West Semitic* (Atlanta, 1999), pp. 26–27, 91. Georges Posener, "Pour une localisation du pays Koush au Moyen Empire," *Kush* 6 (1958) 46, notes that the name Kush is unrelated to any Egyptian root and suggests that if the Egyptian place-name *Kns.t* is a variation of *Kush,* it may indicate a foreign, perhaps Nubian, origin of the name. See also T. Säve-Söderbergh in *Lexikon der Ägyptologie,* ed. Wolfgang Heck, Otto Eberhard, and Wolfhart Westendork (Wiesbaden, 1975–92), 3:888–89, s.v. Kusch.

2. Franz Wutz, *Onomastica Sacra: Untersuchungen zum Liber Interpretationis Nominum Hebraicorum des Hl. Hieronymus* (Leipzig, 1914–15), pp. 427, 740;

Michael Stone, ed., *Signs of the Judgement, Onomastica Sacra, and The Generations from Adam* (Chico, Calif., 1981), p. 133.

3. Origen, *Selecta in Genesim, PG* 12.100: "Ethiopia in Hebrew is Kush which means σκότωσιν." Philo, *Quaestiones in Genesim* 2.81. On Origen, see R.P.C. Hanson, "Interpretations of Hebrew Names in Origen," *Vigiliae Christianae* 10 (1956) 104. On Philo, see R. Marcus in LCL, ad loc., note k; A. Hanson, *JTS* 18 (1967) 138; and V. Nikiprowetzky, *Le commentaire de l'écriture chez Philon d'Alexandrie* (Leiden, 1977), pp. 83–84, n. 36.

4. Philo's (*Legum Allegoriae* 2.67) allegorical comparison of the Kushite in Num 12:1 with the black pupil of the eye is not based on the name "Kush" (contra Wutz, p. 427), but on the skin color of the Kushite. Elsewhere, Philo etymologizes Ethiopian as meaning "lowness" or "cowardice" (*Leg. All.* 1.68), but this is based on the Greek name "Ethiopian" and not the Hebrew "Kush." For both of these Philonic passages, see pp. 46 and 51.

5. E.g., Robin Blackburn, *The Making of New World Slavery* (London, 1997), p. 67; Ephraim Isaac, "Genesis, Judaism and the 'Sons of Ham,'" *Slavery and Abolition* 1 (1980) 7 = J. R. Willis, ed., *Slaves and Slavery in Muslim Africa,* 1:80; Yaacov Shavit, *History in Black,* p. 157.

6. Recently László Török has synthesized the evidence regarding the kingdom of Kush and has written a comprehensive history covering the political, cultural, and intellectual spheres: *The Kingdom of Kush: Handbook of the Napatan-Meroitic Civilization* (Leiden, 1997). An overview sketch of the history of Kush is provided by W. Y. Adams, "The Kingdom and Civilization of Kush in Northeast Africa," in *CANE,* pp. 775–89; Donald B. Redford in *ABD* 4:110a, s.v. Kush; and Timothy Kendall in *OEAE* 2:250–52. See also J. Daniel Hays, "The Cushites: A Black Nation in Ancient History," *Bibliotheca Sacra* 153 (1996) 270–80. More detailed information on the Meroitic period (ca. 274 B.C.E.–370 C.E.) of Kush: L. Török, "Geschichte Meroes: Ein Beitrag über die Quellenlage und den Forschungsstand," in *ANRW* 2.21.1 (1984) 107–341 with a thorough and indexed bibliography. A short history of Kush during the biblical period is found in John D. Currid, *Ancient Egypt and the Old Testament* (Grand Rapids, Mich., 1997), pp. 233–37, and Robert Bennett, "Africa and the Biblical Period," *HTR* 64 (1971) 483–500. See also *ABD* 2:665, s.v. Ethiopia (R. H. Smith); *EI*² 5:521, s.v. Kūsh (D. Cohen); *EB* 4:67–68, s.v. Kush (J. Liver); and, especially for Nubian-Egyptian relations, T. Säve-Söder in *Lexicon der Ägyptologie* 3:888–93, s.v. Kusch, and Derek Welsby in *OEAE* 2:551–57. A collection of articles, including many on Kush in antiquity, has recently been published: *Africa and Africans in Antiquity,* ed. Edwin Yamauchi (East Lansing, Mich., 2001).

7. Pliny, *Natural History* 12.8.19. In the unvocalized Hebrew text of the Bible the name is spelled *swnh;* in the Isaiah scroll from the Dead Sea (1QIs[a] 49:12) it is spelled *swnyym.* On the geographic location of biblical Kush (south of Egypt, i.e., south of Aswan, approximately the region of Nubia = Ethiopia of classical authors), see J. Simons, *The Geographical and Topographical Texts of the Old Testament* (Leiden, 1959), pp. 18–21. See also A. Dihle, *Umstrittene Daten: Untersuchungen zum Auftreten der Griechen am Roten Meer* (Cologne, 1965), pp. 65–79 ("Zur Geschichte des Aethiopennamens"), and G. Posener, "Pour une localisation du pays Koush au Moyen Empire," *Kush* 6 (1958) 39–68.

8. Strabo 17.1.3.

9. The fairly common pairing of Kush and Egypt may derive from the period of the Twenty-fifth (Nubian) dynasty; see Liver, *EB* 4:66. Regarding Nah 3:9 (***kush ʿoṣmah we-miṣrayim***), 4Q385 17a ii 6 (*DJD* 30:155) reads: ***kush miṣrayi*** [***m ʿoṣmah***]. Isa 11:11 also apparently refers to Nubia when it mentions the Jews in Kush. The reference is to the military colony of Jews in Elephantine near Aswan, which we know about through the discovery of their documents dating from the fifth century B.C.E. So according to E. Ullendorff, "Hebraic-Jewish Elements in Abyssinian (Monophysite) Christianity," *JSS* 1 (1956) 217, and H. Wildberger, *CC: Isaiah 1–12,* trans. T. H. Trapp (Minneapolis, 1991; originally in German, 1980), p. 492.

10. According to some scholars, this is one of several places in the Bible where Kush appears as a synonym for, or in place of, Egypt, such usage deriving from the period of the Kushite dynasty in Egypt. See R. H. Smith in *ABD* 2:666a, s.v. Ethiopia; Yair Hoffman, *OhT: 2 Kings,* p. 172c. Smith refers to Amos 9:7, Zeph 2:12, 3:10, 2 Chr 14, as well as 2 Kgs 19:9, and Simons, *Geographical and Topographical Texts,* p. 19, refers to Ezek 30:4, 9. See p. 117 for examples in the rabbinic period of Egyptians being called Kushites. On the title of "king" for Tirhaqa, see M. Cogan and H. Tadmor, *AB: 2 Kings,* p. 248, n. 3.

11. Note also the LXX reading of Σοήνη (i.e., Syene, Aswan) for Seba.

12. On the passages from Isaiah, see p. 32, where also classical references to the Kushites' height are cited.

13. Josephus, *Antiquities* 1.134–35, and cf. 2.249, 8.165; Strabo 16.4.2 and 8. See Abraham Schalit's note 132 in his edition of Josephus, *Qadmoniyot ha-Yehudim* (Jerusalem, 1955–63), ad loc.

14. So the interpretation of Matthew 12:42 (Luke 11:31) in Origen (third century), Gregory of Nazianzus (fourth century), and Arator (sixth century). Origen, *Comm. in Cant.* 2.1, *GCS* 33 (Origen 8) 116; *SC* 375:268; see also his *Hom. in Cant.* 1.6, *GCS* 33 (Origen 8) 37; *SC* 37:37. Gregory, *Discours 38–41, SC* 358:261. Arator is in *De actibus apostolorum,* 1.697–99, *CSEL* 72:54; *Arator's On the Acts of the Apostles (De actibus apostlorum),* ed. and trans. R. J. Schrader, with J. L. Roberts and J. F. Makowski cotranslators (Atlanta, 1987), p. 45. See also Honorius, cited later; Josephus, *Antiquities* 8.165, cited in the previous note; and A. Epstein, "Les Chamites de la table ethnographique selon le Pseudo-Jonathan comparé avec Josèphe et le Livre des Jubilés," *REJ* 24 (1892) 82–98. For the onomastic lists: Wutz, *Onomastica Sacra,* p. 120; note also Theodoret of Cyrrhus, *Interpretatio in Psalmos* 72.9, *PG* 80.1436A, *FC* 101:417: "Sabba is an Ethiopian nation," and similarly Anastasius Sinaita in Juhani Piilonen, *Hippolytus Romanus, Epiphanius Cypriensis and Anastasius Sinaita: A Study of the ΔΙΑΜΕΡΙΣΜΟΣ ΤΗΣ ΓΗΣ* (Helsinki, 1974), p. 19, line 32.

15. W. W. Müller, "Seba," in *ABD* 5:1064; A. Demsky, *OhT: Genesis,* p. 74b–c; Simons, *Geographical and Topographical Texts,* pp. 21, 40–41, 77, 81–85; F. V. Winnett, "The Arabian Genealogies in the Book of Genesis," *Translating and Understanding the Old Testament,* ed. H. T. Frank and W. L. Reed (Nashville, 1970), pp. 173–74. S. Krauss has suggested that the Palestinian targumic (including Targum Chronicles) identification of Sabtah as Semrai may be a reference to Sembritae, south of Meroe ("Die biblische Völkertafel im Talmud, Midrasch und Targum, *MGWJ* 39 [1895] 56).

16. "It is certain that the majority of the names describe people in Arabia"—Claus Westermann, *CC: Genesis 1–11: A Commentary,* trans. John J. Scullion (Minneapolis, 1984; originally in German, 1974), p. 511. Similarly, Gordon J. Wenham, *WBC: Genesis 1–15* (Dallas, 1994), pp. 221–22. I. Ephᶜal argues for two different peoples bearing the name Sheba, one in north and one in south Arabia, but agrees that "most of the names on the list of the sons of Cush relate to South Arabia" (Israel Ephᶜal, *The Ancient Arabs,* Jerusalem, 1992, p. 227). Note that the LXX has ʾΑράβων for MT Sheba in Ps 72/71:10. For the Arabian location of the various descendants of Kush, see further the encyclopedia articles listed in n. 6; Simons, *Geographical and Topographical Texts,* on Kush and the names of the individual descendants; Umberto Cassuto, *A Commentary on the Book of Genesis,* vol. 1: *From Noah to Abraham,* trans. Israel Abrahams (Jerusalem, 1961; originally in Hebrew, 1944), pp. 198–99; S. Hidal, "The Land of Cush in the Old Testament," *Svensk Exegetisk Arsbok* 41–42 (1976–77) 97–106, esp. pp. 103 and 106; B. Moritz, *Arabien: Studien zur physikalischen und historischen Geographie des Landes* (Hannover, Germany, 1923), p. 125; A. Demsky in *OhT: Genesis,* p. 74b–c; A. Jeremias, *The Old Testament in the Light of the Ancient Near East,* trans. from the 2nd German ed. by C. L. Beaumont, ed. C.H.W. Johns (New York, 1911), 1:286; Allen P. Ross, "The Table of Nations in Genesis—Its Content," *Bibliotheca Sacra* 138 (1981) 25; and the literature cited in R. D. Haak, "'Cush' in Zephaniah," in *The Pitcher Is Broken,* ed. S. W. Holloway and L. K. Handy (Sheffield, 1995), p. 242, n. 15. See also KBL (1st ed., 1958), s.v. Kush I.2 citing C. Landberg: "The tribe of Âl ᶜAmrān call the region of Zebid (Yaman) Kūš . . . " and therefore Kūš of Gen 10 and 1 Chr 1 is "the country astride the southern Red Sea"; Landberg is in his *Étude sur les dialectes de l'arabie méridionale,* vol. 2: *Daṯînah* (Leiden, 1909), p. 868, n. 1. See also Landberg's *Glossaire Daṯînois* (Leiden, 1920), p. 1009. Winnett ("Arabian Genealogies," pp. 175–80) would locate Havilah of Gen 10:7 and 2:11 in East Africa (Zeila) but Havilah of Gen 25:18 in East Arabia (Ar-rubᶜ al-ḫāli), and Raamah in Southeast Arabia on the northern border of Yemen (South Arabian inscription *Rgmt*) between Dedan to the north and Sheba to the southeast.

17. See, e.g., J. Desanges, "Arabes et Arabie in terre d'Afrique dans la géographie antique," in *L'Arabie préislamique et son environnement historique et culturel,* ed. T. Fahd (Leiden, 1989), pp. 420–29; J. Hiernaux, *The People of Africa* (New York, 1974), p. 55, and note that inscribed bowls with Arab names were found at a sanctuary at Tell al-Maskhuta in the eastern delta of Egypt (M.C.A. MacDonald, "North Arabia in the First Millennium BCE," *CANE,* p. 1367). See further W. W. Müller, "Seba" in *ABD* 5:1064, who speaks of the immigration to the Ethiopian littoral by settlers from South Arabia and the relations between ancient Yemen and Abyssinia. He refers to South Arabian (Sabean) epigraphic texts found in Ethiopia and a few African toponyms with Sabean foundations. Müller concludes that the biblical Seba and Sheba might thus refer to the names of the two regions in African and Arabia, respectively, the former having been colonized by inhabitants from the latter. See also the similar comments of Abraham Epstein, *Kitvei Avraham Epstein,* ed. A. M. Haberman (Jerusalem, 1950), 1:61.

18. A. N. Tucker, "What's in a Name?" in *Hamito-Semitica,* ed. James Bynon and Theodora Bynon (The Hague, 1975), p. 472. Long ago, the great Semitic linguist Theodor Nöldeke expressed the view that "the connexion between the Se-

mitic languages and the Hamitic appears to indicate that the primitive seat of the Semites is to be sought in Africa" (*Encyclopaedia Britannica*, 11th ed., New York, 1911, 24:620, s.v. Semitic Languages).

19. For Arabia to Africa migration, see W. W. Müller, "Seba," in *ABD* 5:1064; M. Naor, *Ha-Miqra' weha-Areṣ* (Tel Aviv, 1952), 1:8; and Liver, *EB* 4:65. For the opposite direction, see Simons, *Geographical and Topographical Texts*, p. 20. Westermann thinks that behind the biblical genealogy "a geographic association is intended" (*CC: Genesis 1–11*, p. 511). On Kushites in Arabia, S. Krauss already noted that in the biblical view, "the territory on both sides of the Red Sea formed an ethnic unit, which was sharply distinguished from the rest of Africa" (*JE* 1:224b). See the conclusion of M. Weiss, *The Book of Amos* (in Hebrew; Jerusalem, 1992), 1:282, that "the people on both sides of the Red Sea were known as Kushites," a view expressed earlier by G. Hölscher, *Drei Erdkarten: Ein Beitrag zur Erdkenntnis des hebräischen Altertums* (Heidelberg, 1949), pp. 40–41. Devisse (*IBWA* 2/1:49) quotes Honorius Augustodunensis (eleventh–twelfth century), *De imagine mundi* 1.33, to the effect that Ethiopia extended to "the land of the Sabaeans," i.e., to Arabia. But Honorius does not exactly say this. Rather he speaks of the "kingdom of Ethiopia . . . in which is the city of Saba," i.e., in Africa, which is an ancient and common view, as we saw earlier. Honorius has been edited by V.I.J. Flint in *Archives d'histoire doctrinale et littéraire du moyen age* 49 (1982) 7–153.

20. Desanges, "Arabes et Arabie in terre d'Afrique," pp. 413–29; so also H. I. Macadam, "Strabo, Pliny the Elder and Ptolemy of Alexandria: Three Views of Ancient Arabia and Its Peoples," in Fahd, *L'Arabie préislamique et son environnement historique et culturel*, pp. 291–92. This image of Africa in which the Nile divides Africa and Asia (Arabia) "closely follows ancient Greek tradition . . . which would still be prevalent in Pomponius Mela's and Pliny's [works]" (László Török in *FHN* 3:817). See also J. Devisse in *IBWA* 2/1:47–48 ("Roman antiquity regarded Africa as bound by the Nile"); and Pietschmann in *RE* 1:351, Brandis in *RE* 2:343, and the supplement to Liddell and Scott: P.G.W. Glare with A. A. Thompson, *Greek-English Lexicon, Revised Supplement* (Oxford, 1996), p. 49, s.v. Ἀράβαρχης. Jeremias, *The Old Testament in Light of the Ancient Near East*, 1:286, also notes that in classical sources the right bank of the Nile is called the "Arabian desert" and the left bank the "Libyan desert."

21. Targum Pseudo-Jonathan and Targum Neofiti margin to Gen 10:6 and Targum to 1 Chr 1:8. On these traditions, see Epstein, "Les Chamites de la table ethnographique," pp. 82–98, and Krauss, "Die biblische Völkertafel," pp. 56–57.

22. Herodotus 7.69–70.

23. Devisse in *IBWA* 2/1:49, quoting *Liber nominum locorum, ex Actis* (*PL* 23.1298), attributed to Jerome.

24. G. Posener, *Princes et pays d'Asie et de Nubie* (Brussels, 1940), pp. 88–89, E 50 and E 51. According to Mazar, *Eretz Israel* 3 (1954) 20, and "Palestine at the Time of the Middle Kingdom in Egypt," *Revue de l'histoire juive en Egypt* 1 (1947) 37–38 (reprinted in Mazar, *Kena'an we-Yisra'el*, Jerusalem, 1974), these Kushu are mentioned also in the Egyptian Story of Sinuhe (R. B. Parkinson, *The Tale of Sinuhe and Other Ancient Egyptian Poems, 1940–1640 BC*, Oxford, 1997, p. 38, line 220; cf. the translation of John L. Foster, *Thought Couplets in the Tale of Sinuhe*, Frankfurt am Main, 1993, p. 56); so too Y. Aharoni, *The Land of the Bible: A His-*

torical Geography, 2nd ed. (Philadelphia, 1979), pp. 143–44 (bibliography on the execration texts is listed by Aharoni, p. 186, n. 23), and S. Yeivin, *Meḥqarim be-Toledot Yisraʾel we-Arṣo* (Tel Aviv, 1960), p. 37. Yeivin, "Topographic and Ethnic Notes II," *ʿAtiqot* (English Series) 3 (1961) 176–80, thinks that a group of five (probably ethnic) names mentioned in inscriptions of Ramases II and III also refer to the Kushu (so too A. Demsky *OhT: Genesis,* p. 74b). These names are all preceded by the prefix *qʒwś* variously spelled.

25. J. Liver, *EB* 4:69, s.v. Kush; B. Maisler (Mazar), *Untersuchungen zur alten Geschichte und Ethnographie Syriens und Palästinas* (Giessen, 1930), pp. 46–47, n. 1; "Palestine at the Time of the Middle Kingdom in Egypt," pp. 37–38; *Eretz Israel* 3 (1954) 20, n. 16 (reprinted in Mazar, *Kenaʿan we-Yisraʾel,* Jerusalem, 1974); and *EB* 4:70–71, s.v. Kushan; Nadav Naʾaman, "Pastoral Nomads in the Southwestern Periphery of the Kingdom of Judah in the 9th–8th Centuries BCE," *Zion* 52 (1987) 261–64; J. H. Hayes, *Amos, the Eighth-Century Prophet* (Nashville, 1988), p. 219; S. Hidal, "The Land of Cush in the Old Testament," *Svensk Exegetisk Arsbok* 41–42 (1976–77) 100–103; A. Demsky in *OhT: Genesis,* p. 74b, also mentions Zerah and Kushan; for the identification of Kushan in Hab 3:7 as Kush, see also Yeivin, "Topographic and Ethnic Notes II," p. 177, and *Meḥqarim be-Toledot Yisraʾel we-Arṣo,* pp. 36–37, for Zerah, and see the discussion on Moses' Kushite wife in the next chapter. I. Ben-Shem identifies Zerah the Kushite as the head of a Kushite tribe inhabiting the area southeast of the Jordan River, near Petra and Maan in the southern area of Mount Seir. He thinks that the nearby Jebel Kash retains the name of the early inhabitants ("The War of Zerah the Cushite," in *Bible and Jewish History . . . Dedicated to the Memory of Jacob Liver,* ed. B. Uffenheimer, in Hebrew, Tel Aviv, 1971, pp. 52–53; English abstract, p. x). Note that some medieval commentaries had already made the identification of Kush(an) with Midian as being two names for the same people or the former a tribe of the latter; so Tanḥum Ha-Yerushalmi in his commentary to Hab 3:7 and to Zeph 2:12, *Tanḥum Ha-Yerushalmi's (13th Century) Commentary on the Minor Prophets,* ed. Hadassa Shy (in Hebrew; Jerusalem, 1991), pp. 226–27, 250–51. Lastly, my colleague Sol Cohen has suggested to me that the Land of Goshen, which is located by biblical scholars in the eastern delta of the Nile, that is, in the same general area inhabited by the bedouin Kushites, may be related to the name Kushan.

26. Maisler, *Untersuchungen,* pp. 46–47, n. 1; Yeivin, "Topographic and Ethnic Notes II," p. 177. Other candidates: Kushan Rishatayim in Judg 3:8ff. (Maisler; but see J. R. Bartlett in *ABD* 1:1220, and A. Malamat in *EB* 4:71); Isa 45:14 (Jeremias, *The Old Testament in the Light of the Ancient Near East,* 1:286, who also accepts the Zerah identification), and perhaps Ps 87:4 (Liver, *EB* 4:69, s.v. Kush).

27. Ephʿal, *The Ancient Arabs,* p. 78. "Gedor" is the reading in MT; "Gerar" is that of the Septuagint. Y. Aharoni, "The Land of Gerar," *IEJ* 6 (1956) 27, n. 7, argues that "Gerar" is the correct reading.

28. On this Arabian Kush, see EI^2 5:521, s.v. Kūsh (D. Cohen), and the literature cited in R. D. Haak, "'Cush' in Zephaniah," in Holloway and Handy, *The Pitcher Is Broken,* p. 242, n. 15. Also note the Targum to Song 1:5: "When the House of Israel worshipped the Golden Calf, their faces became black as the Kushites who live in the tents of Kedar." As Krauss remarks, "Kushites" here refers not to the African Kush but to the Arabian Kush ("Talmudische Nachrichten über Arabien,"

ZDMG 70 [1916] 323). See further W. F. Albright, "The Land of Damascus between 1850 and 1750 BC," *BASOR* 83 (1941) 34, n. 8; B. Mazar, *EB* 4:70–71, s.v. Kushan; M. Astour, "Sabtah and Sabteca: Ethiopian Pharaoh Names in Genesis 10," *JBL* 84 (1965) 422; Aharoni, *The Land of the Bible,* p. 146, and *Eretz Israel in Biblical Times: A Geographical History* (in Hebrew; rev. ed., Jerusalem, 1987), p. 120; and Eph'al, *The Ancient Arabs,* p. 78. Not everyone agrees that all these biblical references are concerned with the bedouin Kushites. So, for example, G. Rice is of the opinion that the Kushites of 2 Chr 14 and 21 refer to displaced Nubians resulting from an Egyptian (Twenty-fifth, Nubian Dynasty) alliance with Judah against Assyria, or resulting from an even earlier event, in the tenth–eighth century, when Nubians served as mercenaries in the Egyptian army during its invasions of Palestine ("The African Roots of the Prophet Zephaniah," *JRT* 36 [1979] 21–31).

29. R. D. Haak, "'Cush' in Zephaniah," in Holloway and Handy, *The Pitcher Is Broken,* pp. 238–51, esp. 249–50. Similarly Yeivin ("Topographic and Ethnic Notes II"), who thinks that the Kushites mentioned as being in the service of the kings of Judah (2 Sam 18:21ff., Jer 38:7) are descended from Ethiopian tribes that had settled in the Negev and assimilated among the Jews.

30. Jeremias, *The Old Testament in the Light of the Ancient Near East,* 1:286. On the Babylonian-Assyrian use of Miṣir to refer to "part of the desert between southern Palestine and Egypt," see W. Röllig, *RLA* 8:265, s.v. Miṣir. Nadav Na'aman, "The Brook of Egypt and Assyrian Policy on the Border of Egypt," *Tel Aviv* 6 (1979) 77, locates this area as "the territory south of Naḥal Besor (= the Brook of Egypt)."

31. Following E. Speiser in *AB: Genesis* (1964), p. 66, and *IDB* 2:236. The view was earlier expressed by G. Hölscher, *Drei Erdkarten,* p. 43. On the Kassites, see J. A. Brinkman, "Kassiten," *RLA* 5:464–73, and Walter Summerfeld, "The Kassites of Ancient Mesopotamia: Origins, Politics, and Culture," in *CANE,* pp. 917–30.

32. Some scholars—both medieval and modern—would also see other biblical references to Kush to mean the Kassites. Isa 18:1 is understood this way by Ibn Ezra (M. Friedländer, *The Commentary of Ibn Ezra on Isaiah,* London, 1873, p. 85). Gen 2:13 is so understood by Hidal, "The Land of Cush in the Old Testament," pp. 104–5, where earlier literature is cited. Ivan J. Ball, *A Rhetorical Study of Zephaniah* (Berkeley, 1988), p. 141, and, following him, Adele Berlin, *AB: Zephaniah* (1994), p. 134, see Kush in Zeph 3:10, Isa 18:1, and Gen 2:13 as referring to the Kassites. (Ball notes a linguistic and theological relationship between Isa 18:1–7 and Zeph 3:8–13, and specifically relates the "rivers of Kush" to the Garden of Eden tradition in Gen 2:13.)

33. Wildberger, *CC: Isaiah 13–27,* p. 218, ad loc.

34. M. Harel and J. Blau in *OhT: Isaiah,* p. 95c. See also Y. M. Grintz, *Studies in Early Biblical Ethnology and History* (Jerusalem, 1969), pp. 40–41, and Edward Ullendorff, *Ethiopia and the Bible* (London, 1968), p. 2.

35. KBL, s.v. *bz'*. NEB: "scoured by rivers."

36. See, e.g., RSV, NIV, NKJV; George B. Gray, *ICC: Isaiah 1–39* (Edinburgh, 1912), 1:306; Joseph Blenkinsopp, *AB: Isaiah 1–39* (New York, 2000), p. 308.

37. Wildberger, *CC: Isaiah 13–27,* pp. 206, 217–18. On the translation of He-

brew *me'ever le-naharei kush* as "in the region of the rivers of Kush" instead of the more common "beyond the rivers of Kush," see Wildberger, p. 207.

38. Odyssey 1.23 (τοὶ διχθὰ δεδαίατα); Strabo 1.2.25. The plural form of the verb (*baz'u*) referring to a singular subject (the Nile) would not be uncommon, particularly in poetic texts; see P. Joüon, *A Grammar of Biblical Hebrew* (Rome, 1993), trans. and rev. T. Muraoka p. 500, §136a–c; B. Waltke and M. O'Connor, *An Introduction to Biblical Hebrew Syntax* (Winona Lake, Ind., 1990), p. 120, §7.4.1. But see Gray's objection to this interpretation in *ICC: Isaiah 1–39,* 1:317.

39. *Natural History* 37.42.126.

40. J. Vercoutter, "The Gold of Kush," *Kush* 7 (1959) 120–53; quotation on pp. 27–28. A magnificent volume of pictures of surviving gold objects from Egypt and Kush, including also pictures of Egyptian tomb paintings containing gold objects, was published by Hans W. Müller and Eberhard Thiem, *Gold of the Pharaohs* (Ithaca, N.Y., 1999).

41. Vercoutter, "The Gold of Kush," and Hays, "The Cushites: A Black Nation in Ancient History," *Bibliotheca Sacra* 153 (1996) 273, 276. Painting reproduced in Müller and Thiem, *Gold of the Pharaohs,* p. 36.

42. Quoted in Diodorus Siculus 3.12.1. Translation Tormod Eide in *FHN* 2:658, where also László Török cites literature on the precise area meant (p. 659).

43. Pliny, *Natural History* 6.35.189; Strabo 17.2.2. The gold mines of Nubia were well known even into the Islamic period. See, e.g., al-Ya'qūbī (d. 897), *Ya'ḳūbī: les pays,* trans. Gaston Wiet (Cairo, 1937), p. 189.

44. Steffen Wenig, *Lexikon der Ägyptologie,* 4:527, s.v. Nubien. For the Egyptian word, see Rainer Hannig, *Grosses Handwörterbuch Ägyptisch-Deutsch* (Mainz, 1995), pp. 403ff., s.v.

45. On the phrase *tariṣ yadaw* 'stretch out its hands,' see W. F. Albright in *HUCA* 23/1 (1950–51) 34; H. J. Kraus, *CC: Psalms 60–150,* trans H. C. Oswald (Minneapolis, 1989; originally in German, 1978), ad loc.; and D. Boyarin, "Talmudic Lexicon VI," *Meḥqerei Talmud* 2 (1993) 18, n. 14, who points to an Akkadian parallel *qāta tarāṣu* meaning "to entreat in prayer," which is the meaning given to the biblical phrase by the Targum here and at Ps 88:10 (*šaṭaḥ kapayim*). Already Salmon ben Yeruḥam, the Karaite (fl. tenth century), explained the expression as "spreading out his hands to God in prayer and worship" (L. Marwick, *The Arabic Commentary of Salmon Ben Yeruham the Karaite on The Book of Psalms, Chapters 42–72,* Philadelphia, 1956, p. 96).

46. In, respectively, KJV, NJB, REB, NAB, RSV, NJPS, and KBL, s.v. The last translation, "blue-green wool," is mentioned by Muchiki, *Egyptian Proper Names and Loanwords in North-West Semitic,* p. 246, based on Akkadian *ḫašmanu* 'a blue-green (wool)', *ḫušmānu* 'a blue [?] shade (of wool)', although he favors an Egyptian origin for the word (Egyptian *ḥsmn* means "bronze"). He also notes the word's occurence in Ugaritic (*ḫus/ḫasmannu*), but the meaning there is unknown. In regard to the definition "bronze vessels," note should be taken of Herodotus 3.23: "Among these Ethiopians there is nothing so scarce and so precious as bronze." The translation "envoys" or "ambassadors" is found in the LXX and Vulgate. The Peshiṭta has *'yzd',* which I take to be either a mistake for *'izr'* (without the diacritic *d* and *r* are the same in Syriac) 'a linen girdle', or an apocopated form of *'yzgd'* (*'izgado'*) 'ambassador' (from the Persian), thus representing both possibilities of interpretation.

47. R. Harper, *ICC: Amos and Hosea* (Edinburgh, 1905), p. 192, ad loc.

48. Ibid. The same thinking lies behind the common interpretation of the Kushite runner in 2 Sam 18:21 as a despised slave, on which see p. 31.

49. S. R. Driver, *The Cambridge Bible for Schools and Colleges: The Books of Joel and Amos,* 2nd ed. (Cambridge, 1915), p. 224, ad loc. Similarly Erling Hammershaimb, *The Book of Amos: A Commentary,* trans. John Sturdy (New York, 1970; originally in Danish, 1946), p. 134.

50. N. H. Snaith, *Amos, Hosea and Micah* (London, 1956), p. 49. Hughell E. W. Fosbroke in *IB* 6:848 to Amos 9:7, castigated S. R. Driver for thinking that Jer 13:23 indicated a contempt for the dark-skinned Kushites: "[This] passage no more implies disdain for the Ethiopian's skin than it does for the leopard's spots." However, Fosbroke misread Driver (as did Charles Copher, "Racial Myths and Biblical Scholarship: Some Random Notes and Observations," in Copher, *Black Biblical Studies,* Chicago, 1993, p. 125). Driver merely referred to Jer 13:23 as proof of the Kushite's black skin, not as proof that the Kushite was despised.

51. James L. Mays, *OTL: Amos* (Philadelphia, 1969), ad loc., p. 157.

52. Jacob Dyer, *The Ethiopian in the Bible* (New York, 1974), p. 22. The full range of interpretations, medieval and modern of Amos 9:7—whether negative, positive, or neutral—is reviewed by M. Weiss (*The Book of Amos,* 1:282), who provides the most recent thorough discussion of the issue.

53. Matthew Poole, *Synopsis criticorum aliorumque S. Scripturae interpretum* (London, 1673), 3:1874, to Amos 9:7, or "most vile and abject" (1:657, to Num 12:1).

54. Augustine, *Enarrationes in Psalmos* 71.12, English translation in *NPNF1,* 8:330–31.

55. Ullendorff, *Ethiopia and the Bible,* p. 9.

56. Jan de Waard and W. A. Smalley, *A Translator's Handbook on the Book of Amos* (New York, 1979), p. 180. In a review of the literature on this verse, G. Rice ("Was Amos a Racist?" *JRT* 35 [1978] 35–44, p. 35, n. 1) and David Adamo ("The Place of Africa and Africans in the Old Testament and Its Environment," Ph.D. diss., Baylor University, 1986, pp. 156–64) list many of the studies that interpret the reference by Amos to Ethiopians in a derogatory way, e.g., as despised for the color of their skin or for their status as frequent slaves or their lack of civilization.

57. Shalom Paul, *Hermeneia: Amos* (Minneapolis, 1991), pp. 282–83. Similarly Hans W. Wolff, *Hermeneia: Joel and Amos,* trans. W. Janzen, S. Dean McBride, and C. Muenchow (Philadelphia, 1977; originally in German, 1975), p. 347; Francis I. Andersen and David N. Freedman, *AB: Amos* (New York, 1989), pp. 867–69; Jörg Jeremias, *OTL: Amos* (Louisville, 1998), p. 164, although Jeremias's comment about the Israelites seeing the Ethiopians as strange because of their skin color has no basis; see also Hayes, *Amos, the Eighth-Century Prophet,* p. 219; A. Ḥakham, *Daʿat Miqraʾ: Amos* (Jerusalem, 1990), p. 71; and Nahum Rozel, *The Book of Amos* (Haifa, 1987), ad loc. A partial listing of earlier scholars who agreed with this interpretation was compiled by Rice, "Was Amos a Racist?" p. 42, n. 13, who also took the same view. To Rice's list add also: H.E.W. Fosbroke in *IB* 6:848, ad loc.; Robert Bennett, "Africa and the Biblical Period," *HTR* 64 (1971) 498; and Snaith, *Amos, Hosea and Micah,* p. 49. Even S. R. Driver recognized that one of the main characteristics of the Kushites in the eyes of the Israelites was their geographic dis-

tance; see his comment cited earlier and on the word "Kush" in Zeph 3:10, "a type of distant nation" (*The Century Bible: The Minor Prophets,* rev. ed., New York, 1904, 2:135).

58. *Odyssey* 1.23.

59. See Strabo 1.2.27 and Ptolemy, *Tetrabiblos* 2.2.56. Note also the interpretation of the church father Origen that the queen of the South, who "came from the ends of the earth to listen to the wisdom of Solomon" in Matt 12:42 (Lk 11:31), is the queen of Ethiopia *because* Ethiopia is "situated in the farthest place" (see the references above, in n. 14). The tradition that the queen of Sheba (1 Kgs 10:1–10) was the queen of Ethiopia is basic to Christian Ethiopian tradition, which also interprets Lk 11:31 as referring to Ethiopia; see E.A.W. Budge's translation of the Kebra Nagast, *The Queen of Sheba and Her Only Son Menyelek* (London, 1922), pp. xli, 17 (sec. 21), 30 (sec. 28). Budge (p. lx) also records a modern North Abyssinian account according to which the Queen of Ethiopia was a Tigrē girl called "Queen of the South." On the *Kebra* and its date, see p. 343, n. 25.

60. See the references in Frank Snowden, *Blacks in Antiquity: Ethiopians in the Graeco-Roman Experience* (Cambridge, Mass., 1970), p. 262, n. 32, and Thompson, *Romans and Blacks,* pp. 65 and 199, n. 46. For the same phenomenon in rabbinic and Islamic sources, see D. Goldenberg, "Scythian-Barbarian: The Permutations of a Classical Topos in Jewish and Christian Texts of Late Antiquity," *JJS* 49 (1998) 87–102, esp. 91–94.

61. On the substitution of Egyptian or Indian for Ethiopian in classical, Christian, and Jewish sources, see Goldenberg, "Scythian-Barbarian," p. 100, and the literature cited below in Appendix II.

62. Snowden, *Blacks in Antiquity,* pp. 171–77 and 197, quotation on 177. See also Thompson, *Romans and Blacks,* p. 105; and "Observations on the Perception of 'Race' in Imperial Rome," in *Proceedings of the African Classical Associations* 17 (1983) 8; I. Opelt and W. Speyer in *Jahrbuch für Antike und Christentum* 10 (1967) 268; and Goldenberg, "Scythian-Barbarian," p. 93, n. 16.

63. W. Heimpel, "Meluḫḫa" in *RLA* 8:55. See below, p. 260, n. 136.

64. S. P. Vleeming and J. W. Wesselius, "Betel the Saviour," *Jaarbericht Ex Oriente Lux* 28 (1983–84) 111; *Studies in Papyrus Amherst 63,* vol. 1 (Amsterdam, 1985), pp. 88 and 91. The dating follows these authors. R. C. Steiner and C. F. Nims dated the text (papyrus Amherst 63) to the late second century B.C.E. ("A Paganized Version of Psalm 20:2–6 from the Aramaic Text in Demotic Script," *JAOS* 103 [1983] 261). However in a revised view, Steiner would now date the document earlier, to the beginning of the Hellenistic period (personal communication.)

65. First published in Norman de G. Davies, *The Rock Tombs of El Amarna* (London, 1908), 6:30, and found in many collections, e.g., *Ancient Near Eastern Texts,* ed. James B. Pritchard, 3rd ed. (Princeton, 1969), p. 370. See A. Erman and H. Grapow, *Wörterbuch der aegyptischen Sprache* (Leipzig, 1929–31), 3:232, s.v. *ḫ3rw.j:* "Syrians" used "im Gegenstand zum Südländer (*nḥsj*)."

66. R. G. Kent, *Old Persian: Grammar, Texts, Lexicon,* 2nd ed. (New Haven, 1953), pp. 136–37, "Persepolis H."

67. See *bMeg* 11a. Cf. Pseudo-Methodius's (seventh century, Syriac Christian) description of the inhabited world: "from Egypt to Kush and from the Euphrates

to Hendū and from the Tigris to the sea called Fire of the Sun" (Paul Alexander, *The Byzantine Apocalyptic Tradition,* ed. Dorothy deF. Abrahamse, Berkeley, 1985, p. 18). J. Yvan Nadeau has shown that the Mauretanian-Indian merism, indicating the east-west ends of the world, found among several Latin authors, derived from Homer's reference to the two Ethiopian peoples, one in the far east and one in the far west (*Odyssey* 1.23–24). In other words, these writers understood Mauretania to be the western Ethiopia, which is then combined in a merism with India, very much like the passage in Esther. One author, Apuleias (*Metamorphoses* 1.8), comes even closer to the biblical author in using the the phrase "Indians and both kinds of Ethiopians" to indicate the far reaches of the world. See J. Y. Nadeau, "Ethiopians," *Classical Quarterly* 20 (1970) 339–49, esp. 347, and "Ethiopians Again and Again," *Mnemosyne* 30 (1977) 75–78, esp. 76.

68. So, e.g., Ball, *A Rhetorical Study of Zephaniah,* p. 141, to Zeph 2:12; J.M.P. Smith, W. H. Ward, and J. A. Bewer, *ICC: Micah, Zephaniah, Nahum, Habakkuk, Obadiah and Joel* (Edinburgh, 1911), p. 232, to Zeph 2:12; S. R. Driver, *New Century Bible: The Minor Prophets,* 2:128 and 135 to Zeph 2:12 and 3:10. Ball adds Ezek 29:10; Est 1:1, 8:9; Ps 68:32, and our passage in Amos 9:7 as other examples of the biblical use of Kush "to designate a remote region at the end of the earth" (p. 141), and Smith, Ward, and Bewer add Zeph 3:10, Isa 11:11, 18:1, and Ezek 38:5 (p. 232). Driver adds Isa 11:11. Adele Berlin understands Kush in 2:12 and 3:10 as meaning the Assyrian Kush (Kassites), following Ball on Zeph 3:10 (see above, n. 32).

69. John L. McKenzie, *AB: Second Isaiah* (Garden City, N.Y., 1968), pp. 50 and 81. So also Rice, "Was Amos a Racist?" 39, who also notes the connotation of remoteness in Est 1:1, 8:9, and Job 28:19.

70. See F. Field, *Origenis Hexaplorum* (Oxford, 1875), ad loc., p. 211; so also the church fathers dependent upon the LXX, e.g., Cyril of Alexandria, *Explanatio in Psalmos, PG* 69.1187–88. Vulgate: *Biblia sacra: iuxta Vulgatam versionem,* ed. R. Weber, 2nd ed. (Stuttgart, 1975), ad loc. The Peshiṭta's *gzrtʾ* 'islands' must represent a reading of *ʾiyyim* for *ṣiyyim,* probably influenced by the occurrence of *ʾiyyim* in the following verse. The Targum reads *eiparkaya* = ὑπαρχία 'provinces', with no manuscript variants shown in Emanuel White, "A Critical Edition of the Targum of Psalms" (Ph.D. diss., McGill University, 1988), p. 312.

71. André Caquot has suggested that the variant *Aithiopes* is due to an association of Ethiopia, the outer limit of Egypt, with the desert, and thus the desert dwellers with the Ethiopians: "Hébreu *ṣiyyîm,* Grec *Aithiopes,*" in *Mélanges Marcel Cohen,* ed. David Cohen (The Hague, 1970), pp. 219–23. Note also that in Mesopotamian and Ugaritic myth the desert is located at the edge of the earth; see the discussion on Song 8:5 in chapter 5.

72. Is the Peshiṭta's *ʿšynʾ* 'strong', 'powerful' based on an interpretive reading of the Greek influenced by the reputation of the Kushites as a powerful people (see the discussion on Isaiah 18:2 in chapter 2)?

73. *Enarrationes in Psalmos* 71.12 (to v. 9), *CCL* 39:980–81, "Per Aethiopes, a parte totum, omnes gentes significavit, eam ligens gentem, quam potissimum nominaret, quae in finibus terrae est," and 67.40 (to v. 32/31), *CCL* 39:897, "Aethiopia, quae videtur extrema gentium." English translation can be found in *NPNF1* 8:330, sec. 72.12 and p. 298, sec. 68.37.

74. And not therefore as Haak has argued that Kush in Amos refers to the bedouin Kush on the southwest borders of Judah. R. D. Haak, "'Cush' in Zephaniah," in Holloway and Handy, *The Pitcher Is Broken,* p. 249.

75. The quotation is from Jack Sasson, who argues that the biblical compiler integrated all three homonymous Kushes into his genealogy. Sasson understands the references to the descendants of Kush in Gen 10:7 as the compiler's way of tying in the North Arabian Kush as their ancestor ("The Tower of Babel as a Clue to the Redactional Structuring of the Primeval History [Gen. 1–11:9]," in *The Bible World: Essays in Honor of Cyrus H. Gordon,* ed. G. Rendsburg et al., New York, 1980, p. 212). J. Liver is not as certain as Sasson, saying that the Northwest Arabian Kushites may possibly be implied (*EB* 4:65–70, s.v. Kush, esp. 69), and A. Demsky mentions only the Kassite and the Nubian Kushites as elements in the Table of Nations (*OhT: Genesis,* p. 74b). A review of the evidence for three different homonymous Kushes is presented in Weiss, *The Book of Amos,* 1:282.

CHAPTER TWO

1. For this use of *ki,* see A. Aejumelaeus, "Function and Interpretation of כי in Biblical Hebrew," *JBL* 105 (1986) 203. B. L. Bandstra, "The Syntax of Particle *ki* in Biblical Hebrew and Ugaritic" (Ph.D. diss., Yale University, 1982), pp. 159–71, 247 etc., lists Num 12:1 and similar usages under the general category of causal (i.e., either reason or motive) use of *ki.* See also Ziony Zevit, *The Anterior Construction in Classical Hebrew* (Atlanta, 1998), pp. 68–69. Some other examples of this use of *ki:* Gen 20:17–18; 35:18; 38:11, 16; Ex 32:25.

2. *Perushei Rabi Yosef Bekhor Shor ʿal ha-Torah,* ed. Yehoshafat Nevo (Jerusalem, 1994), p. 258, ad loc.

3. Among modern biblicists, see, e.g., Martin Noth, *OTL: Numbers* (London, 1968; originally in German, 1966), p. 91; Jacob Licht, *A Commentary on the Book of Numbers* (in Hebrew; Jerusalem, 1985–91), 2:38 and 42; Yeḥiel Moskovitz in the *Daʿat Miqraʾ* series (Jerusalem, 1988), p. 134; and Rita J. Burns, *Has the Lord Indeed Spoken Only through Moses? A Study of the Biblical Portrait of Miriam* (Atlanta, 1987), p. 68. Among medieval Jewish exegetes, in addition to Bekhor Shor, see Joseph ibn Kaspi (d. 1340) in his commentary to the Pentateuch, *Mishneh Kesef,* ed. I. Lasst (Cracow, 1905), 2:255, and the tosafist R. Aharon (as quoted by Isaac b. Judah ha-Levi [thirteenth century], *Paʿaneaḥ Razaʾ,* Warsaw, n.d., ad loc., p. 348).

4. On the NJPS rendering, see Jacob Milgrom, *JPSC: Numbers* (Philadelphia, 1990), ad loc.; H. Orlinsky, ed., *Notes on the New Translation of the Torah* (Philadelphia, 1970), p. 231; J. Muilenburg, "The Linguistic and Rhetorical Usages of the Particle כי in the Old Testament," *HUCA* 32 (1961) 144; and KBL, s.v. כי II (7).

5. KBL, s.v. כי II (5).

6. Some examples: A. Dillmann, quoted by G. B. Gray in *ICC: Numbers* (Edinburgh, 1903), p. 122; W. Eichhold, "Les noirs dans le livre du prophète Isaie," in *Afrique noire et monde méditerranéen dans l'antiquité: Colloque de Dakar, 19–24 janvier 1976* (Dakar, 1978), p. 281: "[L]e racisme est aussi vieux que l'humanité—exemple classique: l'attitude de Miriam"; Everett Fox, *The Five Books of Moses* (New York, 1995), p. 718: "clearly a racial slur" if Kushite means Ethiopian and not Mid-

ianite (cf. Licht, *A Commentary on the Book of Numbers,* 2:37–38, who understands Kushite in Num 12:1 to mean Ethiopian but says nothing about a "racial slur"); Louis Feldman, "Josephus' Portrait of Isaac," *Rivista di storia e letteratura religiosa* 29 (1993) 22, n. 51; Shlomo Katz, in *Negro and Jew: An Encounter in America,* ed. Shlomo Katz (New York, 1967), p. xii; Cain Hope Felder, *Troubling Biblical Waters: Race Class, and Family* (New York, 1989), p. 42. Felder's proof from the rendering of the LXX, ἕνεκεν τῆς γυναικὸς, does not stand, for this is merely a literal translation of the Hebrew *ʿal odot ha-ishah.*

7. H. Gressmann, *Die Anfänge Israels* (Göttingen, 1922), p. 96. One Christian Syriac commentary (anonymous) explains that Zipporah might have been called "Kushite" as an insult; see S. Brock, "Some Syriac Legends concerning Moses," *JJS* 33 (1983) 247, who dates the commentary possibly to the ninth century.

8. *Dictionary of the Bible,* ed. J. Hastings (New York, 1911), 1:179, s.v. Ethiopian Woman. Similarly John E. B. Mayor, *Thirteen Satires of Juvenal* (London, 1877), 1:254 on Satire 5.53, assumes that the Kushite of Num 12:1 was a slave.

9. Ullendorff, *Ethiopia and the Bible,* p. 8. Similarly, Aage Bentzen, *Introduction to the Old Testament* (Copenhagen, 1948–49), 2:153, assumes that since the name of the father of the biblical prophet Zephaniah was Kushi, the prophet must have come from a slave family, and Henry Smith, *ICC: Samuel* (Edinburgh, 1899), p. 359, makes the same assumption regarding the Kushite runner in 2 Sam 18:21, "naturally, a slave." George Caird (*IB* 2:1142) and J. M. Ward (*IDB* 1:751, s.v. Cushi) are less certain: "probably" and "perhaps" a slave, respectively. For a list of such interpretations where a slave status for a biblical Kushite is assumed, see David Adamo, "The Images of Cush in the Old Testament: Reflections on African Hermeneutics," in *Interpreting the Old Testament in Africa,* ed. Mary Getui et al. (New York, 2001), p. 69.

10. A few examples: Henry Higland Garnet, a Black abolitionist and clergyman, in *The Past and the Present Condition, and the Destiny of the Colored Race* (1848), p. 11; John G. Fee, a nineteenth-century Christian minister from Kentucky, in *An Anti-Slavery Manual,* 2nd ed. (New York, 1851), p. 171; Frank M. Cross, a major Bible scholar of our time, in *Canaanite Myth and Hebrew Epic: Essays in the Religion of Israel* (Cambridge, Mass., 1973), p. 204, followed equivocally by his student Richard Elliott Friedman, *Who Wrote the Bible* (San Francisco, 1987), p. 78; Robert Bennett, "Africa and the Biblical Period," *HTR* 64 (1971) 489–90, 498; Claudia Camp, *Wise, Strange and Holy: The Strange Woman and the Making of the Bible* (Sheffield, 2000), p. 237. See also L. Holden in the following note. Strangely, N. F. Gier understands the leprosy as a "fascinating color reversal" but admits that "it is not clear if Aaron and Miriam objected to Zipporah because she was black, or just because she was a foreigner" ("The Color of Sin/the Color of Skin: Ancient Color Blindness and the Philosophical Origins of Modern Racism," *JRT* 46 [1989] 43–44). If the objection was to her foreignness, color reversal is irrelevant.

11. It is incorrectly included by, e.g., R. K. Harrison, *Numbers: An Exegetical Commentary,* Wycliffe Exegetical Commentary 1990 (Grand Rapids Mich., 1992), ad loc., p. 197; Steven L. McKenzie, *All God's Children: A Biblical Critique of Racism* (Louisville, Ky., 1997), p. 34; Camp, *Wise, Strange and Holy,* p. 237; Blackburn, *The Making of New World Slavery,* p. 69; Randall Bailey, "Beyond Identifi-

cation: The Use of Africans in Old Testament Poetry and Narratives," in *Stony the Road We Trod: African American Biblical Interpretation,* ed. Cain Hope Felder (Minneapolis, 1991), p. 180. For earlier writers, note the comment of John Fee, in *An Anti-Slavery Manual:* "God, in a most signal manner, struck her with the leprosy: 'She became leprous, white as snow.'" L. Holden, *Forms of Deformity* (Sheffield, 1991), p. 272, no. 20, cites *LevR* 17.3 and *NumR* 7.5 as sources for his statement that "Miriam becomes a leper, white as snow, as a punishment for complaining about Moses in connection with the Cushite woman." Neither of these texts says anything about Miriam's affliction being "white as snow," nor do they imply, as does Holden, that "leprosy" was punishment for a racist remark. Snow is used as an example of whiteness in the Hebrew Bible (Ps 51:4, 9), but not here.

12. This description of *ṣaraʿat,* its relationship to leprosy, and the position of biblical scholars on the issue is taken from David P. Wright and Richard N. Jones, *ABD* 4:277–80, s.v. Leprosy. See also Elinor Lieber, "Old Testament 'Leprosy,' Contagion and Sin," in *Contagion: Perspectives from Pre-Modern Societies,* ed. Lawrence Conrad and Dominik Wujastyk (Aldershot, 2000), pp. 99–136. On "like snow" being a reference not to color but to the flaky texture of the snow, see also Athalya Brenner, *Colour Terms in the Old Testament* (Sheffield, 1982), p. 82.

13. On Kushan as a lengthened form of Kush, see P. Neʾeman, *Encyclopedia of Biblical Geography* (in Hebrew; Tel Aviv, 1964), 2:700. Such lengthening is found also with other Biblical Hebrew place-names; note the Naʿaman/Naʿami parallel in Num 26:40 and the Śalmah/Śalmon parallel in Ruth 4:20–21. Francis Andersen, *AB: Habakkuk* (New York, 2001), p. 312, points to the names Teman and Paran in Hab 3:3, which form an inclusio with the name Midian and Kushan in 3:7. On the *-ān* suffix, see Joshua Blau, *A Grammar of Biblical Hebrew* (Wiesbaden, 1976), 40.25.1; Simons, *Geographical and Topographical Texts,* p. 20, who sees the *-ān* ending as common to Arabian ethnographic names. Hidal, "The Land of Cush in the Old Testament," pp. 101–2, notes the *-ān* ending of Arabic *nomina propria* and points to Jokshan, Medan, and Midian (Gen 25:2) as well as Kushan; see also Yeivin, "Topographic and Ethnic Notes II," p. 177, for *Kushan-aram* in an Egyptian inscription. Cyrus Gordon points out that in Ugaritic the *-n* ending for toponyms is very common (*Ugaritic Textbook,* Rome, 1965, p. 63). Lastly, note that the translator of the LXX understood "Kushan" to be the equivalent of "Kush" and therefore rendered the word "Ethiopians." (It is possible, of course, that the Hebrew behind the LXX was "Kush," in which case there would be an even stronger argument for a Kush-Midian identity).

14. J. Liver, *EB* 4:69, s.v. Kush; B. Mazar, *EB* 4:70–71, s.v. Kushan; D. W. Baker, *ABD* 1:1220, s.v. Cushan; Cassuto, *From Noah to Abraham,* pp. 198–99; Aharoni, *The Land of the Bible: A Historical Geography,* 2nd ed., p. 146 = *Eretz Israel in Biblical Times: A Geographical History* (in Hebrew), (rev. ed. Jerusalem, 1987), p. 120; M. Astour, "Sabtah and Sabteca: Ethiopian Pharaoh Names in Genesis 10," *JBL* 84 (1965) 422; Andersen, *AB: Habakkuk,* p. 312. Apparently, W. F. Albright was the first to suggest the Kushan/Midian identification for Kushu in the Egyptian execration texts ("The Land of Damascus between 1850 and 1750 BC," *BASOR* 83 [1941] 34, n. 8), and the idea has since become widely accepted, even if some argue that Habakkuk's Kushan is a reference to Kush in Africa (so Y. Avishur, *Studies in Hebrew and Ugaritic Psalms,* Jerusalem, 1994, pp. 171–72). Also arguing for the identification

of Kush with Midian is the definition "Midianite" for "Kushaya" given by several Syriac dictionaries (cited by R. Payne Smith, *Thesaurus Syriacus,* Oxford, 1879–1901, s.v. Kusha, col. 1716). On the "Midianites, who were related to, if not identical with, the biblical Ishmaelites," see R. H. Smith, *ABD* 1:325 and G. E. Mendenhall, *ABD* 4:815. Note that in Gen 37:36 the Midianites sold Joseph to Potiphar but in the recapitulation at 39:1 it is the Ishmaelites who sold him to Potiphar.

15. Theodoret of Cyrrhus (fifth century) says that the *kushit* is Zipporah, and he explains that the Midianites and the Ethiopians are in geographical proximity and therefore came to be confused. See N. Fernández Marcos and A. Sáenz-Badillos, *Theodoreti Cyrensis: Quaestiones in Octateucham. Editio Critica* (Madrid, 1979), Numbers 22, p. 207. For Jewish-Hellenistic sources, see pp. 52–54. Tanḥum Ha-Yerushalmi (thirteenth century) in his commentary to Hab 3:7 quotes an anonymous opinion that the Kushites are another name for the Midianites or are a Midianite tribe and therefore Zipporah is the Kushite; see above, p. 220, n. 25.

16. E.g., Astour, "Sabtah and Sabteca," p. 422; Cross, *Canaanite Myth and Hebrew Epic,* p. 204; J. Marsh in *IB* 2:201; S. Aḥituv, *Canaanite Toponyms in Ancient Egyptian Documents* (Jerusalem, 1984), p. 85; J. Liver in *EB* 4:69 and 688; B. Mazar in *EB* 4:70–71 and *Eretz Israel* 3 (1954) 20; Weiss, *The Book of Amos,* 1:282; Simons, *Geographical and Topographical Texts,* p. 63 (a "not improbable assumption"); M. Naor, *Ha-Miqraʾ weha-Areṣ,* 1:118; P. Neʾeman, *Encyclopedia of Biblical Geography,* 2:700; S. Abramsky, s.v. Kush, *Encyclopaedia Hebraica* (*Enṣiqlopedyah ha-ʿIvrit*) (Tel Aviv, 1949–81), 20:709; S. Cohen in *IDB* 1:751, s.v. Cushan; Cassuto, *From Noah to Abraham,* pp. 198–99; Y. Elitzur and Y. Kiel, *Atlas Daʿat Miqraʾ* (Jerusalem, 1993), pp. 42–44. See also Howard Jacobson, *The Exagoge of Ezekiel* (Cambridge, 1983), p. 87; G. B. Gray in *ICC: Numbers,* p. 121; M. Elat, "The Economic Relations of the Neo-Assyrian Empire with Egypt," *JAOS* 98 (1978) 28, n. 49; Hidal, "The Land of Cush in the Old Testament," p. 102; Moritz, *Arabien,* p. 125; J. M. Myers, *AB: 2 Chronicles* (Garden City, N.Y., 1965), pp. 85 and 122; and I. Ben-Shem, "The War of Zerah the Cushite," in *Bible and Jewish History,* ed. B. Uffenheimer, p. 52. Among "moderns" the identification of Kush with Arabia and Kushite with Midianite appears as early as Sir Walter Raleigh, who made the argument already in 1614, *The History of the World,* book I, chap. 8, sec. 10. To be sure not all modern biblical scholars agree that Kushite in Numbers means Midian. They would claim that the term here has its more common meaning in Biblical Hebrew, "Ethiopian." One example is Baruch Levine, *AB: Numbers 1–20* (New York, 1993), ad loc. However, as can be seen by the large number of citations in this note, this view is by now exceptional.

17. E.g., Jacob Milgrom, *JPSC: Numbers,* ad loc.; M. Margaliot, "Numbers 12: The Nature of Moses' Prophecy," *Beit Miqra* 25 (1979–80) 136; Jacob Dyer, *The Ethiopian in the Bible,* pp. 14–15. For a review of the generally accepted opinion, see Bernd J. Diebner, "' . . . er hatte sich nämlich eine kuschitische Frau genommen' (Num 12,1)," *Dielheimer Blätter zum Alten Testament* 25 (1988) 75–95; also in English in abridged form: "' . . . for he had married a Cushite woman' (Numbers 12:1)," *Nubica* 1 (1990) 499–504. Diebner himself argues that "Kushite" is a reference to the Jewish colony at Elephantine in Kush. Some scholars long ago objected to the notion that it was the Kushite's blackness, not her foreigness,

that was disturbing to Miriam and Aaron. See, for example, Gray's reaction to this idea in *ICC: Numbers,* p. 122. For a list of non-Israelite marriages in the Hebrew Bible, see V. P. Hamilton, *ABD* 4:564a.

18. H. Wildberger, *CC: Isaiah 13–27,* pp. 205–6.

19. It is not clear whether this alliance was related to the rebellion of the Philistine city of Ashdod against Assyria in 712 B.C.E., which is referred to in Isa 20:1, or to the later rebellion of Hezekiah of Judah against Assyria in 701 B.C.E.; see the discussion in H. Wildberger, *CC: Isaiah 13–27,* pp. 213–14, and cf. Marvin A. Sweeney, *Isaiah 1–39,* Forms of the Old Testament Literature 16 (Grand Rapids, Mich., 1996), p. 257.

20. This interpretation of events behind Isaiah 18 follows most commentators. Some think that Isaiah is sending the Kushite delegation on to Assyria and that the Assyrians are described in verse 2; see John D. W. Watts, *WBC: Isaiah 1–33* (Waco, Tex., 1985), pp. 245–46. It will become clear, however, that the description in this verse accords with other ancient descriptions of the Kushites.

21. Gray, *ICC: Isaiah 1–39,* 1:316; O. Kaiser, *OTL: Isaiah 13–39* (Philadelphia, 1974; originally in German, 1973), pp. 89–90; Wildberger, *CC: Isaiah 13–27,* pp. 206–7, 217; R.B.Y. Scott, *IB* 5:276, ad loc. KBL, s.v. *ṣelāṣal.* In support of the last interpretation, it is interesting to take note of a late first-century B.C.E.–early first-century C.E. Greek inscription from Philae that mentions swift Ethiopian barges (νέας ὠκυπορούσας) sailing on the Nile; see L. Török, "Economy in the Empire of Kush: A Review of the Written Evidence," *Zeitschrift für Ägyptische Sprache und Altertumskunde* 111 (1984) 53; also in *FHN* 2:712. The French translation of the École Biblique, *La Sainte Bible* (Paris, 1955), has "susurrent des ailes." Regarding the connection with locusts, note Strabo's (16.4.12) reference to an Ethiopian people known as Acridophagoi 'Locust-eaters'. A review of the three theories with literature cited is found in M. Lubetski, "Isaiah 18:1—Egyptian Beetlemania," in *Jewish Studies in a New Europe: Proceedings of the Fifth Congress of Jewish Studies in Copenhagen 1994 . . . ,* ed. U. Haxen et al. (Copenhagen, 1998), pp. 512–13, nn. 1–3. Lubetski himself (pp. 513–20) suggests that *ṣilṣel* refers to the divine winged beetle, an emblem found in Upper Egypt. On the translation "shadow," cf. Tosafot, *bBQ* 116b, s.v. *yaḥsenineh.*

22. R. H. Smith in *ABD* 2:666. Cf. Gray, *ICC: Isaiah 1–39,* 1:309, "The land where objects at noon-day sometimes cast a shadow to the N[orth] and sometimes to the S[outh]."

23. See KBL, s.v. *ṣll.*

24. Symmachus (ὁ ἦχος πτερωτὸς) in Field, *Origenis Hexaplorum,* 2:461, ad loc. This translation is mentioned in KBL, s.v. *kanaf;* it is not found under the entry for *ṣelaṣal.*

25. Ahmed M. Moussa, "A Stela of Taharqa from the Desert Road at Dahshur," *Mitteilungen des Deutschen Archeologischen Instituts, Kairo* 37 (1981) 331–37, text on p. 336, line 9'. The text with translation (by R. H. Pierce) is found also in *FHN* 1:158–63.

26. Because the Egyptian expression is used by Tirhaqa to describe an army, Isaiah may have even implied a double entendre, for the Hebrew word *kanaf* was also used to mean "the flank of an army" (so in the Dead Sea text, *War of the Sons of Light* 9.11). Cf. Gesenius and Cheyt quoted in Gray, *ICC: Isaiah 1–39,* 1:309.

27. *Aethiopica* 8.16.4.

28. Ahmed M. Moussa, "A Stela of Taharqa," 331–38; *FHN,* 1:158–63. See D. B. Redford, *Egypt, Canaan, and Israel in Ancient Times* (Princeton, 1992), p. 306, n. 99, and in *ABD* 4:111, s.v. Kush. In general the text praises the army, but the specific concern is with the army's running ability, and the stela is so entitled: "His Majesty ordered to erect a [stela] . . . and to call it "(Stela reporting) the [running of the] [army] of the Son of Re Taharqa may he live eternally."

29. Herodotus 4.183; Pliny, *Natural History* 7.2.31. Strabo 17.1.2 locates the Troglodytes in Ethiopia between the Nile and the Red Sea, but when Isidore, *Etymologies* 9.2.129, refers to the Troglodytes who were swift runners, it is not clear whether he means these Ethiopian Troglodytes or some other people such as those Troglodytes mentioned in the *Periplus of Hanno* (before 400 B.C.E.), who were said to be "quicker than horses in running," but who were located near the Ethiopians of Northwest Africa. Similarly, Sallust (first century B.C.E.) says of the inhabitants of Africa, by which he means North Africa, that they are "swift of foot." Hanno in J. Blomqvist, *The Date and Origin of the Greek Version of Hanno's Periplus with an Edition of the Text and a Translation* (Lund, 1979), §7, pp. 60, 62; on the date, pp. 52–56. Another translation is that of Jacques Ramin, *Le Périple d'Hannon / The Periplus of Hanno* (Oxford, 1976). Sallust, *Jugurtha* 17; LCL, pp. 170–71 (J. C. Rolfe). The original form of the word is "Trogodytes."

30. *Aethiopica* 8.16.4. Text and translation in *FHN* 3:1047, where also information on editions, translations, and dating (fourth century C.E.) is found.

31. Harel and Blau in *OhT: Isaiah,* p. 96a. On the Kushites ability with the bow there is much evidence; see pp. 34–35.

32. Herodotus 3.20.

33. *Periplus* 112. Text in C. Müller, *Geographi Graeci Minores* (Paris, 1855–61), 1:94; see Snowden, *Blacks in Antiquity,* p. 107.

34. *Periplus Maris Erythraei,* text, translation, and commentary by L. Casson (Princeton, 1989), 16, p. 60. On μέγιστοι δὲ ἐν σώμασιν referring to stature, see LSJ, s.v. μέγας I. Cf. also Arrian (second century C.E.), *Anabasis* 5.4.4, and Eusebius (fourth century C.E.), *Vita Constantini* 4.7.1 (*FHN* 3:1081). The LXX renders *anshei midah* in Isa 45:14 similarly: ἄνδρες ὑψηλοὶ (Syro-Hexapla: *gvrʾ rbʾ*—A. Vööbus, *The Book of Isaiah in the Version of the Syro-Hexapla, CSCO* 449, Subsidia 68, Louvain, 1983, f. 31b), as does the Peshiṭta: *gvrʾ dmšwḥtʾ,* on which see Payne Smith, *Thesaurus Syriacus,* col. 2237. On the Sabaeans being in Africa, see p. 18.

35. Pliny, *Natural History* 6.35.190. At 7.2.31 Pliny cites Crates of Pergamum (second century B.C.E.) as his source for the statement. Diodorus is at 2.56. Note also Snowden's remark about "tall slender tribute-bearers in a mural from the tomb of Sebekhotep (ca. 1400 B.C.E.)," in *Before Color Prejudice,* p. 12.

36. For the Muslim writers, see, e.g., Marvazī (twelfth century), *Sharaf al-Zamān Ṭāhir Marvazī on China, the Turks and India,* ed. and trans. Vladimir Minorsky (London, 1942), pp. 53, 54, 57, 58 (English), pp. *41–*42, *47, *48 (Arabic), and p. 156, §2. For the moderns, see G. W. Titherington, "The Raik Dinka of Bahr-el-Ghazal Province," *Sudan Notes and Records* 10 (1927) 178, who described the Raik Dinka as being tall of stature, with the "pure Raik" standing at about 6′ 4″and "men up to seven feet are seen"; and F. M. Deng, *The Dinka of the*

Sudan (New York, 1972), p. 1, who notes that the Dinka of Sudan have been known well into modern times for their height. See also J. Hiernaux, *The People of Africa* (New York, 1974), pp. 80–81, 126ff.

37. The Greek word is regularly translated in Isa 18:2 as "lofty, exalted, uplifted" (see J. Lust et al. ed., *A Greek-English Lexicon of the Septuagint,* Stuttgart, 1996, p. 302, s.v.), but given the evidence presented here, perhaps a literal sense of the word (i.e., "tall") is to be preferred.

38. Wildberger, *CC: Isaiah 13–27,* pp. 206, 218. Cf. NAB and NJB: "bronzed."

39. Dominique Zahan, "White, Red and Black: Colour Symbolism in Black Africa," pp. 389–90.

40. KBL, s.v. *mrṭ*.

41. Diodorus 2.56; Dimashqī is excerpted in N. Levtzion and J.F.P. Hopkins, *Corpus of Early Arabic Sources for West African History* (Cambridge, 1981), p. 213.

42. Grover S. Krantz, *Climatic Races and Descent Groups* (North Quincy, Mass., 1980), pp. 50, 89–90.

43. Gray, *ICC: Isaiah 1–39,* p. 312.

44. J. Skinner, *Cambridge Bible for Schools and Colleges: Isaiah,* rev. ed. (Cambridge, 1915), 1:148, ad loc. See also Walter Reichhold, "Les noirs dans le livre du prophète Isaie," in *Afrique noire et monde méditerranéen dans l'antiquité,* pp. 276–81, who deals with *memušakh u-moraṭ* and comes to the same conclusion.

45. E.g., Wildberger, *CC: Isaiah 13–27,* p. 218; Gray, *ICC: Isaiah 1–39,* p. 312. Herodotus's statement is echoed by Pseudo-Scylax (fourth century B.C.E.) in his *Periplus* 112 (Müller, *Geographi Graeci Minores,* 1:94). See also Mela (first century C.E.) 3.85, drawing on earlier sources.

46. The parallel with Herodotus is noted by, among others, D. von Orelli (in the *Kurzgefasster Kommentar* series, Munich, 1904), ad. loc. Similarly, Diodorus (2.56) describes those near the equator as tall, hairless, and "also remarkably beautiful." Another parallel between Herodotus and Diodorus is their description of these people as living long lives (Herodtus 3.19 and 97, Diodorus 2.57).

47. H. L. Ginsberg, "Reflexes of Sargon in Isaiah after 715 BCE," in *Essays in Memory of E. A. Speiser,* ed. William W. Hallo (New Haven, 1968), p. 48, n. 7. Shalom Paul informed me that the NJPS translation of Isa 18:1–2 is the work of Ginsberg, who, Paul says, in this passage relied on the eleventh-century Hebrew grammarian Ibn Janaḥ (see also below, p. 35, on *ʿam noraʾ*). Ibn Janaḥ says that *memušakh* means "dragged, drawn" and *moraṭ* means "uprooted, plucked out" (*Sefer ha-Shorashim,* ed. W. Bacher, Berlin, 1896, pp. 274 and 276, and A. Z. Rabinovits's compilation of Ibn Janaḥ's biblical interpretations, *Perush le-Khitvei ha-Qodesh,* 2nd ed., Tel Aviv, 1935/36, p. 115). The same translation of *memušakh u-moraṭ* is found in the Peshiṭta, which has *mlyg wʿqyr* 'plucked out and uprooted'.

48. Wildberger, *CC: Isaiah 13–27,* p. 218.

49. Donald B. Redford in *ABD* 4:110a, s.v. Kush. Nahum 3:9 also makes mention of Kush's strength. A recent work suggests that Sennacherib withdrew his siege of Jerusalem in 701 in the face of a Kushite attack against the Assyrian forces, thus explaining the enigmatic biblical account of Sennacherib's sudden retreat (Henry T. Aubin, *The Rescue of Jerusalem: The Alliance between Hebrews and Africans in 701 BC,* New York, 2002). The account is found in 2 Kgs 18:17–19:35 = Isa 36:1–37:36.

50. Snowden, *Before Color Prejudice,* pp. 21–22, 38–40, 72, and see index, s.v. Soldiers; quotation on p. 58. See also J. Daniel Hays, "From the Land of the Bow: Black Soldiers in the Ancient Near East," *Bible Review,* August 1998, pp. 29–33, 50–51.

51. See Snowden, *Blacks in Antiquity,* pp. 121–29, and Henry G. Fischer, "The Nubian Mercenaries of Gebelein during the First Intermediate Period," *Kush* 9 (1961) 78.

52. Fourteenth-century Amarna texts: EA 127.36, 131.13, 133.17, 287.33, 287.72, 288.36, translated in William L. Moran, *The Amarna Letters* (Baltimore, 1992); tenth century: 2 Chr 12:3, cf. 16:8; sixth century: Jer 46:9, Ezek 30:5.

53. Herodotus 7.69–70.

54. Similarly Diodorus Siculus 3.8.4, Pliny, *Natural History* 8.8.26, and Strabo 17.2.3. Cf. Strabo 17.3.7.

55. *Natural History* 6.35.194.

56. Snowden, *Before Color Prejudice,* p. 57, with reference to Heliodorus 9.18. See also Diodorus 3.8.8. Reference to "Nubian archers" is also found in an Egyptian text recording a decree of Ptolemy V Epiphanes dating to 185/4 B.C.E.; text and translation in *FHN* 2:605.

57. Reproduced in several publications, e.g., D. O'Connor, "Ancient Egypt and Black Africa—Early Contacts," *Expedition* 14.1 (Fall 1971) 5; Snowden, *Before Color Prejudice,* ill. 5a–b; Jean Vercoutter in *IBWA* 1:43 and ill. 10–12; Hays, "From the Land of the Bow," pp. 29–33, 50–51; Eugen Strouhal, *Life of the Ancient Egyptians* (Norman, Okla., 1992), p. 202. See also the literature cited by Snowden, *Blacks in Antiquity,* pp. 286–87, n. 55. Other iconographic evidence is cited by Snowden, *Before Color Prejudice,* p. 40. On the use of the bow, see Snowden, "Greeks and Ethiopians," in *Greeks and Barbarians: Essays on the Interactions between Greeks and Non-Greeks in Antiquity and the Consequences for Eurocentrism,* ed. J. E. Coleman and C. A. Walz (Bethesda, Md., 1997), p. 110. H. Last in *Classical Quarterly* 17 (1923) 35–36 interprets μακροβίους in Herodotus 3.17 and 97 as "long-bows" and not "long-lived."

58. Henry G. Fischer, "The Nubian Mercenaries of Gebelein during the First Intermediate Period," *Kush* 9 (1961) 44–80, esp. 56–77.

59. Others are of the opinion that "Land of the Bow" refers to the great bend in the Nile, which to a large extent defined the land to the south. See J. J. Taylor, *Egypt and Nubia* (Cambridge, Mass., 1991), p. 5; Daniel Hays, "The Cushites: A Black Nation in Ancient History," *Bibliotheca Sacra* 153 (1996) 270; W. B. Emery, *Egypt in Nubia* (London, 1965), p. 16.

60. James Bruce, *Travels to Discover the Source of the Nile* (Edinburgh, 1790), 2:438.

61. See also the Vulgate: *in Africam.* See John Bright, *AB: Jeremiah* (Garden City, N.Y., 1965), ad loc., Raphael Giveon, *OhT: Isaiah,* ad loc., and now 4Q385b 3–4 with Devorah Dimant's notes in *DJD* 30:72–74. Incidentally, Giveon errs when saying that the Peshiṭta reads as the LXX; it reads as the MT: Pul.

62. M. Mellink in *IDB* 4:179, s.v. Lud, Ludim, and see Moshe Greenberg, *AB: Ezekiel 21–37* (New York, 1997), p. 552.

63. See W. McKane, *ICC: Jeremiah* (Edinburgh, 1986–96), 2:1117, ad loc. The debate hinges on whether Put is to be identified with Egyptian *pywd, pyyt,* Coptic

phaiat, Persian *putaua,* which refer to a people who became eponymous with Libya, or with Egyptian *pwn.t,* which refers to the area of or near Somalia. The disagreement is of long standing and is not yet resolved, although recent research favors Libya, such as J. Osing in *Lexikon der Ägyptologie,* 3:1015–16; D. W. Baker in *ABD* 4:397 and 5:560; Édouard Lipinski, "Les Chamites selon Gen 10,6–20 et 1 Chr 1,8–16," *Zeitschrift für Althebraistik* 5 (1992) 140; Yair Hoffman in *OhT: Jeremiah,* p. 199; Isaac Avishur in *OhT: Genesis,* p. 76b; Redford, *Egypt, Canaan, and Israel in Ancient Times,* p. 404; Wolf-Dietrich Niemeier, "Archaic Greeks in the Orient: Textual and Archaeological Evidence," *BASOR* 322 (2001) 18. Several ancient sources identify Put with Libya: LXX; Jubilees 9:1; Josephus, *Antiquities* 1.132 (Libya was founded by Phoutes); Jerome: "Up to the present day, Ethiopia is called Chus by the Hebrews, Egypt is called Mesraim, and the Libyans Phuth. So it is, then, that up to the present day the river of Mauretania is called Phut, and all the Libyan territory round about it is called Phuthensis. Many writers, both Greek and Latin, are witnesses to this fact" (C.T.R. Hayward, *Saint Jerome's* Hebrew Questions on Genesis, Oxford, 1995, p. 40). Note should also be made of a ninth-century B.C.E. Phoenician inscription from Cyprus that mentions *pt* and may mean Phoenicia; see Charles Krahmalkov, *Phoenician-Punic Dictionary* (Leuven, 2000), p. 399, s.v. *pn(y)m,* p. 408, s.v. *pt.* Those arguing for an East Africa location include Westermann, *CC: Genesis 1–11,* p. 511; R. Herzog, *Punt,* Abhandlungen des Deutschen Archäologischen Instituts Kairo. Ägyptologische Reihe, Band 6 (Glückstadt, 1968); McKane, *ICC: Jeremiah,* p. 1117; R. H. Smith in *ABD* 2:666a; J. J. Taylor, *Egypt and Nubia,* p. 16; D. T. Potts in *CANE* 3:1460. Exceptional is Diakonoff's opinion ("The Naval Power and Trade of Tyre," *IEJ* 42 [1992] 177–81) that *pwṭ* is the Greek *Pontos* 'sea' = Mediterranean, i.e., the Greek islands. Lastly, in regard to the name Put, it should be noted that the name *Qūṭ,* which often appears in Arabic sources as a son of Ham (e.g., Levtzion and Hopkins, *Corpus,* p. 353), is obviously only a corruption of P/Fut. Without diacritical marks the *q* and *f* are identical in Arabic.

64. See the color reproduction of a painting of Nubian shields found in an Egyptian tomb from *The Tomb of Ḥuy, Viceroy of Nubia in the Reign of Tutʿankhamūn (No. 40),* by Nina de Garis Davies and Alan H. Gardiner (London, 1926), pl. 25; and see p. 22.

65. Strabo 17.1.54; cf. Diodorus Siculus 3.8.4.

66. Ginsberg, "Reflexes of Sargon in Isaiah after 715 BCE," p. 48, n. 7. See above, p. 32, on *memušakh u-moraṭ.*

67. Wildberger, *CC: Isaiah 13–27,* pp. 208, 218. Similarly, *La Sainte Bible* ("peuplade puissante et dominatrice").

68. Blenkinsopp, *AB: Isaiah 1–39,* p. 308.

69. Mela 3.85–86. Herodotus (3.20) says that the Ethiopians chose their leader on the basis of his good looks and superior strength, but he does not say explicitly that the Ethiopians admire bodily strength. This is one of the differences between the two writers that led A. Silberman to note that although this section of Mela derives ultimately from Herodotus, it does so through an intermediary; see Silberman's edition and commentary: *Pomponius Mela: Chorographie* (Paris, 1988), p. 311. A new English translation of Mela has been published by F. E. Romer, *Pomponius Mela's Description of the World* (Ann Arbor, Mich., 1998).

70. See H. Donner, *Israel unter den Völkern,* Supplements to Vetus Testamentum 11 (Leiden, 1964), p. 122, and J. Tigay, "'Heavy of Mouth' and 'Heavy of Tongue': On Moses' Speech Difficulty," *BASOR* 231 (1978) 63, n. 11. Both explanations of *qaw-qaw* (strength and babble) are noted in KBL, s.v. See the note reference in NJPS to Isa 33:19, Deut 28:49 and Jer 5:15. The meaning of "sound" or "call" usually given to *qawam* in Ps 19:5 need not mitigate the onomatopoetic explanation of *qawqaw.* On the contrary, the phonetic and semantic similarity of the word in Psalms would strengthen the development of an onomatopoetic creation. On the meaning "sound" or "call," see H.-J. Kraus, *CC: Psalms 1–59,* trans. H. C. Oswald (Minneapolis, 1993), 1:267–68; M. Dahood, *AB: Psalms* (Garden City, N.Y., 1966–70), 1:122, based on Jacob Barth; and for postbiblical evidence, D. Boyarin, "Towards the Talmudic Lexicon IV," *Te'uda* 6 (1988) 64–66.

71. KBL, s.v. *qaw, qāw* I. See Ibn Janaḥ, *Sefer ha-Shorashim,* ed. W. Bacher, p. 443, who understands the two words, *qaw* and *qawqaw,* to be related and derived from the same root.

72. Ibn Ezra, ad loc. (M. Friedländer, *The Commentary of Ibn Ezra on Isaiah,* p. 85) and KJV respectively.

73. Levtzion and Hopkins, *Corpus,* pp. 21, 94; Joseph Cuoq, *Recueil des sources arabes concernant l'Afrique occidentale du viie au xvi^{e}e siècle (bilād al-Sūdān)* (Paris, 1975), p. 52. For the Arabic sources mentioning the Kawkaw, see the indexes in these two works, pp. 450 and 478 respectively.

74. David Goldenberg, "Rabbinic Knowledge of Black Africa (Sifre Deut. 320)," *JSQ* 5 (1998) 323–24, where literature is cited.

75. Both in personal correspondence to me. Hunwick also suggests that *qawqaw* might be "an inversion of *waqwaq* (or just possibly the reverse), which is a name applied to the southern reaches of Africa, beyond the 'land of the Zanj,' an approriate location for a place that lay 'beyond the rivers of Kush.'" For the Arabic sources mentioning these names, see the indexes in Levtzion and Hopkins, *Corpus,* and in Cuoq, *Recueil.* The Waqwaq are also mentioned by al-Hamadhānī (ninth century), *Kitāb al-buldān,* ed. M. J. de Goeje (Leiden, 1885), p. 7, and Marvazī (twelfth century), *Sharaf al-Zamān Ṭāhir Marzavī on China, the Turks and India,* ed. and trans. V. Minorsky, p. 60 (English), p. *50 (Arabic). On the Waqwaq, see also J. Spencer Trimingham, "The Arab Geographers and the East African Coast," in *East Africa and the Orient: Cultural Synthesis in Pre-colonial Times,* ed. H. Neville Chittick and Robert I. Rotberg (New York, 1975), p. 120.

76. The linguistic justification for such translations seems to be an assumption that *qaw-qaw* is associated with the Hebrew root *qwh* 'to hope.' See Harel and Blau in *OhT: Isaiah,* p. 96b.

77. See KBL 1:115, s.v. *bws.*

78. Fosbroke in *IB* 6:848 to Amos 9:7, and Wildberger, *CC: Isaiah 13–27,* p. 217. Similarly Gray, *ICC: Isaiah 1–39,* 1:311–12. Scott in *IB* 5:276 thinks that Isaiah was not sincere; that his words, rather, reflect "the flattering language of diplomacy." Blenkinsopp thinks that Isaiah was being sarcastic, that far from being "a people feared far and near, a nation strong and conquering," the Kushites were rather a weak nation that could provide Judah no support in an anti-Assyrian alliance (*AB: Isaiah 1–39,* p. 310).

79. Henry G. Fischer, "The Nubian Mercenaries of Gebelein during the First Intermediate Period," *Kush* 9 (1961) 77.

80. Ibid., p. 52.

81. Victor Sasson is of the opinion that *kushi* in this text has the meaning of "dark-skinned person," not necessarily Nubian/Ethiopian; see his "King Solomon and the Dark Lady in the Song of Songs," *VT* 39 (1989) 412.

82. Stanley R. Hopper in *IB* 5:298 to Jer 13:23.

83. A. G. Dunston, *The Black Man in the Old Testament and Its World* (Trenton, N.J., 1992), p. 47. A good example of this sentiment is found in A. A. Roback, *A Dictionary of International Slurs* (Cambridge, Mass., [1944]), p. 283, which, reflecting popular opinion, considers Jeremiah's remark to be a slur against Blacks.

84. Dunston, *The Black Man*, p. 47.

85. "The Instructions of Ankhsheshonqy" 21.5, translated by Miriam Lichtheim, *Late Egyptian Wisdom Literature in the International Context: A Study of Demotic Instructions* (Göttingen, 1983), p. 86. The relationship to the Jeremiah text was noted by B. Gemser, "The Instructions of ʿOnchsheshonqy and Biblical Wisdom Literature," in *Supplements to Vetus Testamentum 7, Congress Volume: Oxford*, ed. G. W. Anderson (Leiden, 1960), p. 126. The Egyptian text is dated to the fifth century B.C.E. (Gemser, p. 106). On the reading "Indian" for "Kushi" in the Peshiṭta and Targum versions of Jeremiah, see Appendix II.

86. Lucian, *Adversus indoctum* 28. See Snowden, *Blacks in Antiquity*, p. 263, n. 36. Cf. Aesop's fable 274 (= 393), Ben E. Perry, *Aesopica* (Urbana, Ill., 1952), 1:481, and *Babrius and Phaedrus*, LCL (Cambridge Mass., 1984), p. 494.

87. On the meaning of *ʿebed* as vassal, see Jonas Greenfield, "Some Treaty Terminology in the Bible," in *Fourth World Congress of Jewish Studies: Papers* (Jerusalem, 1967), 1:117–19, and Ziony Zevit, "The Use of עבד as a Diplomatic Term in Jeremiah," *JBL* 88 (1969) 74–77.

88. Jer 38:7. See B. Kedar-Kopfstein in *TDOT*, 10:344–50, s.v. *saris*; Nili Sacher Fox, *In the Service of the King: Officialdom in Ancient Israel and Judah* (Cincinnati, 2000), pp. 196–203. Cf. Targum *gevar rav* 'important person'. The word is missing altogether in the LXX. Cf. Acts 8:27. Regarding the Peshiṭta's rendering *gbrʾ mhymnʾ*, W. McKane, argues that while "a pious man" or "a believing man" could be the meaning, it is more likely that *mhymnʾ* is a straightforward translation of the Hebrew, since *mhymnʾ* can mean "eunuch" in Syriac (*ICC: Jeremiah*, ad loc., p. 952). The Peshiṭta's rendering may, however, be based on the description of Ebed-melech in Jer 39:18 as one who trusted in God (*baṭaḥta bi*), and thus the meaning "a pious man" or "a believing man" would be apt. Adamo ("Images of Kush," p. 70) calls attention to an underlying racial prejudice in the translation "eunuch." I would add that such a translation may also be the result of an association between the eunuch and the slave or servant.

89. Note that in these three cases Kush(i) is rendered Χουσί in LXX and the Vulgate, and, also in Aquila, Symmachus, and Theodotian to Ps 7:1, where their readings are preserved, i.e., the word was understood not as a gentilic (Ethiopian) but as a personal name. Rodney Hutton, "Cush the Benjaminite and Psalm Midrash," *Hebrew Annual Review* 10 (1986) 123–37, argues that Ps 7:1 refers to the Kushite of 2 Sam 18.

90. László Török in *FHN* 1:43, and *The Kingdom of Kush*, p. 145; Heather D.

Baker, *The Prosopography of the Neo-Assyrian Empire* (Helsinki, 2000), 2/1: 642–44.

91. R. Anderson, "Zephaniah ben Cushi and Cush of Benjamin: Traces of Cushite Presence in Syria-Palestine," in Holloway and Handy, *The Pitcher Is Broken*, pp. 45–70. In the same volume, R. D. Haak discusses the identity of Zephaniah's father but does not come to a conclusion as to whether the name implies an ethnic origin ("'Cush' in Zephaniah," pp. 249–50). See also David W. Baker, *Nahum, Habakkuk and Zephaniah*, Tyndale Old Testament Commentary (Leicester, 1988), p. 91 to Zeph 1:1.

92. Gene Rice, "The African Roots of the Prophet Zephaniah," *JRT* 36 (1979) 21–31. The arrival of the Kushite delegation to Jerusalem is described in Isa 18:1–2, on which see above, n. 19. Rice finds that a number of the biblical Kushites have ties to the royal house of Judah, and he traces this connection to the alliance against Assyria. Thus, Yehudi ben Netaniah ben Shelemiah ben Kushi is employed by Yehoiakim king of Judah; Ebed-Melech "the Kushite," who saves the prophet Jeremiah, is in the service of the Judahite king Zedekiah (Jer 38:7–13); and the prophet Zephaniah's great-grandfather Hezekiah was, according to Rice, the Judahite king of that name. See also G. Rice, "Two Black Contemporaries of Jeremiah," *JRT* 32 (1975) 104–7.

93. R. Giveon, *The Impact of Egypt on Canaan* (Göttingen, 1978), pp. 90–96. Cf. also the line "The Nubians [*nḥs(y)w*] of every foreign country rose up against him [Psammetich II]" in a stele recording the Nubian campaign of the Egyptian king Psammetich II in 593 B.C.E.. Text and translation by R. H. Pierce in *FHN* 1:281. We know of a colony of Nubians in Upper Egypt (Gebelein) as early as the First Intermediate Period, ca. 2258–2040 B.C.E. (Fischer, "The Nubian Mercenaries of Gebelein during the First Intermediate Period," pp. 44–80, esp. 76–77). Inge Hofmann, "Kuschiten in Palästina," *Göttinger Miszellen* 46 (1981) 9–10, argues that Zerah the Kushite (2 Chron 14:8–14, 16:8) was a Nubian born in Palestine. Hofmann also refers to a Zenon papyrus recording a gift of four young slaves, three of whom, he says, are of Nubian origin, from Tobias an Ammonite prince to an Apollonius in the year 257 B.C.E.. Reinhold Scholl, however, claims that from the description of the slaves' features (μελαγχρὴς, μελίχρους, κλαστόθριξ, κτλ.) we cannot determine their ethnicity as Hofmann wishes to do (*Sklaverei in den Zenonpapyri*, Trier, 1983, p. 105).

94. Ehud Ben Zvi, *A Historical-Critical Study of the Book of Zephaniah* (Berlin, 1991), pp. 44ff. Similarly Édouard Lipinski in a review of A. S. Kapelrud, *The Message of the Prophet Zephaniah, Morphology and Ideas*, in *VT* 25 (1975) 688–91, and now in "Les Chamites selon Gen 10,6–20 et 1 Chr 1,8–16," *Zeitschrift für Althebraistik* 5 (1992) 136–39. References to ancient Near Eastern Kushi names are found in Ben Zvi on p. 44, n. 14, and Lipinski, p. 689, as also in N. Avigad, "Six Ancient Hebrew Seals" in *Sefer Shemu'el Yevin*, ed. S. Abramsky et al. (Jerusalem, 1970), pp. 305–6, and W. Kornfeld, *Onomastica Aramaica aus Ägypten* (Vienna, 1978), p. 56. Note also the name *kšy'l* (?) on an Aramaic magic bowl recorded in J. Naveh and S. Shaked, *Magic Spells and Formulae: Aramaic Incantations of Late Antiquity* (Jerusalem, 1993), p. 128, no. 21.9, and the name κασσιε occurring in a Jewish inscription (not before the third century B.C.E.) listed in J. B. Frey, *Corpus Inscriptionum Iudaicarum* (Rome, 1936), 1:488, no. 676. On the name Kushi,

see further Yoshiyuki Muchiki, *Egyptian Proper Names and Loanwords in North-West Semitic* (Atlanta, 1999), pp. 26–27, 91.

95. Literature cited in Rice, "The African Roots of the Prophet Zephaniah," p. 25. Regarding the designation "Kushi" for one of a dark complexion, see R. Zadok, *The Pre-Hellenistic Israelite Anthroponomy and Prosopography* (Leuven, 1988), p. 156 (see also n. 81 above), and in general on the name, index, p. 430.

96. Muchiki, *Egyptian Proper Names*, p. 222. Cf. Henry Fischer's remarks ("The Nubian Mercenaries," p. 75) that the name *Nfr-nḥs-i*, discovered in an Egyptian inscription from the First Intermediate Period, may not necessarily mean "Nfr the Nubian," but may have indicated "some point of resemblance to a Nubian that earned *Nfr* the epithet *Nḥśy*." For the biblical form of the name, see KBL 3:926, s.v. *Pynḥs* with literature cited, plus M. Görg, *Aegyptiaca-Biblica: Notizen und Beiträge zu den Bezeihungen zwischen Ägypten und Israel* (Wiesbaden, 1991), pp. 7 and 183.

97. Kaiser, *OTL: Isaiah 13–39*, p. 93.

CHAPTER 3

1. For the Targum, see p. 19; for the Hellenistic writings, see below pp. 53–54.

2. See Jeremy Silver, *JQR* 64 (1973) 132; Lipinski, "Les Chamites selon Gen 10,6–20 et 1 Chr 1,8–16," pp. 135–39.

3. Josephus, *Antiquities* 1.131. Jerome: Hayward, *Saint Jerome's* Hebrew Questions on Genesis, p. 40.

4. 211. Philip S. Alexander, "The Toponymy of the Targumim" (Ph.D. diss., University of Manchester, 1974), p. 128. The same identity is commonly found in early Christianity as well, where, for example, Kush is translated as "Ethiopia" in the onomastic lists (Wutz, *Onomastica Sacra*, pp. 120, 163, etc.; Stone, *Signs of the Judgement*, pp. 161, 197). Note also the common identification of the Ethiopians with Kush in Augustine (d. 430), *City of God* 16.11; Isidore of Seville (d. 636), *Isidori Hispalensis Episcopi: Etymologianem sive originum*, ed. W. M. Lindsay (Oxford, 1911; repr., 1985) 9.2.39; and in the sources cited by Paul H. D. Kaplan, "Ruler, Saint and Servant: Blacks in European Art to 1520" (Ph.D. thesis, Boston University, 1983), p. 218, n. 81. For an iconographic example from a later period, see the thirteenth-century German miniature depicting Blacks as the descendants of Kush in Ruth Mellinkoff, *Outcasts: Signs of Otherness in Northern European Art of the Late Middle Ages* (Berkeley, 1993), 1:203, 2: fig. x.23.

5. Discussions of *afriqa/i* in rabbinic literature: Solomon Y. Rapoport, *ʿErekh Milin* (Prague, 1852; Warsaw 1914; repr., Jerusalem, 1970), 1:358–64, s.v. *afriqa;* A. Harkavy, "*Afriqa, Afriqi* in Thargum und bei den Rabbinen," *Jüdische Zeitschrift für Wissenschaft und Leben* 5 (1867) 34–39; *Ha-Yehudim u-Śefat ha-Slavim* (Vilna, 1867), pp. 120–25; Adolph Neubauer, *La Géographie du Talmud* (Paris, 1868), pp. 400–405; S. Krauss, "Die biblische Völkertafel im Talmud, Midrasch, und Targum," *MGWJ* 39 (1895) 2–7; Y. Z. Hirshenzohn, *Shevaʿ Ḥokhmot: ha-Giʾografiyah shel ha-Talmud* (in Hebrew; London, 1912), pp. 41–42; H. Z. Hirschberg, *A History of the Jews in North Africa*, 2nd ed. (Leiden, 1974–81), 1:27–28, 40–48. See also the Talmud and Targum dictionaries of Levy, Kohut (below, nn. 8–9), and Jastrow (n. 16), s.v. *afriqa/i.*

6. E.g., four military leaders (*dux*) including one from *afriqa* are mentioned as attacking Jerusalem with Vespesian (*LamR* 1:5.31, ed. Rom = 1.5 in ed. S. Buber, Vilna, 1899, p. 33a). Buber notes, however, that the manuscript reading is *afniqa* (not *afriqa*), which he takes to be Phoenicia. So too A. Oppenheimer, "The Attitude of the Sages towards the Arabs," in *Jewish Studies in a New Europe,* ed. U. Haxen et al. (Copenhagen, 1998), pp. 573–74. On the term *dux,* see below, p. 311, n. 75.

7. *bSan* 94a. R. Ḥanina disagreed with Mar Zuṭra and placed the exiles in the Selug Mountains, which are about sixty miles to the east of Divrigi, on the Turkish-Iranian border near Mosul. This explanation of Babylonia as the location of the Ten Tribes was put forward by Jacob Obermayer, *Die Landschaft Babylonien im Zeitalter des Talmuds und des Gaonats* (Frankfurt am Main, 1929), pp. 11–12, and from there to B. Z. Eshel, *Yishuve ha-Yehudim be-Bavel bi-Tequfat ha-Talmud: Onomasṭikon Talmudi* (Jerusalem, 1979), pp. 26 and 199. Z. Kasdoi's theory that "Africa" in *bSan* 94a (and elsewhere in rabbinic literature) is Iberia/Ibericia, an area in the Caucuses (*Shivṭe Yaᶜaqov u-Neṣure Yisraʾel,* Haifa, 1928, pp. 24–31), was suggested earlier by Harkavy, "*Afriqa, Afriqi.*"

8. Palestinian Targums and *GenR* 37.1 to Gen 10:2 (the territory of Gomer) according to many: see S. Y. Rapoport, *ᶜErekh Milin,* 1:358–64; Jacob Levy, *Chaldäisches Wörterbuch über die Targumim* (Leipzig, 1881), 1:56, s.v. *afriqi;* Alexander Kohut, *ᶜArukh ha-Shalem* (*Aruch Completum*) (1878–92; repr., New York, 1955), 1:244, s.v. *afriqi;* Theodor in his notes to *GenR,* p. 343; M. McNamara and M. Maher in the notes to their translations of the Targum in *The Aramaic Bible: The Targums* ed. K. Cathcart et al. (Wilmington, Del., 1986–), vols. 1A (Neofiti) and 1B (Pseudo-Jonathan); Hayward, *Saint Jerome's* Hebrew Questions on Genesis, pp. 138–39, with cited literature in n. 2; and others. Note also that the text in "*Pirqei Mashiaḥ*" points to a northern location: "I will gather all the nations to war against Jerusalem, and they are Gomer, its branches Togarmah, *ʾfryqy,* Garamit, Garmamiah, Cappadocia, Barbari, Italy. . . ." On this text, see D. Goldenberg, "Geographia Rabbinica: The Toponym Barbaria," *JJS* 50 (1999) 64.

9. For examples of this usage in rabbinic sources, see Rapoport, Levy, and Kohut, loc. cit., and J. Levy, *Wörterbuch über die Talmudim und Midraschim,* nebst Beitragen von H. L. Fleischer, 2nd edition mit Nachträgen und Berichtigungen von L. Goldschmidt (Berlin and Vienna, 1924; originally published in Leipzig, 1876–89), 1:150, s.v. *afriqa.* This is the meaning of the toponym in the rabbinic tradition about the emigration of the Canaanites to Africa in the face of Joshua's conquest of Canaan. The reference is to the Phoenicians of Carthage whose original home was Canaan (Phoenicia). The tradition is in *Mekhilta, Pisḥa* 18 (pp. 69–70); *tShab* 7.25; *bSan* 91a; the glosses to *Megilat Taᶜanit, Siwan* 25, according to MS Parma; *YalqSh,* Genesis 25, sec. 110; and *Midrash ha-Gadol,* 1:415. *Megilat Taᶜanit* and *YalqSh* are here dependent on *bSan* according to Ido Hampel, "Megilat Taᶜanit" (Ph.D. diss., Tel Aviv University, 1976), ad loc. For the identification of *afriqiyim* in this tradition with the Carthaginian descendants of Canaan, see Rapoport, *ᶜErekh Milin;* Louis Ginzberg, *The Legends of the Jews* (Philadelphia, 1925), 6:177, n. 34; Louis Ginzberg in Samuel Krauss, *Tosafot he-ᶜArukh ha-Shalem* (*Additamenta ad librum Aruch Completum*) (Vienna, 1937; published as a supplement to Kohut's *ᶜArukh ha-Shalem*), p. 432a; Saul Lieberman, *Tosefta ki-Fshutah* (New

York, 1955–88) to Shabbat, p. 105. For a discussion of the extrarabbinic sources referring to this tradition, see Johanan Hans Levy, *ʿOlamot Nifgashim* (Jerusalem, 1960), pp. 60–78, and Matityahu Mieses, "After the Destruction of Carthage" (in Hebrew), *Ha-Tequfah* 18 (1923) 228–33; see also Salomo Rappaport, *Agada und Exegese bei Flavius Josephus* (Vienna, 1930), pp. 99–100; P. S. Alexander "Notes on the 'Imago Mundi' of the Book of Jubilees," *JJS* 33 (1982) 200, n. 3; A. Brüll, *Fremdsprachliche Redensarten* (Leipzig, 1869), p. 55; Hirschberg, *A History of the Jews in North Africa,* 1:40–48; and André N. Chouraqui, *Between East and West: A History of the Jews of North Africa,* trans. M. M. Bernet (Philadelphia, 1968), pp. 3–5. Cf. M. Kister, "Mesorot Aggadah we-Gilguleihen," *Tarbiẓ* 60 (1991) 220, n. 109. For the meaning of Ifrīqiya in Arabic sources, see *EI*[2] 2:453–55 (G. Yver). For mythical and philological etymologies of the name, see *EI*[2] 3:1047a–1048b (M. Talbi).

In his edition of *Mekhilta,* 1:158, Jacob Lauterbach says that the original country of the Canaanites was Africa. As far as I could determine, there is no rabbinic tradition regarding an origin for the Canaanites before they were in Israel. It would seem that Lauterbach came to his interpretation by reading, with MS Munich, *be-arṣekha* and *be-arṣekhem,* i.e., God said to the Canaanites, "I will give you a goodly land *in* your own country." Since according to the midrash the Canaanites left Israel for Africa, "I will give you a goodly land in your own country" must mean that Africa had been their country. Lauterbach's decision to accept the reading in MS Munich may have been influenced by the postbiblical tradition in Jubilees 10.29–34, according to which Canaan was given Africa when the world was divided among Noah's descendants. Whether Jubilees influenced Lauterbach or not, it did not influence the rabbinic text, for the Venice and Constantinople editions of *Mekhilta* read, as Lauterbach notes, *ke-arṣekha/khem* 'as your own country' i.e., God will give the Canaanites a land (Africa) as goodly as their own country (Israel), which they had just left. Undoubtedly, the editions represent the correct reading (adopted also by Horovitz and Rabin in their edition of *Mekhilta,* pp. 69–70, although they show no variant reading; so also M. Margulies in his edition of *LevR,* p. 386, s.v. *me-arṣo*), since the midrash is based on an exegesis of Isa 36:17 which has *ke-arṣekhem* (no variants shown in the Hebrew University Bible Project: *The Book of Isaiah,* ed. Moshe Goshen-Gottstein, Jeruslaem, 1981, p. 54). Confusion of *bet* and *kaf* is, of course, common; cf. the parallel in *yShevu* 6.1, 36c.

10. So, e.g., (1) *bSan* 91a ed. *afriqiya* (so in MS Munich abbreviated), but MS Florence *afriqi;* (2) the reading in *Midrash Abba Gurion,* MS Cambridge to the midrash on Est 1:14, which gives Carshena's land of origin as *afriqi* (S. Buber, *Sifre de-Aggadeta ʿal Megilat Esther,* Vilna, 1886, p. 16). The exegetical basis of the midrash is presumably a play on Carshena as Carthage, and not a play on Tarshish as thought by Aaron Bernstein in B. Grossfeld, *The Targum to the Five Megilloth* (New York, [1973]), pp. 121–22. (Levy and Kohut in their dictionaries, s.v. *afriqi,* both understand *afriqi* here as Phrygia.) The midrash appears also in *Midrash Panim Aḥerim B* and *Leqaḥ Tov* on Esther (Buber, *Sifre de-Aggadeta,* pp. 61, 93) as well as in *Targum Sheni.* Incidentally, the reading in MS Sassoon (*The Targum Sheni to the Book of Esther,* ed. B. Grossfeld, Brooklyn, N.Y., 1994, p. 39) is *ʾfrqwy. Targum Sheni* was translated by B. Grossfeld in the Aramaic Bible series, vol. 18, *The Two Targums of Esther* (Collegeville, Minn., 1991), p. 130. Note also the fol-

lowing two cases of *afriqiya* for *afriqa*, although the location is not certain: (3) *bRH* 26a, MS London for the statement made by R. Akiba that in *afriqi* they call a *meʿah* a *qeśiṭah* (see R. Rabbinovicz, *Diqduqe Soferim: Variae lectiones in mischnam et in talmud babylonicum,* Munich and Przemysl, 1868–97, ad loc.); (4) *yBer* 9.1, 13c: R. Levi said that in *afriqiya* they call a menstruous woman a *galmudah*. So in MSS Leiden, Paris, and London; MS Vatican has *afriqi*. Both *bRH* and *yBer* are discussed below, p. 73.

11. Moshe Elat (*EB* 8:943) claims that the most generally accepted opinion today is Tarsus, although he himself ("Tarshish and the Problem of Phoenician Colonisation in the Western Mediterranean," *Orientalia Lovaniensia Periodica* 13 [1982] 55–69) argues for an Iberian location; Edward Lipínski (*CANE* 2:1322) says that most today agree on Tartessos. B. Oded in *OhT: 1 Kings* 10:22 says that there is no consensus. See also Jack Sasson, *AB: Jonah* (New York, 1990), p. 79.

12. Al-Idrīsī, *Description de l'Afrique Septentrionale et Saharienne,* Texte arabe extrait du "Kitāb Nuzhat al-Muchtāq fī Ikhtirāq al-Afāq" d'après l'édition de Leyde (1866), par R. Dozy et J. de Goeje, publié par Henri Peres (Alger, 1957), p. 81. Vater is in his *Commentar über den Pentateuch* (Halle, 1802), 1:107, quoted by Solomon Y. Rapoport, *ʿErekh Milin,* 1:358 (and from there to Kohut, *ʿArukh ha-Shalem,* 1:244).

13. Above, p. 21.

14. Jer 10:9 also refers to the "silver brought from Tarshish and gold from Ophir" in the Peshiṭta, a variant in the Vulgate, and a reading recorded in a rabbinic text (MT has "Uphaz" for "Ophir"). The variants readings are listed in *The Book of Jeremiah,* ed. C. Rabin et al., Hebrew University Bible Project (Jerusalem, 1997), ad loc. Kohut, *ʿArukh ha-Shalem,* 1:244, also suggests that the Targum's *afriqa* might be black Africa but he does so for a different reason: the presumed association of Uphaz with Mount Afura in East Africa.

15. Indeed, an understanding of Africa as the location of Ps 72/71:8–10 is what led the LXX to translate *ṣiyyim* in verse 9 as "Ethiopians," as I have agrued above (pp. 24–25).

16. So Marcus Jastrow, *A Dictionary of the Targumim, the Talmud Babli and Yerushalmi, and the Midrashic Literature* (London, 1886–1903), p. 108, s.v. *afriqi,* and Alexander, *The Toponymy of the Targumim,* p. 128. See also Levy, *Chaldäisches Wörterbuch über die Targumim,* 1:56.

17. See the discussion below, pp. 61–67, 68–69, and 73–74 respectively.

18. J. Devisse in *IBWA* 2/1:47, 216, nn. 75 and 76.

19. Goldenberg, "Geographia Rabbinica."

20. *PesRK* 5.7 (1:89–90), *PesR* 15 (p. 71b), *SongR,* 2:8.2 (ed. Warsaw 2.19). In all the sources the statement is transmitted in the names of mid-second-century sages. For the dating of these works, see Glossary. *Kuthi* is most probably a corruption of either *Skuthi* (Scythian) or *Guthi* (Goth). On this and the following discussion, see my "Scythian-Barbarian," pp. 87–102, the conclusions of which I present here.

21. Louis Ginzberg, *Ginzei Schechter* (New York, 1928), 1:86. Ginzberg does not date the fragment but thinks that it might have served as a source for *LevR,* whose redaction is dated between 400 and 500 C.E.. The fragment is also found in

Jacob Mann and Isaiah Sonne, *The Bible as Read and Preached in the Old Synagogue* (Cincinnati, 1966), 2:212 (Hebrew section). Mann and Sonne omit the line immediately following the text quoted here, which Ginzberg had reconstructed. Indeed, Ginzberg's reconstruction of this line is problematic.

22. *MidPs* 25.14 (p. 108a); *YalqSh,* Psalms 702 end. Although a date of redaction for *Midrash Psalms* is uncertain, most of the material in *MidPs* 1–118 goes back to the talmudic period (see Glossary).

23. *MidPs* 109.3 in the printed editions and some manuscripts, but not in MS Parma and thus not in Buber's edition (based primarily on this manuscript). Krauss, Kohut, and Strack-Billerbeck ("vielleicht") feel that "Shtutia" (*š/śtwtyh*) is a corruption of "Scythia" (respectively: *Griechische und lateinische Lehnwörter im Talmud, Midrasch und Targum,* with commentary by Immanuel Löw, vol. 2 [Berlin, 1899], p. 583, s.v., and "Biblische Völkertafel," p. 8 n. 6; *ʿArukh ha-Shalem,* 2:184; *Kommentar zum Neuen Testament aus Talmud und Midrasch,* Munich, 1926, 3:630).

24. On the other hand, when Origen said, "As long as . . . we adopt Egyptian and *barbaros* morals, we do not merit to be counted before God among the the holy and consecrated" (aegyptios gerimus et barbaros mores, haberi apud Deum in sancto et consecrato numero non meremur) (*Hom. in Num.* 1.3, *GCS* 30 [Origen 7] 4; *SC* 415:34–35), he probably did not mean the proper noun "Barbarian." Because "Egyptian" is commonly allegorized as any people of low moral standards, and Origen in particular shared this interpretation, *barbaros* in this text probably meant "barbaric." For a full discussion of this text as well as Colossians 3:11, see Goldenberg, "Scythian-Barbarian," pp. 96–99.

25. Pp. 22–25.

26. *bTaʿan* 10a, *bPes* 94a. Arabic literature has the same saying, only substituting Sudan (i.e., Land of the Blacks) for Kush: "Egypt is one-sixtieth the size of Sudan which is one-sixtieth of the whole world." So Ibn Khurradādhbih (d. 911), Ibn al-Faqīh (after 903), and Masʿūdī (tenth century), quoted in Levtzion and Hopkins, *Corpus,* pp. 17, 27, 31.

CHAPTER FOUR

1. *Legum Allegoriae* 1.68. This interpretation was commonly accepted in the Christian onomastic lists; see Wutz, *Onomastica sacra,* pp. 154, 427, 677, 792–93 and the indexes under *aithiops* and *kushi.* See also Ambrose, *Paradise* 3.16, "The meaning of Ethiopia in Latin is 'lowly and vile (*abiecta et vilis*).'" *CSEL* 32/1:275–76, *FC* 42:297 (trans. J. J. Savage with an obvious printer's error). On Ambrose's use of Philo, see p. 50.

2. Lester Grabbe, *Etymology in Early Jewish Interpretation: The Hebrew Names in Philo* (Atlanta, 1988), p. 130.

3. *Kbš:* Wutz, *Onomastica Sacra,* p. 427; Y. Amir, *Philo of Alexandria: Writings* (in Hebrew; Jerusalem, 1997), 4:51, n. 86, equivocally. *Qāsa:* C. Siegfried, *Philo von Alexandria als Ausleger des alten Testaments* (Jena, 1875), p. 195; in his earlier *Die hebräischen Worterklärungen des Philo und die Spuren iher Einwirkung auf die Kirchenväter* (Magdeburg, 1863), p. 10, Siegfried didn't know what to make of Philo's etymology. *Śaḥor* > *šaḥ:* Chava Schur, "Etymologies of Hebrew Names in

Philo's Allegorical Exegesis" (in Hebrew; Ph.D. diss., Tel Aviv University, 1991), p. 104.

4. See pp. 43–45.

5. The environmental theory is discussed above, p. 23.

6. Some discussion of the theory will be found in Thompson, *Romans and Blacks,* pp. 100–104, and Snowden, *Blacks in Antiquity,* pp. 170–79. For more sources and an examination of the consequences of this theory, see David Goldenberg, "The Development of the Idea of Race: Classical Paradigms and Medieval Elaborations," *International Journal of the Classical Tradition* 5 (1999) 561–63.

7. *Physiognomonica* 6.812a and b, in *Scriptores physiognomonici graeci et latini,* ed. R. Foerster (Leipzig, 1893), 1:72; translated in the LCL series (W. S Hett) in *Aristotle's Minor Works,* pp. 125–27, 131. Note that Pseudo-Aristotle also thinks that "the excessively fair are also cowardly; witness women" (Hett, p. 127). The *Physiognomonica* dates possibly from the third century B.C.E. The much earlier description of the Nubians as cowards, found in an Egyptian stela from about 1850 B.C.E., is different from the classical examples mentioned here. The Egyptian text is representative of a literary theme of the foreigner, any foreigner, as coward easily subdued by the Egyptian king. The text is found in Miriam Lichtheim, *Ancient Egyptian Literature* (Los Angeles, 1976), 1:119.

8. J. L. Ideler, *Physici et medici graeci minores* (Berlin, 1841), 1:303, translated in R. Klibansky, E. Panofsky, and F. Saxl, *Saturn and Melancholy: Studies in the History of Natural Philosophy, Religion and Art* (London, 1964), p. 59.

9. *De architectura* 6.1.4 and 10.

10. Vegetius is in his *Epitoma rei militaris* 1.2. In addition to the Latin text, an early (1408) English translation of Vegetius has been published from manuscript: G. Lester, ed., *The Earliest English Translation of Vegetius' De Re Militari* (Heidelberg, 1988); our text is on p. 50. Later writers range from Albertus Magnus and Vincent of Beauvais in the thirteenth century, through Ranulph Higden in the fourteenth, to Bodin in the seventeenth. Albertus ("their hearts are made timid" because of evaporation of the hot air) is translated from his *De natura locorum* 2.3, in J. P. Tilmann, *An Appraisal of the Geographical Works of Albertus Magnus and His Contribution to Geographical Thought* (Ann Arbor, Mich., 1971), p. 101; see also C. J. Glacken, *Traces on the Rhodian Shore: Nature and Culture in Western Thought from Ancient Times to the End of the Eighteenth Century* (Berkeley, 1967), pp. 267–69. Vincent of Beauvais, speaking of Ethiopians and Egyptians, is cited by Peter Biller, "Views of Jews from Paris around 1300: Christian or 'Scientific'?" in *Christianity and Judaism,* ed. Diana Wood (Oxford, 1992), p. 201. Biller, p. 200, notes that the idea is repeated in a thirteenth-century Paris *quodlibet.* Higden is in his *Polychronicon,* ed. C. Babington (London, 1865), 1:50–53. An anonymous fifteenth-century English translation of Higden, published together with the original Latin, put it this way: "Therefore . . . men in Europe be . . . moore bolde in herte [*animo audaciores*], more feire in beaute, than in Affrike. For the beame of the sonne beenge continually by contynualle permanence on men of Affrike . . . causethe theyme to be . . . more feynte in herte [*animo defectiores;* var. *sicciores*] by the evaporation of spirits." An earlier, fourteenth-century, translation also published in the same volume is that by Trevisa ("coward of herte" for "feynte in herte"). Bodin and others are in M. J. Tooley, "Bodin and the Mediaeval Theory

of Climate," *Speculum* 28 (1953) 73–77. See also Abrabanel (d. 1508) in his *Commentary to the Pentateuch,* to Gen 10:1, p. 171a, and Wolfdietrich Fischer, *Farb- und Formbezeichnungen in der Sprache der altarabischen Dichtung Wolfdietrich* (Wiesbaden, 1965), pp. 275–76. The connection of cowardice with dark skin in the early Arabic poets, whom Fischer quotes, probably has more to do with the association of dark skin with the the vulgar rabble and people of low character or ignoble origin, for which see below, pp. 118–22.

11. Some years ago Albrecht Dihle had suggested that the commonly held view of Ethiopians' cowardice might have been behind Philo's etymology ("Der Fruchtbare Osten," *Rheinisches Museum für Philologie* 105 [1962] 99, n. 5).

12. *Quaestiones in Genesim* 2.82. Contrary to Marcus (see his note in LCL), Philo is not confused here; see Grabbe, *Etymology in Early Jewish Interpretation,* p. 191.

13. R. Lonis, "Les trois approches de l'Ethiopien par l'opinion gréco-romaine," *Ktema* 6 (1981) 81, with particular reference to Philo's *Quaestiones in Genesim.*

14. Babacar Diop, "La politique africaine de l'etat chrétien romano-byzantin (iv–viième siècle après J-C): héritages hellénistiques, regards chrétiens sur les populations africaines" (These de 3ème cycle, Université de Paris, 1981), pp. 103–25. I am grateful to Prof. Diop for sending me the relevant material from his thesis.

15. Emmanuel Tonguino, "La malediction de canaan et le mythe chamitique dans la tradition juive" (Ph.D. diss., Université de Paris-Sorbonne, 1991), p. 157.

16. *MidPs* 7.14 (p. 70).

17. *SongR* 1:5.1 (ed. Warsaw 1.35): "*I am black but beautiful*—Israel said: I am black in my own eyes but beautiful in the eyes of my Creator, as it is written, *Are you not like Kushites to Me, O Israelites, said the Lord:* 'You are like Kushites' in your own eyes, but 'to Me you are like Israelites, said the Lord.' " It is, however, possible that in *MidPs* 7.14 and this *SongR* passage the Rabbis understood "Kushites" to mean dark-skinned Arabs rather than black Africans. The Targum to Song 1:5 states: "When the House of Israel worshipped the Golden Calf, their faces became black as the Kushites who live in the tents of Kedar." As Samuel Krauss remarked, in this text "Kushites" refers not to the African Kush but to the Arabian Kush ("Talmudische Nachrichten über Arabien," *ZDMG* 70 [1916] 323). In terms of applying the metaphor of blackness to skin color it wouldn't matter whether "Kushites" was understood to mean Africans or dark-skinned Arabs. On the rabbinic view of the Arab as dark-skinned, see pp. 122–23.

18. See p. 84.

19. Origen, *Homilies to Song* 1.6, *Commentary to Song* 2.1, 2.2, *GCS* 33 [Origen 8] 35–38, 113–26; English translation in *ACW* 26:91–107, 276–77 (R. P. Lawson, 1957). Similarly in his *Homilies on Jeremiah* 11.5, "We are black when we begin to believe. Therefore it is said at the beginning of Song 'I am black and beautiful.' At first our soul is compared to an Ethiopian. Then we are cleansed and become all white (bright), as it says 'Who is she who comes up having been made white' " (*GCS* 6 [Origen 3] 84–85; *SC* 232:428–31; German translation: E. Schadel, *Origenes: Die griechisch erhaltenen Jeremiahomilien,* Bibliothek der griechischen Literatur 10 [Stuttgart, 1980], 11.6, p. 130). In his *Homilies on Numbers* 6.4, and similarly in 7.2, Origen again makes the equation of the Ethiopian wife of Moses = the gentile church (and Miriam, Moses' sister = the synagogue,

the Jews); *GCS* 30 (Origen 7) 36, 39; *SC* 415:156–59, 172–73. For an analysis of this theme in Origen's commentary to Song, see J. Chênevert, *L'église dans le commentaire d'Origène sur le Cantique des Cantiques* (Montreal, 1969), pp. 127–29.

20. Dennis Brown, *Vir Trilinguis: A Study in the Biblical Exegesis of Saint Jerome* (Kampen, The Netherlands, 1992), pp. 17, 141, 153–55; J. W. Trigg, *Biblical Interpretation* (Wilmington, Del., 1988), pp. 23, 26; M. Simonett, *Biblical Interpretation in the Early Church: An Historical Introduction to Patristic Exegesis,* trans. J. A. Hughes (Edinburgh, 1994; originally in Italian, 1981), p. 39; J. Daniélou, *Origen,* trans. W. Mitchell (New York, 1955), p. 304; Bertrand de Margerie, *An Introduction to the History of Exegesis. I: The Greek Fathers,* trans. L. Maluf (Petersham, Mass., 1993), pp. 112–13; (originally in French, 1980), p. 132; and for even later influence, see G. R. Evans, "Origen in the Twelfth Century," in *Origeniana Tertia: The Third International Colloquium for Origen Studies,* ed. R. Hanson and H. Crouzel (Rome, 1985), pp. 279–81; J. Danielou, *The Bible and the Liturgy* (Notre Dame, Ind., 1956), pp. 198ff.; H. Riedlinger, *Die Makellosigkeit der Kirche in den lateinischen Hoheliedkommentaren des Mittelalters* (Münster, 1958), pp. 7, 19, 26, 78–79, 126, 155, 400.

21. François de Medeiros, *L'occident et l'Afrique (XIIIe–XVe siècle)* (Paris, 1985), p. 47, n. 45; see also Kaplan, *Ruler, Saint and Servant,* p. 81. It appears that the germ of this exegetical idea preceded Origen, for we find Irenaeus in the second century interpreting the Kushite in Num 12:1 as referring to the gentile church, and Moses' marriage to the Kushite symbolizing the acceptance of the gentiles into the Christian faith (Irénée de Lyon, *Contre les Hérésies* 4.20.12, *SC* 100/2:672–73). Nevertheless, it was Origen who developed the hermeneutical superstructure, which influenced those who followed.

22. J. M. Courtès, *IBWA* 2/1:14–15; Snowden, *Before Color Prejudice,* pp. 101, 114. See also Robert Wilken, "Philo in the Fourth Century," *Studia Philonica* 6 (1994) 101.

23. *GCS* 33 (Origen 8) 26. See also Elizabeth Clark, "The Uses of the Song of Songs: Origen and the Later Latin Fathers," in *Ascetic Piety and Women's Faith: Essays on Late Ancient Christianity,* ed. E. Clark (Lewiston, N.Y., 1986), pp. 387–88 and 411, n. 3.

24. "Those who are altogether reprobate, and unrepentant, who possess the Ethiopian's unchanging skin . . . " (*On Penance,* "Canonical Epistle," Canon 4, quoted by Franz Dölger, *Die Sonne der Gerechtigkeit und der Schwarze* [1918; repr., Munich, 1971], p. 62, from Martin J. Routh, *Reliquiae sacrae* 4.2 [1846] 26; translation is that of James Hawkins in *ANF* 6:270).

25. "Those who have . . . abandoned their life of the Ethiopians, receive immortality and say, full of thanks, 'Let the brightness of the Lord our God be upon us' (Ps 89/90:17 LXX) because having been washed by the Cause of all good we appear bright and white" (*In Zachariam* 3.195, *SC* 83:712–13). MT Ps 90:17, incidentally, does not read "brightness" (LXX: λαμπρότης), but "pleasantness" (*noʿam*).

26. Moses marriage of the Ethiopian represented Jesus' espousal of the gentiles. Apollinaris is in Theodoret of Cyrrhus, *Theodoreti Cyrensis: Quaestiones in Octateucham,* ed. Fernández Marcos and Sáenz-Badillos, Numbers 22, p. 207. See also

R. Devreesse, *Les anciens commentateurs grecs de l'octateuque et des Rois (fragments tirés des chaînes)* (Rome, 1959), pp. 139–40.

27. "We, namely, sinners of the Gentiles, formerly black with sins, and once fruitless, have brought forth from the depth the words of prophecy. . . . And so it is written: 'Ethiopia shall stretch out her hands to God.' In this a figure of Holy Church is signified, which says in the Canticle of Canticles: 'I am black but beautiful O ye daughters of Jerusalem'; black through sin, beautiful through grace" (*De spiritu sancto* 2.10.112, *CSEL* 79:130; trans. R. J. Deferrari, *FC* 44:135); "What is more lowly, what is more like Ethiopia, than our bodies, blackened, too, by the darkness of sin?" (*Paradise* 3.16, *CSEL* 32/1:275–76; trans. J. J. Savage, *FC* 42:297).

28. "The peoples of Ethiopia . . . are not burnt by the sun, but are black with vice, sin giving them the color of night" (*Carmina* 28.249–51, *CSEL* 30:302; trans. P. G. Walsh, *ACW* 40:303).

29. "He that gave light to the Gentiles, both to the Ethiopians and unto the Indians did his bright beams reach. The eunuch of Ethiopia upon his chariot saw Philip: the Lamb of Light met the dark man from out of the water. . . . The Ethiopian was baptized and shone with joy, and journeyed on. He made disciples and taught, and out of black men he made men white. And the dark Ethiopian women became pearls for the Son; He offered them up to the Father, as a glistening crown from the Ethiopians. The Queen of Sheba was a sheep . . . the lamp of truth did Solomon give her. . . . She was enlightened and went away" (*Hymnen de Fide* 83 [= *The Pearl* 3]; trans. J. B. Morris in *NPNF2* 13:295; text and German translation: E. Beck, *Des heiligen Ephraem des Syrers: Hymnen de Fide* (Louvain, 1955), *CSCO* 154–55, Scriptores Syri 73–74; text, pp. 254–55, trans., p. 217. There is also a French translation by Fr. Graffin in *L'Orient Syrien* 12 [1967] 140–41). Regarding Origen's influence in the East, see the comments by Elizabeth Clark, *The Origenist Controversy* (Princeton, 1992), p. 141, and by de Vregille and Neyrand in *SC* 420:76.

30. The black maiden in Song 1:5 together with various scriptural Ethiopians represent those living in idolatry. *Apponii in Canticum Canticorum Expositio* 1.9 and 41, *CCL* 19:6–7, 28–29; *SC* 420:152–53, 204–7; *Apponius: Die Auslegung zum Lied der Lieder*, ed., trans., and commentary H. König (Freiburg, 1992), pp. 12, 40–41 and n. 72. On the question of Origen as a direct source for Apponius, see Riedlinger, *Die Makellosigkeit der Kirche*, p. 50, n. 14; de Vregille and Neyrand in *SC* 420:206–7, n. 3, and their comments on pp. 74–76; and M. McNamara, "Early Irish Exegesis: Some Facts and Tendencies," *Proceedings of the Irish Biblical Association* 8 (1984) 72. On Apponius's dates and nationality, see p. 273, n. 43.

31. "Christ came into the world to make blacks [τοὺς μέλανας] bright"; when those who were dark with sin accept Jesus, "the Ethiopians become light in color"; "the Ethiopians, however, hastened to the faith . . . having washed off their darkness by a mystical washing" (*Gregorii Nysseni opera*, ed. W. Jaeger et al., vol. 6: *Commentarius in Canticum Canticorum* 1.5, ed. H. Langerbeck, Leiden, 1960, pp. 48–49, 205; trans. C. McCambley, *Saint Gregory of Nyssa: Commentary on the Song of Songs*, Brookline, Mass, 1987, pp. 62, 142).

32. "Kush in Hebrew means Ethiopian, that is, black and dark, one who has a soul as black as his body"; "Let Ethiopia extend its hands to God" (Ps 68/67:32)

means "we were black from sin and passion, [but] we have outstripped the Israelites and believe in the Saviour"; "Ethiopia" of Ps 87/86:4 means "black and cloaked in the filth of sin. . . . At one time we were Ethiopians in our vices and sins. How so? Because our sins had blackened us" (trans. M. L. Ewald, *FC* 48:28, 58, 140); "Ethiopia . . . that is the Gentiles" (*Commentarii in Sophoniam prophetam,* ad Zeph 3:10, *PL* 25.1380C). Similarly on Amos 9:7, *CCL* 76:343.

33. "How do I understand 'the Ethiopian peoples' (LXX Ps 74/73:14)? How else than by these, all nations? And properly by black men [*nigros*]: for Ethiopians are black [*nigri*]. They are those called to the faith who were black [*nigri*]; the very same indeed, so that it may be said to them: 'You were sometimes darkness but now you are light in the Lord' (Ephesians 5:8)" (*Enarrationes in Psalmos* 73.16, *CCL* 39:1014; see also 71.12, *CCL* 39:980. English trans. after A. C. Coxe, NPNF1 8:346 and 330–31).

34. "Ethiopia signifies all nations that are black in sin" (*Explanatio in Psalmos* 67.32, *PG* 69.1159–60); similarly on Ps 72/71:9 and 74/73:14, *PG* 69.1187–88; On Num 12:1, the Kushite represents the gentiles: *Glaphyra in Numeros* 1.2, *PG* 69.596A.

35. "We must interpret the Ethiopians as sinning people, for just as the Ethiopians are covered in the foulest [*teterrimo*] skins, so the souls of transgressors are enshrouded in the darkness of wicked deeds" (*Expositio in Psalterium* 71.9, *PL* 70.510; trans. P. G. Walsh, *ACW* 52:189; similarly 73.13, *PL* 70.531, *ACW* 52:218, and 86.4, *PL* 70.619–20, *ACW* 52:339).

36. On Ps 68/67:32, "Ethiopia signifies all nations that are black in sin" (*Explanatio in Psalmos, PG* 69.1159–60); "Ethiopians" of Ps 72/71:9 and 74/73:14 means "those who have dark and unenlightened minds that are not yet illumined and do not have divine light" (*PG* 69.1187–88).

37. The Ethiopians, who represent the gentiles, "preceded the synagogue of the Jews taking off the blackness of sin and putting on the whiteness of faith" (*Sermones* 8, *CSEL* 21:253).

38. "Many weak ones fall from the condition of faith and, after they fall, persecute the faith. What else is exposed other than the blackness of their skin, so that which first seemed beautiful, now appears foul" (*Moralia* 20.40 [77], *CCL* 143/1:1060).

39. "Keep your virginity constant forever. . . . Let not black girls stain your body, and don't lie with them on account of their hellish face" (Sic tibi virginitas mansuro constet in aeuo. . . . Sic tua non maculent nigrantes membra puellae, Nec iaceas propter Tartaream faciem. Epistulae 7.21, *CSEL* 6:189–90; *Monumenta Germaniae Historica* series, Auctorum Antiquissimorum, ed. F. Vogel, 7:246). Thompson, *Romans and Blacks,* p. 42, explains that Ennodius, in arguing for sexual abstention, uses the black person as a metaphor for sin: since the sin is sexual, the metaphor takes on the form of black girls. See also Courtés, *IBWA* 2/1:22. B. Teyssèdre, *Le diable et l'enfer au temps de Jésus* (Paris, 1985), p. 262 and n. 50, and David Brakke, "Ethiopian Demons: Male Sexuality, the Black-Skinned Other, and the Monastic Self," *Journal of the History of Sexuality* 10 (2001) 501–35. Cf. Ambrose's interpretation of the black maiden of Song 1:5, "The soul has been darkened by her union with the body. . . . The passions of the body have attacked me and the allurements of the flesh have given me my color" (*De Isaac vel anima* 4.13, *CSEL* 32/1:651–52, trans. M. P. McHugh, *FC* 65:19).

40. *Theodoreti Cyrensis: Quaestiones in Octateucham,* ed. N. Fernández Marcos and A. Sáenz-Badillos, Exodus 4, p. 101. Recent scholarship has shown that the Antiochene school was not exclusively literalist and often recognizes a level of meaning beyond the literal. See Simonett, *Biblical Interpretation in the Early Church,* pp. 67–68. On the meaning of the terms "Antiochene school" and "Alexandrian school," see Wilken, "Philo in the Fourth Century," p. 101.

41. Thompson, *Romans and Blacks,* pp. 40, 112.

42. J. M. Courtès, "The Theme of 'Ethiopia' and 'Ethiopians' in Patristic Literature," *IBWA* 2/1:9–32.

43. Origen reacted to the Rabbis: Isaac Baer, "Israel, the Christian Church and the Roman Empire from the Days of Septimus Severus to the 'Edict of Toleration' of 313 CE," *Scripta Hierosolymitana* 7 (1961) 99–101, originally in Hebrew in *Zion* 21 (1956) 17–18, repr., Baer, *Meḥqarim u-Masot be-Toledot ʿAm Yiśraʾel* (Jerusalem, 1986); Ephraim E. Urbach, "The Homiletical Interpretation of the Sages and the Expositions of Origen on Canticles, and the Jewish-Christian Disputation," *Scripta Hierosolymitana* 22 (1971) 262–65, originally in Hebrew in *Tarbiẓ* 30 (1960) 159–62, repr., Urbach, *Mi-ʿOlamam shel Ḥakhamim* (Jerusalem, 1988), pp. 514–36, 525–28. The Rabbis reacted to Origen: Reuven Kimelman, "Rabbi Yoḥanan and Origen on the Song of Songs: A Third-Century Jewish-Christian Disputation," *HTR* 73 (1980) 593–94; see also Raphael Loewe, "Apologetic Motifs in the Targum to the Song of Songs," in *Biblical Motifs: Origins and Transformations,* ed. A. Altmann (Cambridge Mass., 1966), p. 175.

44. Fearghus Ó Fearghail, "Philo and the Fathers: The Letter and the Spirit," in *Scriptural Interpretation in the Fathers: Letter and Spirit,* ed. T. Finan and V. Twomey (Cambridge, 1995), pp. 39–59; Wilken, "Philo in the Fourth Century," pp. 100–102; Simonett, *Biblical Interpretation in the Early Church,* pp. 77ff., and David T. Runia, *Philo in Early Christian Literature* (Assen, 1993), pp. 197–204; "Philo of Alexandria and the Beginnings of Christian Thought," *Studia Philonica* 7 (1995) 143–60.

45. Simonett, *Biblical Interpretation in the Early Church,* p. 38, and Annewies van den Hoek, *Clement of Alexandria and His Use of Philo in the "Stromateis": An Early Christian Reshaping of a Jewish Model* (Leiden, 1988).

46. See E. Lucchesi, *L'usage de Philon dans l'oeuvre exégétique de saint Ambrose: une "Quellenforschung" relative aux commentaires d'Ambrose sur la Genèse* (Leiden, 1977).

47. Ambrose, *De Noe* 34.128, *CSEL* 32/1:496. Courtès, *IBWA* 2/1:18. Note D. Runia's remark that in *De Noe* Ambrose closely follows Philo's exegesis of Gen 6–10 as given in *Questions in Genesis* 1.87–2.82 ("A Note on Philo and Christian Heresy," *Studia Philonica* 4 [1992] 72).

48. David Runia, "Philo and Origen: A Preliminary Survey," in Runia, *Philo and the Church Fathers: A Collection of Papers* (Leiden, 1995), p. 122; originally published in *Origeniana Quinta: Papers of the 5th International Origen Congress Boston College 14–18 August 1989,* ed. Robert J. Daly (Leuven, 1992). On Philo's interpretation of Genesis as a source for Origen's allegorical exegesis, see N.R.M. de Lange, *Origen and the Jews* (Cambridge, 1976), pp. 103–32. A exhaustive comparison of Philo-Origen parallels is now found in Annewies van den Hoek, "Philo and Origen: A Descriptive Catalogue of Their Relationship," *Studia Philonica* 12 (2000) 44–121.

49. Thompson, *Romans and Blacks,* p. 110 and literature cited in n. 96.

50. *TDOT* 5:246–47, 252–58 (Mitchel); *TDNT* 7:424–25 (Conzelmann); Thompson, *Romans and Blacks,* pp. 110–13; Snowden, *Before Color Prejudice,* pp. 82ff., the literature cited on p. 139, n. 94, and "Asclepiades' Didyme," *Greek, Roman, and Byzantine Studies* 32 (1991) 251, n. 30. The first two sections of Gershom Scholem's article, "Colours and Their Symbolism in Jewish Tradition and Mysticism," *Diogenes* 108 (1979) 84–111; 109 (1980) 65–76, deal with biblical and rabbinic material. For Arabic literature, note also the tradition recorded by Ṭabarsī (d. 1153) that the Black Stone (*al-ḥajar al-aswad*), which is built into the Kaʿba, was originally white "but it became black because of the sins of the children of Adam" (M. Ayoub, *The Qurʾan and Its Interpreters,* Albany, 1984, 1:158, from Ṭabarsī's commentary on the Qurʾan, Beirut, 1961, 1:460). Surprisingly, the negative symbolism of black in the Hebrew Bible does not extend to the realm of the sacred and cultic. Sin, for example, is symbolized by red, not black; see Athalya Brenner, "On Color and the Sacred in the Hebrew Bible," in *The Language of Color in the Mediterranean,* ed. Alexander Borg (Stockholm, 1999), pp. 200–207. Compare Isaiah's (1:18) "sins like scarlet . . . red like crimson" with its paraphrase "sin redder than scarlet or blacker than sackcloth" in the *Apocryphon of Ezekiel* (*OTP* 1:494, trans. James R. Mueller and S. E. Robinson; J. R. Mueller, *The Five Fragments of the Apocryphon of Ezekiel: A Critical Study,* Sheffield UK, 1994, pp. 101–20; Benjamin Wright, "The Apocryphal Ezekiel Fragments," in *The Apocryphal Ezekial,* ed. Michael Stone et al., Atlanta, 2000, pp. 19–21). *mYoma* 6.8 (R. Ishmael) records a Second Temple practice (*lashon shel zehorit*) that assumes the symbolism used by Isaiah.

51. *SongR* 1:6.3 (ed. Warsaw 1.41), *Midrash Shir ha-Shirim* 1.6 (ed. Wertheimer, p. 29): Israel's sins are temporary as the maiden's suntan is a temporary blackening of the skin. (The passage and its implications are discussed below, pp. 86–87, 126–28.) Hippolytus of Rome (d. ca. 235): The blackness of the maiden in Song 1:5 is an allegorical reference to mankind's loss of glory on account of Original Sin. Thus man became black. He is, however, beautiful through Christ's renewal, which washes away the black of sin (*Commentary on Song, GCS* 1:359). It is possible that Origen knew and was influenced by Hippolytus's commentary, but it remains to be proved; see Riedlinger, *Die Makellosigkeit der Kirche,* pp. 26–27. Clark thinks it likely ("The Uses of the Song of Songs," p. 387).

52. Dölger, *Die Sonne der Gerechtigkeit,* p. 50. I cannot, therefore, agree with B. Kedar-Kopfstein when he says that one can detect Jewish Alexandria in Jerome's allegorical treatment of these matters ("Jewish Traditions in the Wrtitings of Jerome," in *The Aramaic Bible: Targums in Their Historical Context,* ed. D.R.G. Beattie and M. J. McNamara, Sheffield, 1994, pp. 421–22).

53. Cf., however, Origen's description of God who "is called the light in whom there is no darkness" (*Commentary to Song* 2.2, *GCS* 33 [Origen 8] 130, Lawson, *ACW* 26:112) with Philo's description of evil that is dark and "has no participation in light" (*Quaestiones in Genesim* 2.82).

54. Ladislas Bugner, *IBWA* 1:38.

55. Courtès, *IBWA* 2/1:9, 19–21. Similar views in Gay Byron, *Symbolic Blackness and Ethnic Difference in Early Christian Literature* (London, 2002), pp. 122–29, speaking of "the power of symbolic language in shaping attitudes, values,

worldviews, and practices of early Christians" (p. 124), and in Robert Hood, *Begrimed and Black: Christian Traditions on Blacks and Blackness* (Minneapolis, 1994), pp. 73–90, speaking of the associations made by the church fathers between blackness and sin and evil, which "shaped the perception of blacks by Christians" (p. 87).

56. Carolyn Prager, "'If I Be Devil': English Renaissance Response to the Proverbial and Ecumenical Ethiopian," *Journal of Medieval and Renaissance Studies* 17 (1987) 264.

57. J. Devisse in *IBWA* 2/1:61. Devisse is talking specifically about Jerome, but what he says can be applied in general to patristic exegesis of the Ethiopian. Perhaps the most startling example of the effects of the metaphor of the Ethiopian as sin and sinner is an incident that occurred in 1870. At the First Vatican Council, which took place in that year, a group of missionary bishops presented a document to the pope requesting him to release the black race from the Curse of Ham, the eternal curse of slavery on Blacks (see chapter 12), which had been put on it. The petition was unsuccessful, for only by conversion to Christianity could the curse be removed. See Jean-Marc Ela, "L'église, le monde noir et le concile," *Personnalité Africaine et Catholicisme* (Paris, 1962), p. 79; C. Wauthier, *The Literature and Thought of Modern Africa* (New York, 1967; originally published as *L'Afrique des Africains,* 1964); see Pierre Charles, "Les Noirs, fils de Cham le maudit," *Nouvelle Revue Theologique* 55 (1928) 721–39, where the Vatican proceedings are cited as *Acta Concil. recentiorum (Collectio Lacensis),* 7:906. Another startling example of the effects of this metaphor may perhaps be seen by comparing Ennodius's statement "Keep your virginity constant forever. . . . Let not black girls stain your body, and don't lie with them on account of their hellish face" (above, n. 39) with an incident that occurred in Virginia in 1630, when a certain Hugh Davis was "soundly whipped . . . for abusing himself to the dishonor of God and the same of Christians, by defiling his body in lying with a negro" (quoted from the Statutes of Virginia by Carl Degler, "Slavery and the Genesis of American Race Prejudice," in *The Making of Black America,* ed. August Meier and Elliott Rudwick, New York, 1969, pp. 98–99).

58. Devisse, *IBWA* 2/1:80.

59. Ibid.

60. *IBWA* 1/1:14. See also Thompson, *Romans and Blacks,* p. 42. The symbolism impacted not only on black Africans, but on dark-skinned people in general. In Corippus's sixth-century poetic account of the Roman reconquest of North Africa, "the dark skin of the natives is stressed . . . and made a symbol of their depravity. . . . [B]lack and white, clearly racial here, [are used] to symbolize evil and good" (George Shea, *The* Iohannis *or* De Bellis Libycis *of Flavius Cresconius Corippus,* Lewiston, N.Y., 1998, pp. 34–35). A later example, from the *Vienna Genesis* (eleventh–twelfth century), more clearly shows the depiction of black skin color as an external manifestation of internal sinfulness: Adam's offspring included the dogheads, the headless, the large-eared, the single-footed, and some who "completely lost their beautiful coloring; they became black and disgusting, and unlike any people. . . . [They] displayed on their bodies what the forebears had earned by their misdeeds. As the fathers had been inwardly, so the children were outwardly." Text in K. Smits, *Die frühmittelhochdeutsche Wiener Genesis* (Berlin, 1972), lines 1292–

1309, pp. 134–35; J. Diemer, *Genesis und Exodus nach der Millstätter Handschrift* (Vienna, 1862), p. 26; translation is that of John B. Friedman, *The Monstrous Races in Medieval Art and Thought* (Cambridge, 1981), p. 93. See B. Seitz, "Die Darstellung hässlicher Menschen in mittelhochdeutscher erzählender Literatur von der Wiener Genesis bis zum Ausgang des 13. Jahrhunderts" (Ph.D. diss., Eberhard-Karls Universität zu Tübingen, 1967), p. 74.

61. Snowden, *Blacks in Antiquity*, pp. 196–215; *Before Color Prejudice*, pp. 99–108.

62. *Quaestiones in Genesim* 2.35–36, trans. R. Marcus (LCL).

63. *Legum Allegoriae* 2.67, trans. G. H. Whitaker (LCL). For the possible interpretation that black here means unmixed, pure, see Michaelis in *TDNT* 4:550, n. 10; Claude Mondésert's note ad loc. in *Les Oeuvres de Philon d'Alexandrie* (Paris, 1962), 2:140–41; and cf. Plato, *Timeus* 68c. Yehoshua Amir takes the allegory to mean "clearly defined character" (*ofi baʿal qawim nimraṣim*); see his *Philo of Alexandria*, 4:76, n. 70. Note that Plutarch uses the same figure of speech as does Philo: "[The Egyptians] call Egypt, which has the blackest of soils, by the same name as the black portion of the eye 'Chemia' (Χημίαν)." Plutarch, *Isis and Osiris* 33 (364C), ed. J. Gwyn Griffiths, in *Plutarch's De Iside et Osiride* (Cambridge, 1970), p. 170. Cf. a Ptolemaic text that compares Egypt with the pupil of the eye, quoted by Elsa Oréal, "'Noir parfait': Un jeu de mots de l'égyptien au grec," *Revue des études grecques* 111 (1998) 561. C. G. Siegfried thinks that Philo was playing on the double meaning of κόρη 'pupil of the eye' and 'maiden'; see his *Philo von Alexandria als Ausleger des Alten Testament*, p. 195.

64. Text and translation in Carl R. Holladay, *Fragments from Hellenistic Jewish Authors* (Chico, Calif., 1983), 1:75–77; another recent English translation is by J. Hanson in *OTP* 2:852–53. On Demetrius, in addition to these two works, see the discussion and bibliography in Gregory E. Sterling, *Historiography and Self-Definition: Josephos, Luke-Acts and Apologetic Historiography* (Leiden, 1992), p. 152, n. 93, pp. 153–67. See also Erich Gruen, *Heritage and Hellenism: The Reinvention of Jewish Tradition* (Berkeley, 1998), p. 115, who injects a note of caution regarding both the date and place of Demetrius.

65. *Exagoge* 60–65. Text, translation, commentary, and bibliography have appeared in two recent publications: Jacobson, *The Exagoge of Ezekiel*, pp. 52–55, 85–86; and Holladay, *Fragments from Hellenistic Jewish Authors*, 2:358–59, 430–34. In addition there is a new English translation by R. G. Robertson in *OTP* 2:810–11. Translation quoted is that of Jacobson. On the date of Ezekiel, see the discussions in these editions and translations. On Ezekiel in general, see now John J. Collins, *Between Athens and Jerusalem: Jewish Identity in the Hellenistic Diaspora*, 2nd ed. (Grand Rapids, Mich., 2000), pp. 224–30. "Libya" in classical antiquity usually referred to the continent of Africa, as for example in Cleodemus Malchus, the Hellenistic-Jewish writer from before the first century B.C.E. (Robertson, *OTP* 2:810–11; R. Doran, *OTP* 2:884). On this meaning of Libya in classical sources, see also M. Besnier, *Lexique de géographie ancienne* (Paris, 1914), s.v. Africa; J. Devisse, *IBWA* 2/1:216, n. 75; E. Honigmann's article in *RE* 13:149–51; as well as the literature cited by Holladay, p. 432, and J. Gutmann, *The Beginnings of Jewish-Hellenistic Literature* (in Hebrew; Jerusalem, 1963), 2:36–37.

66. See pp. 19–20.

67. See Jacobson, *The Exagoge of Exekiel*, p. 432; E. Gruen, *Heritage and Hellenism*, pp. 129–30; and A. Kerkeslager, "Jewish Pilgrimage and Jewish Identity in Hellenistic and Early Roman Egypt," in *Pilgrimage and Holy Space in Late Antique Egypt*, ed. D. Frankfurter (Leiden, 1998), p. 159.

68. Augustine, *Quaestionum in Heptateuchum* 4.20, *CSEL* 28/2:331, *CCL* 33:247. "Sed nunc eos Aethiopes nemo fere appellat, sicut solent locorum et gentium nomina plerumque uetustate mutari."

69. I am indebted to Daniel Sheerin for help with deciphering Augustine's meaning. If Augustine's text does in fact imply that in his time the name Ethiopian for Midianite was still known, at least to some, it may explain the equation of Midian with Kush/Ethiopia in some fourth- and fifth-century Christian works. The probably fourth-century Syriac *Cave of Treasures* 34.5 says that after killing the Egyptian, Moses "fled to Midian, to Reuel, the Kushite, the priest of Midian" (ed. and trans. Su-Min Ri, *La caverne des trésors: les deux recensions syriaques*, *CSCO* 486–87, Scriptores Syri 207–8, Louvain, 1987, pp. 268–69, 102–103. See below, p. 354, n. 35, for bibliographic information and dating). Basil, bishop of Caesarea (d. 379), says that when Moses fled Egypt he went to Ethiopia, not Midian as in the Bible (S. Giet, ed., *Basile de Césarée: Homélies sur l'Hexaéméron*, 1.2c, *SC* 26:90; cf. the language of *Targum Ps-Jon* quoted later). The insertion of Ethiopia/Kush into the story about Midian is no doubt an attempt to reconcile the story with Num 12:1 (see Giet's note ad loc.). This is particualry obvious in the *Cave of Treasures*, which immediately follows "Reuel, the Kushite, the priest of Midian" with "And Moses married Zipporah the Kushite, daughter of the priest" (or, "daughter of the priest Jethro" in one version, which is yet another attempt at reconciliation). Nevertheless, if the equation of the two names were unknown, the reconciliation would have sounded absurd. Theodoret of Cyrrhus (fifth century C.E.) may have also known of the equation when he said that the Ethiopian of Num 12:1 is Zipporah, even though he provided an explanation: the Midianites and the Ethiopians are in geographical proximity and therefore came to be confused (*Theodoreti Cyrensis: Quaestiones in Octateucham*, ed. Fernández Marcos and Sáenz-Badillos, Numbers 22, p. 207).

70. *Exagoge* 66–67. Translation, Jacobson, *The Exagoge of Ezekiel*, pp. 54–55; Holladay, *Fragments from Hellenistic Jewish Authors*, 2:360–61; Robertson in *OTP* 2:811.

71. Holladay, *Fragments from Hellenistic Jewish Authors*, 2:435–36.

72. Howard Jacobson, "The Identity and Role of Chum in Ezekiel's *Exagoge*," *Hebrew University Studies in Literature* 9 (1981) 139–46, quotation from p. 145.

73. Robertson in *OTP* 2:811.

74. A review of the literature on Josephus's source of the story is found in L. Feldman, "Josephus' Portrait of Moses: Part Two," *JQR* 83 (1992) 15–18, nn. 112–13.

75. Artapanus, whose dates are unknown, is found in citations of Eusebius (d. ca. 340) from the compendium of Alexander Polyhistor (first century B.C.E.). Text, translation, and discussion in Holladay, *Fragments from Hellenistic Jewish Authors*, 1:189ff. Translation with notes, in *OTP* 2:889ff. On Artapanus, see Sterling, *Historiography and Self-Definition*, p. 152, n. 93, pp. 167–86, with bibliography; on

the relationship between Artapanus and Josephus, pp. 268–80. Some would put Artapanus in the third century B.C.E., some ca. 100 B.C.E. For later, medieval, versions of the story, see pp. 162–63.

76. *Perush Rabbenu Ephraim b. Shimshon u-Gedolei Ashkenaz ha-Qadmonim,* ed. E. Korach and Z. Leitner (Jerusalem, 1992), 2:86. The work was published primarily from MS British Museum, or. 10855. The text reads: "In the Sifre R. Eleazar ben R. Yose ha-Galili said, 'Ṣipporah—i.e. look and gaze (*ṣefu u-re'u*) how beautiful is this Kushite. . . .' He [or, it] also said that Ṣipporah died and he married a Kushite wife. . . ."

77. Ibid. (quoted as *ameru ḥazal;* the editors note that they could not find the source).

78. *Sifre Num* 99 and 100 (pp. 98–99), *Sifre Zuṭa* 12.1–3 (p. 274). The midrash speaks of Zipporah in accord with its view that the Kushite is Zipporah. It is not clear to me whether *Targ Ps-Jon* took the element of sexual separation from the midrash and grafted it onto its understanding of the Kushite as Moses' Ethiopian wife, or whether the combination was in the Targum's source. In any case, the idea that Moses separated from his wife out a sense of superiority (as Miriam and Aaron thought) is clearly derived from a reading of the verses, as I show.

79. In the words of *Sifre Zuṭa* 12.3: "*Now the man Moses was very humble:* From here you know that they claimed that Moses was haughty and for this reason would not sleep with his wife, for the verse rebukes them and says *Moses was very humble,* contrary to their claim that he was haughty."

80. See Avigdor Shinan, "From Artapanos to 'The Book of Jashar': Toward the Development of the Moses and the Ethiopian Story" (in Hebrew), *Eshkolot* 9–10, n.s. 2–3 (1977–78) 60 = "Moses and the Ethiopian Woman: Sources of a Story in *The Chronicles of Moses,*" *Scripta Hierosolymitana* 27 (1978) 72, and *Agadatam shel Meturgemanim* (Jerusalem, 1979), p. 170; and see now Shinan, *Targum we-Aggadah Bo* (Jerusalem, 1992), p. 94. Shinan thinks that the enigmatic verse did not produce the story. Similarly, and independently, Redford feels that the Chronicle story derives from a preexistent tale and is not based on the biblical verse (*Egypt, Canaan, and Israel in Ancient Times,* p. 419). For the theory that the verse generated the story, see, for example, Martin Braun, *History and Romance in Graeco-Oriental Literature* (Oxford, 1938), pp. 97–102.

81. It is well known that Josephus wrote for a non-Jewish audience. It is also true, however, that he had Jewish readers in mind, as he himself says on several occasions. See the summaries of this issue in Paul Spilsury, *The Image of the Jew in Flavius Josphus' Paraphrase of the Bible* (Tübingen, 1998), pp. 16–22, and Louis Feldman, *Josephus's Interpretation of the Bible* (Berkeley, 1998), pp. 46–50. The dating of *Targum Ps-Jonathan* is much debated; see the Glossary.

82. See also Philo, *Legum Allegoriae* 2.67.

83. *Sifre Num* 99 (pp. 98–99). On the distinctiveness of "beauty and character," cf. Origen's paraphrase of Song 1:5, "Do not reproach me for my color, then, O daughters of Jerusalem, seeing that my body lacks neither natural beauty, nor that which is acquired by practice [*exercitio quaesita*]" (*Commentary to Song* 2.1, *GCS* 33 [Origen 8] 113, trans., R. P. Lawson, *ACW* 26:91). Lawson notes (p. 329, n. 3) that "*exercitium* (Gk. ἀκησις) in Patristic Latin often means the practice of

the virtues." On the inclusion of nonphysical with physical features in describing the ideal woman, see Shaye Cohen, "The Beauty of Flora and the Beauty of Sarai," *Helios* 8 (1981) 47–48.

84. The midrash is found in various combinations in *Sifre Num* 99 (p. 99); *Sifre Zuṭa* 12.1 (p. 274); *bMQ* 16b; *ARNb* 43 (p. 122); *MidPs* 7.14 (p. 70); *Tanḥuma, Ṣaw* 13; *Yelamedenu* in *YalqSh* (*Be-haʿalotekha*) 738; *bYoma* 75b; Targums Neofiti, Onqelos, and Fragment Targum (especially MS Paris) to Num 12:1; *Midrash ha-Gadol* to Num 12:1; *PRE* 53 (p. 127a; fragment in Solomon A. and Abraham J. Wertheimer, *Batei Midrashot,* 2nd ed., Jerusalem, 1950, 1:239); Targum to Ps 7:1; *Sefer Pitron Torah,* ed. E. E. Urbach (Jerusalem, 1978), p. 148; see also *ExR* 1.27, *PesR* 26 (p. 130b); *YalqSh,* Sam 157 and Jer 326; *Leqaḥ Ṭov,* Num 12:1; *Midrash Aggadah, Be-haʿalotekha,* p. 103; *Yalquṭ Makhiri,* Ps 7.1 and 6, and Amos 9.7; *Midrash Sheloshah we-Arbaʿah* in Wertheimer, *Batei Midrashot,* 2:62. In some sources Ebed-melech is identified with Baruch ben Nuriyah, the attendant of Jeremiah, whose brother held office in the court of King Zedekiah (Jer 51:59). In other sources "the Kushite" is midrashically understood to refer to Zedekiah himself.

85. One amoraic source, *MidPs* 7.18 (p. 71), is exceptional in not giving the metaphor a positive connotation in regard to Israel and Saul. Israel is said to be different from other peoples in its laws as the Kushite is different in skin color. Here the metaphor of differentness would appear to be value-neutral. The meaning of the metaphor in regard to Saul is not as clear, for the midrash quotes 1 Sam 10:8–9, 13:11–12, and 15:3, 9, showing Saul's disobedience of Samuel's orders. While the connotation could certainly be value-negative (Saul sinned), it could also be value-neutral, that is, Saul's actions differed (*meshuneh*) from what he was told to do (as Israel's laws differ from those of other nations). If the connotation is negative, it would significantly differ from the other "Kushite" interpretations of Saul's actions, which are always understood in a positive light, as is clear from the coupling of his actions with his handsome appearance (e.g., *MidPs* 7.14 and elsewhere: "Saul was different/distinct in his actions and handsomeness," *be- maʿaśaw uwe-yofyo; PRE:* "actions and good deeds"). Saul's good looks was a rabbinic commonplace; see Ginzberg, *Legends of the Jews,* 4:65 and 6:274, n. 134; see also David Pardo's (d. 1790) comment, *Sifre Rabbi Dovid Pardo,* ed. Ḥavrei Makhon Lev Śameaḥ (Jerusalem, 1990), ad loc. M. Gruber understands the midrashic take on Saul as possibly indicating sinfulness (*Rashi's Commentary on Psalms 1–89 [Books I–III]* Atlanta, 1998, ad loc., p. 71, n. 7). He translates Rashi's quotation of the midrash as, "Just as an Ethiopian is dark with respect to his skin, so was Saul dark with respect to his deeds" (p. 69). Rashi, however, says: "Just as an Ethiopian is different [*meshuneh*] with respect to his skin so was Saul different with respect to his deeds." Gruber's translation of *meshuneh* as "dark" is based on *panaw yešanne* of Qoh 8:1 and on Gruber's studies showing that "change the face" in various Semitic languages means "make the face dark, gloomy" (see p. 180). But this meaning is restricted to the expression "change the face." "Change" alone simply means "change," or in the passive participial form "changed" or "different," with the following preposition *b-* denoting that which was changed, that is, "different in skin color, different in deeds."

86. For this view and its rebuttal, see Goldenberg, "The Curse of Ham," p. 36 and n. 57. Those who hold this view have overlooked the fact that the Rabbis did

not "interpret away" the Kushi, who was the father of the prophet Zephaniah (Zeph 1:1).

87. See S. Fraade's comments about the "double-facing" character of midrashic commentaries—the need to see these commentaries from both an hermeneutical internal-facing and a sociohistorical external-facing perspective; *From Tradition to Commentary* (Albany, 1991), pp. 14–15.

88. See Isaac Heinemann, *Darkhe ha-Aggadah,* 3rd ed. (Jerusalem, 1970), index, s.v. *beriḥah miha-anonimiyut,* and Shaye Cohen, *Josephus in Galilee and Rome* (Leiden, 1979), p. 38. For another example of a midrashic identification of the unknown (Iscah) with the known (Sarah), see Eliezer Segal, "Sarah and Iscah: Method and Message in Midrashic Tradition," *JQR* 82 (1992) 417–29.

89. *Sifre Num* 99 (p. 99); *Sifre Zuṭa* 12.1 (p. 274).

90. *Sifre Num* 99 (p. 99). The same interpretation of "Zipporah" as "beautiful" is found in Christian onomastic lists (καλλος ὡραιοτητος) and in the fifth–sixth century Procopius of Gaza (*visitatio vel pulchra*). See Wutz, *Onomastica Sacra,* 2:937 and 1069. Also in the Armenian onomastic list published by Stone, *Signs of the Judgement,* pp. 157 and 195.

91. The association of *kushit* of Num 12:1 with *kaśita* of Deut 32:15 is, to my knowledge, not made in rabbinic sources, with one exception. The medieval text mentioned earlier, *Perush Rabbenu Ephraim b. Shimshon u-Gedolei Ashkenaz ha-Qadmonim,* ed. Korach and Leitner, 2:86, quotes *Sifre* (R. Eliezer b. Yose ha-Galilee) as in the editions but then adds the connection to Deut 32:15.

92. Ze'ev Ben-Ḥayyim, *Tibat Marqe* (Jerusalem, 1988), pp. 272–73, sec. 214b (on the dating of Marqe, see Glossary); *ʿIvrit we-Aramit Nusaḥ Shomron* (Jerusalem, 1957–77), 2:496 and nn. 291–92; and "Samaritan Poems for Joyous Occassions," *Tarbiẓ* 10 (1939) 368 and 371. A. Tal, *Ha-Targum ha-Shomroni la-Torah* (Tel Aviv, 1980–83), ad loc. (Tal, 3:104 English section, dates the original Samaritan Targum to not later than the fourth century C.E.). See also S. Lowy, *The Principles of Samaritan Bible Exegesis* (Leiden, 1977), p. 16, who notes that Munajja, a twelfth-century Samaritan exegete takes for granted the "beautiful" interpretation as "an original Samaritan exegesis."

93. Adolf Grohmann, *From the World of Arabic Papyri* (Cairo, 1952), p. 164, line 10. For the references in the *Thousand and One Nights,* see J. Kraemer, H. Gätje, et al., *Wörterbuch der klassischen arabischen Sprache* (Wiesbaden, 1970), 1:493, and R. Dozy, *Supplément aux Dictionnaires Arabes* (Leiden, 1927), 2:505. The *Thousand and One Nights* is a collection of stories that developed gradually and by the twelfth century took the form we have today. The earliest fragment of the work dates from the ninth century (E. Littman in EI^2 1:358ff). Dozy also lists later attestations (note especially his reference to Payne Smith's citation of Bar Bahlul's tenth-century dictionary). For colloquial Arabic, see, e.g., A. Barthélemy, *Dictionnaire arabe-français, dialects de Syrie: Alep, Damas, Liban Jérusalem* (Paris, 1935–54), pp. 731, s.v. *kuse;* 735, s.v. *kwayyes, kwayysat,* 'feminine beauty'.

94. Simon Hopkins, *Studies in the Grammar of Early Arabic* (Oxford, 1984), p. xlvi.

95. J. Perles, "Bemerkungen," *ZDMG* 20 (1866) 447, who prefers to see the exegesis via the Persian *khwash.* This explanation was accepted by Alexander Kohut, who refers also to Saadia's translation of the verse and Rashi's commentary in *bSuk*

53a (*ʿArukh ha-Shalem,* 4:348b). D. Geiger rejects any relationship between Hebrew *kushi* and Persian *khwsh* (in A. Kohut, *Tosafot he-ʿArukh,* ed. S. Krauss, Vienna, 1937, p. 237b), but it is not clear to me whether he rejects the Persian cognate as related to the Biblical Hebrew *kushi* or to the rabbinic interpretation of *kushi* as "beautiful." My colleague Sol Cohen tells me that his teacher, Joshua Finkel, had once suggested in a lecture that the midrash may be based on the Arabic *kuwayyis.* B. Barry Levy makes the same suggestion in print, *Targum Neophyti 1: A Textual Study* (Lanham, Md., 1987), 2:86.

96. E.g., *GenR* 36.1 and 79.7; see, however, p. 946, n. 3 (ed. Theodor-Albeck).

97. See, e.g., A. Geiger, *Urschrift und Uebersetzungen der Bibel* (Breslau, 1857), p. 199, and S. Kohn, *Samaritanische Studien* (Breslau, 1868), p. 15.

98. Stephen J. Lieberman has shown that the hermeneutic device of *gemaṭriya* is found as early as Assyrian cuneiform literature of the eighth–seventh century B.C.E. See his "A Mesopotamian Background for the So-Called *Aggadic* 'Measures' of Biblical Hermeneutics?" *HUCA* 58 (1987) 157–225, esp. 193ff. For literature on *gemaṭriya,* see Günter Stemberger, *Introduction to the Talmud and Midrash,* trans. and ed. M. Bockmuehl, 2nd ed. (Edinburgh, 1996), p. 29. Regarding the rabbinic and patristic interpretations of the 318 slaves of Abraham's household on the basis of *gemaṭriya,* see Burton Visotsky, *Fathers of the World: Essays in Rabbinic and Patristic Literatures* (Tübingen, 1995), pp. 14–15. The gnostic teaching of Marcus the Magician is full of *gemaṭriya;* see Irenaeus, *Adv. Haer.* 1.13.1–1.21.5 = Epiphanius, *Panarion* 34.2.1–34.20.12, in W. Foerster, *Gnosis: A Selection of Gnostic Texts,* trans. and ed. R. McL. Wilson (Oxford, 1972–74; originally in German, 1971), 1:198–221.

99. *Tanḥuma, Ṣaw* 13.

100. T. Siebers, *The Mirror of Medusa* (Berkeley, 1983), p. 58; see also p. 66. Siebers (p. 42) provides examples from various cultures of one manifestation of the fear of praise, that is, the custom of addressing children by opprobious names. On the phenomenon of language circumlocution in the rabbinic world, see Jacob Z. Lauterbach, "The Belief in the Power of the Word," *HUCA* 14 (1939) 288–92 (= his *Studies in Jewish Law, Custom, and Folklore,* New York, 1970, pp. 154–58).

101. See chapter 5 for the preference for light skin in women (and young children).

102. Alberto Morabia, "Lawn," in EI^2 5:705b.

103. E.g., Ullendorff, *Ethiopia and the Bible,* p. 8, and Gray, *ICC:Numbers,* p. 122.

104. Buber's remarks are in his edition of *Tanḥuma, Wa-Yiqraʾ,* p. 1a, n. 1; *Ṣaw,* p. 6a, n. 1; and his introduction, pp. 10–19, esp. 18 (on our passage). The *gemaṭriya* and the evil-eye explanations are found in Rashi's commentary to Num 12:1. Subsequent citations: e.g., Jacob b. Asher, *Perush Baʿal ha-Ṭurim ʿal ha-Torah,* ed. Jacob Rainitz, 3rd ed. (Benei Beraq, 1974), ad loc., and Ephraim b. Shimshon, *Commentary,* 2:76 (*gemaṭriya*); *Zohar, Terumah,* p. 130a, and R. Baḥye, *Commentary* to Num 12:1 (evil eye). See also Ibn Ezra to Song 1:5.

105. Benveniste, *Ot Emet* (Salonika, 1565; repr., Jerusalem, 1970), p. 67b. In addition to Benveniste and Buber, Jacob Reifmann (*Bet Talmud* 3 [1883] 184) also noted the Rashi origin of the *gemaṭriya* on Num 12:1, and see lately I. Avinery, *Hekhal Rashi* (Jerusalem, 1979–85), vol. 2, sec. 2, col. 509.

106. The *gematriya* explanation may even derive from a source later than Rashi, because the first printed edition of Rashi's *Commentary to the Pentateuch* (Reggio de Calabria, 1475; repr., Jerusalem, 1970, unpaginated) does not have the line. Thus, A. Berliner brackets the line in his edition of the commentary, *Rashi ʿal ha-Torah* (Frankfurt am Main, 1905) and so, following him, does C. D. Chavel, *Perushei Rashi ʿal ha-Torah,* 2nd ed. (Jerusalem, 1982). Until we have a critical edition of the *Commentary,* which may show the statement in reliable manuscripts (other than those that served the editor of the editio princeps), it is reasonable to conclude that it was absent in Rashi's original work and was added to it some time between 1475, when the first edition of the *Commentary* appeared, and 1520–22, when the first edition (Constantinople) of *Tanḥuma* appeared and may have drawn on it. See also Kohut's comment, *ʿArukh ha-Shalem,* 4:348b. The Yemenite manuscript of Rashi published by M. Lehman (New York, 1981) is late—about the time of the first print—and thus its inclusion of the *gematriya* is irrelevant to my argument.

107. For the ancient view, see pp. 32–33.

108. Translation, Bruce D. Chilton in *The Aramaic Bible,* ed. K. Cathcart et al., 11:37, ad loc.

109. See pp. 29–37.

110. See *Miqra'ot Gedolot Haketer: Isaiah,* ed. Menachem Cohen (Ramat Gan, Israel, 1996), ad loc., pp. 124–25.

111. Chilton, in *The Aramaic Bible,* 11:37

112. See Appendix II.

113. *4 Baruch* (also called *Paraleipomena Jeremiou)* is found in English translation by S. E. Robinson in *OTP* 2:413ff. and by Robert Kraft and Ann Purintun, *Paraleipomena Jeremiou* (Missoula, Mont., 1972), the latter of which provides the Greek text with variant readings. The relevant parts of *4 Baruch* are 3:12–14; 5:1–2, 28; 7:26, 32. Scholarly consensus considers the work to be of Jewish origin with Christian interpolations and additions (not affecting the parts referring to Abimelech); see Robinsion's introduction and J. H. Charlesworth, *The Pseudepigrapha and Modern Research with a Supplement* (Ann Arbor, Mich., 1981), pp. 88–89.

114. Both statements are found in many later midrashic collections, anthologies, and medieval writings; see Ginzberg, *Legends,* 6:412 and index, s.v. Ebed-melech, and M. Higger, *Mesekhtot Zeʿirot* (New York, 1929), pp. 74, 129–32. Several of the rabbinic texts are collected in Judah D. Eisenstein's *Oṣar ha-Midrashim* (New York, 1915), pp. 50a (*Alpha-beta de-Ben Sira*), 437a (*ʿAktan de-Mar Yaʿakov*), 513b (*Pirqei Rabbenu ha-Qadosh*). The secondary literature on the Ebed-melech stories contains an unfortunate example of compounded misunderstanding. Louis Ginzberg refers to "Ebed-melech, a 'white raven,' the only pious man at court" (*Legends of the Jews,* 4:299). Ginzberg used an expression of his day ("white raven") to indicate ironically that the black-skinned Ebed-melech was the "only 'white,' i.e. pious, man at the court of King Zedekiah" (*Legends of the Jews,* 6:412). Harold Brackman, searching for anti-Black rabbinic sentiment, drew on Ginzberg's statement, without acknowledgment, and declared: "The Sages actually nicknamed 'Ebed-melech the Ethiopian' the 'white raven' in order to emphasize that the 'true' meaning of his national designation had nothing to do with skin color" (Brackman,

"The Ebb and Flow of Conflict: A History of Black-Jewish Relations through 1900," Ph.D. diss., UCLA, 1977, 1:84–85). The Sages never nicknamed Ebed-melech "the white raven." The expression was Ginzberg's, drawn from his own time (see, e.g., John S. Farmer and W. E. Henley, *Slang and Its Analogues,* London, 1890–1904, s.v. white-crow); it is not in rabbinic literature despite Brackman's desire to find it there.

115. Sources in Ginzberg, *Legends of the Jews,* 6:412. On the identification with Baruch, see J. Edward Wright, "Baruch: His Evolution from Scribe to Apocalyptic Seer," in *Biblical Figures Outside the Bible,* ed. Michael Stone and Theodore Bergen (Harrisburg, Pa., 1998), pp. 282–83.

116. *bMeg* 15a.

117. For a recent discussion of geographic ethnocentrism and the parallel tradition of "inverse ethnocentrism" in the classical world, see James S. Romm, *The Edges of the Earth in Ancient Thought* (Princeton, 1992), pp. 45–60. The two concepts are related. Wiedemann notes that the edges of the world are also where utopias are found. This is where we find paradigms of morality and bestiality. See T.E.J. Wiedemann, "Between Man and Beast: Barbarians in Ammianus Marcellinus," in *Past Perspectives: Studies in Greek and Roman Historical Writing,* ed. I. S. Moxon, J. D. Smart, and A. J. Woodman (Cambridge, 1986), pp. 191–92.

118. *LevR* 27.1 (pp. 618–21) and *PesRK* 9.1 (pp. 148–49). The translation is adapted from William Braude and Israel Kapstein, *Pesikta de-Rab Kahana* (Philadelphia, 1975), pp. 171–72. Parallels sources are noted by Margulies in his edition of *LevR* and Theodor in his edition of *GenR* 33.1 (pp. 301–2). Note also the manuscript of *Tanḥuma* quoted by S. Buber in his edition of *Tanḥuma,* introduction, p. 152. *Tanḥuma,* ed. Buber, *Emor* 9 (p. 88), lacks mention of King Qaṣya. Both *qṣyʾ* and *qrṭygniʾ* are variously spelled in the sources. *Afriqi* is termed a *medinah* also in a geonic variant to *bSan* 4b; see the literature in n. 202, below.

119. Dennis Kratz, trans., *The Romances of Alexander* (New York, 1991), pp. xi–xvii. E. Baynham, "Who Put the 'Romance' in the Alexander Romance?: The Alexander Romances within Alexander Historiography," *Ancient History Bulletin* 9 (1995) 2, with literature cited. Baynham (n. 3) provides bibliography on the sources and evolution of the romance.

120. The Greek is from 1 Macc 1:3. This theme even extended to the third dimension, as Alexander was said to have devised mechanisms that allowed him to travel above and below the earth, in the air and to the depths of the seas (Richard Stoneman, *The Greek Alexander Romance,* London, 1991, 2.38 and 41, pp. 118, 123).

121. Stoneman, *The Greek Alexander Romance,* p. 14.

122. Ibid., 3.26–27, pp. 145–46. The version in Ibn Makīn (d. 1273/4) puts it where the sun rises (E.A.W. Budge, *The Alexander Book in Ethiopia,* London, 1933, p. 226). Also the version in Yosippon has an eastern setting (*Sefer Yosippon,* ed. David Flusser, Jerusalem, 1978, 2:59). The ends-of-the-earth location is unspecified in the Syriac, Ethiopic, and some Persian versions: G. J. Reinink, *Das Syrische Alexanderlied: Die drei Rezensionen,* CSCO 454–55, Scriptores Syri 195–96 (Louvain, 1983), pp. 26–27; Budge, *The Alexander Book in Ethiopia,* p. 102; *Iskandarnamah: A Persian Medieval Alexander-Romance,* trans. Minoo Southgate (New York, 1978), p. 59. See also Stoneman's comments in his *Legends of Alexan-*

der the Great (London, 1994), p. xviii. Stoneman (*Legends of Alexander*, p. ix), also notes that in the fourteenth-century French romance, *Perceforest*, Alexander reaches Britain.

123. Reinink, *Das Syrische Alexanderlied*, pp. 21, 26–27, 29, 44–45; Southgate, *Iskandarnamah*, pp. 53–54, 172, 177, 180, 192; Budge, *The Alexander Book in Ethiopia*, pp. 146, 227. See also *Alexander's Letter to Aristotle* 10, in Stoneman, *Legends of Alexander*, p. 11.

124. *Sefer Yosippon*, ed. Flusser, 2:59. On the reading *ṣalmei ḥoshekh* in some manuscripts of *GenR* instead of *harei ḥoshekh*, see Theodor's note, ad loc. The Mountains of Darkness and their location in Kush are found in two later midrashic accounts not related to the Alexander cycle (J. D. Eisenstein, *Oṣar ha-Midrashim*, p. 434, and *NumR* 16.25, cf. *PesR* 31, p. 147a) and in the medieval travel diary of the ninth-century Eldad ha-Dani (Epstein, *Kitvei Avraham Epstein*, 1:94). Another travel diary—this the thirteenth-century account (fiction?) of a Jacob ha-Nasi of Persia—puts the Mountains of Darkness on the way to Kush (A. Harkavy, "Ḥadashim Gam Yeshanim," in *Ha-Gat*, ed. L. Rabinowitz, St. Petersburg, 1897, pp. 66–67).

125. Budge, *The Alexander Book in Ethiopia*, p. 146; Reinink, *Das Syrische Alexanderlied*, pp. 46–47, but Reinink, against C. Hunnius, prefers to vocalize *ṭwr'* as *ṭawrā* 'distance' rather than *ṭūrā* 'mountain'; see his comment on p. 47.

126. Southgate, *Iskandarnamah*, pp. 58–59. Similarly Ibn Makīn (Budge, *The Alexander Book in Ethiopia*, pp. 226–27).

127. Para. 15, in Stoneman, *Legends of Alexander*, p. 13. This work, originally in Greek, was already incorporated into Pseudo-Callisthenes; see ibid., p. xviii. Cf. the "mountain where there are black men" in *On the Wonders of the East* 28 (Stoneman, *Legends of Alexander*, p. 24).

128. Wayne Horowitz, *Mesopotamian Cosmic Geography* (Winona Lake, Ind., 1998), pp. 97–100, 330–32; Utukku Lemnutu in W. Heimpel, "The Sun at Night and the Doors of Heaven in Babylonian Texts," *JCS* 38 (1986) 145; Gilgamesh IX ii and iii–v in R. Campbell Thompson, *The Epic of Gilgamish* (Oxford, 1930), pp. 50–52; translation in Pritchard, *Ancient Near Eastern Texts*, p. 88. See also M. J. Geller, *Forerunners to Udug-hul* (Stuttgart, 1985), pp. 36–37, lines 285–86: "[He] does not enter the foot of the mountain, nor will he cross over the path of the Netherworld." "Mashu" is understood to be the Akkadian word *māšu* 'twin', presumably because the mountain is perceived as being at the eastern and western horizons guarding sunrise and sunset (Heimpel, pp. 143–46).

129. The Baal Cycle 4 viii 1–7; trans. Mark Smith in *Ugaritic Narrative Poetry*, ed. S. B. Parker (Atlanta, 1997), p. 138. On these lines, see Michael Astour, "The Nether World and Its Denizens at Ugarit," in *Death in Mesopotamia*, ed. B. Alster (Copenhagen, 1980), p. 229.

130. See Mark Lidzbarski, *Ginzā: Der Schatze oder das grosse Buch der Mandäer* (Göttingen, 1925), p. 21 and n. 3; *bTam* 32b.

131. See Ginzberg, *Legends of the Jews*, 5:170, for sources.

132. Budge, *The Alexander Book in Ethiopia*, p. 136; Reinink, *Das Syrische Alexanderlied*, pp. 38–39, and see Reinink's n. 64.

133. The Book of Watchers comprises chapters 1–36 of *1 Enoch*. The lines quoted are at 17:2, 5–6 (cf. 32:2). Milik is in his *The Books of Enoch* (Oxford, 1976),

pp. 15 and 38. Cf. Mieses, "After the Destruction of Carthage," pp. 225–26. The dating of the Book of Watchers is based on James C. VanderKam, *Enoch and Growth of an Apocalyptic Tradition* (Washington, D.C., 1984), pp. 111–14, who thinks it likely that the work is a third-century B.C.E. composition, but at any rate almost certainly pre-Maccabean. Cf. also "the seven regions of the earth" in Ibn Makīn (Budge, *The Alexander Book in Ethiopia,* p. 226) with *1 Enoch* 77:4–8 and 4Q Enastr^{b} xxiii 9 in Milik, pp. 15, 289, 291. The notion of a Land of Darkness at the ends of the earth, where the world-encircling Great River or Ocean exists, is found also in the first to fourth-century C.E. Syriac *History of the Rechabites* (or *The Narrative of Zosimus*) 2.8, where the Island of the Blessed is found at the end of the earth, beyond a dense wall of a cloud that extends from the midst of the Great Ocean to the top of heaven (J. H. Charlesworth in *OTP* 2:451).

134. For another echo of Gilgamesh in the Alexander romance, see Stephanie Dalley, "The Tale of Bulūqiyā and the *Alexander Romance* in Jewish and Sufi Mystical Circles," in Reeves, *Tracing the Threads,* pp. 239–69.

135. Reinink, *Das Syrische Alexanderlied,* p. 45, n. 83. For the translation of *hmt,* see J. P. Margoliouth, *Supplement to the Thesaurus Syriacus of R. Payne Smith* (Oxford, 1927), p. 101, s.v. The word *hmt* may possibly be derived from Hebrew *hmwn* in Ezek 39:15–16; see Reinink, p. 45, n. 3, and Geiger, "Jüdische Begriffe und Worte innerhalb der syrischen Literatur," *ZDMG* 21 (1867) 491. Reinink thinks that *ymtʾ* derives from an original *hmt* etc. (p. 29, note to recension III). For the Syriac *hmn,* see Payne Smith, *Thesaurus Syriacus,* col. 1020–21.

136. The correlation between the ends of the earth and the dark mountains may explain the shift of the place-name Meluḫḫa, which in third-millennium Sumerian texts apparently refers to the Indus Valley and in first-millennium (perhaps earlier), Assyrian texts to Kush/Nubia. The earlier texts mention "Meluḫḫans, people of the black mountains [or, black land; *kur*]," or Meluḫḫa as the "black *kur.*" The later, Assyrian, material clearly identifies Meluḫḫa with Kush/Nubia (e.g., "the land of Kus, the black Meluḫḫans"). Although some scholars believed that even in the earlier texts the term refers to Kush, the consensus today is that in the earlier texts Meluḫḫa means the Indus Valley. Why was the Indus Valley called Black Mountain or Black Land and why was that name transferred to Kush at a later date? Sumerian scholars believe that the name derived from some aspect of the land, perhaps from the fact that the land supplied diorite stone and ebony wood, both of which are black. The transference of the name to Nubia, it is believed, came about because Meluḫḫa was considered to be at the (eastern) extreme of the known world; when Nubia was later discovered at the (southern) extreme of the world, the name was then applied to that land. Additionally, the following may be suggested. The term "Black Mountain" of the third-millennium texts may be the same as the Mountains of Darkness, which, we recall, were situated at the ends of the world. In other words, the name Black Mountain (or Black Land) may derive from neither a natural resource nor from the skin color of the inhabitants, but from the mythic-geographic location of the Black Mountain/Land at the ends of the earth, where Meluḫḫa was considered to lie. Because, when Nubia was discovered, it was considered to lie at the extreme ends of the earth, it too was considered to be the location of the Black Mountain and thus was called Meluḫḫa. (For discussion and literature on the location of Meluḫḫa, see D. T. Potts, "Distant Shores: Ancient Near Eastern Trade with South

Asia and Northeast Africa," in *CANE* 3:1452–59 with bibliography; see also John Hansman, "A *Periplus* of Magan and Meluḫḫa," *Bulletin of the School of Oriental and African Studies* 36 [1973] 574–81; I. J. Gelb, "Makkan and Meluḫḫa in Early Mesopotamian Sources," *Revue d'Assyriologie* 64 [1970] 1–2; Wayne Horowitz, *Mesopotamian Cosmic Geography*, pp. 79, 94, 328–29; W. F. Leemans, "Old Babylonian Letters and Economic History," *Journal of the Economic and Social History of the Orient* 11 [1968] 226; A. Leo Oppenheim, *Ancient Mesopotamia*, rev. ed. by Erica Reiner [Chicago, 1977], pp. 64, 408; Danièle Michaux-Colombot, "Magan and Meluḫḫa: A Reappraisal through the Historiography of Thalassocratic Powers," in *Proceedings of the XLVe Recontre Assyriologique Internationale: Historiography in the Cuneiform World*, ed. Tzvi Abusch et al. [Bethesda, Md., 2001], pp. 329–55. My thanks to Jacob Klein for his help with the Sumerian material.) Although the etymology of Meluḫḫa is unknown, Romila Thapar has suggested a proto-Dravidian original **mēlukku* with the meaning "up, high, the extremity." Thapar notes further that a Sanskrit translation of **mēlukku* is *aparānta*, which also means "extremity." See "A Possible Identification of Meluḫḫa, Dilmun and Makan," *Journal of the Economic and Social History of the Orient* 18 (1975) 10 and see also 11, n. 36 (now reprinted in Romila Thapar, *Cultural Pasts: Essays in Early Indian History*, Oxford, 2000). This etymology would accord perfectly with my suggestion.

137. Stoneman, *The Greek Alexander Romance*, p. 21.

138. Contra, e.g., Joseph Schwarz, *A Descriptive Geography and Brief Historical Sketch of Palestine*, trans. Isaac Leeser (Philadelphia, 1850), pp. 448–53, and Jacob Shavit, "Ma hi' Afriqa sheba-Talmud?" in *Studies in Geography and History in Honour of Yehoshua Ben-Arieh*, ed. Y. Ben-Artzi et al. (Jerusalem, 1999), pp. 75–91, esp. 82–83, who assume that the talmudic account must represent Alexander's actual intinerary. Irrespective of this wrong assumption, Shavit's conclusion—that *afriqi* is the result of the ancient confusion between Ethiopia and India—is not incompatible with the explanation of *afriqi* I have put forward here. On the contrary, there are a number of features, which the Alexander stories attribute to India, that are commonly found associated with Ethiopia, such as the ten-foot-high stature and pointed teeth of some inhabitants, or the dearth of bronze but plethora of gold of the land, or the reference to Candace as ruler of Inner India, or Axum as the seat of the king of India (respectively: *Alexander's Letter to Aristotle* 17 and 19; *Chronicle of George the Monk;* Palladius, *On the Life of the Brahmans* 4; all in Stoneman, *Legends of Alexander*, pp. 14, 17, 29, 35; for parallels to Ethiopian height, bronze, and gold, see above, pp. 21 and 32–33). On the confusion of India and Ethiopia beginning in antiquity, see Appendix II.

139. Lucan 10.272–75. Alexander in Ethiopia: Firdawsī (tenth–eleventh century), al-Dīnāwarī (ninth century), and Ibn Hishām (d. 829) who quotes Wahb ibn Munabbih (d. 732); see Southgate, *Iskandarnamah*, pp. 172 ("Alexander reached the land of Habash and fought its gigantic, black inhabitants"), 180, 192 (Ethiopia, Sudan, Yemen), 200 ("he conquered Ethiopia and went to Sudan"). See also the Ethiopian accounts: Budge, *The Alexander Book in Ethiopia*, p. 40 ("The countries of Egypt and Nubia and Ethiopia were opened out before him without fighting, and many of the inhabitants of the countries of Tenkēyā and Africa, and of the region of the west brought out [gifts] to him").

140. Stoneman, *The Greek Alexander Romance,* 3.18–23, 33, pp. 135–42, 176. Upon their meeting, the queen says to Alexander "Do not despise us for the colour of our skin" (p. 136). So also the Armenian version, Albert Wolohojian, trans., *The Romance of Alexander the Great by Pseudo-Callisthenes: Translated from the Armenian Version with an Introduction* (New York, 1969), pp. 132ff.

141. See also the reference to Ethiopians in *On the Wonders of the East* 24 (Stoneman, *Legends of Alexander,* p. 23).

142. Wout Jac. van Bekkum, trans., *A Hebrew Alexander Romance according to MS London, Jews' College no. 145* (Leuven, 1992), pp. 194–95; and *A Hebrew Alexander Romance according to MS Héb. 671.5 Paris, Bibliothèque nationale* (Groningen, 1994), pp. 132–33, 146–47.

143. Quoted in David G. White, *Myths of the Dog-Man* (Chicago, 1991), p. 53.

144. *Sibylline Oracles* 3:319–20 (*OTP* 1:369). On the Third Sibyl in general, see now J. J. Collins, *Between Athens and Jerusalem,* 2nd ed., pp. 83–97, 160–65.

145. White, *Myths of the Dog-Man,* p. 63; see also 32, 34, 237.

146. The first story alone is found in *bTam* 32a–b, and the second story in *yBM* 2.5, 8c, *GenR* 33.1 (pp. 301–2), and *YalqSh,* Ps 727 with various crossovers of narrative elements. MSS Florence for *bTam,* Escorial for *yBM,* Vatican 60 and Genizah fragments for *GenR* present no relevant variants. Theodor and Margulies are in their respective editions of *GenR* and *LevR* (p. 618). Only the first story is paralleled in the Greek Alexander romance, which is found in the translation of Stoneman, *The Greek Alexander Romance,* p. 144: "If we conquer the enemy or put them to flight, that is regarded as a humiliation for them for the rest of time; but if they conquer us, it is only women that they have defeated." Similarly, in a different recension translated by E. H. Haight, *The Life of Alexander of Macedon* (New York, 1955), p. 118, and the fifth-century Armenian version, Wolohojian, *The Romance of Alexander . . . Translated from the Armenian,* p. 142. Another English translation based primarily on the same recension as Stoneman's translation is that of Ken Dowden in B. P. Reardon, *Collected Ancient Greek Novels* (Berkeley, 1989), pp. 650–735.

147. For references, see pp. 41–42 and notes.

148. So S. Y. Rapoport, *ʿErekh Milin,* 1:131; S. Krauss "Die biblische Völkertafel," *MGWJ* 39 (1895) 4; Kohut, *ʿArukh ha-Shalem,* 1:244, s.v. *afriqi;* Levy, *Chaldäisches Wörterbuch über die Targumim,* 1:56, s.v. *afriqi,* and *Wörterbuch über die Talmudim und Midraschim,* 1:150, s.v. *afriqa;* Buber, ed. *Tanḥuma, ʾEmor* 9 (p. 88); Jastrow, *Dictionary,* p. 108, s.v. *ʾafriqi;* p. 511, s.v. *ḥoshekh;* p. 1416, s.v. *qarṭigni.*

149. W. Blake Tyrrell, *Amazons: A Study in Athenian Mythmaking* (Baltimore, 1984), p. 57.

150. V. Y. Mudimbe, *The Idea of Africa* (Bloomington, Ind., 1994), p. 90.

151. Ibid. The Amazons are discussed on pp. 80–92.

152. See Aharon Oppenheimer, *Babylonia Judaica in the Talmudic Period* (Wiesbaden, 1983), pp. 485–86, with cited literature.

153. Ḥanokh Zundel b. Joseph (d. 1867), in his commentary *ʿEṣ Yoseph* to *Tanḥuma, Emor* 6 (cf. *Tanḥuma,* ed. Buber, *Emor* 9, p. 88, n. 85); Israel Lévi in *JE* 1:343; M. Mieses, "After the Destruction of Carthage," p. 225.

154. Strabo, 17.1.22; Pliny, *Natural History* 5.9.49.

155. S. Lieberman in *PesRK* (2:474) and in *Yerushalmi Neziqin Edited from the Escorial Manuscript,* ed. E. S. Rosenthal with S. Lieberman (Jerusalem, 1983), p. 136. So too H. Freedman in his translation of *GenR,* Soncino edition (London, 1939), 1:258. Oppenheim, "Zur talmudischen Geographie," *MGWJ* 17 (1868) 383–85, has also argued that *afriqi* means black Africa although his main proof is not from the name Qaṣya, but from the Mountains of Darkness, which he associates with the Mountains of the Moon, mentioned by Arabic writers as existing at the source of the Nile. Oppenheim notes that there is uncertainty on the vocalization of the second word of the *jibāl al-qmr,* and some reject its derivation from *qamaru* 'moon'. He thinks that the word is related to the Syriac root *kmr* 'to be dark, black, gloomy, sad'. In other words, the *jibāl al-qmr* at the source of Nile are the Mountains of Darkness. Dimashqī (d. 1327) also refers to the *qmr* mountain and J. M. Couq, *Recueil des sources arabes concernant l'Afrique occidentale du viiie au xvie siècle (bilād al-Sūdān)* (Paris, 1975), pp. 240–41, n. 5, notes that some read *qamar* (moon), i.e., white, and some read *qumr* referring to certain people in India.

156. Diodorus 3.52.1, 3.53.1–4. Cf. Aeschylus's (*Suppliants* 277–89) description of the Danaids who look like the "nomad women . . . dwelling in a land neighbouring the Aethiopians" and who, had they been armed with a bow, would have looked like the "mateless, flesh-devouring Amazons." The western Ethiopians are mentioned by Homer, *Odyssey* 1.22–24.

157. Lieberman, *PesRK* 2:474 and *Yerushalmi Neziqin,* p. 136. Could the early-centuries Jewish and Christian identity of the queen of Sheba with Ethiopia (p. 18) derive from her reputation as a wise woman (1 Kgs 10:1–13)?

158. Snowden, *Blacks in Antiquity,* pp. 144–50 and 180–81; *Before Color Prejudice,* p. 56; Thompson, *Romans and Blacks,* pp. 88–93 and literature cited at nn. 9 and 14. (The reference to Stobaeus in *Blacks in Antiquity,* p. 148, is really to Nicolaus of Damascus, late first century B.C.E., whom Stobaeus quotes; see *FHN* 2:683–85.) See Agatharchides in Diodorus Siculus 3.2.2 and H. Freedman in the Soncino edition of *GenR,* 1:258, n. 3.

159. R. Jahnke, ed., *Lactantii Placidi Commentarios in Statii Thebaida* (Leipzig, 1898) 427, p. 284; quoted in translation from Friedman, *Monstrous Races,* p. 250.

160. Some have argued against the explanation of Qaṣya as derived from *qeṣ.* L. Wallach, "Alexander the Great and the Indian Gymnosophists in Hebrew Tradition," *PAAJR* 11 (1941) 75, says: "The etymologies suggested by the Midrash and pointing to a derivation from *qeṣ* are, of course, untenable and of no scholarly value whatsoever," a statement for which he provides no support. The idea of remoteness could certainly be incorporated into a proper name, cf. *al-Masjid al-Aqṣā,* 'the remotest sanctuary' in Qur'an 17:1; see O. Grabar in *EI*^{2} 6:707a. Another argument against this derivation was made by Matityahu Mieses in *Ha-Tequfah* 18 (1923) 226, who claimed that in the rabbinic period the word *qeṣ* was only used in a temporal and not a spatial sense. But *GenR* 44.7 (Abraham lived at one end/*qeṣ* of the world and Shem at the other) would show that argument to be ill-founded.

161. *yShevi* 9.2, 38d; translation Alan Avery-Peck, *The Talmud of the Land of Israel,* ed. J. Neusner (Chicago, 1982–91), 5:306. MS Leiden: *arʿaʾ de-raḥiqaʾ;* MS Vatican: *arʿaʾ raḥiqah.* On the story, see the commentary of Yehuda Feliks, *Talmud Yerushalmi: Tractate Sheviʿit* (Jerusalem, 1986), 2:241–42.

162. The *Muktār al-ḥikam wa-maḥāsin al-kalim* by Abu ʾl-Wafāʾ al-Mubashshir

ibn Fātik. The work was then translated into various Western languages beginning with the thirteenth-century Spanish *Bocados de Oro.* The trial story is also found, with the ending missing, in the Chronicle of St. Hubert (composed in 1118) incorporated in the *Chronicon Andaginensis Monasterii* (*Monumenta Germanica Scriptores,* 8:599). See Israel Lévi in *JE* 1:343; Friderich Pfister, "Das Nachleben der—berlieferung von Alexander und den Brahmen," *Hermes* 76 (1941) 157–58; reprinted in *Kleine Schriften zum Alexanderroman* (Meisenheim am Glan, 1976), pp. 67–68. See also Pfister's "Eine orientalische Alexandergeschichte in mittelenglischer Prosabearbeitung," *Englische Studien* 74 (1940) 25–26; *Kleine Schriften,* pp. 210–11. Pfister is unsure about the source for the Chronicle of St. Hubert.

163. A similar story is said of Solomon, who rendered the same judgment, in the *Qiṣaṣ al-anbiyā'* of Kisā'ī. See W. M. Thackston Jr., *The Tales of the Prophets of al-Kisa'i* (Boston, 1978), p. 292. Cf. Philostratus, *Life of Appolonius of Tyana* 2.39. In the *Iskandarnamah* (p. 54), although there is no trial, we find a story that shares many of the same characteristics of the rabbinic trial story—that is, justice, piety, and sharing of wealth as attributes of those who live at the ends of the world.

164. Literature on the rabbinic story is found in L. Wallach, "Alexander the Great and the Indian Gymnosophists in Hebrew Tradition," *PAAJR* 11 (1941) 53–54, 81–82, and Israel J. Kazis, *The Book of the Gests of Alexander of Macedon* (Cambridge, Mass., 1962), pp. 16–20, 184–85. Further on the Alexander stories in rabbinic literature, see van Bekkum, *A Hebrew Alexander Romance according to MS London, Jews College, no. 145,* pp. 7–12, and the studies mentioned there. Wallach, pp. 63–75, thinks, against others, that the story originally derived from a Greek source. See further Kazis, pp. 20–23, 185, and van Bekkum, pp. 7–12.

165. *GenR* 60.2 (p. 640). *GenR*'s final redaction is put in the fifth century (probably the first half). Another reference to "*kushi* or *barbari*" occurs in some variant readings of *GenR* 60.3, as listed in the Theodor-Albeck edition (p. 642) and in M. Sokoloff, *The Genizah Fragments of Bereshit Rabba* (Jerusalem, 1982), p. 147. However, I have shown that the reading is not original but was copied from the immediately preceeding section, *GenR* 60.2; see my "Scythian-Barbarian," p. 98, n. 24, and Appendix I, below.

166. Cf. Origen, *Comm. in Cant. Cantic.,* Prologue, *GCS* 33 (Origen 8) 78, "For Abraham declares moral philosophy through obedience" (Abraham numquam moralem declaret philosophiam per oboedientiam), and Philo, *De Abrahamo* 4, who, speaks of the patriarchs' "good and blameless lives" as being a model for others to follow.

167. *Yelamedenu* to Num 8:6 (or 3:45) quoted in Nathan b. Yeḥiel's *ʿArukh,* s.v. *smrtyn,* in Kohut, *ʿArukh ha-Shalem,* 6:78a. On this text, see further Goldenberg, "Scythian-Barbarian," p. 87.

168. *Leqaḥ Ṭov,* ed. S. Buber, Genesis 1.14, p. 13.

169. *bShab* 31a and *ARNa* 15 (p. 60), *ARNb* 29 (p. 61). Jastrow, *Dictionary,* p. 108, s.v. *afriqi,* understands *afriqiyim* to mean black Africans.

170. Pp. 41–43, 61–67.

171. Text and translation by R. H. Pierce in *FHN* 1:280.

172. Derek A. Welsby, *The Kingdom of Kush: The Napatan and Meroitic Empires* (London, 1996), pp. 58, 70. So too T. H. Corcoran's note in his translation

of Seneca in the LCL series, and L. P. Kirwan, "Rome beyond the Southern Frontier," *Geographical Journal* 123 (1957) 16–17.

173. The *Virgilian Appendix:* Moretum 35, in the LCL *Virgil* at 2:454–55. Cf. the "web-footed men" (στεγανόποδας) mentioned by Alcman, the Greek lyric poet of the seventh century B.C.E. (quoted in Strabo 1.2.35 and 7.3.6), although it is not clear where he places these people. Plautus's (in *Pseudolus* 1218) description of a slave as having red hair, dark complexion (*subniger*), and very big feet (*admagnis pedibus*) does not, presumably, refer to a black African. On the Moretum passage and the designation *Afer,* see Snowden, *Blacks in Antiquity,* pp. 6, 9, and 11.

174. Thaʿlabī, *Qiṣaṣ al-anbiyāʾ* (ed. Cairo, n.d.), pp. 193–94; (ed. Cairo, 1928) p. 243. I am indebted to William Brinner for the translation of this passage. G. Sale is in his translation of the Qurʾan, Sura 31 "Lukmān," *The Koran* (repr., London, 1910), p. 336. Levtzion and Hopkins (*Corpus,* p. 406, n. 47), however, translate "split feet."

175. Masʿūdī, *Murūj al-dhahab,* following the translation of de Meynard and de Courteille, *Les prairies d'or* (Paris, 1861–77), 1:163. There is, however, disagreement as to the correct translation of this word. Charles Pellat translates "les crevasses" (*Les prairies d'or,* Paris, 1962, 1:69). Similarly, Dimashqī's quotation of Galen has *tashaqquq al-aṭrāf,* which is rendered "split extremities" in Levtzion and Hopkins, *Corpus,* p. 214. (Pellat notes, as a possiblity, such a reading in Masʿūdī, which he would, however, translate "slenderness.") Galen is also quoted in Qazwīnī (Levtzion and Hopkins, p. 406, n. 48: "split hands and heels"). Musa Kamara quotes from *Tuḥfat al-ʿarūs wa-nuzhat al-nufūs* that Black women have "chapped hands and feet." See Constance Hilliard, "Zuhur al-Basatin and Taʾrikh al-Turubbe: Some Legal and Ethical Aspects of Slavery in the Sudan as Seen in the Works of Shaykh Musa Kamara," in Willis, *Slaves and Slavery in Muslim Africa,* 1:171.

176. Snowden, *Blacks in Antiquity,* pp. 9–10 and 264, n. 44. Julius Preuss notes that the observation of Blacks having flat feet is correct, although the physiology is not: *Biblisch-talmudische Medizin* (Berlin, 1911), p. 268; English edition: *Biblical and Talmudic Medicine,* trans. and ed. F. Rosner (New York, 1978), pp. 231–32.

177. A medieval manuscript, *Liber complexionum,* attributed to John of Paris (d. 1306), apparently also referred to Blacks' characteristically broad feet. L. Thorndike, in her article "De Complexionibus," *Isis* 49 (1958) 402, quotes only the "feet and thighs slender" of those living in the cold northern countries; presumably the manuscript said something about the broad feet of the "Egyptians and Ethiopians" living in the hot southern climates, which would have produced the opposite physiological characteristics.

178. *I Know Why the Caged Bird Sings* (New York, 1969), p. 2.

179. "Rabbinic Knowledge of Black Africa," pp. 318–28.

180. *Sifre Deuteronomy* 320 (p. 367). Parallels and citations: *bYev* 63b, *Midrash Tannaim,* ad loc. (ed. D. Hoffman, Berlin, 1908–09, p. 196), *Midrash ha-Gadol,* ad loc. (p. 717), *Leqaḥ Ṭov,* ad loc. (ed. Buber, Vilna, 1884), p. 115. Variant readings are recorded in the critical editions of *Sifre* and *bYev.* M. Kahana's *Manuscripts of the Halakhic Midrashim: An Annotated Catalogue* (Jerusalem, 1995) lists no extant fragments covering the relevant lines in *Sifre.* The question of redaction, which is generally put in the early amoraic period (230–280), is separate from the dating

of Sifre's contents, which stem from the tannaitic period. According to Saul Lieberman ("Palestine in the Third and Fourth Centuries," *JQR* 36 [1946] 355), "those who come from among the nations and kingdoms" is a reference to the *socii populi Romani,* the auxiliary (*blwy* = bi-leway) troops drafted by the Romans. (Cf. the commentary of Moses David Treves Ashkenazi [d. 1856], *Toledot Adam,* Jerusalem, 1974, p. 359, for a similar idea based on an exegesis of *blwy* = mixture.) My translation of Deut 32:21 follows NJPS with minor modification.

181. Given the history of Blemmyan and Nobaean raids into Roman Egypt, it is possible that the unnamed people who are "expelled from their homes" may be the Romans, although in my article, "Rabbinic Knowledge of Black Africa," I assumed them to be the Jews.

182. For the land of Barbaria in East Africa, see pp. 43–45.

183. *bʿEr* 96a; *yBer* 2.3, 4c; *yʿEr* 10.1, 26a; *Mekhilta, Pisḥa* 17 (p. 68); *PesR* 22 (p. 112b); *Tractate Tefilin* 3.

184. Thus the reading in *yʿEr* is not necessarily a "revision [which] is clearly an attempt by the *Palestinian Talmud* to distance this woman into the mythical past thus making her actions unique and inimitable" as Tal Ilan, *Mine and Yours Are Hers: Retrieving Women's History from Rabbinic Literature* (Leiden, 1997), p. 188, believes. The midrash on Ps 7:1 is discussed earlier, p. 56.

185. The tradition contains three distinct elements: (1) Michal the daughter of Kushi used to wear phylacteries; (2) the wife of Jonah used to make pilgrimage; and (3) the Sages did not object. The historical impossiblity of the third element, that the Sages controlled religious practice at the time of Saul (as "Kushi" was understood) and Jonah, does not necessarily invalidate the historicity of the first two elements. The necessary agreement of the Sages is the later rabbinic take on two earlier events, but are independent of them.

186. S. Krauss comes to a similar conclusion for different reasons: see "Le-ḥeqer ha-Shemot weha-Kinuyim," *Leshonenu* 1 (1929) 339. See pp. 38–39, for the possibility of the personal name Kushi indicating place of origin.

187. *Sibylline Oracles* 3.512–17 in *OTP* 1:373, trans. J. J. Collins; and V. Nikiprowetzky, *La troisième Sibylle* (Paris, 1970), pp. 316–17. The inscription is in E. Bernand, *Inscriptions métriques de l'Egypte gréco-romaine,* Annales littéraires de l'Université de Besançon 98 (Paris, 1969), p. 593, line 24. It is dated between the end of the first and the end of third century.

188. This fragment of the Hebrew *Testament of Naphtali* is preserved in quotation in the *Chronicles of Jerahmeel,* which has recently been published by Eli Yassif, *Sefer ha-Zikhronot, huʾ Divrei ha-Yamim li-Yraḥmeʾel* (Tel Aviv, 2001), p. 146, and in translation by M. Gaster, *Chronicles of Jerahmeel* (London, 1899; repr., New York, 1971), p. 92. For literature, see Haim Schwarzbaum's prolegomenon in the 1971 reprint, pp. 49–50 (note that M. Gaster's edition of the Hebrew text in *Proceedings of the Society of Biblical Archaeology* 16 [1893–94] 109–17 was preceded by his translation on pp. 44–49). See also the two versions of the Hebrew *Naphtali* that Wertheimer published from manuscript, *Batei Midrashot,* 2nd ed. (Jerusalem, 1950), 1:196 and 203. Ginzberg's translation is in *Legends of the Jews,* 2:215; H. W. Hollander and M. De Jonge's in *The Testament of the Twelve Patriarchs: A Commentary* (Leiden, 1985), p. 449.

189. *MidPs* 7.13. A manuscript of *MidPs* published by S. A. Wertheimer, *Batei Midrashot,* 1:295, provides no variant on this point, nor does the quotation of *MidPs* in *Yalquṭ Makhiri,* Psalms 7.5 (p. 41). As seen earlier (p. 56), the Rabbis understood Kush of Ps 7:1 to mean Saul.

190. Herodotus 4.183. Pliny, *Natural History* 5.8.45; cf. 7.2.24. Are Herodotus and Pliny referring to the unique sound of the click languages of East Africa?

191. Diodorus Siculus 3.8.3.

192. Edward Ullendorff, "C'est de l'Hébreu pour moi!" *JSS* 13 (1968) 130–31; the article has now been reprinted in E. Ullendorff, *Is Biblical Hebrew a Language?* (Wiesbaden, 1977). Ullendorff quotes a later recorded instance, that of the fifteenth-century Andalusian-Jewish poet Saadia ibn Danan: "Is the Hebrew language like the tongue of Kush and Put? / Is the voice of Jacob like the voice of strangers?"

193. There is another Hebrew quotation of *Naphtali* in Moshe ha-Darshan's eleventh-century *Midrash Bereʾshit Rabbati* (ed. Ḥ. Albeck, Jerusalem, 1940, p. 119), and it is paralleled in the Greek *Testament of Naphtali.* It was suggested, however, that this was a medieval translation from the Greek; so M. Himmelfarb, "R. Moses the Preacher and the Testaments of the Twelve Patriarchs," *AJS Review* 9 (1984) 55–78.

194. M. Stone, "The Genealogy of Bilhah," *Dead Sea Discoveries* 3 (1996) 20–36. The Qumran fragment was published by Stone in *DJD* 22:73–82. Stone's conclusion has now been corroborated by Menahem Kister, "Some Observations on Vocabulary and Style in the Dead Sea Scrolls," in *Diggers at the Well: Proceedings of a Third International Symposium on the Hebrew of the Dead Sea Scrolls and Ben Sira,* ed. T. Muraoka and J. F. Elwolde (Leiden, 2000), p. 144, n. 54. Note Solomon Wertheimer's comment (*Batei Midrashot,* 1:191) that Joseph Halévy had seen an Ethiopic version of *Naphtali.* To my knowledge there is no known Ethiopic version of the *Testament of Naphtali* or of the *Testament of the XII Patriarchs.* If Halévy was not mistaken, could this be be an indication of the transmission between late antiquity and the Middle Ages? Yassif's discussion (p. 479) on the relationship between the medieval and pseudepigraphal works is not up-to-date.

195. For a later, medieval, Jewish reference to Kushite speech, see p. 366, n. 23.

196. *bRH* 26a (MSS Munich and London have *afriqiya*). A variant reading of "sea towns" (*kerakei ha-yam,* Jastrow: "mercantile ports") instead of *afriqi* is found in two eleventh-century quotations of the talmudic text, Nathan b. Yeḥiel's *ʿArukh* (ed. Kohut), 7:224b, s.v. *qeśiṭah,* and Rashi in his commentary to Gen 33:19, as Kohut notes. Cf. *bSoṭ* 42a, below (n. 199), and see R. Rabbinovicz, *Diqduqei Soferim,* ad loc.

197. *yBer* 9.1, 13c; MSS Leiden, Paris, and London have *afriqiya;* MS Vatican has *afriqi.*

198. Arabian: *GenR* 79.7, following the reading of the *ʿArukh;* see Theodor's note ad loc. Biblical Hebrew: Gen 33:19, Josh 24:32, Job 42:11 (KBL, 3:1150). Samaritan Aramaic: Abraham Tal, *A Dictionary of Samaritan Aramaic* (in Hebrew; Leiden, 2000), 2:804, s.v. *qśṭ*[2]. Neo-Syriac: Payne Smith, *Thesaurus Syriacus,* 2:3678, s.v. *qsyṭʾ.* On the meaning of the word as a value of exchange (given variously as a coin, weight, sheep, or camel), see D. Talshir, "Anaqa she-hiʾ Gamala,"

in *Hebrew Language Studies Presented to Prof. Zeev Ben-Ḥayyim,* ed. M. Bar-Asher, Aron Dotan, et al. (Jerusalem, 1983), pp. 219–36, where earlier literature is cited. Note also Talshir's comment (p. 236) that the word *qešitah* meaning "fruit-stone" in Babylonian Jewish Aramaic and in Syriac may be behind the definition of *meʿah* as *qešiṭah.*

199. Galia: *bRH* 26a in the name of R. Akiba; Arabia: *GenR* 79.7; sea towns: *bSoṭ* 42a and *GenR* 31.12 in some readings recorded by Theodor.

200. Biblical Hebrew: Isa 49:21, Job 3:7, 15:34, 30:3 (KBL 1:194). Palestinian Amoraic Hebrew: *GenR* 31.12, *yTaʿan* 1.6, 64d. Ethiopic: W. Leslau, *Comparative Dictionary of Geʿez (Classical Ethiopic)* (Wiesbaden, 1987), p. 191, s.v. *galamota.* In addition to the dictionaries, see also A. Brüll, *Fremdsprachliche Redensarten und ausdrücklich als fremdsprachlich bezeichnete Wörter in den Talmuden und Midraschim* (Leipzig, 1869), p. 55.

201. On pp. 41–43 and 61–67 I discuss in greater detail the meaning of *afriqa/i* in rabbinic sources.

202. *bSan* 4b, *bZev* 37b, *bMen* 34b. Variants: *gdpy* for *ktpy, ṭyṭ* and *ṭwṭ* for *ṭṭ,* and *pwṭ* for *pṭ;* see Zwi Taubes, *Oṣar ha-Geʾonim le-Masekhet Sanhedrin* (Jerusalem, 1966), p. 25; Mordechai Sabato, *Ketav-yad Temani le-Masekhet Sanhedrin (Bavli) u-Meqomo be-Masoret ha-Nusaḥ* (Jerusalem, 1998), p. 128; and Kohut, *ʿArukh ha-Shalem,* 4:23, s.v. *ṭaṭ.*

203. S. Y. Rapoport's attempt to transpose *ktpy* to *kpty,* i.e., Coptic, doesn't help because *pt* in Coptic does not mean "two." Neubauer's suggestion that *pat* is a scribal error for *aft* doesn't help either because *aft* in Coptic (Egyptian *jfdw, fdw*n) means "four," not "two." For these suggestions, see A. Neubauer, *La géographie du Talmud,* p. 418. Kohut, *ʿArukh ha-Shalem,* ad loc., suggests that *afriqi* is Iberica/Iberia. As for *ṭṭ,* the word does occur in several South Arabian languages, such as Mehri, but it means "one," not "two"; see T. M. Johnstone, *Mehri Lexicon* (London, 1987), p. 406, s.v. *ṭd.*

204. J. J. Collins, and following him, R. Doran, argue that Demetrius's motive in showing that Zipporah descended from Abraham was precisely to show that Moses did not marry a non-Jew. See Collins, *Between Athens and Jerusalem,* 2nd ed., pp. 33–34; R. Doran "Jewish Hellenistic Historians before Josephus," in *ANRW* 2.20.1 (1987) 250.

205. In contrast, because in Christian exegetical tradition color symbolism and the image of the Ethiopian played such a large role, the blackness of Moses' wife is highly relevant. Two examples illustrate the point: Cyril of Alexandria (d. 444) said, "[Moses] married an Ethiopian, not only of a foreign [non-Israelite] nation, but black too" (τὴν Αἰθιόπισσαν ἐπεγάμει, καὶ ἀλλογενῆ καὶ μέλαιναν; *Glaphyra in Numeros* 1.2, *PG* 69.593D). While Cyril's statement was meant allegorically, the same cannot be said for the *Kebra Nagast,* the (Christian) Ethiopian national epic, where the queen of Ethiopia says to King Solomon concerning their son: "Thy son whom thou hast begotten, who springeth from an alien people into which God hath not commanded you to marry, that is to say, from an Ethiopian woman, who is not of thy color, and is not akin to thy country, and who is, moreover, black" (E.A.W. Budge, *The Queen of Sheba and Her Only Son Menyelek,* p. 102, sec. 64; similar sentiments on p. 156, sec. 90. On the date of *Kebra,* see below, p. 343, n. 25). The Ethiopian Christians see themselves as ethnically dis-

tinct from the surrounding black African population. They consider themselves to be descendants of Shem, and the surrounding population as descendants of Ham. In color terms, they see themselves as red and the surounding people as black (Richard Pankhurst, "The History of Bareya, Šanqella and Other Ethiopian Slaves from the Borderlands of the Sudan," *Sudan Notes and Records* 58 [1977] 2, 4–5, 30–32; see also Budge, *A History of Ethiopia,* London, 1928, p. 190). The Ethiopic Christian interpretation of Num 12:1 does not contain a similar sentiment. Miriam and Moses spoke against Moses, "because he married a woman from the land of Midian, a heathen, while he forbade such an association to the Israelites" (Getatchew Haile in a private communication, quoting an Ethiopic biblical commentary at the Hill Monastic Manuscript Library). The same explanation of the complaint, that Moses had married a non-Israelite, is also found in two Syriac Christian writers on Num 12:1, Ishō bar Nūn (d. 828), Catholicus of the Nestorian Church, and Ishodad (ninth century). Ishō bar Nūn is in E. G. Clarke, *The Selected Questions of Ishō Bar Nūn on the Pentateuch* (Leiden, 1962), question 50, p. 41, in the name of anonymous others. Ishodad is in *Commentaire d'Išo'dad de Merv sur l'Ancien Testament,* 2. Exode-Deutéronome. Translation, C. Van Den Eynde, *CSCO* 179, Scriptores Syri 81 (Louvain, 1958), text, pp. 93–94; translation, p. 126. On the Christian allegorical tradition regarding the Ethiopian, see above, pp. 48–51.

206. There may have even been a black African Jew mentioned in the Talmud as one who transmitted a rabbinic tradition, if one scholar's reconstruction of *yBer* 2.6, 5b is correct. David Rosenthal would read "Benjamin *zngʾy*" for "Benjamin *gnzkyyh*" by metathesis (*Tarbiẓ* 60 [1991] 439–41). *Zngʾy* is a form of Zanj, a word that is apparently etymologically related to "Zanzibar," and referred originally to East Africans south of Ethiopia, and then, more generally, to black Africans (see Bernard Lewis, *Race and Slavery in the Middle East,* New York, 1990, p. 50; François Renault, *La traite des noirs au proche-orient médiéval: viie–xive siècles,* Paris, 1989, p. 60; Alexandre Popovic, *The Revolt of African Slaves in Iraq in the 3rd/9th Century,* trans. Léon King [Princeton, 1999; originally in French, 1996, pp. 14–15]); further on the etymology, see Dan Shapira, "Zoroastrian Sources on Black People," *Arabica* 49 [2002] 118). S. Krauss, "Die biblische Völkertafel im Talmud, Midrasch und Targum," *MGWJ* 3 (1895) 57, emends *dngʾy* in the Targum to 1 Chr 1:9 to *zngʾy,* i.e., Zanj, but could *dngʾy* be Dinka?

CHAPTER FIVE

1. Isaacs, "Blackness and Whiteness," p. 13.

2. All Old Greek witnesses read "and," in a wooden translation of the Hebrew. See J. C. Treat, "Lost Keys: Text and Interpretation in Old Greek Song of Songs and Its Earliest Manuscript Witnesses" (Ph.D. diss., University of Pennsylvania, 1996), p. 82. While most manuscripts of the Vulgate translate the Hebrew *shezafatni* 'the sun has darkened me' as *decoloravit me sol* 'the sun has discolored me', thus giving the text a pejorative connotation (see above, pp. 110–11), some manuscripts read *decoravit* 'to add beauty, adorn'. See *Biblia sacra iuxta Vulgatam versionem,* ed. R. Weber, 2nd ed., ad loc. *Decoravit,* however, is probably a copyist's error for *decoloravit* and does not reflect an interpretive tradition.

3. The particle *waw* (*we-*) does not *mean* "but"; it's only meaning is copulative, i.e., it joins ideas or clauses. Those ideas may be contrastive and adversative, as in Song 1:5, but that is expressed by other means, such as word order, and not by the *waw*. See Richard Steiner, "Does the Biblical Hebrew Conjunction -ו Have Many Meanings, One Meaning, or No Meaning At All?" *JBL* 119 (2000) 249–60.

4. As a representative example of this interpretation, see Michael Fox, *The Song of Songs and the Ancient Egyptian Love Songs* (Madison, Wis., 1985), p. 101. Others translating this way are listed by M. T. Elliott, *The Literary Unity of the Canticle* (Frankfurt am Main, 1989), p. 293, n. 16, and add J. M. Munro, *Spikenard and Saffron: The Imagery of the Song of Songs* (Sheffield, 1995), pp. 37–38.

5. J. Cheryl Exum, "Asseverative *ʾal* in Canticles 1,6?" *Biblica* 62 (1981) 419.

6. Marvin H. Pope, *AB: Song of Songs* (Garden City, N.Y., 1977), pp. 191, 291, 307–28.

7. Othmar Keel, *CC: Song of Songs*, trans. Frederick Gaiser (Minneapolis, 1994; originally in German, 1986), pp. 43–45. Roland Murphy, *Hermeneia: Song of Songs* (Minneapolis, 1990), pp. 84, 124, 126. Both Pope and Keel list examples of black goddesses and madonnas to buttress their positions.

8. Dahood, *AB: Psalms*, 1:302.

9. Dianne Bergant, *Berit Olam: Song of Songs* (Collegeville, Minn., 2001), p. 13.

10. Exum, "Asseverative *ʾal* in Canticles 1,6?" pp. 416–19. Exum's summary of the scholarship succintly presents the issues.

11. Murphy, *Hermeneia: Song of Songs*, pp. 126 and 128; Michael Fox, *The Song of Songs and the Ancient Egyptian Love Songs*, p. 101. Despite Kim Hall, *Things of Darkness: Economies of Race and Gender in Early Modern England* (Ithaca, N.Y., 1995), p. 111, there is no "link between the Bride's darkness and Africa."

12. Brenner, *Colour Terms in the Old Testament*, pp. 95–99, 181, citing Tur-Sinai.

13. Ibid., pp. 98–99. See also KBL 4:1466, s.v. *shaḥor:* "perhaps swarthy or suntanned." The Peshiṭta captured the point by translating *sheḥorah* and *sheshezafatni* with the same root: *ʾwkmʾ ʾnʾ . . . dʾwkmny šmšʾ*. Cf. Chaim Rabin, "The Nature and Origin of the Šafʿel in Hebrew and Aramaic," *Eretz-Israel* 9 (1969) 155, who thinks that Hebrew and Aramaic *šḥr* is a *shafʿel* form of *ḥrr* 'to be hot, to burn'. For the meaning of *ḥrr*, see Leslau, *Comparative Dictionary of Geʿez*, p. 243.

14. Henry G. Fischer, "Varia Aegyptiaca," *Journal of the American Research Center in Egypt* 2 (1963) 17–20, the Naga el-Deir tomb 248 (Eighth Dynasty).

15. Henry G. Fischer, "The Nubian Mercenaries of Gebelein during the First Intermediate Period," *Kush* 9 (1961) 59, n. 27. The tombs are from the Eleventh Dynasty. The lighter skin of the upper classes of the cities is seen in Lam 4:7, which speaks of the lighter, radiant skin of Jerusalem's elect (*nezireha*). See chapter 6 for a discussion of this verse.

16. Fischer, *Farb- und Formbezeichnungen*, p. 276.

17. Paul Haupt, *The Book of Canticles* (Chicago, 1902), p. 30. The book is a reprint of *American Journal of Semitic Languages and Literatures* 18 (1902) 193–245 and 19 (1902) 1–32. Similarly Keel, *CC: Song of Songs*, pp. 46–47, quoting G. Dalman. See also Pope's quotations of Stephan and Horst (*AB: Song of Songs*, pp. 63 and 67–68).

18. For the first view, see Fox, *The Song of Songs and the Ancient Egyptian Love*

Songs, p. 101; for the second, Brenner, *Colour Terms in the Old Testament*, pp. 98–99, and *The Song of Songs* (Sheffield, 1989), pp. 54–55.

19. M. Falk, *Love Lyrics from the Bible: A Translation and Literary Study of the Song of Songs* (Sheffield, 1982), pp. 13, 110–11. Similarly Bergant, *Berit Olam: Song*, p. 13. In truth, one can convey the same sense even while translating *we-* adversatively (as Y. Zakovitch has done), with "but" indicating a change of perspective from urban to rural dweller. Although, says Zakovitch, the maiden is excusing her blackness, there is sense of pride embedded within her excuse. The maiden is deliberately inciting the jealousy of the daughters of Jerusalem with declarations of her rural beauty and her different life-style (Yair Zakovitch, *Miqraʾ le-Yisraʾel: Shir ha-Shirim*, Tel Aviv, 1992, pp. 49–50).

20. Erik Hornung, *The Valley of the Kings*, trans. D. Warburton (New York, 1990; originally in German, 1982), p. 42; see also pp. 192–93, pl. 146. Fischer, "Varia Aegyptiaca," p. 17. Irwin argues that the Greek color distinction was adopted from the Egyptian convention (*Colour Terms in Greek Poetry*, Toronto, 1974, p. 112, n. 1). An excellently preserved example of the Egyptian color distinction is the (ca. 2640 B.C.E.) painted reddish brown limestone statue of Rahotep sitting next to his yellowish white wife Nofret. See the reproduction and the comments of Frank J. Yurco, "Were the Ancient Egyptians Black or White," *Biblical Archaeology Review* 15 (Sept.–Oct. 1989) 29. The statues are reproduced in various publications, e.g., J. Baines and J. Málek, *Atlas of Ancient Egypt* (New York, 1980), p. 132, or Strouhal, *Life of the Ancient Egyptians*, p. 53.

21. *The Generation of Animals* 1.20 (727b).

22. W. Boer, *Epistola Alexandri ad Aristotelem* (Meisenheim am Glan, 1973), p. 57; translation: L. Gunderson, *Alexander's Letter to Aristotle about India* (Meisenheim am Glan, 1980), p. 156. According to Gunderson, the letter was written between 308 and 296 B.C.E. (p. 119).

23. K. J. Dover, *Theocritus: Select Poems* (Bristol, 1971), p. 169, on *Idyll* 10.27.

24. Wiltrud Neumer-Pfau, *Studien zur Ikonographie und gesellschaftlichen Funktion hellenistischer Aphrodite-Stauen* (Bonn, 1982), pp. 93–94. Regularly, but not always. Pausanius records that in some places Aphrodite has the title "Black One" because she is the goddess of love and people make love in the dark; see below, p. 296, n. 80.

25. For some examples, see H. J. Kunst, *The African in European Art* (Bad Godesberg, 1967), p. 8; R. S. Folsom, *Attic Black Figured Pottery* (Park Ridge, N.J., 1975), pp. 9, 12, and the plates in T. H. Carpenter, *Dionysian Imagery in Archaic Greek Art: Its Development in Black-Figure Vase Painting* (Oxford, 1986). In red-figure vase paintings, however, both men and women are generally painted reddish-brown (K. J. Dover, *Greek Homosexuality*, Cambridge, Mass., 1978, p. 77). This may indicate an artistic convention unique to this genre of vase painting, due perhaps to the lack of different colored clay.

26. Irwin, *Colour Terms in Greek Poetry*, p. 112. Dover, *Greek Homosexuality*, p. 77, notes that in these vase paintings young men too, even when seen as sexual objects, are painted the same black as the older men; see also plates B51, B53, and B634; but Irwin, speaking of Greek literature, says that men might be depicted white if they were considered effeminate (p. 132). Cf. the example of fair (*candidi*) skin being considered a mark of beauty in young boys (*pueros*) in the writings of

Bede, *Bede's Ecclestiastical History of the English People,* ed. B. Colgrave (trans.) and R.A.B. Mynors (Oxford, 1969; repr., 1991), 2.1, pp. 132–33.

27. Reproduced in E. C. Keuls, *The Reign of the Phallus* (New York, 1985), p. 163.

28. Irwin, *Colour Terms in Greek Poetry,* p. 111. See also Alice Kober, *The Use of Color Terms in the Greek Poets* (New York, 1932), pp. 2–3, 26.

29. H. Blümner, *Die Farbenbezeichnungen bei den römischen Dichtern* (Berlin, 1892), p. 19.

30. Thompson, *Romans and Blacks,* pp. 32, 35, 51, 131–34. In an unpublished paper Peter Frost collected numerous examples of Greco-Roman literature showing an association of white skin with beauty and dark skin with ugliness. I am grateful to him for putting his paper at my disposal and sharing with me the results of his work, which have been very helpful.

31. Thompson, *Romans and Blacks,* p.132.

32. *Anthologia Palatina* 5.210; trans. W. R. Paton, *The Greek Anthology* (LCL), 1:233. See the discussion by A. Cameron in *Greek, Roman, and Byzantine Studies* 31 (1990) 287–92, and F. Snowden in 32 (1991) 239–53. Cameron thinks that the dark beauty is an Egyptian, but Snowden's arguments for an Ethiopian are convincing.

33. Theocritus, *Idyll* 10.26–29, trans. A.S.F. Gow (Cambridge, 1965), 1:83. For "the explanation of the nickname ['Syrian'] by the two adjectives which follow," see Gow, 2:199. Irwin comes to the conclusion that μελίχλωρος 'honey-colored' is an intermediate shade between black and white and is thus used by classical writers hypocoristically for someone who is either too dark or too light (*Colour Terms in Greek Poetry,* pp. 57–59).

34. *Eclogues* 10.35–39. Translation is that of E. V. Rieu, *Virgil: The Pastoral Poems* (Hammondsworth, 1954), pp. 114–15, except for "hyacinths" (LCL, trans. H. R. Fairclough) rather than Rieu's "blueberries." Another early Roman poem conveying the same sense of apology is found in the *Anthologia Palatina* 5.121 (Philodemus): "Philaenion is short and rather too dark, but . . ." (LCL, trans. Paton). On these "apologetic references to swarthy beauty," see Thompson, *Romans and Blacks,* pp. 32 and 182, n. 61. Presumably Pliny's comment (*Natural History* 6.35.189) that certain Ethiopian peoples smear their body with red ochre "because they are ashamed of their black color" comes from the same Roman aesthetic.

35. See also below, p. 276, n. 65.

36. For the Old Greek (λελευκανθισμένη) and Old Latin (*candida; dealbata*) readings, see Treat, "Lost Keys," pp. 68 and 328–29; on the Latin versions, see also Eva Schulz-Flügel, "Interpretatio. Zur Wechselwirkung von Übersetzung und Auslegung im lateinischen canticum canticorum," *Vetus Latina,* 24/1 (Freiburg, 1993), pp. 131–49. Aquila, Symmachus, and Theodotian have as the Hebrew (F. Field, *Origenis Hexaplorum,* 2:422). For the Ethiopic version: C. Gleave, *The Ethiopic Version of the Song of Songs* (London, 1951), pp. 36–37; for the Russian: M. Altbauer, *The Five Biblical Scrolls in a Sixteenth-Century Jewish Translation into Belorussian (Vilnius Codex 262)* (Jerusalem, 1992), p. 189. Origen is in his *Homilies to Song* 1 and *Commentary to Song* 2, *GCS* 33 (Origen 8) 36, 125–26, *ACW* 26:106–7, 276–77); and his *Commentary to Psalms,* ed. René Cadiou, *Commen-*

taires inédits des Psaumes (Paris, 1936), p. 83. Jerome: *Against Jovinianus* 1.30, *PL* 23.253B, *NPNF2* 6:369; *To Pammachius against John of Jerusalem* 34, *PL* 23.386A, *NPNF2* 6:441; *Epistulae* 22 ("To Eustochium") 1.5, *CSEL* 54:145, *ACW* 33:134 (also *NPNF2* 6:23 and LCL, p. 57); and see Treat, p. 329 ("LaH"). Augustine: *On Grace and Free Will* 6 (13), *PL* 44.890, *FC* 59:265, *NPNF1* 5:449; *Sermons* 95.5, *PL* 38.583, *NPNF1* 6:407; *On the Gospel of St. John* 65.1, *PL* 35.1808, *NPNF1* 7:318; *On the Psalms* 45.24, *CCL* 38 (Ps 44, par. 26), *NPNF1* 8:153. Ambrose: *On the Mysteries* 7.35, *CSEL* 73:103, *NPNF2* 10:322; *Isaac, or the Soul* 8.72, *CSEL* 32:692, *FC* 65:58; *The Prayer of Job and David* 4.16, *CSEL* 32/2:278, *FC* 65:401; and see Treat, p. 329. Cyril: *Catechesis on Baptism* 3.16, *PG* 33.448B.

37. Littledale notes "the stress laid by the Greek Fathers on the LXX reading, *made white*" (Richard F. Littledale, *A Commentary on the Song of Songs: From Ancient and Mediaeval Sources,* London, 1869, ad loc., p. 350). For a discussion of the patristic exegetical tradition, see pp. 48–51.

38. Treat, "Lost Keys," p. 18. Treat estimates that the translation was done in the first century B.C.E. or the first century C.E. See his "Aquila, Field, and the Song of Songs," in *Origen's Hexapla and Fragments,* ed. A. Salvesen (Tübingen, 1998), p. 137.

39. Pope, *AB: Song of Songs,* pp. 661–62.

40. Ariel Bloch and Chana Bloch, *The Song of Songs: A New Translation with an Introduction and Commentary* (New York, 1995), p. 159. The Ethiopic version of Song made the association explicit, for in its translation of 8:5 it repeats the first part of 6:10. See Gleave, *The Ethiopic Version of the Song of Songs,* ad loc., pp. 36–37. The metaphor of dawn or the rising sun to indicate human beauty is found in Ps 19:4–5 but in referring to a bridegroom. The metaphor is applied to a woman in an anonymous, fifth/sixth-century Syriac homily (*memra*), where Sarah's beauty is compared to the sun when it rises. See S. Brock and S. Hopkins, "A Verse Homily on Abraham and Sarah in Egypt: Syriac Original with Early Arabic Translation," *Le Muséon* 105 (1992) 116–17, line 86; see also pp. 124–26, lines 137 and 146.

41. *IDB,* Supplementary volume, p. 946, s.v. wilderness. See also Shemaryahu Talmon, "The 'Desert Motif' in the Bible and in Qumran Literature," in *Biblical Motifs: Origins and Transformations,* ed. A. Altmann (Cambridge, Mass., 1966), pp. 31–64. Similarly Gary Anderson, *A Time to Mourn, a Time to Dance: The Expression of Grief and Joy in Israelite Religion* (University Park, Pa., 1991), pp. 64–67, and Pope, *AB: Song of Songs,* p. 424. On the Ugaritic sources where the *mdbr* is at the edge of the underworld, see Mark Smith, *The Origins of Biblical Monotheism* (Oxford, 2001), pp. 28–30. See also "the great desert," which exists at the ends of the world before the expanse of dark emptiness, mentioned in 4QGiants and in 4QEnastr^{b} (Milik, *The Books of Enoch,* pp. 15 and 288–91, 306).

42. See, e.g., Wolfgang Heimpel, "The Sun at Night and the Doors of Heaven in Babylonian Texts," *JCS* 38 (1986) 127–51.

43. Apponius is in B. de Vregille and L. Neyrand, eds., *Apponii in Canticum Canticorum Expositio, CCL* 19 (Turnhout, 1986), 1.40, p. 27, lines 657–59. On Apponius's dates and country of origin, see M. McNamara in *Scriptural Interpretation in the Fathers: Letter and Spirit,* ed. T. Finan and V. Twomey (Cambridge, 1995), p. 259, and "Early Irish Exegesis: Some Facts and Tendencies," *Proceedings*

of the Irish Biblical Association 8 (1984) 72, who cites two opinions, one that he was a seventh-century Irishman and the other ("a more commonly held opinion") that he was a Syrian convert to Christianity who wrote in Latin about 391–415. Against a seventh-century dating (and against the thesis that Apponius was a converted Jew), see also P. S. Alexander, "The Song of Songs as Historical Allegory: Notes on the Development of an Exegetical Tradition," in *Targumic and Cognate Studies,* FS Martin McNamara, ed. K. J. Cathcart and M. Maher (Sheffield, 1996), p. 27. As for the onomastic lists, the etymology is found in Jerome's *Liber interpretationis hebraicorum nominum,* ed. P. de Lagarde (Göttingen, 1887), 70.14, and in two other onomastica (Lagarde 196.96; Wutz, *Onomastica Sacra,* p. 396). The *Liber interpretationis* is Jerome's translation of a work no longer extant in its original form. Jerome believed that Philo wrote it and Origen revised it. Modern scholars do not accept the Philonic authorship; possibly it is of Alexandrian Jewish-Greek origin. See Hayward, *Saint Jerome's* Hebrew Questions on Genesis, p. 18.

44. König, *Apponius: Die Auslegung zum Lied der Lieder;* B. de Vregille and L. Neyrand, *Apponius: Commentaire sur le Cantique des Cantiques* (Paris, 1997), *SC* 420.

45. It is even possible that once the description in Song 8:5 was brought to bear on 1:5, Apponius et al. deliberately punned on the Aramaic *ukma* 'black' as *uqma,* based on the root *qwm* 'to arise'. According to the "more commonly held opinion," Apponius came from Syria; his mother tongue would have therefore been Aramaic. Aramaic sources may have been familiar also to Jerome. Hayward has shown that in his *Hebraicae quaestiones in libro Geneseos* Jerome used the Aramaic Targums. "Indeed, there are many passages in *QHG* which appear to presuppose Targumic tradition, and some which may even preserve Targumic language and terminology. . . . These renderings reflect almost exactly the Aramaic translation. . . . These examples, and the many others . . . strongly suggest that Targums in particular may have been the ultimate source of some of Jerome's knowledge of the Haggadah" (Hayward, *Saint Jerome's* Hebrew Questions on Genesis, pp. 21–22). Just as the Targums may have served as a source for the *Hebrew Questions,* it is not unreasonable to assume that they may have played a similar role in Jerome's *Liber interpretationis.*

46. Thompson, *Romans and Blacks,* pp. 134–36, quotations on 136.

47. Joseph A. Fitzmyer, *The Genesis Apocryphon of Qumran Cave I,* 2nd ed. (Rome, 1971), p. 63: *wkmʾ špyr lh kwl lbnhʾ drʿyhʾ mʾ špyrn.* Fitzmyer notes (p. 121) that fair skin was "greatly admired among dark-skinned Mediterranean races," and G. R. Driver commented on the preference for light-skinned women as expressed by the Greek poets and as depicted by Greek vase painters (Driver, *JTS* 18 [1967] 186). The date of the *The Genesis Apocryphon* is determined to be between 100 B.C.E. and 70 C.E.; see Fitzmyer, p. 15. The scroll itself has been dated between 73 B.C.E. and 14 C.E. on the basis of carbon-14 tests; see G. Bonani et al., "Radiocarbon Dating of the Dead Sea Scrolls," *ʿAtiqot* 20 (1991) 30.

48. See LSJ, s.v. λευκώλενος.

49. *Aeneid* 8.387.

50. For other examples, see M. B. Ogle, "Classical Literary Tradition in Early German and Romance Literature," *Modern Language Notes* 27 (1912) 240 and n. 49, and Irwin, *Colour Terms in Greek Poetry,* pp. 112–29. Conversely, but less frequently, dark skin signified manliness; Irwin, pp. 129–35, 155.

51. *mNed* 9.10 and the talmudic discussion in *bNed* 65b–66a.

52. *GenR* 40.4 (p. 384) to Gen 12:11. See also *GenR* 40.5 (anonymous): "Sarah's light brightened Egypt" (*hivhiqah ereṣ miṣrayim me-ʾorah*). Rashi to this verse quotes *GenR* regarding the Egyptians being "black and ugly" and is quoted, in turn, by Genebrard, *Chronographiae . . . universae historiae speculum* (Paris, 1580), p. 28, but Naḥmanides' (to Gen 12:13) quotation of Rashi does not have "ugly." On Egyptians as dark-skinned, see pp. 107–9.

53. *SongR* 1:6.3; 6:6.1 (ed. Warsaw 1.41; 6.12).

54. *bMQ* 9b, *bShab* 80b. This account is based on the reading in MS Munich *bMQ* and on MS *YalqSh* (R. Rabbinovicz, *Diqduqe Soferim* to *bMQ* 9b, p. 26, n. *mem,* and to *bShab* 80b, n. *kaf*) that have: *barta ukhmeta* 'a dark daughter'. The other witnesses do not have the word *ukhmeta.* The effect of the oil is said (ibid.) to remove hair and smooth (*meʿaden*) the skin.

55. *bKet* 59b.

56. *GenR* 18.5 (p. 167); see also *The Mishnah of Rabbi Eliezer, or the Midrash of Thirty-two Hermeneutic Rules,* ed. H. G. Enelow (New York, 1933), ch. 18, p. 327, where the story is given in greater detail and it is clear (as it is not in *GenR*) that the women accompanied Nehemiah on his return. On R. Ḥanan, see Wilhelm Bacher, *Agadat Amoraʾe Ereṣ-Yiśraʾel,* trans. A. Z. Rabinovits (Tel-Aviv, 1924/25–36/37), 3/1:88–89.

57. *bTaʿan* 23b. Other references speak of the incandescent beauty of some women. E.g., Ḥoma, Abaye's wife, "uncovered her arm and the room was lit up" (*bKet* 65a); or a beautiful woman passed by a house and light fell through the opening to the room (*bQid* 81a; Rashi: the radiance from her face lit up the room). Even R. Yoḥanan's radiant (*ziharurei*) beauty, the light from which would light up a room (*nafal nehoraʾ*) when he uncovered his arm (*bBer* 5b), is an indication of the feminine light-skin equation, for R. Yoḥanan's appearance is explicitly compared with that of a woman (*bBM* 84a, especially following MS Hamburg: *ḥazyeh Resh Laqish sevar itetaʾ hawaʾ*). Cf. *PesRK* 11.23, pp. 198–99, regarding Elazar b Shimʿon.

58. See also pp. 126–28 and 137 where the third parable is also discussed.

59. *Qartani* is a an inhabitant of a *qarta* 'town, village', as opposed to a city dweller. See Margulies's note to *LevR* 24.3 in his edition (p. 553); Y. Kutscher, *Milim we-Toledotehen* (Jerusalem, 1961), p. 20; Michael Sokoloff, *A Dictionary of Jewish Palestinian Aramaic of the Byzantine Period* (Ramat Gan, 1990), pp. 505–6, s.v. *qiryah, qarta.* Economically, a *qartani* is a person of substance, one who owns, and does not work, the land (Samuel Krauss, *Qadmoniyot ha-Talmud,* 2nd ed. [Berlin and Vienna, 1923; Tel Aviv, 1929], 1/1:43–44). Socially, a *qartani* is situated in the upper classes, occupying a position close to the nobility (*ben palaṭin*), as we see in *LevR* 24.3, where the only difference between them is that the *ben palaṭin* is familiar with royal procedure and the *qartani* is not. Similarly in *Tanḥ, Haʾazinu* 2, the *qartani* is on the same social level as the ruler who addresses him as "my friend." But cf. *ExR* 6.3 with Avigdor Shinan's note in his edition, *Midrash Shemot Rabba, Chapters I–XIV* (Jerusalem, 1984), p. 187.

60. *SongR* 1:6.3 (ed. Warsaw 1.41), *Midrash Shir ha-Shirim,* ed. Joseph H. Wertheimer, 2nd ed. (Jerusalem, 1971), p. 29; *YalqSh,* ad loc.; see also *Leqaḥ Ṭov ʿal Megilat Shir ha-Shirim,* ed. A. W. Greenup (London, 1909), pp. 21–22, where the polemic seems to be directed at Christianity, a view held by several scholars (see

above, p. 248, n. 43). R. Isaac is R. Isaac Nafḥa, the student of R. Yoḥanan—so W. Bacher, *Aggadot Amora'e Ereṣ Yisra'el,* 2/1:187 and 265, followed by M. Margulies, *Encyclopedia le-Ḥakhme ha-Talmud weha-Geonim* (Tel Aviv, 1969), 2:578. A. Hyman thinks that the name R. Isaac is generally a reference to R. Isaac b. Pinḥas but admits that at times it may refer to R. Isaac Napaḥa (*Toledot Tanna'im we-Amora'im,* Jerusalem, 1964, 2:782 and 800). In any case, the dating and location are the same.

61. *NumR* 16.23; *Tanḥ, Shelaḥ* 13; *TanḥB, Shelaḥ* 25 (4:71); *YalqSh, Malachi* 591. The parable is transmitted without attribution. Chapters 15–23 of *NumR* are considered to have been redacted between 600 and 800 C.E. (see Glossary).

62. See Saul Lieberman, *Greek in Jewish Palestine* (New York, 1942), pp. 39–43. The term *maṭronah* is found on a Jewish tomb inscription written in Greek from third- or fourth-century Israel as a title of honor indicating high social position. See M. Schwabe, "Greek Inscriptions Found at Beth She'arim in the Fifth Excavation Season, 1953," *IEJ* 4 (1954) 251–52.

63. Jastrow, *Dictionary,* p. 769, s.v. *maṭronah. OLD,* s.v., gives two meanings: (1) "a married woman, matron . . . ([also] applied familiarly to young girls of superior rank)," and (2) "a wife." The latter definition would not appear to apply in these parables; see my subsequent discussion.

64. *Yelamedenu* quoted in *YalqSh,* Malachi 591 (cited by Buber in his notes to *TanḥB*) and in the addendum to *YalqSh,* ed. pr. (Salonika, 1527), p. 377c, no. 18, directly after the quotations from the Jerusalem Talmud (published separately by A. Jellinek, *Bet ha-Midrasch* (Leipzig, 1853–77), 6:81; see his comments on pp. xxiii–xxiv). The last line of the story is found only in the addendum.

65. Samuel Krauss, *Talmudische Archäologie* (Leipzig, 1910–12), 2:85–86; Salo Baron, *Social and Religious History of the Jews,* 2nd ed. (New York, 1952), 2:238.

66. Pelagia of Antioch 4–5, *Holy Women of the Syrian Orient,* trans. Sebastian P. Brock and Susan Ashbrook Harvey (Berkeley, 1998), pp. 42–43. The Syriac reads: *glywt' dgwšmh ltlg' dmy' hwt* (Ioannes Gildemeister, ed. *Acta S. Pelagiae Syriace,* Bonn, 1879, p. 2, lines 7–8).

67. On Theodore's commentary on Song, see Dimitri Z. Zaharopoulos, "Theodore of Mopsuestia's Critical Methods in Old Testament Study" (Ph.D. diss., Boston University, 1965), pp. 59, 75ff; on Theodore and the Antioch school of literal Bible interpretation, see pp. 145–54. Solomon's marriage to Pharaoh's daughter is recorded in 1 Kgs 3:1.

68. So in quotation from Ishodad published by J.-M. Vosté, "L'oeuvre exégétique de Théodore de Mopsueste au iie concile de Constantinople," *RB* 38 (1929) 395. The relevant text in the records of the Council of Constantinople (553) is in *PG* 66.699B. The maiden's "smallness" refers to her height; it would seem that short stature was not a desirable feature. In a story from the Christian desert fathers, fornication is represented by a "foul, black and small girl" (quoted from the Ethiopic *Collectio monastica,* ed. V. Arras, *CSCO* 238 [Louvain, 1963], 14, 27, by David Brakke, "Ethiopian Demons: Male Sexuality, the Black-Skinned Other, and the Monastic Self," p. 520. It is also quoted in Lucien Regnault, *Les sentences des peres du desert: nouveau recueil; apophtegmes inedits ou peu connus,* 2nd ed., Solesmes, 1977, p. 320). Note the tannaitic antitheses of various desirable and non-

desirable human physical characteristics, in which shortness and blackness are included among the negative features (*tSoṭ* 2.3; the passage is discussed on p. 96. See also *mNed* 9.10, discussed above, pp. 85–86). Note also Philodemus quoted earlier (n. 34), "Philaenion is short and rather too dark," and the deprecating lines in *Priapea* 46: "Girl no whiter than the Moors (*Mauro*), . . . shorter than some Pygmy crane bait" (Richard Hooper, *The Priapus Poems,* Urbana, 1999, pp. 76–77), and, from a Muslim text, a woman of beauty is described as "white-skinned and tall" (*Fathnamah-i Sind,* ed. N. A. Baloch, Islamabad, 1983, p. 65; my thanks to Ephraim Dardashti for the translation. In Mirza Kalichbeg Fredunbeg's translation, *The Chachnamah,* Delhi, 1900, the passage is on p. 70). For examples of a negative evaluation of short stature in men, see Augustine, *Enarrationes in Pslamos,* 2nd discourse on Ps 33:15, *CCL* 38, *ACW* 30:173–174; Eusebius, *History of the Martyrs in Palestine,* ed. and trans. William Cureton (London, 1861), pp. 24 (trans.) and 26 (text); Alexander, *The Byzantine Apocalyptic Tradition,* p. 155 (see also p. 177, n. 90); Anthony Corbeill, *Controlling Laughter: Political Humor in the Late Roman Republic* (Princeton, 1996), pp. 28–29, 39 n. 47, 42; and Ruth Mazo Karras, *Slavery and Society in Medieval Scandinavia* (New Haven, 1988), p. 56.

69. Thompson, *Romans and Blacks,* pp. 134–35. Both Theodore's and Origen's interpretations played influential roles in Christian biblical exegesis that followed. "Theodore's scriptural commentaries became the foundation for much subsequent interpretation, particularly in the east-Syrian church of the fifth and later centuries and, through Jerome and Junilius Africanus (d. ca. 551), of the western, Latin church. Just as Origen represents the most consistent and thoroughgoing application of figurative interpretation in the Alexandrian tradition, Theodore represents the most consistent and thoroughgoing application of historical interpretation in the Antiochene tradition" (Trigg, *Biblical Interpretation,* p. 32).

70. *Explanatio in canticum canticorum, CCL* 69:176. Cf. the same statement in *Song Zuṭa* 1.5 (ed. Buber, p. 11), a work dated to the tannaitic period according to Hirshman (see Glossary). See also *ExR* 49.2, and an anonymous medieval commentary published by S. Hübsch, *Ḥamesh Megillotʿim Targum Suri . . . we-ʿod Perush ha-Miqraʾ ʿal ha-Megillot* (Prague, 1866), ad loc.

71. Thompson, *Romans and Blacks,* p. 134.

72. Jerome, *Epistulae* 22, 1.5, *CSEL* 54:145, *ACW* 33:134 (also found in *NPNF2* 6:23 and LCL, p. 57).

73. Augustine, *In Joannis epistolam ad Parthos, PL* 35.2051.

74. Peter Frost, "Attitudes toward Blacks in the Early Christian Era," *Second Century* 8 (1991) 7–8.

75. Ibid., 8–9.

76. Ibid. On the translation, see Byron, *Symbolic Blackness and Ethnic Difference,* p. 166, n. 117. The unpleasantness associated with the Ethiopian is increased with the remark that Pachomius "boxed her on the ear and for two years could not bear the smell of his hand." Other such examples can be cited.

77. For some examples, see Dronke, "Tradition and Innovation in Medieval Western Color-Imagery," pp. 57 and 59; Walter C. Curry, *The Middle English Ideal of Personal Beauty; as Found in the Metrical Romances, Chronicles, and Legends of the XIII, XIV, and XV Centuries* (Baltimore, 1916), pp. 80–88; K. Hall, "I Rather Would Wish to Be a Black-Moor: Beauty, Race, and Rank in Lady Mary Wroth's

Vrania," in *Women, "Race," and Writing in the Early Modern Period,* ed. M. Hendricks and P. Parker (London, 1994), pp. 178–79.

78. William Lipscomb, *The Armenian Apocryphal Adam Literature* (Atlanta, 1990), pp. 112 and 122 for the first source; pp. 177 and 194 for the second. On the dating (between the eighth and fourteenth centuries) of these compositions, which are part of the "Armenian Adam Cycle of Four Works," see p. 33.

79. Bernard Lewis, *Islam from the Prophet Muhammad to the Capture of Constantinople* (New York, 1974), 2:274.

80. Thackston, *Tales of the Prophets,* p. 31. The identity and dates of Kisāʾī are uncertain. Thackston (p. xix) thinks that the *Qiṣaṣ* was written not long before 1200, whereas T. Nagel cautions against searching for a specific author at a specific date. Rather, he sees the *Qiṣaṣ* materials as belonging to the "popular narrative tradition of medieval Islam" (*EI*^{2}, s.v. Kisāʾī). Aviva Schussman, on the other hand, has found that "Kisāʾī's work is not an accidental collection of folktales, but a very definite and systematic work" by a specific—although unidentified—author who she thinks may have lived before the tenth century. She also does not rule out the identification (first made in the seventeenth century) of Kisāʾī with the eighth-century grammarian ʿAlī b. Ḥamza al-Kisāʾī. See A. Schussman, "Stories of the Prophets in Muslim Tradition: Mainly on the Basis of 'Kisas al-Anbiya' by Muhammad b. ʿAbdallah al-Kisaʾi" (Ph.D. diss., Hebrew University of Jerusalem, 1981), pp. viii–x of English abstract.

81. Levtzion and Hopkins, *Corpus,* p. 68. See similarly the quotation from Ibn Baṭṭūṭa on p. 301, and from the *Darabnamah* in Minoo Southgate, "The Negative Images of Blacks in Some Medieval Iranian Writings," *Iranian Studies* 17 (1984) 13.

82. *Al-Shuʿarāʾal-Sūd wa-Khaṣāʾiṣuhum fiʾl-Shiʿr al-ʿArabī* (Cairo, 1973), p. 21, as translated by B. Lewis in "The Crows of the Arabs," *Critical Inquiry* 12 (1985) 89–90; reprinted in H. L. Gates, ed., *"Race," Writing and Difference* (Chicago, 1986), pp. 108–9.

83. Arthur Jeffrey, *The Foreign Vocabulary of the Qurʾān* (Baroda, 1938), pp. 117–20, s.v. *ḥūr.* See also A. J. Wensinck and Ch. Pellat, *EI*^{2} 3:581, s.v. *ḥūr.* Note Kisāʾī's description of the "beautiful, white-skinned, dark-eyed houris" (Thackston, *Tales of the Prophets,* p. 17).

84. K. Vollers, "Ueber Rassenfarben in der arabischen Literatur," in *Centenario della nascita di Michele Amari* (Palermo, 1910), 1:91–92. See also the *Chachnamah* quoted above, n. 68.

85. Peter Frost, "Human Skin Color: A Possible Relationship between Its Sexual Dimorphism and Its Social Perception," *Perspectives in Biology and Medicine* 32 (1988) 39, 49–52. See also Frost's article at http://www.quebectel.com/gt/usagers/pfrost/, containing more anthropological information and expanded bibliography.

86. Degler, *Neither Black nor White,* p. 210. H. Wagatsuma, "The Social Perception of Skin Color in Japan," in *Color and Race,* ed. J. H. Franklin, pp. 129–32. See also Harold Isaacs, "Group Identity and Political Change: The Role of Color and Physical Characteristics," *Daedalus* 96 (1967) 370, who notes that "dazzling white" arms and hands are common descriptions in ancient Chinese poetry, and that such descriptions continue into the 1940s.

87. Peter Frost, "Fair Women, Dark Men: The Forgotten Roots of Colour Prejudice," *History of European Ideas* 12 (1990) 669–79.

88. See, for example, folktale type 403 ("The Black and White Bride") or 463B ("The Black Princess") in A. Aarne and S. Thompson, *The Types of the Folktale,* 2nd ed. (Helsinki, 1981), and in R. Haboucha, *Types and Motifs of the Judeo-Spanish Folktales* (New York, 1992), pp. 66–69.

89. Eva Tegner, "Sex Differences in Skin Pigmentation Illustrated in Art," *American Journal of Dermatopathology* 14 (1992) 283–87.

90. P. L. van den Berghe and P. Frost, "Skin Color Preference, Sexual Dimorphism, and Sexual Selection: A Case of Gene-Culture Co-evolution?" *Ethnic and Racial Studies* 9 (1986) 92–95, 103–5. For modern Egypt, see also Devin Stewart, "Color Terms in Egyptian Arabic," in Borg, *The Language of Color in the Mediterranean,* p. 116, who notes that "one of the most famous wedding songs in Egypt is *il-bint^i bēḍa* 'The Girl is White,' i.e., beautiful and of fair complexion."

91. Zahan, "White, Red and Black: Colour Symbolism in Black Africa," pp. 385–86. With men, however, black skin color is preferred and is associated with maturity (p. 389). Regarding the lighter-skin preference for newborns, cf. *tSoṭ* 2.3 treated above, p. 96.

92. E. W. Ardener, "Some Ibo Attitudes to Skin Pigmentation," *Man* 54 (1954) 71–73, and M. Searle-Chatterjee, "Colour Symbolism and the Skin: Some Notes," *New Community* 9 (1981–82) 31–35. On how the universal preference for lighter-skinned women has led some to question theories of culture contamination from a white society, whether in the African American community or in Africa, see Noni Jabavu, *Drawn in Colour: African Contrasts* (London, 1960), pp. 85–86, about South Africa, and K. Russell, M. Wilson, and R. Hall, *The Color Complex: The Politics of Skin Color among African Americans* (New York, 1992), esp. chs. 3 and 7, and p. 57, about the African American world. Note John Gage's reference to "a rather slight modification of the traditionally negative interpretation of 'black' among Afro-Americans" (*Color and Meaning,* Berkeley, 1999, p. 273, n. 6).

93. For the most recent scientific studies on sexual difference in skin color, see N. G. Jablonski and G. Chaplin, "The Evolution of Human Skin Coloration," *Journal of Human Evolution* 39 (2000) 78. Frost and Tegner are cited above, nn. 87 and 89–90.

CHAPTER SIX

1. "Whiter than milk" is found in the Peshiṭta, KJV, NKJV, NJPS, RSV, NRSV, REB, NAB, NJB, NIV. Delbert Hillers: "Her Nazirites were whiter than snow; lighter than milk" (*AB: Lamentations,* 2nd ed., New York, 1992, p. 135). For blackness, cf. Job 30:28, 30.

2. LXX, KJV, NKJV.

3. See Pope, *AB: Song,* p. 531, for a discussion of the meaning of the word. Cf. Hippocrates' (*Airs, Waters, Places* 5) description of a healthy complexion as "bright" (ἀνθηρὰ). Jones's literal translation (LCL) "blooming" does not capture the sense of brightness or brilliance. Note that Galen's quotation of Hippocrates, as transmitted in the thirteenth-century Hebrew translation (via Arabic) of Solomon ha-Meʾati has "bright and shining" (*uriyim u-mavhiqim*). See Abrahm

Wasserstein, *Galen's Commentary on the Hippocratic Treatise Airs, Waters, Places in the Hebrew Translation of Solomon ha-Meʾati* (Jerusalem, 1982), pp. 38–39; originally published in *Proceedings of the Israel Academy of Sciences and Humanities* 6.3 (1982) 222–23.

4. "Radiant": Symmachus (λαμπρός, Field, *Origenis Hexaplorum,* 2:419; also for Hebrew *ṣaḥu* in Lam 4:7, λαμπρότεροι, Field, p. 758), RSV, NIV, Pope, *AB: Song,* p. 531; "dazzling": NASB; "gleaming, shiny": KBL, Keel, *CC: Song;* "clear-skinned": NJPS. Note also LXX Lam 4:7, "radiant" (ἔλαμψαν).

5. *CAD* N 1:244, s.v. *namru;* W. von Soden, *Akkadisches Handwörterbuch* (Wiesbaden, 1965–81), 2:771, s.v. *nawru(m);* see also J. J. Stamm, *Die akkadische Namengebung* (Darmstadt, 1968), p. 248. For the older interpretation of this word ("white-skinned" or "blond-haired"), see e.g. A. L. Oppenheim, *Catalogue of the Cuneiform Tablets of the Wilberforce Eames Babylonian Collection* (New Haven, 1948), p. 24, with cited references. See Brenner, *Colour Terms in the Old Testament,* pp. 118–20, for a discussion of the development of the meaning of *ṣaḥ* from radiant to white. See also Brenner, "Dodi Ṣaḥ we-Adom," *Beit Miqraʾ* 27 (1982) 168–73. The same meaning of "healthy" for "white" should thus be given to the reading λευκήν in Aristophanes' description of the ideal youth at the gymnasium (*Clouds* 1012). Some manuscripts have λαμπράν 'clear, radiant'. See K. J. Dover's remarks in his edition and commentary (Oxford, 1968), ad loc., p. 222.

6. *Bellum* 6.55.

7. *LevR* 19.2 (p. 423) and *SongR* 5:11.5 (ed. Warsaw 5.11) (see Margulies's note in *LevR* and commentaries to *LevR* and *bSan* 100a), *bʿEr* 21b–22a, *bKet* 10b, *ExR* 1.17, 23.10. See Eliezer Ben-Yehuda, *Milon Ha-Lashon ha-ʿIvrit ha-Yeshanah weha-Ḥadashah* (repr., Jerusalem, 1948–59), p. 7035, s.v. *šḥr.* Note also the Aramaic *ḥashikh* 'emaciated' describing one who fasts, e.g., *LamR* 1:5.31 (ed. Buber, p. 68), although this word may derive from a different root (see Kohut, *ʿArukh ha-Shalem,* 3:513).

8. Peter Schäfer with M. Schlütter and H. G. von Mutius, *Synopsis zur Hekhalot-Literatur* (Tübingen, 1981), p. 70, sec. 159.

9. See Fischer, *Farb- und Formbezeichnungen,* p. 277. Note also Kisāʾī's *Qiṣaṣ al-anbiyāʾ:* "[t]heir bodies became emaciated and their faces black" (Thackston, *Tales of the Prophets,* p. 207; cf. p. 199 and Job 10:22). An interesting reversal of this color-health relationship is recorded by Marvazī (twelfth century), who says that black Africans find beauty in black skin and consider white skin unhealthy; see *Sharaf al-Zamān Ṭāhir Marzavī,* ed. and trans. V. Minorsky, p. 54 (English), p. *42 (Arabic). For Christian literature, see the story of Pelagia of Antioch, whose complexion, through ascetic fasting and emaciation, had become "course and dark like sackcloth" (*Holy Women of the Syrian Orient,* trans. S. Brock and S. Harvey, p. 60).

10. Soṭah: *mSoṭ* 3.4; pregnancy: *ARNa* 1, p. 4a; cf. *GenR* 45.4, p. 451; Naomi: *RuthR* 3.6; bloodletting: *bShab* 129a.

11. For dark/black see Job 30:28, 30 and p. 181. For white/pale: Jer 30:6 (*yrq*); Syriac *Ben Sira* 25.20 (*yrq,* for which the Hebrew is *šḥr* 'black'); *bBM* 58b–59a etc. (*lbn*); see also *bYev* 60b (fear) and *GenR* 42/43.2 (anger, defiance). See further Shalom Paul, "Decoding a 'Joint' Expression in Daniel 5:6, 16," *JANES* 22 (1993) 124, n. 30. Similarly in Akkadian; see Mayer Gruber, *Aspects of Nonverbal Communication in the Ancient Near East* (Rome, 1980), 1:362, and Paul, p. 125. Brenner notes the opposite ways of depicting embarrassment (dark face, pale face), the

"difference in deep structure between the two idioms notwithstanding" (*Colour Terms in the Old Testament*, p. 181). Note also that the sadness of Cain (Gen 4:5), commonly described by imagery of blackness in postbiblical sources (see chapter 13), is also described in pale colors ("his face was dressed in pale colors") in the fifth- or sixth-century Symmachus, *Life of Abel*, para. 5, ed. S. P. Brock as "A Syriac Life of Abel," *Le Muséon* 88 (1974) 472–85; quoted in J. B. Glenthøj, *Cain and Abel in Syriac and Greek Writers (4th–6th centuries)* (Louvain, 1997), p. 135. In light of the fact that these emotions can be depicted by both dark and pallid face, it is probably best to translate the Biblical Hebrew and Biblical Aramaic expression "changed face" without reference to any particular color. See the translations to Dan 5:9–10, 7:28 made by NJPS ("darkened face") and L. F. Hartman and A. A. Di Lella ("ashen, pale, blanched") in the Anchor series (1978) as contrasted with RSV ("changed color") or, even better, J. J. Collins ("changed countenance") in the Hermeneia series (1993). Cf. Lam 5:17 "his eyes became black" to indicate the same emotion.

CHAPTER SEVEN

1. Rudyard Kipling, *The English Flag:* "What should they know of England / who only know England?"

2. *mNeg* 2.1; *Sifra, Negaᶜim* 1.4–5 (p. 60a). For the translation of *kushi* and *germani* as "very dark skinned person" and "very light skinned person," see the discussion in chapter 8, esp. examples 3, 4, and 8. For "may I be like an expiatory sacrifice for them" (*ani kaparatan*) as an expression of love, see, e.g., Maimonides in his *Commentary to the Mishnah,* ad loc., ed. Yosef Qapeḥ (Kafah) (Jerusalem 1968), 6/1:343. The expression has its parallel in Arabic *juᶜiltu fidāka;* see the geonic commentary to this mishnah with Epstein's note in J. N. Epstein, *Perush ha-Geonim le-Seder Toharot,* ed. E. Z. Melamed (1921–24; Jerusalem, 1981), p. 95, and Edward W. Lane, *An Arabic-English Lexicon* (London, 1863), 1:2354b. Cf. also Lane, 1:11b *fudīta bi-ʾābī* 'may my father be a ransom for you'.

3. The date given is that for R. Ishmael, but in any case the statement appears in the Mishnah, a document redacted shortly after the close of the second century. This middle-range color description is found also in later (seventh–eighth century) Jewish and Arabic self-descriptions; see pp. 183–87. There are rabbinic texts that depict the Jews as dark-skinned, but they express a non-Jewish perception of the Jewish physiognomy and I, therefore, exclude them from this discussion. I intend to deal with these texts and this issue in a separate study.

4. Yehuda Feliks, *The Song of Songs: Nature, Epic and Allegory* (in Hebrew; Jerusalem, 1974), p. 43, for the color of boxwood. Preuss, *Biblisch-talmudische Medizin,* p. 88, English edition, trans. F. Rosner, p. 79: "yellowish." It is interesting that this intermediate way of describing the Jewish complexion relative to the non-Jewish is found also in modern times. Nahum Stutchkoff, *Der Otzar fun der Yiddisher Shprach* (New York, 1950), p. 168, sec. 236, records two Yiddish terms for non-Jews: *gelhoitiker* 'light-skinned' and *tunkelhoitiker* 'dark-skinned'.

5. See Shaye J. D. Cohen, *The Beginnings of Jewishness* (Berkeley, 1999), pp. 29–30, who lists fourteen descriptions of Jews from the papyri. Thirteen of them have "honey-colored" (μελίχρως et sim.) complexion and one is "dark-colored" (μελάγχρως); see also I. F. Fikhman, "The Physical Appearance of Egyptian Jews

according to the Greek Papyri," *Scripta Classica Israelica* 18 (1999) 134. Another people who were apparently considered honey colored were the Syrians. Theocritus writes of his "charming Bombyca" that because of her sun-scorched color everyone calls her Syrian, but that he prefers the term "honey-colored" (*Idyll* 10.26–29); see A.S.F. Gow's edition (Cambridge, 1950), 2:199. For "honey-colored," as an intermediate shade between black and white, see Irwin, *Colour Terms in Greek Poetry,* pp. 57–59. See also Goldenberg, "The Development of the Idea of Race," p. 565, for this description as a common term of human complexion.

6. Snowden, "Asclepiades' Didyme," p. 248; Frank Snowden, "Attitudes toward Blacks in the Greek and Roman World," in *Africa and Africans in Antiquity,* ed. Yamauchi, pp. 256–57, and Thompson, *Romans and Blacks,* p. 131.

7. Thompson, *Romans and Blacks,* p. 131. The sociologist H. Hoetink seems to have introduced the term "somatic norm image," which he defined as "the complex of physical (somatic) characteristics which are accepted by a group as its norm and ideal"; it is "the yardstick of aesthetic evaluation and ideal of the somatic characteristics of members of the group." See his *The Two Variants in Caribbean Race Relations* (Oxford, 1967), pp. 120–21 (originally in Dutch, 1962).

8. It would go beyond the evidence of the rabbinic text to say that R. Ishmael "was extremely proud the Jews were neither as fair as Germans nor as dark as Negroes, but of an intermediate color," as Baron does in *A Social and Religious History of the Jews,* 2:238 (see also Snowden, *Before Color Prejudice,* p. 134, n. 56). Baron has misread the mishnaic text. The biblical *baheret* is described in the immediately preceding mishnah as a skin discoloration that is "bright white as snow." This description gave rise to the obvious objection that the color of the diseased skin would appear relative to the color of the surrounding healthy skin: "An intensely bright white spot [*baheret*] appears faint on the very light skinned [*germani*], while a faint spot appears bright on the very dark skinned [*kushi*]." To this objection, R. Ishmael answers that the brightness of the discoloration is to be based on the relative skin color of the Jews, for whom the biblical laws were prescribed and whose skin color is "neither black nor white, but intermediate." R. Ishmael's statement, therefore, is a legal qualifier and says nothing of chromatic preference. Furthermore, "May I be like an expiatory sacrifice for them" as an expression of love is said of the Jews collectively, or of individuals, in other, nondermatological, contexts. For sources, see the Talmud dictionaries of Levy and Jastrow, s.v. *kaparah,* and add: *Seder Eliyahu Rabba* 5, 18, 26, and 29 (ed. Ish-Shalom, pp. 25, 105, 141, 159), and *YalqSh, We-Etḥanan* 837.

9. Sextus, *Against the Ethicists* 43. Sextus's view does not contradict the transcultural aesthetic of men's preference for lighter-skinned women, a view discussed earlier in chapter 5. His point is a relative one: ethnocentrism extends to skin color as well. Presumably he would agree with Aristotle that the ideal female is light-skinned. As we have seen, the preference for lighter-skinned women seems to be unrelated to the concept of a people's somatic norm, which I discuss in this chapter.

10. Snowden, *Before Color Prejudice,* pp. 75–79, and *Blacks in Antiquity,* pp. 171–79; Thompson in *Romans and Blacks* (see his index entry, "somatic norm image").

11. *mBekh* 7.6; cf. *Sifra, Emor, pereq* 3.1–7 (pp. 95c–d). For a discussion of the terms used this text (*kushi, giḥor, lbkn/lwkn,* etc.), see pp. 113–14.

12. E. C. Wertlieb, "Attitudes towards Disabilities as Found in the Talmud," *Journal of Psychology and Judaism* 12 (1988) 192–96.

13. *tBer* 6/7.3. The terms used in this text too are discussed at pp. 113–14.

14. *tSoṭ* 2.3. Although the dark-fair clause is missing in some Talmud (*bSoṭ*) manuscripts and medieval anthologies, it is found in several other—including the tannaitic—compositions that cite this tradition. I therefore take the clause as authentic. Not all the textual witnesses include the ugly-beautiful clause, but whether this clause is or is not original to the tradition does not change the fact that a dark-fair antithesis is presented with other bad-good value judgments of human physical characteristics. Clearly fair skin is the preferred complexion in this tradition. For a listing of parallel sources and variant readings, see *bSoṭ* 26a in the edition of the Institute for the Complete Israeli Talmud (Jerusalem, 1977). The tradition is quoted in the name of R. Judah b. Bathyra who recounted it in the name of Eleazar b. Matya (*Tosefta*), or in the name of R. Ishmael (e.g., *Sifre Num*), or in the name of R. Judah (*Sifre Zuṭa*ʾ). The unique reading of *NumR* 9.25 that opposes ugliness to lightness is the result of a scribal error of homoioteleuton. The term *meluban* found in *bSan* 70b, *NumR* 10.4 (*meluban u-mezuraz*) does not mean "fair-skinned" but "refined" or "hardened" as in a furnace. Cf. the play on the name Laban, who was "refined in wickedness" (*GenR* 60.7, p. 647, and parallels). For the semantic development, see Kohut's discussion in *ʿArukh ha-Shalem,* 5:11.

15. See chapter 5, esp. the discussion of *mNed* 9.10 (pp. 85–86).

16. See above, p. 91.

17. See p. 86. The expression *shaḥor we-khaʿor* 'dark/black and ugly,' is commonly found for a number of inanimate things (pots, tent coverings, etc.) as well. See, e.g., *SongR* 1:5.1 (ed. Warsaw, 1.38).

18. *bBer* 50a, *bPes* 88a, *bMeg* 14b, *bAZ* 16b. Translation follows geonic traditions; see Epstein, *Perush ha-Geonim le-Seder Toharot,* pp. 28–29 of introduction (p. 25 in ed. Berlin) and p. 10 of text.

19. *bNed* 50b.

20. Sokoloff (*Dictionary,* s.v. *pḥm*), however, is mistaken when he says that the word *pḥm* 'coal' is used as a "euphemism for an ugly person." His source is the statement in *GenR* 36.2 (p. 336) that explains "the father of Canaan" (Gen 9:18) as "father of *pḥmh*" (*ʾbwy dpḥmh*). Although the printed edition of *GenR* has *pḥth,* Sokoloff relies on Kutscher's observation that MS Vatican 30 (Makor reproduction, p. 40a), which has *pḥmh* (contrary to Theodor's notes), preserves the correct reading. Vatican 30, however, is the only source for the reading *pḥmh;* all other witnesses listed by Theodor, as well as MS Vatican 60 (Makor, p. 124), have *pḥth* or *pḥt*ʾ 'curse', an apt description for Canaan, who was cursed. Furthermore, Sokoloff identified this section of Vatican 30 ("Scribe 2") as based on a linguistically inferior *Vorlage* of *GenR,* influenced by the language of the Babylonian Talmud ("The Hebrew of *Genesis Rabba* according to MS Vat. Ebr. 30," *Leshonenu* 33 [1968] 35–42; introduction to Vatican 60 reproduction). As Menahem Moreshet notes (*A Lexicon of the New Verbs in Tannaitic Hebrew,* in Hebrew, Ramat Gan, 1980, p. 275, s.v. *pḥm*), the correct reading is undoubtedly *pḥth,* and *pḥmh* is probably a scribal error influenced by the description of Ham as blackened (*mefuḥam*) that is found a few sections later in *GenR* (36.7; p. 341). The unfamiliar root *pḥt* was corrupted in some later quotations. Thus *TanḥB, Noaḥ* 19, p. 46, has *prwḥ,* but MS

Vatican 44 of the text reads *pḥ'*; see J. Adler in *Qoveṣ ʿal Yad*, n.s., 8 (1975) 29. *Leqaḥ Ṭov* has *avi shel shefaḥot*, which is probably either an attempt to make sense—Canaan *was* the father of *shefaḥot* 'female slaves, maidservants'—of the unusual word, or the result of a scribal error: *shel paḥot* (aut sim.) > *shel shefaḥot*. See L. Ginzberg, "Die Haggada bei den Kirchenvätern und in der apokryphischen Literatur," *MGWJ* 43 (1899) 462, n. 2. Sokoloff's entry may be misleading in referring to a Syriac parallel. In Syriac *paḥama* indeed means "coal," but it is not a euphemism for an ugly person. For the meaning of *pḥth* as "curse," see Saul Lieberman, *Hellenism in Jewish Palestine* (New York, 1950), pp. 12–13 n. 59, and *JQR* 36 (1945–46) 346.

21. E.g., Aristotle, *Problemata* 10.66, 898b, *Generation of Animals* 5.3.782b; Pliny the Elder (first century), *Natural History* 2.189–90; Ptolemy (second century), *Tetrabiblos* 2.2.56–58; Galen (second century), *De temperamentis* 2.5 and 6. Literature on the theory in Greco-Roman, Islamic, and Jewish sources will be found in Goldenberg, "The Development of the Idea of Race," p. 562, n. 3.

22. In the classical sources the northern and southern peoples are indicated by a shorthand reference to the "Ethiopians and Scythians," which has its parallels in rabbinic and early Christian literature and accounts for several otherwise enigmatic texts. See Goldenberg, "Scythian-Barbarian," where references to literature on the classical, Christian, and Islamic sources may also be found (pp. 92–94). Incidentally, in regard to skin color, the Greco-Roman environmental theory is not far removed from modern scientific theory, for most physical anthropologists believe that pigmentation is related to climate. See V. Barnouw, *An Introduction to Anthropology*, Vol. 1: *Physical Anthropology and Archaeology*, 4th ed. (Homewood, Ill., 1982), pp. 326–27, and Jablonski and Chaplin (above, p. 279, n. 93).

23. In discussions on the history of racist thinking, insufficient attention is given to this ancient link between physical and the nonphysical characteristics, which we find as early as Herodotus and Hippocrates, and which are explicitly or implicitly given an inferior-superior ranking. Such a link later became a crucial component of racist thinking. I have discussed this to some extent in "The Development of the Idea of Race," pp. 561–63.

24. Ovid (d. 17 C.E.), *Metamorphoses* 2.235–36. The story is mentioned as early as Theodectes (fourth century B.C.E.) apud Strabo 15.1.24.

25. For an explanation of, and literature on, etiological myths, see Åke Hultkrantz, chief editor, *International Dictionary of Regional European Ethnology and Folklore* (Copenhagen, 1965), 2:16–19.

26. There are also linguistic etiologies to explain names of peoples or places ("folk etymologies"). An example from the Bible is the name Moses explained as based on a Hebrew root meaning "to draw"—"for I drew him out of the water" (Ex 2:10). See Naftali Zvi Yehuda Berlin (d. 1893), *Haʿameq Davar* to Ex 2:10, who recognized that the name Moses is not a Hebrew, but an Egyptian, word. On the Egyptian etymology of Moses, see A. Cody, *A History of Old Testament Priesthood* (Rome, 1969), pp. 39–41.

27. Stanley Gevirtz, "Curse Motifs in the Old Testament and the Ancient Near East" (Ph.D. diss. University of Chicago, 1959), p. 258.

28. David Neiman, "The Date and Circumstances of the Cursing of Canaan" in Altman, ed., *Biblical Motifs*, pp. 116–18, reviews the literature while he himself is

of the opinion that the curse of Canaan represents a hope or wish; similarly—an optative connotation—V. P. Hamilton, *The Book of Genesis, Chapters 1–17* (Grand Rapids, Mich., 1990), 1:324. On Gen 9:25 as an etiology for the state of the Canaanites, see further J. Rogerson, *Genesis 1–11* (Sheffield, 1991), pp. 72–73.

29. Westermann, *CC: Genesis 1–11*, pp. 490–91; see also Lloyd R. Bailey, *Noah: The Person and the Story in History and Tradition* (Columbia, S.C., 1989), pp. 159–61; Neiman "The Date and Circumstances," pp. 113–34; A. Van Selms, "Judge Shamgar," *VT* 14 (1964) 308; Frederick W. Bassett, "Noah's Nakedness and the Curse of Canaan: A Case of Incest?" *VT* 21 (1971) 232. For interpretations of the meaning of the biblical story, see M. Vervenne, "What Shall We Do with the Drunken Sailor? A Critical Re-Examination of Genesis 9.20–27," *JSOT* 68 (1995) 33–55, esp. 37–38.

30. *Biblical Antiquities* 7.5: "Divisit Deus linguas eorum et mutavit eorum effigies, et non cognovit unusquisque fratrem suum nec audiebant singuli quique linguam proximi sui." The text was edited by Guido Kisch, *Pseudo-Philo's Liber Antiquitatum Biblicarum* (Notre Dame, Ind., 1949), p. 132. Another edition (D. J. Harrington) plus translation (J. Cazeaux) and notes (C. Perrot and E. M. Bogaert) appeared in the Sources Chrétiennes series 229–30, *Pseudo-Philon: Les Antiquités Bibliques* (Paris, 1976), 1:98–99. English translations were done by M. R. James, *The Biblical Antiquities of Philo* (London, 1917), reprinted with prolegomenon by Louis H. Feldman (New York, 1971), pp. 95–96, and by D. J. Harrington in *OTP*, 2:297ff. Howard Jacobson has recently published a new edition and translation (on which, see his preface) of Pseudo-Philo: *A Commentary on Pseudo-Philo's Liber Antiquitatum Biblicarum* (Leiden, 1996); our text is on pp. 11, 101. On the dating of Pseudo-Philo, Feldman (pp. xxviii–xxxi) ranges from the end of the first to the beginning of the second century, Harrington (p. 299) pushes the date back to the first century before 70 C.E., and Jacobson (pp. 199–210) argues for a date between 70 and the mid-second century. See further the literature cited in George Nickelsburg, *Jewish Literature between the Bible and the Mishnah* (Philadelphia, 1981), p. 273, n. 106, and Jacobson.

31. Ginzberg, *Legends of the Jews*, 5:203, n. 88. Jacobson, *Commentary*, p. 384.

32. Frederick J. Murphy, *Pseudo-Philo: Rewriting the Bible* (New York, 1993), pp. 89–90.

33. Perrot and Bogaert, *Pseudo-Philon*, 2:99 (*SC* 230); Feldman, "Prolegomenon," *Biblical Antiquities*, p. lxxxix; D. C. Harlow *The Greek Apocalypse of Baruch (3 Baruch) in Hellenistic Judaism and Early Christianity* (Leiden, 1996), p. 110; similarly C. Uehlinger, *Weltreich und "eine Rede": Eine neue Deutung der sogenannten Turmbauerzählung (Gen 11, 1–9)* (Göttingen, 1990), p. 125, following D. J. Harrington, *The Hebrew Fragments of Pseudo-Philo's Liber Antiquitatum Biblicarum Preserved in the Chronicles of Jeraḥmeel* (Missoula Mont., 1974), p. 32. The basis given for this interpretation is either *3 Baruch* 2.3–3.8 or later, medieval, literature such as the *Sefer ha-Zikhronot* (*Chronicles of Jerahmeel*) or *Sefer ha-Yashar*. See also the same notion in al-Dīnawarī (ninth century), translated in Levtzion and Hopkins, *Corpus*, p. 23.

34. Jacobson, *Commentary*, p. 384.

35. For this text and another, similar, one from Qumran, see pp. 114–15.

36. This is also how the the biblical text was understood in a medieval Christian

painting. Miniatures from four eleventh- or twelfth-century Byzantine octateuchs show both black and white figures in the depiction of the punishment of sinful humanity at the Tower of Babel incident. As Paul Kaplan says, the point is that God's punishment "consists of the introduction of *racial* as well as linguistic variation" (*Ruler, Saint and Servant,* p. 73, Kaplan's emphasis; see also J. Devisse, *IBWA* 2/1:100 and 230, n. 57, and Arno Borst, *Der Turmbau von Babel,* Stuttgart, 1957, 1:285–86). Note also that a Mandaic text reporting the history of the Mandaeans mentions a period of prosperity in Babylonia "followed by divisions, many races, tongues and wars" (E. S. Drower, *The Mandaeans of Iraq and Iran,* Oxford, 1937, p. 8).

37. For bibliography, see p. 44, where also, as well as in p. 116, the text is discussed. The Isaiah passage is one of several depicting the idea of a messianic reversal to humanity's original state ("*Urzeit-Endzeit*").

38. This and other Egyptians texts are fully discussed in p. 114.

39. Some discussion of this topic will be found in Gerhard Rotter, "Die Stellung des Negers in der islamisch-arabischen Gessellschaft bis zum XVI Jahrhundert" (Ph.D. diss., Friedrich-Wilhelms Universität, Bonn, 1967), pp. 141–52; Susanne Enderwitz, *Gesellschafticher Rang und ethnische Legitimation: Der arabische Schriftsteller Abū ʿUthmān al-Ǧāḥiẓ (gest. 868) über die Afrikaner, Perser und Araber in der islamischen Gesellschaft* (Freiburg im Breisgau, 1979), pp. 25–27; and Lewis, *Race and Slavery,* pp. 123–25, n. 9.

40. The catena is found in MS Leiden, Scaliger Arab. 230, which bears the title *Kitāb takwīn al-khalāʾiq wa-tafsīruhū* and is dated to 1528 (author unknown). It was published in Paul de Lagarde's *Materialien zur Kritik und Geschichte des Pentateuchs* (Leipzig, 1867), part II. In part I, Lagarde published another Leiden manuscript, containing an Arabic Pentateuch, Genesis and Exodus being Saadia's translation and the remainder being an Arabic translation of a Syriac Pentateuch (see Paul Kahle, *Die arabischen Bibleübersetzungen,* Leipzig, 1904, pp. viii–ix). In his introduction, Lagarde describes the two manuscripts, providing an index of the patristic quotations (pp. xv–xvi). A short discussion of the catena is found in G. Graf, *Geschichte der christlichen arabischen Literatur* (Vatican City, 1944–51), 2:284–89; A. Götze, "Die Nachwirkung der Schatzhöhle," *Zeitschrift für Semitistik und verwandte Gebiete* 3 (1924) 169ff.; and H. Achelis, *Hippolytstudien,* Texte und Untersuchungen zur Geschichte der Altchristlichen, n.F. 1.4 (Leipzig, 1897), pp. 118–19. The catena was originally written in Syriac and then translated into Arabic (Götze, p. 170), although it was written in Syriac characters ("Qarshuni") and probably dates from the thirteenth century. By far the most quoted author in this manuscript—at least in Genesis—is Ephrem.

41. The text is on 2:87 in Lagarde's edition and is cited by Max Grünbaum, *Neue Beiträge zur semitischen Sagenkunde* (Leiden, 1893), p. 86.

42. Nor is it found in the Armenian commentary on Genesis attributed to Ephrem, which is anyway, according to its editor, not the work of Ephrem in Armenian translation. See E. G. Mathews, *The Armenian Commentary on Genesis Attributed to Ephrem the Syrian, CSCO* 573, Scriptores Armeniaci 24 (Louvain, 1998), pp. ix–lii.

43. Lagarde, *Materialien,* 2:79; Grünbaum, *Neue Beiträge,* p. 83. This story, incidentally, is found in modern Arabic folklore. See Philip Baldensperger, "Peasant

Folklore of Palestine," *Palestine Exploration Quarterly* 25 (1893) 213, and G. Weil, *Biblische Legenden der Muselmänner* (Frankfurt am Main, 1854), p. 51. The motif of the raven, originally white, being punished with blackness is much older than Ephrem; it is found in Ovid's (d. 18 C.E.) *Metamorphoses* 2.531ff. What is unique about the Near Eastern sources is the setting in Noah's ark. Another Near Eastern source that puts the raven-cursing story in Noah's ark is the Mandaean *Ginza* ("Noah cursed the raven and blessed the dove"), but we are not told the content of Noah's curse. See Lidzbarski, *Ginzā*, p. 410. This legend is, to my knowledge, not found in Jewish sources. Correct, therefore, the caption in *Biblical Archaeologist* 47 (1984) 232 ("According to a Jewish legend the raven's feathers were originally white but turned black when it did not return to the ark"), which was inserted not by the author, Jack P. Lewis, but by one of the journal's editors (communication from Lewis). For medieval and modern stories about the raven turning black, see P. J. Heather, "Colour Symbolism," *Folklore* 59 (1948) 208–9; Paul Freedman, *Images of the Medieval Peasant* (Stanford, Calif., 1999), p. 332, n. 6; Oskar Dähnhardt, *Natursagen: Eine Sammlung naturdeutender Sagen, Marchen, Fabeln und Legenden,* with contributions by V. Armhaus et al. (Leipzig and Berlin, 1907–12), 1:283–85, 286 n. 1, 287 (for more examples, see index "Rabe"); E. S. McCartney, "Folk Tales Which Account for the Blackness of the Raven and the Crow," *Papers of the Michigan Academy of Science, Arts and Letters* 12 (1930) 137–48, and "Noah's Ark and the Flood: A Study in Patristic Literature and Modern Folklore," ibid. 18 (1932) 86. Anna B. Rooth also quotes many such stories of a raven turning black, most of them similar to Ephrem's, found in Russian, Irish, and North American Indian folktales. See her *The Raven and the Carcass: An Investigation of a Motif in the Deluge Myth in Europe, Asia, and North America* (Helsinki, 1962), pp. 85, 121–22, 152–53, 166, 176, 180, 200–202, 207, 221, 225–26, 233. Add also J. Mooney, "The Jicarilla Genesis," *American Anthropologist,* o.s., 11 (1898) 200, and F. L. Utley, *The Devil in the Ark consisting of "some sample texts of the Noah story" now being compiled,* Ohio Valley Folk Research Project, Ohio Valley Folk Publications, n.s., 32 (Chillicothe, Ohio, 1959), p. 6.

44. As noted by Yeshaya Maori, *The Peshitta Version of the Pentateuch and Early Jewish Exegesis* (in Hebrew; Jerusalem, 1995), p. 108, n. 30. See now also M. P. Weitzman, *The Syriac Version of the Old Testament* (Cambridge, 1999), p. 144.

45. Freedman, *Images of the Medieval Peasant,* p. 333, n.15, quoting Brock in an oral communication. So too Ignatius Ortiz de Urbina lists the Ephrem citations in the catena under "opera dubia" (*Patrologia Syriaca,* Rome, 1965, p. 74).

46. *Commentaire d'Išoʿdad de Merv sur l'Ancien Testament.* Genèse: text, ed. J.-M. Vosté and C. Van Den Eynde, *CSCO* 126, Scriptores Syri 67 (Louvain, 1950), pp. 128–29; translation, C. Van Den Eynde, *CSCO* 156, Scriptores Syri 75 (Louvain, 1955), p. 139.

47. On the dating of Marqe, see Glossary.

48. Zeʾev Ben-Ḥayyim, *Tibat Marqe,* pp. 288–89, sec. 232a. "To wear" or "to put on" an attribute is a common metaphor, of which there are many examples in ancient Near Eastern literature, including the Bible (e.g., Judg 6:34, Job 8:22, 10:11, Ps 93:1, 104:1, 109:17–19, 29). Marqe elsewhere uses the metaphor: "clothed in God's name" (*Tibat Marqe,* pp. 154–55, sec. 104b); "clothed in prophecy" (pp. 330–31, sec. 267b); and note especially "wearing a curse" (pp. 344–

45, sec. 275a), which is the same metaphor used by Ephrem in one of his hymns about Ham, for which see below, p. 341, n. 10. Marqe's usage is echoed by an early black African poet, Suḥaym (d. 660): "I am covered with a black garment, but under it there is a lustrous garment with white skirts" (trans. Lewis, *Race and Slavery,* p. 29). In Christian literature the metaphor is found in Galatians 3:27 ("as many of you as have been baptized into Christ have clothed yourselves in Christ [ἐνεδύσασθε]"), and Hippolytus (d. 235) uses a similar expression for Jesus who "put on human garments" (ἀλλ᾿ εἰ καὶ ἐκ τῆς παρθένου τὸ ἀνθρώπινον ὄργανον ἀναλαβὼν ἐφόρησε; *In Lucam* 2; *PG* 10.701A). The metaphor is particularly common to describe the body as clothing a person, as in Job 10:11; see Sebastian Brock, "Clothing Metaphors as a Means of Theological Expression in Syriac Tradition," in *Typus, Symbol, Allegorie bei den östlichen Vätern und ihren Parallelen im Mittelalter,* ed. M. Schmidt with C. F. Geyer (Regensburg, 1981), pp. 11–38, esp. 17–18 and nn. 23, 29; reprinted in S. Brock, *Studies in Syriac Christianity: History, Literature and Theology* (Hampshire, 1992). For the Armenian liturgy, see *Liturgies Eastern and Western,* trans. and ed. F. E. Brightman (Oxford, 1896), 1:412–14. For Mandaean literature, see Foerster, *Gnosis,* 1:118, 2:191, 201, 231, 233, 252, 255. In light of all this, perhaps there is no need to emend the apocryphal *Acts of Peter* 8, where Peter says to the devil, who is black, "Keep thou to thyself thy garments [*tunicas*] of darkness" (so James, *ANT,* p. 312; Elliott, *ANT,* p. 406) to "thy gates [*ianuas*] of darkness" (so Schneemelcher in *NTA* 2:295).

49. Ben-Ḥayyim: "i.e., Ham, who is the father of Kush." So too M. Heidenheim, *Der Commentar Marqah's des Samaritaners,* Bibliotheca Samaritana Bd. 3, Heft 5–6 (Weimar, 1896), p. 201, n. 707.

50. *Tibat Marqe,* pp. 344–45 (275b); pp. 262–63 (203a); and pp. 372–73 (304b).

51. Quoted by Ibn Qutayba (d. 889), *Kitāb al-maʿārif,* ed. Tharwat ʿUkāsha (Cairo, 1960), p. 26; *Ibn Coteibas Handbuch der Geschichte,* ed. F. Wüstenfeld (Göttingen, 1850), p. 14. Translation is that of Lewis in *Race and Slavery,* pp. 124–25, and *Islam,* 2:210, except for "Barbars," where Lewis has "Berbers"; also translated in Levtzion and Hopkins, *Corpus,* p. 15. On the Barbars, see my article "Geographia Rabbinica." ʿUkāsha has the name partially vocalized *barbr.* On a reading "Qazan" (possibly for "Fazzan") instead of "Qaran," see Levtzion and Hopkins, *Corpus,* p. 376, n. 1. According to later Arabic sources, Wahb was a convert from *ahl al-kitāb,* i.e., Judaism or Christianity, or specifically from Judaism, but the earliest sources know nothing of this. He was probably born a Muslim (see R. G. Khoury in *EI*[2] 11:34). This is also the opinion of A. A. Duri, *The Rise of Historical Writing among the Arabs,* ed. and trans. L. I. Conrad (Princeton, 1983; originally in Arabic, 1960), p. 123; R. G. Khoury, "Quelques réflexions sur la première ou les premières bibles arabes," in *L'Arabie préislamique et son environnement historique et cultural,* ed. T. Fahd (Leiden, 1989), p. 561; R. G. Khoury "Ibn Khaldūn et quelques savants des deux premiers siècles islamiques," *Jerusalem Studies in Arabic and Islam* 10 (1987) 196; and Camilla Adang, *Muslim Writers on Judaism and the Hebrew Bible: From Ibn Rabban to Ibn Hazm* (Leiden, 1996), pp. 10–12. On Ibn Qutayba and his sources, see Adang, pp. 30ff., 112–17.

52. A *ḥadīth* recorded by al-Kisāʾī in his *Qiṣaṣ al-anbiyāʾ,* ed. Isaac Eisenberg, *Vita prophetarum auctore Muḥammed ben ʿAbdallāh al-Kisāʾi* (Leiden, 1923), p. 101;

translation is that of Thackston, *Tales of the Prophets,* pp. 107–8, except for "Barbars," where Thackston has "Berbers"; see my article, "Geographica Rabbinica." On Kaʿb, said to be a Jewish Yemini convert to Islam, see the literature cited by Adang, *Muslim Writers on Judaism,* p. 8, nn. 45–46. "The very existence of Kaʿb al-Aḥbār is far from certain. Historians such as al-Ṭabarī make no mention of him. Even if he was historical there seems little doubt that his name was slavishly or spuriously quoted whenever a storyteller or interpreter of a folk-tale was demanded" (H. T. Norris, "Fables and Legends in Pre-Islamic and Early Islamic Times," in *Cambridge History of Arabic Literature: Arabic Literature to the End of the Umayyad Period,* ed. A.F.L. Beeston et al., Cambridge, 1983, p. 384).

53. Hermann Zotenberg, ed. and trans. *Chronique de Abou-Djafar-Mo'hammed-ben-Djarir-ben-Yezid Tabari traduite sur la version persane d'Abou-'Ali Mo'hammed Bel'ami* (Paris, 1867–74), 1:115.

54. A *ḥadīth* transmitted by Aḥmad Baba (d. 1627), which he found in a work by Suyūṭī (d. 1505): "Noah took a bath and his son [Ham] looked at him and Noah said, 'You look at me when I am washing, may Allah change your color,' and it became black and thus, came the Sudan." See B. Barbour and M. Jacobs, "The Miʿraj: A Legal Treatise on Slavery by Ahmad Baba," in Willis, *Slaves and Slavery in Muslim Africa,* 1:132. See also John Hunwick, "Islamic Law and Politics over Race and Slavery in North and West Africa (16th–19th Century)," in *Slavery in the Islamic Middle East,* ed. Shaun E. Marmon (Princeton, 1999), p. 48, and Mahmoud Zouber, *Ahmad Bābā de Tombouctou (1556–1627): sa vie et son oeuvre* (Paris, 1977), pp. 140–41, where the story is also quoted. A bath scene is a natural development from the biblical "Noah uncovered himself." Perhaps too there was influence from the Arabic *ḥamm, istaḥamm* 'to take a bath' (Lane, *Lexicon,* 1:636; Dozy, *Supplément aux Dictionnaires Arabes,* 1:319).

55. "They say that he [Noah] sent Ham to the regions of Hindustan because he was black. That was because one day, seeing his father's nakedness exposed, he laughed; the Exalted King blackened his face" (*Qiṣaṣ al-anbiyāʾ,* ed. Ḥabīb Yaghmāʾī, Persian Texts Series, no. 6; Teheran, 1961), p. 39. I am indebted to Vera Moreen for the English translation.

56. *Tanwīr al-ghabash fī faḍl al-sūdān waʾl-ḥabash* ("The Illumination of the Darkness: On the Merits of the Blacks and the Ethiopians"), trans. Akbar Muhammad, "The Image of Africans in Arabic Literature: Some Unpublished Manuscripts," in Willis, *Slaves and Slavery in Muslim Africa,* 1:56. Another English translation, based on a different manuscript, shows no significant differences at this point (E. van Donzel, "Ibn al-Jawzi on Ethiopians in Baghdad," in *The Islamic World from Classical to Modern Times,* ed. C. E. Bosworth, Charles Issawi, Roger Savory, and A. L. Udovitch, Princeton, 1989, p. 114).

57. *Athār al-bilād wa-akhbār al-ʿibād,* ed. F. Wüstenfeld (Beirut, 1960), p. 22.

58. Cf. Abū al-ʿAlāʾ al-Maʿarrī (d. 1057): "Ham wasn't black because he sinned; God wished it" (G.B.H. Wightman and A. Y. al-Udhari, eds. and trans., *Birds through a Ceiling of Alabaster: Three Abbasid Poets,* Hamondsworth, 1975, p. 116).

59. *Kitāb nukhbat al-dahr fi ʿajāʾib al-barr waʾl-baḥr,* ed. A. F. Mehren (St. Petersburg, 1866; repr., 1923), p. 266; trans., Mehren, *Manuel de la cosmographie du moyen age* (1874; repr., Amsterdam, 1964), p. 385. An English translation of this section is found in Levtzion and Hopkins, *Corpus,* p. 212. Incidentally, these

stories continue into modern times. Edward Westermark notes the belief in modern-day Morocco that "the Negroes . . . have become black in consequence of the curse which Sīdan Nōḥ (Noah) pronounced upon his son Ham, their ancestor" (*Wit and Wisdom in Morocco: A Study of Native Proverbs,* London, 1930, p. 131). Such stories are even found in black African (Islamic) societies. A creation myth of the Lamu (a people living in the archipelago off the East African coast below the Somali border) says that Noah cursed Ham, asking God to make his descendants black (Abdul Hamid M. El Zein, *The Sacred Meadows: A Structural Analysis of Religious Symbolism in an East African Town,* Evanston, 1974, p. 201).

60. Trans. Richard Burton, ed. L. C. Smithers (London, 1894), 3:364–65 (the 335th night).

61. *Fakhr al-sūdān ʿala al-bidan* ("The Boasts of the Dark-Skinned Ones over the Light-Skinned Ones"), ed. G. van Vloten in *Tria opuscula auctore* (Leiden, 1903), pp. 81–82; reedited by ʿAbd al-Salām Hārūn in *Rasāʾil al-Jāḥiẓ* (Cairo, 1964), 1: 219–20; and by T. Khalidi in *The Islamic Quarterly* 25 (1981) 23–24 (text), with translation on p. 48. O. Rescher translates the last line as "Veränderung und Strafe, Verunstaltung und (Bevorzugung bezw.) Benachteiligung" in *Orientalische Miszellen* (Istanbul, 1926), 2:180–81. The English translation used here is that of Lewis, *Islam,* 2:215–16, whose questioning of the word "blackness" follows Rescher's suggested emendations from *asrar* to *aswad.* Another English translation is based on Charles Pellat's French version of selected texts, *The Life and Works of Jāḥiẓ,* trans. D. M. Hawke (Berkeley, 1969), pp. 196–97.

62. For sources on the prohibition of sex in the ark, see Ginzberg, *Legends of the Jews,* 5:188, n. 54; Menaḥem Kasher, *Torah Shelemah* (Jerusalem, 1927–), 2:408, n. 200, 2:418, n. 31; and M. Grünbaum, *Semitische Sagenkunde,* pp. 85–86. Philo, referred to in *Legends,* is now found in the Loeb edition, Supplement 1, pp. 129–30 (*Quaestiones in Genesim* 2.49), on which see S. Belkin, "Maqor Qadum le-Midreshei Ḥazal," in *The Abraham Weiss Jubilee Volume,* ed., Samuel Belkin et al. (New York, 1964), pp. 607–9. On the question of a relationship between the Philonic and rabbinic traditions, see Naomi G. Cohen, *Philo Judaeus: His Universe of Discourse* (Frankfurt am Main, 1995), pp. 46–65, and David Winston's review in *JQR* 86 (1996) 510–11. The prohibition is commonly mentioned in medieval Jewish, Christian, and Islamic literature. For Christian sources, in addition to Ginzberg's *Legends* and his "Die Haggada bei den Kirchenvätern," *MGWJ* 43 (1899) 415–16, see A. Guillaumont, "A propos du célibat des esséniens," *Hommages à André Dupont-Sommer* (Paris, 1971), p. 401, and de Lange, *Origen and the Jews,* p. 205, nn. 48–50. For more on the prohibition of sex in later sources, see Jack P. Lewis, *A Study of the Interpretation of Noah and the Flood in Jewish and Christian Literature* (Leiden, 1968), p. 144, n. 10; M. Grünbaum, *Neue Beiträge,* p. 85; Paul Kaplan, *Ruler, Saint and Servant,* pp. 172, 218 nn. 85–86; and J. B. Friedman, "Nicholas's 'Angelus ad Virginem' and the Mocking of Noah," *Yearbook of English Studies* 22 (1992) 177. For the possibility that Theophilus of Antioch (second century) refers to the same tradition with his remark that "some call [Noah] a eunuch," see Stephen Gero, "The Legend of the Fourth Son of Noah," *HTR* 73 (1980) 321, n. 2. Regarding Islamic sources, the legend is noted by Zamakhsharī (quoted in H. Gätje, *The Qurʾān and Its Exegesis,* English translation by Alford T. Welch, London, 1976, p. 104), Ibn Hishām, *Kitāb al-tījān an fī mulūk*

Ḥimyar (Haydarabad, 1928–29), p. 24, and others. Finally, regarding the origin of the legend of sexual continence, which in the midrash and Philo is exegetically derived, Rooth, *The Raven and the Carcass,* p. 150, thinks that these stories have their origin in an attempt to explain the problem of increase and lack of space in the ark. Of course, this explanation is not incompatible with the exegetical derivation; the two are not mutually exclusive.

63. *pTaʿan* 1.6, 64d. MS Leiden has *mefursam* for ed. pr. *mefurṣam,* the same word with an interchange of sibilants. J. Neusner (*The Talmud of the Land of Israel,* 18:169), understands *mefurṣam* as if from the root *prṣ* and translates "dissolute"; see Jastrow, *Dictionary,* s.v. *paraṣ.* So too S. Buber, *Tanḥuma, Noaḥ,* p. 46, n. 199. In context the legend is quoted as tannaitic material (*teninan*) by R. Ḥiyya who lived in the third and beginning of the fourth centuries. The date for the redaction of the Palestinian Talmud is not later than 370 (see Glossary). *GenR* 36.7 (p. 341) also records this legend in the name of R. Ḥiyya, but without the element of the raven. (In addition to the readings recorded by Theodor in his critical edition of *GenR,* by Sokoloff in his edition of the Genizah fragments, and in the published facsimile of MS Vatican 60, I checked the manuscripts at the Institute of Microfilmed Hebrew Manuscripts at the Israel National Library, Jeruslaem—all with no significant variants). The *GenR* version is quoted in the later anthologies *YalqSh, Noaḥ* 61, ed. Heiman et al., 1:223, and *Yalquṭ Talmud Torah,* Gen 9:25, ed. Elazar Hurvitz, "The Nature and Sources of Yalkut Talmud Torah by Rabbi Jacob Sikily" (Ph.D. diss., Yeshiva University, 1965), 2:182, and in the eleventh-century dictionary of Nathan b. Yeḥiel of Rome, *ʿArukh ha-Shalem,* ed. Kohut, 6:308b, s.v. *peḥam.* The quotation in the sixteenth-century *Sefer Reʾshit Ḥokhma* of Elijah de Vidas, which has Canaan cursed with blackness (sec. *Ahava* 6.8, ed. Ḥ. Y. Waldman, *Reʾshit Ḥokhma ha-Shalem,* Jerusalem, 1984, 1:456) would appear to be an error; see the text there.

64. *bSan* 108b. The redaction of the Babylonian Talmud is dated from the end of the fifth to the mid-sixth century (Stemberger, *Introduction,* pp. 192–97). The manuscripts show no significant variants. Unfortunately MS Karlsruhe of *bSan* is missing this particular page of the tractate; see *Die Handschriften der grossherzoglich Badischen Hof- und Landesbibliothek in Karlsruhe,* ed. Badische Landesbibliothek Karlsruhe (Karlsruhe, 1891–1901), 2:17. The text is quoted in Latin translation in the Paris MS Bibliotheque Nationale Lat. 16558 (a work compiled between 1245 and 1248 to serve as a source book for the church in its polemic against Judaism): "The teachers say that three copulated with their females in the ark: the dog, the crow, and Ham, and all were punished. The dog because it is stuck to its female when it copulates, the crow spits [and] copulates spitting, Ham because of this was cursed" (Dicunt magistri tres coierunt in archa cum feminis suis. canis. corvus et cham. et omnis puniti fuerunt. Canis quia colligatur cum femina sua. quando coit. corcus spuit. spuendo coit cham quia propter hoc maledictus fuit). The strange lack of a punishment for Ham is probably due only to a misreading of the Hebrew (*be-ʿado* or *baʿavuro* for *beʿoro*), either by the scribe of the Latin manuscript or the scribe of the Talmud text which served as the translator's *Vorlage.* The text is on folios 69b and 181a of the manuscript; see Ḥ. Merḥavia, *Ha-Talmud bi-Reʾi ha-Naṣrut* (Jerusalem, 1970), p. 410. A succinct description of the manuscript, with references to literature dealing with it, can be found in Jeremy Cohen, *The Friars and*

the Jews: The Evolution of Medieval Anti-Judaism (Ithaca, N.Y., 1982), p. 65. My thanks are due to Ann Matter both for deciphering the Latin and for the translation.

65. The sources that provide these explanations, in part or in whole, are *Tanḥuma, Noaḥ* 12; the medieval Ben Sira cycle of stories, published by Eli Yassif, *Sipurei Ben Sira bi-Ymei ha-Beinaiyim* (Jerusalem, 1985), pp. 246–49, for versions A and B; and by David Z. Friedman and Samuel Loewinger in *Ha-Ṣofeh le-Ḥokhmat Yisra'el* 10 (1926) 265, offprinted separately (Vienna, 1926), p.15, for version C; *Pirqei de-Rabbenu ha-Qadosh,* 3.97, in *Sheloshah Sefarim Niftaḥim,* ed. Samuel Schönblum (Lemberg, 1877), p. 32b (but not found in another manuscript of the work published by E. Grünhut in *Sefer ha-Liqquṭim,* Jerusalem, 1898–1903, 3:33ff.); *Ḥupat Eliyahu Rabba,* quoted in al-Naqawah, *Menorat ha-Ma'or,* ed. H. G. Enelow (New York, 1929), 6:465, and from there to Elijah de Vidas, *Re'shit Ḥokhmah,* ed. Ḥ. Y. Waldman, *Re'shit Ḥokhmah ha-Shalem,* 3:225. See also H. M. Horowitz, *Kevod Ḥupah* (Frankfurt, 1888), p. 25; Rashi to *bSan* 108b ; *ʿArukh,* ed. Kohut, 7:226a, s.v. *qashar.* From the eleventh century onward: Ṭoviah b. Eliezer (eleventh century), *Leqaḥ Ṭov* to Gen 6:20, ed. S. Buber, p. 40; *YalqSh* (twelfth/thirteenth century), *Noaḥ* 58, ed. Heiman et al., 1:199; David b. Amram of Aden (thirteenth/fourteenth century), *Midrash ha-Gadol,* Gen 8.7, p. 175; Nathaniel b. Yeshaʿya (fourteenth century), *Me'or ha-Afelah* (fourteenth century), ed. Yosef Qapeḥ (Kafah), Jerusalem, 1957, p. 61; Zechariah ben Solomon ha-Rofé (fourteenth century), *Midrash ha-Ḥefeṣ,* ed. Meir Ḥavaṣelet (Jerusalem, 1990–92), 1:97; *Haggadot ha-Talmud* (Constantinople, 1511), p. 102a.

66. Pliny, *Natural History* 10.83.174. See also Aristotle, *Historia animalium* 5.2. Given these parallels and the sexual framework of the story, I cannot accept the explanation of "connected" offered by Meir ha-Levi Abulafia (d. 1244) in his commentary *Yad Ramah* to *bSan* 108b, that the dog is usually tied to a leash. Clearly the sexual punishment is the correct explanation; otherwise the measure-for-measure (sexual punishment for a sexual sin) nature of the etiology is lost. See Reuben Margaliot, *Margaliot ha-Yam* (Jerusalem, 1977), p. 194. A unique reading (*mzbzh*) of the dog's punishment is found in *Pirqei de-Rabbenu ha-Qadosh,* 3.97. I have no idea what this word means if it is not a scribal corruption.

67. Aristotle, *De generatione animalium* 3.6; Aristophanes, *Excerptorum Constantini De natura animalium* etc. as cited by John Boswell, *Christianity, Social Tolerance, and Homosexuality* (Chicago, 1980), p. 138, n. 4; Psuedo-Clement, *Recognitions* 8.25 (*ANF* 8:172). Note also the tenth-century Abū Ḥayyān al-Tawḥidi: "The crow [*ghudāf*] lays eggs and has chicks not as a result of copulation." See Conway Zirkle, "Animals Impregnated by the Wind," *Isis* 25 (1936) 112, and L. Kopf, "The Zoological Chapter of the *Kitāb al-Imtāʿ wal-Mu'ānasa* of Abū Ḥayyān al-Tauḥīdī(10th Century)," *Osiris* 12 (1956) 447. On the rabbinic sources, see Ginzberg, *Legends of the Jews,* 5:55, n. 177, and L. Lewysohn, *Die Zoologie des Talmuds* (Frankfurt am Main, 1858), sec. 205, p. 173.

68. Boswell, *Christianity,* p. 138, n. 4. The belief in the oral insemination of some birds may be a result of the belief that these birds give birth through the mouth. A medieval rabbinic text, *Pereq Zeraʿim* (date uncertain) claims that "the raven is different from other creatures because it conceives through the mouth and lays its eggs through the mouth" (*Pereq Zeraʿim,* ed. Y. Feliks, Jerusalem, 1973,

p. 193). A causal connection between two similar beliefs was made by Aristotle in regard to the weasel, which was also thought to conceive and give birth through the mouth. Aristotle suggested that the fact that it carried its young in its mouth gave rise to the notion that the weasel was orally inseminated (Aristotle, *De generatione animalium* 3.6 quoting Anaxagorus). Perhaps, on the basis of the *Pereq Zeraᶜim* text, we can make the same causal connection for the belief in oral insemination for the raven and other birds.

69. Hippocrates, *Airs, Waters, Places* 14. On the ancient theory of "pangenesis," see Iain Lonie, *The Hippocratic Treatises "On Generation," "On the Nature of the Child," "Diseases IV"* (Berlin, 1981), pp. 115–17.

70. *Commentary to Song of Songs* 2.2, *GCS* 33 (Origen 8) 125. R. P. Lawson translates: "natural blackness inherited by all" and "bodies that have once been scorched and darkened, transmit a congenital stain to their posterity" for the bracketed words (*ACW* 26:107).

71. Herodotus 3.101; cf. 3.97. Aristotle, *De generatione animalium* 2.736a, 10–15. Despite Aristotle the idea had staying power, for we find Peter Heylyn in 1627 arguing against the "foolish supposition" that "the generative seed of the africans to be blacke" (Heylyn, *ΜΙΚΡΟΚΟΣΜΟΣ* [1627], p. 771, quoted in Jordan, *White over Black,* p. 20).

72. Qatādah (d. 736) quoted by Thaᶜlabī, *Qiṣaṣ al-anbiyā᾿* Cairo, 1954), p. 57; Ibn Jurayj (d. ca. 766) quoted by Ṭabarī, *Annales quos scripsit Abu Djafar Mohammed ibn Djarir at-Tabari,* ed. M. J. de Goeje (Leiden, 1964), 1:196, trans. F. Rosenthal, *The History of Tabari,* vol. 1 (Albany, 1989), p. 365; Dimashqī (thirteenth century), *Nukhbat al-dahr,* ed. Mehren, p. 266; trans., Mehren, *Manuel de la cosmographie,* p. 385; excerpted in Levtzion and Hopkins, *Corpus,* p. 212. See also Balᶜamī's (tenth century) Persian version of Ṭabarī ("May God change the semen of your loins. After that all the people and fruit of the country of Ham became black"), *Chronique de Abou-Djafar-Mo'hammed-ben-Djarir-ben-Yezid Tabari,* ed. and trans. Zotenberg, 1:115. Balᶜamī's setting is the biblical account in Genesis, not the rabbinic story of sex-in-the-ark. Similarly, al-Rabghūzī (fourteenth–fifteenth century) quoting Abū Isḥaq Nishābūrī: *Al-Rabghūzī, The Stories of the Prophets: Qiṣaṣ al-Anbiyā᾿, An Eastern Turkish Version,* trans. H. E. Boeschoten, J. O'Kane, M. Vandamme (Leiden, 1995), 2:67. Other Islamic writers adopted the rabbinic story without the explanatory gloss, e.g., Ibn ᶜAbd al-Ḥakam (d. 870/1): "Canaan was the one who was ensnared in sin in the ark and Noah cursed him and he emerged black [*aswāda*]" (*Futūḥ Miṣr,* ed. Charles C. Torrey, *The History of the Conquest of Egypt, North Africa and Spain Known as the Futūḥ Miṣr of Ibn ᶜAbd al-Ḥakam,* New Haven, 1922, p. 8). Al-Ḥakam's report may be part of a lengthy *isnad* (chain of tradition) going back ultimately to ᶜAbd Allāh ibn ᶜAbbās (d. 686/8), a contemporary of the prophet of Islam. So too did Syriac Christians adopt the story. Ishodad of Merv (ninth century) mentions it: "According to others . . . the black color [came to] Ham, who engaged in conjugal relations in the ark, despite his father's prohibition" (*Commentaire d'Išoᶜdad de Merv sur l'Ancien Testament,* Genèse, text: *CSCO* 126, S. Syri 67, pp. 128–29; translation: *CSCO* 156, S. Syri 75, p. 139). On the other hand, when D. L. Jeffrey writes that the talmudic legend is followed by Philo, the Book of Adam and Eve, the Evangel of Seth, and Origen (*A Dictionary of Biblical Tradition in English Literature,* Grand Rapids, Mich.,

1992, s.v. Ham [Cham]), he is mistaken. What these sources report is the common tradition of a prohibition of sex on the ark. They do not mention the talmudic legend of a transgression.

73. *GenR* 36.7 (pp. 341–42). The manuscripts present no significant variations. It is not clear whether the last sentence of the quotation is R. Levi's or whether it is a gloss of the *GenR* editor(s), who worked Levi's comment into the framework of *GenR*. Cf. *Mekhilta, Ba-ḥodesh* 8 (p. 233), where the process of invalidating coins by defacing the image is described as "reducing/diminishing [*miʿatu*] the image of the king."

74. The metaphor of the dyecast for human procreation is found, e.g., in *GenR* 37.5 (pp. 347–48). The classic expression of this metaphor is found in *mSan* 4.5 where God is compared to man, "for man stamps many coins in one diecast and they are all alike; but God stamped all men in the diecast of Adam, yet no two are alike." Samuel Yaffe Ashkenazi's (sixteenth century) unusual interpretation of the parable as referring to slavery rather than dark skin (*Yefeh Toʾar* [Jerusalem, 1989 = reprint of Ferrara, 1692], p. 226a, s.v. *sheqavaʿ*) is a consequence of his view that black skin is a climatically, and not a genetically, engendered characteristic (ibid., s.v. *kaʾur*). See also Zeʾev Wolf Einhorn (d. 1862), *Perush Maharzaw* to *GenR* 37.5.

75. In recent years some have written about these rabbinic accounts, although they misread and misunderstood them, even in English translation, with at times laughable results. So, for example, "Ham and the dog copulated in the Ark" in a popular English translation of the Talmud became "Ham commits bestiality on the boat by copulating with a dog" (see my "The Curse of Ham," pp. 49–50, n. 54, and add also Emmanuel Tonguino, *La malediction de canaan et le mythe chamitique dans la tradition juive,* p. 12, and Lynn Holden, *Forms of Deformity,* Sheffield, 1991, pp. 49, 71, who made the same mistake). Paul Carranza, a graduate student at the University of Pennsylvania, points out to me that the error of Ham copulating with a dog was made seven hundred years ago in the anonymous *Libro del caballero Zifar,* which incorporated the rabbinic story and said: "For he [Ham] erred in two ways; the first, that he lay with his wife in the ark. . . . And also the Jews say that Ham was cursed because he lay with a dog [*cadiella*] while he was in the ark." Carranza refers to a note by D. S. Blondheim suggesting that the resemblance in Spanish between *Cam* and *can* 'dog' (which at a later stage became *cadiella* 'a bitch') brought about the confusion (Blondheim, "A Rabbinical Legend in the Cavallero Cifar," *Modern Language Notes* 27 [1912] 250–51). But that is not all, for Carranza notes that Charles Nelson then compounded the error by translating the relevant line as "the Jews say that Canaan was cursed because he lay with the wife of the leader in the ark" (*The Book of the Knight Zifar,* Lexington, Ky., 1983, p. 23). Nelson read *Cam* as *Can,* interpreting it as Canaan, and *cadiella* as *cabdiella,* a female form of *cabdiello* 'leader'. Errors have a life of their own. Even the Tuareg, a Berber people, believe that in the ark Ham copulated with an animal, and "chastised for his carnal sin, Ham turned black" (G. Gerster, "River of Sorrow, River of Hope," *National Geographic* 148 [August 1975] 174). And if Ham copulating with a dog were not enough, another scholar claims that according to the Rabbis Ham copulated with a raven on the ark (Albert Friedman, "When Adam Delved . . . ," in *The Learned and the Lewed,* ed. Larry D. Benson, Cambridge, Mass., 1974, p. 229). This claim too has an interesting history. While it is not clear

from Friedman's citation whether his source is the medieval *Sachsenspiegel* or Oskar Dähnhardt's *Natursagen,* Marc Shell assumed the former in "Marranos (Pigs), or From Coexistence to Toleration," *Critical Inquiry* 17 (Winter 1991) 328, n. 73 = *Children of the Earth: Literature, Politics, and Nationhood* (New York, 1993), p. 218, n. 92; from Shell the attribution to the *Sachsenspiegel* found its way to Werner Sollors, *Neither Black nor White Yet Both: Thematic Explorations of Interracial Literature* (Oxford, 1997), p. 101; and from Sollors to Stephen Haynes, *Noah's Curse: The Biblical Justification of American Slavery* (Oxford, 2002), p. 25. But there is nothing to this effect in the *Sachsenspiegel.* Friedman was rather referring to Dähnhardt's *Natursagen,* 1:229, but he misread Dähnhardt who accurately records the rabbinic midrash. In short, just as there is no rabbinic statement that Ham copulated with a dog, so there is no rabbinic statement that Ham copulated with a raven, despite the persistence of such reports in modern scholarship.

76. Hippocrates, *Airs, Waters, Places* 23, trans. W.H.S. Jones (LCL). A variant reading preserved in a medieval Arabic translation of Hippocrates has: "Appearances differ greatly at the formation of the semen, and because of the differences of the seasons" (*Kitāb Buqrāṭ fi'l-amrāḍ al-bilādiyya,* ed. and trans. J. N. Mattock and M. C. Lyons, Cambridge, 1969, pp. 151–52). Galen's *Commentary on Airs, Waters, Places,* as paraphrased by Maimonides, has: "Semen and blood are of one composition in the summer and a different constitution in the winter. Therefore, variations in fetuses occur in these [different] times" (Suessman Muntner, *The Medical Aphorisms of Moses Maimonides,* trans. Fred Rosner, Brooklyn, 1970, 1:59; Hebrew edition: *Pirqei Moshe [bi-Rfu'ah],* Jerusalem, 1959, pp. 40–41).

77. On this incorrect etymology of Ham, see chapter 10. In the Palestinian version the etymology would seem to be implicit in the statement "Ham [*ḥam*] went forth darkened [*mefuḥam*]."

78. An ancient myth concerning Ham's act (done to cover up his wife's pregnancy resulting from her indiscretion with Shemḥaza'el, one of the "sons of God," who are mentioned in Gen 6:1–4) may also be behind the sex-in-the-ark story. This myth is preserved only in medieval quotation (Baḥya, *Commentary to the Pentateuch,* ed. Charles B. Chavel, Jerusalem, 1966–68, 3:159, to Num 21:34; Abraham Re'uven Hacohen Sofer, *Yalquṭ Re'uveni,* Jerusalem, 1972, *Noaḥ,* p. 130 to Gen 7:7), but it seems to go back to the Giants cycle of stories now uncovered at Qumran; see John C. Reeves, *Jewish Lore in Manichaean Cosmogony: Studies in the Book of Giants Traditions* (Cincinnati, 1992), esp. pp. 86 and 143 for medieval Jewish parallels. The rabbinic sources on Shemḥaza'e and Aḥiyah are collected in R. Margaliot, *Mala'khe 'Elyon* (Jerusalem, 1964), p. 292. A new assessment of the Qumran materials and a reconstruction of the Book of Giants is offerred by Loren T. Stuckenbruck, *The Book of Giants from Qumran* (Tübingen, 1997).

79. The statement is transmitted by R. Joseph via R. Huna, his student (fourth century), who is known as a proponent of the measure-for-measure principle. See *GenR* 9.11 (p. 73): "R. Huna in the name of R. Jose: From the beginning of creation, God foresaw that man would receive measure for measure. Therefore Scripture says, 'And behold it was very good [*hineh tov me'od*]'—behold *midah* is good [*hineh tov midah*]." On R. Huna, see Theodor's note ad loc.; Hyman, *Toledot Tannaim we-Amoraim,* 1:345–46; and Margulies, *Encyclopedia le-Ḥakhme ha-Talmud weha-Geonim,* 1:233–36.

80. *GenR* 36.7 (p. 341). In the twelfth- or thirteenth-century anthology *YalqSh* 61 (1:223), the text is transmitted by the fourth-century R. Joseph via R. Huna (MS Paris 749 reads "Joshua" for "Joseph"). In place of "may you be" (or euphemistically "may that man be"), MS London reads "may your descendants be," a difference discussed later (n. 98). Other variant readings as recorded by Theodor and as found in MS Vatican 60 yield no substantial differences. MS JTS Rab.1672, f. 6a has "ugly as coal" (*kaʾur kepeḥam*) for "ugly and dark." On the question of whether the original spelling of *kaʾur* is with *alef* or *ʿayin,* see S. Sharvit, "Gutturals in Rabbinic Hebrew," *Studies in the Hebrew Language and the Talmudic Literature: Dedicated to the Memory of Dr. Menaḥem Moreshet,* ed. M. Z. Kaddari and S. Sharvit, Ramat-Gan, 1989, p. 227; see also Kister, "Some Observations on Vocabulary and Style in the Dead Sea Scrolls," pp. 140–41, for other attestations of the word and for the possibility of a meaning "shameful" rather than "ugly." Cf. "Ham lost all sense of shame and he became black and was called shameless all the days of his life, forever" (*Cave of Treasures*), quoted on p. 173. As to the midrash itself, note that precisely the same idea lies behind the title "Black One" (Μελαινίς) given to Aphrodite, the goddess of love, according to Pausanius, the Greek geographer of the second century C.E.: people make love in the dark (*Description of Greece* 8.6.5; "black Aphrodite" is also mentioned at 2.2.4 and 9.27.5).

81. The authenticity of Rashi's commentary to *bSan,* chapter *Ḥeleq,* has been questioned (see M. Kasher and J. Mandelbaum, *Sarei ha-Elef,* New York, 1959, 1:288, 2:618), but Yonah Frenkel has shown that the essential part of the commentary, including our section, is indeed Rashi's (*Darko shel Rashi be-Ferusho le-Talmud ha-Bavli,* 2nd ed., Jerusalem, 1980, pp. 304–35). Although Shama Friedman's recent study of Rashi supports J. N. Epstein's view that the commentary on *Ḥeleq* was edited by Rashi's student Yehudah b. Nathan (Rivan), nevertheless the content of the commentary, says Friedman, is Rashi's work ("Perush Rashi le-Talmud—Hagahot u-Mahadurot," in *Rashi: ʿIyyunim bi-Yṣirato,* ed. Z. A. Steinfeld, Ramat Gan, 1993, pp. 164–66). S. H. Pick and S. Munitz, *A Tentative Catalogue of Manuscripts of the Rashi Commentary to the Talmud* (Ramat Gan, 1988), p. 44, do not record any extant manuscript fragments of Rashi to this chapter of *bSan.*

82. M. D. Herr, *EJ* 16:1516, and *Sefer ha-Meqorot I: Ha-Milon ha-Hisṭori le-Lashon ha-ʿIvrit shel ha-Aqademiah le-Lashon ha-ʿIvrit,* ed. Hebrew Language Academy (Jerusalem, 1963), p. 38.

83. Horowitz, *Kevod Ḥupah,* p. 9. On the "probably" earlier dating of *Ḥupat Eliyahu Rabba,* see J. Theodor in *JE* 8:575; *Sefer ha-Meqorot,* p. 27, on the other hand, puts it within the years 600 to 800. The Ben Sira cycle of stories is in Yassif, *Sipurei Ben Sira bi-Ymei ha-Beinaiyim,* pp. 246–49, versions A and B. Yassif dates the relevant part of the Ben Sira stories ("Toledot Ben Sira") to a period from the end of the ninth to the beginning of the tenth century (pp. 27–29). For the Ben Sira cycle in this instance as the source for *Pirqei,* see p. 89, n. 58. *Pirqei de-Rabbenu ha-Qadosh* is the name of one version of a genre of midrashic literature known collectively as *Midrash Sheloshah we-Arbaʿah.* Of the other versions of this genre that I have seen in print (many are still in manuscript), only *Ḥupat Eliyahu Rabba* includes the story of sex-in-the-ark. Thus *Pirqei de-Rabbenu ha-Qadosh* found in a Yemenite manuscript and published by M. Higger (*Ḥoreb* 6 [1942] 115–49), *Pirqei de-Rabbenu ha-Qadosh* published by E. Grünhut, *Sefer ha-Liqquṭim,* 3:33–

93, *Midrash Maᶜaseh Torah* published by Jellinek, *Bet ha-Midrasch* 2 (1853) 92–101, and *Midrash Sheloshah we-Arbaᶜah* published by S. A. Wertheimer in *Batei Midrashot,* 2:45–73, do not have this story.

84. Abd al-Malik ibn Hishām, *Kitāb al-tījān an fī mulūk Ḥimyar* (Haydarabad, 1928–29), p. 24. My thanks are due to Barbara von Schlegell for her translation of this passage.

85. Material found only in the "printed" *Tanḥuma,* not paralleled in Buber's edition, as is the case with the midrash under discussion, is considered to derive from the Islamic period; see Glossary.

86. Benjamin b. Eliezer Ha-Kohen Vitale (d. 1730, Italy), *Gevul Binyamin* (Amsterdam, 1727; repr., New York, 1992), part 1, p. 8b. Vitale is quoted by Henokh Zundel b. Joseph (d. 1867), in his commentaries *ᶜAnaf Yosef* (to *GenR,* ad loc., in the Romm-Vilna edition) and *ᶜEṣ Yoseph* (in Jacob ibn Ḥabib, *ᶜEin Yaᶜaqov* to San. 108b, ed. Vilna, 1922), who attempts to bring Rashi in line with the plain meaning of the story by emending Rashi's words to read: "Ham was punished in his skin *and* Kush descended from him." See also *ᶜEṣ Yoseph* to *Tanḥuma, Noaḥ* 12.

87. *Yalquṭ Shimᶜoni, Noaḥ* 58, ed. Heiman et al., 1:199 (so also *Haggadot ha-Talmud,* p. 102a); David B. Amram, *Midrash ha-Gadol,* 1:175 (Gen 8:7); for the Chrisitan writers, see Peter Fryer, *Staying Power: Black People in Britain since 1504* (Atlantic Highlands, N.J.), pp. 142–43; *Entdecktes Judenthum* ([Frankfurt], 1700), 1:448, "Der Cham ist an seiner Haut gestraffet worden; dieweil der schwartze Cus darvon hergekommen ist." As far as modern works are concerned, in addition to the *Encyclopedia Judaica,* s.v. Ham (A. Rothkoff) and the *Jewish Encyclopedia,* s.v. Ham (J. Jacobs), the "Kush" explanation is found in: David Brion Davis, *Slavery and Human Progress* (New York, 1984), p. 87, on the basis of E. Isaac (see next note); J. Preuss, *Biblisch-talmudische Medizin,* p. 537 (English edition, trans. F. Rosner, p. 460); and Frost, "Attitudes toward Blacks in the Early Christian Era," p. 3. MS Jerusalem, Yad ha-Rav Herzog, of *bSan,* a late Yemenite manuscript, has incorporated the explanation into the talmudic text, a common phenomenon. The process of incorporation can clearly be seen by comparing the manuscript with *Haggadot ha-Talmud,* an anthology of talmudic legends, which quotes *bSan* as "Ham was smitten in his skin—*explanation:* Kush descended from him." Eliezer Diamond has shown that MS Jerusalem has elsewhere (*bTaᶜan* 2a) incorporated into the talmudic text an explanation of "Rashi" (as found in manuscripts, not the printed text of "Rashi" to this section; see his "A Model for a Scientific Edition and Commentary for 'Bavli Taᶜanit,' Chapter I with a Methodological Introduction," Ph.D. diss., Jewish Theological Seminary, 1990, pp. 146–47). I put "Rashi" in quotes because the commentary attributed to him is actually a combination of R. Gershom's commentary (the first three pages of *bTaᶜan*) and the School of Rashi; see D. Halivni, "The First Three Pages of the Commentary Attributed to Rashi on Taᶜanit" (in Hebrew), *Sinai* 43 (1958) 211–22. See A. Grossman, *Ḥakhmei Ṣarfat ha-Rishonim* (Jerusalem, 1995), p. 216, n. 275, for further bibliography on this commentary. On the phenomenon of Rashi's explanations migrating into the talmudic text—noted already by the Rishonim (eleventh–fifteenth century)—see Yeḥiel Y. Weinberg, *Meḥqarim ba-Talmud* (Berlin, 1937/38), pp. 166–69. Diamond also shows (p. 126) that in another place on *bTaᶜan* 2a the reading of MS Jerusalem is similar to the style of abridgment used by the geonim and

R. Ḥananel. (A description of MS Jerusalem is found in Y. Kara, *Babylonian Aramaic in the Yemenite Manuscripts of the Talmud* [in Hebrew; Jerusalem, 1983], pp. 8–9. The passage is not mentioned in Mordechai Sabato, *Ketav-yad Temani le-Masekhet Sanhedrin.*)

88. This point was recognized by Tonguino, *La malediction de canaan,* p. 139, but unfortunately not by Isaac, "Genesis, Judaism and the 'Sons of Ham,'" p. 84; Isaac makes the same error again—mistaking Rashi for the Talmud—in his discussion of *bSuk* 53a on p. 81.

89. See the sources listed above in n. 72. It is clear that the Islamic accounts of Ham's sin in the ark derive from the Jewish tale, which is first recorded in rabbinic literature. Further proof of this can be found in al-Kalbī's (d. 763) statement recounting a second element of the Jewish story, the dog's transgression (in Thaʿlabī, *Qiṣaṣ al-anbiyāʾ,* Cairo, 1954, p. 57): "Al-Kalbī said: 'Noah commanded that no male should approach a female during the time in the ark. But the male dog mounted (*wathaba ʿalā*) the female dog, so Noah cursed him and said 'May God make it difficult for you [*allāhumma jʿalhu ʿasrān*).'" On Muḥammad ibn al-Sā'ib al-Kalbī, see Thackston, *Tales of the Prophets,* p. xxvii.

90. ʿUthmān Sayyid-Ahmad Ismaʾil al-Beily, "'As-Sudan' and 'Bilad as-Sudan' in Early and Medieval Arabic Writing," *Majallat Jāmiʿat al-Qāahirah bi-al-Khartūm* (Bulletin of Cairo University in Khartoum) 3 (1972) 33–47; quotation on p. 39. *Brbr* may refer to the Berbers of North Africa or the Barbars south of Ethiopia depending on the context; see my article "Geographia Rabbinica."

91. So Akbar Muhammad speaking of Jāḥiẓ (d. 869): "'Sudan' . . . is not consonant with 'black' and 'Negro.' . . . [Jāḥiẓ] applies it to African and Arab peoples, including the Coptic Egyptians, as well as to Indians and other Asians. . . . Therefore, it seems appropriate to render *sudan* as 'dark-skinned' peoples" (Muhammad, "The Image of Africans in Arabic Literature," p. 49). See also J. L. Triaud in EI^2 9:752b, s.v. Sūdān (Bilād al-Sūdān 'land of the blacks' refers to the "Saharo-Sahelian sector of Africa"). Rotter, *Die Stellung des Negers,* pp. 20–21, is a notable exception: while the singular *aswad,* especially in the earlier period, can describe any dark-skinned person, the plural *sūdān,* when used as a substantive, "steht dabei fast ausschliesslich für die schwarzen Afrikaner."

92. For ʿUbāda see Ibn ʿAbd al-Ḥakam, *Futūḥ Miṣr,* ed. Torrey, p. 66, and Lewis, *Race and Slavery,* p. 26. For "the red and the black," see Ignaz Goldziher, *Muslim Studies* (ed. S. M. Stern, translated from the German, 1889–90, by C. R. Barber and S. M. Stern, Albany, N.Y., 1966), 1:243–44, citing al-Tabrīzī, al-Māwardī, and Ibn Hishām, who use the expression. See also A. Fischer, "Ausdrücke per Merismum im Arabischen," *Streitberg Festgabe* (Leipzig, 1924), p. 48, and Lane, *Lexicon,* p. 642a (who translates "the white and the black," taking *aḥmar* when referring to complexion to mean "white"; however, Fischer, *Farb- und Formbezeichnungen,* pp. 338–39, argues against this interpretation). On Jāḥīẓ's (eighth–ninth century) use of the same expression, see Lewis, *Islam,* 2:215–16. Regarding ʿUbāda's description, cf. Rotter, *Die Stellung des Negers,* p. 20: "Nur in dem stereotypen Ausdruck 'al-aswad wa'l-aḥmar' . . . sah man wohl den Araber als 'aswad' an im Vergleich zu Byzantinern und Persern."

93. Translation from Lewis, *Islam,* 2:215–16. On editions and translations of Jāḥiẓ's work, *Fakhr al-sūdān ʿala al-bidan,* see above, n. 61.

94. Recorded by al-Kisāʾī in his *Qiṣaṣ al-anbiyāʾ*, cited above, n. 52.

95. For references, see above, pp. 101 and 288, n. 51.

96. Quoted in *Ṭabarī, Tarikh,* ed. M. J. de Goeje, 1:212; translation, William M. Brinner, *The History of al-Ṭabarī,* vol. 2 (New York, 1987), p. 11.

97. Published by B. Carra de Vaux as *L'abrégé des merveilles* (Paris, 1898, 1984). On the authorship and date, see below, p. 350, n. 14. The quotation is from Levtzion and Hopkins, *Corpus,* p. 35. Also in later writers reporting earlier material, e.g., Halabi (b. 1567): "Noah invoked God against Ham that God should make his son the color black. God answered his prayer and his son became black and he is the father of the Sūdān" (quoted from the *Sirat al-Halabiya* by Musa Kamara [d. 1945], *Zuhur al-Basatin,* trans. Constance Hilliard in Willis, *Slaves and Slavery,* 1:165). I am indebted to Prof. Hilliard for sending me a copy of the relevant page of the *Zuhur al-Basatin* manuscript.

98. With one exception, all textual witnesses to this passage as recorded by Theodor (as well as MS Vatican 60 and the *Yalquṭ Talmud Torah* anthology to Gen 9:25, ed. Hurvitz, 2:182) state that the curse fell on Ham ("may you be," literally and euphemistically "may that man be"). The exception is MS London ("may your descendants be," lit. "may his seed be"), which served as the basis for the Theodor-Albeck edition of *Genesis Rabba* (which, in turn, served as the basis for the English translation of the Soncino edition). In his notes, Theodor states his preference for the reading "your descendants," found in MS London, but his reasoning seems to be based on Rashi's interpretation that sees the punishment of blackness beginning with Kush, an interpretation also found in the commentary to *GenR* found in MS Oxford 147 (see Theodor's note). Clearly the weight of textual evidence is in favor of the reading that Ham himself was cursed with blackness. The scribe of MS London (or his Vorlage) was probably influenced by Rashi's interpretation just as was Theodor.

99. Biblical "Put" is either modern-day Libya or Somalia; see above, pp. 233–34, n. 63.

100. See p. 117, regarding Potiphar's wife and the *piyyuṭ* "A Complete Salvation" (*Tešuʿah šelemah*).

101. *GenR* 40.4 (p. 384), *maqom keʿurim u-sheḥorim.* MS Stuttgart omits "black"; the quotation in *Midrash Ha-Gadol* (to Gen 12:11) has "ugly and despised"; in David ben Abraham Maimuni (d. 1300), *Midrash David Ha-Nagid,* ed. Abraham Katsh (Jerusalem, 1964), ad loc., 1:58, it is "ugly and steeped in sin."

102. See p. 21.

103. *MidPs* 68.15. The passage is found only in MSS Parma and Halberstam. I have put the last four words of the text in parentheses following the glosses of A. Provençal, which are based on manuscript evidence; see A. Jellinek, *Bet ha-Midrasch* 5 (1873) xxix–xxxii, 75. Buber brackets the entire section in his edition; see his note ad loc. William Braude translates *ʾashmanim* as "burnished by the sun" (?), *The Midrash on Psalms* (New Haven, 1959), 1:549. For my translation "dark" for *sheḥorim,* see above, pp. 81 and 185.

104. See Ben-Yehudah's *Dictionary,* 1:424, s.v. Similarly the Vulgate (*tenebris*), and the Old French gloss (*an ècurtèç* 'in obscurity') in M. Banitt, ed., *Le glossaire de Bâle* (Jerusalem, 1972), 2:384.

105. E.g., Akkadian *zīmu* and *zīwu* (Aramaic/Hebrew *zīw*); Akkadian *(w)araḫsamna* and Hebrew/Syriac *marḥešwan;* Akkadian Awīl Marduk and Amīl Marduk

(Hebrew Ewil-Merodakh); Hebrew *argaman,* Ugaritic *argmn,* Akkadian *argamannu* as opposed to Aramaic *argewan* and Arabic *urjuwān.* See Édouard Lipiński, *Semitic Languages: Outline of a Comparative Grammar* (Leuven, 1997), pp. 110–11 (*m* > *w*), 470–71 (*w* > *m*).

106. See p. 18.

107. While for the Hebrew *ḥashmanim* the standard printed Targum has "the children of Ham *ḥusmanaya*" (*benoi de-ḥam ḥusmanayya*), apparently taking the word as a proper noun (cf. LXX Gen 10:14, 1 Chr 1:12 Χασμονιεὶμ as a son of Egypt), most manuscripts as well as the Antwerp 1569–72 Polyglot have "the black children of Ham" (*benoi de-ḥam ukhmayya,* aut sim.), which clearly reflects the midrashic "dark men." The same can be said for the reading in the Genoa 1516 Polyglot: *datrayen ukkamana,* whatever *datrayen* may mean ("two"? "twice"?). Note that two Targum manuscripts have *usmana* (*usmanin*) instead of *ukhmayya,* and one adds *asmana* in the margin to *ukhmayya,* readings that may lend support to the suggested association with the place-name Aswan. For the manuscript readings, see White, *A Critical Edition of the Targum of Psalms,* p. 289; see also Jastrow, *Dictionary,* p. 31, s.v. *usmana,* and Levy, *Wörterbuch über die Targumim,* p. 27, s.vv. *ukam* and *ḥusmanayya.* The reading *bbwdḥ* (*bbdwḥ*) in two manuscripts is probably a corruption of *bnwy dḥm.*

108. Dölger, *Die Sonne der Gerechtigkeit,* p. 54. As far as I am aware, there are no biblical references to the Egyptian skin color. The term *shiḥor,* mentioned in regard to Egypt (Josh 13:3, Isa 23:3, Jer 2:18, 1 Chr 13:5), is the Egyptian *š(y)-ḥr* 'the pond of Horus', not the Hebrew *šḥr* 'black'; see KBL 4:1477.

109. Herodotus 2.104 (μελάγχροες; cf. Pindar, *Pythian Odes* 4.212); Aeschylus, *Suppliants* 154–55 (μελανθὲς), 530 (μελανόζυγ᾽), 719–20 (μελαγχίμοις), 745 (μελαγχίμῳ), cf. 279–86, *Prometheus* 851 (κελαινὸν); Martial 10.12 (*niger*); Ammianus Marcellinus 22.16.23 (*subfusculi et atrati*). See also Herodotus 2.55–57, who thinks that a story about a black dove is actually about an Egyptian priestess and that the dove's black color "signifies that the woman was Egyptian." Finally, note Adespota F 161 in Bruno Snell, *Tragicorum graecorum fragmenta* (Göttingen, [1971]).

110. *Works and Days* 527; he may have meant Ethiopians, see H. G. Evelyn-White's note in LCL, and P. R. Helm, "Races and Physical Types in the Classical World," in *Civilization of the Ancient Mediterranean: Greece and Rome,* ed. M. Grant and R. Kitzinger (New York, 1988), 1:147, where also reference is made to Minoan and Mycenaean palace frescoes that depict dark-skinned Egyptians or Ethiopians.

111. Pseudo-Aristotle, *Physiognomonica* 6.812a; Manilius, *Astronomica* 4.722–730; Arrian, *Indica* 6.9. On the classical and later depiction of the Egyptian as dark-skinned, and for more examples, see Snowden, "Asclepiades' Didyme," pp. 242–44; and "Bernal's 'Blacks,' Herodotus, and Other Classical Evidence," *Arethusa Special Issue* (Fall 1989), 83–93; Thompson, *Romans and Blacks,* pp. 111–12; Kober, *The Use of Color Terms in the Greek Poets,* p. 36; and Dölger, *Die Sonne der Gerechtigkeit,* pp. 52–53, with the comments of Jan den Boeft and Jan Bremmer in "Notiunculae Martyrologiae II," *Vigiliae Christianae* 36 (1982) 390, and Gokey in *The Terminology for the Devil and Evil Spirits in the Apostolic Fathers,* p. 113, n. 9, regarding the Egyptian devil in the *Passion of Perpetua.* The fullest treat-

ment of the Egyptian dark color in Greek and Roman sources is found in "Exkurs 4. Der Schwarze" (esp. pp. 144–48) of Peter Habermehl, *Perpetua und der Ägypter oder Bilder des Bösen in frühen afrikanischen Christentum* (Berlin, 1992). Mention should also be made of the name of ancient Egypt in some mythological accounts: "the country of the blackfooted ones" (LSJ, s.v. μελαμπόδων; Apollodorus 2.1.4, LCL, p. 136, n. 4; W. C. Greene, *Scholia Platonica,* Haverford, Pa., 1938, p. 287, ad *Timaeus* 25b). For the related usage of "Egyptian" as a synonym for "Ethiopian," see Thompson, pp. 96; 113; 202, n. 90; 206–7, nn. 37, 38; 213 n. 114.

112. J.-M. Vosté, "L'oeuvre exégétique de Théodore de Mopsueste au iie concile de Constantinople," *RB* 38 (1929) 395. See p. 88 for a discussion of the passage.

113. *Homilies on Genesis* 16.1, *GCS* 29 (Origen 6) 136–37. I deal with this passage in detail later, pp. 168–69. Note also that Apponius's exegesis assumes that Joseph's Egyptian wife, Aseneth (Gen 41:45), was dark-skinned (*Apponii in Canticum Canticorum Expositio, CCL* 19, 1.41, pp. 28–29; *SC* 420:204–7; ed. H. König, pp. 40–41). On Apponius's dates, see above, pp. 273–74, n. 43. Dark-skinned depictions of Egyptians continue in later Christian literature and iconography, and by the mid-Byzantine period it had become a relatively common motif; see Kaplan, *Ruler, Saint and Servant,* pp. 4–7.

114. See p. 183, above, and H. G. Fischer, "Varia Aegyptiaca," *Journal of the American Research Center in Egypt* 2 (1963) 17.

115. See E. Lobel, *The Oxyrhynchus Papyri* (London, 1956), 23:55–59, a fragment of Sophocles' *Inachus.* Lobel understands that κάρβανος αἰθός means that Zeus looked like an Egyptian, but Stephanie West thinks that it indicates Ethiopian, not Egyptian ("Io and the Dark Stranger [Sophocles, *Inachus* F 269a]," *Classical Quarterly* 34 [1984] 292–97); so also Richard Carden, *The Papyrus Fragments of Sophocles,* Berlin, 1974, pp. 70–71 ("negro Zeus"), and Dana Sutton, *Sophocles' Inachus,* Meisenheim am Glan, 1979, p. 43 ("Negro . . . or perhaps 'sunburnt'"). Lobel notes that αἰθός means "burnt black, sooty" and that κάρβανος, "is thought to mean 'foreign'and is used by Aeschylus, in two out of the three places where he has it, with reference to the Egyptian descendants of Io." The derivation of the non-Greek κάρβανος is disputed (see Carden); it may be the Latin *carbo* 'coal' (so LSJ), which would well fit the view that Zeus disguised himself as a black African.

116. Aeschylus, *Suppliants* 312–16; Apollodorus, *Bibliotheca* 2.1.4. The description of Epaphus as κελαινός is in Aeschylus, *Prometheus* 851. In classical sources Libya means the continent of Africa; see above, p. 251, n. 65. Euripides is quoted in Apollodorus. For Phineus meaning Nubia, see p. 39 and Konrat Ziegler, *RE* 20/1:216.

117. R. Merkelbach and M. L. West, *Fragmenta Hesiodea,* Oxford, 1967, p. 74, frag. 150 (= *POxy* XI 1358 frag. 2), who take "Blacks" as a proper name, and understand Zeus's son to be "Scythia." Other readings have been proposed; see Snowden in *Lexicon Iconographicum Mythologiae Classicae,* ed. John Boardman et al. (Zurich, 1981–), 1/1: 414.

118. West, "Io and the Dark Stranger," p. 295.

119. Ibid., p. 297. West thinks that the etiology is meant to account for national character as well because Zeus is depicted in terms (master of charms or drugs, sly, crafty) that were said to be characteristic of the Egyptians.

120. Snowden, "Asclepiades' Didyme," pp. 242–44.

121. See above, p. 9.

122. Veronika Görög-Karady, "Noirs et blancs: a propos de quelques mythes d'origine vili," in *Itinérances—en pays peul et ailleurs* (Paris, 1981), 2:82–83, 88–89. For examples of black African skin color etiologies, in addition to those listed in Görög-Karady, see Goldenberg, "The Curse of Ham," pp. 40–41, n. 15, and add the following: Eduard Pechuel-Loesche, *Volkskunde von Loango* (Stuttgart, 1907), p. 268; M. J. and F. S. Herskovitz, *Dahomean Narrative* (Evanston, Ill., 1958), pp. 407–9; Sollors, *Neither Black nor White Yet Both,* p. 41, citing a Dogon etiology; R. R. Earl, *Dark Symbols, Obscure Signs: God, Self, and Community in the Slave Mind* (Maryknoll, N.Y., 1993), pp. 49–50, quoting an etiology told by an American ex-slave. Some skin color etiologies are recorded also in Native American traditions: John R. Swanton, *Myths and Tales of the Southeastern Indians,* Bureau of American Ethnology, Bulletin 88 (Washington, D.C., 1929), pp. 74–75; Hartley B. Alexander in *The Mythology of All Races,* vol. 11: *Latin America,* ed. Louis H. Gray (New York, 1964), p. 271; R. Erdoes and A. Oritz, ed., *American Indian Myths and Legends* (New York, 1984), pp. 46–47; Sollors, p. 39 (see literature cited there). See also Dähnhardt, *Natursagen,* 1:157, for a folktale from Brazil.

123. David Wiesen, "Juvenal and the Blacks," *Classica et Mediaevalia* 31 (1970) 142–43. See, e.g., Claudian, *War against Gildo* 193, who in referring to the children of Ethiopians or Nasamonians and Roman women, says: "[T]he discolored infant frightens its crib [*exterret cunabula discolor infans*]." Thompson agrees with Wiesen's interpretation of *decolor,* although he understands Juvenal to be expressing sensory aversion to black skin rather than race prejudice (*Romans and Blacks,* pp. 26–28, 130).

124. Cohen, *The French Encounter with Africans,* p. 13; similarly, 82, 83, and see 236–37.

125. Jean Devisse in *IBWA* 2/1:221, n. 179. The point was also made by John Hunwick, "A Region of the Mind: Medieval Arab Views of African Geography and Ethnography and Their Legacy," an unpublished lecture given at the Program of African Studies, Northwestern University, 15 February 1993, p. 19. My thanks to Professor Hunwick for the copy of his talk.

126. *Politics* 7.6.1, trans. H. Rackham (LCL).

127. Another difference between the environmental theory and the etiology (rabbinic or Greek) is of interest. The theory directly links physical and nonphysical characteristics, both of which are explicitly or implicitly considered as inferior or superior, while the etiology has no reference to nonphysical characteristics. On this point and its relationship to racist thinking, see David Goldenberg, "The Development of the Idea of Race," pp. 561–70.

CHAPTER EIGHT

1. Ran Zadok cited above, p. 238, n. 95; see also p. 236, n. 81.

2. In the following listing I do not include the Greek *Life of Adam and Eve* (*Apocalypse of Moses*) 35:4–36:3. In this text, Eve has a vision and sees the sun and moon praying to God over Adam's dead body. "Who are the two Ethiopians as-

sisting at the prayer for your father?" she asks Seth. She calls them Ethiopians because they cannot shine when standing before "the Light of All Things, the Father of Light" (text and translation with Georgian and Slavonic parallels in Gary Anderson and Michael Stone, *A Synopsis of the Books of Adam and Eve,* 2nd rev. ed., Atlanta, 1999, pp. 80–81). Clearly, the text is not speaking specifically of ethnic Ethiopians, as can be seen in M. D. Johnson's translation "dark-skinned persons" (*OTP* 2:289). If there is a Semitic Jewish *Vorlage* to the Greek *Life* (dated before 400 C.E.), as some presume, it would argue for a Jewish use of *kushi* meaning "dark-skinned person" or even "dark-skinned thing." However, proofs for both propositions (Semitic and Jewish) have recently been called into question. See the discussion by Michael Stone and Gideon Bohak in M. Stone, *A History of the Literature of Adam and Eve* (Atlanta, 1992), pp. 53–61.

3. *mBekh* 7.6; cf. *Sifra, Emor, pereq* 3.1–7 (pp. 95c–d). For an explanation of the law, see above, p. 96.

4. *bBekh* 45b.

5. So also the dictionaries of Ben-Yehuda and Yaʿakov Kenaʿani, *Oṣar ha-Lashon ha-ʿIvrit li-Tequfoteha ha-Shonot* (Tel-Aviv, 1960–87), s.v. *kushi.* Along the same lines, David Qimḥi (d. 1235) suggested that the Kushite in King David's army (2 Sam 18:21) may have been a very dark-skinned Jew (in Kimḥi's commentary to the passage).

6. *tBer* 6/7.3. The reading *bohaq,* and its translation, which is not certain, follow Lieberman, *Tosefta ki-Fshuṭah,* ad loc., 1:106, where also parallels are cited. After *nanas,* the parallel in *bBer* 58b adds *hdrnyqws* (many variants in spelling), which is translated "dropsical" in the English translations of Maurice Simon (Soncino Press) and Jacob Neusner. This seems to be based on Jastrow (*Dictionary,* p. 335, s.v. *hidroqan*), who derives the word from ὑδρωπικόν or ὑδερικόν. Levy (*Wörterbuch über die Talmudim,* 1:262) reads *bardanikos* for *wardanikos* deriving it from ῥοδινικός and translating "rose-red complexion." Lieberman cites geonic traditions (also in *ʿArukh*) that the word means "very tall" and thinks that the corresponding Greek may be either ἀνδρογίγας or δράκων. The "dropsical" translations, despite the resemblance to the Greek, would seem to be wrong since the list of extremes are not symptoms of diseases. Regarding, *bohaq* and *giḥor,* Alex Thein, a graduate student at the University of Pennsylvania, calls my attention to Plutarch's description of Sulla's complexion as "covered with coarse blotches of red, interspersed with white" (*Lives,* Sulla 2.1) and to Ovid, *Fasti* 6.149–50.

7. So, e.g., Tzvee Zahavy translates "Negro" in *The Tosefta,* ed. Jacob Neusner and Richard Sarason (New York, 1986), 1:36, although in his translation of the Tosefta in *pBer* (Neusner, ed., *The Talmud of the Land of Israel,* 1:319) Zahavy has "black-skinned person." Similarly giving a black African meaning are C. Horowitz in his translation of the Tosefta in *pBer* 9.2, 13b (*Der Jerusalemer Talmud in deutscher Übersetzung,* Tübingen, 1975, 1:225), and William Braude in his translation of Hayim Nahman Bialik and Yehoshua Hana Ravnitzky's *Sefer ha-Aggadah, The Book of Legends (Sefer Ha-Aggadah): Legends from the Talmud and Midrash* (New York, 1993), p. 535, no. 259, but see their comment to the text. Some early-modern rabbinic authorities who thought that *kushi* meant black African and who understood the blessing as praising God for His creation of the unusual (cf.

Braude's translation of *meshaneh ha-beriyot* as "strange creatures") declared the tannaitic law invalid when the Black was no longer an unusual part of the human landscape in the Jewish world. See Jacob b. Samuel Ḥagiz (seventeenth-century, Israel), *Halakhot Qeṭanot* (Jerusalem, 1981), part 1, sec. 240, and Isaac Lampronti's (1679–1756, Italy), *Paḥad Yiṣḥaq,* 1813 (repr., Jerusalem, n.d.), s.v. *kushi.* The much-discussed view of the Rabad (as cited by Jacob b. Asher [d.1340], *Ṭur Oraḥ Ḥayyim* 225, and others) that the blessing indicates sympathy for the "afflicted" refers not to the blessing under discussion but to another that is pronounced upon seeing the crippled, the blind, the leprous, etc. See *Ṭaz, Magen Abraham,* the Gaon of Vilna (to *Shulḥan ʿArukh*), *Baḥ* (to *Ṭur*), and Yeruḥam b. Meshullam (as cited by *Magen Abraham*), ad loc.

8. Cf. the language used in the *Yelamedenu* fragment in L. Ginzberg, *Ginzei Schechter,* 1:54, *levarekh ule-qales* 'to bless and to praise'.

9. S. Sauneron collected those Egyptian texts that differentiate humanity by language. The Hymn to Amun-Re is one of three such texts which also include skin color with language as markers of difference (some include as well diet and physical appearance). See S. Sauneron, "La différenciation des langages d'après la tradition égyptienne," *Bulletin. Institut français d'archéologie Orientale* 60 (1960) 31–41. My translation is of Sauernon's French. See also E. Cruz-Uribe, *Hibis Temple Project,* vol. 1: *Translations, Commentary, Discussions and Sign List* (San Antonio, 1988), p. 128.

10. The translation of the Egyptian text is a combination of John L. Foster, *Hymns, Prayers, and Songs: An Anthology of Ancient Egyptian Lyric Poetry* (Atlanta, 1995), pp. 104–5, and Hellmut Brunner in Walter Beyerlin, *Near Eastern Religious Texts Relating to the Old Testament* (Philadelphia, 1978; originally in German, 1975), p. 18. The Egyptian word *ynm* is translated as "color of skin," or "complexion" (de Garis Davies, *The Rock Tombs of El Amarna,* 6:30; see Erman and Grapow, *Wörterbuch,* 1:96). Others translate "skins" with, obviously, the same meaning; see John A. Wilson in Pritchard, *Ancient Near Eastern Texts,* 3rd ed., p. 370; James H. Breasted, *The Dawn of Conscience* (New York, 1933), p. 284; A. Erman, *The Literature of the Ancient Egyptians* (New York, 1927; originally in German, 1923), p. 290; D. W. Thomas, *Documents from Old Testament Times* (London, 1958), p. 147; M. Lichtheim, *Ancient Egyptian Literature,* 2:98; cf. also Foster, pp. 60–61 (Papyrus Boulaq XVII). The word *qd* can mean either "nature" or "form" (*Wörterbuch,* 5:72) and is translated variously in the editions cited here. My thanks to David Silverman for help with the Egyptian text. The hymn is ascribed to Akhenaton (1350–1334 B.C.E.).

11. Reading and translation follow J. M. Baumgarten in *DJD* 18:76–77. The words ברוכ את are written above the line in the manuscript fragment. Incidentally, recognition of this topos in the Qumran fragment confirms Baumgarten's reconstruction of [ע]מים as opposed to [ש]מים, which had been proposed in earlier readings and translations. 4Q266 is the oldest of the Qumran fragments of this work having been written in the Hasmonaean period (*DJD* 18:2).

12. Y. Yadin, *The Scroll of the War of the Sons of Light against the Sons of Darkness* (Oxford, 1962), pp. 304–9, whose translation I adopt, with the exception of my "peoples" for his "nations" and "lands" for "countries"; in Yadin's original Hebrew edition, the text is on pp. 316–20.

13. Cf. Moshe Greenberg's remark in a different context examining Jewish (primarily, biblical and rabbinic) views toward different peoples: "Individual differences are esteemed as testimonies to the creative greatness of God" ("Mankind, Israel and the Nations in the Hebraic Heritage," in *No Man is Alien: Essays on the Unity of Mankind,* ed. J. R. Nelson, Leiden, 1971, p. 19).

14. E.g., Rashi (d. 1104) to *bBer* 58b; Meiri (d. 1306), *Bet ha-Beḥirah,* ed. Samuel Dikman, 2nd ed. (Jerusalem, 1965), ad loc., p. 207; Israel b. Joseph al-Naqawah (d. 1391), *Menorat ha-Maʾor,* ed. H. G. Enelow, 4:463; David Abudarham (fourteenth century), *Abudarham ha-Shalem,* ed. S. Werthheimer (Jerusalem, 1963), p. 343; Y. Abramsky; *Ḥazon Yeḥezkiel* (Vilna, 1925), 1:25, to *tBer* 6.1.

15. *mNeg* 2.1; *Sifra, Negaʿim* 1.4–5 (p. 60a–b).

16. So, e.g., Israel Lifschitz (d. 1860) in *Tifʾeret Yisraʾel* (Vilna, 1927), *Yakhin,* ad loc.; Ḥ. Albeck, in his edition of the Mishnah (Jerusalem, 1952–58), ad loc.; J. Neusner, *The Mishnah: A New Translation* (New Haven, 1988), p. 983, and *Sifra: An Analytical Translation* (Atlanta, 1988), 2:260; and Preuss, *Biblisch-talmudische Medizin,* p. 382 (English edition, trans. Rosner, p. 332).

17. Hai Gaon (d. 1038), *Perush ha-Geʾonim le-Seder Toharot,* ed. J. N. Epstein, p. 94; Nathan b. Yeḥiel (d. ca. 1110), *ʿArukh,* ed. Kohut, 2:368, s.v. *grmn;* Maimonides (d. 1204) in his *Commentary to the Mishnah,* ad loc., ed. Y. Qapeḥ (Kafah), 6/1:343; and Rabad (d. 1198), *Commentary to Sifra,* ed. I. M. Weiss in his edition of *Sifra,* ad loc., p. 60a. It would appear that this translation of *germani* as "white skinned," rather than "German," constrained Maimonides and others to provide a forced etymology of the word from *grm* 'bone', i.e., 'very white'. So also Hillel b. Eliakim of Greece (twelfth century), *Commentary to Sifra,* ed. S. Koleditzky (Jerusalem, 1961), 1:190; and Shimshon of Sens (twelfth–thirteenth century) published in the Jerusalem, 1955 edition of *Sifra,* p. 52b. The etymology is given also by Nathaniel b. Yeshaʿya of Yemen (fourteenth century) for both *Germayah* 'Germany' and *Togarmah* 'Turkey' (*Meʾor ha-Afelah,* ed. Qapeḥ, pp. 62 and 72). Note also Brenner, *Colour Terms in the Old Testament,* p. 188, who, in referring to our mishnah, sees "*germa(o)ni* (= 'German') as a general denotation for 'white-skinned man.'"

18. See above, p. 44.

19. The Barbari are a people who lived in black Africa, in the area of today's Sudan and Somalia; see the discussion above, pp. 43–45.

20. So, e.g., Ben-Yehudah, *Dictionary,* 5:2308, s.v. *kushi;* Brenner, *Colour Terms in the Old Testament,* p. 190; *ʿArukh,* ed. Kohut, 4:348a, s.v. *kush.*

21. *mSuk* 3.6.

22. See *bSuk* 36a and the discussion in *pSuk* 3.6, 53d.

23. The text reads "a citron that comes from the *kushi*" but seems to mean "a citron that comes from Kush" as noted by Menaḥem b. Solomon ha-Meiri, *Beit ha-Beḥirah,* ad loc., and Aryeh Leib Yellin, *Yefei ʿEinayim,* ad loc., and as translated by Jacob Neusner in *The Talmud of the Land of Israel,* 17:78.

24. Alfasi, R. Ḥananel, Meiri, ad loc., Ibn Ghiyyat, *Shaʿare Simḥah* (Furth, 1861), *Hilkhot Lulav,* p. 106, Maimonides, *Mishneh Torah, Lulav* 8.8, Joseph Karo, *Shulkhan ʿArukh, Oraḥ Ḥayim,* 648.17. See further *Oṣar Meforeshei ha-Talmud,* ed. S. Kivelevitz et al. (Jerusalem, 1988), col. 280, n. 63.

25. *tMen* 9.9. ἡλιάζω means "to bake in the sun" (LSJ, s.v.). Note the quotation in LSJ from the anonymous *De incredibilibus* 17 to the effect that wine left in the sun results in a mature and strong product, contrary to the rabbinic implication. See also *ʿArukh,* ed. Kohut, 1:92a.

26. *bBB* 97a–b.

27. *Shaʿarei Simḥah, Hilkhot Qiddush,* p. 2. See also Samuel Krauss, *Talmudische Archäologie,* 2:239 Note Homer's αἴθοπα οἶνον (*Iliad* 4.259 etc.), although this is usually translated as "fiery wine," based on the meaning of αἰθός as "burnt"; see LSJ, s.v. αἴθιοψ, and Kober, *The Use of Color Terms in the Greek Poets,* p. 105. E. Mveng compares the modern Greek *mauros,* which means "black," "Negro," and "red wine." See his *Les sources grecques de l'histoire négro-africaine; depuis Homère jusqu'à Strabon* (Paris, 1972), p. 85.

28. *MidPs* 7.3. Although the passage is missing in ed. pr. and in five manuscripts (Florence, Bibl. Nat. Cod.13; Vat. Heb.76; Vat. Heb.81; London, Or. Ginsburg; Paris 152—see ed. Buber, p. 44, n. 20; the passage is found in MSS Parma and Halberstam), it would seem to have been originally part of the text, for it forms a crucial linguistic connection (*kush*) to the verse in Ps 7:1.

29. First published by J. Mann, "Genizah Fragments of the Palestinian Order of Service," *HUCA* 2 (1925) 294, and now found in E. Fleischer, *Ha-Yoṣerot: be-Hithawutam we-Hitpatḥutam* (Jerusalem, 1984), p. 54. My thanks to Sol Cohen who alerted me to this *piyyuṭ*. The Hebrew reads: *tešuʿah šelemah raʾu qedošim / ṣahalu peduyim ʿal śonʾehem / noraʾ miher lenaʿer / kušim yaḥad ṭibeʿam. . . .* Line 1 *tešuʿah* probably has Ex 15:2 *yeshuʿah* in mind; line 2 is based on Isa 24:14 *ṣahalu mi-yam* with a probable echo of Ex 15:10 *ṣalalu;* line 3 is based on Ex 14:27 (Ps 136:15) and 15:11 (*noraʾ*); line 4 *ṭibeʿam* plays on Ex 15:4 *ṭubeʿu be-yam.* See also the remark of Zechariah ben Solomon ha-Rofé (fourteenth century), *Midrash ha-Ḥefeṣ,* ed. Meir Ḥavaṣelet, 1:110, "Kush is Egypt."

30. Above, p. 18.

31. See above, chapter 7, esp. pp. 107–9.

32. *GenR* 86.3 (p. 1055), which see for parallel sources. In addition to the references listed by Theodor-Albeck, M. Bialik Lerner calls to my attention the reading of an Oxford manuscript of *Tanḥuma* (quoted by Buber in his edition of *Tanḥuma,* Introduction, p. 128, sec. 16): "The *germani* sells the *kushi,* the *kushi* doesn't sell the *germani;* for the Midianites are darker [*sheḥorim yoter*] than the Ishmaelites." The statement is transmitted anonymously. *Genesis Rabba* was probably redacted in the first half of the fifth century.

33. Theodor, ad loc., with reference to *Perush ha-Geonim le-Seder Toharot,* ed. J. N. Epstein, p. 94; *ʿArukh,* s.v. *german;* also note the comments of Issachar Berman Ashkenazi, *Matenot Kehunah,* and Z. W. Einhorn, *Perush Maharzaw* to *GenR* 86.3. The *ʿArukh,* ed. Kohut, 4:348a, s.v. *kush,* also defines *kushi* in *GenR* 41/42.4 ("Amrafel had three names: Kush, Nimrod, and Amrafel. Kush because he was a real *kushi.*") as referring to skin color, not ethnicity; cf. Theodor ad loc., and below, n. 96. It is probable that a Germanos ben Judah, who appears as the scribe of one of the Babatha documents, was given his name because of his light skin. The document was published by N. Lewis and J. C. Greenfield, *The Documents from the Bar Kokhba Period in the Cave of Letters: Greek Papyri* (Jerusalem, 1989), p. 117, no. 27. To assume, otherwise, that his name indicates his origin (see

above, p. 131 regarding the name Meroe), would require us to consider him a Jewish slave (his father's name was Judah) from Germany, a less likely proposition at that time. "Germani" who is a slave of R. Judah Nesi'ah (*yShab* 8, 8c; *yYoma* 8.5, 45b), on the other hand, may be named after his country of origin. Germanus (Germanicus, Germana) are common Roman slave names, which derive from the country of origin; see J. Baumgart, Die römischen Sklavennamen (Ph.D. diss., University of Breslau, 1936), pp. 22–23, 61.

34. Quoted by Karras, *Slavery and Society,* pp. 56–57.

35. This tripartite division of society by complexion is found in the Old Norse "Eddic" poem, the *Rigsthula* (scholars vary in dating the work from the ninth to the thirteenth century), and in several other medieval texts: an Old English work from the ninth century, the twelfth-century *Imago mundi* of Honorius Augustodnensis, the thirteenth-century *Weltchronik* of Jansen Enikel, and the fourteenth-century *Cursor mundi.* See Thomas D. Hill, "*Rígsþula:* Some Medieval Christian Analogues," *Speculum* 61 (1986) 79–89; Mellinkoff, *Outcasts,*1:149; Sarah M. Horrall, ed., *The Southern Version of Cursor Mundi* (Ottawa, 1978), 2133–36, 1:102–3. See also Thomas Gamkrelidze and Vjačeslav Ivanov, *Indo-European and the Indo-Europeans: A Reconstruction and Historical Analysis of a Proto-Language and a Proto-Culture* (Berlin, 1995), 1:689 and n. 18, and 1:690, n. 20, for the association of social classes with color in ancient India and Iran. Jan de Vries collected numerous stories, legends, poems, songs, etc.—mostly from the Indo-European world—showing a tripartitie color scheme of black, red, white. De Vries's article, originally written in 1942, is summarized by G. Dumézil, "'Tripertita' fonctionnels chez divers peuples indo-européens," *Revue de l'Histoire des Religions* 131 (1946) 57–60, from which I draw. Dumézil later expanded these ideas in his *Rituels indo-européens a rome* (Paris, 1954), pp. 44–61. In his material white often symbolizes the priestly caste, red the warrior caste, and black the agriculturalists. Note also Romila Thapar's comment that the word *varna,* which is used to designate the different castes in India, derives from a root meaning "color" and designates "social differentiation symbolized in colours [as] is not unusual in the traditions of many early societies" ("Durkheim and Weber on Theories of Society and Race Relating to Pre-colonial India," in Thapar, *Cultural Pasts: Essays in Early Indian History,* p. 26; the article originally appeared in *Sociological Theories: Race and Colonialism,* ed. Marion O'Callaghan, Paris, 1980, 93–116). Another common scheme saw the division of society into three classes deriving from the three sons of Noah. On this, see Freedman, *Images of the Medieval Peasant,* pp. 99ff.; cf. Freedman, "Sainteté et sauvagerie: deux images du paysan au moyen age," *Annales. Économies, sociétés, civilisations,* May–June 1992, no. 3, pp. 549–50. See also Cristopher Hill, *The English Bible and the Seventeenth-Century Revolution* (London, 1993), p. 118.

36. Karras, *Slavery and Society,* pp. 56–68.

37. Kristen Hastrup, *Culture and History in Medieval Iceland* (Oxford, 1985), pp. 107–8, regarding the references in Icelandic literature to slaves as "blackish" (*hörfi svartan*).

38. John Lindow, "Supernatural Others and Ethnic Others," *Scandinavian Studies* 67/1 (1995) 12–28. The terms used for "blackman," *blámaðr* (Icelandic) and *blamaþær* (Old Swedish), actually mean "blue man" but Lindow notes that

blár was only used to indicate an ethnic difference since *svartr* was used for swarthy Nordic people. The meaning of the term, however, was "black" as can be seen by the descriptions of a *blámaðr*, "who is black as coal on his body" (*som er kolblár á sinn líkama*), or of another as "blacker than pitch" (*biki svartari*), or another as "black and stout as a bull" (*svartr ok digr sem naut*), or "black as hell" (*blár sem hel*).

39. *De parasito* 41, trans. A. M. Harmon (LCL).

40. See chapter 9, esp. nn. 1 and 45.

41. A. M. Devine, "Blacks in Antiquity? (The Case of Apollonios ὁ μέλας)," *Ancient History Bulletin* 2 (1988) 9.

42. Keith Bradley, *Slavery and Society at Rome* (Cambridge, 1994), pp. 142–43. See also the fifth-century Syriac Christian *Euphemia and the Goth,* where Euphemia's appearance as "fair and comely" (*špyrʾ wpʾyʾ*) is "witness that she is not like the slave-girls" (F. C. Burkitt, ed. and trans., *Euphemia and the Acts of Martyrdom of the Confessors of Edessa,* London, 1913, pp. 137 of the translation and 53–54 of the text). Burkitt dates the text to between 430 and 506 (pp. 57–60).

43. *LevR* 4.1 (p. 76) and parallels. For the variants and different interpretations, see Margulies's note, ad loc. Sokoloff, *Dictionary of Jewish Palestinian Aramaic,* p. 473, s.v. *qblʾy,* says that the meaning is "uncertain." The expression "dark one" (*bar qiblʾai, bar qibloy*), found in *LevR* 25.5 (p. 578) = *QohR* 2:20, apparently means "stupid," "fool," i.e., unenlightened. The Hebrew parallel, *ben afelah,* lit. "son of darkness," is found in *ARNb* 32, p. 35a, according to the medieval citation of Shimʿon Duran, *Magen Avot* 3.10 (quoted by Saul Lieberman, *Hellenism in Jewish Palestine,* p.12). A Syriac parallel, *brt ḥšwkʾ* 'daughter of darkness', is found in P. Bedjan, *Acta martyrum et sanctorum* (Paris and Leipzig, 1890–97; repr., Hildesheim, 1968), 2:596.

44. Fischer, *Farb- und Formbezeichnungen,* p. 275. Perhaps too because of the association of light skin with nobility, the prophet of Islam, Muḥammad, is traditionally described as having light skin color. On Muḥammad's skin color, see Vollers, "Ueber Rassenfarben in der arabischen Literatur," p. 90.

45. In his commentary to Isa 34:12. My thanks to my colleague Sol Cohen for this reference, as well as the reference to the *piyyuṭ* and Speier's article mentioned below (n. 49).

46. Curry, *The Middle English Ideal of Personal Beauty,* p. 87.

47. Kim F. Hall, *Things of Darkness: Economies of Race and Gender in Early Modern England* (Ithaca, N.Y., 1995), pp. 1–7; quotation on 6–7.

48. Nederveen Pieterse, *White on Black: Images of Africa and Blacks in Western Popular Culture,* p. 215.

49. *Pace* Baron, *A Social and Religious History of the Jews,* 2:238. An illustration of the Selling of Joseph in the fourteenth-century Sarajevo Haggadah depicts the Ishmaelites as Blacks with negroid features (reproduced in facsimile, *The Sarajevo Haggadah,* New York, 1963, with introduction by Cecil Roth, folio 13; see p. 19). It is tempting to see in this a misunderstanding of the term *kushi* in *GenR* 86.3, but the origin of this depiction may lie elsewhere. Paul Kaplan writes that in Christian iconography Midianites (Ishmaelites) are repeatedly depicted as Black, both in Byzantium and the West, and this is primarily so in the story of Joseph. See his "The Rise of the Black Magus in Western Art" (revised Ph.D. diss., Boston University,

1985), p. 8, and *Ruler, Saint and Servant,* pp. 4–8, where he mentions several examples from the eleventh to the fourteenth century, and pp. 71–74, 174–81, for the depiction of Arabs, in general, in Christian Byzantine art as Black. Such representation goes back earlier than the eleventh century. A Christian Coptic tapestry from the seventh–eighth century, depicting the Selling of Joseph, shows the Midianite/Ishmaelite as a black African surrounded by white figures. See E. Kitzinger, "The Story of Joseph on a Coptic Tapestry," *Journal of the Warburg Institute* 1 (1937–38) 266–68, who notes the similarity to the illustrations in the Byzantine Seraglio Octateuch, which "also imagined the Ishmaelites to look like Nubians or Ethiopians." In other words, the Sarjevo Haggadah may be representative of this iconographic tradition. On the other hand, the midrash was clearly the basis for the characterization of Joseph as a *germani* in the land of Ham in Benjamin b. Zeraḥ's eleventh-century liturgical poem, *Omeret ani maʿaśai la-melekh.* See S. Speier, "Critical Remarks on the Text of the Additional Portion for Sabbath Hagadol according to the Ashkenazic Ritual," *JQR* 38 (1948) 461, n. 1, for literature on this text. And it may have been the source for Moses Arragel's Castilian translation (1433) of "Moors" for Ishmaelites in Gen 37:27–28, 39:1 and for Midianites in 37:36 (I cite Arragel from M. McGaha, *Coat of Many Cultures: The Story of Joseph in Spanish Literature, 1200–1492* [Philadelphia, 1997], pp. 15, 17).

50. *Testament of Joseph* 11.2–3; translation H. C. Kee in *OTP* 1:822. Kee and Charlesworth are of the opinion that the *Testaments* is basically a Jewish document (second century B.C.E.) with later Christian interpolations, while M. de Jonge thinks it is a Christian composition (second century C.E.) built upon Jewish traditions (*OTP* 1:777–78; Hollander and de Jonge, *The Testaments of the Twelve Patriarchs: A Commentary,* pp. 83–85).

51. Ὄψις is the reading according to both recensions of the Greek text; see R. H. Charles ed., *The Greek Versions of the Testaments of the Twelve Patriarchs* (Oxford, 1908), p. 199, and M. de Jonge, ed., *The Testaments of the Twelve Patriarchs: A Critical Edition of the Greek Text* (Leiden, 1978), p. 157. For the meaning of the word, see LSJ, s.v. and William F. Arndt and F. Wilbur Gingrich, *A Greek-English Lexicon of the New Testament and Other Early Christian Literature,* 2nd ed., rev. Frederick W. Danker (Chicago, 1979), s.v.; for the Armenian, see Michael E. Stone, ed., *The Armenian Version of the Testament of Joseph* (Missoula, Mont., 1975), p. 39.

52. Aubrey Diller, *Race Mixture among the Greeks before Alexander* (Westport, Conn., 1937), pp. 143–47, provides a discussion of the various slave classes in Greece.

53. Philo, *De Iosepho* 106.

54. E. Isaac, "The Ethiopic History of Joseph: Translation with Introduction and Notes," *JSP* 6 (1990) 52–53.

55. McGaha, *Coat of Many Cultures,* pp. 87, 95; see also Ginzberg, *Legends of the Jews,* 2:15, 5:329, n. 49. On the date of *Sefer ha-Yashar,* see below, p. 346, n. 47.

56. McGaha, *Coat of Many Cultures,* p. 175 (see also 185). Cf. the Jewish Palestinian Aramaic poem that refers to Joseph as having "the appearance (*demut*) of a king . . . he is of royalty" (Joseph Yahalom and Michael Sokoloff, *Shirat Benei Maʿarava,* Jerusalem, 1999, pp. 136–37.

57. McGaha, *Coat of Many Cultures,* p. 346.

58. Ibid., p. 430.

59. In his *Midrash ha-Ḥefes,* ed. Meir Ḥavaṣelet, 1:232.

60. On the theme of Joseph's good looks and its development in postbiblical literature, see James Kugel, *In Potiphar's House* (New York, 1990), pp. 28–33, 66–75, 86–89, and Shalom Goldman, *The Wiles of Women, the Wiles of Men: Joseph and Potiphar's Wife in Ancient Near Eastern, Jewish and Islamic Folklore* (Albany, N.Y., 1995), pp. 81–83, 89. In addition, note that *Testament of Simeon* 5.1 and Josephus, *Antiquities* 2.9 make reference to Joseph's beauty, as does, from a later period, the Middle English *Iacob and Iosep,* where Joseph's face shone bright (F. Faverty, "Legends of Joseph in Old and Middle English Literature," *Publications of the Modern Language Association of America* 43 [1928] 79), recalling the "gleaming countenance" of Saxo Grammaticus.

61. The association of dark skin with slave, as found in *GenR* 86, may lie behind an enigmatic text in Menaḥem b. Solomon's twelfth-century work, *Midrash Sekhel Ṭov* (provenance unknown). The text interprets the name *Ḥori* (Seir the Horite) in Gen 36:20 as "manumitted [*meshuḥrarin*], for in the words of our rabbis a manumitted person [*meshuḥrar*] is called white [*ḥiwer*], and they are called *trpwly* for they are free but not completely free," and goes on to explain that the Horites were included in the curse of slavery imposed on Canaan but during the confusion of languages at the Tower of Babel, the Horites fled to Seir (ed. S. Buber, Berlin, 1900–1901, 1:207). The word *trpwly,* not found elsewhere in rabbinic literature to my knowledge, must be related to the Greek θεράπων 'servant' (as opposed to δοῦλος 'slave'), that is, one who is "free but not completely free." If the reading of *ḥywr* is correct (I have not seen the single manuscript of *Sekhel Ṭov*) and if its translation is indeed "white," then the text may possibly be explained by reference to the association of dark skin with slave as evinced in *GenR* 86. If a slave is seen as dark, upon manumission he or she may have been considered metaphorically whitened.

62. *NumR* 9.34; *TanḥB, Naso*ʾ 13 (p. 31); *Tanḥuma, Naso*ʾ 7. The story as found in *GenR* 73.10 according to the printed edition and one manuscript (see ed. Theodor-Albeck, p. 854) has a nondescript "king" without any further identification.

63. Ullendorff, "Hebraic-Jewish Elements in Abyssinian (Monophysite) Christianity," pp. 220–21, and *Ethiopia and the Bible,* p. 17; S. Krauss, "Talmudische Nachrichten über Arabien," *ZDMG* 70 (1916) 325–26 and n. 3. Similarly, Preuss translated *kushi* here as Ethiopian ("Mohr") in his *Biblisch-talmudische Medizin,* p. 454; Rosner's English translation, *Biblical and Talmudic Medicine,* however, renders the word "black" (p. 392).

64. G. Rentz in *EI*^{2} 1:548b–549a, s.v. Djazīrat al-ʿArab; ʿAbd al-Muhsin Madʿaj M. al-Madʿaj, *The Yemen in Early Islam 9–233/630–847* (London, 1988), pp. 2–3. Philip Hitti, *History of the Arabs,* 8th ed. (London, 1963), p. 60.

65. For examples from the classical world, see Balsdon, *Romans and Aliens,* p. 218; Snowden, *Before Color Prejudice,* pp. 95–96; Thompson, *Romans and Blacks,* p. 197, n. 17; Owsei Temkin, *Soranus' Gynecology* (Baltimore, 1956; 1991), pp. 37–38, n. 17. For the Middle Ages: Kaplan, *Ruler, Saint and Servant,* p. 240, n. 267; Lynn Thorndike, "De complexionibus," *Isis* 49 (1958) 400. For the early

modern period and later: Barker, *The African Link,* pp. 86–87 (who cites Thomas Browne and notes that in eighteenth-century England this was a common belief); Jordan, *White over Black,* p. 12 and note; J. A. Rogers, *Sex and Race* (New York, 1940), 1:2–4, 137, 261. See also Ch. M. Horowitz, *Tosfata ʿAtiqata* (Frankfort am Main, 1890), 4:4; Theodor's note to *GenR* 73.10; and *Sefer Niṣaḥon* 238, ed. D. Berger, pp. 159 (Hebrew), 224 (English). Medieval Jewish tales about a white child of black parents (the R. Akiba story), as well as a black child of white parents, are found in Moses Gaster, ed., The *Maʿaseh Book* (Phildelphia, 1934), pp. 648–49, no. 248, for the former case, and pp. 240–44, no. 134, for the latter; see also "Baraita de-Masekhet Nidah," in Horowitz, *Tosfata ʿAtiqata,* 5:56; J. Trachtenberg, *Jewish Magic and Superstition* (New York, 1939), p. 187 and note; and *Kalah Rabbati* 3.6, ed. Higger (New York, 1936), p. 231; cf 1.11, p. 181. As late as the nineteenth century: Ṣevi Hirsch Chajes, *Darkhe ha-Horaʾah* (Zolkiew, Galicia, 1848) now reprinted in *Kol Sifre Maharaṣ Chajes* (Jerusalem, 1958), 1:216.

66. E.g., Steven Kaplan, *The Beta Israel (Falasha) in Ethiopia: From Earliest Times to the Twentieth Century* (New York, 1992), p. 31, following Ullendorff, *Ethiopia and the Bible,* p. 17. Ch. Z. Hirschberg, *Israel in Arabia* (in Hebrew; Tel Aviv, 1946), p. 40, is more circumspect, citing the story merely as evidence of a visit by R. Akiba to Arabia, which is mentioned elsewhere (*bRH* 26a). On the idea and uses of maternal impression throughout history, see M. Reeve, "Conception," *Proceedings of the Cambridge Philological Society* 215 (1989) 81–112.

67. See p. 136.

68. *Kitāb al-Jāmiʿ al-sahīh: Le recueil des traditions mahométanes par Abou Abdallah Mohammed ibn Ismaīl el-Bokhāri,* ed. M. L. Krehl and T. W. Juynboll (Leiden, 1862–1908), 4:431. French translation in O. Houdas and W. Marçais, *El-Bokhâri: les traditions islamiques traduites de l'arabe* (Paris, 1903–14), 3:628. An English translation of the passage is found in John A. Williams, *Islam* (New York, 1962), pp. 83–84.

69. Rotter, *Die Stellung des Negers,* p. 20. See also above, pp. 106–7.

70. P. Mayerson, "A Confusion of Indias: Asian India and African India in the Byzantine Sources," *JAOS* 113 (1993) 169–74.

71. George F. Hourani, *Arab Seafaring in the Indian Ocean in Ancient and Early Medieval Times,* 2nd ed., rev. and expanded by John Carswell (Princeton, 1995), p. 39.

72. See Jehan Desanges, "L'Afrique noire et le monde méditerranéen dans l'Antiquité (Éthiopiens et Gréco-Romains)," *Revue francaise d'histoire d'outre-mer* 62 (1975) 404.

73. On the Ethiopian/Indian confusion, see the literature cited in Appendix II.

74. J. B. Segal, *Encyclopaedia Iranica,* ed. Ehsan Yarshater (London, 1985–), 1:211a.

75. *Annals* 12.12–14. Not surprisingly, therefore, *LamR* 1.5.31 ed. Romm (= ed. Buber, p. 63), refers to a certain Abgar as a *dux* (military leader) of Arabia under the command of Vespasian. On Abgar in this text, see Y. Baer, "Yerushalayim bi-Ymei ha-Mered," *Zion* 34 (1971) 171–72. (My thanks to Paul Mandel for this reference.) M. Hadas-Lebel has noted that use of the term *dux* is indicative "of the military organization of the late empire and thus confirms that the midrash is narrating past events in language of its own time (4th century)" ("Emprunts Grecs et

Latins dans la langue du Talmud et du Midrash," *Journées d'études de l'E.H.E.J.*, Clichy, 1987, p. 29); see also Hirschberg, *A History of the Jews in North Africa,* 1:35. Hans Zucker had expressed this opinion fifty years earlier in his *Studien zur jüdischen Selbsverwaltung in Altertum* (Berlin, 1936), p. 127, note. The *Biblical Antiquities* (6.13) of Pseudo-Philo, a Palestinian text dating from the first or second century, already uses *dux* (*SC* 229:98–99; *OTP,* 2:297ff.; James, *The Biblical Antiquities of Philo,* pp. 95–96; Jacobson, *A Commentary on Pseudo-Philo's Liber Antiquitatum Biblicarum,* pp. 11, 101). On the dating of Pseudo-Philo, see above, p. 285, n. 30. A discussion of the use of *dux* in rabbinic literature is found in S. Krauss, *Persia and Rome in the Talmud and Midrash* (in Hebrew), pp. 194–95. See also above, p. 239, n. 6.

76. So G. Phillips (*The Doctrine of Addai, the Apostle,* London, 1876, p. 1), noting that another king of Edessa was known as Abgar the Red (Sumaqa). A third king of this dynasty is called Abgar the Fair in an unpublished Syriac manuscript, the *Chronography of Elia of Nisibis* (Sebastian Brock and David Taylor, *The Hidden Pearl,* Rome, 2001, 1:157; Brock, "Some Basic Annotation to *The Hidden Pearl,*" *Hugoye: Journal of Syriac Studies* 5.1 [January 2002] note to 2:253). Payne Smith (*Thesaurus Syriacus,* 1:182, s.v. *ʾukāmāʾ*) cites Joannes D. Michaelis that the name derives from the effects of leprosy on Abgar's skin, but he also cites Bar Hebraeus to the contrary, that the leprosy made Abgar's skin white, and therefore the name "the black" must derive from antiphrastic substitution. So also A. Guillaumont, "La désignation des couleurs in hébreu et en araméen," in *Problèmes de la couleur,* ed. I. Meyerson (Paris, 1957), p. 341. Michaelis's theory actually has a much earlier pedigree, for Georgius Cedrenus (fl. ca. 1100) writes that Abgar sufferred from *black* leprosy, λέπρᾳ μελαίνῃ (*Compendium Historiarum,* ed. Immanuel Bekker, Corpus Scriptorum Historiae Byzantinae 34; Bonn, 1838, p. 310, lines 15–16), i.e., that his disease turned his skin color black. Another explanation has it that Abgar may have been blind and takes *ukkama* as realted to Syriac *kmh,* which can mean blind as well as black. So J. B. Segal, *Edessa: "The Blessed City"* (Oxford, 1970), p. 72.

77. *Bellum* 2.520 and 566.

78. Iiro Kajanto, *The Latin Cognomina* (Helsinki, 1965), p. 228 and index; see also L. R. Dean, *A Study of the Cognomina of Soldiers in the Roman Legions* (Princeton, 1916), p. 67. Such color nicknames were often used to distinguish two people of the same name (F. Münzer, *RE* 17/1:200). See for example "Apollonius the black [μέλας]" and "Apollonius the white [λευκὸς]" (as well as "Apollonius the baggage-carrier") mentioned side by side in a second-century B.C.E. papyrus, *The Amherst Papyri,* ed. Bernard P. Grenfell and Arthur S. Hunt (London, 1900–1901), no. 62, and Cleitus the white (λευκός) and Cleitus the black (μέλας), noted by A. M. Devine, "Blacks in Antiquity? (The Case of Apollonios ὁ μέλας)," *Ancient History Bulletin* 2 (1988) 9.

79. Arndt and Gingrich, *Lexicon,* s.v. Niger. In light of the evidence marshaled by Snowden (*Blacks in Antiquity,* pp. 3–5) that *niger* is often the equivalent of *Aethiops,* we cannot rule out the possibility that Niger of Peraea (or Simeon, for that matter) was an African. But see Devine, cited in the previous note, and Alan Cameron, "Black and White: A Note on Ancient Nicknames," *American Journal of Philology* 119 (1998) 113–17.

80. Addai Scher, "Notice sur la vie et les oeuvres de Yoḥannan bar Penkayê," *Journal Asiatique,* ser. 10, 10 (1907) 163 (text), 165 (translation). See also E.A.W. Budge, ed. and trans., *The Book of Governors: The Historia Monastica of Thomas Bishop of Margā A.D. 840* (London, 1893), 1:37 (Syriac) and 2:66–67 (English): a monk in a Mesopotamian monastery of the sixth–seventh century was called Ūkhāmā. See also Margoliouth, *Supplement to the Thesaurus Syriacus of R. Payne Smith,* p. 18, s.v. *ʾukamaʾ*. On the other hand, we cannot assume that every nickname "the black" originated from the color of one physiological feature or another, such as skin or hair. Paul the Black, patriarch of Antioch (564–81), for example, had this designation because of his association with Beth Ukkame; he is also known as Paul of Beth Ukkame. See *Encyclopedia of the Early Church,* ed. A. Di Berardino (New York, 1992), 2:662; on Paul in general, see W. Smith and H. Wace, *A Dictionary of Christian Biography* (London, 1887), 4:254–55; Payne Smith, *Thesaurus Syriacus,* 1:183.

81. A St. Elbod the Black (Elbod Ddu) mentioned in Nennius's version of the Historia Britonum is so called because of either his hair color or his swarthy complexion. See *Leabhar breathnach annso sis: The Irish Version of the Historia Britonum of Nennius,* ed. and trans. J. Henthorn Todd with additional notes by A. Herbert (Dublin, 1848), p. 6. The original Historia is dated to ca. 822 and Nennius's edition to ca. 858 (p. 18). Another example, this one Jewish but from a later period, is the name Samuel (ha-Nagid) ibn Nagrela, which means "son of a dark woman" (S. M. Stern, "Le-Toledot Rabbi Shmuʾel ha-Nagid," *Zion* 15 [1950] 135, n. 2, accepted by E. Ashtor, *The Jews of Moslem Spain,* Philadelphia, 1973; originally in Hebrew, 1960, 2:311, n. 10). For the possiblity of such usage also in ancient Egypt, see Hermann Grapow, *Die bildlichen Ausdrüdke des Aegyptischen* (Leipzig, 1924), p. 44.

82. Perhaps an association of dark skin with the Arab can explain the unique reading *kushi* in MS Munich of *GenR* 48.9 (p. 486). In the passage three names for Arabs are mentioned: Saracen, Nabatean, and Arab. MS Munich, however, replaces Nabatean with *kushi.* Is this due to a scribal assumption of dark-skinned Arabs? Cf. al-Dimashqī who lists the Nabateans (*nbṭ*) among the descendants of Ham together with the Copts, the *Brbr,* and the *Sūdān* (ed. Mehren, p. 266; trans., Mehren, *Manuel de la Cosmographie,* p. 385, excerpted in Levtzion and Hopkins, *Corpus,* p. 212), and the *Akhbār al-zamān* which lists the Nabīṭ among the children of Canaan, and continues, "Nabīṭ signifies 'black'" (see below, p. 352, n. 23). I have no other explanation for this strange reading, unless we assume a late echo of the name Kush (Kushu) for the peoples who lived at the southern border of Judaea (see above, pp. 19–20).

83. E. Fleischer, "A Historical Poem Describing Some Military Events in Syria and Ereẓ Israel in the Early 11th Century," *Zion* 52 (1987) 417–26 [in Hebrew]. My thanks to Menahem Ben-Sasson for the reference to this article.

84. Ibid., pp. 425–26.

85. The tosafist Jacob of Vienna, quoting anonymous others, *Sefer Peshaṭim we-Perushim ʿal Ḥamishah Ḥumshei Torah,* ed. M. Grossberg (Mainz, 1888), p. 151; and the Karaite Aaron b. Elijah, *Keter Torah* (Gozlow/Eupatoria, 1866–67), 4:16b. Similarly, Ibn Ezra, *Commentary to the Pentateuch,* ed. Asher Weiser [Vaizer] (Jerusalem, 1977), 3:147, and Baḥya, *Commentary to the Pentateuch,* ed. Chavel,

3:70. On Jacob of Vienna, his work, and the location of "Vienna," see Jacob Gellis, *Sefer Tosafot ha-Shalem* (Jerusalem, 1982), 1:19. Bar Hebraeus cites Ibn Ezra's explanation (anonymously: "others say") among a few interpretations (M. Sprengling and W. C. Graham, *Barhebraeus' Scholia on the Old Testament,* Chicago, 1931, pp. 196–97). S. Pincus, while drawing attention to Ibn Ezra, considers him to be the source of a different interpretation in Bar Hebraeus; see Pincus's "Die Scholien des Gregorius Abulfarag Barhebräus zum Buche Numeri" (Ph.D. diss, Friedrich-Wilhelms-Universität zu Breslau, 1913), pp. 12, 36.

86. Turkish: *Redhouse yeni Türkçe-İngilizce sözlük,* ed. V. Bahadir Alkim et al., 10th ed. (Istanbul, 1968), p. 69; see also Pertev N. Boratav, "The Negro in Turkish Folklore," *Journal of American Folklore* 64 (1951) 83; and Ehud R. Toledano, *The Ottoman Slave Trade and Its Suppression: 1840–1890* (Princeton, 1982), p. xiv. In Turkish, the same word also means "Arab," so that when it is necessary to distinguish Arab from Black, the Arab is called *ak-arap* "white-Arab" (*Redhouse,* p. 31). For modern Greek: *The Oxford Dictionary of Modern Greek,* ed. J. T. Pring (Oxford, 1982), p. 26, s.vv. ἀράπης, ἀραπίνα; the word for Arab is Ἄραψ. Russian: *Elsevier's Russian-English Dictionary,* ed. P. Macura (Amsterdam, 1990), 1:62, s.v. арап. Confusion of the meaning of this word presumably lies behind the strange statement in the Slavic *Chronicle of Moses* that Moses became king of the Saracens, rather than the Ethiopians (see Melissa Lee Farrall, "A Jewish Translator in Kievan Rus: A Critical Edition and Study of the Earliest Redaction of the Slavic 'Life of Moses,'" [Ph.D. diss., Brown University], 1981, pp. 23 and 47). In Yiddish the word is found in a manuscript of the sixteenth-century *Tze᾿ena u-Re᾿ena,* where *narap* appears as a variant for *kushi* and *shvartze* (Jacob ben Isaac Ashkenazi of Yanow, *Tze᾿ena u-Re᾿ena,* ed. with Hebrew translation by Israel M. Hurwitz, New York, 1985, p. 57). The word is clearly derived from *an arap/b,* a derivation suggested by Mordechai Schechter in a personal communication to Sol Cohen, to whom I owe some of the following information in this note. On the b/p change, cf. Palestinian Yiddish *arapish* for *arabish* (Alexander Harkavy, *Yiddish-English Dictionary,* 2nd ed., New York, 1928, p. 322, and Mordecai Kosover, *Arabic Elements in Palestinian Yiddish,* Jerusalem, 1966. On the b>p shift in Yiddish in general, see M. Weinreich, *The History of the Yiddish Language* (Chicago, 1980; originally in Yiddish, 1973), pp. 36, 436–37. Nahum Stutchkoff lists *narap* as a term for non-Jew, and he groups the word with other terms for Black; see his *Otsar fun der Yiddisher Shprach,* p. 168, sec. 236.

87. The text was published by Ginzberg in *Ginzei Schechter,* 1:313–23, and Yehuda Even-Shemuel, *Midreshei Ge᾿ulah,* 2nd ed. (Jerusalem, 1954), pp. 232–52, 408–11, but see Bonfils's comment on *Midreshei Ge᾿ulah,* in *Zion* 44 (1979) 111, n. 3. Andrew Sharf produced a study and English translation of the fragment in *Byzantinisch-neugriechische Jahrbücher* 20 (1970) 302–18, now reprinted in A. Sharf, *Jews and Other Minorities in Byzantium* (Jerusalem, 1995), pp. 119–35; see also his *Byzantine Jewry: From Justinian to the Fourth Crusade* (London, 1971), pp. 201–4. On the dating, see Ginzberg's comments and those of Even-Shemuel, pp. 244–45.

88. Samuel Krauss, "Ein neuer Text zum byzantinisch-jüdischen Geschichte," *Byzantinisch-Neugriechische Jahrbücher* 7 (1928–29) 67–68; the article also appeared in French in *REJ* 87 (1929), relevant pages 10–11. Similarly Robert Bon-

fils, who lately dealt with this text in "The 'Vision of Daniel' as a Historical and Literary Document" (in Hebrew), *Zion* 44 (1979) 111–147 and 56 (1991) 87–90, also accepts the Zaoutzes identification (44:128). I am indebted to Y. Sussman for bringing Bonfils's articles to my attention.

89. E. Kurtz, "Zwei griechische Texte über die heilge Theophano, die Gemahlin Kaisers Leo VI," in *Mémoires de l'Académie Impériale des Sciences de St.-Pétersbourg,* 8th series, Historical-philological section, vol. 3, no. 2 (St. Petersburg, 1898), pp. 11 (line 28) and 56. Ginzberg, Even-Shemuel, and Sharf also attempted to identify the *kushi,* but they were not aware of the Byzantine text. The first, as far as I could tell, to rely on the Greek text to explain the Hebrew was Romilly J. H. Jenkins, "The Chronological Accuracy of the 'Logothete' for the Years AD 867–913," *Dumbarton Oaks Papers* 19 (1965) 107, n. 72; reprinted in his *Studies on Byzantine History of the 9th and 10th Centuries* (London, 1970), ch. 3.

90. Steven Runciman, *The Byzantine Theocracy* (Cambridge, 1977), pp. 97 and 180, n. 39.

91. Romilly Jenkins, *Byzantium: The Imperial Centuries, AD 610–1071* (1966; repr., Toronto, 1987), p. 200.

92. Patricia Karlin-Hayter, *Vita Euthymii Patriarchae Cp.* (Brussells, 1970), p. 149. Shaun Tougher, *The Reign of Leo VI (886–912)* (Leiden, 1997), p. 90, n. 6. Sharf assumed as much for the Genizah text, translating *kushi* as "dark one." Tougher also refers to L. Rydèn's suggestion in "The Portrait of the Arab Samonas in Byzantine Literature," *Graeco-Arabica* 3 (1984) 107, that the apocalypse *Andrew the Holy Fool,* a tenth-century composition, also refers to Zaoutzes as an Ethiopian.

93. Epstein, *Kitvei Avraham Epstein,* 1:50; reprinted in Eisenstein, *Oṣar ha-Midrashim,* p. 22a.

94. Lemuel A. Johnson, *The Devil, the Gargoyle, and the Buffoon: The Negro as Metaphor in Western Literature* (Port Washington N.Y., 1969), p. 36; see also J. D. Forbes, *Africans and Native Americans: The Language of Race and the Evolution of Red-Black Peoples,* 2nd ed. (Urbana, 1993), pp. 67–68.

95. Desange, "L'Afrique noire et le monde méditerranéen dans l'Antiquité," p. 409, and "The Iconography of the Black in Ancient North Africa," *IBWA* 1:247 and 308, n. 20. Thompson, *Romans and Blacks,* pp. 60–62. Cf. also the tenth-century Arabic writer Iṣṭakhrī, who refers to the "white Zanj," who differed from other peoples of East Africa by their lighter skin (Tadeusz Lewicki, *Arabic External Sources for the History of Africa to the South of Sahara,* London and Lagos, 1969, p. 35).

96. On the other hand, the expression *kushi wad'ai* 'a real Kushite' used in *GenR* 41/42.4 (p. 408), if it is original (it is missing in several manuscripts including Vat. 30), does not represent a similar development, i.e., an ethnic Kushite as opposed to a dark-skinned person. Rather, as Theodor notes, it means a literal Kushite as opposed to a metaphoric interpretation of the word *kushi.* See above, n. 33.

97. This meaning of the term *kushi* in rabbinic texts was obvious to those operating within traditional boundaries, and it accounts for explanations such as that by a nineteenth-century rabbi, Joseph Guggenheimer, to explain why David ibn Zimra (sixteenth century) considered the Ethiopian Jews to be ethnically Jewish. The term

"Kushite" used by Ibn Zimra, said Guggenheimer, simply meant dark-skinned "as in the Bible (Jer 13:23), the Talmud (*bSuk* 36a), and rabbinic literature." See Michael Corinaldi, *Ethiopian Jewry: Identity and Tradition* (in Hebrew; Jerusalem, 1988), p. 156, where Guggenheimer's text is quoted.

98. Lloyd Thompson, "Eastern Africa and the Graeco-Roman World (to A.D. 641)," in *Africa in Classical Antiquity,* ed. L. A. Thompson and J. Ferguson (Ibadan, Nigeria, 1969), p. 26.

99. In *Lexicon Iconographicum Mythologiae Classicae,* ed. Boardman et al., 1/1:413.

100. Desanges, "L'Afrique noire et le monde méditerranéen dans l'Antiquité," pp. 400–404, 408–9. See also Desanges's *Catalogue des tribus africaines de l'antiquité classique à l'ouest du Nil* (Dakar, 1962), p. 95: "The term 'Ethiopian' does not at all imply total negritude." Mveng, *Les sources grecques de l'histoire négro-africaine,* p. 84, similarly, based on the conclusions of Snowden and Desange. As long ago as 1833, that view, in an even more widely extended form, was made by Michael Russell. In his book *Nubia and Abyssinia: Comprehending Their Civil History, Antiquities, Arts, Religion, Literature, and Natural History* (Edinburgh, 1833), Russell wrote that the term "Ethiopian" was used by the Greeks "not so much to denote a country bounded by certain geographical limits, as to describe the complexion of the inhabitants, whatever might be their position with respect to other nations" (p. 23). See also n. 2, above.

101. de Medeiros, *L'occident et l'Afrique (XIIIe–XVe siècle),* pp. 158–59. Note also that on an ostracon found in Upper Egypt, Aphrodite, the Greek goddess of love, is called "the Ethiopian," apparently a development of her nickname "Black One," given to her because people make love in the dark; see Snowden, *Blacks in Antiquity,* p. 18, and above, p. 296, n. 80.

102. J. W. Gardner, "Blameless Ethiopians and Others," *Greece and Rome* 24 (1977) 185.

103. Homer (above, n. 27); cicada: Meleager (first century B.C.E.) in the *Anthologia Palatina* 7.196; crow-fish: Oppian (second–third century C.E.), *Halieutica* 1.133; ivy: Proclus (fifth century C.E.) in the *Appendix nova epigrammatum* 3.166 of the *Anthologia Graeca* (references quoted from LSJ, s.v. Aἰθίοψ, αἶθοψ`); Indians: Nonnus (probably fourth–fifth century C.E.), *Dionysiaca* 16.254, 17. 114. Alexander, *The Toponymy of the Targumim,* p. 128, recognized the development of the term *kushi* in Jewish sources to "denote anyone of dark complexion whether or not of negroid stock." He claimed a similar development for Ἄιθιοψ, but he cited Lucian, *Adv. Ind.* 28 and Juvenal 2.23, neither of which provides proof for the claim.

104. See pp. 86–88 with notes for all source and bibliographic references.

105. *ExR* 3.4; ed. Shinan, p.124; cf. A. Brüll, *Trachten der Juden in nachbiblischen Alterthume* (Frankfurt am Main, 1873), p. 4, n. 3. The parable is transmitted by R. Joshua b. Levi (mid-third century).

106. Michael Sachs, *Beiträge zur Sprach- und Alterthumsforschung: aus jüdischen Quellen* (Berlin, 1852–54), 2:109.

107. See Annalisa Rei, "Villians, Wives, and Slaves in the Comedies of Plautus," in *Women and Slaves in Greco-Roman Culture,* ed. Sandra Joshel and Sheila Murnaghan (London, 1998), p. 95.

108. Shinan notes (so too Maharzaw) that the relationship between the parable

and that which it is supposed to illustrate is weak. One would indeed expect the *kushit* to be the servant of the *maṭronah,* just as in the previous parable, which would correspond to Moses as the servant of God.

109. Fischer, *Farb- und Formbezeichnungen,* p. 276. Thus the early Arabic use of "blackness" and "black face" to describe people of low or ignoble character appears as well in describing unpleasant, unkind women (p. 248).

110. See p. 90.

111. See p. 81.

CHAPTER NINE

1. Stanley M. Burstein, *Graeco-Africana: Studies in the History of Greek Relations with Egypt and Nubia* (New Rochelle, N.Y., 1995), p. 196. Davis, *Slavery and Human Progress,* pp. 8, 34–35. See also E. W. Bovill, *The Golden Trade of the Moors* (London, 1958), p. 46. A extensive, but difficult to use, bibliography of articles on slavery is J. C. Miller, *Slavery and Slaving in World History: A Bibliography, 1900–1991* (Millwood, N.Y., 1993).

2. Burstein, *Graeco-Africana,* pp. 195–99.

3. Ibid., pp. 197–98.

4. *Periplus* 13, ed. Casson, p. 59. Sec. 8 (p. 55) also reports that at another location on the Horn (Malao) slaves are exported on rare occasions. See also the literature cited in van Donzel, "Ibn al-Jawzi on Ethiopians in Baghdad," p. 119, n. 13. Burstein, *Graeco-Africana,* mistakenly says that the *Periplus* also mentions Adulis and Massawa as slave-exporting locations. On the date of the *Periplus,* see Gervase Mathew, "The Dating and Significance of the *Periplus of the Erythrean Sea,*" in Chittick and Rotberg, *East Africa and the Orient,* pp. 155–58.

5. *Natural History,* 6.34.172–73.

6. Burstein, *Graeco-Africana,* p. 198, citing Baumgart, "Die römischen Sklavennamen," p. 64.

7. Friedrich Preisigke, "Ein Sklavenkauf des 6. Jahrhunderts (P. gr. Str. Inv. nr. 1404)," *Archiv für Papyrusforschung* 3 (1906) 415–24.

8. Burstein, *Graeco-Africana,* pp. 199–205; and *Ancient African Civilizations: Kush and Axum* (Princeton, 1998), pp. 119, 151. See also Rotter, *Die Stellung des Negers,* pp. 23–24, who speaks of a large-scale Black slave trade existing, at the latest, in the second half of the first millennium B.C.E.

9. Kathryn Bard and Rodolfo Fattovich, "Some Remarks on the Processes of State Formation in Egypt and Ethiopia," in *Africa and Africans in Antiquity,* ed. Yamauchi, pp. 280–81. On the "Semitic Colonization in Abyssinia," see also J. Spencer Trimingham, *Islam in Ethiopia* (London, 1952), pp. 32–34.

10. W. W. Müller in *ABD* 5:1064, s.v. Seba. See also Epstein, *Kitvei Avraham Epstein,* 1:61.

11. *Periplus* 16, ed. Casson, p. 61, and see Casson's comments, pp. 134–35. "On the East African shore Arab merchants were found everywhere, as far south as Rhapta, near Zanzibar" (Hourani, *Arab Seafaring,* p. 33).

12. Thompson, "Eastern Africa and the Graeco-Roman World (to A.D. 641)," p. 32. Regarding the Arab settlements in East Africa, see also Gervase Mathew in *History of East Africa,* ed. R. Oliver and G. Mathew (Oxford, 1963–76), 1:102;

A.M.H. Sheriff, "The East African Coast and Its Role in Maritime Trade," in *General History of Africa,* vol. 2: *Ancient Civilizations of Africa,* ed. G. Mokhtar (London, 1981), p. 566; and R. Coupland, *East Africa and Its Invaders: From the Earliest Times to the Death of Seyyid Said in 1856* (Oxford, 1938), pp. 15–40; H. Neville Chittick, "The Peopling of the East African Coast," in Chittick and Rotberg, *East Africa and the Orient,* pp. 34–35. See also E. Cerulli and G.S.P. Freeman-Grenville, *EI*^{2} 6:128a, s.v. Maḳdishū, and E. Ullendorff, *EI*^{2} 3:3a–b, s.v. *Ḥabash, Ḥabasha.*

13. Tadeusz Lewicki, "External Arabic Sources for the History of Africa to the South of the Sahara," in *Emerging Themes of African History,* ed. T. O. Ranger (Nairobi, 1968), pp. 14–15.

14. Chang Hsing-lang, "The Importation of Negro Slaves to China under the T'ang Dynasty (A.D. 618–907)," *Bulletin of the Catholic University of Peking* 7 (1930) 37–59, and L. C. Goodrich, "Negroes in China," *Bulletin* 8 (1931) 137–39; Paul Wheatley, "Analecta Sino-Africana Recensa," in Chittick and Rotberg, *East Africa and the Orient,* pp. 76–85, 109; Graham W. Irwin, *Africans Abroad* (New York, 1977), pp. 168–69; C. Martin Wilbur, *Slavery in China during the Former Han Dynasty, 206 B.C. to A.D. 25* (Chicago, 1943), p. 93 and literature cited there. But see Edward Schafer, *The Golden Peaches of Samarkand: A Study of T'ang Exotics* (Berkeley, 1963), pp. 46–47, 290 n. 48, who questions Chang's proofs. Note also the ninth-century Chinese work, the *Yu-yang-tsa-tsu,* which says that "the people of this country [= East African coast] make their own countrymen prisoners whom they sell to strangers" (quoted in F. Hirth and W. W. Rockhill, *Chao Ju-kua* [St. Petersburg, 1911; repr., 1966], p. 128). Javanese sources from 813 and 860 also mention black African (Zanj) slaves; see J. Spencer Trimingham, "The Arab Geographers and the East African Coast," in Chittick and Rotberg, *East Africa and the Orient,* p. 133, n. 52.

15. Y. M. Kobishanov, "Aksum: Political System, Economics and Culture, First to Fourth Century," in Mokhtar, *Ancient Civilizations of Africa,* p. 391; R. W. Beachey, *The Slave Trade of East Africa* (New York, 1976), pp. 1–10; Chittick and Rotberg, *East Africa and the Orient,* p. 8; Vinigi Grottanelli, "The Peopling of the Horn of Africa," in Chittick and Rotberg, *East Africa and the Orient,* pp. 70–71.

16. F. Løkkegaard in *EI*^{2} 1:966a–b, s.v. *baqṭ.* In addition to the 360 another 40 were sent annually, either for the Arab officials handling the transaction (Løkkegaard) or to compensate for an estimated 10 percent loss during the transport (Otto Meinardus, "The Christian Kingdoms of Nubia," *Cahiers d'histoire égyptienne* 10 [1967] 146).

17. The quote is R. Brunschvig's, *EI*^{2} 1:32a, s.v. *ʿabd.* Similarly, Yūsuf F. Hasan, *The Arabs and the Sudan* (Edinburgh, 1967), p. 42. See also Renault, *La traite des noirs,* pp. 10ff.

18. See E. Ashtor, *A Social and Economic History of the Near East in the Middle Ages* (Berkeley, 1976), p. 106.

19. The conquest of Zanzibar is reported by Masʿūdī (d. 956); see Masʿūdī, *Murūj al-dhahab,* ed. C. Barbier de Meynard (Paris, 1861), 1:205; ed. Charles Pellat (Paris, 1965–74), text, 1:112, trans., 1:84.

20. Rotter, *Stellung des Negers,* p. 25, thinks that the Zanj importation into Iraq preceded the Muslim conquest of that country in 649. Similarly Trimingham, "The

Arab Geographers and the East African Coast," pp. 117–18. See also Grottanelli, "The Peopling of the Horn of Africa," p. 72. Note, however, a Zoroastrian text studied by Dan Shapira, "Zoroastrian Sources on Black People," *Arabica* 49 (2002) 119, which indicates that "the Blacks appeared on the Iranian borders, in southern ʿIrāq, after the Muslim Arab invasion of Iran."

21. S. A. Riavi, "'Zenj': Its First Known Use in Arabic Literature," *Azania* 2 (1967) 200–201.

22. *The Chachnamah,* trans. Mirza Kalichbeg Fredunbeg, pp. 69–70, cited in H. M. Elliot, *The History of India,* ed. John Dowson, 2nd ed. (Allahabad, [1963]), 1:429. The Persian text is in *Fathnamah-i Sind,* ed. N. A. Baloch, p. 64. Cf. Minoo Southgate, "Negative Images of Blacks," p. 6, quoting ʿAlī Akbar Dihkhudā, *Lughat-nāma* (Tehran, 1946–79), 1/6:2603, col. 3: "In [A.D. 713] Musa ibn Nasir took 300,000 captives from Africa, of whom he sent one-fifth, i.e. 60,000, to the Caliph Walid ibn ʿAbd al-Malik."

23. Trans. B.T.A. Evetts, *PO* 5.1 (1909) excerpted in Giovanni Vantini, *Oriental Sources Concerning Nubia* (Heidelberg, 1975), p. 44. This source is quoted by Hasan, *The Arabs and the Sudan,* p. 45. Hasan also quotes Nā ṣir-ī Khusraw (eleventh century): "Muslims and others stole Bejāwī children and sold them in Muslim towns." Similarly, the tenth-century *Kitab al-Ajaib al-Hind* reports how the visitors to Africa from Oman would "steal their children enticing them away by offering them fruits. They carry the children from place to place and finally take possession of them and carry them off to their own country" (ed. P. A. van der Lith, Leiden, 1883–86, p. 22, quoted by R. W. Beachey, *A Collection of Documents on the Slave Trade of Eastern Africa,* London, 1976, p. ix; see also p. 2 quoting the twelfth-century Chinese work, the *Ling-wai-tai-ta* referring to the East Africans: "They are enticed by (offers of) food and then captured and sold as slaves to the Arabic countries. . . . Thousands of them are sold as foreign slaves." Al-Idrīsī (d. 1165), speaking of peoples in the Sūdān, also mentions this practice: "Peoples of the neighboring countries continually capture them, using various tricks. They take them to their own lands, and sell them in droves to the merchants" (*Nuzhat al-Mushtāq fī Ikhtirāq al-Āfāq,* in Levtzion and Hopkins, *Corpus,* p. 109; see also Lewis, *Race and Slavery,* pp. 51 and 121, n. 6).

24. See Lewis, *Race and Slavery,* pp. 51 and 121, n. 6. See also Trimingham, "The Arab Geographers and the East African Coast, pp. 132–33.

25. J. L. Triaud in *EI*² 9:752b, s.v. *Sūdān.*

26. Hasan, *The Arabs and the Sudan,* p. 8.

27. Ibid., p. 42. See also R. Brunschvig, *EI*² 1:32a; J. O. Hunwick, "Black Africans in the Islamic World: An Understudied Dimension of the Black Diaspora," *Tarikh* 5 (Historical Society of Nigeria, published in London, 1978) 20–40; W. D. Phillips, *Slavery from Roman Times to the Early Transatlantic Trade* (Minneapolis, 1985), pp. 114–27; E. Cerulli and G.S.P. Freeman-Grenville, *EI*² 6:128b, s.v. Maḳdishū; Samir Zoghby, "Blacks and Arabs: Past and Present," *Current Bibliography on African Affairs* 3.5 (May 1970) 6.

28. For North Africa, see E. Savage who traces the development of the Black African slave trade by the Muslim Berber tribes beginning in the eighth century ("Berber and Blacks: Ibāḍī Slave Traffic in Eight-Century North Africa," *Journal of African History* 33 [1992] 351–68). A later version of the article was published

as chapter 4 in Savage's *A Gateway to Hell, a Gateway to Paradise: The North African Response to the Arab Conquest* (Princeton, 1997). For a discussion of the black African slave trade in North Africa during the ninth–twelfth century, see M. Brett, "Ifrīqiya as a Market for Saharan Trade from the Tenth to Twelfth Century AD," *Journal of African History* 19 (1969) 354ff.

29. Paul E. Lovejoy, *Transformations in Slavery: A History of Slavery in Africa* (Cambridge, 1983, 2000), pp. 15–16; and S. Labib, "Islamic Expansion and Slave Trade in Medieval Africa," *Mouvements de populations dans l'Ocean Indien* (Paris, 1979), p. 33. For West Africa, see J. O. Hunwick, *West Africa and the Arab World* (Accra, 1991), pp. 22–23.

30. R. Brunschvig, *EI*[2] 1:24b; see also van Donzel, "Ibn al-Jawzi on Ethiopians in Baghdad," p. 115.

31. Brunschvig, *EI*[2] 1:24b; W. ʿArafat, "The Attitude of Islam to Slavery," *Islamic Quarterly* 10.1–2 (1966) 12.

32. Apparently Brunschvig's source for his claim is the thesis of P. H. Lammens that the *Aḥābīsh,* a confederacy of tribes or clans, to a large extent consisted of Abyssinian (*Ḥabash*) and other black African slaves. W. Montgomery Watt, however, claims that Lammens's hypothesis is unjustified for several reasons, including the following: (a) Brunschvig gives too much weight to the meaning "Abyssinians" and neglects another possible meaning of *Aḥābīsh* deriving from *uḥbūsh* or *uḥbūsha* 'companies or bodies of men, not all of one tribe' (Lane); (b) there is no reason to assume that the tribes or clans of the *Aḥābīsh* are not Arab; (c) the *Aḥābīsh* are said to be confederates (*ḥulafāʾ*), not slaves, of Quraysh, and the first time they are mentioned they appear as confederates of the enemies of Quraysh (*EI*[2] 3:7b–8a, s.v. *Ḥabash, Ḥabasha*). Rotter, *Stellung des Negers,* p. 26, also speaks of Lammens's "exaggerated claims."

33. Bernard Lewis, "The Crows of the Arabs," in Gates, *"Race," Writing and Difference,* pp. 111–12; the article originally appeared in *Critical Inquiry* 12 (1985) 88–97; see also Lewis's *Race and Slavery,* pp. 23 and 41. Similarly, Rotter, *Stellung des Negers,* p. 26.

34. Of course, the numbers of other people whom the Muslims conquered also increased. But Lewis shows (*Race and Slavery,* p. 53) how the religious strictures against enslaving those converted to Islam were not readily observed when it came to black Africans.

35. For Greece and Rome, see Thompson, *Romans and Blacks,* p.156; Snowden, *Blacks in Antiquity,* p.186.

36. *Satyricon* 102. See also Thompson's remarks (*Romans and Blacks,* p. 196, n. 189) about the mental association of Blacks with slaves in Roman society, which is seen in "satirical comments on adultery between Roman ladies and black men, where the writers' disapproval rests entirely on the *assumption* that realism demands representing the black paramour of an upper-class woman as a slave (or, at best, a free man of low rank)."

37. *Acts of Peter* 22 in W. Schneemelcher, *NTA* 2:305; J. K. Elliott, *ANT,* p. 415. For the dating (ca. 190), see Schneemelcher, p. 283; for provenance ("an open question, although Rome or Asia Minor remain the likeliest"), see Elliott, p. 392.

38. The text is discussed in detail on pp. 172–74.

39. *IBWA* 2/1:62. See also Vincent Wimbush, "Ascetic Behavior and Color-ful

Language: Stories about Ethiopian Moses," *Semeia* 58 (1992) 81–92, who questions the historicity of the Abba Moses stories.

40. The life and sayings of Abba Moses are recorded in various sources, the earliest of which is Palladius's *Historia Lausiaca,* written in 420. Four versions, including Palladius's, were recently collected and published by K. O'Brien Wicker in *Ascetic Behavior in Graeco-Roman Antiquity,* ed. Vincent Wimbush (Minneapolis, 1990), pp. 329–48. For discussion and information on other sources of the Abba Moses story, see Devisse *IBWA* 2/1:225, nn. 256–57, 261. The Abba Moses stories are usually quoted in scholarly literature to show an early example of racial prejudice; see, e.g., Wicker, p. 334; Peter Frost, "Attitudes toward Blacks in the Early Christian Era," *Second Century* 8 (1991) 5–6; and Philip Mayerson, "Anti-Black Sentiment in the *Vitae Patrum,*" *HTR* 71 (1978) 304–11. An Ethiopian slave is encountered also in a story of another desert Father, Arsenius (d. 450); see the *Apophthegmata Patrum,* Arsenius 32 in *PG* 65.100B (παιδίσκη τις Αἰθιόπισσα).

41. A. Sanda, *Oposcula Monophysitica Johannes Philoponi* (Beirut, 1930), pp. 29, 55 (Syriac text), and 66, 96 (Sanda's Latin translation). In the first quotation Philoponus actually has "Indian" and not "Ethiopian" (Syriac, p. 29), but this only reflects the Ethiopian/Indian confusion of antiquity (on which, see the literature cited in Appendix II), and Sanda translates "Ethiopian."

42. Translation from Lewis, "The Crows of the Arabs," p. 113.

43. Rotter, *Die Stellung des Negers,* pp. 25–26. In particular he refers to several pre-Islamic Arabic poets known as the "crows of the Arabs," whose mothers were Black slaves (on these poets, especially ʿAntara, see Lewis, *Race and Slavery,* pp. 24–25); to the report of Ibn Saʿd (d. 845) that of nineteen slaves or freed slaves belonging to Muḥammad, six were Black or part Black; and to a listing of freed slaves who participated in the Battle of Badr in 624, of whom one-third were Blacks.

44. The Coptic texts and an Arabic version were published by A. Amélineau, *Monuments pour servir à l'histoire de l'Egypte chrétienne,* Mémoires publiés par les membres de la mission archéologique française au Caire; the complete Bohairic text is in vol. 4, part 1 (Paris, 1888), pp. 1–91, the Arabic on pp. 289–478, and the Sahidic fragments on p. 247 and vol. 4, part 2 (1895), pp. 633–49. The relevant passages are at 4/1:444, where Amélineau translates the Arabic *ʿabd aswad* as "nègre abyssinien" (presumably reflecting the meaning of *ʿabd* in his time) and at 4/2:646–47 (Sahidic). The Bohairic version, does not have this section at all. An English translation of the *Life,* based on the complete Coptic, together with introduction and notes, was done by David N. Bell, *Besa, the Life of Shenoute* (Kalamazoo, Mich., 1983). My discussion of the relationship between the Coptic and Arabic versions follows Bell, p. 4; on Shenoute's dates, see p. 7; on the Arabic version published by Amélineau, see p. 26, n. 21, where Bell says that there are other manuscripts of the Arabic version that differ from Amélineau's text as well as from each other. Bell also provides a bibliography including a listing of the Coptic editions and translations of the *Life* (pp. 115–16). See also the entries "Besa" and "Shenute" by K. H. Kuhn in *The Coptic Encyclopedia,* general ed., Aziz S. Atiya (New York, 1991), 2:378–79 and 7:2131–33, where bibliographies are found. An earlier, and shorter, discussion of the *Life* is found in J. Leipoldt, *Schenute von Atripe und die Entstehung des national ägyptischen Christentums* (Leipzig, 1903), pp. 12–16. In his introduction to the translation volume, G. Colin, *La version éthiopienne de la*

vie de Schenoudi (Louvain, 1982), *CSCO* 444–45, Scriptores Aethiopici 75–76, discusses the various versions and editions (Coptic, Syriac, Ethiopic, Arabic) of the *Life of Shenoute.* For the dating of the Arabic, see A. Amélineau, 4/1:li–lii. On the later Arabic additions to the Coptic, Leipoldt, pp. 14–15. On the early Arabic translations of Coptic literature, see Khalil Samir, "Arabic Sources for Early Egyptian Christianity" in *The Roots of Egyptian Christianity,* ed. B. A. Pearson and J. E. Goehring (Philadelphia, 1986), pp. 82–97; see also J. Timbie, "The State of Research on the Career of Shenoute of Atripe," in the same volume, pp. 261–62, for discussion of the dates of Shenoute and editions of the Coptic *Life.* Incidentally, the same phenomenon as we see in the Arabic version of *Shenoute* may be behind a MS reading "Ethiopian" in Cicero, *Post reditum in senatu* 6.14. Cicero compares Piso to "a dolt of an Ethiopian [*stipite Aethiope*], devoid of all sense, insipid, unable to speak, retarded, barely human, a Cappadocian only just removed from a band of slaves [*Cappadocem modo abreptum de grege venalium*]." Modern scholarship has shown that "Ethiopian" is not the original reading but a medieval corruption (*stipite>stipe>Etiope>Aethiope*); see Desanges, "L'Afrique noire et le monde méditerranéen dans l'Antiquité," p. 410, and in *Afrique noire et monde méditerranéen dans l'antiquité,* pp. 283–284. Perhaps the error came about, even partly (after all, Cappadocian and Ethiopian can hardly stand together), due to the association of slave with Black.

45. Davis, *Slavery and Human Progress,* p. 33. So too Thompson, *Romans and Blacks,* pp. 147, 156; and Snowden, *Blacks in Antiquity,* p. 186.

46. Lewis, "The Crows of the Arabs," p. 112. For the use of the term with this meaning, see Lewis, *Race and Slavery,* pp. 125–126, n. 10.

47. Thompson, *Romans and Blacks,* p. 79.

48. See the discussion above (pp. 38–39) regarding Ebed-Melech in Jer 38 and Yehudi in Jer 36. Whether *saris,* said of Ebed-Melech, means "court official" or "euncuh" presumably would not change his status as servant of the king. In regard to Yehudi, if the name of his great-grandfather, Kushi, does not indicate land of origin, we cannot claim him as a Black slave in Israel. A good review of the scholarship on Jewish ownership of, and practice toward, slaves from the biblical through the talmudic period is found in E. Leigh Gibson, *The Jewish Manumission Inscriptions of the Bosporus Kingdom* (Tübingen, 1999), pp. 56–94, "Judaism, Slavery, and Manumission."

49. For the date (after the redaction of both the Babylonian and Palestinian Talmuds, but before the Islamic conquest) and the Palestinian provenance, see P. S. Knobel's introduction to his translation in *The Aramaic Bible* (Collegeville, Minn., 1991), 15:2–15.

50. *ExR* 10.2 (ed. Shinan, pp. 227–28). Similarly *ExR* 13.4 (p. 258) states that the plague of locusts affected Egypt "in your borders (Ex 10:4) . . . and not in the borders of the Hamites [*bnei ḥam*]." The variant readings in 10.2, "Kushim" or "others" for "Hamites" (MS Paris and ed. pr.), seems to derive from a lack of understanding of the term *bnei ḥam.* Meir Benvenisti suggested emending the text of 13.4 to read "Kushites" (*bnei kush*) in place of "Hamites" (Benvenisti in *Ot Emet,* Salonika, 1565, as cited by Shinan in his edition, ad loc.).

51. Rotter, *Die Stellung des Negers,* p. 141, citing a poem attributed to the daughter of Labīd (d. 660/1), recorded by Iṣfahānī, as well as other material. A

translation of the verse is found in C. J. Lyall, "The Moʿallaqah of Lebīd, with the Life of the Poet as Given in the Kitāb-el-Aghānī," *Journal of the Asiatic Society of Bengal* 46, pt. 1 (1877) 69–70 and see 81, n. 27.

52. Benjamin refers to "the black slaves, the sons of Ham" (*ha-ʿavadim ha-sheḥorim bnei ḥam*)." See M. N. Adler, ed., *The Itinerary of Benjamin of Tudela* (London, 1907), pp. 62 (text), 68 (translation). Maimonides, *Mishneh Torah, Matenot ʿAniyim* 10.17: "The Sages commanded that one should employ the poor and the orphaned rather than use slaves in one's home. It is better to employ the former and thus benefit the descendants of Abraham, Isaac, and Jacob, rather than benefit the descendants of Ham [*zera ʿ ḥam*]." Given Maimonides' world—twelfth-century Egypt—he is clearly speaking of Black slaves.

53. In his Long Commentary to Ex 8:22 (ed. Asher Weiser [Vaizer], 2:58) Ibn Ezra says that the Hindus are *bnei ḥam* and are vegetarians.

54. For *kushi(t)* as a dark-skinned person, see chapter 8; for slaves as dark-skinned, pp. 118–22.

55. See p. 248, n. 43.

56. On Origen's Ethiopian exegesis, see pp. 48–51, 168–69, and Thompson, *Romans and Blacks,* p. 196, n. 189.

57. As in Greece, Rome, and Arabia, to say that most Blacks in the Land of Israel were slaves is not to say that most slaves were Black. There is no evidence that that was the case. Unfortunately, William M. Evans misread the secondary literature on this issue and concluded, to the contrary, that "most [non-Jewish slaves] were in fact either Syrians or *Kushim* from black Africa." On Evans's misreading, which undermines the entire thesis of his article about the "shifting ethnic identities of the 'sons of Ham,'" see my "The Curse of Ham," p. 49.

58. See p. 68 where the text is fully discussed.

59. In the fourteenth century the king of Mali had Turkish slaves (Phillips, *Slavery from Roman Times to the Early Transatlantic Trade,* pp. 125–26).

60. Goldenberg, "Rabbinic Knowledge of Black Africa."

61. Of course, not all Blacks in Israel were slaves. Consider the Ethiopian eunuch, minister of the queen of Ethiopia, who went to Jerusalem to worship (Acts 8:27–40), and, if the comments of a Nestorian synod held in 585 are historically correct, the eunuch was not the only Ethiopian to come to Jerusalem to pray. The synod stated: "The minister of Qandaq [= Candace], queen of the Ethiopians . . . following an ancient custom, went to Jerusalem to worship the God of the Hebrews. . . . He had come up from his country not as a heathen . . . but as a Jew" (quoted by Jean Devisse, *IBWA* 2/1:223, n. 228). See also J. Schneider in *TDNT* 2:768, n. 26, and Kaplan, *Ruler, Saint and Servant,* p. 56.

CHAPTER TEN

1. *The Works of Sir William Jones* (1799), 3:199–200, quoted by Thomas Trautmann, *Aryans and British India* (Berkeley, 1997), p. 46.

2. The last lines are translated variously. NJPS has "Blessed be the Lord, the God of Shem; let Canaan be a slave to them. May God enlarge Japheth, and let him dwell in the tents of Shem; and let Canaan be a slave to them."

3. J. J. Flournoy, *A Reply to a Pamphlet . . .* (Athens, Ga., 1838), p. 16.

4. Edward Blyden, "The Negro in Ancient History" *Methodist Quarterly Review* (January 1869) 75. See also his "Noah's Malediction" (1862) reprinted in *Slavery and Abolition* 1 (1980) 18.

5. From an anonymous work, *African Servitude,* printed in 1860.

6. Thomas V. Peterson, *Ham and Japheth: The Mythic World of Whites in the Antebellum South* (Metuchen, N.J., 1978), pp. 42, 45–47, and 149; quotation from p. 102. On p. 96 Peterson cites Gayraud S. Wilmore, *Black Religion and Black Radicalism* (New York, 1972), pp. 163–67, who has shown that "black clergymen, not infrequently, accepted their race's descent from Ham"; see also pp. 7 and 46 where Peterson refers to the work of an escaped slave who shared this view. On the use of the Curse of Ham in antebellum America, see also Caroline L. Shanks, "The Biblical Antislavery Argument of the Decade, 1830–1840," *Journal of Negro History* 16 (1931) 137–38, reprinted in *Religion and Slavery* ed. P. Finkelman (New York, 1989), pp. 621–22; Jordan, *White over Black,* p. 201, n. 48; Larry E. Tise, *Proslavery: A History of the Defense of Slavery in America, 1701–1840* (Athens, Ga., 1987), p. 189 and n. 10. On the Curse of Ham in America more generally, see Forest Wood, *The Arrogance of Faith* (New York, 1990), pp. 84–111. L. R. Thomas, *Biblical Faith and the Black American* (Valley Forge, Pa., 1976), pp. 27–28, provides discussion and sources on the Curse of Ham in American writings. Sollors, *Neither Black nor White Yet Both,* pp. 78–111, 438–57, does so generally in literature.

7. Peterson, *Ham and Japheth,* p. 46.

8. *The Selling of Joseph* (Boston, 1700), reprinted in Louis Ruchames ed., *Racial Thought in America* (Amherst, Mass., 1969), 1:49.

9. Joseph Koranda, "Aftermath of Misinterpretation: The Misunderstanding of Genesis and Its Contribution to White Racism" (B.D. thesis, Concordia Theological Seminary, 1969), pp. 1–2, 52, and 55.

10. James Baldwin, *The Fire Next Time* (New York, 1964), pp. 45–46.

11. *Slavery as It Relates to the Negro, or African Race* (Albany, N.Y., 1843), pp. 27–28; repeated in his *Bible Defence of Slavery* . . . (Glasgow, 1852), pp. 33ff. On Priest's popularity, Peterson, *Ham and Japheth,* pp. 42–43, 60, notes that his *Slavery* was reprinted five times in eight years.

12. H. P. Eastman, *The Negro; His Origin, History and Destiny* (Boston, 1905), p. 307. Italics in original.

13. *The Great Question Answered; or Is Slavery a Sin in Itself (Per Se?) Answered According to the Teaching of the Scriptures* (Memphis, Tenn., 1857), p. 60.

14. H. Shelton Smith, *In His Image, But . . . Racism in Southern Religion, 1780–1910* (Durham N.C., 1972), p. 131. Cartwright is quoted in W. S. Jenkins, *Pro-Slavery Thought in the Old South* (Chapel Hill, N.C., 1935), p. 206. Cf. also John G. Fee, *The Sinfulness of Slaveholding* (New York, 1851), p. 16: "All this talk we have about the word Ham meaning black, and made so by the curse of the Almighty."

15. Peterson, *Ham and Japheth,* p. 43. To Peterson's examples, add also Buckner H. Payne ("Ariel"), *The Negro: What Is His Ethnological Status* (1840; Cincinnati, rev. 1867), p. 5. See also Eastman, *The Negro; His Origin, History and Destiny,* pp. 285, 288, 293, 308, 330; James Buswell, *Slavery, Segregation and Scripture* (Grand Rapids, Mich., 1964), pp. 16–17, 64–65; and Jenkins, *Pro-*

Slavery Thought in the Old South, p. 206. Even those who believed that black skin began with Cain—a minor position in the literature of the time—held that through marriage with Ham's line the complexion was transmitted to Ham's descendants. On Cain's blackness, see below, chapter 13.

16. Ron Bartour, "American Views on Biblical Slavery: 1835–1865, A Comparative Study," *Slavery and Abolition* 4 (1983) 41–55. For a discussion of how Christian Blacks at the time reinterpreted the Curse by means of hermeneutical inversion, see Michael G. Cartwright's remarks in his "Ideology and the Interpretation of the Bible in the African-American Christian Tradition," *Modern Theology* 9.2 (1993) 141–58.

17. Ed. John M'Clintock and James Strong (New York, 1872), 4:34.

18. Hill, *The English Bible*, pp. 118, 398. See also Jean-Louis Hannemann writing in 1677, quoted in J. Lécuyer, "Le père Libermann et la malédiction de Cham," in *Libermann 1802–1852: un pensée et une mystique missionnaires*, ed. Paul Coulon and Paule Brasseur (Paris, 1988), p. 603.

19. Peterson cites Bishop Thomas Newton, chaplain to King George II, as the intermediary between Calmet and the American writers, although he notes that at least one American author cited Calmet directly (*Ham and Japheth*, pp. 43–44, 61). See below, p. 176.

20. Albright's review of *HUCA* 16 (1941) in *JBL* 64 (1945) 294.

21. J. Lewy, "The Old West Semitic Sun God Ḥammu," *HUCA* 18 (1944) 473–76. "Allegedly" because there is no clear evidence that *Ḥammu* was the name of a deity; see I. Nakata, "Deities in the Mari Texts" (Ph.D. diss., Columbia University, 1974), p. 191. The *Ḥammu* theory is mentioned as one of two uncertain etymological possibilities for the name of Ham in KBL 1:325 (the other is *ʿamm* 'kinsman, paternal uncle'); it is rejected by K. van der Toorn in *Dictionary of Deities and Demons in the Bible*, 2nd ed., ed. Karel van der Toorn et al. (Leiden, 1999), p. 383, s.v. Ham.

22. R. S. Hess, *Studies in the Personal Names of Genesis 1–11* (Neukirchen-Vluyn, 1993), p. 30. So too F. L. Benz, *Personal Names in the Phoenician and Punic Inscriptions* (Rome, 1972), p. 311. Both Hess and Benz cite earlier literature.

23. S. A. Loewenstamm in *EB* 3:164. On the meaning "father-in-law," see KBL 1:324, s.v. *ḥam I.*

24. See J. K. Stark, *Personal Names in the Palmyrene Inscriptions* (Oxford, 1971), p. 89. To his list of sources, add now S. D. Ricks, *Lexicon of Inscriptional Qatabanian* (Rome, 1989), p. 63.

25. See John Skinner, *ICC: Genesis*, 2nd ed. (Edinburgh, 1930), pp. 192–96, and August Dillmann, *Genesis, Critically and Exegetically Expounded*, trans. W. B. Stevenson (Edinburgh, 1897; originally in German, 1892), 1:317–23. Note also E. Reuveni in *Leshonenu* 3 (1930–31) 128. Even as late as G. Castellino in *Enciclopedia cattolica* (Vatican City, 1949–54), 3:419, s.v. Cam.

26. Hess, *Personal Names*, p. 30, and Gary Rendsburg, "Word Play in Biblical Hebrew: An Eclectic Collection," in *Puns and Pundits: Word Play in the Hebrew Bible and Ancient Near Eastern Literature*, ed. Scott Noegel (Bethesda, 2000), pp. 143–44. The connection between Ham and the Egyptian *ḥm* 'servant' was suggested by A. S. Yahuda, *The Language of the Pentateuch in Its Relation to Egyptian* (London, 1933; originally in German, 1929), p. 267, who thus explained the curse

of slavery on Ham's son as a wordplay on the name. This derivation is also mentioned as a possibility by Loewenstamm in *EB* 3:164.

27. Cyrus Gordon, "Notes on Proper Names in the Ebla Tablets," in *Eblaite Personal Names and Semitic Name-Giving,* ed. Alfonso Archi (Rome, 1988), p. 154: "The divine Pharaoh is often called *ḥm.f* 'His Majesty.'" Gordon thus sees Shem, Ham, and Japhet as representing divine progenitors of humanity, since "*šum* 'name' was applied to many gods in the Ancient Near East" and "Japheth . . . is borne by the Titan *Iapetos* in Greek mythology." Gordon's etymology is entertained as a possibility by van der Toorn, *Dictionary of Dieties,* p. 383, s.v. Ham.

28. Philo, *Quaestiones in Genesim* 2.65 and 77. Countrary to S. Krauss's implication (*JE* 1:224b, s.v. Africa), Jubilees 8:30 does not assume a connection between the name Ham and the hot southern countries. Jubilees merely says that, "[the land of Japheth] is cold, and the land of Ham is hot, but the land of Shem is not hot or cold because it is mixed with cold and heat." The author no more assumes that the name Ham is associated with heat than that the name Japheth is assocated with cold.

29. The root *ḥmm* occurs with the sense of sexual heat in regard to animals (Gen 30:38, 39) and humans (Isa 57:5), as already noted by Saadia (and from him to Ibn Janaḥ), as cited by S. Abramson, *Mi-pi Baᶜale Leshonot* (Jerusalem, 1988), p. 287. In Amoraic Hebrew the verb in its *hitpaᶜel* form means "to be sexually aroused" and/or "to conceive" (*GenR* 24.6, p. 236; *PesRK,* Supplements 3, 2:460), while the *hifᶜil* form in Babylonian Talmudic Aramaic also has a sexual meaning, "to excite" (*bNid* 43a). For postbiblical (Qumran etc.) evidence, see David Clines, *Dictionary of Classical Hebrew* (Sheffield, 1993–), 3:255–56, s.v. *ḥmm.* Ugaritic *ḥmḥm* and the derived noun *ḥmḥmt* have the meaning "sexual ardor" or "being pregnant." The root occurs in *Aqhat* 17 i 41, 42, and in *Shachar and Shalim* 51, 56; see Stanislav Segert, *A Basic Grammar of the Ugaritic Language* (Berkeley, 1984), p. 186, who suggests "ardor"; and J.C.L. Gibson, *Canaanite Myths and Legends* (Edinburgh, 1977), pp. 104 and 126, who stays with "pregnant, pregnancy"; see also K.-M. Beyse, *TDOT* 4:473, s.v. *ḥmm.* The root *yḥm* serves a double meaning of "arousal" and "conception" in Jewish Palestinian Aramaic while Arabic *waḥama* indicates "sexual desire" and *waḥamit* that "she was compliant to the male." See F. Brown, S. R. Driver, and C. A. Briggs, *A Hebrew-English Lexicon of the Old Testament* (Oxford, 1953), Albert de Biberstein-Kazimirski, *Dictionnaire Arabe-Français* (Paris, 1860), and the dictionaries of Sokoloff, Jastrow, Levy, and Lane (Supplement).

30. See Jordan, *White over Black,* p. 18.

31. KBL, s.v. *ḥūm* following R. Gradwohl, *Die Farben im Alten Testament* (Berlin, 1963), pp. 50–51, although an earlier view—that *ḥūm* in Gen 30 means "in heat"—is mentioned, against which see H. Janssens, "Les couleurs dans la Bible hébraïque," in *Annuaire de l'Institut de Philologie de d'Histoire Orientales et Slaves* 14 (1954–57) 149.

32. See, e.g., *TDNT* 4:549 (Michaelis), and 4:475 (Beyse). See also, e.g., Y. Z. Hirshenzohn, *Shevaᶜ Ḥokhmot,* p. 21. Among medieval grammarians, Judah ben Quraysh, David b. Abraham Alfasi, Ibn Janaḥ, Ibn Barun, David Qimḥi, and Salomon Parḥon (all between the tenth and twelfth centuries) agree that *ḥum* means "black." Sources: Quraysh, *The Risāla of Judah ben Quraysh,* ed. Dan Becker (Tel

Aviv, 1984), p. 258; see also S. Eppenstein, *ʿIyyun we-Ḥeqer* (Jerusalem, 1976; originally in German), p. 241. Alfasi, *The Hebrew-Arabic Dictionary of the Bible Known as Kitāb Jāmiʿ al-Alfāẓ (Agrōn)* . . . , ed. S. Skoss (New Haven, 1936), 1:558–59, 2:91. Ibn Janaḥ, *Sefer ha-Shorashim,* ed. W. Bacher (Berlin, 1896), p. 146. Ibn Barun, *Yeter ha-Peleṭah min Kitāb al-Muwāzana bayn al-Lugha al-ʿIbrāniyya wa-al-ʿArabiyya* (St. Peterburg, 1890), ed. P. Kokovtsov, p. 44; *Ibn Barun's Arabic Works on Hebrew Grammar and Lexicography,* ed. P. Wechter (Philadelphia, 1964), p. 82. Qimḥi (Kimhi), *Sefer ha-Shorashim,* ed. J.H.R. Biesenthal and F. Lebrecht (1847; repr., Jerusalem, 1967), cols. 196, 214; Parḥon, *Maḥberet he-ʿArukh* (1844; repr., Jerusalem, 1970), p. 19b. Some medievals, as Alfasi, define *ḥum* as "black" based on the assumed blackness of Ham (*ḥām*). On the often close semantic relationship in Hebrew between middle hollow roots (i.e., roots whose second radical is either *w* or *y*), such as *ḥwm,* and geminated roots (i.e., roots whose second and third radical are the same), such as *ḥmm;* see Joüon and Muraoka, *A Grammar of Biblical Hebrew,* 1:219 §80 o, 1:233 §82 o ("contamination"); J. Blau, "Studies in Hebrew Verb Formation," *HUCA* 42 (1971) 147–51; Blau, *A Grammar of Biblical Hebrew,* p. 61 §35.1: both II *w/y* and geminated roots were expanded from biliteral to triliteral roots; J. Kurylowicz, *Studies in Semitic Grammar and Metrics* (Wroclaw, 1972), ch. 1, esp. pp. 8–13 (§§5–12). My thanks to Steven Fassberg for these last few bibliographic references.

33. Geʿez *ḥəmmat* 'soot, charcoal, black liquid, blackness', *taḥammata* 'burn, become charcoal'; Arabic *ḥamma* 'become black', *ḥumam* 'charcoal, ashes'; Datina *ḥumum* 'soot'; South Arabian dialects Śaḥri, Yemenite *ḥum(m)* 'charcoal', Soqoṭri *ḥemḥom* (W. Leslau, *Lexique Soqoṭri,* Paris, 1938, pp. 180–81; Leslau, *Comparative Dictionary of Geʿez [Classical Ethiopic],* p. 235, where Leslau lists also the related words in the various Ethiopic dialects. Incidentally, there is a typo in this entry where Leslau adds "perhaps also Heb. *ḥūm* 'black and white.'" This presumably derives from KBL's "undefined color between black and white.") Similarly, Highland East Cushitic grouping *hem-* 'be black' (Hadiya *heem-*); Dahalo *himm-aṯe* 'black' (V. E. Orel and O. V. Stolbova, *Hamito-Semitic Etymological Dictionary: Materials for a Reconstruction,* Leiden, 1995, p. 273, no. 1232). See also A. Murtonen, *Hebrew in Its West Semitic Setting: A Comparative Survey of Non-Masoretic Hebrew Dialects and Traditions* (Leiden, 1986–88), 3:176–77 XWM, 185 XM(M). The biblical story of Jacob and the sheep is clearly playing on the relationship between the words *ḥum* 'black, dark' and *ḥmm* 'to be in heat, to conceive'.

34. J. J. Finkelstein, "An Old Babylonian Herding Contract and Genesis 31:38f," *JAOS* 88 (1968) 33. This point was already made by A. Dillmann, *Genesis,* 2:246.

35. Athalyah Brenner, who studied colors in the Bible, concluded that *ḥum* denotes a color "within the sector governed by *šaḥor*" (but not equal to biblical *šaḥor* 'black'), perhaps having a meaning close to that of modern Hebrew *ḥwm* 'brown' (*Colour Terms in the Old Testament,* pp. 122–23). Following her, Clines, *Dictionary of Classical Hebrew,* 3:172, s.v. has "brown."

36. See Skinner, *ICC: Genesis,* pp. 192–93. Dillmann, *Genesis,* pp. 319–20. This theory had its counterpart in popular writings of the antebellum South in America, thus explaining the origins of the Europeans, Blacks, and Native Americans; see Peterson, *Ham and Japheth,* pp. 42–43. It is wrong to suggest, as M. Harl does

in *La Bible d'Alexandrie*. vol. 1, Genesis (Paris, 1986), p. 143 to Gen 9:27, that rabbinic literature records the opinion that the Greeks, descendants of Japhet, were considered the most beautiful. The rabbinic texts are concerned with the language of Japhet, and the targumic texts with the borders of Japhet; neither with the pigmentation of Japhet. See the collection of sources quoted by Kasher in his *Torah Shelemah* to Gen 9:27, and Borst, *Der Turmbau von Babel,* 3/1:1306.

37. *Kmt* is a feminine form literally meaning "black," with "land" or something similar being understood, and the adjective deriving from the color of the alluvial soil of the Nile after it deposits its silt. See Erman and Grapow, *Wörterbuch,* 5:126–27; Werner Vycichl, *Dictionnaire étymologique de la langue copte* (Leuven, 1983), p. 81; see also H. Kees, *Ancient Egypt* (Chicago, 1961), p. 36, and *Farbensymbolik in ägyptischen religiösen Texten,* Nachrichten von der Akademie der Wissenschaften in Göttingen: Philologisch-historische Klasse, Jahrgang 1943, nr. 11 (Göttingen, 1943), p. 417; and Theodor Hopfner, *Plutarch über Isis und Osiris* (Hildesheim, 1974), 2:155. The Egyptian name for the land was taken over into ancient Greek as "The Black Land" in one form or another (τῆς μελάνης γῆς, μελάγγαιος, μελάμβωλος, τὸ μέλαν πέδον Αἰγύπτοιο, μελανῖτις γῆ, κτλ.); see David Bain, "Μελανῖτις γῃ an Unnoticed Greek Name for Egypt: New Evidence for the Origins and Etymology of Alchemy?" in *The World of Ancient Magic,* ed. David Jordan et al. (Bergen, Norway, 1999), pp. 205–26. The term is also used in modern Egyptian Arabic (*samra*) to mean "Egypt"; see Stewart, "Color Terms in Egyptian Arabic," p. 112. As Gary Rendsburg points out to me, an ancient term for Egypt was "The Black and the Red Land," i.e., the black land of the Nile valley (*kmt*) and the red land of the desert (*dšrt*). On this term for Egypt, see James H. Breasted, *Ancient Records of Egypt* (Chicago, 1906), 2:245, 3:471; see also Erman and Grapow, *Wörterbuch,* 5:126; Kees, *Farbensymbolik,* p. 417; and compare Alessandra Nibbi, "A Contribution to Our Understanding of *kmt,*" *Discussions in Egyptology* 16 (1990) 70, who argues that *dšrt* in the parallel of *kmt* and *dšrt* does not refer to the desert but to part of the delta where the soil has a red color. (My thanks to Jeffrey Gaillard for referring me to the Nibbi article.) Cf. the Hebrew toponym Edom, which may derive from the word *adom* 'red'; see KBL 1:12.

The word *kmt* meaning "Egypt" has become popular in works having an Afrocentric focus, where it is argued that since the Egyptian root *km* means black, *kmt* means "black [people]" not "black [land]," thus indicating that the ancient Egyptians were black. See, e.g., Cheikh Anta Diop in *The General History of Africa,* vol. 2: *Ancient Civilizations of Africa,* ed. G. Mokhtar (Berkeley, 1981), pp. 27–57. Reactions (negative) to Diop's thesis by several scholars are found in the same volume of *The General History of Africa* on pp. 61–75. Note especially the points made by S. Sauneron (p. 64): the grammatical form of the Egyptian word cannot refer to people; the Egyptians never used the term to refer to Blacks to their south; the Egyptians did not use color terms to designate different peoples. Diop's original work on this subject (*Nations, negres et culture,* 1955) was critiqued by Raymond Mauny in *Bulletin de l'Institut Français d'Afrique Noire* 22 series B (1960) 544–51. Both Diop and Mauny were translated into English in *Problems in African History,* ed. R. O. Collins (Englewood Cliffs, N.J., 1968), pp. 10–23; reprinted in *Problems in African History: The Precolonial Centuries,* ed. R. O. Collins et al. (New York, 1993), pp. 32–49. Arguments against the blackness of the ancient Egyptians, including a discussion on the untenability of Diop's thesis, are presented by David H. Kelly, "Egyptians and Ethiopians: Color, Race, and Racism," *Classical Outlook* 68.3 (Spring 1991) 77–82. See also Snowden, "Bernal's 'Blacks,' Herodotus, and Other Classical Evidence," pp. 89–90. Diop's theories, their critiques and ramifications have recently been exhaustively examined by Stephen Howe as part of his study of the history of Afrocentrism, *Afrocentrism: Mythical Pasts and Imagined Homes* (London, 1998), pp. 163–92. Incidentally the debate over the blackness of the Egyptians is not new. It already took place in America in the nineteenth century; see Dickson Bruce, "Ancient Africa and Early Black American Historians, 1883–1915," *American Quarterly* 36 (1984) 684–99. Afrocentrism itself is a valid methodological approach to scholarly research that "attempts to avoid the values and assumptions imposed by the European tradition, and, where possible, to look at questions from an African perspective" (Ann M. Roth in *OEAE* 1:29). In other words, it is based on "the premise that it is valid to posit Africa as a geographical and cultural starting base in the study of peoples of African descent" (Keto, *The Africa Centered Perspective,* p. 1); see also Kwesi Otabil, *The Agonistic Imperative* (Bristol, Ind., 1994). Despite the fact that Diop's writings have been instrumental to the development of this methodology, his claim for the word *kmt* cannot be sustained. On this point, and for a good and balanced treatment of the subject in general, see Roth's article (pp. 29–32).

38. See Vycichl, *Dictionnaire étymologique,* p. 81, s.v., and Antonio Loprieno, *Ancient Egyptian* (Cambridge, 1995), p. 42.

39. Plutarch, *Isis and Osiris* 33 (364C), ed. J. Gwyn Griffiths, p. 170. Some three hundred years later, Jerome (d. 420 C.E.) said pretty much the same thing. In explaining why the LXX rendered Hebrew Ḥam (with *ḥ*) as Cham (with Greek χ), he says that the χ was meant to indicate rough breathing (*duplex adspiratio*), since there is no Greek equivalent to the *ḥ* sound, and then he adds: "So in this verse [Gen 9:18] they translate *Cham* for what is actually Ham—from which the word 'Egyptian' is pronounced as 'Ham' in the language of the Egyptians up to the present day" (Unde et in praesenti colo Cham transtulerunt pro eo quod est Ham, a quo et Aegyptus usque hodie Aegyptiorum lingua Ham dicitur); *CCL* 72:10–11, translation Hayward, *Saint Jerome's* Hebrew Questions on Genesis, p. 38. On the other hand, when Jerome says, in his *Liber interpretationis hebraicorum nominum* (ed. P. de Lagarde, 66.28), that "Egypt" means darkness or tribulation (*tenebrae vel tribulatio*), he is referring to the Hebrew word for Egypt (*miṣrayim*), as the title of his book implies, not the Egyptian word, and the meaning is exegetical, not etymological. So also Apponius (fourth–fifth or seventh century) says that "Egypt" in Hebrew means darkness (*tenebrae*): B. De Vregille and L. Neyrand, eds., *Apponii in Canticum Canticorum Expositio* 1.40 and 10.29, *CCL* 19:27, line 659, and 249, line 378, or "obscurity and gloom" (*obscuritas vel caligo*) (12.92, [epilogue], *CCL* 19:309, line 1367), *SC* 420:202–3. H. König, *Apponius: Die Auslegung zum Lied der Lieder* (Freiburg, 1992), p. 40. Apponius (1.40, p. 27) thus associates the Egyptians in Ex 11:4 allegorically with demons, the "Lords of Darkness."

40. This point has been noted at least as early as W. Spiegelberg's *Aegyptologische Randglossen zum Alten Testament* (Strassburg i. E., 1904), p. 10. Mazar's name is most closely associated with the explanation that Ham in Gen 10:6 refers

to Egypt's empire in fifteenth–twelfth century. See B. Mazar (Maisler) in *Eretz Israel* 3 (1954) 31–32. On the identification of Put as either Somalia or Libya, see above, pp. 233–34, n. 63.

41. Today, with the discovery of the Dead Sea Scrolls, we can add another source that uses "Ham" to mean Egypt: 1Q20 19 13, ed. Fitzmyer, *The Genesis Apocryphon,* p. 110. Two other documents from Qumran may also refer to Egypt and the Egyptians in their use of "Ham" but the text is too fragmentary to tell for sure: 6Q19 1 (*DJD* 3:136) has *dy bny ḥm* and 4Q454 3 (*DJD* 29:405) has *bʾrṣ ḥm wngwʿy.* Note also J. M. Myers's comment that the reference to the Hamites in 1 Chr 4:40 is explained by the fact that the "lands were in the hands of Egyptian puppets" (*AB: 1 Chronicles,* Garden City, N.Y., 1965, p. 31). On the passage, see further above, p. 20. The expression "the Land of Ham" for Egypt is sometimes encountered in later texts, e.g. *Pirqei Rabbi Eliezer* 39 (p. 92a) or *Sefer ha-Zikhronot (Chronicles of Jerahmeel),* ed. Eli Yassif, p. 166.

42. Hess, *Personal Names,* pp. 29–35, 118–23. Iapetos is the name of one of the Greek Titans. In arguing for the Japhet-Iapetos connection, Hess says that Japhet has no onomastic environment. There may, however, be some parallels to "Japhet." First, an Old South Arabian (Ḥaḍramout) inscription may record such a name. It reads *YWS BYN YPT / [H]QNY ʿŚTRM,* which the editor has translated as "Yaws(?) Bayyim Yafût / has dedicated to Aśtarum" (G. Ryckmans, "Inscriptions Sud-Arabes," *Le Museon* 45 [1932] 286–95 d. In his *Les noms propres sud-sémitiques* [Louvain, 1934–35], 1:399, Ryckmans questions whether the name should perhaps be read as *YPŠ̌*). G. L. Harding, *An Index and Concordance of Pre-Islamic Arabian Names and Inscriptions* (Toronto, 1971), p. 678, suggests a connection with the Arabic *fatta* 'to crush'. Second, the personal name *YPTN* is found in a Phoenician inscription: *[LRBT LT]NT PN BʿL WL / [ʾDN LBʿ]L ḤMN ʾŠ ND / [R ʿ]ZRBʿL BN YPTN* (N. Slouschz, *Thesaurus of Phoenician Inscriptions,* Tel-Aviv, 1942, p. 318, no. 501). Finally, cf. an Aramaic seal inscription with the name *YBT* (Nahman Avigad, *Corpus of West Semitic Stamp Seals,* revised and completed by Benjamin Sass, Jerusalem, 1997, p. 299, no. 800, p. 501).

43. See above, n. 27.

44. I am indebted to Richard Steiner for his patient clarification of several linguistic laws underlying the explanation that follows, part of which was anticipated more than one hundred years ago by Bähler, "De dienst van de Septuaginta in de etymologie van de Hebreeuwsche eigennamen, door de etymologie van den eigennaam חם opgehelderd," *Theologische Studiën Tijdschrift* 2 (1884) 115–22. (My thanks to Elizabeth Hollender for her help with reading the Dutch.)

45. Cf. Rendsburg, "Word Play in Biblical Hebrew," p. 145, n. 30.

46. This phenomenon is not as uncommon as one might think. It occurs in English as well: our *th* sign represents two different sounds, one as in the word *thin* and one as in *the.* The two sounds were represented by two different signs in Old English. Although modern English has only the one *th* sign, we readily recognize and distinguish the two sounds.

47. Wevers, "*Ḥeth* in Classical Hebrew," in *Essays on the Ancient Semitic World,* ed. J. W. Wevers and D. B. Redford (Toronto, 1970), pp. 101–12; Blau, "On Polyphony in Biblical Hebrew," *Proceedings of the Israel Academy of Sciences and Humanities* 6 (1982) 144–78; internal enumeration, 40–74. See also F. W.

Knobloch, "Hebrew Sounds in Greek Script: Transcriptions and Related Phenomena in the Septuagint, with Special Focus on Genesis" (Ph.D. diss., University of Pennsylvania, 1995), pp. 398–99. A summary of the realization of pharyngal and velar fricatives in Semitic languages is found in Lipinski, *Semitic Languages,* pp. 141–51.

48. See, e.g. (regarding the existence of an original *ḫ* merging with *ḥ* in Hebrew and Aramaic): Joüon and Muraoka, *A Grammar of Biblical Hebrew,* 1:26–27 §5k; Gary Rendsburg, "Ancient Hebrew Phonology," in *Phonologies of Asia and Africa,* ed. Alan Kaye (Winona Lake, Ind., 1997), 1:71–74 §5.4.9, 10; 5.5.2; J. Huehnergard, "Semitic Languages," in *CANE* 4:2117; R. Steiner, *The Case for Fricative-Laterals in Proto-Semitic* (New Haven, 1977), p. 120, n. 28, and 2x; James E. Hoch, *Semitic Words in Egyptian Texts of the New Kingdom and Third Intermediate Period* (Princeton, 1994), pp. 484–85; and Anson Rainey, "Grammar and Syntax of Epigraphic Hebrew," *JQR* 91 (2001) 419–20. For Aramaic: K. Beyer, *Die aramäischen Texte vom Toten Meer* (Göttingen, 1984), pp. 102–3; Stanislav Segert, "Old Aramaic Phonology," in Kaye, *Phonologies of Asia and Africa,* 1:118.

49. Leslau (*Comparative Dictionary of Geʿez,* p. 233) lists: Arabic *ḥamma* 'heat', *ḥumma* 'have a fever', Datina *ḥmy* 'be hot', Epigraphic South Arabian *ḥmm* 'hot season' (?), Saḥri *ḥmm,* Hebrew *ḥam* 'be warm, be hot', Aramaic *ḥămam,* Syriac *ḥam,* Ugaritic *ḥm* 'heat', Akkadian *emēmu* (derived from *ḥememu*) 'be warm, be hot', Geʿez *ḥmm* 'be in pain, suffer illness, have a fever'. Add also North Yemenite *ḥmm* 'to heat' (P. Behnstedt, *Die nordjemenitischen Dialekte* 2/1, Wiesbaden, 1992, p. 283); cf. Orel and Stolbova, *Hamito-Semitic Etymological Dictionary,* p. 283, no. 1285; and C. Ehret, *Reconstructing Proto-Afroasiatic (Proto-Afrasian)* (Berkeley, 1995), p. 371, no. 749: *ḥam* 'to warm up'. The reference in Gradwohl, *Die Farben im Alten Testament,* p. 50, to Ugaritic *ḫm* is a mistake for *ḥm.*

50. See Leslau, *Comparative Dictionary of Geʿez,* p. 235, who also lists Akkadian *emu.*

51. Behnstedt, *Die Nordjemenitische Dialekte* 2/1, p. 300.

52. Lane, *Lexicon,* 1:635–37. On the semantic relationship between middle hollow verbs (e.g. *ḥwm*) and geminated verbs (e.g. *ḥmm*), see above, n. 32. Note that just as *ḥmm* covers the semantic fields of "heat" and "dark," so too in the Northern Yemenite dialect of Arabic *ḥawm* (from the root *ḥwm*) means "heat." The reading *yaḫmūmu* meaning "dark" listed in Thomas Bauer, *Altarabische Dichtkunst* (Wiesbaden, 1992), 2:400, line 63, is a mistake, as can be seen from Bauer's index (p. 465), where the word is recorded as *yaḥmūmu.*

53. The fact that the Egyptian element *ḥm* appears as *ḫm* in the name Pa-ḫa-am-na-ta (the servant of god) found in the Amarna archives (see Hess, *Personal Names,* p. 30) is irrelevant, for Akkadian usually realized *ḥ* as *ḫ*. For the phenomenon, see Lipiński, *Semitic Languages,* pp. 141–51, esp. 144; Ran Zadok, *On West Semites in Babylonia during the Chaldean and Achaemenian Periods: An Onomastic Study* (Jerusalem, 1977), pp. 244–45.

54. Contra Hess, *Personal Names,* p. 30 (see also his *Amarna Personal Names,* Winona Lake, Ind., 1993, p. 234). The confusion between *ʿamm* and *ḥam* led Hess to say that "the West Semitic word for 'paternal kinsman, uncle' . . . appears in Hebrew with the same spelling as Ham" (*Personal Names,* p. 30). That is not the case. The word that appears in Hebrew with the same spelling as Ham, i.e., *ḥam,* means

"father-in-law." Jeaneane Fowler (*Theophoric Personal Names in Ancient Hebrew,* Sheffield, 1988, p. 280), although not confusing the two words, once translates Hebrew *ḥm* as "paternal uncle."

55. The entry in the 1911 edition was written by D. S. Margoliouth; in the 1963 edition (ed. F. C. Grant and H. H. Rowley) it was written by A. H. McNeile and T. W. Thacker. Similarly the entry "Ham, Land of" in the 1911 edition of Hasting's *Dictionary* (p. 289) offered *kmt* as one of two possibilities although concluding that the derivation is improbable, while the entry in the later edition (written by the same author, F. L. Griffith) explicitly rejects the possibility. So also rejecting the derivation from *kmt:* Loewenstamm, *EB* 3:164, and W. Gesenius, *Hebraïsches und aramaïsches Handwörterbuch über das Alte Testament,* 17th ed., ed. F. Buhl (Leipzig, 1921), p. 238, s.v. *ḥam* III. Jerome Lund in *The New International Dictionary of Old Testament Theology and Exegesis* (Grand Rapids, Mich., 1997), 4: 693, s.v. Ham: "most unlikely." A review of the *kmt* theory and its rejection can be found in Dillmann *Genesis,* 1:321–22; or in Hölscher, *Drei Erdkarten,* p. 42, n. 1. The older scholarship perpetuating the *kmt-ḥam* connection continues to make an appearance now and then; see, e.g., D. Neiman "The Two Genealogies of Japhet," in *Orient and Occident,* FS Cyrus Gordon, ed. H. A. Hoffner (Neukirchen-Vluyn, 1973), p. 122; E. Isaac in *ABD* 3:31, s.v. Ham; and Tonguino, *La malediction de canaan,* p. 251. So also O. Bimwenyi-Kweshi, *Discours théologique négro-africain* (Paris, 1981), pp. 118–21, and R. Drew Griffith, "Homer's Black Earth and the Land of Egypt," *Athenaeum* 84 (1996) 252.

56. On this poetic usage, see KBL 1:325, s.v. *ḥām* III.2. Cf. Latin *Aethiops* for "Egyptian" in poetic texts (*OLD,* s.v. Aethiops, 1b, citing only Horace, *Carmina* 3.6.14), although this for different reasons than that given for Egypt-Ham. See the discussion above, pp. 107–9, where also instances of the reverse phenomenon, "Egyptian" as a synonym for "Ethiopian," are noted (p. 301, n. 111). For the ethnic-geographic explanation, see Mazar, above, n. 40.

57. Muchiki, *Egyptian Proper Names and Loanwords in North-West Semitic,* p. 263; similarly Egyptian *k* is realized as *k* in Phoenician, Aramaic (also as *q*), and Akkadian (Amarna). Not one instance is cited of Egyptian *k* becoming *ḥ* or *ḫ* in a Northwest Semitic language (p. 314).

58. Ryckmans, *Les noms propres,* 1:104, 230. A. van den Branden, *Les inscriptions thamoudéenes* (Louvain-Heverlé), pp. 255, 106, 154.

59. Ryckmans and van den Branden, ibid. See also F. V. Winnett, W. L. Reed, et al., *Ancient Records from North Arabia* (Toronto, 1970), p. 110; and J. C. Biella, *Dictionary of Old South Arabic, Sabaean Dialect* (Chico, Calif., 1982), p. 198. Among modern Arabic dialects, the Syriac and the South Arabian Mehri, Jibbāli, and Ḥarsusi preserve the root *ḫmm* with the same range of meanings: Barthélemy, *Dictionnaire arabe-français,* p. 218; Johnstone, *Mehri Lexicon,* p. 443. Regarding *Ḫimmān,* note also, *ḫummān* and *ḫammān* 'refuse, low, ignoble, bad, base, weak' (Lane, *Lexicon,* p. 807; see Ryckmans, *Les noms proprés,* 1:104, 230). A.F.L. Beeston et al., *Dictionnaire sabéen* (Louvain-la-Neuve, 1982), p. 198, shows *ḫwm* with the meaning "sickness, plague."

60. Blau, "On Polyphony in Biblical Hebrew," p. 168 (internal enumeration, p. 64). Similar conclusion ("no sure etymology") by van der Toorn, "Ham," in *Dictionary of Deities and Demons in the Bible,* p. 383, s.v. Ham.

61. *ICC: Genesis*, p. 195. See also Nahum Sarna's similar comment in *JPSC: Genesis* (Philadelphia, 1989), p. 44 to 5:32.

62. Rendsburg fixes the phonological merging of *ḫ* with *ḥ* around 200 B.C.E. See his "Ancient Hebrew Phonology," pp. 73–74.

63. See Wutz, *Onomastica Sacra*, pp. 259, 289, 426, 765, 801, 835; Stone, *Signs of the Judgement*, p. 133.

64. *De sobrietate* 44–47, trans. F. H. Colson and G. H. Whitaker (LCL) except for my rendering of "evil" for κακία. To today's readers, Colson and Whitaker's "vice" conveys the impression of sexual immorality, and while "vice" may have this meaning, it need not be so restricted; it has a wider semantic range of moral imperfection in general. The meaning of Philo's κακία is not restricted to sexual immorality. C. D. Yonge provides a clearer translation of the last part of Philo: "In effect he is cursing his son Ham through the medium of Canaan; for Ham being moved to commit sin does himself become Canaan. For there is one subject, namely wickedness, of which one kind is comtemplated in a stationary condition, and the other in motion" (*The Works of Philo*, trans. C. D. Yonge, Peabody, Mass., 1993, p. 231). In his *Quaestiones in Genesim* 2.65 and 77 Philo also says that Ham means "heat" or "hot." See Grabbe, *Etymology in Early Jewish Interpretation*, p. 216. The wide range of interpretations given to Ham-Heat can be seen by comparing *Midrash ha-Neʿelam* (R. Margaliot, ed., *Zohar, Tiqqune ha-Zohar, Zohar Ḥadash*, Jerusalem, 1940–53, 1:21b)—Ham symbolizes desire, which heats the body—with Augustine: Ham signifies the "hot breed of heretics" (*haereticorum genus calidum*), [f]or heretical hearts are wont to be fired not by the spirit of wisdom, but by that of impatience, and thus to disturb the peace of the saints" (*City of God* 16.2, trans. E. M. Sanford and W. M. Green, LCL).

65. D. Dawson, *Allegorical Readers and Cultural Revision in Ancient Alexandria* (Berkeley, 1992), p. 100. Much has been written on the topic of Philo's allegorical reading of the Bible, its sources in the Greek and/or Jewish world, and its influences on Christian allegory. For some discussion of the first two topics, see Harry Wolfson, *Philo: Foundations of Religious Thought in Judaism, Christianity, and Islam* (Cambridge, 1947), 1:115–38, and Burton Mack, "Philo Judaeus and Exegetical Traditions in Alexandria," in *ANRW* 2.21.1 (1984) 227–71, esp. part II, "Exegetical Methods in Philo's Commentaries," pp. 249ff. Menahem Kister has recently shown how Qumran *pesher* exegesis "could indeed lead to allegorical interpretations, which may be considered Palestinian antecedents to Philo's hellenistic allegories"; see his "A Common Heritage: Biblical Interpretation at Qumran and Its Implications," in *Biblical Perspectives: Early Use and Interpretation of the Bible in Light of the Dead Sea Scrolls*, ed. M. Stone and E. Chazon (Leiden, 1998), pp. 109–11 and n. 37. A survey of recent scholarship on Philo's allegorization is provided by Peder Borge, "Philo of Alexandria: A Critical and Synthetical Survey of Research since World War II," *ANRW* 2.21.1 (1984) 128–32. Earle Hilgert, "Philo Judaeus et Alexandrinus: The State of the Problem," in *The School of Moses: Studies in Philo and Hellenistic Religion in Memory of Horst R. Moehring*, ed. J. P. Kenney (Atlanta, 1995), pp. 1–15. See also Mack, pp. 250–57; D. I. Brewer, *Techniques and Assumptions in Jewish Exegesis before 70 CE* (Tübingen, 1992), pp. 199–212; A. A. Long, "Allegory in Philo and Etymology in Stoicism: A Plea for Drawing Distinctions," *Studia Philonica* 9 (1997) 198–

210; and David Winston, "Philo and the Hellenistic Jewish Encounter," *Studia Philonica* 7 (1995) 124–42.

66. A modern Bible scholar has read the story of Ham and Canaan, without resort to allegory, in a way strikingly similar to Philo. Allen Ross shows how the stories in Genesis portray the characteristics of contemporary peoples as originating in eponymous ancestors, thus anticipating the future histories of these peoples. In this way, he says, when the Bible portrays Ham as evil and then says that "Ham was the father of Canaan," it means to say that "Ham, acting as he did, revealed himself as the true father of Canaan." See Allen P. Ross, "The Curse of Canaan," *Bibliotheca Sacra* 137 (1980) 225.

67. The texts and their authorship are fully discussed in pp. 54, 251, n. 65 (Ezekiel) and 171 (Pseudo-Eupolemus).

68. B. Z. Wacholder, "Pseudo-Eupolemus' Two Greek Fragments on the Life of Abraham," *HUCA* 34 (1963) 95.

69. Howard Jacobson, "The Identity and Role of Chum in Ezekiel's *Exagoge*," *Hebrew University Studies in Literature* 9 (1981) 139–46, quotation from 145.

70. The independent composition, which scholars call the Book of Dreams, actually constitutes chapters 83–90; the Animal Apocalyse consists of the second dream vision of the Book of Dreams. On the dating, see Patrick Tiller, *A Commentary on the Animal Apocalypse of I Enoch* (Atlanta, 1993), pp. 78–79; VanderKam, *Enoch and the Growth of an Apocalyptic Tradition*, pp. 161–63; D. Dimant, "History according to the Animal Apocalypse" (in Hebrew), *Jerusalem Studies in Jewish Thought* 2 (1982) 19; D. Bryan, *Cosmos, Chaos, and the Kosher Mentality* (Sheffield, 1995), pp. 38–39.

71. Bryan, *Cosmos*, p. 40.

72. *1 Enoch* 89:9. Recent translations of *1 Enoch* are those of Matthew Black, *The Book of Enoch, or 1 Enoch* (Leiden, 1985), Ephraim Isaac in *OTP* (see, however, Sebastian Brock's important review in *JJS* 35 [1984] 202), and Siegbert Uhlig, *Das äthiopische Henochbuch* (Jüdische Schriften aus hellenistischen-römischer Zeit 5–6, Gütersloh, 1984). George Nickelsburg has just published a new translation and commentary of parts of the work, *Hermeneia: 1 Enoch, Chapters 1–36, 81–108* (Minneapolis, 2001). The Ethiopic text has been edited, with a translation, by Michael A. Knibb, *The Ethiopic Book of Enoch* (Oxford, 1978). Tiller's *Commentary* provides a synoptic (Ethiopic, Greek, Aramaic) edition, with translation, of the Animal Apocalypse. The final words of the quotation, "and one black," are missing in one manuscript. However, the context clearly requires a third color, and the passage is thus translated by Black and Uhlig. Unfortunately, 89:9 is not preserved among the Aramaic Enoch fragments from Qumran (Milik, *The Books of Enoch*, pp. 241, 358; Tiller, *Commentary*, p. 165).

73. See Tiller, *Commentary*, p. 267; Bryan, *Cosmos*, p. 75.

74. Black, *Book of Enoch*, pp. 75, 257, 264; Uhlig, *Äthiopische Henochbuch*, p. 684, following G. Beer in E. Kautzsch, *Die apokryphen und Pseudepigraphen des Alten Testaments* (Tübingen, 1900), 2:291, note b. See also Black, "The New Creation in I Enoch" in *Creation, Christ, and Culture*, ed. R.W.A. McKinney (Edinburgh, 1976), pp. 20–21, and Gerald Friedlander, *Pirḳê De Rabbi Eliezer* (London, 1916), p. xxxii.

75. Dimant, "History according to the Animal Apocalypse," p. 24. (She is unsure about what to do with Japhet's red color.)

76. As already remarked by Bryan, *Cosmos,* p. 76. Bryan also presents other arguments against the pigmentation theory.

77. See Bryan, *Cosmos,* pp. 74–79; Tiller, *Commentary,* pp. 225–26, 267, 380, 385; and Nickelsburg, *Hermeneia: 1 Enoch,* pp. 371, 358, 376. Also: R. H. Charles, *APOT* 2:250–251; G. Reese, "Die Geschichte Israels in der Auffassung des frühen Judentums: Eine Untersuchung der Tiervision und Zehnwochenapokalypse des äthiopiscen Henochbuches, der Geschichtsdarstellung der Assumptio Mosis und der des 4 Esrabuches" (Ph.D. diss., Ruprecht-Theologischen-Universität zu Heidelberg, 1967), p. 28; and E. R. Goodenough, *Jewish Symbols in the Graeco-Roman Period* (New York, 1958), 7:24–25.

78. Based on the four horses in Zech 6:2–3 (cf. 1:8). Less well known is the vision of the four colors on the head of the beast in the *Shepherd of Hermas* (second century C.E.), vis. 4.1.10 and 4.3.3. In these three apocalyptic texts we find the grouping of red, white, black, plus a fourth color. See Martin Dibelius, *Die Hirt des Hermas,* Handbuch zum neuen testament: die apostolischen väter 4 (Tübingen, 1923), pp. 484–85; Carolyn Osiek, *Hermeneia: Shepherd of Hermas* (Minneapolis, 1999), p. 93. Although these colors are obviously meant symbolically, their usage as a group may have originated in the real-life color variation among animals ("red" being a reddish brown; cf. the biblical red heifer). This is indicated clearly in the pharonic Egyptian ceremony of driving (or, striking) the calves, in which the king drives four calves, white, red, black, and speckled, to a depiction of a divinity. See A. M. Blackman and H. W. Fairman, "The Significance of the Ceremony Ḥwt Bḥsw in the Temple of Horus at Edfu," *Journal of Egyptian Archaeology* 35 (1949) 98–112; 36 (1950) 63–81. Note also the use of red, black, white, "and so forth" to signify the variety of animal skin color in the medieval (thirteenth-century) *Zohar:* "As for the lower creatures, they are produced from the moisture of the earth under the influence of the heavens, which brings forth creatures of various kinds, some with skins and some with shells—red, black, or white, and so forth" (ed. R. Margaliot, 3:10a; English translation, M. Simon and P. P. Levertoff, *The Zohar,* 4:346). It is possible that the animal context in the *Animal Apocalypse* suggested the same three colors.

79. J. Massyngberde Ford, *AB: Revelation* (1975), p. 98: black is mourning, affliction; white is purity, conquest. *Shepherd of Hermas,* vis. 4.3.3 provides its own explanation: black is this world, white is the world to come. See also the commentary by Osiek, *Hermeneia: Shepherd of Hermas,* p. 93.

80. See both sources in the previous note, as well as Revelation 12:3 with J. Massyngberde Ford's commentary, p. 190. Cf. Pseudo-Dionysius Areopagita, *Celestial Hierarchy* 15.337A (ed. G. Heil, Stuttgart 1986, p. 69); C. Luibheid, *Pseudo-Dionysius: The Complete Works,* New York, 1987, p. 189; R. W. Thomson, trans., *The Armenian Version of the Works Attributed to Dionysius the Areopagite, CSCO* 489, Scriptores Armeniaci 18, Louvain, 1987, p. 36), who interprets the red as fiery and energetic, active. (Pseudo-Dionysius was from the East, probably Syria, fourth–sixth century.) For Arabic sources, see *EI*² 5:706b (A. Morabia).

81. In the tomb of Ramasses IX enemies are painted red for this reason. See Hornung, *The Valley of the Kings,* p. 161, pl. 119–20; also p. 164, pl. 125. See also Gay Robins in *OEAE* 1:292, s.v. color symbolism. Red representing blood is also found in the Harranian temple of Mars (Sinasi Gündüz, *The Knowledge of Life,* Oxford,

1994, p. 148). In rabbinic literature, R. Abba b. Kahana commented on Esau's ruddiness (Gen 25:25): "As if a murderer. And when Samuel saw that David was ruddy (1 Sam 16:12), he was afraid that David too might be a murderer" (*GenR* 63.8; p. 688). "As if [*ke'ilu*] a murderer" follows a reading represented by several manuscripts. Alternatively: "Completely [*kulo*] a murderer." This latter reading, is complicated by the biblical lemma "completely ruddy" (*admoni kulo*); see Theodor's apparatus. Whether or not we read "as if," it is clear that Esau's color is understood symbolically by R. Abba (contra, e.g., Samuel Yaffe Ashkenazi, *Yefeh To'ar*, ad loc.). A Syriac *Life of Abel* says that Abel realized Cain's murderous intentions when "he saw his brother's eyes, and how they looked like blood, and his face clothed in green [*yrqn'*]." See S. P. Brock, "A Syriac Life of Abel," *Le Muséon* 87 (1974) 474, ch. 5. Brock dates the work to the late fifth or early sixth century. The same symbolism is applied by Mani (b. 216) to Cain, according to Ibn al-Nadīm's tenth-century report (Bayard Dodge, ed. and trans., *The Fihrist of al-Nadīm*, New York, 1970, 2:784).

82. See Ruth Mellinkoff, *Outcasts*, 1:147–59 and *Journal of Jewish Art* 9 (1982) 31–46; John Friedman, *Monstrous Races*, p. 98; Peter Dronke, "Tradition and Innovation in Medieval Western Color-Imagery," in Portmann and Ritsema, *The Realms of Colour*, p. 89; reprinted in P. Dronke, *The Medieval Poet and His World* (Rome, 1984). This may be the origin of "the red Jews," who appear in German-language writings between the twelfth and sixteenth centuries (Andrew Anderson, *Alexander's Gate, Gog and Magog, and the Inclosed Nations*, Cambridge, Mass., 1932, p. 72, and A. C. Gow, *The Red Jews: Antisemitism in an Apocalyptic Age, 1200–1600*, Leiden, 1995, esp. pp. 4, 66–69). Gow remarks that a contributing factor in the designation "red Jews" may have been the secondary meaning of *rot* (red) in Middle High German, "duplicitous, wicked, faithless, cunning" (see below, p. 376, n. 39). Other Christian use of red symbolizes Jesus' passion or Christian martydom in general. A modern parallel to these symbolic meanings of red, white, and black is found in Jacob Grimm's discussion of these colors: "Red stands for the wounds of the Savior—white for the purity of Jesus—black for the baseness of the Jews" (Maria Tatar, *Off with Their Heads: Fairy Tales and the Culture of Childhood*, Princeton, 1992, p. 264, n. 32 quoted from Grimm's *Altdeutsche Wälder*, ed. W. Schoof, Darmstadt, 1966, 1:1–30).

83. For Abel, see Black, *The Book of Enoch*, p. 257, and Tiller, *Commentary*, p. 226. For Japhet, see Gabriele Boccaccini, "Jewish Apocalyptic Tradition: The Contribution of Italian Scholarship," in *Mysteries and Revelations: Apocalyptic Studies since the Uppsala Colloquium*, ed. J. J. Collins and J. H. Charlesworth (Sheffield, 1991), p. 42.

84. Above, n. 81.

85. Tiller (*Commentary*, p. 267) admits that the red-violence interpretation does not apply to Japhet, but he does not offer another explanation. Bryan's interpretation of the symbolic meaning of red (*Cosmos*, pp. 77–79) fails to convince, because he assigns it two meanings: positive for Abel, negative for Japhet.

86. *Quaestiones in Genesim* 1.88, 2.71, 2.79, trans. R. Marcus (LCL). The text is extant only in Armenian translation. See also 2.76 with Marcus's note e. A.F.J. Klijn, "From Creation to Noah in the Second Dream-Vision of the Ethiopic Henoch," in *Miscellanea Neotestamentica I*, ed. T. Baarda, A.F.J. Klijn, and W. C.

van Unnik (Leiden, 1978), pp. 157–58, mentions the Philonic passage but does not use it to explain the Animal Apocalypse. Tiller (*Commentary,* p. 267) also mentions the passage in Philo but rejects it as an explanation for Japhet's red color, since, he thinks, Philo's "indifference" relates to a Stoic notion and is irrelevant for determining the meaning in the Animal Apocalypse.

87. A middle position can be attained either by being equally unidentified with two opposing positions or by being equally identified with two opposing positions. An example of the first case would be the Stoic notion of "indifference" that is neither good nor bad, or indifference to food, sex, etc. that is, neither desiring nor not desiring something. The middle position in the second case, illustrated by several examples of color symbolism cited later, consists of being identified with both positive and negative, or good and bad. It seems that Philo had the latter case in mind, since the Armenian word *anoros* means "unbounded, limitless," i.e. not identified exclusively with any one position (good or bad) but with both. It is unlikely that Philo meant to play on the commonly understood etymology of Japhet as "broad" (πλάτος, *QG* 2.80), based on Gen 9:27, "May God broaden the territory of Japheth," i.e., "unbounded," since he would have made the etymology explicit if he had, as he does elsewhere. Marcus's translation of *anoros* as "indifferent" is probably based on Ambrose, who is clearly quoting Philo: *Sem Cham Iapheth quae nomina significant "bonum" et "malum" et "indifferens"* (*De Noe* 2.3, *CSEL* 32:414). But Marcus is unhappy with that translation, as he notes to the passage, because *indifferens* usually translates ἀδιαφόρον while the Armenian *anoros* usually translates Greek ἀόριστος 'unbounded, limitless'. As I indicated earlier, however, "unbounded, limitless" is exactly what Philo meant to say. As to Ambrose, his *indifferens* is also accurate because it undoubtedly did translate ἀδιαφόρον, as Marcus surmised, but ἀδιαφόρον means both "indifferent," i.e., neither good nor bad, as well as "absence of difference, equivalence," i.e., both good and bad, or "unbounded" (see LSJ, pp. 22–23, and G.W.H. Lampe, *A Patristic Greek Lexicon,* Oxford, 1961, p. 36, s.vv. ἀδιαφόρον, ἀδιαφορία). In short, Philo wrote ἀδιαφόρον with the meaning of "unbounded," as he often uses the word (e.g., *Conf.* 62, 81; *Migr.* 39, 47, 80, 129; *Mos.* 1.123, etc.; see P. Borgen et al., *The Philo Index* [Grand Rapids, Mich., 2000], p. 5, for more instances of Philo's use of the word). Cf. A. Méasson and J. Cazeaux, "From Grammar to Discourse: A Study of the *Questiones in Genesim* in Relation to the Treatises," in *Both Literal and Allegorical: Studies in Philo of Alexandria's "Questions and Answers on Genesis and Exodus,"* ed. D. M. Hay (Atlanta, 1991), p. 172: "Japeth is a combination of bad and good."

88. Gay Robins in *OEAE* 1:293b.

89. Alexander Borg, "Linguistic and Ethnographic Observations on the Color Categories of the Negev Bedouin," in Borg, *The Language of Color in the Mediterranean,* p. 140.

90. Ibid., p. 122; see p. 363, n. 13.

91. Thackston, *Tales of the Prophets,* p. 335. The work, based on early traditions, tells that Jesus had a vision of three men, one with a white face, one with a face the color of saffron, and one with a black face. The first went to Paradise, the second was tormented in his grave, and the third—who did not believe in God—after death "was seized by grapples of blazing fire and . . . was given a draught of hot water." Presumably, the second was punished in his grave but did not go to Hell, while the

third received the more severe punishment in Hell. Another passage in the *Qiṣaṣ al-anbiyā'* (p. 115) describes white, red, and black clouds and tells how the black clouds brought torment and death. We are not told the nature of the red and white clouds, but it is likely that they represent neutral and good things or values respectively. Note that in another passage in the *Qiṣaṣ* white clouds bring rain that resurrects (p. 144).

92. Anita Jacobson-Widding, *Red-White-Black as a Mode of Thought: A Study of Triadic Classification by Colours in the Ritual Symbolism and Cognitive Thought of the Peoples of the Lower Congo* (Uppsala, 1979), p. 369. See also Jacobson-Widding's "Colors and the Social Order: Symbolic Classification in Central Africa," in Borg, *The Language of Color in the Mediterranean,* pp. 234–39.

93. Victor Turner, "Colour Classification in Ndembu Ritual," *Anthropological Approaches to the Study of Religion,* ed. Michael Banton (Edinburgh, 1966), p. 64, and *The Forest of Symbols,* p. 70.

94. Pauline M. Ryan, "Color Symbolism in Hausa Literature," *Journal of Anthropological Research* 32 (1976) 141–60, esp. 144–47.

95. Above, pp. 118–19 and 307, n. 35.

96. Brenner, "On Color and the Sacred in the Hebrew Bible," p. 203.

97. *bShab* 114a. Note the reading (*kelim*) *adumim* in the Oxford manuscripts of *GenR* 96.5 (p. 1198), although the text as it stands is corrupt (*lo' adumim* should probably be read as *ela' adumim*). Other parallels have different readings, on which, see *GenR* 100.2, p. 1285. On the term *'wlyyryn,* see Saul Lieberman, "Interpretations in Mishna," *Tarbiẓ* 40 (1970) 14–16, and Sachs, *Beiträge zur Sprach- und Alterthumsforschung aus jüdischen Quellen,* 1:129–30.

98. Note, incidentally, that in the *Zohar* (ed. R. Margaliot, 1:73a), "Shem [represents] the right side, Ham the left side, Japheth is purple which includes them" i.e., encompasses both Shem-right and Ham-left. I do not mean to draw a parallel to the color symbolism of the Animal Apocalypse (purple is not red, and in zoharic symbolism in any case red has negative symbolic value) but to the symbolism of Shem as good (right), Ham as evil (left), and Japhet as encompassing both good and evil (Shem and Ham).

99. Tiller, *Commentary,* p. 268; see also pp. 225–26, 380, 385.

100. The manuscripts were published by Lagarde in 1892 and incorporated by Wutz in his *Onomastica Sacra,* p. 754. On the dating, see p. 7.

101. Pseudo-Jerome, *Expositio quattuor Evangeliorum, PL* 30.537A. On dating (eighth century), see Eligius Dekkers and Aemilius Gaar, eds., *Clavis Patrum Latinorum,* 3rd ed. (Steenbrugis, 1995), p. 219, no. 631.

102. Kaplan, *The Rise of the Black Magus,* pp. 23–24. Kaplan quotes a second passage from Hilary in which he "again alludes to Ethiopia while discussing the Magi."

103. Ibid., p. 25. Similarly, Friedman, *Monstrous Races,* p. 251, n. 27, and see V.I.J. Flint in *Archives d'histoire doctrinale et littéraire du moyen age* 49 (1982) 7–153. One of the three who is quoted is Sedatus. The text (*CSEL* 21:253, *CCL* 104:787), however, is falsely attributed to Sedatus, and probably comes from the eighth century. See Iohannis Machielsen, *Clavis patristica pseudepigraphorum medii aevi* (Turnhout, 1990), 1B: 931, no. 6420.

104. For Origen's exegesis, see above, pp. 48–51 and 168–69.

105. Pseudo-Sedatus, *CSEL* 21:253, *CCL* 104:787.

106. This would, incidentally, coincide with the iconographic evidence, which does not depict a Black magus until much later, in the fourteenth century. So Hugo Kehrer, *Die heiligen drei Könige un Literatur und Kunst* (Leipzig, 1909), 2:224, and Kaplan, *Rise of the Black Magus,* p. 71. Kaplan mentions a single visual image of a Black magus in a twelfth-century manuscript (no longer extant), but admits that the image is "of an extremely doubtful nature" (p. 30). Henri Baudet's statement in regard to the magi should be modified. Baudet wrote that "Otto von Freising (1150) established a relationship between the Ethiopian royal family and Caspar who, according to the later Evangelists, was the King of India (which included Ethiopia) and one of the Three Magi" (*Paradise on Earth: Some Thoughts on European Images of Non-European Man,* trans. Elizabeth Wentholt, 2nd ed., Middleton, Conn., 1988, p. 17). As far as I can tell, however, Otto said that Prester John, who lived, "beyond Persia and Armenia in the uttermost East" was a descendant of the the magi (*The Two Cities: A Chronicle of Universal History to the Year 1146 A.D. by Otto, Bishop of Freising,* trans. Charles C. Mierow and ed. Austin Evans and Charles Knapp, New York, 1928, p. 443).

107. See pp. 102–5.

108. For the redaction date of the Palestinian Talmud, see Glossary.

109. Tibat Marqe 33b, ed. Ben-Ḥayyim, pp. 78–79. John MacDonald, *Memar Marqah: The Teaching of Marqah* (Berlin, 1963), 2:26, renders *ḥm* as "heat" in the passage. M. Heidenheim, *Der Commentar Marqah's,* p. 17 (text), 26 and 166 (translation), reads *šwʿpyw bḥm,* which he translates as "devastation of Ham." This section of *Tibat Marqe* (Book 1) is dated by Ben-Ḥayyim to the time of Marqe (see Glossary).

110. On the *Samareitikon,* see now the review of the literature by Alan Crown, *Samaritan Scribes and Manuscripts* (Tübingen, 2001), pp. 7–10, 15–17.

111. Tal does not list this passage in his new *Dictionary of Samaritan Aramaic,* either under *ʿrb* or under *ḥm.* The association of the raven with Ham would be even closer if Marqe knew of, and was referring to, the traditions transmitted by Ephrem of both Ham and the raven turning black (see above pp. 99–100), but there is no indication that this is the case in this passage.

112. *Tibat Marqe* 59a (pp. 114–15); this section is part of Book 2 of *Tibat Marqe,* which, according to Ben-Ḥayyim, like Book 1 is basically from Marqe himself or contemporaneous with him (see Glossary). The definition of *ʿarob* as "mixed birds" is found in rabbinic literature, as is the definition "mixed birds and wild animals," and the definition "a mixture of flying insects" (respectively: *MidPs* 78.11 to Ps 78:45, "eagles, falcons, the *daʾah* [meaning unknown], ravens, and fowl," following Buber's notes ad loc. in his edition, and see *YalqSh,* ad loc., sec. 820; *MidPs,* 78.11 and *ExR* 11.2; *ExR* 11.3: "hornets and mosquitoes/gnats"). The last is somewhat similar to the definition "dog-flies" found in LXX Ex 8:15 and in Philo (*De Vita Mosis* 1.130, κυνομυία).

113. *bʿEr* 22a; *LevR* 19.1 (p. 415) and sources cited, to which add: *Midrash Samuel,* ed. S. Buber (Cracow, 1893), 5.2, p. 57; *yPeʾah* 1.1, 15d; *PRE* 21 at the end. Because of the reference to "destroyer of his children," I prefer translating *ʿrb* as "raven" rather than "evening" or "sunset," another meaning of the word. Although this meaning is also found in rabbinic literature (*MidPs* 78.11 and *YalqSh,* Psalms, 820), it would not account for the expression "destroyer of his children."

114. The raven commonly appears as a metaphor for dark-skinned people. For classical antiquity, see the references in Franz Bömer, *P. Ovidius Naso, Metamorphosen: Kommentar* (Heidelberg, 1969), 1:371. Early Arabic poets, from the pre-Islamic and early Islamic periods, who were African or partly African were known as *aghribat al-ʿArab,* "the crows of the Arabs"; see Lewis, "The Crows of the Arabs," and *Race and Slavery,* pp. 28ff. In ninth-century Baghdad a military corps of Ethiopians bore the title *ghurābīya* 'crows'; see E. van Donzel, "Ibn al-Jawzi on Ethiopians in Baghdad," p. 115 citing Ṭabarī (d. 923). Several Persian-Islamic poets refer to Blacks as crows and, vice-versa, to crows as Zangi; see Southgate, "Negative Images of Blacks," p. 11. In Biblical Hebrew "raven" is used in a "be black" connotation; see Brenner, *Colour Terms in the Old Testament,* p. 158.

CHAPTER ELEVEN

1. The variant readings of "Cham" ("Chan"), including Old Latin translations, are listed in the Göttingen edition of the Greek Bible: *Genesis,* ed. John W. Wevers (1974), p. 131. In addition to the Fathers cited there, add Irenaeus (end second century), in his *Proof of the Apostolic Teaching* 20–21 to this verse as well as to 9:26–27. The text (Armenian) was edited and translated by Karapet ter Mekerttschian et al., *The Proof of the Apostolic Preaching with Seven Fragments: Armenian Version, PO* 12.5 (Paris, 1919); translation and annotation by J. A. Robinson, *St. Irenaeus: The Demonstration of the Apostolic Teaching* (London, 1920), pp. 87–88, and by J. P. Smith, *St. Irenaeus: Proof of the Apostolic Preaching,* in *ACW* 16:59; see Smith's note on pp. 156–57, as well as L. M. Froidevaux's note in his translation in *SC* 62:60–61. Also add to Göttingen, Eutychius, "Annales," *PG* 111.917B (sec. 41–43), and *The Book of the Demonstration* (*Kitāb al-Burhān*), pt. 2, ed. P. Cachia (Louvain, 1961), *CSCO* 209–10, Scriptores Arabici 22–23, pp. 48 (text), 32 (English trans., W. M. Watt). Regarding the sixth-century *Dialogue of Timothy and Aquila* 31.12, cited by Wevers from manuscript, see now the Ph.D. dissertation of R. G. Robertson "The Dialogue of Timothy and Aquila" (Harvard, 1986), pp. lxv and 204. For the Latin readings, which include the Old Latin text of Ambrose (fourth century) and several fourth- to sixth-century writers, see B. Fischer, *Vetus Latina,* vol. 2: *Genesis* (Freiburg, 1951–54), pp. 131–32. "Cham" also appears in an Old English version of the Bible (Aelfric) in an eleventh-century manuscript, as noted in S. J. Crawford, *The Old English Version of the Heptateuch, Aelfric's Treatise on the Old and New Testament and His Preface to Genesis* (London, 1922), p. 108. For a review of modern biblical scholarship on the problem that "Ham sinned and Canaan was cursed?!," as the editor(s) of *GenR* 36.7 put it, see Claus Westermann, *CC: Genesis 1–11,* pp. 481–94, who notes also that the reading of "Ham" in 9:25 found in the manuscripts and quotations is obviously a change meant to harmonize the narrative. See also J. W. Wevers, *Notes on the Greek Text of Genesis* (Atlanta, Ga., 1993), p. 124, and Beno Jacob, *The First Book of the Bible: Genesis* (abridged), ed. and trans. E. I. Jacob and W. Jacob (New York, 1974), p. 68, to Gen 9:23.

2. *De sobrietate* 44–48. The interpretations of Ham as vice in potential and Canaan as vice in action are based on Philo's etymology of Ham as "heat" and Canaan as "tossing." For a full discussion of the passage, see above, pp. 150–51.

Cf. Philo's comments in *Quaestiones in Genesim* 2.65 with Marcus's note *a* in LCL.

3. Καὶ Νῶ χηος αἰσθόμενος τοῖς μὲν ἄλλοις παισὶν εὐδαιμονίαν εὔχηεται, τῷ δὲ Χάμᾳ διὰ τὴν συγγένειαν αὐτῷ, μὲν οὐ κατηράσατο, τοῖς δ' ἐγγόνοις αὐτοῦ· καὶ τῶν ἄλλων διαπεφευγότων τὴν ἀρὰν τοὺς Χαναναίου παῖδας μέτεισιν ὁ θεός (*Antiquities* 1.142; trans. Thackeray, LCL).

4. See, e.g., Samuel Yaffe Ashkenazi (sixteenth century), *Yefeh To'ar* (Jerusalem, 1988–89 = reprint of Ferrara, 1692), p. 225b.

5. T. W. Franxman, *Genesis and the "Jewish Antiquities" of Flavius Josephus* (Rome, 1979), pp. 112–13.

6. *Dialogue with Trypho* 139.1. Text in *Iustini Martyris: Dialogus cum Tryphone,* ed. Miroslav Marcovich (Berlin, 1997), p. 309. Translation is that of A. C. Coxe, *ANF* 1:269; another English translation is by A. Lukyn Williams, *Justin Martyr: The Dialogue with Trypho* (London, 1930), pp. 283–84. On the passage and its relationship to Jewish sources, see Louis Ginzberg "Die Haggada bei den Kirchenvätern," *MGWJ* 43 (1899) 463–64, and Oskar Skarsaune, *The Proof from Prophecy: A Study in Justin Martyr's Proof-Text Tradition* (Leiden, 1987), pp. 341–44.

7. Another early work, the Pseudo-Clementine *Recognitions* may refer to a curse on all of Ham's descendants but we cannot be sure. The text reads: "[Ham] abused his father and his offspring (τὸ σπέρμα, Syr. *zr*ʿʾ) was accursed to slavery" (1.30.2). See F. Stanley Jones, *An Ancient Jewish Christian Source on the Homily of Christianity: Pseudo-Clementine Recognitions 1.27–71* (Atlanta, 1995), p. 56, and cf. Thomas Smith's translation in *ANF* 8:85. The word "offspring" is ambiguous and may refer only to Canaan. Jones considers *Recognitions* 1.27–71 to be a Jewish-Christian work composed around 200 C.E. "quite possibly in Judaea or Jerusalem" (p. 166). The Greek and Syriac texts are found in W. Frankenberg, *Die syrischen Clementinen mit griechischem Paralleltext,* Texte und Untersuchengen zur Geschichte der altchristlichen Literatur 48.3 (Leipzig, 1937), pp. 36–37.

8. 4Q252 *Pesher Genesis*[a] 1 ii 6–7, *DJD* 22:185–207; F. García Martínez and E. Tigchelaar, *The Dead Sea Scrolls Study Edition* (Leiden, 1997), 1:502–3.

9. *GenR* 36.7; similarly *Tanḥuma, Noaḥ* 15 = *Tanḥuma,* ed. Buber 21, p. 49. *GenR* is cited by Tosafot, *bSan* 70a, s.v. *qilelo.*

10. R.-M. Tonneau *Sancti Ephraem Syri in Genesim et in Exodum Commentarii, CSCO* 152, Scriptores Syri 71 (Louvain, 1955), p. 64 (text). See also Ephrem, *Nisibene Hymns* 57.6: "Not Noah was damaged, but your instrument (*m'nk*) [Ham]. / He dressed himself in curses, as you had clothed yourself in him, and he became a servant" (translation Tryggve Kronholm, *Motifs from Genesis 1–11 in the Genuine Hymns of Ephrem the Syrian,* Uppsala, 1978, p. 208). A different translation is that of J. T. Sarsfield Stopford, *NPNF2* 13:210, Hymn 57.7: "Noah was not harmed, but thy garment, wherewith thou clothedst him: even cursings, he put on, and became a slave." Also in another poem, Ephrem has the curse fall on Ham; see Edmund Beck, *Nachträge zu Ephraem Syrus, CSCO* 363–64, Scriptores Syri 159–60 (Louvain, 1975), Auszug 4:97–109, pp. 55 (text), 74 (translation).

11. *Adversus haereses* 4.31.1, *SC* 100:786–87.

12. *Blessings of Isaac and Jacob* 5, *PO* 27.1–2:16–17.

13. *Pachomian Koinonia,* trans. A. Veilleux, Cistercian Studies 45–47 (Kalamazoo, Mich., 1980–82), 3:64, Letter 5.5.

14. *De patriarchis* 5.29; *CSEL* 32/2:141, *FC* 65:258.

15. *Letters* 27.12, ed. G. Banterle, *Sant' Ambrogio: Lettere (1–35)*. Sancti Ambrosii episcopi Mediolanensis opera 19 (Milan, 1988), pp. 258–59, *CSEL* 82/1:185, *FC* 26:147. Ambrose's biblical text had Canaan as the recipient of the curse as can be seen in *De Noe* 32.120, *CSEL* 32/1:493–94. It is possible that the shame mentioned by Ambrose refers to dark skin color rather than to slavery; for this possibility see p. 173 (cf. 94 and 181).

16. *Panarion* 63.3.9; trans. F. Williams, *The Panarion of Epiphanius of Salamis* (Leiden, 1994), 2:130.

17. *Commentarius in epistulas Paulinas ad Phillippenses* 2.7, *CSEL* 81/3:140. On authorship, see the list of suggestions by A. Pollastri in *Encyclopedia of the Early Church,* 1:30.

18. *Homilies on Matt* 6.8 (but cf. 8.5) and *Homilies on 1 Thess* 4; English translation in *NPNF1* 10:41 and 13:342.

19. Severus, *Chronica* 1.4, *CSEL* 1:6, *NPNF2* 11:72. Vincent, *Commonitoria* 7, ed. Reginald S. Moxon, *The Commonitorium of Vincentius of Lerins* (Cambridge, 1915), pp. 28–29, *FC* 7:279, *NPNF2* 11:136. Augustine, *De civitate Dei* 16.2: "Ideo Cham in filio suo maledictus est." And again in 16.3: "Chanaan . . . in quo filio maledictus est Cham." Also in 16.3 Augustine says that Noah's middle son, i.e., Ham, was cursed.

20. Caedmon is in K. W. Bouterwek, *Caedmon's der Angelsachsen biblische Dichtungen* (Gütersloh, 1854), p. 64, line 1590. The text of *Genesis* is in G. P. Krapp, *The Junius Manuscript* (New York, 1931), p. 49, and the translation in C. W. Kennedy, *The Caedmon Poems* (London, 1916), pp. 56–57. It is unclear whether Caedmon authored *Genesis,* which is traditionally dated to the early eighth century. See K. O'Keeffe, "The Book of Genesis in Anglo-Saxon England" (Ph.D. diss., University of Pennsylvania, 1975), p. 217, n. 1. Aaron Mirsky attempted to show rabbinic sources for the additions to, and deviations from, the Bible as paraphrased in *Genesis* ("On the Sources of the Anglo-Saxon *Genesis* and *Exodus,*" *English Studies* 48 [1967] 385–97). He did not comment on this deviation.

21. "Enim vero demum ex tribus liberis, unus effectus atrox cham tunc videlicet, quod non tuta vidisset patris pudentia. maledictus a patre . . ." (F. Blatt, *Die lateinischen Bearbeitungen der Acta Andrea et Matthiae apud Anthropophagos,* Giessen, 1930, p. 126, quoted in Friedman, *Monstrous Races,* p. 102). This reading is, as far as I could tell, not found in the other versions of the work. The *Recensio* is a poetic version of the original *Acts,* which varies so greatly from the textual tradition of the other versions of the work that its unique readings cannot be dated to the time of the *Acts* itself. See Robert Boenig, *The Acts of Andrew in the Country of the Cannibals* (New York, 1991), p. iii, and, for the dating, Dennis R. MacDonald, *The Acts of Andrew and the Acts of Andrew and Matthias in the City of the Cannibals* (Atlanta, 1990), p. 10.

22. S. C. Malan, *The Book of Adam and Eve,* also called *The Conflict of Adam and Eve with Satan* (London, 1882), p. 160. For literature and dating, see Stone, *A History of the Literature of Adam and Eve,* pp. 98–100.

23. *Leabhar breathnach annso sis,* ed. and trans. J. Henthorn Todd, p. 35. Also in T. Mommsen, *Chronica minora saec. iv, v, vi, vii* (Berlin, 1892–98), 3:151.

24. W. Wilmanns, "Ein Fragebüchlein aus dem neunten Jahrhundert," *Zeit-*

schrift für deutsches Altertum und deutsche Literatur 15 (1872) 169 (no. 37), p. 82. A later example is found in "The Dialogue of Adrian and Epictetus": "Unde sunt servi?—Ex Cam." See Walther Suchier, *L'Enfant Sage (Das Gespräch des Kaisers Hadrian mit dem klugen Kinde Epitus)* (Dresden, 1910), p. 267, no. 30 (line 65), and *Das mittellateinische Gespräch Adrian und Epictitus* (Tübingen, 1955), pp. 33, 55, 60, 110, 126.

25. *Kebra Nagast* 9, ed. Budge, *The Queen of Sheba and Her Only Son Menyelek,* pp. 6 and 126 (sec. 73). While the final redaction of the *Kebra Nagast* is dated to the first half of the fourteenth century, much of the material dates from the sixth–seventh century (Budge, p. xvi; D. A. Hubbard, "The Literary Sources of the *Kebra Nagast*" [Ph.D. diss., University of St. Andrews, Scotland, 1957], pp. 351–57; David Johnson, "Dating the *Kebra Nagast,*" in *Peace and War in Byzantium,* ed. Timothy S. Miller and John Nesbitt, Washington, 1995, pp. 197–208). According to the *Kebra,* the Ethiopians saw themselves as descendants of Shem and the surrounding peoples as descendants of Ham (see above, pp. 268–69, n. 205). The Jews of Ethiopia (Beta Israel) accepted this view and the corresponding version of the biblical story that has Ham cursed with slavery (Hagar Salamon, *The Hyena People: Ethiopian Jews in Christian Ethiopia,* Berkeley, 1999, p. 75).

26. *Adv. Marcion* 3.13.10, *CCL* 1/1:525–26, *SC* 399:128–29, *ANF* 3:332.

27. *Homilies on Genesis* 16.1, *GCS* 29 (Origen 6) 136–37, *SC* 7:373–74. Translation is that of R. Heine in *FC* 71:215. Graham Gould notes that this passage implies that the curse fell on all the descendants of Ham, not just on Canaan; see his "The Influence of Origen on Fourth-Century Monasticism: Some Further Remarks," in *Origeniana Sexta: Origène et la Bible / Origen and the Bible, Actes du Colloquium Origenianum Sextum, Chantilly 30 août–3 septembre 1993,* ed. Giles Dorival and Alain Le Boulluec with Monique Alexandre et al. (Leuven, 1995), p. 596.

28. Josephus, *Contra Apionem* 2.128, says that the Egyptians have always been enslaved to some power, but his statement is presumably unconnected to the biblical curse of Ham.

29. *PesR* 21 (p. 110a–b). Thus the reading in ed. pr., which is problematic since it would be difficult for Tanḥum b. Ḥanilai, who lived in the third century, to quote Berakhiah, who lived in the fourth. Manuscript evidence, however, provides different readings. MSS Dropsie and Casanata have Tanḥum b. Ḥusa, and MS Parma and the Vienna fragments have Tanḥum b. Ḥum (Rivka Ulmer, *Pesiqta Rabbati: A Synoptic Edition,* Atlanta, 1997, 1:510–11). A. Hyman, *Toledot Tannaim we-Amoraim,* 3:1242, suggests that the similar reading (Tanḥum b. Ḥanilai in the name of R. Berakhiah) found in *Tanḥuma, Tazriaʿ* 11, be reversed to read "Berakhiah in the name of Tanḥum b. Ḥanilai." Sections 21–24 of *PesR* stem from an independent *Midrash of the Ten Commandments* (Stemberger, *Introduction,* p. 299).

30. While this exegesis of Ex 20:2 appears in the amoraic *Pesiqta Rabbati,* we can assume its existence much earlier, even earlier than the authorities mentioned in the text, for a tannaitic midrash to the verse argues against it: "'Who brought you out of the land of Egypt, out of the house of slavery [lit. house of slaves]'—They [the Hebrews] were slaves to kings. You say that they were slaves of kings, but perhaps it means that they were slaves of slaves ['Out of the house of slaves']?

When it says, however, 'And He redeemed you from the house of slavery, from the hand of Pharaoh, king of Egypt' (Deut 7:8), it implies that they were slaves of kings and not slaves of slaves" (*Mekhilta, Ba-ḥodesh* 5, p. 222). The same interpretation of Ex 20:2 may be behind the statement that the Israelites "were driven out of Egypt in war by their own servants" found in the late third-century or early fourth-century Christian work known as the *Dialogue of Adamantius* (2.10); see Robert A. Pretty, *Adamantius: Dialogue on the True Faith in God,* ed. Garry W. Trompf (Leuven, 1997), p. 52; on the dating, see xvii and 17.

31. *LamR* 5.8 (Buber's edition reads differently).

32. The *yelamedenu* text, published by Ginzberg in *Ginzei Schechter,* 1:49, is paralleled in *ExR* 3.14 (in the name of R. Pinḥas the Priest, fourth century). The redaction of the first part of *Exodus Rabba,* i.e., chs. 1–14, is considered to date from no earlier than the tenth century; see Glossary.

33. *Wa-ʾerah* 10.

34. *PRE* 39 according to some manuscripts and ed. pr.; see Gerald Friedlander, *Pirḳê De Rabbi Eliezer,* p. 303, n. 3, and M. Ish-Shalom (Friedmann), *Nispaḥim le-Seder Eliyahu Zuṭa,* p. 50, n. 2, reprinted with *Seder Eliyahu Rabba we-Seder Eliyahu Zuṭa,* ed. Ish-Shalom. So also in MS HUC 2043. Some manuscripts add "for all the descendants of Ham are slaves" at the end, but this is missing in most witnesses to *PRE* 39 (see below to *PRE* 24). Some manuscripts don't even have "among slaves, the children of Ham"; see ed. Higger, *Ḥorev* 10 (1948) 214–15.

35. David b. Amram of Aden, *Midrash ha-Gadol,* 1:190.

36. *PRE* 24, ed. pr. (p. 56b). The manuscripts read: "Are not all the descendants of Ham (*bnei ḥam*) slaves?" in place of "for all the descendants of Ham are slaves." See ed. Higger, *Ḥorev* 9 (1946) 155 and Friedlander, *Pirḳê De Rabbi Eliezer,* p. 174.

37. See David Luria's *Commentary* to *PRE* printed in ed. Weiss, p. 56b, n. 15.

38. *Tanḥuma, Noaḥ* 15 = ed. Buber, *Tanḥuma* 21, p. 50 (see Buber's n. 232).

39. *Pitron Torah,* ed. E. E. Urbach, p. 68.

40. David Luria, *Commentary* to *PRE,* p. 56b, n. 15.

41. *TanḥB, Shemini* 7 (p. 25). The parallel in *NumR* 10.2 and 8 continues with: "and it says, 'Cursed be Canaan'—this was Ham who was his third son and he is called 'the father of Canaan.'" This, it seems to me, is an addition to the original text (as preserved in *TanḥB*), which attempts to reconcile the text with the biblical curse on Canaan, not Ham. Cf. *Tanḥuma, Shemini* 5, which parallels *TanḥB,* but adds, a bit further on in the text: "He cursed his son, as it says, 'And he said: Cursed be Canaan.'"

42. *Tanḥuma, Qedoshim* 15 (= *Tanḥuma,* ed. Buber, *Qedoshim* 15, p. 40a). MS Munich 224, f. 11b reads *nistares* instead of *nitraheq* (influenced by *bSan* 70a?). The *Tanḥuma* passage is quoted in *YalqSh,* Proverbs 959, s.v. *ube-taḥbulot,* without variant. This *Tanḥuma* text is dated to sixth–seventh century; see below, Glossary.

43. *ExR* 30.5. Such is the reading in "all good manuscripts of *ExR,* e.g. MS Jerusalem and MS Oxford" (Avigdor Shinan, personal correspondence). The second part of *Exodus Rabba* (i.e., from ch. 15 onward) belongs to the *Tanḥuma-Yelamedenu* family of midrash literature. "Ham the father of Canaan" is a quote from the biblical verse (Gen 9:22) and is undoubtedly used by the rabbinic author

deliberately, rather than simply saying "Ham," in order to implicitly justify the curse of slavery which he mentions next and which affected only Canaan in the biblical account.

44. The language of distance that occurs with slavery, as used in *Tanḥuma,* is found also in *Esther Rabba* 5.1 (a work dated after ca. 500; Stemberger, *Introduction,* p. 319): "Wine caused the separation [*hifrish*] of Noah from his children in regard to slavery . . . for on account of it he said 'Cursed be Canaan, a slave of slaves.'" These rabbinic texts speaking of slavery as a distancing from the social environment provide a striking early confirmation of Orlando Patterson's explanation of slavery as social death. "The second constituent element of the slave relation [was] the slave's natal alienation. . . . The definition of the slave [was] as a socially dead person. . . . He ceased to belong in his own right to any legitimate social order. . . . Not only was the slave denied all claims on, and obligations to, his parents and living blood relations but by extension . . . on his more remote ancestors and on his descendants. He was truly a genealogical isolate." The condition of the slave is one of "natal alienation . . . the loss of ties of birth in both ascending and descending generations," of which the slave's social death was the "outward conception." As others have noted, "the slave will remain forever an unborn being (non-né)." See Orlando Patterson, *Slavery and Social Death* (Cambridge, Mass., 1982), pp. 5, 7–8, 38. On this notion, see also C. Meillassoux, *The Anthropology of Slavery,* trans. A. Dasnois (Chicago, 1991; originally in French, 1986), pp. 99–107. On its application in Rome: Bradley, *Slavery and Society at Rome,* p. 27; in rabbinic Judaism: Paul Flesher, *Oxen, Women, or Citizens: Slaves in the System of the Mishnah* (Atlanta, 1988), pp. 94–101. The sixteenth-century Judah Loew of Prague (d. 1609) well understood this concept when he remarked, perhaps having the *Tanḥuma* text in mind: "[Ham's] progeny was cursed and was distanced from society" (*nitqalel zarʿo we-nitraḥeq mi-bnei adam*); see his *Ḥiddushe Aggadot,* ed. Ch. Hoenig et al. (London, 1960), 3:258, to *bSan* 108b.

45. Ginzberg, *Ginzei Schechter,* 1:164. Ginzberg considers this a late, post-talmudic text.

46. For the Hellenistic-Roman versions of the campaign, see above p. 55. The *Chronicles of Moses* was edited from thirteen manuscripts by Avigdor Shinan in *Ha-Sifrut* 24 (1977) 100–116; see secs. 8–12. On the dating, see p. 102, and Shinan's comments in "From Artapanos to 'The Book of Jashar,'" p. 65 and "Moses and the Ethiopian Woman," pp. 74, 76. On the *Chronicles of Moses,* in addition to Shinan see Tessa Rajak, "Moses in Ethiopia: Legend and Literature," *JJS* 29 (1978) 111–22; Donna Runnalls, "Moses' Ethiopian Campaign," *JSJ* 14 (1983) 135–56; and, especially for information on manuscripts, editions, and translations, Meyer Abraham, *Légendes juives apocryphes sur la Vie de Moïse* (Paris, 1925), pp. 12–22, 46–74. A study of Russian manuscripts of the the *Chronicles of Moses* was undertaken by E. Turdeanu "La 'Chronique de Moïse' in russe," *Revue des étude slaves* 46 (1967) 35–64; reprinted in his *Apocryphes slaves et roumains de l'Ancien Testament* (Leiden, 1981), pp. 276–305. These manuscripts also refer to the Kushite as "this female descendant of the cursed race of Ham" (Turdeanu, p. 45 [= 286]). I assume that the "Cham" that is mentioned by Turdeanu (p. 287) in describing the story of Moses pulling out the staff from Raguel's garden and thereby being eligible to marry Raguel's daughter—the staff that had been passed down from Adam

to Noah to Cham to Abraham to Isaac to Jacob and to Joseph—is really "Shem," as it is in Farrall's translation, "A Jewish Translator in Kievan Rus," p. 54. The story of Moses' Ethiopian campaign is also found in the Christian Byzantine chronicle *Palaea Historica,* which drew on Jewish aggadic material. In the *Palaea Historica,* as in some of the other accounts, Moses' marriage to the queen is omitted. The *Palaea Historica* was published by A. Vassiliev, *Anecdota Graeco-Byzantina* (Moscow, 1893), pp. 188–291; the section on Moses and Ethiopia is at pp. 228–29. The work is studied by D. Flusser in *Scripta Hierosolymitana* 22 (1971) 28–79; the relevant section is at pp. 67–68. The *Palaea* is dated not earlier than the ninth century (*Oxford Dictionary of Byzantium,* 3:1557). Flusser puts it after 953, "the year when the *Book of Yosippon* was composed" (p. 64, n. 62), while S. Lieberman, in a study of the *Palaea* as a source for Jewish aggadic material, accepts the ninth-century date put forward by earlier scholars ("Neglected Sources," *Tarbiẓ* 42 [1972–73] 42). The story is also recorded by the Syriac Christian writers, Jacob of Edessa (seventh century) and Ishᶜodad of Merv (ninth century): *Commentaire d'Išo'dad de Merv sur l'Ancien Testament* Exode-Deutéronome: C. Van Den Eynde, *CSCO* 176, Scriptores Syri 80 (Louvain, 1958), pp. 4–5; W. Wright, "Two Epistles of Mār Jacob, Bishop of Edessa," *Journal of Sacred Literature* 10 (1867) 9 of the Syriac enumeration (= p. 452); Jacob of Edessa, *Commentary to the Old Testament,* quoted by S. Brock from manuscript, "Some Syriac Legends concerning Moses," *JJS* 33 (1983) 243.

47. *Sefer ha-Yashar,* ed. Joseph Dan (Jerusalem, 1986), pp. 293–98; Dan's text is based on ed. Venice, 1625, the presumed first edition (but see Moshe Lazar, *Sēfēr Ha-Yāšār: First Ladino Translation,* Lancaster Calif., 1998, p. xiv), which has been published in facsimile by the Centre de Recherches sur la Culture Rabbinique under the direction of J. Genot-Bismuth, *Sefer hayašar (libro retto)* (Paris, 1986). *Sefer ha-Zikhronot,* ed. Eli Yassif, pp. 162–66; trans. M. Gaster, *Chronicles of Jerahmeel,* pp. 113–22. A consensus on the dating and provenance of these works is emerging: *Sefer ha-Yashar*—end fifteenth to beginning of sixteenth century, Italy or Spain; *Sefer ha-Zikhronot*—fourteenth century, Italy. *YalqSh* (twelfth–thirteenth century) is at Exodus, sec. 168 (in ed. Hyman et al., sec. 166, p. 38).

48. On the name of the Kushite king, compare "Kirki," the name of the great Nubian ruler ("king" in Arabic sources) of the ninth century C.E.; see, e.g., Giovanni Vantini, "Le roi Kirki de Nubia à Baghdad: un ou deux voyages?" in *Kunst und Geschichte Nubiens in christlilcher Zeit,* ed. Erich Dinkler (Recklinghausen, 1970), pp. 41–48.

49. I have chosen the text from *Sefer ha-Yashar* (p. 298) because the *Chronicles of Moses* text, as Shinan has published it (p. 12), conveys the impression that it is quoting a nonexistent biblical verse: "But Moses feared the Lord, the God of his fathers, and he did not come into her, for he remembered the oath that Abraham had sworn his servant, Eliezer, to take saying 'Do not take a wife for my son from among the daughters of the Canaanites' (Gen 24:3). And Isaac did similarly when Jacob was fleeing form Esau, and he commanded him and said 'Do not marry with the descendants of Ham,' for he remembered that Noah had enslaved the descendants of Ham to the descendants of Shem and the descendants of Japheth." Since there is no verse that says "Do not marry with the descendants of Ham," it would appear that the text derives from a form similar to that preserved in *Sefer ha-Yashar.*

The version in the *Sefer ha-Zikhronot* and *Yalquṭ Shimʿoni* is the same as that of Shinan's *Chronicles of Moses*. A different version of the *Chronicles of Moses* was published in 1516 and reprinted by A. Jellinek in his *Bet ha-Midrasch* 2 (1853) 6, which has none of the biblical references: "And they gave Moses the noblewoman, the [former] wife of Niqanos. But Moses remembered the covenant of the Lord, his God, and he did not approach her. And he put his sword between himself and her and he did not sin with her."

50. The earlier explanation of Moses' abstinence is discussed above, pp. 55–56.

51. See p. 68 where the text is discussed.

52. Eli Yassif, *Sipurei Ben Sira bi-Ymei ha-Beinaiyim*, p. 256.

53. Ṭabarī, *Taʾrīkh*, ed. M. J. de Goeje, 1:212; translation, Brinner, 2:11–12. Masʿūdī, *Murūj al-dhahab* (*Les praires d'or*, ed. de Meynard and de Courteille 1:76; ed. Charles Pellat, Beirut, 1965–74, 1:32); English translation by Aloys Sprenger, *El-Masʾūdī's Historical Encyclopaedia, Entitled "Meadows of Gold and Mines of Gems"* (London, 1841), p. 75. Dimashqī, *Kitāb nukhbat al-dahr*, ed. Mehren, p. 266; trans., Mehren, *Manuel de la cosmographie*, p. 385. In Ṭabarī, Ham is cursed in addition to Canaan: "Cursed be Canaan . . . May Ham be a slave."

54. Rotter, *Die Stellung des Negers*, p. 146. Apparently, after Yaʿqūbī some writers were influenced by him and refer to the curse on Canaan alone. See Enderwitz, *Gesellschaftlicher Rang und ethnische Legitimation*, p. 26.

55. Aharon b. Yose Hakohen, *Sefer ha-Gan* in *Tosafot ha-Shalem*, ed. Gellis, 1:277.10; also 277.12 citing Abraham ibn Ezra. In the Islamic world we find Yaʿqūbī, doing the same thing (Rotter, *Die Stellung des Negers*, p. 146). For Christianity, see Eike von Repgow (thirteenth century), who, in the *Sachsenspiegel*, records and refutes those who say that servitude derives from Ham (Landrecht, 3.42.3. In the modern German edition of C. Schott et al., Zurich, 1984, p. 189; in the edition of C. G. Homeyer, Berlin, 1842, 3:334). See Guido Kisch, *Sachsenspiegel and Bible* (Notre Dame Ind., 1941), pp. 137–38. On pp. 159–61, 170–79 (earlier in *Jewish Thought in the Sachsenspiegel*, New York, 1938, pp. 7–8, 14–17), Kisch shows a close similarity between this passage in Eike and the biblical commentary of Abraham ibn Ezra to Gen 9:25. He thinks it possible that Eike, here and elsewhere, was dependent upon Jewish oral traditions.

56. *Perushei R. Saʿadya Gaʾon li-Bereʾshit*, ed. Moshe Zucker (New York, 1984), p. 353 with Zucker's n. 100; see also Qapeḥ's edition (rev. Jerusalem, 1984), p. 31, and n. 9, and Ḥananel Mack, "Prolegomena and Example to an Edition of Midrash Bemidbar Rabba Part I" (Ph.D. diss., Hebrew University, 1991), p. 127. Qapeḥ says that Saadia's explanation follows Arabic custom.

57. *NumR* 10.2. As pointed out by D. Luria, ad loc., the parallel in *NumR* 10.8 is missing the statement "this is the way they used to curse." In Luria's commentary (ad loc.) the phrase "This is the way . . ." (*we-khen*) is replaced with "They cursed all of them" (*we-khulam*). To this, Luria remarks: "All the descendants of Ham." In light of Luria's thesis, expressed elsewhere, that all the desendants of Ham were cursed (see his *Commentary* to *PRE* 23, p. 55a, n. 59, and 24, p. 56b, n. 15), it may be that the reading *we-khulam* is Luria's own tendentious "correction." *NumR*, chs. 1–14, were redacted probably in the twelfth century; see Glossary. Saadia's interpretation was also accepted by Ibn Janaḥ (eleventh century), *Kitāb al-Lumaʿ*, ed. Joseph Derenbourg, *Le livre des parterres fleuris* (Paris, 1886),

p. 250, in the Hebrew translation of Ibn Tibbon, *Sefer ha-Riqmah,* ed. M. Wilensky, 2nd ed. (Jerusalem, 1964), p. 265; Samuel Masnut (thirteenth century), *Midrash Bere'shit Zuṭa',* ed. Mordekhai Hacohen (New York, 1962), p. 41, ad loc.; David b. Amram of Aden, *Midrash ha-Gadol,* Genesis, ed. M. Margulies, ad loc.; and the Karaite Aaron b. Joseph (fourteenth century), *Ha-Mivḥar weha-Mishar,* ad loc., although Ibn Ezra (to Gen 9:26) was quick to reject it.

58. V. Aptowitzer, "Asenath, the Wife of Joseph: A Haggadic Literary-Historical Study," *HUCA* 1 (1924) 239–41, n. 5. Most of the rabbinic and patristic sources that I cited in this chapter were already listed in Aptowitzer's one footnote.

59. *Yefeh To'ar* (Jerusalem, 1989), p. 225b.

60. Cf. the interpretation, found in some of the medieval tosafists, that "a slave of slaves" implies two enslavements, that of Ham to his brothers and that of Canaan to his brothers (*Da'at Zeqenim,* in *Sefer Tosafot ha-Shalem* 1:275.1; see also the manuscript commentary to *GenR* cited by Theodor, ad loc.). This interpretation seems to have its origin in R. Berakhiah's statement in *GenR* 36.7: "Ham sinned and Canaan was cursed?! . . . R. Berakhiah said . . . when Ham committed that act, he [Noah] said: 'You prevented me from having a young son to serve me. Therefore may that man be a slave to his brothers,'" with the understanding that "that man" means Ham. However, with the exception of MS London of *GenR* all text witnesses cited by Theodor (as well as MS Vatican 60) apparently took "that man" to refer to Canaan (as did the English translation in ed. Soncino) and therefore added "for they serve me" to the end of Berakhiah's statement, i.e., Canaan's brothers served their grandfather, Noah. Such apparently was the understanding of other tosafists, who took *a slave of slaves* to mean that Canaan will be a slave to his brothers, who will also be slaves, i.e., all of Ham's descendants were cursed, although Ham himself was apparently unaffected (Jacob of Vienna, Bekhor Shor, *Sefer Tosafot ha-Shalem,* 1:276.4, 5; similarly David Qimḥi [twelfth–thirteenth century], *Commentary,* ad loc.; see also Maharzaw to *GenR* 60.2, s.v. *shema' yavo' kushi*). This also seems to be the understanding of R. Berakhiah's statement, quoted earlier (p. 160), in *PesR* 21 (*Midrash of the Ten Commandments*). According to the reading of MS London ("that man" = Ham), R. Berakhiah's point is that Ham did not escape punishment for his sin, thus answering, at least partially, the Midrash's original question "Ham sinned and Canaan was cursed?!"

61. Section division follows W. Wright in his editon of the Syriac text: *The Homilies of Aphraates, the Persian Sage* (London, 1869), pp. 252, 290, and 56 respectively. Neither the French translation by M.-J. Pierre (*SC* 359:617, 672; 349:285), nor the German by Peter Bruns (*Fontes Christiani* 5/1:131, 5/2:338, 377), nor the Armenian edition by G. Lafontaine (*CSCO* 382–83, Scriptores Armeniaci 7–8, sec. 3.13; *CSCO* 386, Scriptores Armeniaci 8, sec. 13.10; *CSCO* 424, Scriptores Armeniaci 12, sec. 13.40) shows any variants to our texts. Robert Owens deduced from the contradiction in the *Demonstrations* that Aphrahat's biblical text read "Canaan" and that the reading "Ham" is interpretive (Robert J. Owens Jr., *The Genesis and Exodus Citations of Aphrahat the Persian Sage,* Leiden, 1983, pp. 108–9).

62. David George, "Narsai's Homilies on the Old Testament as a Source of Exegesis" (Ph.D. diss., Dropsie College, 1972), pp. 270–76.

63. *Book of the Demonstration (Kitāb al-Burhān), CSCO* 192–93, 209–10,

Scriptores Arabici 20–21, 22–23 (Arabic, ed. P. Cachia; English translation, W. Montgomery Watt), Louvain, 1960–61, para. 482. "Canaan" follows MS Vatican, which Cachia takes as the correct reading; see his note ad loc.

64. L. Cheikho, ed., *Eutychii patriarchae Alexandrini: Annales* (Beirut, 1906), *CSCO* 50, Scriptores Arabici 6 (= MS Beirut ar. 1), p. 14, lines 19–21. For "Ham," MS Florence has "Ḥeyaʿan . . . ," which Breydy thinks is dependant upon the biblical "Canaan." The readings of the various manuscripts are found in M. Breydy, *Études sur Saʿīd ibn Baṭrīq et ses sources, CSCO* 450, Subsida 69 (Louvain, 1983), p. 118, lines 14–17. Possibly the reading in the *Annales* derives from the *Cave of Treasures,* which was a source for the work (F. Micheau, EI^2 8:854a).

65. The *CSCO* edition follows MS Sinai and thus prints "Ham," but Cachia notes (ad loc.) that the reading of MS Sinai has been altered, and (vol. 192, p. 14) that in such a case the original reading is that represented by MS Vatican.

66. Baḥya, *Commentary to the Pentateuch,* Gen 9:24 and Ex 20:2, ed. Chavel, 1:123–24 and 2:187. The commentary on Ex 20:2 reads: "'From the house of slaves'—your masters were slaves, for the Egyptians were descendants of Ham."

67. G[ustav] Gottheil, *Moses versus Slavery, Being Two Discourses on the Slave Question* (London, 1861), p. 16.

68. Mahmoud Zouber, *Ahmad Bābā de Tombouctou (1556–1627),* p. 139.

69. Michael Banton, *Racial Theories* (Cambridge, 1987), p. 1; 2nd ed. (1998), p. 17, cf. p. 4. Robert Graves and Raphael Patai, "Some Hebrew Myths and Legends," *Encounter* 20.2–3 (1963) 5. Anthony Pagden, *The Fall of Natural Man: The American Indian and the Origins of Comparative Ethnology* (Cambridge, 1982), p. 42.

70. See chapter 9.

71. See above, pp. 106–7, and Rotter, *Stellung des Negers,* p. 144.

72. See above, pp. 105 and 150–56. Although Ham was originally pronounced as *ḫam* and the Arabic language has the *ḫ* sound (see pp. 147–49), the Muslims learned the name of Noah's son Ham from Jews who had long since been pronouncing Ham as if were written with *ḥ,* thus coinciding with other *ḥ*-based Arabic words connoting darkness, such as *ḥamamu* 'to become black,' *ḥumamu* 'charcoal,' *aḥammu* 'black,' etc. (Lane, *Arabic-English Lexicon,* 1:635–38).

CHAPTER TWELVE

1. See chapter 7.

2. See above, pp. 98–99.

3. *GenR* 36.7 (p. 341); see above, p. 105, where this text is partially discussed. The pericope in *GenR* deals with the question of why the curse of slavery was pronounced against Canaan if Ham was the one who sinned. An etiology of dark skin is logically out of place in this pericope and was apparently included because it was transmitted by the same R. Huna in the name of R. Joseph who transmitted the curse-of-slavery tradition. On the character of expositional midrashim such as *Genesis Rabba* as anthologies of various unconnected interpretations, see Joseph Heinemann, "Profile of a Midrash: The Art of Composition in Leviticus Rabba," *Journal of American Academy of Religion* 39 (1971) 142–43; this article is an English abridgment of Heinemann's Hebrew article that appeared in *Hasifrut* 2 (1971) 808–34. See also Heinemann's *Aggadot we-Toldoteihen* (Jerusalem, 1974), p. 181;

David Stern, "Midrash and the Language of Exegesis: A Study of Vayikra Rabbah, Chapter 1," in *Midrash and Literature,* ed. Geoffrey Hartman and Sanford Budick (New Haven, 1986), p. 106; James Kugel, "Two Introdutions to Midrash," *Prooftexts* 3 (1983) 146–47, repr. in *Midrash and Literature,* pp. 94–95; and Richard Sarason, "Toward a New Agendum for the Study of Rabbinic Midrashic Literature," in *Studies in Aggadah, Targum and Jewish Liturgy in Memory of Joseph Heinemann,* ed. J. J. Petuchowski and E. Fleischer (Jerusalem, 1981), p. 64, n. 21.

4. *Homilies on Genesis* 16.1, *GCS* 29 (Origen 6) 136–37, *SC* 7:373–74. Translation is that of R. Heine in *FC* 71:215. The *Homilies on Genesis* are not extant in the original Greek (except for a few sections) but are transmitted to us via Rufinus's (d. 411) Latin translation. The word translated "discolored" is the Latin *decolor,* which can have two meanings: "discoloration" or, in a derived sense, "degenerate" (*Thesaurus Linguae Latinae* [Leipzig, 1900–], s.v. *decolor*). The first meaning is the correct one in this text and is chosen in the translations of Louis Doutreleau in *SC* and Ronald Heine in *FC.*

5. P. 160.

6. For the common view of the Egyptians as dark skinned, see pp. 107–109.

7. *Commentary to Song* 2.2, *GCS* 33 (Origen 8), 126, and 114 respectively.

8. See pp. 48–51, 168–69 where this is treated at length.

9. Some discussion of this topic will be found in Rotter, *Die Stellung des Negers,* pp. 141–52; Enderwitz, *Gesellschafticher Rang und ethnische Legitimation,* pp. 25–27; and Lewis, *Race and Slavery,* pp. 123–25, n. 9.

10. Al-Kisāʾī, *Qiṣaṣ al-anbiyāʾ,* ed. Isaac Eisenberg, p. 99; trans. Thackston, *Tales of the Prophets,* p. 105. The identity and dates of Kisāʾī are uncertain; see above, p. 278, n. 80.

11. Ṭabarī, *Tarikh,* ed. M. J. de Goeje, 1:223. Translation in Brinner, *The History of al-Ṭabarī,* 2:21, "Ham begat all those who are black and curly-haired. . . . Noah prayed that the hair of Ham's descendants would not grow beyond their ears, and that wherever his descendants met the children of Shem, the latter would enslave them."

12. Thaʿlabī *Qiṣaṣ al-anbiyāʾ* (Cairo, 1954), p. 61: "Ham is the father of the Blacks (*al-sūdān*). . . . ʿAtāʾ said that Noah cursed Ham that the hair of his descendants should not grow below their ears, and wherever his offspring be, they would be slaves to the descendants of Shem and of Yafeth." Thaʿlabī is quoted in turn by Musa Kamara (d. 1945), *Zuhur al-basatin,* trans. Constance Hilliard in *Slaves and Slavery in Muslim Africa,* ed. J. R. Willis, 1:165.

13. *Tarikh,* 1:215. Brinner, *The History of al-Ṭabarī,* 2:14, "He prayed that Ham's color would be changed and that his descendants would be slaves to the children of Shem and Japheth." On Ṭabarī, see Adang, *Muslim Writers on Judaism,* pp. 39ff., 120ff.

14. Published in translation by B. Carra de Vaux as *L'abrègè des merveilles.* It is not certain who the author is. Carra de Vaux (introduction, pp. xxviii–xxxv) discusses whether it is Masʿūdī (tenth century) or Ibrāhīm ibn Waṣīf Shāh (d. before 1209), and tends toward authorship by the former; Levtzion and Hopkins (*Corpus,* pp. 33–34), the latter. There are two relevant statements in this work, the first of which reads: "The traditionists say that Noah cursed Cham and asked God that his descendants become ugly and black and that they be subject to serve the de-

scendants of Shem" (ch. 6, pp. 99–100 in ed. 1898; p. 105 in ed. 1984). The second speaks of Nimrod, who, so it says, was the first black man. He had "black color, red eyes, deformed body, and horns on his forehead. . . . He was born thus because of the curse pronounced by Noah on his son Ham. . . . Noah cursed Ham and asked God to make his descendants black and deformed and slaves to the sons of Shem" (pp.137–38 in ed. 1898; p. 129 in ed. 1984).

15. "Negroes are the children of Ham, the son of Noah, and . . . they were singled out to be black as the result of Noah's curse, which produced Ham's color and the slavery God inflicted upon his descendants (*Muqaddimah,* ed. Etienne Quatremère, Paris, 1858, 1:151; trans. F. Rosenthal, *Ibn Khaldun: The Muqaddimah,* 2nd ed., London, 1967, 1:169–70; see also 171–72). Ibn Khaldūn himself disagrees with this opinion, citing the Bible, which mentions only slavery. On the importance of genealogy and the institution of genealogists in Arab (pre-Islamic and Islamic) culture, see F. Rosenthal in EI^2 7:967–68, s.v. *nasab;* Walter J. Fischel, "Ibn Khaldūn: On the Bible, Judaism, and the Jews," in *Ignace Goldziher Memorial Volume,* ed. S. Löwinger et al. (Jerusalem, 1958), 2:157; and W. Montgomery Watt, "The Materials Used by Ibn Isḥāq," in *Historians of the Middle East,* ed. B. Lewis and P. M. Holt (London, 1962), p. 26.

16. "Cham was most beautiful in face and form, but God changed his color and that of his progeny because of the curse of Noah. [Noah] cursed Cham blackening his appearance and that of his progeny, and that they be made slaves to the sons of Shem and Japheth." My translation follows the Italian of Enrico Cerulli, *Somalia* 1 (Rome, 1957), p. 254, text on p. 234. The *Kitāb al-Zunūj* is a late nineteenth-century redaction of earlier manuscripts. On the work, see Prins in the *Journal of East Africa Swahili Committee* 28 (1958) 26–40, and G.S.P. Freeman-Grenville, *The Swahili Coast, 2nd to 19th Centuries* (London, 1988), sec. II, pp. 8–9, originally published as *Uganda Museum Occasional Papers, No. 4: Discovering Africa's Past* (Kampala, 1959).

17. A version found in modern Arabic folklore is recorded by Samuel Romanelli in the account of his travels (around 1790) through Morocco. Speaking of a black African he met, he says: "I asked him about the palms of his hands and the soles of his feet which were white. He informed me that the blacks are the descendants of Ham. When Noah, Ham's father, cursed him, his skin turned black. He wept and pleaded with him, and his father out of compassion, took pity on him so that his palms and soles became white again. On account of this, however, they were subjugated and sold into slavery, thus fulfilling their forefather's curse—'Cursed be Canaan, the lowest of slaves shall he be to his brothers'" (Samuel Romanelli, *Travail in an Arab Land,* ed. and trans. Y. K. Stillman and N. A. Stillman, Tuscaloosa and London, 1989, pp. 69–70). See also below, n. 19.

18. Karl Jahn, ed., *Die Geschichte der Kinder Israels des Rašīd ad-Dīn* (Vienna, 1973), p. 33 (translation), pl. 9 (text).

19. C. Snouck Hurgronje, *Mekka in the Latter Part of the 19th Century,* transl. J. H. Monahan (Leiden, 1931), p. 107, n. 1; in the German edition, *Mekka* (Haag, 1888–89), 2:133.

20. Probably the same historical situation is behind the Islamic revision of the rabbinic sex-in-the-ark story, which has Canaan, rather than Ham, becoming black (*aswāda*) in the ark. See Ibn ʿAbd al-Ḥakam (d. 870/1), *Futūḥ Miṣr,* ed. Torrey, *The History of the Conquest of Egypt,* p. 8. Al-Ḥakam's report may go back to ʿAbd

Allāh ibn ʿAbbās (d. 686–88), a contemporary of the prophet of Islam; see above, p. 293, n. 72.

21. Joannes C. J. Sanders, *Commentaire sur la Genèse, CSCO* 274–275, Scriptores Arabici 24–25 (Louvain, 1967), 1:56 (text), 2:52–55 (translation). Sanders's translation at this point does not literally follow the Arabic.

22. For Ishodad, see above, p. 100. Bar Hebraeus: "'And Ham, the father of Canaan, saw the nakedness of his father and showed [it] to his two brothers.' That is . . . that Canaan was accursed and not Ham, and with the very curse he became black (*ʾwkm*) and the blackness (*ʾwkmwtʾ*) was transmitted to his descendants. . . . And he said, 'Cursed be Canaan! A servant of servants shall he be to his brothers'" (Sprengling and Graham, *Barhebraeus' Scholia on the Old Testament,* pp. 40–41, to Gen 9:22).

23. Wahb ibn Munabbih: The Nubians, Zanj, Zaghawa (quoted in Ṭabarī, *Tarikh,* 1:212; Brinner, 2:1); or "the descendants of Kush and Canaan are the races of the Sūdān: the Nūba, the Zanj, the Qazān, the Zaghāwa, the Ḥabasha, the Qibṭ and the Barbar" (quoted in Ibn Qutayba [d. 889], *Kitāb al-maʿārif,* ed. Tharwat ʿUkāsha, p. 26; ed. F. Wüstenfeld, p. 14. English trans., Lewis, *Race and Slavery,* pp. 124–25, and *Islam,* 2:210; Levtzion and Hopkins, *Corpus,* p. 15. On a reading "Qazan"—possibly for "Fazzan"—instead of "Qaran," see Levtzion and Hopkins, p. 376, n. 1). Ibn ʿAbd al-Ḥakam (ninth century): Canaan is the father of the blacks (*sūdān*) and the Abyssinians (*Futūḥ Miṣr,* p. 8). Yaʿqūbī (d. 897): "The posterity of Kush ben Ham and Canaan ben Ham are the Nuba, the Zanj, and the Ḥabasha" (*Tārīkh,* ed. M. Th. Houtsma, *Ibn Wādhih qui dicitur al-Ja'qubī Historiae,* Leiden, 1883, 1:13; translation in Levtzion and Hopkins, *Corpus,* p. 20. On Yaʿqūbī, see Adang, *Muslim Writers on Judaism,* pp. 117–20). *Akhbār al-zamān:* "Among the children of Canaan are the Nabīṭ, Nabīṭ signifies 'black.' . . . Among the children of Sūdān, son of Canaan, are . . . the Zanj" (Carra de Vaux, *L'abrégé des Merveilles,* ed. 1898, pp. 99–101; ed. 1984, pp. 105–7. English translation in Levtzion and Hopkins, *Corpus,* pp. 34–35. On the authorship of the work, see above, n. 14). In Maqdisī's (tenth century) *Kitāb al-badʾ waʾl-taʾrīkh,* ed. and trans. C. Huart (Paris, 1903), text 3:27, translation 3:28–29, Canaan is the father of, among several African peoples, "the Sūdān [and] the Nūba." The *Book of the Zanj* states that the Nūba, the Ḥabash, and the Zanj are the descendants of Canaan (Cerulli, *Somalia,* p. 234, text; p. 254, trans.).

24. Maqrīzī (d. 1442): "The Nubians are descended from Nuba son of Kush son of Canaan son of Ham" (Gaudefroy-Demombynes, *Ibn Faḍl Allah al-ʿOmarī: Masālik el Abṣār fi Mamālik el Amṣār* (Paris, 1927), appendix I, p. 85; excerpted in English translation in Levtzion and Hopkins, *Corpus,* p. 353. Maqrīzī's reference to Qūṭ b. Ḥām is probably only the result of a scribal error for Fūṭ ben Ḥām, the biblical genealogy (see above, p. 234, the end of n. 63). Ṭabarī quotes Ibn Masʿūd (tenth century) and "some of the companions of the Prophet" to say that Canaan was the son of Kush (Brinner, *The History of al-Ṭabarī,* 2:50). Ṭabarī himself says several times that Kush was the son of Canaan (Brinner, pp. 105, 109, etc.) as does Ibn Saʿd (*Kitāb al-ṭabaqāt al-kabīr,* vol. 1/i, ed. E. Mittwoch, Leiden, 1905, p. 19; trans. S. Moinul Haq and H. K. Ghanzafar, Karachi, 1967, 1:33). Masʿūdī refers to Kush as the son of Canaan, or as the great-grandfather of Canaan (*Murūj al-dhahab,* ed. Charles Pellat, *Praires d'or,* 2:321, 418, n. 1. English translation, Levtzion and Hopkins, *Corpus,* p. 31. Quoted by Ibn Khaldun; see *Corpus,*

p. 332. On Masʿūdī, see Adang, *Muslim Writers on Judaism,* pp. 44ff., 122ff.). Kaʿb al-Aḥbar has Canaan as the son of Kush (as quoted by Kisāʾī; Thackston, *Tales of the Prophets,* p. 129) as also Dimashqī (*Kitāb nukhbat al-dahr,* ed. and trans. Mehren, p. 266, text; p. 385, trans.) Note also that Ibn Ḥawqal (tenth century) in his *Kitāb ṣurat al-arḍ* (ed. J. H. Kramers, Leiden, 1938–39, p. 245; trans. J. H. Kramers and G. Wiet, *Configuration de la terre (Kitab surat al-ard),* Paris, 1964, p. 237), makes Nimrod, the biblical son of Kush, a son of Canaan.

25. The text has come down to us in a quotation twice removed—Eusebius quoting Alexander Polyhistor quoting "Eupolemus." Indeed, we know of a Jewish-Hellenistic historian by this name, and he is generally identified with the Eupolemus who was an ambassador for Judas Maccabeus mentioned in 1 and 2 Maccabees. Nonetheless, the generally accepted view—until recently, at any rate—is that this text could not have been authored by Eupolemus and that the author was an unknown Samaritan living in the mid-second century B.C.E. During the past several years, however, some have argued against this once almost unanimous consensus. R. Pummer, "Αργαζιν: A Criterion for Samaritan Provenance?" *JSJ* 18 (1987) 18–25, has cast doubt on the main piece of evidence for the Samaritan attribution. R. Doran, who translated the fragment anew in *OTP,* argued that the author is the genuine Eupolemus. His argument is presented in "The Jewish Hellenistic Historians before Josephus," *ANRW* 2.20 (1987) 270–74. More recently Erich Gruen and J. J. Collins have expressed reservations about the Samaritan attribution. See Gruen, *Heritage and Hellenism,* p. 147, and Collins, *Between Athens and Jerusalem,* 2nd ed., pp. 47–50. A review of the debate is found in Gregory E. Sterling, *Historiography and Self-Definition*, pp. 187–206, with bibliography (add Gutmann, *The Beginnings of Jewish-Hellenistic Literature,* 2:95–96).

26. Text in Holladay, *Fragments from Hellenistic Jewish Authors,* 1:174–75. Doran (*OTP* 2:881) reads the text somewhat differently. Some think that the second Belus is a dittographic error, in which case the genealogy would be Belus > Canaan > Chum instead of Belus > Belus > Canaan > Chum; see Holladay's note 32 on p. 186.

27. See Holladay, *Fragments from Hellenistic Jewish Authors,* 1:186, n. 35; Doran, *OTP* 2:877, n. 32. B. Z. Wacholder argues that the change from Chus to Chum was a deliberate attempt to play on the Hebrew *ḥmm* or *ḥwm* 'dark' ("Pseudo-Eupolemus' Two Greek Fragments on the Life of Abraham," *HUCA* 34 [1963] 95). See above, p. 151.

28. Cf. the description of a demon who appeared in the form of an Ethiopian as black as soot (Αἰθίοπα μαῦρον ὡς ἡ ἀσβόλη) in *Passio Bartholomaei* 7 (R. A. Lipsius and M. Bonnet, *Acta Apostolorum Apocrypha,* Hildesheim, 1959, 2:146, line 23), and the similar term, "an ash-skinned black" (σποδόδερμε μελανέ), describing the fourth-century black African, Christian monk, Abba Moses (*Apophthegmata Patrum, PG* 65.284B).

29. See Sterling, *Historiography and Self-Definition,* p. 194, n. 281. But R. V. Huggins, "Noah and the Giants: A Response to John C. Reeves," *JBL* 114 (1995) 105, notes that even this emendation does not solve all the difficulties.

30. *OTP* 2:881.

31. René Dussaud, "Cham et Canaan," *Revue de l'histoire des religions* 59 (1909) 221–30.

32. See above, p. 301, nn. 116–17, for source references.

33. Note that the Kronos legend, which is unlike Greek mythology, is considered to be pre-Hellenic and to have derived from Asia Minor. See H. J. Rose and H. W. Parke in *The Oxford Classical Dictionary,* ed. N.G.L. Hammond and H. H. Scullard 2nd ed. (Oxford, 1970), s.v. Kronos. The confusion of the relationship of Canaan and Ham as seen in the two genealogies may be behind the biblical crux of Canaan being punished for Ham's sin; see Dussaud, "Cham et Canaan."

34. Moses Gaster has argued for Samaritan influences on Islamic traditions; see EI^1 7:124–28, s.v. Samaritans, esp. 124b.

35. The *Cave of Treasures* exists in several versions. The relevant section is 21.16. The original Syriac has been edited by Su-Min Ri, *La caverne des trésors,* pp. 162–63 (text), 62–63 (translation); earlier edition: C. Bezold, *Die Schatzhöle* (Leipzig, 1883), pp. 108–9 (Syriac and Arabic texts), 25 (translation); English trans., E.A.W. Budge, *The Book of the Cave of Treasures* (London, 1927), pp. 120–21. The Arabic version, known as *Kitāb al-Magāll* (Book of the Rolls) was published by Margaret Dunlop Gibson, *Apocrypha Arabica* (London, 1901), pp. 29–30 (text) and 30–31 (translation). Besides Bezold's edition, the Arabic version (with Italian translation and commentary) was published by A. Battista and B. Bagatti, *La caverna dei tesori* (Jerusalem, 1979). An Ethiopic version (also known as *Qalēmentos,* "Pseudo-Clementine") was published by S. Grébaut, "Littérature Éthiopienne Pseudo-Clemintine," *Revue de l'Orient Chrétien* 17 (1912) 22. For "Musdaye" variants abound: Muṣraye, Musaye, Musnaye, Mysians (*mūsīn*), and Mosirawiens. The Ethiopic also has Kuerbawiens. The *Cave of Treasures* in its present form dates from the sixth century at the latest, but it originally goes back to the fourth or, according to Su-Min Ri (pp. xxii–xxiii), the third. It derives from the Orient, originally composed in Syriac, possibly from the school of Ephrem. On the dating, see also Stone, *A History of the Literature of Adam and Eve,* pp. 54–55.

36. See p. 134.

37. See n. 35. Ri takes the Syriac here to be the adjective *musraya* 'abominable, odious' (Payne Smith, *Thesaurus Syriacus,* 2:2044, via the Greek μυσαρός).

38. Ibid. On the Arabic translation, "often a type of midrash on the Syriac," done around 750 C.E., see G. Anderson, "Celibacy or Consummation in the Garden? Reflections on Early Jewish and Christian Interpretations of the Garden of Eden," *HTR* 82 (1989) 147, n. 62; see also Ri, *La caverne des trésors,* p. xv.

39. A slightly different reading of the Ethiopic is quoted by Bezold, *Schatzhöle,* p. 76, n. 94.

40. L. Cheikho, ed., *Eutychii patriarchae Alexandrini: Annales,* p. 14, lines 19–21. Pococke's Latin translation (1658–59) of the *Annales* published in *PG* 111.917B (sec. 41–43) has "the Egyptians, the Nigritae, the Ethiopians and (it is said) the Barbari." Pococke's translation was based on three seventeenth-century Arabic manuscripts. MS Florence and MS London read "the Egyptians, the Sūdān, and all of that race." The readings of the various manuscripts are found in Breydy, *Études sur Saʿīd ibn Baṭrīq et ses sources,* p. 118, lines 14–17. On the black African Barbari, see my article, "Geographia Rabbinica." Regarding the origin of this passage, note that one of the major sources of the *Annales* was the *Cave of Treasures* (F. Micheau, EI^2 8:854a citing Breyde, *Études,* ch. 2).

41. *La caverne des trésors: version Géorgienne,* ed. Ciala Kourcikidzé, trans. Jean-

Pierre Mahé, *CSCO* 526–27, Scriptores Iberici 23–24 (Louvain, 1992–93), ch. 21, pp. 54–55 (text), 38–39 (translation). The Georgian is based on a no-longer extant Arabic redaction of the original Syriac (Mahé, pp. xxv–xxvi). For the ninth–eleventh-century dating of the Georgian, see Ri, *La caverne des trésors,* p. vi.

42. In addition to 21.16, the curse of slavery on Canaan is mentioned elsewhere in the document: 21.7–8, 16, 21, 32.11, pp. 158–59, 164–65, 256 (text), pp. 60–63, 98 (translation).

43. Michael Stone lists the literature documenting the "extensive influence on Oriental Christianity" of the *Cave of Treaures.* See his *A History of the Literature of Adam and Eve,* p. 92 et passim (Index, s.v.), as well as J.-B. Frey in *Dictionnaire de la Bible, Supplément,* ed. L. Pirot et al. (Paris, 1928), 1:115–16.

44. Anderson, "Celibacy or Consummation in the Garden?" p. 146, n. 60. For Chiekho, see Khoury's remarks in "Quelques réflexions sur la première ou les premières bibles arabes," p. 551. See also Thackston, *Tales of the Prophets,* pp. xiii–xiv, xxii–xxiv.

45. Adang, *Muslim Writers on Judaism,* pp. 2, 16, 38, 114, 117, 120–21. See also the articles by A. Götze, "Die Nachwirkung der Schatzhöhle," *Zeitschrift für Semitistik und verwandte Gebiete* 2 (1923) 51–94, and 3 (1924) 53–71, 153–77, in which he surveys use of the *Cave of Treasures* by later writers including some Muslims. See also D. Bundy, "Pseudepigrapha in Syriac Literature," in *Society of Biblical Literature: 1991 Seminar Papers* (Atlanta, 1991), pp. 759–62.

46. *Chrónica dos feitos notáveis que se passaram na conquista da Guiné por mandado do Infante D. Henrique,* ed. Torquato de Sousa Soares (Lisbon, 1978–81), ch. 16, vol. 1, p. 77 and see 2:103. French translation: L. Bourdon and R. Ricard, eds. *Chronique de Guinée* (Dakar, 1960), p. 90; English translation, C. R. Beazley and E. Prestage, *The Chronicle of the Discovery and Conquest of Guinea* in the Hakluyt first series, no. 95 (London,1896), 1:54. Zurara wrote his work in 1453. For the reading "Cham," see Beazley and Prestage's note ad loc., 2:319. On the confusion between Cham and Cain in medieval literature, see Ruth Mellinkoff, "Cain's Monstrous Progeny in *Beowulf*: Part II, Post-Diluvian Survival," *Anglo-Saxon England* 9 (1980) 194. Further cause for confusion is due to the fact that in medieval orthography the *m* could be read as an *i* and an *n*. "This confusion occurred widely in English, French, and Latin spellings. Ranulf Higden in the *Polychronicon* was alluding to this familiar identification when he spoke of 'Cain, who is commonly called Cham'" (Friedman, *Monstrous Races,* p. 100). Perhaps such confusion can account for the line in *Adam and His Descendants,* a medieval Irish apocryphon, which refers to Cain as "the decrepit creature of bondage" (M. Herbert and M. McNamara, eds., *Irish Biblical Apocrypha* [Edinburgh, 1989], p. 17), but see below, chapter 13.

47. *Biblia de Alba,* ed. Antonio Paz y Meliá (Madrid, 1899, 1918–21), ad loc.: "E Chanaan fue siervo de siervos. Algunos dizen que son los moros negros, que do quier que cativos son." Arragel's translation and commentary was completed in 1433. On the work and its author, see Sonia Fellous, "Moïse Arragel, un traducteur juif au servise des chrétiens," in *Transmission et passages en monde juif,* ed. Esther Benbassa (1997), pp. 119–36. A short history of the *Biblia de Alba* is found in A. A. Sicroff, "The Arragel Bible: A Fifteenth Century Rabbi Translates and Glosses the Bible for His Christian Master," in *Américo Castro: The Impact of His Thought,* ed. Ronald Surtz et al. (Madison, 1988), pp. 180–81, n. 1.

48. I do not find a Curse of Ham in Jewish writings before the fourteenth (in the East) or the fifteenth (in the West) century. Charles, "Les Noirs, fils de Cham le maudit," pp. 732–33, believes that Cassian (d. ca. 435), in *Collationes* 8.21, preserves an echo of a rabbinic Curse of Ham. Cassian, however, is not talking about a Curse of Ham, but a tradition that the wickedness and evil magic that existed before the Flood (in the line of Cain) was preserved through the Flood by Ham, who wrote these magical formulae on metal plates and hard rocks. This is, of course, another matter, one that may be related to the gnostic belief that Ham carried the seed of wickedness from antedeluvian to postdeluvian times. *Collationes* 8.21 can be found in *CSEL* 13:239–40; *SC* 54:30–31; English translation in *NPNF2* 11:384. As to the gnostic belief, it can be found in the writings of the Sethians, an early Christian sect, as recorded in Epiphanius, *Adv. Haer.* 39.3.2–3, trans. Frank Williams, *The Panarion of Epiphanius of Salamis: Book I (Sects 1–46)* (Leiden, 1987), p. 257.

49. Ibn Ezra, *Commentary to the Torah,* ed. Asher Weiser (Vaizer), to Gen 9:25.

50. Nathaniel ibn Yeshaʿya, *Meʾor ha-Afelah,* ed. Qapeḥ, p. 72. Zechariah b. Solomon ha-Rofe, *Midrash ha-Ḥefeṣ,* ed. Ḥavaṣelet, 1:111.

51. John Weemse, *The Portraiture of the Image of God in Man* (London, 1627), p. 279, quoted in Vaughan, *Roots of American Racism,* p. 164.

52. Peterson, *Ham and Japheth,* pp. 47 (citing Theodore Weld, 1838) and 102.

53. Alexander Crummell, "The Negro Race Not under a Curse: An Examination of Genesis IX. 25," in *The Future of Africa, being Addresses, Sermons, etc., etc., Delivered in the Republic of Liberia* (New York, 1862), pp. 327–28. An earlier version of the article had been published in 1850. Crummell was educated at Cambridge and spent sixteen years in Liberia.

54. Sloan, *The Great Question Answered; or, Is Slavery a Sin in Itself,* pp. 75, 78, 80 (emphases in the original).

55. Ariel [Buckner H. Payne], *The Negro: What Is His Ethnological Status* (Cincinnati, 1867), pp. 4–5 (emphases in the original).

56. In a one-act play, *The First One,* of the biblical story, Zora Neale Hurston has Noah curse Ham and his descendants with blackness and slavery. See *Ebony and Topaz: A Collectanea,* ed. C. S. Johnson (1927; repr., Freeport, N.Y., 1971), pp. 53–57. As late as 1966, some were still expounding the belief in a dual curse. A biblical commentary by L. Thomas Holdcroft, a Pentecostal writer, who taught at Western Bible College in British Columbia, states: "The descendants of Canaan became the black races who for long centuries furnished the world's supply of slaves" (L. T. Holdcroft, *The Pentateuch,* Oakland, Calif., 1951, 4th printing 1966, p. 18). See Nzash U. Lumeya, "The Curse on Ham's Descendants: Its Missiological Impact on Zairian Mbala Mennonite Brethren" (Ph.D. diss., Fuller Theological Seminary, 1988), p. 32.

57. Peterson, *Ham and Japheth,* pp. 43–44.

58. Quotation is from the London, 1800 edition, *Calmet's Dictionary of the Holy Bible,* ed. C. Taylor, s.v. Ham. The work was first published in French in 1722–28. Peterson's mistaken identification of Ṭabarī as a rabbinic source apparently derives from Albert Perbal, "La race nègre et la malédiction de Cham," *Revue de l'Université d'Ottawa* 10 (1940) 160, n. 8. See my article, "The Curse of Ham," p. 49, n. 54.

59. Cited by Perbal, "La race nègre," p. 174.

60. Circular reasoning was not limited to Catholic theologians. The nineteenth-century rabbinic scholar, Ze'ev Wolf Einhorn (Maharzaw) wrote: "Since we see that all of Ham's descendants are ugly and black, and the Torah says that Ham was cursed with slavery, apparently then the blackness was part of the curse" (*Commentary to GenR,* 36.7).

61. For this point as it pertained to antebellum America, see Peterson, *Ham and Japheth,* pp. 6–8, 44, 48, 110, etc.

62. Translated and published from the Inquisition proceedings in the Madrid Historical Archives, by Marcel Bataillon in J. Friede and B. Keen, *Bartolomé de Las Casas in History* (DeKalb, Ill., 1971), p. 417. See the similar attitude of de la Cruz's fellow Dominican, Bartolomé de Las Casas (1474–1566), in Juan Friede, "Las Casas and Indigenism in the Sixteenth Century," and Juan Comas, "Historical Reality and the Detractors of Father las Casa," in the same volume. Some others from this period who know of a dual curse are Gilbert Génébrard and Augustin Tornielli, and a century later, Jean-Louis Hannemann; see Lécuyer, "Le père Libermann et la malédiction de Cham," pp. 601–2.

63. Perbal, "La race nègre," p. 157, and see above, pp. 268–69, n. 205. The Ethiopian Jews, who, according to most scholars, are a fourteenth- or fifteenth-century offshoot from the Ethiopian Christian community, share the same view and practice. See Salamon, *The Hyena People,* p. 75. For the origins of the Beta Israel, see Ken Blady, *Jewish Communities in Exotic Places* (Northvale, N.J., 2000), pp. 347–90, and the literature cited by Steven Kaplan in *Between Africa and Zion: Proceedings of the First International Congress of the Society for the Study of Ethiopian Jewry,* ed. Steven Kaplan, Tudor Parfitt and Emanuela Trevisan Semi (Jerusalem, 1995), pp. 14–15.

CHAPTER THIRTEEN

1. *An Appeal to the Coloured Citizens of the World* (Boston, 1829), excerpted in Joanne Grant, ed., *Black Protest* (Greenwich, Conn., 1968), pp. 85–86, and in Thomas, *Biblical Faith and the Black American,* pp. 48–49.

2. Some examples: Elihu Coleman, *A Testimony against the Antichristian Practice of Making Slaves of Man* (Boston, 1733), reprinted in Ruchames, *Racial Thought in America,* 1:94. David Child, *Oration in Honor of Universal Emancipation in the Britsh Empire* (Boston, 1834), p. 10. See Shanks, "The Biblical Anti-slavery Argument of the Decade," p. 137, n. 13 (reprinted in Finkelman, *Religion and Slavery,* p. 621); Theodore D. Weld, *The Bible against Slavery* (New York, 1837, 1838), pp. 47 and 66. John Fletcher, *Studies on Slavery, in Easy Lessons* (Natchez, Miss., 1852), pp. 248–52, 443–49. "The Rev. Dr. Mensor of Dublin," in a paper read before the Philosophical Society, Trinity College, Dublin, reported in *The American Israelite,* 13 July 1855, p. 2. (My thanks to Shlomit Yahalom for bringing this source to my attention and providing me a transcription of it.) Samuel A. Cartwright, *Slavery in the Light of Ethnology,* in E. N. Elliot, ed., *Cotton is King, and Pro-Slavery Arguments* (Augusta, Ga., 1860), p. 711, and "Unity of the Human Race Disproved by the Hebrew Bible," *De Bow's Review* 29 (August 1860) 134. See Naomi Woodbury, "A Legacy of Intolerance: Nineteenth Century Pro-

Slavery Propoganda and the Mormon Church Today" (M.A. thesis, University of Nevada, 1966), pp. 82–83, 151, and George M. Fredrickson, *The Black Image in the White Mind: The Debate on Afro-American Character and Destiny, 1817–1914* (New York, 1971), pp. 87–89. William W. Brown, *The Rising Son* (Boston, 1874), p. 46. In 1883, George W. Williams referred to the Curse of Cain as "the generally accepted theory" explaining black skin, in his *History of the Negro Race in America: From 1619 to 1880* (New York, 1883), 1:19. In 1894 the idea was expressed in a poem by George Cossins, who, speaking of Africa, wrote: "She to whom fell the dark disgrace, / Cain's evil brood to bear!" ("Africa" quoted in Philip Foner, *History of Black Americans,* Westport Conn., 1975, pp. 90–91).

3. Quoted by St. Clair Drake, *The Redemption of Africa and Black Religion* (Chicago, 1970), p. 47. Wheatley's *Poems on Various Subjects* (London, 1773) was the first published book by an African American.

4. As shown by Coleman, *A Testimony,* in 1733.

5. E.g., John Fletcher and Samuel Cartwright (see above, n. 2). Nathan Lord, the president of Dartmouth College in 1860, also mentioned Ham's marriage with a descendant of "the previously wicked and accursed race of Cain" as a partial reason for the biblical curse on Canaan (cited by Shelton Smith, *In His Image, but . . . ,* p. 131, n. 7).

6. Newell G. Bringhurst, *Saints, Slaves, and Blacks: The Changing Place of Black People within Mormonism* (Westport, Conn., 1981), pp. 41–42. Woodbury, "A Legacy of Intolerance," pp. 14–27. Mormon foundational documents were written during the 1830s.

7. Newell Bringhurst, "The 'Descendants of Ham' in Zion: Discrimination against Blacks along the Shifting Mormon Frontier, 1830–1920," *Nevada Historical Society Quarterly* 24 (1981) 311. See Woodbury, "A Legacy of Intolerance," pp. 2–18, 23–27, 36, 49–51, 54, 60. A summary of the Mormon view is provided by Ruth Mellinkoff, *The Mark of Cain* (Berkeley, 1981), pp. 78–80, and "Cain's Monstrous Progeny in *Beowulf:* Part II," pp. 195–96.

8. For some twentieth-century echoes of the Curse of Cain, see C. W. Scruggs, "The Mark of Cain and . . . Jean Toomer's *Cane,*" *American Literature* 44 (1972) 277, and Buswell, *Slavery, Segregation and Scripture,* p. 65.

9. Peyton is quoted in Prager, "'If I Be Devil,'" p. 263, n. 9; Isert is in S. A. Winsnes, *Letters on West Africa and the Slave Trade: Paul Erdmannn Isert's Journey to Guinea and the Caribbean Islands in Columbia (1788)* (Oxford, 1992), p. 120. See also the *Athenian Oracle* in 1704: "Some have believed that Cain's Mark was black," quoted in Jordan, *White over Black,* p. 242; Thomas Astley's reference to Cain's mark of blackness as an opinion held in his day, in his *A New General Collection of Voyages and Travels,* 1745–47 (London, 1749), 2:269; and Thomas Clarkson, *An Essay on the Slavery and Commerce of the Human Species Particularly the African; Translated from a Latin Dissertation . . .* (London, 1788), p. 126. An allusion to the belief is found also in the work of the former slave, Ottobah Cugoano, *Thoughts and Sentiments on the Evil of Slavery* (London, 1787), p. 33. Regarding the devil and Cain, a similar notion was also known—that Cain was born of the union of Eve and the devil; see Ricardo J. Quinones, *The Changes of Cain* (Princeton, 1991), p. 53.

10. The unpublished "dissertation" is cited from the manuscript in Paris by

Cohen, *The French Encounter with Africans,* pp. 11 and 298, n. 51. Labat is quoted by Carson Ritchie, "Notes et documents: Deux textes sur le Sénégal (1673–1677)," *Bulletin de l'Institut français d'Afrique noire* 30 (1968) 309, n. 4; Bergier is quoted by Charles, "Les Noirs," p. 732. On this belief in French writing of the 1730s, see Roger Mercier, *L'Afrique noire dans la littérature française: les premièrs images (xviie et xviiie siècle)* (Dakar, 1962), p. 71. It continued into the nineteenth century: note the report that in Paris in 1856 "on the stage . . . a pure South African . . . played Cain in the drama of 'Le Paradis Perdu,' in the theatre L'Ambigu Comique" (George S. Blackie in a letter to R. A. Young, which was then incorporated in Young's *The Negro: A Reply to Ariel* [Nashville, 1867], p. 45), and see also Raoul Allier, *Une énigme troublante: la race nègre et la malédiction de Cham,* Les Cahiers Missionnaires no. 16 (Paris, 1930), pp. 20 and 24–25, who quotes A.-L. Montandon, a nineteenth-century Protestant minister.

11. C. R. Boxer, "Negro Slavery in Brazil," *Race* (1964) 38–41; also in Boxer's *Race Relations in the Portuguese Colonial Empire, 1415–1825* (Oxford, 1963), where it is noted that in the 1620s, the Curse of Cain had been used in the Portuguese empire to justify the enslavement of American Indians, who were believed to be descendants of Cain (pp. 96 and 104). See also A.J.R. Russell-Wood, "Iberian Expansion and the Issue of Black Slavery: Changing Portuguese Attitudes, 1440–1770," *American Historical Review* 83 (1978) 40. For eighteenth-century Portugal, see Freedman, *Images of the Medieval Peasant,* p. 333, n. 27. In nineteenth-century Brazil, some clergy taught that black Africans were the condemned descendants of Cain (David Brion Davis, *The Problem of Slavery in Western Culture* [Ithaca, N.Y., 1966], p. 236; see also 171).

12. See E. Bökeln, *Adam und Qain in Lichte der vergleichenden Mythenforschung* (Leipzig, 1907), pp. 112, 114.

13. D. Greene and F. Kelly, *The Irish Adam and Eve Story from Saltair Na Rann* (Dublin, 1976), 1:91, lines 1959–1960. On the date and bibliography, see M. McNamara, *The Apocrypha in the Irish Church* (Dublin, 1975), pp. 14–16, and J. E. Caerwyn Williams and Patrick K. Ford, *The Irish Literary Tradition* (Cardiff, Wales, 1992), p. 111, n. 56. Williams and Ford note James Carney's view that the work is much earlier than the tenth century. See also J. A. Kenney, *The Sources for the Early History of Ireland: Ecclesiastical,* 2nd ed. (Dublin, 1968), pp. 736–37. Note the medieval Irish reference to Cain as a "creature of bondage" (Herbert and McNamara, ed. *Irish Biblical Apocrypha,* p. 17), quoted earlier.

14. K. Smits, *Die frühmittelhochdeutsche Wiener Genesis,* pp. 134–35, lines 1292–1309; Diemer, *Genesis und Exodus nach der Millstätter Handschrift,* p. 26; translation from Friedman, *The Monstrous Races,* p. 93. The lineage through Cain is not so clear in the section translated by Friedman but it is in Oliver F. Emerson, "Legends of Cain, Especially in Old and Middle English," *Proceedings of the Modern Language Association* 21 (1906) 884; see also Mellinkoff, *Mark of Cain,* pp. 77 and 128, n. 185, and Freedman, *Images of the Medieval Peasant,* pp. 91 and 333.

15. Mellinkoff, *Mark of Cain,* pp. 75–76, and *Outcasts,* 1:134, 2: fig. vi.50.

16. E. H. Gombrich, "Bosch's 'Garden of Earthly Delights': A Progress Report," *Journal of the Warburg and Courtauld Institutes* 32 (1969) 164–65. The descent from Cain follows Augustine, *City of God* 15.22.

17. F. H. Marshall, ed. and trans., *Old Testament Legends: From a Greek Poem on Genesis and Exodus by Georgios Chumnos* (Cambridge, 1925), pp. 8–9. Marshall's translation—"changed were his colour and might"—sacrifices literalness for poetry. Does "loss of power" refer to servitude? On Chumnos's poem, see Stone, *A History of the Literature of Adam and Eve,* p. 88.

18. See pp. 152–54.

19. For a full recent discussion of this text and the Latin parallel, *Life of Adam and Eve,* see Johannes Tromp, "Cain and Abel in the Greek and Armenian/Georgian Recensions of the *Life of Adam and Eve,*" in *Literature on Adam and Eve: Collected Essays,* ed. G. Anderson, M. Stone, and J. Tromp (Leiden, 2000), pp. 278–82. Tromp thinks that the meaning of ἀδιάφωτος is "the unenlightened one" or "the obscure one" or even "the one with a dark soul."

20. *The History of Abel and Cain* 10, in Lipscomb, *The Armenian Apocryphal Adam Literature,* pp. 145, 250 (text) and 160, 271 (translation); an older translation is that of Jacques Issaverdens, *The Uncanonical Writings of the Old Testament Found in the Armenian Mss. of the Library of St. Lazarus* (Venice, 1901), pp. 54–55. The quotation on the dating is from Stone, *A History of the Literature of Adam and Eve,* who discusses the apocryphal Adam-books in their various languages and versions (for the Armenian versions, see pp. 12–13). Lipscomb (p. 33) dates the Adam-books to sometime between the eighth and the fourteenth centuries. On *The History of Abel and Cain,* see Stone, p. 102.

21. See Mayer I. Gruber, "The Tragedy of Cain and Abel: A Case of Depression," *JQR* 69 (1978) 89–97, and *Nonverbal Communication,* 1:365–79; Yoḥanon Muffs, "Tefilatam shel Nevi᾿im," *Molad* 7 (1975) 205–6; and Sasson, *AB: Jonah,* pp. 273–75.

22. The Vulgate translated *iratusque* 'he was angry,' confusing the idiom *ḥarah le-* with *ḥarah af;* see Gruber, *Nonverbal Communication,* 1:357, 491–502.

23. Gruber, *Nonverbal Communication,* 1:358–65; Paul, "Decoding a 'Joint' Expression in Daniel 5:6, 16," pp. 122–125. To the sources cited by these authors add the following: 1QapGen 2.17 (J. Fitzmyer, *The Genesis Apocryphon of Qumran Cave 1,* pp. 52–53): "Your face is so changed [*šn᾿*] and deformed, your spirit is so depressed [*ʿlyb᾿*]"; the *Mandaean John-book:* When Christ saw Anoš "he changed colour" (W. Foerster, *Gnosis,* 2:301–2, bis); the Syriac *Euphemia and the Goth:* when the Goth saw his wife who he thought was dead, "the color of his face changed, and like a dead man so he became . . . for shame and for the fear and terror that fell on him" (F. C. Burkitt, ed. and trans., *Euphemia and the Acts of Martyrdom of the Confessors of Edessa,* London, 1913, p. 150 trans. and 70 text; the Arabic *Qiṣaṣ al-anbiyā᾿* of Kisā᾿ī: When Joseph's brothers found his cup in Benjamin's saddlebag "their complexions changed," and again, when Joseph produced the contract of sale which the brothers had written to the merchants of the passing caravan when they sold Joseph, Reuben's "countenance was altered. . . . Turning to his brethren in fright and shame, he said, 'This is the paper we wrote the day we sold Joseph at the well' " (Thackston, *Tales of the Prophets,* pp. 184 and 186).

24. *GenR* 22.6 (p. 209). If my explanation of the exegesis (*me-᾿od/mi-᾿ud*) is right, the variant reading *ke-᾿or* 'like a fire' for *ke-ʿud* has no basis; see Theodor's note, ad loc. Ginzberg thinks that the exegesis is based on the word *wyplw* = *wy᾿plw,* i.e., *᾿plh* 'darkness' (*Legends of the Jews,* 5:137, n. 13).

25. *bSoṭ* 35a; *NumR* 4.20.

26. Theodor and Ginzberg (see above, n. 24). See also Mellinkoff, *Mark of Cain*, pp. 76–77.

27. The quote is Lipscomb's, *The Armenian Apocryphal Adam Literature*, p. 34, although he does not include this passage in his examples of Jewish influence on the Adam-books in "Foreign Influences on the Armenian Apocryphal Adam Books," in *Classical Armenian Culture*, ed. T. J. Samuelian (Philadelphia, 1982), pp. 102–12. Similarly, Frey does not include this passage in his discussion of rabbinic parallels to the Armenian Adam books (*Dictionnaire de la Bible. Supplément*, 1:127–28.

28. For the possibility that Nah 2:11 and Joel 2:6 employ the same imagery, if not the same language, see Brenner, *Colour Terms in the Old Testament*, pp. 163–64.

29. *Ben Sira* 25:17 (Hebrew). The Greek and Syriac versions have a different reading, referring the dark face to the woman, but 25:23 would seem to support the Hebrew, although P. Skehan and A. Di Lella, *AB: Sira* (Garden City, N.Y., 1987), pp. 346–48, and Charles, *APOT* 1:402, understand two different referents in the two verses. Other lines in Sira, which describe the shining face of the husband, would also seem to support the Hebrew of 25:17: "Happy the husband of a good wife. . . . Be he rich or poor, his heart is content and his face lights up [*panaw urim*]" (26:1–4); "A woman's beauty makes her husband's face light up" (30:27; see Di Lella's note, p. 427). Mayer has shown that a "shining face" is opposed to a "darkened face" and indicates joy in Biblical Hebrew, Aramaic, Akkadian, and Ugaritic; see Gruber, *Nonverbal Communication*, p. 362, n. 2, pp. 554–96. For later literature, see esp. *Mekhilta, Wa-yasa* 2 (p. 162): "With a lit face [*panim me'irot*] was the mana given to Israel [for they asked for it properly] but with a darkened face [*panim ḥashekhot*] was the quail given to them for they asked for it on a full stomach." On the "bear" in *Ben Sira* 25.17, see M. Kister, "Be-Shulei Ben Sira," *Leshonenu* 47 (1983) 134, and "Genizah Manuscripts of Ben Sira," in *The Cambridge Genizah Collections: Their Contents and Significance*, ed. Stefan Reif (Cambridge, 2002), p. 40. *Ben Sira* is dated to the second century B.C.E.

30. אנחה ויגון יסובבוני ובושת על פני ... יחשך מאור פני לאפלה והודי נהפך למשחור ... ואוכלה בלחם אנחה ושקוי בדמעות אין כלה ... (*Thanksgiving Hymns* 5:32–35 [1QH xiii 32–35]). García Martínez and Tigchelaar, *The Dead Sea Scrolls Study Edition*, 1:172–75.

31. *1 Enoch* 62:10 (trans. Michael Knibb, *The Ethiopic Book of Enoch*, 2:151). This part of *1 Enoch* belongs to the Similitudes, a Jewish work whose date is debated; perhaps early second century C.E. (J. C. Hindley in *NTS* 14 [1967–68] 551–65); see the discussion in Michael Stone, "Apocalyptic Literature," in *Jewish Writings of the Second Temple Period*, ed. M. Stone (Assen, 1984), pp. 398–400.

32. *bShab* 30a. Other cases: *Mekhilta, Wa-yasa* 2 (p. 162); *ARNa* 25 (p. 40a); *pḤag* 2.2, 77d; *pShab* 10.5, 12c; *bShab* 152a; *bBM* 59a; *PesR* (p. 95b; cf. p. 203a); further examples, see Sokoloff, *Dictionary*, p. 547, s.v. *šiḥur*. The term as found in the printed editions of *LamR* 1.1.13, whatever it may mean in context, is not found in the manuscript published by Buber, *Midrash Eikhah Rabba* (Vilna, 1899), p. 51.

33. For Akkadian, see Gruber, *Nonverbal Communication*, 1:364; Paul, "Decoding a 'Joint' Expression," p. 123, n. 24; and *CAD* Ḫ 189. For Arabic, see the Qur'an 3:102–16, 16:58, 39:60, 43:17 (where also a white face indicates joy), and

Fischer, *Farb- und Formbezeichnungen,* pp. 275–76 (black face describing the grief and sorrow of the mourner).

34. Lipscomb, *The Armenian Apocryphal Adam Literature,* p. 34.

35. Payne Smith, *Thesaurus Syriacus,* col. 1757.

36. Recently, Weitzman has noted that " 'dark' is a stock epithet for a sad face" in the Peshiṭta (*The Syriac Version of the Old Testament,* p. 33). On the linguistic association of sadness, mourning (which is also an associated meaning of the Syriac *kmr*), and blackness, see Anderson, *A Time to Mourn,* p. 52, n. 116. E. Levine understood the Peshiṭta *ethkamaru* in the sense of "became black" as part of his theory that the Peshiṭta represents a view that saw Cain as symbolizing Satan. There is, indeed, such a view in Syriac writings (as we shall presently see), but the meaning of of the word in our passage is "became sad," as Y. Maori has rightly noted. See Étan Levine, "The Syriac Version of Genesis IV 1–16," *VT* 26 (1976) 70ff.; Maori, "Midrashic Influence on the Peshiṭta's Choice of Words," *Tarbiẓ* 46 (1977) 225, n. 64 (Hebrew). Indeed, in the reflexive forms *kmr* only means "to be sad," not "to be black" according to Payne Smith.

37. The description of Ephrem's interpretation and the quotations are taken from Kronholm, *Motifs from Genesis 1–11,* pp. 135–42. Similarly Isaac of Antioch: darkness characterizes Satan and Cain (quoted by Glenthøj, *Cain and Abel,* p. 108, from manuscript).

38. Another Syriac interpretation of the Peshiṭta's *ethkamaru* is that of the Christian writer Jacob of Serug (d. 521), who says that Cain changed his color/appearance (*gwnh*); his face (*prṣwfh*) was covered with great wrath; he became black in his pride with that hidden pain of jealousy (quoted in Glenthøj, *Cain and Abel,* pp. 108–9, 135, 285). This is in addition to his interpretation that Cain's reaction was one of sorrow (pp. 107–8).

39. Ignaz Goldziher, *Mythology among the Hebrews,* trans. from the German, with additions by the author, by R. Martineau (New York, 1967), pp. 347–50. So also Georges Vajda in *EI*² 3:14.

40. André Miquel, *La géographie humaine du monde musulman jusqu'au mileiu du 11ᵉ siècle,* 2nd ed. (Paris, 1973), 2:142, n. 7.

41. To be sure, this misunderstanding was limited even in the Armenian interpretations. See, e.g., the Armenian work called *History of the Forefathers,* which has "And Cain was very sad and his face became sullen and fell" (M. Stone, *Armenian Apocrypha Relating to Adam and Eve,* Leiden, 1996, pp. 183–84).

CHAPTER FOURTEEN

1. Erik Hornung with A. Brodbeck and E. Staehelin, *Das Buch von den Pforten des Jenseits.* Aegyptiaca Helvetica 7–8 (Basel, 1979–80), 2:134–36. See also F. J. Yurco, "Two Tomb-Wall Painted Reliefs of Ramesses III and Sety I and Ancient Nile Valley Population Diversity," in *Egypt in Africa,* ed. Theodore Celenko (Indianapolis, 1996), p. 109, where earlier literature is cited. The word *ʿ3mw* can also mean "Canaanite"; cf. the biblical four sons of Ham: Egypt, Kush, Libya (?; see pp. 233–34, n. 63), and Canaan. The specific colors of the Asian and Libyan differ in the various descriptions given in the scholarly literature. See the works cited here and also the following: Stuart Smith in *OEAE* 3:31 and 112; Hornung, *The Valley*

of the Kings, p. 147, pl. 105; p. 148, pl. 107–9; Taylor, *Egypt and Nubia,* p. 7 and the reproductions on the title page and on pp. 33–34.

2. N. M. Davies with A. H. Gardiner, *Ancient Egyptian Paintings* (Chicago, 1936), 2:80, 81, 1:28, 2:60. See also the following plates where the different colored peoples are not identified: 1:48, 2:61, 63, 71, 73, 98. These paintings come from various dynasties between 1475 and 1225 B.C.E.

3. For color symbolism, see, e.g., Lise Manniche, "The Complexion of Queen Ahmosi Nefertere," *Acta Orientalia* (Copenhagen) 40 (1979) 11–19. For artistic conventions, see, e.g., H. G. Fischer, "Varia Aegyptiaca," *Journal of the American Research Center in Egypt* 2 (1963) 17; I. Sachs, "L'image du Noir dans l'art européen," *Annales* 24 (1969) 885, note; K. Bard, "Ancient Egyptians and the Issue of Race," *Bostonia* (Summer 1992) 41–43, 69; see also the conventions used in depicting gender difference in both Egypt and Greece, above, pp. 81–82.

4. Lewis, *Race and Slavery,* pp. 22 and 26.

5. Hall, *Things of Darkness,* pp. 2–4.

6. See J. Cooper, *The Commentary on the Qur'ān by Abū Jaʿfar Muḥammad B. Jarīr al-Ṭabarī being an abridged translation of Jāmiʿ al-bayān ʿan taʾwīl āy al-Qurʾān* (Oxford, 1987), pp. 228–29 on Sura 2:31, and Rotter, *Die Stellung des Negers,* pp. 140–41. In Ṭabarī the attribution goes back to the Companions of the prophet of Islam.

7. *PRE* 11 (p. 27b), according to the first printed edition (Constaninople 1514) and some manuscripts; *Targum Ps-Jon* to Gen 2:7. See M. Higger's edition of *PRE* in *Ḥorev* 9 (1946) 96, and Gerald Friedlander's translation, *Pirḳê De Rabbi Eliezer,* pp. 76–77, for variant readings.

8. See Friedlander for the suggestion that the Jewish tradition was originally the same as the Islamic. See also Avigdor Shinan, *Agadatam shel Meturgemanim,* p. 136, n. 75.

9. A redaction date between the eighth and ninth centuries is generally given for *Pirqei R. Eliezer,* and there is a growing consensus that *Targum Pseudo-Jonathan* in its present form also was composed in the Islamic period. See further, Glossary.

10. *PRE* 24. The translation is based on ed. Warsaw, 1852 (repr., New York, 1946), p. 55b, except for the addition of "and beautiful" after *levanim,* which has almost no manuscript support. The readings in the various manuscripts, as well as in the quotation in *Midrash ha-Gadol,* 1:191 (Gen 9:27), are presented in the table on the next page. The *Pirqei* text is probably based on Deut 32:8 ("When God apportioned the inheritances for the nations and when he divided humanity"), as David Luria (d. 1855) notes in his commentary, printed in the Warsaw edition. On the dating of *Pirqei* (mid-eighth century), see Dina Stein, "Yesodot ʿAmamiyim ba-Midrash ha-Meʾuḥar: Pirqei de-Rabbi Eliezer le-ʾOr Meḥqar ha-Sifrut ha-ʿAmamit" (Ph.D. diss., Hebrew University of Jerusalem, 1998), pp. 1–2.

11. Brenner, *Colour Terms in the Old Testament,* pp. 81–94, 180; quotations on pp. 84, 90, 93.

12. Ibid., pp. 95–99, 181, citing Tur-Sinai.

13. Ibid., p. 84. Note, incidentally, the same meaning of "white" and "black" in early Arabic and the Arabic of the Negev (ʿAzāzmih) bedouin, a dialect that "between the pre-Islamic period and the present day . . . has occasioned only minimal change at the level of basic categorization of the color continuum" (Borg, "Lin-

Pirqei Rabbi Eliezer 24 (p. 55b)

11	10	9	8	7	6	5	4	3	2	1	
[ ] כשרים ונאים	לבנים ונאים	לבנים ונאים	טובים ונאים	צדיקים כשרים ונאים	גבורים ונאים	ולבש שחורים	שחורים וטוים	שחורים ונאים	שחורים ונוים	שחורים ונאים	**שם**
שחורים כעורב		כולם שחורים כעורב	שחורים כעורב	שחורים כעורב	שחורים כעורב	שחורים כעורב	שחורים כעורב	שחורים כעורב	שחורים כעורב	שחורים כעורב	**חם**
		כולם לבנים	כולם לבנים	לבנים כגבינה	כולם לבנים	כולם לבנים	כולם לבניו	כולם לבנים	כלם לבנים	כלם לבנים ויפים	**יפת**

1. MS Alliance Israèlite Universelle, Paris 178; MS BM Or. 9952; printed editions. So ed. Venice 1544, 20a–b (for Shem and Ham; apparently nothing for Japhet) but on contents page (2b) it has לבנות for Shem and שחרות for Ham. So too שחורים ונאים and שחורים כעורב in MS JTS 5041B.
2. MS Rome-Casanatense 174 (= Higger MS א), MS HUC 75.
3. MS Rome-Casanatense 175 (= Higger MS ג), MS Parma 1203/3 (2454).
4. MS Moscow-Ginzberg 111 (f. 30b); so too MS Rome-Casanatense 173 (= Higger MS ב), which however reads כלם for כולם לבניו.
5. MS Warsaw 240.
6. MS Paris, BN 710 (f. 50b).
7. MS Lehman 300.
8. MS Leningrad Saltykov-Shchedrin, MS Parma 566, MS Oxford 911 (כ׳ ל׳ ויפים); see also Horowitz's note in ed. Makor, p. 83. So ed. Constantinople 1514, ch. 24 (no pagination) [apparently only Shem and Ham].
9. MS JTS 3847 (= Enelow 866) (f. 109a), MS Sassoon 944, MS HUC 2043 (f. 17a), MS Dropsie 329, *MidHag* Gen 9:27, p. 191 (see ed. Schechter).
10. MS Oxford Bodl. 2495 (Opp. Add. 167), cited by Friedlander; MS Yemenite, cited by M. Margulies, ed., *MidHag* ad loc.
11. MS JTS R1657 (= Enelow 374). [ ] = word erased and difficult to read.

guistic and Ethnographic Observations, pp. 122, 128–29, 133–34, citing Fischer, *Farb- und Formbezeichnungen,* for the early material).

14. P. 81.

15. As noted by Luria in his *Commentary* to *PRE,* p. 55b, nn. 3 and 5.

16. *Tarikh al-Ṭabarī,* ed. M. J. de Goeje, 1:199. A little later (p. 220) Ṭabarī repeats this tradition, again in the name of Ibn ʿAbbas, but this time has "tawny with hardly any whiteness" (*udma wa-bayāḍ qalīl*) for Ham instead of "black with hardly any whiteness." My translation of Ṭabarī's color terms follows Lane, who notes that applied to human complexion *adam* means "tawny or dark-complexioned, syn. *asmar,*" *ḥumra* means whiteness, and *šuqra* implies some mix of red and white, the common classification for a light-skinned complexion (Lane, *Lexicon,* pp. 37a, 640c [see also 642a, *aḥmar*], and 1581b). In their English translations, Franz Rosenthal and William Brinner render *adma* 'brown or red,' *šuqra* 'red,' and *ḥumra* 'brown' (*The History of al-Ṭabarī,* 1:368, 2:19). The tradition is repeated by Ibn al-Jawzī (d. 1208); see the translation by van Donzel, "Ibn al-Jawzī on Ethiopians in Baghdad," p. 114.

17. Bar Hebraeus's father was a Jewish convert to Christianity (thus the name). The quotation is from J. B. Segal, *EI*^{2} 3:805, s.v. Ibn al-ʿIbrī.

18. Sprengling and Graham, ed., *Barhebraeus' Scholia on the Old Testament,* pp. 34–35 and 44–45. My translation of "red" for *smqryʾ* follows Payne Smith, *Thesaurus Syriacus,* col. 2666. Sprengling and Graham prefer "fair." See C. Brockelmann, *Lexicon Syriacum,* 2nd ed. (Halis Saxonum, 1928), p. 482, who gives "flavus," but notes that the Peshiṭta translates Hebrew *admoni* (Gen 25:25 and 1 Sam 16:2) with *smqryʾ.* So does the Fragment Targum to Gen 25:25 (see Sokoloff, *Dictionary,* p. 383). Bar Hebraeus gives Japhet's color once as red and once as white, but there is no contradiction; both terms refer to the same light skin of those people living in the north. That the two terms mean the same as far as skin color is concerned can be seen from the Arabic description (*šuqra*) in Bar Hebraeus' *Tāʾrīkh,* quoted later. The Arabic root *šqr* means red, but applied to the coloring of humans it has the meaning "ruddy complexion combined with fairness, or of a clear ruddy complexion, with the outer skin inclining to white, or having a red, or ruddy, tinge, over a white, or fair, complexion" (Lane, *Lexicon,* p. 1581). In descriptions of complexion, "red is used . . . of lighter color in general" (Goldziher, *Muslim Studies,* 1:243). Note the combination "clear skinned [*ṣaḥ*] and ruddy" in Song 5:10 and Lam 4:7, discussed in chapter 6, and for a period closer to Bar Hebraeus's time, the statement in a medieval work, *Liber complexionum,* attributed to John of Paris, that one of the signs of an equally balanced body is that its color is a compound of white and red (quoted by L. Thorndike, "De Complexionibus," *Isis* 49 [1958] 401–2). Sprengling and Graham have attempted to convey this idea by their translation "fair." Note also that the Negev bedouin, preserving early Arabic color categorization, "attribute redness to the human skin in race classification" (Borg, "Linguistic and Ethnographic Observations," pp. 122, 130).

19. *Tāʾrīkh mukhtaṣar ʾal-duwal,* ed. A. Ṣāliḥānī (Beirut, 1890; repr., 1983), p. 15. Ed. Pococke with Latin translation: Gregorio Abul Pharajio [= Bar Hebraeus], *Historia Compendiosa Dynastiarum,* Oxford, 1663, 1:14 (text) and 2:9 (translation). This work is Bar Hebraeus's own abbreviated translation into Arabic of the first part of his Syriac *Chronicon.* For the biblical period, Bar Hebraeus added much

to the the Arabic version, including the section quoted earlier, not found in the Syriac. In E.A.W. Budge's edition and translation of the Syriac work, *The Chronography of Gregory Abū'l Faraj [=Bar Hebraeus] 1225–1286* (London, 1932), the relevant section occurs at 1:6–7 (translation), 2:2v–3r (text); the translation is based on a different Syriac manuscript than the one reproduced and consequently differs from the Syriac at times.

20. Pp. 105–6.

21. For a discussion of ancient notice of such features, see Snowden, *Blacks in Antiquity*, pp. 2–11.

22. *Tanḥuma, Noaḥ* 13. The passage is not paralleled in the Buber edition of *Tanḥuma*. Twenty-two manuscripts or manuscript fragments checked at the Institute for Microfilmed Hebrew Manuscripts (Jerusalem) show no significant variants. For "crooked," ed. pr. (Constantinople, 1520–22) and several manuscripts read *ʿaqushot*, e.g., Oxford 2337, Columbia x843, Sassoon 641; so also quoted in Samuel b. Nissim Masnut (thirteenth century), *Midrash Bereʾshit Zuṭaʾ*, ed. Mordekhai Hacohen, p. 41, and in Zechariah ben Solomon ha-Rofé (fourteenth century), *Midrash ha-Ḥefeṣ*, ed. Meir Ḥavaṣelet, 1:110, and see Ḥavaṣelet's note referring to other Yemenite sources: *Yalquṭ Midreshei Teiman* to Ex 21:26 and *Meʾor ha-ʾAfelah*. The second edition of *Tanḥuma* (Mantua, 1563) and other manuscripts read *ʿaqumot* (e.g., Vat. 44, Parma 3254). Both Hebrew words mean "crooked." The only witnesses I could find recording significantly different readings of any sort apparently do not represent true variants. The citation of *Tanḥuma* in a seventeenth-century work, *Historia sacra patriarcharum* (Amsterdam, 1667), p. 627, by Johann Heinrich Heidegger, which omits *nimshekahah ʿarlato*, is probably due to Heidegger's sense of propriety more than to a *Vorlage* that lacked the words. "His foreskin withered" (*we-kamshah*), recorded by Masnut in his *Midrash Bereʾshit Zuṭaʾ*, is no doubt due to the graphic similiarity of *w* and *n* and metathesis of *k* and *mš*, i.e., *nmškh* > *wkmšh*. Other "variants," which I list later, appear to be interpretive glosses.

23. So, for example, Luria in his *Commentary* to *PRE*, p. 56, *Hagahot*, note b. Some writers glossed the text according to this understanding, such as Masnut who added "swollen" to "crooked," referring to Ham's lips, or David Maimuni (d. 1300) who substituted "thick and large" for "crooked" (*Midrash David ha-Nagid*, ed. A. Katsh, 1:42). Some moderns did the same thing in their translations, such as M. Grünbaum "Beiträge zur vergleichenden Mythologie aus der Hagada," *ZDMG* 31 (1877) 192, and Robert Graves and Raphael Patai, *Hebrew Myths: The Book of Genesis* (Garden City, N.Y., 1964), p. 121. Maimuni also adds "and their speech is a stammer [?, *ʿlgt*] and not understandable." On the unique speech patterns of the Kushites, see above, pp. 71–73.

24. Goldenberg "The Curse of Ham," pp. 28–30.

25. The reading *nśr* in Maimuni appears to be shortened from *niśraf (śeʿar roʾsham)*, which may be a more readily understood substitution for *Tanḥuma*'s "singed" (*nitḥarekh*).

26. See above, p. 97. Of course, the very name "Ethiopian" (Αἴθιοψ) is traditionally said to derive from αἴθω and ὄψ meaning "burnt face," although this etymology has been called into question; see Bruno Snell, *Lexikon des frühgriechischen Epos* (Göttingen, 1979), 1:296. So also Ullendorff, *Ethiopia and the Bible*, p. 5, n. 2, and J. Forsdyke, *Greece before Homer* (London, 1956), p. 97.

27. For Arabic authors, see, e.g., Masʿūdī (tenth century), cited later, or Dimashqī (d. 1327) quoted in Levtzion and Hopkins, *Corpus*, p. 213; see also Jāḥiẓ quoted in Rotter, *Die Stellung des Negers*, p. 153. For Christian material from the early modern period, Best's "Discourse" will serve as an example: "The people of Africa, especially the Ethiopians, are so cole blacke, and their haire like woole curled short, which blacknesse and curled hair they [i.e. Englishmen] suppose to come onely by the parching heat of the Sunne" (Richard Hakluyt, *The Principal Navigations Voyages Traffiques & Discoveries of the English Nation . . .*, London, 1589; repr., New York, 1969, 5:180).

28. Sources are listed in my "Rabbinic Knowledge of Black Africa," pp. 326–27, nn. 29–31, to which add also the quotation of Marco Polo at n. 35, below, and Kaplan, *The Rise of the Black Magus*, p. 53.

29. See my "The Curse of Ham," p. 29.

30. *bSuk* 32a.

31. *bSan* 91a. Note that the same expression found in this source ("I'll straighten out your hump") is paralleled in *Megillat Taʿanit*, 15 Av (ed. H. Lichtenstein, *HUCA* 8–9 [1931–32] 330), with the Hebrew word *gevihah* 'hump' appearing in place of the Aramaic *ʿaqmumita*. Perhaps the Biblical Hebrew *ʿaqom* (Isa 40:4) has the same meaning of "hump," "hill."

32. Epstein, "Les Chamites de la table ethnographique," p. 89.

33. Galen is found in quotation in the Arab historian Masʿūdī, *Murūj al-dhahab*, ed. Pellat, 1:91; and *Les prairies d'or*, ed. Pellat, 1:69. In the earlier edition and French translation of de Meynard and de Courteille, 1:163–64. Regarding Arab writers, Rotter, *Die Stellung des Negers*, p. 156, mentions Al-Kindī (d. 883) and the Ikhwān al-Ṣafāʾ (tenth century); see also p. 154. Hunwick, "Black Africans in the Islamic World," p. 35, refers to al-Mutanabbī's statement concerning "a black man, one half of whom is lip." Among Christian writers, see the quotations from Marco Polo and Albertus Magnus in the following paragraph. Snowden, *Before Color Prejudice*, pp. 114–15, n. 37, questions the attribution to Galen, arguing that most of the Black characteristics attributed to Galen are found in Arabic and Muslim, but not classical, sources.

34. For the references to these quoted sources and others, see my "The Curse of Ham," p. 43, n. 28. Albertus is in his *Liber de natura locorum* 2.3, translated by Tilmann, *An Appraisal of the Geographical Works of Albertus Magnus*, p. 101.

35. H. Yule, *The Book of Ser Marco Polo*, 3rd ed. (London, 1903), 2:422; in R. E. Latham's translation, *The Travels of Marco Polo* (London, 1958), pp. 275–77.

36. Yonah David, *The Love Stories of Jacob Ben Eleazar (1170–1233?)* (in Hebrew; Tel Aviv, 1992/93), p. 82, line 288; p. 51, line 86. Maimuni's gloss ("red and *puzelot*") is not clear because the root *pzl* occurs only once in the rabbinic corpus, in *PesR* 14 (ed. Friedman, p. 56a), where it parallels another difficult term, *pilbel*, which means "to move from one side to the other." See H. Yalon, "*pll* and *plpl* in Hebrew and Aramaic," *Tarbiẓ* 6 (1935) 226 (= *Pirqei Lashon*, Jerusalem, 1971, p. 92), and Tur-Sinai in Ben-Yehuda's *Dictionary*, 6:4865 and 4927.

37. This usual meaning of *nimshekhah ʿorlah* is found, e.g., in *yYev* 8.1, 8d; *ySan* 10.1, 27c and parallel *yPeʾah* 1.1, 16b. Other examples may be found in Nissan Rubin, "On Drawing Down the Prepuce and Incision of the Foreskin" (in Hebrew), *Zion* 54 (1989) 105–17. For *mashukh*, with *ʿorlah* understood, see the

sources cited by S. Lieberman in *Tosefta ki-Fshutah* to *tShab* 15/16.9, and *Sifre Deut* 321 (p. 369) with A. Perles's note in *Bet Talmud* 1 (1881) 115.

38. Perhaps for this reason Maimuni substitued "and they are not ashamed" (*we-lo᾽ yitbosheshu*) for *nimshekhah ᶜorlato* in the *Tanḥuma*.

39. *QohR* 9.15.4.

40. So the term is understood by A. Cohen in the Soncino edition, *Midrash Rabba* (London, 1939), 8:251, Z. W. Einhorn (Maharzaw) in his commentary, ad loc., and A. Z. Brilliant and P. Barzel in *Midrash Rabba ha-Mevo᾽ar,* ed. Abraham Steinberger et al. (Jerusalem, 1983), ad loc., 8:513.

41. No longer practiced circumcision: *ExR* 1.8; *LevR* 23.2 (p. 528); were prohibited from practicing circumcision: *PRE* 29 (pp. 64b–65a). See David Luria in *PRE,* ad loc., n. 31, and Gerald Friedlander, *Pirḳê De Rabbi Eliezer,* pp. 209–10, n. 6, for additional sources recording this tradition.

42. *PesRK* 28.1 ("Ba-yom ha-Shemini"; p. 422); The passage is also found in *PesR*—in the edition of M. Friedman on p. 200a as an appendix, on which see William Braude's introduction to his translation, *Pesiqta Rabbati* (New Haven, 1968), 1:28, n. 41. There are no manuscript variants recorded by Mandelbaum or Rivka Ulmer, *Pesiqta Rabbati: A Synoptic Edition,* 2:1094–95.

43. *Megaddel lo ᶜorlah* is found in MS Oxford of *PesRK,* ed. Mandelbaum, 2:418–19 (also in *YalqSh, Tazriᶜa* 547, ed. D. Heiman et al., Leviticus 1:372). *Megaddel śeᶜar* meaning to let the hair grow is commonly found, e.g., *GenR* 98.15 (p. 1266) and *bᶜEr* 100b. According to Mandelbaum (p. 418, n. 1) the text of MS Oxford at this point is not original to *PesRK* but derives from a *Tanḥuma-Yelamedenu* midrash or from *PesR*. Incidentally, the translations by Braude and Kapstein of both texts are mistaken. They were influenced by the usual meaning of *mashakh ᶜorlah,* which is clearly not the case here. See Braude and Kapstein, *Pesikta de-Rab Kahana,* p. 433; and Braude's translation of *Pesiqta Rabbati,* 2:872. It is possible that this text is referring to the Greek practice of infibulation, that is, pulling the foreskin down and tying the ends with a string (κυνοδέσμη) or to the Roman practice of bringing the ends together with a ring. But these practices were done by a youth to himself later in life, not by a father to a newborn, which is implied in the midrash. On the Greco-Roman customs, see Jüthner in *RE* 9:2543–48, s.v. *infibulatio;* Eric J. Dingwall, *Male Infibulation* (London, 1925); Thomas Scanlon, *Eros and Greek Athletics* (New York, 2002), pp. 234–36; and Eva Keuls, *The Reign of the Phallus* (New York, 1985), pp. 68–70. The only example I know of that is done in infancy is that mentioned by Soranus (first–second century), who recommends in the case of a newborn who appears to have no foreskin that the nurse gradually and continuously stretch the foreskin until it assumes its normal length (*Gynecology* 2.34 [103], trans. Owsei Temkin, Baltimore, 1991, p. 107). However, this clearly points to an unusual occurrence and would not likely be described as "the way of the gentiles."

44. Note also the reading *ᶜarel* 'uncircumcised' in *YalqSh, Tazriaᶜ* 547, for *mashukh* in *tShab* 15/16.9. The meaning of the term in this text is clearly "extended foreskin" (i.e., restoration), but could the *Yalquṭ* version have been influenced by the meaning "uncircumcised" as found in the two passages quoted?

45. This supposition would be made irrespective of whether black Africans ac-

tually practiced circumcison or not. Early classical evidence shows that many did (a fifth-century B.C.E. vase painting from Greece, Herodotus 2.104, Josephus, *Contra Apionem* 2.141 probably dependant on Artapanus; see Snowden, *Blacks in Antiquity,* pp. 23, 272, n. 4; *Before Color Prejudice,* p. 115, n. 39). It was the practice in ancient Egypt (not everywhere, however) and was widespread among peoples in Africa, including East Africa: Bantu speakers, Maasai, Coptic Christians, and Ethiopians (T. O. Beidelman, "Circumcision," in *The Encyclopedia of Religion,* ed. M. Eliade, New York, 1987, 3:511). And yet rabbinic literature refers to the Egyptians as "the uncircumcised Hamites" (*ʿarelim bnei ḥam*); see M. Ish-Shalom (Friedmann), *Nispaḥim le-Seder Eliyahu Zuṭaʾ,* p. 50, reprinted with *Seder Eliyahu Rabba we-Seder Eliyahu Zuṭa,* ed. Ish-Shalom.

46. *bShab* 149b. The figure is deduced by numeric exegesis (*gemaṭriya*) of the Hebrew word *(he)ʿarel* in Hab 2:16, which can be vocalized to read 'uncircumcised.'

47. So was the term translated by H. Freedman in the Soncino edition, ed. I. Epstein, and by Lazarus Goldschmidt in his German translation (1897). Freedman, incidentally, mistranslated *meḥazeret* as "wagged," while it is correctly "surrounded," "umgab" (Goldschmidt).

48. On macrophallic Blacks in classical iconography, see Snowden, *Blacks in Antiquity,* pp. 23, 272–73, and the literature cited by Thompson, *Romans and Blacks,* p. 210, n. 85.

49. J. Desanges in *IBWA* 1:312, n. 131. See also *IBWA* 1:221 (Snowden), 278f. (J. Leclant); and J. Clarke, "Hypersexual Black Men in Augustan Baths," in *Sexuality in Ancient Art: Near East, Egypt, Greece, and Italy,* ed. N. Boymel Kampen et al. (Cambridge, 1996), p. 189.

50. Galen quoted by Masʿūdī (above, n. 33). Aesop, who is said to have had "a flat nose, prominent lips and black (μέλας) [skin], on account of which he has his name, for *Aesop* is the same as *Aethiop*" (Ben Perry, *Aesopica,* 1:215, from Planude's *Prooemium Vitae Aesopi*), is described also as having a "long and thick" penis (*The Life of Aesop* 75, translated in L. M. Wills, *The Quest of the Historical Gospel,* London, 1997, p. 201). Cf. Jane E. Lewis, *The English Fable: Aesop and Literary Culture, 1651–1740,* Cambridge, 1996, p. 82.

51. For Islam, see Lewis's comment (*Race and Slavery,* p. 52) about how Masʿūdī's quotation of Galen is "repeated, with variations, by later writers" (e.g., Dimashqī, d. 1327; translated in Levtzion and Hopkins, *Corpus,* p. 214), and his remark concerning the sexual stereotype of the "superbly endowed and sexually inexhaustible black slave" (p. 94). Rotter, *Die Stellung des Negers,* p. 156, n. 3, cites several Arab authors who quote Galen. For examples of this belief in Blacks' "large Propagators" among Christian writers in Europe of the fifteenth–eighteenth century, see Jordan, *White over Black,* pp. 29–30, 34–35, 158–59, 501, and note his remarks at 159. Clearly there is a relationship between belief in the hypersexuality of the Black and images of an exaggerated phallus. References to the hypersexuality of the black African are very common in Greco-Roman and Islamic writings. For this stereotype in ancient Rome, see Balsdon, *Romans and Aliens,* p. 218; Clarke, "Hypersexual Black Men in Augustan Baths," pp. 184–98, and *Looking at Lovemaking: Constructions of Sexuality in Roman Art 100 B.C.–A.D. 250* (Berke-

ley, 1998), pp. 120–29; Thompson, *Romans and Blacks,* pp. 105, 107–9, see also p. 113. According to Thompson, the stereotype continued in Christianity. For the Islamic world, see Lewis, *Race and Slavery,* pp. 34, 45–46, 52, 60, 93–94, 97; Miquel, *La géographie humaine,* 2:44; Southgate, "Negative Images of Blacks," pp. 24–25; W. Eberhard and P. N. Boratav, *Typen Türkischen Volksmärchen* (Weisbaden, 1953) p. 238 and index, s.v. Neger, natürlich. See also Davis, *Slavery and Human Progress,* p. 44 (cf. Lewis, *Race and Slavery,* pp. 75–76). The image of a hypersexual Black, as far as I can tell, is not found in biblical or rabbinic literature. There may, however, be such an image of the Egyptian in the Bible. Some have argued that Ezekiel's descriptions of the Egyptian as "big fleshed" (Ezek 16:26) and as having "flesh like that of asses and a discharge like that of horses" (Ezek 23:20) are metaphorical representations of the belief in the Egyptian hypersexual powers, with "flesh" (*baśar*) in both verses being understood as a euphemism for "penis" as in Gen 17:13, Lev 15:2f. Not only the size of the penis but also the seminal discharge express "a popular notion of [the Egyptians'] lewdness" (Moshe Greenberg, *AB: Ezekiel 21–37,* p. 480; similarly *LevR* 25.7). Others, as Greenberg notes, connect *zirma* (discharge) with *zemorah* (vine branch) and take it as another euphemism for penis.

52. The reference to "disfigured" lips and nose is from a letter written in 1579, Hakluyt, *Principal Navigations* 6:384 quoted by R. R. Cawley, *The Voyagers and Elizabethan Drama* (Boston, 1938), p. 86n. There are many such examples; see, e.g., Marco Polo quoted above at n. 35. For Arabic literature, see Rotter, *Die Stellung des Negers,* pp. 153–57.

53. Ginzberg, *Legends of the Jews,* 1:169. Thomas Peterson (*Ham and Japheth,* p. 44) quotes Ginzberg's paraphrase but omits "through Canaan therefore," replacing it with ellipsis. By adding these words Ginzberg clearly understood the passage as not referring to Blacks, who are descended from Kush, not from Canaan. By removing this explanatory gloss, Peterson has Ginzberg say precisely what he took pains not to say.

54. MS Vat 44/1 (f. 27a); in the margin to ed. Venice, 1545 at the Hebrew University library; and in Masnut (or his source).

55. See Snowden, *Blacks in Antiquity,* p. 8.

56. Above, n. 51.

57. Marc Bregman, "The Tanhuma-Yelamedenu Literature: Studies in the Evolution of the Versions" (Ph.D. diss., Hebrew University of Jerusalem, 1991), p. 188. The text of *Tanḥuma* under discussion belongs to the stratum (found only in the "printed" *Tanḥuma*) that was redacted in Babylonia after the conquest of Islam. See the Glossary for a summary of Bregman's views on the development of the *Tanḥuma* genre.

58. Allan D. Kensky, "'Midrash Tanhuma Shmot': A Critical Edition of 'Midrash Tanhuma Shmot' (Standard Edition) through Beshallah, Based on Manuscripts and Early Editions with an Introduction and Commentary" (Ph.D. diss., Jewish Theological Seminary, 1990).

59. Steven Wasserstrom, "Who were the Jewish Sectarians under Early Islam," in *Jewish Sects, Religious Movements, and Political Parties,* ed. Menachem Mor (Omaha, 1992), pp. 101–12.

60. Rotter, *Die Stellung des Negers,* p. 116, and quoted with approval also in Susanne Enderwitz, *Gesellschaftlicher Rang und ethnische Legitimation,* p. 26.

CONCLUSION

1. Jon D. Levenson, "The Universal Horizon of Biblical Particularism," in *Ethnicity and the Bible,* ed. M. G. Brett (Leiden, 1996), p. 159.

2. Galatians 3:28.

3. Thompson, *Romans and Blacks,* p. 19.

4. Gayraud S. Wilmore, "The Black Messiah: Revising the Color Symbolism of Western Christology," *Journal of the Interdenominational Theological Center* 2 (1974) 9.

5. Hall, *Things of Darkness,* p. 4.

6. Audrey Smedley, *Race in North America: Origen and Evolution of a Worldview* (Boulder, Colo., 1993), pp. 6–7. See also Dante Puzzo "Racism and the Western Tradition," *Journal of the History of Ideas* 25 (1964) 579–86.

7. Smedley, *Race in North America,* pp. 303–4. But Smedley's contrast of England with the Mediterranean countries "where populations of great diversity in physical features . . . had interacted and developed a familiarity with one another" (p. 304) must be qualified. There was enough of a difference in physical features between black African and Arab to allow for the development of ideas of "race" when the political climate was ripe.

8. Lewis, *Race and Slavery,* p. 41.

9. In addition to their works, quoted extensively throughout this study, see Snowden's "Attitudes toward Blacks in the Greek and Roman World," pp. 265–66.

APPENDIX I

1. Moses Gaster, "The Apocalypse of Abraham from the Roumanian Text, Discovered and Translated," *Transactions of the Society of Biblical Archaeology* 9 (1893) 197. Gaster actually writes Δρυα τῆς Μαμβρης, presumably taking the first word as neuter; as far as I know it appears only as a masculine. I have given the form in the dative (δρυὶ), which appears in the Greek text at Long Recension 20.11, rather than the nominative or accusative (δρυὸς, δρῦν), which occurs elsewhere (1.2, 2.1, 6.4), because it seems to come closer to Driea in sound. See Francis Schmidt, *Le testament grec d'Abraham* (Tübingen, 1986), p. 166.

2. Émile Turdeanu agrees with Gaster's explanation (*Apocryphes slaves et roumains de l'Ancien Testament,* p. 235), but the most recent editor of the text, Nicolae Roddy, thinks that Dreia the Black derived from the location of Abraham's residence, according to the Romanian text, near the Black Sea (N. Roddy, *The Romanian Version of the Testament of Abraham: Text, Translation and Cultural Context,* Atlanta, 2001, pp. 76–77).

3. *bSuk* 53a (*kusha'e*); so in ed. pr., MSS London 400 (*kushi*), Oxford, and Munich Hebr. 140/41, while MS Munich 95 is missing the word *kusha'e* altogether and MS Vatican Ebr. 134 (facsimile by Makor Press, *Osef Kitvei ha-Yad shel ha-*

Talmud Bavli be-Sifriyat ha-Vatican be-Roma, Jerusalem, 1972, 2:144) has *safre* 'scribes,' over which a later hand has written *kushi.*

4. *pKet* 12.3, 35b reads *ʾysqryṭwry* and *pKil* 9.4, 32c has *ʾysqbṭyryy* (in Sirillo: *ʾsqrbṭwry*), readings which are also preserved in the *ʿArukh,* s.v. *ʾysqryṭry* (cf. *sqbṭr* s.v.), and other works. On the reading of the word in the Palestinian Talmud, and on the secondary literature, see D. Sperber, *A Dictionary of Greek and Latin Legal Terms in Rabbinic Literature* (Bar Ilan, 1984), pp. 38–39, s.vv. *ʾysqbṭryy, ʾysqypṭwryn,* and *ʾysqryṭwr.* Marc Hirshman has noted that this tradition is found in the manuscripts of *Qohelet Rabba,* but not the printed editions ("Midrash Qohelet Rabba, Chapters 1–4," Ph.D. diss., Jewish Theological Seminary, 1982, part 1, pp. 93–94). Hirshman points out that while the text in two manuscripts (*ʾysq mn ṭwry* and *ʾysqwmṭmy*) is similar to, and may be based upon, the Palestinian Talmud, a third manuscript reading has *hawan min saboi safroi di-shelomoh* 'they were of the elder scribes of Solomon.' If this reading is not merely a corruption of "secretaries," or "secretaries" of it (*mn ṭwry </> mn/sbwy*), then we have a third variant of the word.

5. *Sofer* is elsewhere translated as *scriptor:* so at any rate in Musafia's (Kohut, *ʿArukh,* s.v. *ʾysqryṭry*) corrected reading of *QohR* 9.18 explaining 2 Kgs 18:37 (the text in *QohR* reads *sqywwy pṭryy*). Regarding *secretarii* as a straightforward translation of "scribes," cf. *YalqSh,* Esther 1057, quoting *PRE* 50 (p. 122b) but replacing the latter's "scribes" (*soferim*) with "secretaries" (*sqryṭwryn*). The reading *sqryṭwryn* aut sim. follows Ginzberg's suggestion (*Legends of the Jews,* 6:477, n. 176) for the reading in the *Yalquṭ: swnqṭryn* (ed. pr.) or *sqndryn* (ed. sec.). It is much more difficult to accept his emendation of *Midrash Abba Gorion* (ed. Buber, p. 41). On *PRE*'s reading, cf. *ʿArukh,* ed. Kohut, 5:385b, s.v. *nrqʾyn,* and *Targum Sheni* to Est 6:1. The story of Solomon's scribes is found also in later anthologies, see Gaster, *Exempla of the Rabbis,* no. 139A, and the literature cited on p. 215.

6. *Legends of the Jews,* 6:303.

7. For secretaries, black and white, in the Roman Empire, see J. Christes, *Sklaven und Freigelassene als Grammatiker und Philologen im antiken Rom* (Wiesbaden, 1979), index, s.v. *Sekretäre;* see also Snowden, *Blacks in Antiquity,* p. 191.

8. Aḥiyah the son of Shemḥazaʾe is mentioned in *bNid* 61a as the father of Siḥon and ʿOg. Baḥya b. Asher b. Ḥlava (thirteenth century) quotes an anonymous midrash (no longer extant) that Shemḥazaʾel was one of the divine beings ("sons of God") who cohabited with the "daughters of men" according to Gen 6:2–4 (cf. Rashi at *bNid* 91a), and had intercourse with Ham's wife (*Commentary to the Pentateuch,* ed. C. B. Chavel, 3:159, to Num 21:34). The citation in Baḥye was apparently unknown to Milik in his discussion on the Book of the Giants in midrashic literature; see his *The Books of Enoch,* pp. 320ff. The rabbinic sources on Shemḥazaʾe and Aḥiah are collected in R. Margaliot, *Malaʾkhe ʿElyon,* p. 292.

9. Cf. Origen: "Ethiopia in Hebrew is Kush which means σκότωσιν" (*Selecta in Genesim, PG* 12.100) and note the use of σκότος to describe skin color in *Testament of Solomon* 13.5, where it is said of a female demon that "her body was darkness" (σκότος τὸ σῶμα αὐτῆς ὑπῆρχε); C. C. McCown, ed., *The Testament of Solomon* (Leipzig, 1922), ad loc., p. 44*. English translation in *OTP* 1:974. Qoh 2:7 reads, "I acquired male and female slaves," to which the Targum adds "from the children of Ham and other foreign peoples." Since Qohelet is traditionally attributed to Solomon, the tragumic addition would imply that Solomon had Nubian slaves,

which would agree with the statement in the Babylonian Talmud that Solomon's scribes were Kushites. Is there a relationship between the statements in *bSuk* 53a and *TgQoh* 2.7 (*TgQoh* probably dates from the seventh century according to Peter Knobel in *The Aramaic Bible,* 15:2–15) or the sources of these sources? *TgQoh* 2.7 is treated above, pp. 136–37.

10. For the physical dangers of the bathhouse in Jewish sources, see M. R. Hanoune, "Thermes romains et Talmud," Colloque Histoire et Historiographie Clio, ed. R. Chevallier (Paris, 1980), pp. 255–62, and Daniel Sperber, *The City in Roman Palestine* (New York, 1998), pp. 65–66.

11. Katherine Dunbabin, "*Baiarum Grata Voluptas:* Pleasures and Dangers of the Baths," *Papers of the British School in Rome* 57 (1989), 33–46, and Clarke, *Looking at Lovemaking,* pp. 129–42, discuss the Greco-Roman evidence; Campbell Bonner, "Demons of the Bath," *Studies Presented to F. Ll. Griffith* (London, 1932), pp. 203–8, the Christian evidence. Both mention the nocturnal proclivity of demons, and Campbell cites as well medieval and modern examples of the "diabolical haunting of baths" in Egypt (207).

12. Dunbabin, "*Baiarum Grata Voluptas,*" and Clarke, *Looking at Lovemaking.*

13. MS Vatican 111 seems to have the same reading as the printed edition, *nośeʾei qeisar* (*Osef Kitvei ha-Yad shel ha-Talmud Bavli be-Sifriyat ha-Vatican be-Roma,* 6:216), as does MS Oxford 367 (my thanks to Benjamin Richler of the Institute of Microfilmed Hebrew Manuscripts in Jerusalem for reading this manuscript passage for me); MS Munich, apparently by metathesis, has *nśwʾy qysr.* Israel ibn al-Nakawa, *Menorat ha-Maʾor* records *dwśy qysr* (ed. H. G. Enelow, 3:124 with the note; incidentally, Enelow errs in citing the *ʿArukh*). *Haggadot ha-Talmud* (printed edition, p. 56a, and MS British Museum 2419, f. 39b): *kushaʾei de-qeisar;* MS Parma 3010 (f. 88a): *qwšʾy dqysr!* Obviously the reading of Aramaic *kushaʾei* influenced the following *de-*.

14. On the litter, its use, and history, see *RE* 12:1056–1108 (H. Lamer). On knowledge of litters in Roman Palestine, see *Mekhilta, Neziqin* 1 (p. 248): "*furion, kiseʾ, leqṭiqa,*" i.e., φορεῖον, *sella, lectica;* and S. Krauss, *Talmudische Archäologie,* 2:331–33, 675–76. It is possible, but I think less likely, that *nośeʾei* refers to those who, for fear of floor collapse, supported the bather in the bathhouse, such as two servants did for R. Abahu (*bKet* 62a). The explanation of *nośeʾei* as "[armor] bearers" offered by H. Freedman in the Soncino English translation has no warrant. Presumably Freedman was thinking of the ὑπηρέται, who indeed acted as armor bearers, but the word "armor" is not in the text. The talmudic story is transmitted by Rava, who died in 352.

15. *bQid* 49b.

16. See Jastrow's and Levy's comments in their dictionaries (s.v. *šaḥarut*) regarding *NumR* 10.8, and my comments in the Introduction (pp. 6–7).

17. Nehemiah Brüll in his *Jahrbücher* 1 (1874) 164 notes that Samuel b. Moses Avila (seventeenth century), *Keter Torah* (Amsterdam, 1725), p. 101b, quotes the tosafot with this reading; see also the note in *Hagahot ha-Tosafot* in the "Nehardea" edition of the Talmud published by Vagshal (Jerusalem, 1992), which records the same reading in early versions of the Talmud, the tosafot, and Rashi.

18. *Diqduqei Soferim,* ad loc., records the reading *goyim;* M. Friedmann in his critical edition of this tractate (Vienna, 1888), p. 67, notes the reading in *ʿEin Yaʿaqov.*

19. *Diqduqei Soferim,* ad loc.

20. See Levy, *Wörterbuch über die Talmudim,* 2:310–311; Kohut in *ʿArukh* 4:348a.

21. According to Rabbinovicz and Popper, both *kuthi* and *kushi* were introduced as censors' substitutions for the word *goy* in the Basel edition of the Talmud (1578). See R. Rabbinovicz, *Maʾamar ʿal Hadpasat ha-Talmud,* ed. A. M. Habermann, 2nd ed. (Jerusalem, 1965), p. 77; W. Popper, *The Censorship of Hebrew Books* (1899; New York, 1969), p. 59. M. Jastrow believes that *kushi* was a deliberate substitution for *kuthi,* after the latter was commonly understood to mean "Christian" (Jastrow, "The History and the Future of the Text of the Talmud," in *Publications of the Gratz College,* Philadelphia, 1897, pp. 95–96). Arguing for scribal error, against Jastrow, are the cases where textual corruption occurs in the opposite direction, from *kushi* to *kuthi,* as in *bMQ* 16b in ed. Venice 1538, which quotes Amos 9:7 *kushim* as *kuthim* (ed. pr., Venice, 1520–26, has *kushim*), and in the quotation of *tBer* 6/7.3 (discussed above, p. 114) *kushi* as *kuthi* by Elijah of London (thirteenth century), for which see M.Y.L. Sacks, ed., *The Writings of Rabbi Elijah of London* (Jerusalem, 1956), p. 125 to *mBer* 9.4. Note also the (non-African) *kush/kuth* variants in *The Itinerary of Benjamin of Tudela,* ed. Marcus N. Adler (London, 1907), Hebrew section, p. 54.

22. *LevR* 37.4 (pp. 864–65), *GenR* 60.3 (pp. 641–42). A different version, including only Eliezer and Saul, is found in *bTaʿan* 4a, where the tradition is transmitted in the name of Samuel b. Naḥmani (third–fourth century), who quotes it in the name of R. Jonathan (b. Eleazar; early third century), or in the name of R. Yoḥanan (third century) in *Haggadot ha-Talmud* (Constantinople, 1511; facsimile, Jerusalem, 1961), p. 49a; in the other sources the midrash is quoted anonymously. Later compositions quoting this midrash in one form or another (see table on p. 205): *Midrash Aggadah,* p. 57; *Midrash ha-Gadol,* 22:14(1:396); *YalqSh,* Gen 107 (1/2:484); *YalqSh,* Josh 25 (p. 75); *Sefer We-Hizhir,* ed. Israel Meir Freimann (Leipzig, 1873; Warsaw, 1880), 2:260–61; *Leqaḥ Ṭov,* 24:13(1:55a); *Pirqei de-Rabbenu ha-Qadosh* in ed. L. Grünhut, *Sefer ha-Liqquṭim,* 3:41 and (from a different manuscript) in ed. S. Shönblum, *Sheloshah Sefarim Niftaḥim* (Lemberg, 1877), p. 32b, sec. 99. The last cited work quotes the midrash in the name of R. Ishmael; *YalqSh,* Gen (ed. pr.) cites the source of the midrash as *bTaʿan,* but it is *GenR* (at least, in the sources as we have them today). On *We-Hizhir,* see M. Kasher and J. Mandelbaum, *Sarei ha-Elef,* p. 44; A.N.Z. Roth, "Qetaʿ mi-Midrash we-Hizhir," *Talpioth* 7 (1957) 89–91, 98; Y. Sussman in *Meḥqarim be-Sifrut ha-Talmudit: Yom ʿIyun le . . . Shaʾul Lieberman* (Jerusalem, 1983), p. 20, n. 47 and p. 24, n. 72; and Stemberger, *Introduction,* p. 312, for further literature.

23. The original order of the various elements has not been maintained in order to present a table in which comparison can be readily seen.

24. Goldenberg, "Scythian-Barbarian," p. 98, n. 24.

25. Sokoloff, *The Genizah Fragments of Bereshit Rabba,* p. 21.

26. The author and date of *We-Hizhir* are not known. See Y. Sussman's comment and cited literature, in *Meḥqarim be-Sifrut ha-Talmudit,* p. 20 and n. 47. S. Asaf (*Tequfat ha-Geonim we-Sifrutah,* Jerusalem, 1955, pp. 161–63) places the composition in tenth-century Palestine. Lately R. Brody has assigned a dating between 850 and 1000, and a location "on the cultural border between Babylonia

and Israel, although the geographical meaning of this description is unclear" (*Le-Toledot Nusaḥ ha-She'iltot,* New York, 1991, pp. 111–12). N. Danzig, however, thinks it possible that *We-Hizhir* was composed in southern Italy as originally suggested by Zunz. See his "The First Discovered Leaves of *Sefer Ḥefeṣ,*" *JQR* 82 (1991) 107–8, n. 175.

27. Menahem Kahana has shown that this section of *GenR* MS Vatican 60 is dependent on *LevR*. See his "Genesis Rabba MS Vatican 60 and Its Parallels" (in Hebrew), *Te'udah* 11 (1996) 42–45.

28. Similar to the reading *'eved, kushi, goy* in the *GenR* manuscripts is the reading in *Leqaḥ Ṭov: 'eved* (for Caleb) + *kushi, 'akum/*idolater (for Saul).

29. *'akum* could have easily derived from *'eved,* the scribe having read *'eved* as an abbreviation for *'ovdei [kokhavim u-mazalot],* i.e., *'akum.*

30. The reading "Saul ben Kush" in *Pirqei de-Rabbenu ha-Qadosh,* ed. Shönblum is, as noted by Grünhut in his edition, only a scribal error for "Saul b. Qish," King Saul's patronymic. It is possible that this error was influenced by the rabbinic tradition that identifies Saul with Kush of Ps 7:1 (see above, p. 56).

31. Gil, *Ereṣ Yisra'el bi-Tequfah ha-Muslamit ha-Ri'shonah, 634–1099* (Tel Aviv, 1983), 1:662; now in English translation as *A History of Palestine 634–1099* (Cambridge, 1992), p. 821. Gil thinks that the name "Kushan," which is found only in Arabic sources, derives from "Kuthi."

32. See Rashi on *bAZ* 31a: "'Ein Kushi: a Samaritan place [*maqom kuthim*]"; see Kohut in *'Arukh,* 4:348a, s.v. *kš.*

33. *mNed* 3.8; *GenR* 59.1 (pp. 630–31) and parallels.

34. Cf. Qoh 11:10, *ha-yaledut weha-shaḥarut* "youth and black hair" (NJPS). Regarding the tannitic meaning, see also *bNed* 30b.

35. *CAD* Ṣ 75f, s.v.; von Soden, *Akkadisches Handwörterbuch,* 3:1077f., s.v.

36. Wolf Leslau, "Vocabulary Common to Akkadian and South-East Semitic (Ethiopic and South-Arabic)," *JAOS* 64 (1944) 56, based on D. H. Müller, "Mehri- und Soqoṭri-Glossen," *ZDMG* 58 (1904) 780–81. Müller notes that Soqoṭri *ber-ḥoriš* translates *ben adam* in Ezek 37:3, 9.

37. See the Yiddish manuscript published, with introduction, by Isaac Rivkin in the YIVO *Filologishe Shriften* 3 (Vilna, 1929) 1–42, and two Hebrew texts published by Eli Yasif in *Biqoret u-Farshanut* (English title: *Criticism and Interpretation*) 9–10 (1976) 214–28. In other versions of the story that I have checked, the antagonist—cleric or not—is not depicted as black. This is the case in: the first Yiddish printed text (Furth 1694) published by Rivkin; five Hebrew texts published by Joseph Dan in *Biqoret u-Farshanut,* pp. 197–213 (one of which was originally published by Louis Ginzberg, "Haggadot Qetu'ot," *Ha-Goren* 9 [Berlin, 1922] 43–45); an oral tradition told by Moses Attias of Greece in Dov Noy, ed., *Noṣat ha-Zahav* (Haifa, 1976), pp. 149–53; an earlier version (by about two hundred years) of the folktale published by J. Dan, "An Early Hebrew Source of the Yiddish 'Aqdamoth' Story," *Hebrew University Studies in Literature* 1 (1973) 39–46; see also the last paragraph of Rivkin's article in *Ha-Do'ar* 9 (New York, 1929) 507. English translations of the story: I. M. Lask translation of M. J. Bin Gorion (Berdyczewski), *Mimekor Yisrael* (Bloomington, Ind., 1976), 1:335–37; Howard Schwartz, *Miriam's Tambourine* (New York, 1984), pp. 335–48 and 388–90. See also the English summaries in M. Gaster, *The Exempla of the Rabbis,* no. 369

(p. 137) and no. 445 (p. 178). For discussion on the literary development of the folktale, see Dan, and see Noy, pp. 190–91, for further bibliography and sources.

38. On *der shvartz kuntzter,* see Rivkin's introduction, p. 4; the term appears on p. 13.

39. A. C. Gow, *The Red Jews,* especially pp. 4, 66–69. The notion of the "Red Jews," says Gow, is the end product of (a) an imaginative conflation of Christian traditions about the lost Ten Tribes and the nations of Gog and Magog, (b) the secondary meaning of *rot* (red) in Middle High German, "duplicitous, wicked, faithless, cunning," and (c) the earlier Greco-Roman and then Christian association of red hair and beard with evil or sin. The term appears exclusively in German-language writings between the twelfth and sixteenth centuries. The Jews of this time and place adopted the usage of "Red Jews" without, however, the negative and hostile associations found in Christian writings. The "little red Jew" of our story, then, may be such an adoption.

40. See the *The Catholic Encyclopedia,* ed. C. G. Herbermann et al. (New York, 1907–14), 2:591 and the individual entries. Cf. David Qimḥi's explanation of the Hebrew *komer* 'idolatrous priest' as if from the root *kmr* 'to be black' because priests wear black vestments (*Commentrary* to 2 Kings 23:5). See also Yule's reference to the Black Sect of Tibetan lamas called such because of the color of their clothing, in his edition of Marco Polo, *The Book of Ser Marco Polo,* 1:324. Note, finally, J. Harvey's comment that Buddhist and Taoist monks during the Qing Dynasty in China (1644–1911) wore black and, "as in Russia, monks would be referred to as 'men in black'" (*Men in Black,* Chicago, 1995, p. 261, n. 2). Harvey also notes that the "Black Prince was so-named, in some accounts, because his armour was black" (p. 82). In general, on the black clothes of monastic orders, see Harvey, pp. 44–49, 84.

41. The *Maʿaseh Book* was first published in 1602 by Jacob b. Abraham of Mezeritch. The edition quoted from is that by Bertha Pappenheim ed., *Allerlei Geschichten: Maase-Buch* (Frankfort am Main, 1929), p. 95, no. 103, based on the Amsterdam, 1723 edition of the *Maʿaseh-Buch.* The translation is by M. Gaster, *Maʿaseh Book* (Philadelphia, 1934), 1:178–79.

42. *bTaʿan* 20a–b (ed. Malter, p. 80), *ARNa* 41 (p. 131), *Derekh Ereṣ Rabba* 4 (ed. Higger, pp. 166ff.), and *Kalah Rabbati* 7 (ed. Higger, pp. 310–11).

43. R. Ḥananel, found in the standard editions of the Talmud, has now been published from extant manuscripts by David Metzger, *Perush Rabbenu Ḥananʾel ben Ḥushiʾel le-Talmud* (Jerusalem, 1995), 7:51. *Sefer ha-Yuḥasin,* ed. H. Filipowski and Abraham H. Freimann, 2nd ed. (Frankfurt, 1924), p. 77; *Haggadot ha-Talmud,* p. 52b; *ʿEin Yaʿaqov,* ad loc. See also the similar story told by Thaʿlabī about Luqmān, an Ethiopian (above, p. 265, n 174).

44. "Paronomasia in Aggadic Narratives," *Scripta Hierosolymitana* 27 (1978) 44.

45. I am indebted to my father, Rabbi Bernard Goldenberg, for bringing the Maharsha (found in standard editions of the Talmud) to my attention.

46. See, e.g., Aaron, "Early Rabbinic Exegesis," p. 727.

47. *Sefer ha-Musar,* ed. Y. Ratzaby (Jerusalem, 1965), p. 130.

48. *The Itinerary of Benjamin of Tudela,* ed. Adler, English section, pp. 63–64 and Hebrew section, p. 58. The text has been generally understood by the various translators of Benjamin to mean black Africans. So A. Asher, *The Itinerary of Rabbi*

Benjamin of Tudela (New York, 1900), p. 138; Ignacio González Llubera, *Viajes de Benjamin de Tudeal 1160–1173* (Madrid, 1918), p. 105; A. Martinet, *Reissetagbuch des Rabbi Binjamin von Tudela* (Berlin, 1918), p. 24; Rolf Schmitz, *Benjamin von Tudela: Buch der Reissen (Sefār ha-Massaʿot)* (Franfurt am Main, 1988), p. 40. Adler, however, recognized that *kush* in this case could not refer to Africa (see his note on p. 60), although his explanation of the term is unacceptable.

APPENDIX II

1. The literature on the Ethiopia/India "confusion" is extensive. Some bibliography: E. H. Warmington, s.v. Ethiopia in *The Oxford Classical Dictionary,* ed. G. L. Hammond and H. H. Scullard, 2nd ed. (Oxford, 1970); Snowden, *Blacks in Antiquity,* pp. 11, 263 n. 36, 258 n. 10, 277–79 n. 1, 336 n. 80; *Before Color Prejudice,* pp. 113–14, n. 32; Balsdon, *Romans and Aliens,* p. 217; Thompson, *Romans and Blacks,* p. 192, n. 164; Dihle, *Umstrittene Daten,* pp. 37ff., and "Der Fruchtbare Osten," pp. 100–1, n. 6; U. P. Arora, "India vis-à-vis Egypt-Ethiopia in Classical Accounts," *Graeco-Arabica* 1 (1982) 131–40; Jacobson, *Exagoge of Ezekiel,* p. 198, n. 10; Friedman, *The Monstrous Races,* pp. 8 and 213, nn. 13–14; R. Wittkower, "Marvels of the East: A Study in the History of Monsters," *Journal of the Warburg and Courtauld Institutes* 5 (1942) 161, n. 4; R. Wittkower, *Allegory and the Migration of Symbols* (London, 1977), p. 197, n. 13; Kaplan, *The Rise of the Black Magus,* pp. 12–13, 225–26 n. 38, 104, 244 n.153, and 248 n. 200; S. Krauss in *Tarbiẓ* 8 (1937) 218; G. Fiaccadori, *Studi classici e orientali* 33 (1983) 295–300, and 34 (1984) 273f; Jeffrey, *The Foreign Vocabulary of the Qurʾān,* p. 18; Theodore Papadopoullos, *Afrocanobyzantina: Byzantine Influences on Negro-Sudanese Cultures* (Athens, 1966), pp. 26–27; Epstein, "Les Chamites de la table ethnographique," pp. 92–93; Epstein, *Kitvei Avraham Epstein,* pp. 58ff., n. 19.

2. Herodotus 3.17–23, 7.69–70.

3. Ed. John J. Collins, *The Sibylline Oracles of Egyptian Judaism* (Missoula, Mont., 1972), pp. 79–80 (= *OTP* 1:373).

4. Noted by C. Burchard in his translation in *OTP* 2:238. On the dating and provenance (Egypt), see p. 194. Recently Ross Kraemer has proposed a later date, not earlier than the third–fourth century C.E. (*When Aseneth Met Joseph,* New York, 1998, pp. 237–39). On the work in general, see Collins, *Between Athens and Jerusalem,* 2nd ed., pp. 230–39.

5. *SC* 124:152, cited by V. Christides, "The Image of the Sudanese in Byzantine Sources," *Byzantinoslavica* 43 (1982) 12, who also notes that John Malalas, the Byzantine chronicler of the sixth century, calls the Yemenites "Indians" (Malalas, *Chronographia,* Bonn, 1831, p. 457).

6. R. H. Charles, trans., *The Chronicle of John, Bishop of Nikiu* (London, 1916), pp. 16–17.

7. A. Vassiliev, *Anecdota Graeco-Byzantina,* pp. 228–29; D. Flusser in *Scripta Hierosolymitana* 22 (1971) 67–68. See above, pp. 345–46, n. 46.

8. Epstein, "Les Chamites de la table ethnographique," pp. 92–93. These identifications are of one piece with the common and widespread confusion between India and Ethiopia and there is therefore nothing wrong with the text of Rashi, contra I. Avinery, *Hekhal Rashi,* vol. 2, sec. 2 (*Milon*), col. 289. (Elsewhere, to Jer

13:23, Rashi identifies the biblical Kush as "Moor.") On these references, and others in rabbinic literature, see Hirshenzohn, *Shevaᶜ Ḥokhmot,* pp. 102–3.

9. See Yule's note in his edition of Marco Polo, *The Book of Ser Marco Polo,* 2:431–32, n. 1, and Adler, *The Itinerary of Benjamin of Tudela,* 1:95.

10. Yona Sabar, *Targum de-Targum: An Old Neo-Aramaic Version of the Targum on Song of Songs* (Wiesbaden, 1991), p. 79; E. Z. Melamed, *Shir ha-Shirim: Targum Arami, Targum ᶜIvri, Tafsir bi-Leshon Yehude Paras* (Jerusalem, 1971), p. 15. On the other hand, the reading of another Judeo-Persian translation—this of the biblical text—substituting "tan" for "black" (*sheḥorah*) in 1:5 seems to be an attempt at interpretive explanation (J. P. Asmussen and H. Paper, *The Song of Songs in Judeo-Persian,* Copenhagen, 1977, p. 61 MS S). A similar attempt at explanation is made by the same manuscript when it substitutes "do not belittle me" for "do not look at me" (ibid.). My thanks to E. Dardashti for his translation of the Judeo-Persian.

11. Edward Ullendorff, "Candace (Acts 8:27) and the Queen of Sheba," *NTS* 2 (1955) 53 and n.2.

12. Alphonse Mingana, "The Early Spread of Christianity in India," *BJRL* 10 (1926) 443–46.

13. Weitzman, *The Syriac Version of the Old Testament,* p. 109, says that the Peshiṭta's translation of "Indian" for "Kushi" is due to an oral tradition that is also expressed by the early amoraic statement (*bMeg* 11a) that Kush bordered on India. This statement is part of a dispute between Rav and Samuel, with one claiming that India (Hodu) and Kush lie at opposite ends of the world and the other claiming that the two countries border one another. These two opinions correspond with a view of India's geography held by some early-century Christian authors, according to which the country is divided into three parts: North India borders Parthia or Media, South India is connected with Ethiopia, and Further India lies at the end of the world (Albrecht Dihle, "The Conception of India in Hellenistic and Roman Literature," *Proceedings of the Cambridge Philological Society* 190, n. s. 10 [1964] 16–17). Dihle further notes that the perception of India bordering Ethiopia is found in Christian literature until the sixth century at least. Apparently the perception continued for some time, for it is found in the *Libro del Caballero Zifar* (ca. 1300), English translation by Charles Nelson, *The Book of the Knight Zifar,* pp. 22 and 24.

14. Alexander, *The Byzantine Apocalyptic Tradition,* pp. 17–18, 38–40. G. Reinink, *Die syrische Apokalypse des Pseudo-Methodius, CSCO* 541 (1993) 11, n. 1.

15. A few examples: The Portuguese referred to the whole of maritime East Africa and Asia as "the state of India" (Boxer, *Race Relations in the Portuguese Colonial Empire,* p. 41). Thomas Bacon, in mid-sixteenth-century England paraphrased the proverb in Jer 13:23 ("Can the Ethiopian change his skin?") as "[Can] the man of Ind change his skin?" (quoted in Prager, "'If I Be Devil,'" p. 262). A. G. Barthelemy noted a lack of distinction between black Africans and Indians in some English pageant writers of the seventeenth century (*Black Face Maligned Race: The Representation of Blacks in English Drama from Shakespeare to Southerne,* Baton Rouge, La., 1987, p. 47).

GLOSSARY OF SOURCES AND TERMS

This glossary consists of sources and terms that are likely to be unfamiliar to the average reader. For the most part, this means rabbinic literature and related terminology, although some other terms and literature are included as well. The source entries provide a short description of the individual work, its date of composition or redaction, the provenance, the edition used, bibliography on English translations when available, and some references for further readings. More detailed information on rabbinic literature may be found in Günter Stemberger, *Introduction to the Talmud and Midrash,* 2nd ed. Dates of the redaction of various rabbinic works that are used in this study generally follow Stemberger, who presents the scholarly consensus.

Aggadah, aggadic—Traditional Jewish non-halakhic exegesis or teaching.

Amora, amoraim, amoraic—The Rabbis who followed the tannaim and who lived in Israel and Babylonia during the third to fifth century. Their traditions and teachings are recorded in the Babylonian and Palestinian (Jerusalem) Talmuds, and in the aggadic midrashim, such as *Genesis Rabba.*

Anthologies of midrash—Medieval collections of earlier midrashic material. While much of their contents is preserved in the earlier midrashic works, from which the anthologies drew, their value lies in material that is not found in the earlier extant sources and in variant readings of texts that are found in the earlier sources. The most important of the anthologies is *Yalquṭ Shimʿoni* (see entry).

ʿArukh—By Nathan b. Yeḥiel (1035– ca. 1110) of Rome. A dictionary of rabbinic literature. Alexander Kohut published an expanded edition that included Benjamin Mussafia's (seventeenth century) annotations, known as *Musaf he-ʿArukh* (first published in the Amsterdam 1655 edition of Nathan's work), and his own extensive notes, *Arukh ha-Shalem* [*Aruch Completum*] in 1878–92 (repr., New York, 1955). Samuel Krauss added a supplementary volume of notes, *Tosafot he-ʿArukh ha-Shalem* [*Additamenta ad librum Aruch Completum*] (Vienna, 1937).

Avot de-Rabbi Natan—In two recensions (thus, *ARNa* and *ARNb*), published by Solomon Schechter (1887; corrected repr., Hildesheim, 1979). English translation of *ARNa* by Judah Golden, *The Fathers according to Rabbi Nathan* (New Haven, 1955); of *ARNb* by Anthony Saldarini, *The Fathers according to Rabbi Nathan (Abot de Rabbi Nathan) Version B* (Leiden, 1975).

Babylonian Talmud—Redaction is put at the end of the fifth to the mid-sixth century (Stemberger, *Introduction,* pp. 192–97). Standard editions follow Vilna, 1880–86, which is based on Venice, 1520–23. Critical editions exist for some tractates. Critical editions of *Yev, Ket, Soṭ, Ned,* and *Giṭ* (chs. 1–2) have been published by the Institute for the Complete Israeli Talmud: *Talmud Bavli . . . be-Shem Diqduqe Soferim ha-Shalem,* (Jerusalem, 1986–). Variant readings (partial) for the other tractates were collected by R. Rabbinovicz, *Diqduqe Soferim: Variae lectiones in mischnam et in talmud babylonicum* (Munich-Przemysl, 1868–97). For other editions of individual tractates, see Stemberger, p. 213, and add Shabtai Frankel's edition of *BQ* (Jerusalem, 1996). Extra-canonical ("minor") tractates are quoted in this study from the various editions of Michael Higger (New York, 1929–37). For *Avot deR. Natan,* see the separate entry. An English translation of the Babylonian Talmud was published by the Soncino Press under the editorship of I. Epstein, *The Babylonian Talmud* (London, 1935–52); the minor tractates under the editorship of A. Cohen (1965).

Baraita, baraitot—See *Tanna.*

Exodus Rabba—Essentially consists of two different compositions. Chapters 1–14 constitute a rewriting of the *Tanḥuma-Yelamedenu* corpus in the style of exegetical midrash. Chapter 15 until the end also belongs to the *Tanḥuma-Yelamedenu* family of midrash literature. The first part has been edited by A. Shinan, *Midrash Shemot Rabba* (Jerusalem, 1984), who dates its redaction to the tenth century; it is certainly no earlier (p. 23).

Gaon, geonim, geonic—Heads of the rabbinic academies in Babylonia (and Israel) after the amoraic period until the eleventh century when Jewish intellectual/religious leadership migrated west. A history of the geonim is provided by Robert Brody, *The Geonim of Babylonia and the Shaping of Medieval Jewish Culture* (New Haven, 1998).

Genesis Rabba—Redacted probably in the first half of the fifth century (Stemberger, p. 279). A good short description of what we know of the work is that of Ofra Meir, *The Darshanic Story in Genesis Rabba [Ha-Sipur ha-Darshani bi-Vere'shit Raba]* (Tel Aviv, 1987), pp. 70–75. Critical edition: J. Theodor and Ḥ. Albeck (1912–36; repr., Jerusalem, 1965, with corrections). Two manuscripts have been reproduced in facsimile by Makor Press in Jerusalem: *Midrash Bereshit Rabba: Ms. Vat. Ebr. 30,* with introduction and index by M. Sokoloff (1971) and *Midrash Bereshit Rabba: Codex Vatican 60 (Ms. Vat. Ebr. 60),* with page index by A. P. Sherry (1972). MS Vat. 60 was not known to Theodor in his critical edition. Genizah fragments were edited by Michael Sokoloff, *The Genizah Fragments of Bereshit Rabba* (Jerusalem, 1882). For English translation, see *Midrash.*

Genizah—Literally "storage," the place where worn-out ritual or religious materials are temporarily stored, generally in a synagogue, until they can be properly disposed. At the end of the nineteenth century, a Genizah was discovered in the attic of the Ben Ezra synagogue in Old Cairo. While the materials in most Genizahs have been lost to history and the environment, the dry climate in Egypt assured the preservation of over 200,000 fragments of texts in the Cairo synagogue. Because most Jewish writing was in Hebrew characters, all manner of texts were preserved in the Genizah, whether they had a religious status or not. These materials, covering almost a thousand years, are now dispersed among the world's great university libraries (some 140,000 are at Cambridge University) and have been mined by scholars over the past century to reconstruct Jewish history and culture. A history of the Cairo Genizah discoveries and their importance has recently been published by Stephan Reif, *A Jewish Archive from Old Cairo: The History of Cambridge University's Genizah Collection* (Richmond, Surrey, 2000).

Ḥadīth—Arabic, literally "narrative, talk." A tradition of what Muḥammad, the prophet of Islam, said or did.

Haggadot ha-Talmud—Anonymous anthology of aggadic sections in the Talmud published in Constantinople, 1511. Facsimile: Jerusalem, 1961. Manuscripts of the work exist in Parma and London; see M. Hirshler in the Talmud edition of the Institute for the Complete Israeli Talmud (*Babylonian Talmud*), *Ketubot,* 1:70–71. For a description of the work, see Raphael N. Rabinovicz, *Maʿamar ʿal Hadpasat ha-Talmud,* rev. ed. by A. M. Habermann (Jerusalem, 1965), pp. 257–58, and Ezra Z. Melamed, *Midreshei Halakhah shel ha-Tannaʾim be-Talmud Bavli* (Jerusalem, 1943), pp. 71–78.

Halakhah, halakhic—Jewish religious law.

Hebrew Bible—The standard critical edition of the masoretic text of the Hebrew Bible is *Biblia Hebraica Stuttgartensia,* 2nd ed. (1984), which is based on MS Leningrad. The other major masoretic manuscript is MS Aleppo but most of the Pentateuch has been lost. The Hebrew University Bible Project, which is producing a critical edition based on MS Aleppo, has therefore thus far produced only the books of Isaiah and Jeremiah. The traditional masoretic text (MT) with targum and rabbinic commentaries has been published since the sixteenth century as *Miqraʾot Gedolot* (*Biblia Rabbinica*). Two new editions of *Miqraʾot Gedolot* include the rabbinic commentaries revised according to manuscript evidence: *Torat Ḥayim* covers the Pentateuch (Jerusalem, 1986–94) and *Miqraʾot Gedolot ha-Keter* (Jerusalem, 1992–) covering the entire Bible has thus far published Gen, Josh, Judg, 1–2 Sam, 1–2 Kgs, Isa, and Ezek. These two editions, which are based on MS Aleppo, have reconstructed the text of this manuscript for the vast missing parts of the Pentateuch.

Kalah Rabbati—One of the minor talmudic tractates. A Babylonian geonic work of about the eighth century (A. Aptowitzer in *REJ* 57 [1909] 245–48). Ed. Michael Higger, *Masekhtot Kalah, we-hen, Masekhet Kalah, Masekhet Kalah Rabati* (New York, 1936).

Leqaḥ Ṭov—Also known as *Pesiqta Zuṭrata,* of Ṭoviah b. Eliezer (eleventh–twelfth century, Bulgaria). An anthology of midrash with commentary, on the Pentateuch (ed. S. Buber, Vilna, 1880–84) and the five scrolls (ed. A. W. Greenup, London, 1909) (see *Midrash Rabba*).

Leviticus Rabba—Redaction is dated between 400 and 500. Critical edition: ed. M. Margulies, *Midrash Wayyikra Rabba* (Jerusalem, 1953–60). For English translation, see *Midrash Rabba.*

LXX—Shorthand for the Septuagint, the Greek translation of the Bible, begun on the Pentateuch as early as the third century B.C.E. and continued over several centuries. The critical edition is *Septuaginta: Vetus Testamentum Graecum,* Academia Scientiarum Gottingensis (Göttingen, 1954–). There is considerable confusion in scholarly literature regarding the precise meaning of the term "Septuagint." In this study I have adopted the usage proposed in *ABD* 5:1093, s.v. Septuagint: Where the Göttingen edition exists for a biblical book, "Septuagint" refers to the text in that edition (but not to readings in the apparatus); where the Göttingen edition has not yet published the text of a particular biblical book, "Septuagint" refers to the text in Rahlfs' (1935) edition. The exception to this usage occurs with regard to Song of Songs, for which I used Jay Treat's dissertation, "Lost Keys," and adopted his terminology, "Old Greek," with reference to any reading in that book. Books without known Hebrew equivalents are not referred to as "Septuagint" but as "apocrypha" or "pseudepigrapha."

Marqe—The Samaritan sage and author of *Tibat Marqe,* which has been published in a scholarly edition with Hebrew translation and annotation by Z. Ben-Ḥayyim (Jerusalem, 1988). *Tibat Marqe,* "a midrash containing much of Samaritan knowledge, i.e. of the exegetical tradition and their theology," is actually a collection of various materials (Ben-Ḥayyim, *ʿIvrit we-Aramit Nusaḥ Shomron,* 3/2:15). Books 1–2 of the work are from Marqe himself or are contemporaneous with him, while Books 3–6 reflect a linguistic world later than Marqe conforming, rather, to the language of the sixth–ninth century. Therefore, if these latter books were composed by or at the time of Marqe, they have been reworked over the centuries. In any case, these linguistically later texts are likely to contain older concepts and traditions drawn from early sources (Ben-Ḥayyim, *Tibat Marqe,* introduction, pp. 23–27). Until recently the flourit of Marqe was considered to be the latter half of the fourth century, but a dating a hundred years earlier has now been advanced and is accepted by some Samaritan scholars (*Tibat Marqe,* p. 14, n. 16). Abraham Tal opts for either the third or fourth century (in A. Crown, *A Companion to Samaritan Studies,* Tubingen, 1993, pp. 152, 235). Rudolph Macuch and Sylvai Powels favor a fourth-century date (*The Samaritans,* ed. Alan Crown, Tübingen, 1989, pp. 540 and 715; see also Tal on pp. 451–53), and Nathan Schur the end of the fourth century (*History of the Samaritans,* Frankfurt am Main, 1989, p. 74). These works all list earlier studies, as does de Lange, *Origen and the Jews,* p. 166, n. 92. English translation (unreliable): Macdonald, *Memar Marqah: The Teaching of Marqah* (Berlin, 1963).

Matenot Kehunah—See *Midrash Rabba.*

Mekhilta de-Rabbi Shimʿon bar Yoḥai—Ed. J. N. Epstein and E. Z. Melammed (Jerusalem, 1955). See *Midrash.*

Mekhilta de-Rabbi Ishmael—Ed. H. S. Horovitz and I. A. Rabin, 2nd ed. (Jerusalem, 1960). English translation (with text): Jacob Lauterbach (Philadelphia, 1933–35). See *Midrash.*

Midrash—Exegetical interpretation of Scripture. The term is used for both individual interpretations and a work comprising such interpretations, such as *Midrash Genesis Rabba.* Midrashic literature is divided into halakhic (tannaitic) midrashim, and aggadic (amoraic) midrashim. The former contain tannaitic and, in some cases, first-generation amoraic teachings and so are thought to have been redacted shortly after the close of the tannaitic period ca. 220 C.E. Thus most scholars accept a mid-third-century date for the redaction of these texts. For other suggestions, see Jay Harris, *How Do We Know This? Midrash and the Fragmentation of Modern Judaism* (Albany, N.Y., 1995), pp. 266–67, n. 12, and Daniel Boyarin, "On the Status of the Tannaitic Midrashim," *JAOS* 112 (1992) 460. The date of redaction of these works should not be confused with the date of the individual tradition units that comprise the contents of the work (on this issue, see what I have written in the Introduction, p. 12). The halakhic midrashim include the *Mekhilta*s on Exodus, *Sifra* on Leviticus, and the *Sifre*s on Numbers and Deuteronomy. (Some scholars put the redaction of *Mekhilta de-Rabbi Shimʿon bar Yoḥai* later, in the fourth or fifth century.) Genesis, containing no legal material, does not have a corresponding halakhic midrash. Although the framework of these works is halakhic, they contain also aggadic material. The aggadic midrashim, containing the teachings of the amoraim as well as the tannaim, were redacted at different times after the close of the amoraic period. Those used in this study include the "Rabba" midrashim and others, such as *PesRK, PesR.* English translations of midrashic literature have been made by Jacob Neusner, and of *Midrash Rabba* by Soncino Press under the editorship of H. Freedman and Maurice Simon (London, 1939). For more information and the critical editions used, see under the individual entries of the works.

Midrash ha-Gadol—Attributed to David B. Amram of Aden (thirteenth or fourteenth century). Ed. Jerusalem, 1947–75: M. Margulies (Genesis-Exodus), A. Steinsaltz (Leviticus), S. Fisch (Numbers), Z. M. Rabinowitz (Deuteronomy).

Midrash Psalms—Ed. S. Buber, *Midrash Tehilim* (Vilna, 1891). "A definite date of composition [for *MidPs*] cannot be given. . . . Most of the material [in *MidPs* 1–118] certainly dates back to the Talmudic period" (Stemberger, *Introduction,* pp. 322–23). An English translation of *MidPs* was published by William Braude, *The Midrash on Psalms* (New Haven, 1959).

Midrash Rabba—The body of texts known as *Midrash Rabba* is an artificial creation of sixteenth-century printers, who sought to produce a collection of midrash for the biblical books read regularly throughout the year, that is the Pentateuch and the five scrolls (Song of Songs, Ruth, Lamentations/*Eikhah,* Ecclesiastes/*Qohelet,* Esther). Some of the midrashic works they collected are early, redacted probably at the beginning of the fifth century (*Genesis Rabba, Leviticus Rabba, Lamentations Rabba*) and some were redacted late (e.g., *Exodus Rabba, Numbers Rabba*). See the individual entries. Where critical editions of the individual works were not available, I used ed. Romm (Vilna, 1878) of *Midrash Rabba.* The following commentaries, printed in most editions of *Midrash Rabba,* were used in this study: the abridged version of *Yefeh To'ar* by Samuel Yaffe Ashkenazi's (sixteenth century); *Matenot Kehunah* by Issachar Baer b. Naftali Ha-Kohen, also known as Berman Ashkenazi (sixteenth century); and *Perush Maharzaw* by Ze'ev Wolf Einhorn (d. 1862). The original version of *Yefeh To'ar* (Ferrara, 1692; repr., Jerusalem, 1989) was also used. On Samuel Yaffe Ashkenazi and his work, see Meir Beneyahu, "R. Shmu'el Yafe Ashkenazi: Miqṣat Devarim ʿalaw we-ʿal Sefaraw we-ʿal Mefareshim Aḥerim shel ha-Rabot," *Tarbiẓ* 42 (1973) 419–460; on Berman Ashkenazi and his work, Jacob Reifmann, "Toledot R. Yisakhar Ha-Kohen Baʿal Matenot Kehunah we-Qorot Sefaraw," *Beit Oṣar ha-Sifrut* 1 (1887), *Ohel Issachar* 2–20.

Midrash Shir ha-Shirim—Ed. Eliezer H. Grünhut (Jerusalem, 1897); 2nd ed., Joseph H. Wertheimer (Jerusalem, 1971). Grünhut (p. 21) and Wertheimer (pp. 18–19) date the work to Palestine of the eighth–ninth and not later than the tenth century respectively (but see the objections to Wertheimer's arguments advanced by M. B. Lerner in his review, *Kiryat Sefer* 48 [1973] 547). In a linguistic study of this composition, Ch. Magid confirms the location of Palestine, but radically revised the dating to the period of *GenR, LevR,* and *PesRK,* at the latest to the mid-fifth century (Channa Magid, "The Language of *Midrash Shir Hashirim* in the A.H. Grünhut Edition," M.A. thesis, Tel Aviv Univ., 1987 [in Hebrew], pp. 354–61). For English translation, see *Midrash Rabba.*

Mishnah—A compilation of Jewish law (mostly), whose final redaction was made by R. Judah the Patriarch, ca. 200 C.E., and on which the Talmud is based. English translations were made by Herbert Danby (London, 1933) and Jacob Neusner (New Haven, 1988).

Numbers Rabba—A composite text consisting of two separate parts, chs. 1–14 (= *Be-midbar* and *Naso'*) and the remainder of the work. Whereas the second part has a close relationship to *Tanḥuma,* and is often identical to it, the first part is considered to be a late composition with a close relationship to the work of Moses Ha-Darshan of Narbonne (eleventh century), redacted not before the twelfth century, probably in Provence. See Ḥananel Mack, "Prolegomena and Example to an Edition of Midrash Bemidbar Rabba Part I" (Ph.D. diss., Hebrew University of Jerusalem, 1991), and "Zemano, Meqomo, u-Tefuṣato shel Midrash Be-Midbar Rabba," *Teʿudah* 11 (1996) 91–106. The redaction date of the second part is put between 600 and 800; see *Sefer Meqorot,* p. 27, and Stemberger, *Introduction,* p. 311. There is no critical edition except for sections 5.1 and 11.5–6 done by Mack as part of his dissertation.

Onomastica—Lists of biblical names of peoples and places in Hebrew, Greek, and Latin, with etymologies. Compiled by some early church fathers.

Palestinian Talmud—Redacted not later than 370 (Y. Sussman, "We-Shuv le-Yerushalmi Neziqin," *Meḥqerei Talmud* 1 (1990) 132–33 (cf. Stemberger, *Introduction,* pp. 170–71). Ed. pr. Venice, 1523–24. The single complete manuscript was published in facsimile (Jerusalem, 1971). Synoptic edition of manuscripts and early prints: Peter Schäfer and Hans-Jürgen Becker, *Sinopsis la-Talmud ha-Yerushalmi* (Tübingen, 1991). Solomon b. Joseph Sirillio's (d. ca. 1558) commentary, with talmudic text, was published in Jerusalem (1934–67) and covers the orders of *Zeraʿim* and *Sheqalim.* English translation: Jacob Neusner et al., *The Talmud of the Land of Israel* (Chicago, 1982–94). Critical annotations by various scholars: *In the Margins of the Yerushalmi: Glosses on the English Translation,* ed. J. Neusner (Chico, Calif., 1983). Edition used in this study is the editio princeps.

Palestinian Targum—Various Palestinian targums to the Pentateuch exist: *Targum Pseudo-Jonathan, Fragment Targum* (only on selected verses), *Targum Neofiti,* and fragments found in the Cairo Genizah. *Targum Ps-Jon* was reedited from the single extant manuscript and provided a Hebrew translation by D. Reider, *Targum Yonatan ben ʿUziʾel ʿal ha-Torah* (Jerusalem, 1984). An updated edition of the *Fragment Targum* is M. Klein's *The Fragment Targums of the Pentateuch according to Their Extant Sources* (Rome, 1980). Targum Neofiti was discovered and published by A. Diez Macho, *Neophyti 1: Targum Palestinense MS de la Biblioteca Vaticana* (Madrid, 1968–78). Diez Macho (et al.) has also produced a synoptic edition of the various Palestinian targums (including Genizah manuscripts) to the Pentateuch: *Targum Palaestinense in Pentateuchem (Biblia Polyglotta Matritensia)* (Madrid, 1977). There is a growing consensus that *Ps-Jon* in its present form derives from the Islamic period, i.e., not before the seventh–eighth century; see P.S. Alexander in *ABD* 6:322–23.

Perush Maharzaw—See *Midrash Rabba.*

Peshiṭta—Syriac Christian translation of the Bible. According to M. P. Weitzman, *The Syriac Version of the Old Testament: An Introduction* (Cambridge, 1999), the date of composition was 150–200. This date is generally accepted. Lucas van Rompay thinks it might go back to the first century: "The Christian Syrica Tradition of Interpretation," *HBOT* 1:614. A critical edition of the Peshiṭta is now being published by the Peshiṭta Institute in Leiden, *The Old Testament in Syriac according to the Peshitta Version,* edited on behalf of the International Organization for the Study of the Old Testament (Leiden, 1972–).

Pesiqta de-Rav Kahana—A homiletic midrash for festivals and special Sabbaths. Ed. B. Mandelbaum, *Pesikta de-Rav Kahana ʿal pi Ketav Yad Oxford, we-Shinuye Nusaḥot . . .* (New York, 1962). Most would date it in the fifth century or shortly thereafter. Provenance: Palestine. English translation by William G. Braude and Israel J. Kapstein, *Pesikta de-Rab Kahana* (Philadelphia, 1975).

Pesiqta Rabbati—A homiletic midrash for festivals and special Sabbaths. Editions used: M. Friedmann (= Ish-Shalom), *Midrash Pesiqta Rabbati ʿim Tosafot Meʾir ʿAyin . . .* (Vienna, 1880), and Rivka Ulmer, *Pesiqta Rabbati: A Synoptic Edition of Pesiqta Rabbati Based upon All Extant Manuscripts and the Editio Princeps* (Atlanta, 1997). English translation by William G. Braude, *Pesikta Rabbati* (New Haven, 1968). Opinions on the date range from the fourth to the ninth century. Provenance: Palestine.

Pirqei de-Rabbi Eliezer—The edition used is that published in Warsaw, 1852 (reprinted since then), containing the commentary of David Luria (d. 1855). C. M. Horowitz prepared a critical edition and, although never printed, his manuscript was published in facsimile by Makor Press (Jerusalem, 1972). Michael Higger published another Horowitz manuscript, which is an edition of *PRE* based on three Casanatense manuscripts, in *Ḥorev* 8 (1944) 82–119; 9 (1946) 94–166; 10 (1948) 185–294. English translation: Gerald Friedlander, *Pirḳê De Rabbi Eliezer* (London, 1916). The most recent discussion of the work, including a list of manuscripts and fragments and a digitized form of ed. pr. (Constantinople, 1514) and two manuscripts, is that of Lewis Barth, Pirqe Rabbi Eliezer: Electronic Text Editing Project (www.usc.edu/dept/huc-la/pre-project/agendas.html). The date of redaction is put between the eighth and ninth centuries and the provenance in Palestine. M. Pérez Fernández, *Los Capítulos de Rabbí Eliezer: Pirqê Rabbî 'Elî'ezer* (Valencia, 1984), pp. 20–21, would extend the dating to between the seventh and ninth centuries.

Pitron Torah—A ninth-century Babylonian collection of midrash with interpretations, author unknown. Ed. Ephaim E. Urbach (Jerusalem, 1978). An English version of Urbach's introduction, in which he discusses dating and provenance, appeared as "A Preliminary Report on an Unknown Yalkut," *Proceedings of the Seventh World Congress of Jewish Studies* (Jerusalem, 1981), 3:21–27.

Piyyuṭ—Liturgical poem.

Qohelet Rabba—No critical edition exists, excepting Mark Hirshman's Ph.D. dissertation, "Midrash Qohelet Rabba, Chapters 1–4" (Jewish Theological Seminary, 1983). Edited in Palestine between the sixth and eighth centuries according to most scholars; Hirshman opts for the sixth or possibly the seventh century ("The Greek Fathers and the Aggada on Ecclesiastes: Formats of Exegesis in Late Antiquity," *HUCA* 59 [1988] 137, and *A Rivalry of Genius: Jewish and Christian Biblical Interpretation in Late Antiquity,* trans. Batya Stein, Albany, N.Y., 1996, p. 107).

Qumran—The site where the Dead Sea scrolls were found. The Qumran fragments, numbering in the thousands, apparently represent the library of a Jewish sect, generally believed to be the Essenes, which existed from the second century B.C.E. until the Roman conquest of Judaea in 68 C.E. The documents found at Qumran, some of which predate the founding of the sect, are invaluable in reconstructing Jewish history and literature of the Second Temple period. In addition to containing the oldest manuscripts of the books in the Hebrew Bible, the materials also include lost or unknown pseudepigrapha and sectarian writings. A new *Encyclopedia of the Dead Sea Scrolls,* ed. Lawrence H. Schiffman and James C. VanderKam (New York, 2000) provides useful summaries of the latest scholarship. The letter 'Q' is used to designate the materials from Qumran, with the number before it referring to the Dead Sea cave in which the particular item was found; thus 4Q188 refers to fragment 188, which was found in cave 4.

Responsa—A genre of literature consisting of the responses of rabbinic authorities to questions put to them on, mostly, matters of religious law (halakhah).

Second Commonwealth, Second Temple Period—Dating from the return from the Babylonian exile (539 B.C.E.) and the construction of the second temple to the destruction of the temple (70 C.E.).

Seder Eliyahu Rabba—Together with *Seder Eliyahu Zuṭa,* it is also known as *Tanna de-Vei Eliyahu.* One of the ethical midrashim (Stemberger, *Introduction,* pp. 340–43) whose date and place of publication is not certain. Some think that the work, or at least its core, is earlier than the redaction of the Babylonian Talmud, which drew on it, and some think it later. It was certainly composed before the ninth century (see Y. Elbaum in *EJ* 15:803–4). Published by Meir Ish-Shalom (Friedmann), *Seder Eliyahu Rabba we-Seder Eliyahu Zuṭa* (Vienna, 1902). The Jerusalem reprint (1960, 1969) contains also Ish-Shalom's *Nispaḥim le-Seder Eliyahu Zuṭa* (Vienna, 1904), which consists of unrelated material, most of which had gone under the name of *Seder Eliyahu Zuṭa* and was thus included. A facsimile of *Tanna de-Vei Eliyahu* in MS Vatican 31 was published by Makor Press (Jerusalem, 1972). Translation: W. G. Braude and I. J. Kapstein, *Tanna Dĕḇe Eliyyahu: The Lore of the School of Elijah* (Philadelphia, 1981).

Sifra—Also known as *Torat Kohanim,* it is the tannaitic (halakhic) midrash to Leviticus. The oldest rabbinic manuscript, MS Assemani 66, which is dated by scholars variously to the eighth, ninth, or tenth century, contains this work (facsimile with introduction by L. Finkelstein: *Sifra, or, Torat Kohanim according to Codex Assemani,* New York, 1956). A facsimile of MS Vatican 31 was published by Makor Press (Jerusalem, 1972). Three editions of Sifra on the basis of manuscripts have been published, all incomplete: by M. Friedmann (Breslau, 1915; repr., Jerusalem, 1967) containing *Nedavah* 1–19, Lev 1:1–3:9; by L. Finkelstein (New York, 1983–91) on *Nedavah* and *Ḥovah,* Lev 1:1–5:26; by A. Shoshana (Jerusalem, 1991) on *Baraita deR. Ishmael, Nedavah,* and *Ḥovah.* The edition used in this study is that of I. H. Weiss (Vienna, 1862). For English translation, see *Midrash.*

Sifre Deuteronomy—Critical edition: ed. Louis Finkelstein (Breslau and Berlin, 1935–39; New York, 1969). English translation: Reuven Hammer, *Sifre: A Tannaitic Commentary on the Book of Deuteronomy* (New Haven, 1986). Redaction is generally put in the early amoraic period (230–80); see the discussion in S. Fraade, "Sifre Deuteronomy 26 (ad Deut. 3:23): How Conscious the Composition?" *HUCA* 54 (1983) 296–98, and add: Fraade, *From Tradition to Commentary* (Albany, N.Y., 1991), pp. 17 and 185, n. 56; Hammer, *Sifre,* p. 8 (all date the work to the mid-third century); and S. Lieberman "Palestine in the Third and Fourth Centuries," *JQR* 36 (1946) 355 (beginning of the third century). Among those who opt for a later dating add D. Boyarin, who, speaking of tannaitic midrashim in general, considers the redaction to have been done in "probably the late third and fourth centuries" ("On the Status of the Tannaitic Midrashim," *JAOS* 112 [1992] 460).

Sifre Numbers—Ed. H. Horovitz (Leipzig, 1917). Redaction recently dated to before the third century on the basis of the Greek and Latin words in the work; see Shifrá Sznol, "Addenda a Sifre-Números," *Emerita* 63

(1995) 117–28. Stemberger (*Introduction*, p. 267): "after the middle of the third century." For English translation, see *Midrash*.

Sifre Numbers Zuṭa—Published together with *Sifre Numbers*, ed. H. Horovitz (Leipzig, 1917). According to Saul Lieberman (as also J. N. Epstein), Bar Kappara, of the last generation of tannaim, was the final redactor of *Sifre Zuṭa*, thus dating the work to the early third century; see Lieberman, *Sifre Zuṭa (Midrashah shel Lud)*, New York, 1968, pp. 99–124, esp. 115 and 122. I know of no English translation of the work.

Sifre Zuṭa—See *Sifre Numbers Zuṭa*.

Song of Songs Rabba—Also called *Midrash Ḥazita*. No critical edition exists of the entire work. Samuel Lachs's Ph.D. dissertation (Dropsie College, 1958) included a critical edition of the first chapter, "A Critical Edition of Canticles Rabba—Chapter One, Edited on the Basis of Three Manuscripts and Early Editions." The organization of the sections in ed. Vilna of *Midrash Rabba* is confusing and sometimes in error. I, therefore, cite *SongR* by both ed. Vilna and ed. Warsaw. S. Dunsky's popular edition (Montreal, 1973; Jerusalem, 1980) generally follows ed. Warsaw. Critical editions are said to be in preparation but to my knowledge have not yet appeared. See Luis Giron (Ḥiron) Blanc "A Preliminary Description of the Language of Canticles Rabba: Sample Edition," *Meḥqarim be-Lashon* 4 (1990) 129–60, and H. E. Steller in *Rashi 1040–1990: hommage à Ephraïm E. Urbach*, ed. Gabrielle Sed-Rajna (Paris, 1993). A description of manuscripts and editions is in Steller, "Shir Hashirim Rabba 5.2–8: Towards a Reconstruction of a Midrashic Block," in *Variety of Forms: Dutch Studies in Midrash*, ed. a. Kuyt, E.G.L. Schfijver, N. A. van Uchelen (Amsterdam, 1990), pp. 110–11, nn. 1–2. For a summary of views on the dating of *SongR* (ranging from 300 to 1100), see Louis Feldman "Abba Kolon and the Founding of Rome," *JQR* 81 (1991) 249, n. 28. Giron's examination of *SongR* from a linguistic standpoint came to the tentative conclusion that the work exhibits a dialect of Hebrew spoken during the tannaitic period, and if it derives from a later period as is generally assumed, it must stem from a non-Galilean locale whose dialect resembles the Hebrew of the tannaim.

Song of Songs Zuṭa—Published twice, once by Solomon Schechter in *JQR*, o.s., 6–8 (1894–96) and reprinted as *Agadath Shir Hashirim* (Cambridge, 1896); and once by Solomon Buber as *Midrash Zuṭaʾ* (Berlin, 1894), on which see Schechter's review in *JQR*, o.s., 8 (1896) 179–84. Schechter dates *Song Zuṭaʾ* to the end of the tenth century (reprint, pp. 100–104) but Z. M. Rabinovitz would place it much earlier—in the Roman period (*Ginzei Midrash*, Tel Aviv, 1976, pp. 252–53). *Sefer ha-Meqorot:* 800–1000 C.E. M. Hirshman assigns an early, tannaitic dating to the work (*Ha-Miqraʾ u-Midrasho bein Ḥazal le-Avot ha-Knesiyah*,

p. 116, n. 13 = *Rivalry of Genius: Jewish and Christian Biblical Interpretation in Late Antiquity,* p. 148 (n. 13).

Talmud—See *Babylonian Talmud* and *Palestinian Talmud.*

Tanḥuma-Yelamedenu—These midrashim constitute a literary genre which began probably in late Byzantine (fifth–seventh century) Israel and quickly developed a multitude of versions in various locations. The following works belong to this family: *Tanḥuma, Tanḥuma* (ed. Buber), *DeutR, DeutR* (ed. Lieberman), *ExR* 2 (= chap. 15ff.), *NumR* 2 (= chap. 15ff.), parts of *PesR,* etc. The most recent discussions on this body of literature are by Allen D. Kensky, "Midrash Tanhuma Shmot," 1:1–78, and Marc Bregman, "The Tanhuma-Yelammedenu Literature." Bregman dates *Tanḥuma* according to the following development: The earliest stratum (the "Vorlage") is characterized by material shared by both editions of *Tanḥuma* ("printed" and "Buber"); this stratum dates from between the sixth and seventh centuries in Palestine, receiving definite form as the midrash *Tanḥuma* in the late Byzantine period toward the end of the seventh century; the Buber edition of *Tanḥuma,* apparently known only in Ashkenaz, derives from the western Roman Empire, perhaps northern Italy, during the period of the Lombards between 559 and 774; the "accretion-prone" final version, that is the "printed" *Tanḥuma,* was redacted in Babylonia after the conquest of Islam (pp. 166–67, 186, 188; see also *Tarbiẓ* 60 (1991) 269ff.). First edition: Constantinople, 1521; 2nd ed.: Venice, 1545. The third edition (Mantua, 1563) incorporated many additions and became the standard for all subsequent editions. The first and third editions were reprinted by Makor Press (Jerusalem, 1971). The edition used in this study is Warsaw, 1879. The Buber edition, *Midrash Tanḥuma ha-Qadum,* was published in Vilna, 1885. Kensky (1:96–160) finds that the extant manuscripts break down into three groups: Eastern/Mediterranean (represented best by MS Cambridge), Ashkenazic (represented best by MS Parma), and Yemenite (of which MS Oxford 2491 is the best representative). He finds that of the extant manuscripts Cambridge comes closest to the "original" *Tanḥuma* text. An English translation of *Tanḥuma* to Genesis and Exodus was done by Samuel A. Berman, *Midrash Tanhuma-Yelammedenu* (Hoboken, N.J., 1996), and of the Buber edition to Genesis and Exodus by John T. Townsend, *Midrash Tanhuma: S. Buber Recension* (Hoboken, N.J., 1989–).

Tanna, tannaim, tannaitic—The name given to authorities of the rabbinic movement who lived in Israel during the first two centuries of the Common Era. The tannaitic period came to a close with the publication of the Mishnah by R. Judah the Patriarch, who died around 220. Other tannaitic works include the Tosefta, a compendium of Jewish law parallel to the Mishnah, but not traditionally authoritative as is the Mishnah, and the halakhic midrashim (see Midrash). Non-mishnaic tannaitic materials incorporated into the Talmuds are known as *baraitot* (sg. *baraita*).

Targum—The Aramaic Jewish translation and/or paraphrase of the Bible. Recent overview of targumic literature and the state of Targum studies: Paul V. M. Flesher in *Judaism in Late Antiquity*, ed. J. Neusner (Leiden, 1995), 1:40–63; Philip S. Alexander, "Jewish Aramaic Translations of Scripture," in *Mikra*, ed. Martin J. Mulder (Assen, 1988), pp. 217–53, and "Targum," in *ABD* 6:320–331; Étan Levine in *HBOT* 1 (1996) 323–331; and J. Neusner, *Introduction to Rabbinic Literature* (New York, 1994), pp. 611–21. A good history of targumic scholarship is the introductory chapter in Edward Cook's dissertation, "Rewriting the Bible: The Text and Language of the Pseudo-Jonathan Targum" (Ph.D. diss., UCLA, 1986). The dating of targumic literature is much debated, with no agreed-upon conclusions at this point. Flesher gives the following dates and provenances. *Targum Neofiti* and the Genizah fragments: second–third or early fourth century (Palestine). *Targum Onqelos* originated before 135 in Palestine and was reworked in Babylonia before 400. *Targum Jonathan* to the Prophets, like *Onqelos*, originated in Palestine, probably between 70 and 135, and was revised in Babylonia between the third and fourth centuries. *Fragment Targums* originated in Palestine after the fourth century. *Pseudo-Jonathan* to the Pentateuch also originated in Palestine but its date of composition is debated with opinions raging from the fourth to the eighth century. The Targums to the various books of *Ketuvim* (Hagiographa) range in date between the sixth and ninth centuries. Stephen Kaufman suggests both *Targum Onqelos* and the Palestinian Targums derive from one proto-targum of the first century ("Dating the Language of the Palestinian Targums and Their Use in the Study of First Century CE Texts," in *The Aramaic Bible*, ed. D.R.G. Beattie and M. J. McNamara, Sheffield, 1994, pp. 118–41). An English translation of targumic literature, with introductions, is now coming out under the editorship of K. Cathcart et al., *The Aramaic Bible: The Targums* (Wilmington, Del., 1986–). See the individual Targum entries.

Targum Chronicles—An edition based on a Vatican manuscript was published by R. Le Déaut and J. Robert, *Targum des Chroniques (cod. vat. urb. 1)* (Rome, 1971). Now in translation in Cathcart et al., *The Aramaic Bible: The Targums,* vol. 19. The editor of this text, S. McIvor, provides an introduction dealing with extant manuscripts and editions, provenance (Israel), dating (basis, fourth century or earlier; final redaction perhaps eighth century), relationship to other targumim, etc. See also S. Friedman in *Meḥqerei Talmud* 2 (1993) 413, n. 9.

Targum Jonathan—The common name for the Targum to the Prophets.

A survey of scholarship on this Targum is found in Robert P. Gordon, *Studies in the Targum to the Twelve Prophets* (Leiden, 1994), pp. 5–39, and more recently and more extensively in Willem F. Smelik, *The Targum of Judges* (Leiden, 1995), pp. 1–112. Palestinian origin, probably fourth- or fifth-century redaction (P. S. Alexander, *ABD* 6:325).

Targum Lamentations—Critical edition with commentary and translation by Étan Levine, *The Aramaic Version of Lamentations* (New York, 1976). An earlier English translation: A. W. Greenup, *The Targum on the Book of Lamentations* (Sheffield, 1893), reprinted in *The Targum to the Five Megilloth,* ed. B. Grossfeld (New York, 1973). Grossfeld dates the work to the end of the fourth century (p. vii). The Yemenite manuscripts have been critically edited and studied by A. van der Heide, *The Yemenite Tradition of the Targum of Lamentations* (Leiden, 1981).

Targum Onqelos—Originated in Palestine, probably first–second century; redacted in Babylonia, probably fourth–fifth century (P. S. Alexander, *ABD* 6:321). On the language of *Targum Onqelos,* see Hannu Juusola, *Linguistic Peculiarities in the Aramaic Magic Bowl Texts* (Helsinki, 1999), pp. 14–15.

Targum Qohelet—There is general agreement that this targum is of Palestinian origin, and probably dates from the seventh century. See P. S. Knobel's introduction in his translation of the targum in *The Aramaic Bible: The Targums,* 15:2–15. An earlier translation with facsimile of MS Vatican Urb. 1 was produced by Étan Levine (based on the translation of C. D. Ginsburg), *The Aramaic Version of Qohelet* (New York, 1978), and *The Targum to the Five Megillot* (Jerusalem, 1977).

Targum Song—Translation together with a facsimile of MS Vatican Urb.1 was published by Étan Levine, *The Targum to the Five Megillot.* An earlier translation, which served as the basis for Levine, was made by Hermann Gollancz in *The Targum to the Five Megilloth* (London, 1908), ed. Bernard Grossfeld (New York, 1973). A critical edition was published by R. H. Melamed, *The Targum to Canticles according to Six Yemen Mss* (Philadelphia, 1921); originally in *JQR* 9 (1919) 377–410; 11 (1920) 1–20; and 12 (1921) 57–117. On the two distinct text traditions of the Targum—western and Yemenite—see Philip Alexander, "Textual Criticism and Rabbinic Literature: The Case of the Targum of the Song of Songs," *BJRL* 75.3 (1993) 164–65. The general consensus holds to a late, possibly seventh-century, date, although Alexander comes to the conclusion that it is impossible to date the work or to determine whether it is originally Babylonian or Palestinian ("The Aramaic Version of the Song of Songs," in *Traduction et traducteurs au moyen âge,* ed. G. Contamine, Paris, 1989, pp. 129–31; *ABD* 6:327).

Tosafist, tosafot—Rabbinic authorities in Ashkenaz (France–Germany) during the twelfth–fourteenth century who developed a school of talmudic study and commentary.

Tosefta—See *Tanna*. Where available, the critical edition used is that of Saul Lieberman, *Tosefta: ʿal pi Ketav Yad Vinah we-Shinuye Nusḥaʾot mi-Ketav Yad Erfurt, Ketaʿim min ha-Genizah u-Defus Venesyah* (New York, 1955–88), with his commentary, *Tosefta ki-Fshuṭah* (New York, 1955–88). Otherwise K. H. Rengstorf, *Die Tosefta* (Stuttgart, 1967–2001), or M. S. Zuckermandel, *Tosefta ʿal pi Kitvei Yad Erfurt u-Vinah* with a supplement by Saul Lieberman (1973; repr., Jerusalem, 1970). English translation: Jacob Neusner, *Tosefta* (Atlanta, 1999).

Vulgate—Latin translation of the Hebrew Masoretic Bible by Jerome (d. 420). Edition used: *Biblia sacra: iuxta Vulgatam versionem,* adiuvantibus Bonifatio Fischer et al. Recensuit et brevi apparatu instruxit Robertus Weber (Stuttgart, 1983).

Yalquṭ ha-Makhiri—An anthology of midrashim on various books of the Prophets and Ketuvim by Makhir b. Abba Mari of Spain or Southern France (?), thirteenth or fourteenth century (?). The volume on Psalms was edited by S. Buber (1899; repr., Jerusalem, 1964).

Yalquṭ Shimʿoni—An anthology of earlier midrashic material compiled by Shimʿon ha-Darshan (twelfth–thirteenth century). Edition used: D. Heiman, D. N. Lerrer, and I. Shiloni, eds. (Jerusalem, 1973–91).

Yalquṭ Talmud Torah—By Jacob of Sicily (fourteenth century). Ed. Eliezer Hurvitz, "The Nature and Sources of Yalkut Talmud Torah by Rabbi Jacob Sikily" (in Hebrew) (Ph.D. diss., Yeshiva University, 1965).

Zohar—Edition used: *Zohar, Tiqqune ha-Zohar, Zohar Ḥadash,* ed. R. Margaliot (Jerusalem, 1940–53). English translation: M. Simon and P. P. Levertoff, *The Zohar* (London, 1934). For an introduction to this body of literature, see I. Tishby, *The Wisdom of the Zohar,* trans. D. Goldstein (Oxford, 1989).

SUBJECT INDEX

INDEX OF ANCIENT SOURCES

1. Hebrew Bible (413–16) 2. Targum (416–17) 3. Ancient Near East (417) 4. Qumran (417–18) 5. Apocrypha and Pseudepigrapha (418) 6. Greek and Latin Literature (418–21) 7. Hellenistic Jewish Writings (421–22) 8. New Testament (422) 9. Rabbinic Literature (422–26) 10. Christian Literature (426–29) 11. Samaritan Literature (429) 12. Islamic Literature (429–30). Works infrequently cited or not treated at length are listed in the General Index.

1. **HEBREW BIBLE**

Genesis

1:31 295n79
2:13 20, 221n32
3:17 162
4:5 180–81, 281n11
4:15 178
5:32 186
6–10 248n47
6:1–4 295n79
6:2–4 372n8
6:18 103, 105
7:7 103, 105
8:16 103, 105
9 99, 105, 169
9:1 158, 185
9:18 329n39
9:18–25 1
9:18–27 142
9:22 157, 164, 344n43
9:22–23 187
9:23 191, 340n1
9:24 162
9:24–25 157
9:25 68, 98, 141, 160, 162, 163, 165, 285n28, 340n1
9:25–27 143
9:27 328n36, 337n87
10 25, 146, 192
10:6 330n40
10:6–8 (LXX) 19
10:7 18, 226n75
10:8–9 47
10:8–12 20
10:14 (LXX) 300n107
10:32 186
11 98–99
12:10ff. 108
12:11 85, 86, 275n52
17:13 370n51
20:17–18 226n1
24:3 163, 346n48
24:13–14 204
25:25 336n81
25:25 (Peshiṭta) 365n18
28:1 163
30:25–43 145
30:38 326n29, 31
30:39 326n29, 31
33:19 267n198
35:18 226n1
36:20 310n61
37:27–28 309n49
37:36 229n14, 309n49
38:11 226n1
38:16 226n1
39 117
39:1 229n14, 309n49
39:6 122
41:12 121
41:45 301n113
46:4 127

Exodus

2:10 284n26
2:21 28, 53
3:10 127
3:11 127
4:6 27
7:27 136
8:2 136
8:15 (LXX) 339n112
8:17 155
8:20 155
10:4 322n50
10:6 160
11:4 329n39
13:16 73

3. ANCIENT NEAR EAST

4. QUMRAN

7. **HELLENISTIC JEWISH WRITINGS**

10. **CHRISTIAN LITERATURE**

11. SAMARITAN LITERATURE

12. ISLAMIC LITERATURE

INDEX OF MODERN SCHOLARS

JEWS, CHRISTIANS, AND MUSLIMS
FROM THE ANCIENT TO THE MODERN WORLD

SERIES EDITORS
R. Stephen Humphreys, William Chester Jordan, and Peter Schäfer

Imperialism and Jewish Society, 200 B.C.E. to 640 C.E.
by Seth Schwartz

A Shared World: Christians and Muslims in the Early Modern Mediterranean
by Molly Greene

Beautiful Death: Jewish Poetry and Martyrdom in Medieval France
by Susan L. Einbinder

Power in the Portrayal: Representations of Jews and Muslims in Eleventh- and Twelfth-Century Islamic Spain
by Ross Brann

Mirror of His Beauty: Feminine Images of God from the Bible to the Early Kabbalah
by Peter Schäfer

In the Shadow of the Virgin: Inquisitors, Friars, and Conversos *in Guadalupe, Spain*
by Gretchen D. Starr-LeBeau

The Curse of Ham: Race and Slavery in Early Judaism, Christianity, and Islam
by David M. Goldenberg